TRUTH FOR TODAY
COMMENTARY

EDDIE CLOER, D.MIN.
GENERAL EDITOR

DAVID STEWART, M.A.R.
MANAGING EDITOR

DON SHACKELFORD, TH.D.
ASSOCIATE OLD TESTAMENT EDITOR

DUANE WARDEN, PH.D.
ASSOCIATE NEW TESTAMENT EDITOR

TRUTH FOR TODAY
COMMENTARY

AN EXEGESIS & APPLICATION OF THE HOLY SCRIPTURES

ACTS 15–28

DAVID L. ROPER

RESOURCE □
PUBLICATIONS
2205 S. Benton
Searcy, AR 72143

Truth for Today Commentary
Acts 15—28
Copyright © 2001 by Resource Publications
2205 S. Benton, Searcy, AR 72143

ISBN: 0-945441-37-1

CONTENTS

EDITOR'S PREFACE

With this volume on Acts 15—28, we continue a series of commentaries on the Holy Scriptures that we hope will eventually cover every book in God's divine revelation to us. This undertaking is ambitious, to be sure, but one that we believe is needed. May the Lord in His gracious providence allow us to complete the effort that is planned. More importantly, may the work of it be as faithful and true to His will as we can humanly make it.

No one can spend his or her allotted time upon this earth more nobly than in an earnest study of the Scriptures. A handy assistant in such a pursuit is a reliable commentary. Any study of the Scriptures, however, should be predicated upon the realization that the Word of God and the Word of God alone is our guide from earth to heaven. A commentary must never be seen as taking the place of God's precious Word; it must be viewed as a printed teacher that seeks to guide the reader to a better understanding of the Word that God has given.

The author of a commentary does not intend for his comments on the sacred Word to be regarded as infallible; he knows that he is subject to mistakes as is everyone else. Consequently, we must admit at the start that perfection is beyond our reach. This commentary is not perfect, and no commentary ever will be. In writing a commentary, the author only wishes to share with others the fruits of his life-long study of the Scriptures, with the hope that this sharing will aid and encourage the reader in his or her pursuit of the knowledge of God as revealed in the sacred Scriptures.

I have known David Roper for many years. He has proven himself to be one of God's finest servants. Many have read and reread his study of Acts and have found it to be a faithful study of that book. We believe it will bring anyone who reads it to a better understanding of the inspired Book of Acts.

So far as we know, the churches of Christ have never completed a multi-authored commentary series on the entire Bible. Surely, the time for producing such a set is here. We can leave to the generations that will follow no finer legacy than presentations on every book of the Scriptures that have resulted from our faithful scholarship and responsible handling of these Scriptures.

A project of this magnitude will require many faithful laborers, much time, and a great, enduring persistence. Let us join together, as brothers and sisters bought by Christ's blood, and work together until the task is completed.

May all of us, through a diligent study of God's Word, walk in God's will for us and for the world.

EDDIE CLOER
General Editor

ABBREVIATIONS

OLD TESTAMENT

Genesis	Gen.	Ecclesiastes	Eccles.
Exodus	Ex.	Song of Solomon	Song
Leviticus	Lev.	Isaiah	Is.
Numbers	Num.	Jeremiah	Jer.
Deuteronomy	Deut.	Lamentations	Lam.
Joshua	Josh.	Ezekiel	Ezek.
Judges	Judg.	Daniel	Dan.
Ruth	Ruth	Hosea	Hos.
1 Samuel	1 Sam.	Joel	Joel
2 Samuel	2 Sam.	Amos	Amos
1 Kings	1 Kings	Obadiah	Obad.
2 Kings	2 Kings	Jonah	Jon.
1 Chronicles	1 Chron.	Micah	Mic.
2 Chronicles	2 Chron.	Nahum	Nahum
Ezra	Ezra	Habakkuk	Hab.
Nehemiah	Neh.	Zephaniah	Zeph.
Esther	Esther	Haggai	Hag.
Job	Job	Zachariah	Zech.
Psalms	Ps.	Malachi	Mal.
Proverbs	Prov.		

NEW TESTAMENT

Matthew	Mt.	1 Timothy	1 Tim.
Mark	Mk.	2 Timothy	2 Tim.
Luke	Lk.	Titus	Tit.
John	Jn.	Philemon	Philem.
Acts	Acts	Hebrews	Heb.
Romans	Rom.	James	Jas.
1 Corinthians	1 Cor.	1 Peter	1 Pet.
2 Corinthians	2 Cor.	2 Peter	2 Pet.
Galatians	Gal.	1 John	1 Jn.
Ephesians	Eph.	2 John	2 Jn.
Philippians	Phil.	3 John	3 Jn.
Colossians	Col.	Jude	Jude
1 Thessalonians	1 Thess.	Revelation	Rev.
2 Thessalonians	2 Thess.		

ASV   American Standard Version

KJV   King James Version

NASB   New American Standard Bible

NCV   New Century Version

NEB   New English Bible

NIV   New International Version

NKJV   New King James Version

RSV   Revised Standard Version

TEV   Today's English Version

CHAPTER 15

A CONFERENCE IN JERUSALEM— AND PAUL'S SECOND MISSIONARY JOURNEY (PART 1)

At the end of chapter 14, Paul and Barnabas returned, full of excitement, from their first missionary journey. Enthusiastically, they told how the Lord "had opened a door of faith to the Gentiles" (14:27). Some Jews had believed (14:1), but the converts were predominantly Gentile (14:1, 21). Congregations had been established in Antioch of Pisidia, Iconium, Lystra, and Derbe (14:20, 21, 23). Whether or not congregations were established in any other places Paul and Barnabas visited on the first journey, we are not told. Paul and Barnabas had shown that Gentiles in faraway places were receptive. A lost world awaited; a vast harvest of souls was imminent. Surely every Christian would rejoice! Unfortunately, not everyone *was* happy that the Lord "had opened a door of faith to the Gentiles." It was not long until men showed up at Antioch, determined to slam that door shut.

We may possibly have another account of this controversy in the Book of Galatians. The traditional view of conservative scholars is that Galatians 2:1–10 tells of the same events as Acts 15:1–35. As one writer expressed it, "In the two narratives the same people go up at the same time, from the same place, for the same object, in consequence of the same interference by the same agitators, and with the same results."[1] Some difficulties are involved in reconciling the two accounts. For this reason, some conservative writers have decided that Galatians 2:1–10 is

---

[1] F. W. Farrar, *The Life and Work of St. Paul*, vol. 1 (London: Cassell, Petter, Galpin & Co., 1879), 406, n.

speaking of Paul's visit to Jerusalem in connection with the benevolent help for Christians in Judea (11:30; 12:25).[2] One difficulty with the traditional view is that in Acts, the chapter 15 visit was Paul's third visit to Jerusalem, while in Galatians, the chapter 2 visit appears to have been his second visit. However, Paul did not actually say that the Galatians 2 visit was his second visit. He said, "After an interval of fourteen years [after the Galatians 1 visit, a few years after his conversion] I went up *again* . . . " (Gal. 2:1; emphasis added). The word "again" does not rule out the possibility of an additional brief visit to Jerusalem, mentioned in passing in 12:25, at which time he probably had no opportunity to visit with any of the apostles because they were either in hiding or in jail. Difficulties exist regardless of where one places the events of Galatians 2 in the life of Paul. Since the two accounts tell of similar incidents, if not the same incident, we will include a few details from Galatians 2 in the comments on Acts 15.

Most people do not like controversy. We do not like heated exchanges and raised voices. Controversy makes some people physically ill. Nevertheless, controversy is a fact of life—even among God's people (Mt. 10:34–36; Lk. 12:51–53; 1 Cor. 11:18, 19). In Acts 15, there are two classic examples of controversy in the church: In verses 1 through 35, we see a doctrinal disagreement; in verses 36 through 41, we see a difference of opinion. The first controversy involved a congregation. If it had not been handled correctly, this controversy would have spread to many congregations. The second involved two Christians. The question is not "Will we have controversy in the church?" but "How will we deal with controversy when it comes?"

A DISPUTE ABOUT BINDING THE LAW ON GENTILES (15:1, 2)

¹Some men came down from Judea and began teaching the brethren, "Unless you are circumcised according to the cus-

---

[2]See F. F. Bruce, *Paul: Apostle of the Heart Set Free* (Grand Rapids, Mich.: Wm. B. Eerdmans, 1977): 148–59.

2

tom of Moses, you cannot be saved." ²And when Paul and Barnabas had great dissension and debate with them, the brethren determined that Paul and Barnabas and some others of them should go up to Jerusalem to the apostles and elders concerning this issue.

Verse 1. During the "long time" that Paul and Barnabas labored at Antioch after their first journey (14:28), word evidently reached Jerusalem concerning the work they had done—and some Jews were disturbed. This is one of the most reasonable explanations of why the Judaizing teachers showed up in Antioch when they did; but since Luke did not give us the details, we cannot know for sure what prompted these men to go to Antioch at that time. The question of taking the gospel to Gentiles had arisen in Jerusalem about ten years earlier, when Peter converted the household of Cornelius; and it had apparently been settled at that time (11:1–18). When a predominantly Gentile congregation had been established in Antioch of Syria, the church in Jerusalem had even sent Barnabas to help them (11:20–22)—in a sense, giving that work its blessing.

The efforts of Paul and Barnabas, however, awakened old fears. It was obvious that Gentiles would be more receptive than Jews had ever been—and for every Jew in the world, there were thousands of Gentiles. Many could see the church overrun with Gentiles—Gentiles with their heathen cultures, heathen mindset, heathen practices—and the possibility scared them to death. Cornelius had been a God-fearer, and the Gentiles in Antioch had been under strong Jewish influence from the beginning of the work there (11:19–21; 13:1); but some of the Gentiles converted by Paul had little or no Jewish influence at all. This frightened some Jewish Christians. The ungodliness in some Gentile churches—such as the one at Corinth—might illustrate what Jewish Christians feared. They believed that something had to be done to ensure that Gentiles were properly indoctrinated and oriented before they were accepted into full fellowship.

To some, the solution was obvious: Gentiles needed what Gentiles had always needed; they needed to become Jews. The law of Moses would smooth off the Gentiles' rough edges so that conscientious, Law-abiding Jewish Christians could tolerate their presence. Maybe there were some who had been disturbed at the time of the conversion of Cornelius (11:2, 3) saying, "We *told* you that no good would come of accepting uncircumcised Gentiles. Now a disaster is in the making!"

The obvious place for the Jews to start undoing "the damage" was the center of Gentile evangelism, the congregation in Antioch that had sent out Paul and Barnabas. **Some men came down from Judea and began teaching the brethren** in Antioch, **"Unless you are circumcised according to the custom of Moses, you cannot be saved."**

Notice those who arrived: **Some men came . . . from Judea**—specifically, men from Jerusalem (vv. 2–4). These were probably the same as those identified in verse 5 as "some of the sect of the Pharisees who had believed." The Western Text adds to verse 1, "of the party of the Pharisees, who were believers." This is the first time we are told that Pharisees other than Paul had become Christians. (Paul's conversion is first recorded in chapter 9, but Luke did not actually record that Paul was a Pharisee before his conversion until 23:6.) We may be surprised to find that they had become Christians, but we are not surprised "to find them on the wrong side of an important question."[3] Keeping in mind the religious background of the Pharisees (see comments on 5:34), it is easy to see them as ringleaders of an everyone-must-keep-the-Law movement. When they came to Antioch, they probably claimed to be official representatives of the Jerusalem church (v. 24). At any rate, the fact that they were from Jerusalem, which still served as home base for the work of the Twelve, gave their words added weight.

Most commentators like to speak of the church in Jerusalem as "the mother church." Care should be taken not to leave the impression that God established one congregation that had the oversight of other congregations. The *apostles* had a unique relationship to *all* congregations as the primary source of God's revelation for the church—a privilege not passed on to others—

---

[3]J. W. McGarvey, *New Commentary on Acts of Apostles*, vol. 2 (Delight, Ark.: Gospel Light Publishing Co., n.d.), 58.

4

but *the church* in Jerusalem did not have the oversight of other congregations. Each congregation was autonomous, that is, self-governing. Regarding Jerusalem's being "the mother church," note Galatians 4:26: "The Jerusalem *above* [that is, heaven; not the Jerusalem on this earth]" is our spiritual mother.

Next, notice what these men taught: **"Unless you are circumcised according to the custom of Moses, you cannot be saved."** The rite of circumcision had been an essential part of God's covenant with Abraham two thousand years earlier (Gen. 17:10–14, 23–27). However, the men from Jerusalem did not tie circumcision to Abraham; rather, they linked the rite to *Moses*, whose law had been given about five hundred years after the Abrahamic covenant. Their concern was not simply that Gentile men should submit to circumcision; their aim was to convert Gentiles to the Jewish religion and subject them to *all* the Law. Circumcision was the central requirement in a Gentile male's becoming a proselyte (see comments on 2:9–12).

Verse 2. Paul and Barnabas saw their teaching for what it was: a direct attack on the work they had done among the Gentiles—specifically, an attack on their practice of accepting Gentiles on the basis of faith in Jesus without requiring them also to become proselyte Jews. The two missionaries knew the position was false. They also understood the far-reaching consequences of the doctrine: If it became accepted, Christianity would never be anything but a "new-and-improved version" of Judaism. Those who had come from Jerusalem were determined to slam the door of faith that had been opened to the Gentiles as they opened the door of Law-keeping. They said, in effect, "If you want to become a Christian, you have to come in *this* door and first become a Jew." Paul and Barnabas knew this contagion could spread through all the churches they had established. It was heresy and had to be *stopped*. Therefore, **Paul and Barnabas had great dissension and debate with them.** Galatians 2:13 may indicate that Paul believed more strongly about this than Barnabas did. Paul may even have taken the lead in opposing the Judaizing brethren, but the text is clear that Barnabas also opposed the false teachers. Note the word "we" in Galatians 2:5.

Regarding the incident in Galatians 2:1–10, Paul described those who came to Antioch as "false brethren . . . who had sneaked in to spy out our liberty which we have in Christ Jesus, in order to bring us into bondage" (Gal. 2:4). Whether or not that occasion is the same as the one in Acts, the same people with the same mindset were involved. Note the contrast between the words "liberty" and "bondage" in Galatians 2:4: "our *liberty* which we have in Christ Jesus," "to bring us into *bondage*." Paul and Barnabas had brought liberty to the Gentiles; the Judaizing teachers (or Judaizers) wanted to bring them back to the bondage of the Law. Paul implied that these were not true Christians—that they had decided they could not destroy the church from the outside, so they would try from the inside. Some difficulty occurs in reconciling Galatians 2:4 with Acts 15:5, which says that the Pharisees who confronted Paul had "believed," which would imply true conversion. Since we do not have all the details, we must leave the matter in the hands of the Lord, who knows the hearts of all men (v. 8) and who, therefore, knows whether or not these were genuine Christians.

In opposing the false teachers, Paul had spoken as an inspired apostle; that should have settled the matter. Since Paul was not one of the original Twelve, however, some Christians did not believe that his words were as authoritative as the teachings of the other apostles. Throughout his life, Paul's enemies attacked the validity of his apostleship, and he had to defend it (see 2 Cor. 10—13). It is also possible that in Antioch, Paul suffered from the prophet-in-his-own-country syndrome (Jn. 4:44). Whatever their thinking, **the brethren** in Antioch **determined that Paul and Barnabas and some others of them should go up to Jerusalem to the apostles and elders concerning this issue.** Understand that Paul did *not* go to Jerusalem to find out what the truth on the issue was. Of course, the decision of the Jerusalem church vindicated him and his position.

Among the **some others** who traveled with Paul and Barnabas was probably a young man named Titus (Gal. 2:3). Since, according to uninspired tradition, Antioch was Luke's hometown, some have speculated that Titus was Luke's brother. If true, this might explain why Luke never mentioned Titus in spite of the facts that (1) Paul probably converted Titus and felt close to him (Tit. 1:4), (2) Titus was a coworker with Paul on the third missionary journey (2 Cor. 2:13; 7:13, 14; 8:6, 16, 23; 12:18), (3) Titus was a coworker with Paul after his release from his first imprisonment in Rome (Tit. 1:5), and (4) Titus was with Paul during his second imprisonment in Rome (2 Tim. 4:10).

This is an appropriate place to stress that the events of Acts 15 do *not* justify the establishment of *extra-church organizations* to settle church matters. Denominations use Acts 15 to justify their churchwide conferences and conventions. The Catholic Church calls the meeting in Jerusalem "the first Ecumenical Council." However, the situation in chapter 15 was not that many congregations sent delegates to a conference to vote on church issues. Rather, men from one congregation went to another congregation. Even denominational writers understand that this was not an extra-church conference or council:

> The gathering was not a "church council" in the denominational sense. . . . each local church was autonomous.[4]

> The so-called Council of Jerusalem in no way resembled the General Councils of the Church, either in its history, its constitution, or its object. It was not a convention of ordained delegates, but a meeting of the entire Church of Jerusalem to receive a deputation from the Church of Antioch.[5]

A CONFERENCE IN JERUSALEM; A LETTER IS WRITTEN (15:3–29)

Paul and Barnabas Travel to Jerusalem (15:3–5)

3Therefore, being sent on their way by the church, they were passing through both Phoenicia and Samaria, describing in

---

[4]Warren W. Wiersbe, *The Bible Exposition Commentary*, vol. 1 (Wheaton, Ill.: Victor Books, 1989), 461–62.

[5]Farrar, 431.

detail the conversion of the Gentiles, and were bringing great joy to all the brethren. ⁴When they arrived at Jerusalem, they were received by the church and the apostles and the elders, and they reported all that God had done with them. ⁵But some of the sect of the Pharisees who had believed stood up, saying, "It is necessary to circumcise them and to direct them to observe the Law of Moses."

Verse 3. Here we have an illustration of one who was willing to swallow his pride. When the church in Antioch decided to send men to Jerusalem to see what the leaders there thought about the issue (v. 2), this was a slap in Paul's face. He was as qualified as any apostle in Jerusalem to speak on the subject. He later emphasized that when he went to Jerusalem, none there contributed anything to his understanding of biblical truths (Gal. 1:17; 2:6). Why, then, did Paul agree to go to Jerusalem? In Galatians 2:2 he noted that "it was because of a revelation that [he] went up." Some way or another, God told the apostle that, for the sake of unity, he needed to go to Jerusalem as the brethren in Antioch had asked—and Paul did.

Sent on their way indicates that **the church** furnished needed supplies for the trip as well as giving Paul, Barnabas, and the others its blessings. **They were passing through both Phoenicia and Samaria, describing in detail the conversion of the Gentiles, and were bringing great joy to all the brethren.** The brethren in Phoenicia and Samaria did not have the prejudice against Gentile Christians that some of the brethren in Jerusalem had. The churches in these areas were the result of the evangelistic efforts of Hellenistic Jewish Christians (8:5–25; 11:19).

Verse 4. At last **they arrived at Jerusalem.** It was about a three hundred mile trip, so it would have taken some time. **They were received by the church and the apostles and the elders.** Note that the leadership of the Jerusalem church continued to move from the temporary office of apostles to the permanent position of elders. In chapter 15, the elders were involved in every aspect of the decision-making process (vv. 2, 4, 6, 22, 23).

While addressing the church, Paul and Barnabas **reported all that God had done with them.** Earlier the two men had reported to the church in Antioch "all things that God had done with them" (14:27) to give God the glory. This time their purpose in reporting "all . . . that God had done with them" was not merely to give God the glory, but to show that God *approved* of their mission to the Gentiles.

Verse 5. It was not long before **some of the sect of the Pharisees who had believed stood up.** Evidently, this was a public meeting in which Paul and Barnabas were allowed to tell about their work—and during which the Judaizing teachers were also permitted to speak. They said, **"It is necessary to circumcise them** [Gentiles] *and* **to direct them to observe the Law of Moses"** (emphasis added). These men were not saying it would be *good* if Gentiles studied the Law; they were not arguing the *value* of obeying the Law; rather, they were teaching the *essentiality* of becoming a Jew. They had told the Gentiles in Antioch, "Unless you are circumcised according to the custom of Moses, *you cannot be saved.*" The words **it is necessary**, translated from δεῖ (*dei*), emphasize that they did not consider their proposal to be optional (see 1:21; Rom. 13:5; Heb. 8:3). They knew that if being circumcised were simply an option, few Gentiles would be circumcised. Few had been in the past; there was no reason to believe that situation would change without powerful motivation. Therefore, they taught that circumcision was indispensable for salvation. If Galatians 2 describes the same trip, these Judaizers even tried to force Titus, a Gentile Christian, to be circumcised—probably trying to make that a requirement before he was allowed to sit in their meetings—but Paul would not hear of it (Gal. 2:3).

Paul and Barnabas used every opportunity to talk about the problem. If Galatians 2 tells of the same event as in Acts 15, between the public meeting of verse 5 and the public meeting described in verses 6 through 29, Paul and Barnabas met privately with the leaders of the Jerusalem church. As they freely discussed the issues, they found that they were in agreement, as we would expect when inspired men discussed doctrinal matters. Then ". . . James and Cephas and John . . . gave to [Paul] and Barnabas the right hand of fellowship . . . ." (Gal. 2:9). They were on their way to restoring peace to the church, largely because of Paul and Barnabas' willingness to talk freely about the problem.

Peter's Speech (15:6–11)

⁶**The apostles and the elders came together to look into this matter.** ⁷**After there had been much debate, Peter stood up and said to them, "Brethren, you know that in the early days God made a choice among you, that by my mouth the Gentiles would hear the word of the gospel and believe.** ⁸**And God, who knows the heart, testified to them giving them the Holy Spirit, just as He also did to us;** ⁹**and He made no distinction between us and them, cleansing their hearts by faith.** ¹⁰**Now therefore why do you put God to the test by placing upon the neck of the disciples a yoke which neither our fathers nor we have been able to bear?** ¹¹**But we believe that we are saved through the grace of the Lord Jesus, in the same way as they also are."**

Verse 6. The issues were clear; the lines had been drawn. A second public meeting was held to bring the controversy to a satisfactory conclusion: **The apostles and the elders came together to look into this matter.** This was a public meeting, with "the whole church" present (v. 22; see v. 12).

Verse 7. After there had been much debate, Peter stood up. The word **debate** is from the same Greek word ζήτησις (zētēsis), translated "debate" in verse 2. The rhetoric was heated; the meeting was noisy. Before the formal speeches of Peter, Paul, Barnabas, and James, everyone had apparently had an opportunity to speak. Harmony cannot be achieved by muzzling those who are in disagreement. Each one should be allowed to express what is on his mind—with this understanding: *"Every man has his say; no man has his way."*

After each one had expressed himself, **Peter** stood and began to speak. The Judaizing teachers may have thought Peter, raised as a Palestinian Jew, would be sympathetic with their position. If so, they would have been surprised to hear him side with Paul and Barnabas. Peter began, **"Brethren, you know that in the early days God made a choice among you, that by my** mouth the Gentiles would hear the word of the gospel and believe." Peter's speech (vv. 7–11) revolved around his experiences with Cornelius and his household (chs. 10, 11). Peter said that God had chosen him to open the door of salvation to the Gentiles in the first place (see comments on 10:5–8), and that God had *not* made circumcision or keeping the Law a requirement for Gentiles to pass through that door. Peter's arguments were powerful.

Verse 8. Peter's first argument was that **"God, who knows the heart, testified to them giving them the Holy Spirit, just as He also did to us"** (see comments on 10:44–48; 11:15–18). This occurrence is the second time in Acts that God has been called the "heart-knower" (καρδιογνώστης, *kardiognōstēs*) (see 1:24). God does not look at the outward appearance, but looks at the heart (1 Sam. 16:7). The Judaizers looked at the superficial characteristics of uncircumcised Gentiles and pronounced them unfit for the kingdom, but God looked at their *hearts* and announced them as fit as, if not more fit than, the Jews.

Verse 9. Second, Peter argued that God **"made no distinction between us and them."** Compare this statement to Paul's phrase "there is no distinction" in Romans 3:22. God accepted Gentiles, **cleansing their hearts**—just as the hearts of Christian Jews had been cleansed. Observe that their hearts had been cleansed **by faith**, not by being circumcised and keeping the Law. Peter had told Cornelius, ". . . God is not one to show partiality" (10:34); he told this group that God "made no distinction." As the Jews on the Day of Pentecost had to believe and be baptized (2:37, 38), so did Cornelius and his household (10:43, 48).

Verse 10. Peter's third argument was that when the Judaizers tried to bind circumcision on Gentiles, they were putting **God to the test**. The Law-binders thought they were challenging Paul and Barnabas, but in reality they were questioning God's judgment and trying His patience (see comments on 5:9).

Fourth, by attempting to bind Law-keeping on Gentiles, they were **placing upon the neck of the disciples a yoke which** no Jew had ever **been able to bear.** The purpose of a yoke across the neck of an ox was good: to distribute evenly the weight of the load to be pulled. Peter, however, implied that the **yoke** of the Law was heavy, adding to the burdens of the Jews. Jesus also referred to His teachings as a "yoke" (Mt. 11:30), but He said that His yoke is light; therefore, it is able to fulfill the true purpose of a yoke, which is to make burdens easier to bear. Every honest Jew had to admit, as much as he might love the Law (Ps. 119:97), that he always fell short of fulfilling its demands. Day by day, the burden of guilt upon his soul increased until he was exhausted and ready to collapse. Peter asked, in essence, "Why would you want to place that soul-crushing load on anyone else?"

It should be understood that the fault was not with the Law, but with man's failure to keep its demands perfectly. That is why we must have a *grace* arrangement, not a law arrangement. The only One who ever kept the Law perfectly was Jesus Christ (2 Cor. 5:21; Heb. 4:15; 1 Jn. 3:5).

Verse 11. Peter's final words were his most powerful: **"But we believe that we are saved through the grace of the Lord Jesus, in the same way as they also are."** We are saved *by grace*—the unmerited favor of the Lord—and that is the only way we can be saved. The Jews could not perfectly keep the law of Moses; we cannot perfectly keep any law (Rom. 3:23). If we are not saved by grace, we will not be saved at all. Notice the unusual way Peter emphasized that both Jews and Gentiles were saved by grace. We would expect him to say, "*They* are saved by grace just as *we* are." Instead he said, "*We* are saved through the grace of the Lord Jesus, in the same way as *they* also are." In other words, "God has decreed that Gentiles are saved by grace, not Law-keeping; and if we Jews are to be saved, we must learn that we also are saved by grace, not Law-keeping."

The Speeches of Paul, Barnabas, and James (15:12–21)

[12]**All the people kept silent, and they were listening to Barnabas and Paul as they were relating what signs and wonders God had done through them among the Gentiles. [13]After they had stopped speaking, James answered, saying, "Brethren, listen to me. [14]Simeon has related how God first concerned**

Himself about taking from among the Gentiles a people for His name. ¹⁵With this the words of the Prophets agree, just as it is written,

¹⁶'After these things I will return,
And I will rebuild the tabernacle of David which has fallen,
And I will rebuild its ruins,
And I will restore it,
¹⁷So that the rest of mankind may seek the Lord,
And all the Gentiles who are called by My name,'
¹⁸Says the Lord, who makes these things known from long
ago.

¹⁹Therefore it is my judgment that we do not trouble those who are turning to God from among the Gentiles, ²⁰but that we write to them that they abstain from things contaminated by idols and from fornication and from what is strangled and from blood. ²¹For Moses from ancient generations has in every city those who preach him, since he is read in the synagogues every Sabbath."

Verse 12. Peter's speech quieted the crowd. Then **Barnabas** and **Paul** told of their missionary journey. Luke listed Barnabas first because in Jerusalem, Barnabas was more respected. Luke did not record their words, for he had already given the details in chapters 13 and 14. Once more Paul and Barnabas related "what . . . God had done through them." This time, however, their emphasis was on **what** *signs and wonders* **God had done through them** (emphasis added). These miracles were proof that God was with them (Heb. 2:4) and, therefore, that their Gentile ministry was God-approved.

Verse 13. After Barnabas and Paul spoke, it was James' turn— **James**, the half-brother of the Lord (Mt. 13:55; Acts 12:17; 21:18; 1 Cor. 15:7; Gal. 1:19; Jas. 1:1). We know this James was the half-brother of Jesus by the process of elimination. The only other well-known James was the brother of John, and we read of his beheading in chapter 12. The James of Acts 15 was a pillar in the church in Jerusalem (Gal. 2:9). The Judaizing teachers probably thought if they could count on anyone to champion their cause, James would be that one. In a related event, some troublemakers came to Antioch claiming to be "from James" (Gal. 2:12). If they were from James, they probably overstepped their commission. Perhaps they just used his name to give credibility to their position. At any rate, their use of James' name indicates that they thought of James as holding a similar position to their own. James began his speech by capturing the attention of his audience: **"Brethren, listen to me."**

Verse 14. James reviewed what had been said: **"Simeon has related how God first concerned Himself about taking from among the Gentiles a people for His name."** James used the Hebrew form of the name of Simon (Peter), **Simeon.** This, plus the fact that James did not mention what Barnabas and Paul said, may have been calculated to appeal to the Jews who led the "circumcision party." His terminology probably shocked some. The Jews had always been "the people for God's name"—in contrast to the Gentiles. Now God was "taking from among the Gentiles a people for His name" (emphasis added).

Once more the Judaizers were disappointed. James showed by the Scriptures that God intended that the Gentiles should be part of His plans and purposes, and that God had *not* prophesied that to do so, Gentiles would need to first become Jews.

Verse 15. James then turned to God's Word to show that the conversion of Cornelius and his household was a fulfillment of prophecy. **"With this the words of the Prophets agree,"** he said, quoting from Amos 9:11, 12 (see vv. 16–18). James could have quoted many prophecies, such as Isaiah 2:2–4; 49:6 and Micah 4:1–4—and he may have, since Luke recorded an abbreviated version of every sermon. When controversy arises in the church, we must stay close to the Book. Even when the disagreement is not doctrinal, principles given in the Bible will help solve the problem and help assure that we stay in the center of God's will.

Verses 16–18. James quoted from Amos 9:11, 12 to show that the conversion of Cornelius and his household was a fulfillment of prophecy:

"After these things I will return, and I will rebuild the tabernacle of David which has fallen, and I will rebuild its ruins, and I will restore it, so that the rest of mankind

may seek the Lord, and all the Gentiles who are called by My name," says the Lord, who makes these things known from long ago.

The prophecy spoke of the restoration of the dynasty of David, which took place in the ascension and glorification of Jesus, and said that this would happen so that **the rest of mankind** could seek the Lord. In Amos 9:12 in English translations of the Old Testament, which are based on the Hebrew text, there is a reference to the Edomites. The Septuagint (Greek translation) has a more general reference to all mankind. James was apparently quoting from the Septuagint. "The rest of mankind" is specifically identified as **all the Gentiles who are called by My name.** F. F. Bruce defined this group of people as "'all the Gentiles over whom my name has been invoked' (i.e., in baptism)."[6] The rebuilding of **the tabernacle of David** was understood by the Jews to refer to the restoration of Israel's fortunes by the Messiah. As we have seen, the Old Testament prophecies concerning the restoration of the throne of David and the kingdom were fulfilled in Jesus (see comments on 1:6; 2:30; 3:21).

Most premillennialists teach that Amos 9:11, 12 will be fulfilled in the future, when Jesus returns to the earth. James, however, used the passage to prove that God intended for the gospel to be preached to Gentiles. If Amos 9:11, 12 has *not* been fulfilled as James taught, then no Gentile should be allowed to become a Christian—and that includes most of us.

Verse 19. James then said, **"Therefore it is my judgment that we do not trouble those who are turning to God from among the Gentiles."** In other words: "We should not trouble Gentile Christians by binding circumcision and the Law on them." James had proved that God included Gentiles in His plans and purposes for the Christian Age, but how did this relate to the issue of whether or not Gentiles needed to be circumcised and keep the Law? James' argument was based on silence: Amos

---

[6]F. F. Bruce, *The Book of the Acts,* The New International Commentary on the New Testament, gen. ed. F. F. Bruce, rev. ed. (Grand Rapids, Mich.: Wm. B. Eerdmans Publishing Co., 1988), 294.

had stressed that Gentiles were included in God's plans, but the prophet had not stated or implied that Gentiles would first have to become Jews to be part of those plans.

The order of the speakers had probably been decided in the private meeting of Galatians 2:2–10, with James speaking last because his word would carry the greatest weight with those who insisted that Gentiles should be circumcised. For the same reason, it was probably predetermined that he should be the one to say boldly that Gentiles did *not* have to keep the Law.

James did not announce, "Therefore, this is the way it will be." Rather, he said, **"Therefore it is *my judgment* [that we should do thus and so]."** He did not force the decision on the assembly; he showed respect for those who held the opposing view, giving them the opportunity to yield with dignity. This sensitivity for the feelings of others continues through the story.

Verse 20. For all practical purposes, the doctrinal aspect of the issue had been resolved; Peter, Paul, Barnabas, and James had all come to the same conclusion. A problem still had to be faced, however—the practical side of the issue: How could Jewish Christians who had kept the Law all of their lives coexist with Gentile Christians who had never kept the Law? As James prepared to wrap up his speech, he told those present that it was also his judgment **"that we write to them that they abstain from things contaminated by idols and from fornication and from what is strangled and from blood."**

Most agree that the last two items are related to each other and that James basically mentioned three prohibitions: The first was **things contaminated by idols**. Later identified as "things sacrificed to idols" (v. 29), this restriction referred to the meat sacrificed on pagan altars. Only a fraction of this meat was actually burned on the altar. That which remained was either eaten by the pagan priests or by the worshiper. Some of it was sold in the marketplace, where it brought top prices since it was prime quality. Most Gentile Christians had eaten this meat all of their lives, but Jewish Christians had not—and to do so was highly offensive to them.

The second prohibition was **fornication** (πορνεία, *porneia*), or illicit sexual relationships. Fornication had always been condemned by God, but it was considered harmless recreation by most Gentiles until they were taught differently. (Most of those who produce books, movies, and TV programs around the world today seem to hold the same hedonistic view.) Seneca wrote concerning the sexual immorality of his day, "Innocence is not rare; it is non-existent."[7] Since the other two items relate specifically to Jewish-Gentile relationships, some believe that the word "fornication" here especially refers to specialized prohibitions in the Law regarding marrying close relatives, etc. (Lev. 18:6–18). This common practice among Gentiles, perhaps even Gentile Christians, would be extremely offensive to those with a Jewish background. Today many governments of the world recognize the genetic problems involved in close relatives marrying and prohibit it by law.

The third prohibition was **from what is strangled and from blood.** In later centuries, commentators took the word "blood" to refer to murder, but in Acts 15 the terms "what is strangled" and "blood" probably referred to the common Gentile practice of eating flesh with the blood in it, as well as drinking the blood of animals and eating food that uses blood as an ingredient. When an animal was sacrificed to an idol, sometimes part of the blood was drunk by the worshiper. In addition, it was customary among some Gentiles to drink the blood of a strong animal, for by doing so these people believed they would gain the prowess of the animal. Some even drank the blood of fallen enemies for the same reason. However, when the Jews slaughtered an animal, they drained the blood from it. (This method is the common slaughtering practice in America today, and in most other societies.) If they slaughtered an animal for a sacrifice, the blood was poured on the altar. If they slaughtered an animal for meat, they poured the blood on the ground (Lev. 17:10–14; Deut. 12:16, 23–25)—for God taught that "the life of the flesh is in the blood" (Lev. 17:11). A conscientious Jew would be suspicious of any meat prepared by a Gentile.

We cannot be certain why James singled out these three items

---

[7]Quoted by John Waddey, "The Discussion Over Circumcision and the Law," *Studies in Acts* (Denton, Tex.: Valid Publications, 1985), 171.

for prohibition, but we can make some educated guesses: First, the prohibitions represented common practices by the Gentiles, practices that probably continued to be part of the lifestyle of Gentile Christians until they were taught differently. Gentile congregations were still struggling with these sins near the end of the first century (Rev. 2:14, 20). Second, all three practices prohibited by James affected Jewish-Gentile fellowship in the church. Two of the three affected "table fellowship," an important practice in the family of God (see comments on 2:46). Third, none of the three restrictions was exclusively Jewish. Idolatry, fornication, and eating blood had all been wrong before Moses received the Law. (For the prohibition on eating blood, see Gen. 9:4.) Laws concerning these areas had been bound on Gentiles at least from the time of the Flood, so James could urge Gentiles to abstain from these three practices without being accused of inconsistency when he also said that Gentiles did not have to keep the Law.

James was, in effect, saying to Gentile Christians, "We Jewish Christians have decided in your favor regarding Gentiles' keeping the Law. Now do *us* a favor by abstaining from practices that make us uncomfortable." When we disagree with brethren, we need to be sensitive regarding their feelings.

Verse 21. James closed by reminding his listeners that many Gentiles were already aware of what the Law required regarding these issues: **"For Moses from ancient generations has in every city those who preach him, since he is read in the synagogues every Sabbath."** (Concerning synagogues, see comments on 6:9.) It is also possible that he was reassuring them that the Law would continue to be taught.

The Letter from the Council (15:22–29)

²²**Then it seemed good to the apostles and the elders, with the whole church, to choose men from among them to send to Antioch with Paul and Barnabas—Judas called Barsabbas, and Silas, leading men among the brethren, ²³and they sent this letter by them,**

"The apostles and the brethren who are elders, to the

18

brethren in Antioch and Syria and Cilicia who are from the Gentiles, greetings. [24]Since we have heard that some of our number to whom we gave no instruction have disturbed you with their words, unsettling your souls, [25]it seemed good to us, having become of one mind, to select men to send to you with our beloved Barnabas and Paul, [26]men who have risked their lives for the name of our Lord Jesus Christ. [27]Therefore we have sent Judas and Silas, who themselves will also report the same things by word of mouth. [28]For it seemed good to the Holy Spirit and to us to lay upon you no greater burden than these essentials: [29]that you abstain from things sacrificed to idols and from blood and from things strangled and from fornication; if you keep yourselves free from such things, you will do well. Farewell."

Verse 22. When James finished, a remarkable and wonderful thing happened: The whole congregation came to an agreement. **It seemed good to the apostles and the elders,** *with the whole church* to write the letter to the church at Antioch as James recommended (emphasis added). In the letter, they noted that "it seemed good to us, *having become of one mind*" to do this (v. 25; emphasis added). It is possible that the circumcision-binders left the meeting after seeing the way it was progressing, and so were not present when the unanimous decision was reached. It is also possible that the term **the whole church** is intended to convey the idea of a general consensus rather than agreement by each individual. The most natural way to understand the text, however, is that everyone stayed for the whole meeting and that everyone agreed with the final decision. Apparently, the circumcision-binders conceded to the inspired judgment of Peter, Paul, Barnabas, and James. If that is the case, then they were bigger men than many today who insist on having their way "or else." Unless an issue involves a spiritual principle that we cannot compromise, when the majority's preference differs from our personal preferences, we should defer to the majority and make the decision unanimous. (This principle applies only to matters of personal preference. In matters of faith, the position of "the majority" is often wrong [Ex. 23:2; Mt. 7:13, 14].)

Having determined to send the letter, "the apostles and the elders, with the whole church" chose **men from among them to send to Antioch with Paul and Barnabas—Judas called Barsabbas, and Silas**. We can see the wisdom in that decision. If Paul and Barnabas had returned alone with a letter, doubters might have said they had written the letter themselves. Sending representatives eliminated that possibility.

Two men were chosen to carry the letter. The first was **Judas called Barsabbas**. We know nothing else about this man. Since his nickname was Barsabbas ("son of the Sabbath"), some have speculated that he might be the brother of "Joseph called Barsabbas" (see comments on 1:23). However, we cannot imagine why two brothers would have the same nickname. The second man chosen was **Silas**. This reference is our introduction to Silas, who will become the traveling companion of Paul. Luke described Judas and Silas as **leading men among the brethren**. The Greek word translated "leading" is from the same root word ἡγέομαι (*hēgeomai*) as the word translated "leaders" in Hebrews 13:17 and 24, causing some to speculate as to whether or not Judas and Silas were elders at Jerusalem. It would make sense for the church at Jerusalem to send two of its elders to represent it. These men were also prophets (v. 32).

Verse 23. A model of sensitivity, the letter began with the common greeting of that day: **"The apostles and the brethren who are elders, to the brethren in Antioch and Syria and Cilicia who are from the Gentiles, greetings."** The letter was addressed **to the brethren**; the Christians in Jerusalem first acknowledged a family relationship with the recipients. The letter was first sent to the Christians in **Antioch**, where the controversy had begun. The letter was also sent to the regions surrounding Antioch, which was the largest, most influential city of the provinces of **Syria and Cilicia**. Paul later also shared the letter with the churches in Galatia and Phrygia (16:4–6). How much farther it was taken at that time, we do not know. Of course, Luke's inclusion of it in Acts ultimately sent the letter all over the brotherhood.

Verse 24. The letter next emphasized that those who had come to Antioch did not represent the Jerusalem church and expressed concern for the trouble caused by them: "... **we have heard that some of our number to whom we gave no instruction have disturbed you with their words, unsettling your souls."** The Greek words translated **disturbed** (from ταράσσω, *tarassō*) and **unsettling** (from ἀνασκευάζω, *anaskeuazō*) indicate the intense nature of the controversy in Antioch. It was a controversy that threatened to tear the congregation apart.

Verses 25, 26. The letter continued: **"It seemed good to us, having become of one mind, to select men to send to you with our beloved Barnabas and Paul, men who have risked their lives for the name of our Lord Jesus Christ."** Again, **Barnabas** was mentioned first because of his preeminence in Jerusalem. The two missionaries had **risked their lives** for the cause of Christ on numerous occasions. Paul had escaped death in the city of Damascus, being lowered in a basket through a window in the city wall (9:23–25). He had been sent away to Tarsus by the Jerusalem brethren, avoiding a plot to kill him (9:29, 30). On the first missionary journey, Paul and Barnabas were driven out of cities (13:50; 14:5). Paul was even stoned and left for dead (14:19). The high regard shown for the person and work of Paul and of Barnabas in this letter would strike a conciliatory note with the church in Antioch, who had sent them out (13:1–3).

Verse 27. The letter explained why two leading men from the Jerusalem church were sent: **"Therefore we have sent Judas and Silas, who themselves will also report the same things by word of mouth."** These men could confirm that the letter was genuine and also answer questions people had. The brethren in Jerusalem did not depend on the letter alone; they sent two men with the letter. They made sure their response had *the personal touch.*

Verse 28. Notice that the letter was inspired. Near the end of the letter, we have these words: **"For it seemed good *to the Holy Spirit* and to us to lay upon you no greater burden . . ."** (emphasis added). This letter is the first known inspired epistle. This fact is another proof that the meeting in Jerusalem was unlike denominational councils and conferences of today: Those sessions cannot and do not produce Holy Spirit-inspired documents.

Verse 29. The letter also made clear that God did *not* require Gentiles to be circumcised and keep the law of Moses. The letter closed with the prohibitions recommended by James: **". . . that you abstain from things sacrificed to idols and from blood and from things strangled and from fornication; if you keep yourselves free from such things, you will do well."** The letter closed with the greeting **"Farewell"** (see 23:30, KJV).

PAUL AND BARNABAS TAKE THE LETTER TO ANTIOCH (15:30–35)

³⁰So when they were sent away, they went down to Antioch; and having gathered the congregation together, they delivered the letter. ³¹When they had read it, they rejoiced because of its encouragement. ³²Judas and Silas, also being prophets themselves, encouraged and strengthened the brethren with a lengthy message. ³³After they had spent time there, they were sent away from the brethren in peace to those who had sent them out. ³⁴[But it seemed good to Silas to remain there.] ³⁵But Paul and Barnabas stayed in Antioch, teaching and preaching with many others also, the word of the Lord.

Verse 30. Paul and Barnabas, along with the representatives from Jerusalem, **went down to Antioch.** One always went "down" from Jerusalem (8:5, 15; 9:30, 32; 11:27; 12:19) or "up" to Jerusalem (24:11; 25:1) due to the city's high elevation. **And having gathered the congregation together, they delivered the letter.** It was commonplace for letters to be read in the assemblies of the early church (Col. 4:16; 1 Thess. 5:27; Rev. 1:3).

Verse 31. When they had read it, they rejoiced because of its encouragement. The brethren at Antioch were encouraged because the decision had been made that Gentiles did not have to keep the Law; they were encouraged because the controversy was over; they were encouraged because the requests made were not difficult. The Gentile Christians were happy to comply with the requests. If controversies are to be resolved, *both* sides must be ready to "give" a little.

Verse 32. Judas and Silas, also being prophets themselves, encouraged and strengthened the brethren with a lengthy message. Lengthy messages are sometimes in order (see 20:7). In addition to the letter, the words of Judas and Silas strengthened relationships between the Jews and the Gentiles.

Verse 33. After Judas and Silas **had spent time there, they were sent away from the brethren in peace.** A common farewell was "Go in peace." These men were returned **to those who had sent them out** (v. 22, 27). To be sent "in peace to those who had sent them out" indicated that the brethren in Antioch appreciated the men who had come and those who had sent them.

Verse 34. Some manuscripts include the words of verse 34, **[But it seemed good to Silas to remain there]**, but most Greek manuscripts do not have these words. They were probably added later by a scribe to explain how Silas was available when Paul chose him to go on the second journey (v. 40). Other possibilities exist, however: Silas may have left and later returned, Paul may have sent to Jerusalem for him, or Paul may have gone to Jerusalem himself to get him.

Verse 35. But Paul and Barnabas stayed in Antioch, teaching and preaching with many others also, the word of the Lord (see 13:1). We do not know how long they stayed in Antioch after the Jerusalem meeting. Possibly, Paul wrote his letter to the Christians in Galatia during this period.[8] The event of Galatians 2:11–16—when Paul had to rebuke Peter for withdrawing himself from table fellowship with Gentile brethren—may also have occurred during this time. If that is the case, a phrase in Galatians 2 becomes significant to our study: "The rest of the Jews joined him in hypocrisy, with the result that *even Barnabas* was carried away by their hypocrisy" (Gal. 2:13; emphasis added). Paul must have been disappointed by Barnabas' behavior—and deeply hurt. It is possible that Paul and Barnabas' friendship was already strained before the events of verses 36 through 39.

---

[8]For an analysis of Galatians, see David Roper, "Galatians: Liberty in Christ," *Truth for Today* 14 (July 1993): 19–20.

A DISAGREEMENT BETWEEN
PAUL AND BARNABAS (15:36–39)

[36]After some days Paul said to Barnabas, "Let us return and visit the brethren in every city in which we proclaimed the word of the Lord, and see how they are." [37]Barnabas wanted to take John, called Mark, along with them also. [38]But Paul kept insisting that they should not take him along who had deserted them in Pamphylia and had not gone with them to the work. [39]And there occurred such a sharp disagreement that they separated from one another, and Barnabas took Mark with him and sailed away to Cyprus.

The end of Acts 15 comes as something of a shock to the reader. For most of the chapter, Paul and Barnabas unselfishly struggled to resolve differences in the church, to keep the church from splitting. Then, in the closing verses, we read that Paul and Barnabas, unable to resolve their personal differences, parted company.

If we were in Luke's position, it would have been tempting to leave out the fact that Paul and Barnabas had "a sharp disagreement." We might have said that when they decided to revisit the churches established on the first journey, Paul and Barnabas concluded that they could do twice as much good if they formed two mission teams instead of one—and this is what they did. Luke did not succumb to that temptation. As usual, we see Bible characters—even heroes of the Bible—depicted as they were, not as they should have been.

Why did Luke record the disagreement between Paul and Barnabas? It surely was not to embarrass either man. (Barnabas was probably still alive when Luke wrote Acts, and Paul almost certainly was.) Rather, Luke recorded the incident to allow brethren to learn how to settle disagreements.

Verse 36. After the two men worked for a while at Antioch, Paul decided that it was time to get on the road again. **After some days** is an indefinite period of time. It has been suggested that Paul and Barnabas worked in Antioch during the winter months, when travel was difficult, and Paul's decision came in the spring, when travel was once again possible. No doubt the Holy Spirit had a vital part in Paul's decision. **Paul said to Barnabas, "Let us return and visit the brethren in every city in which we proclaimed the word of the Lord, and see how they are."** We cannot baptize people and then ignore them. The Great Commission declares that until we are prepared to nurture new Christians, we are not ready to take the gospel to the lost. Most former missionaries return periodically to their fields of labor to nurture the souls of those they baptized.

The only item on Paul's agenda, at least the only item mentioned, was strengthening the churches already established. The letter to the Galatians reveals that he was concerned about Judaizing teachers, such as those who disturbed the church in Antioch. As is evident from chapters 16 through 18, the simple encouraging visit developed into a significant evangelistic venture.

Verse 37. Barnabas was agreeable to Paul's suggestion, but added a suggestion of his own: **Barnabas wanted to take John, called Mark, along with them also.** John Mark, who was Barnabas' cousin (Col. 4:10), had started with Paul and Barnabas on the first journey, but had turned back at Perga in Pamphylia (13:13). What prompted Barnabas' desire to take Mark on the second journey? Perhaps Mark had come to Barnabas with an apology: "I'm sorry I turned back. I know it was wrong, but I'd like a second chance. I promise I won't let you down this time." Whatever the reason, the Son of Encouragement (4:36) was happy to give Mark another chance.

Verse 38. Paul was *not* happy. He was not convinced that Mark had matured sufficiently to risk taking him again. Therefore, **Paul kept insisting that they should not take him along who had deserted them in Pamphylia and had not gone with them to the work.** The Greek verb ἠξίου (*ēxiou*, from ἀξιόω, *axioō*), translated **kept insisting**, is in the imperfect tense which indicates continuous action. Barnabas kept insisting that they should take Mark, while Paul kept insisting that they should not.

Verse 39. And there occurred . . . a *sharp disagreement* between them (emphasis added). The RSV calls it "a sharp contention." Another translation has "an angry feeling,"[9] while another refers to "a sharp clash of opinions."[10] In both English and Greek, the words suggest a heated exchange—perhaps a loss of temper, almost certainly loud voices and cutting words. Paul later wrote, "Love is patient . . . and . . . not provoked . . ." (1 Cor. 13:4, 5). He may have blushed a little as he dictated those words, remembering the altercation with his friend Barnabas a few years earlier. Undoubtedly, Paul was provoked on this occasion.

After a while, it became apparent that Paul and Barnabas could not resolve their differences—at least for the moment. They decided to split the task of visiting the churches which had been established. Since Barnabas was a native of Cyprus (4:36), he would follow up that work. If Paul and Barnabas had many responses in Cyprus or established any congregations, Luke did not record the fact (see comments on 13:6). Perhaps Barnabas returned to follow up contacts. Paul would go to Asia Minor. **They separated from one another, and Barnabas took Mark with him and sailed away to Cyprus.** Paul and Barnabas did not let their differences keep them from doing the will of the Lord. Their disagreement resulted in two missionary efforts, instead of one. This reference is the last mention of Barnabas in Acts. Like the rest of us, Barnabas had his imperfections, but all in all what a marvelous Christian he was! We need more Sons of Encouragement in the church today.

PAUL AND SILAS START ON THE SECOND MISSIONARY JOURNEY (15:40, 41)

⁴⁰But Paul chose Silas and left, being committed by the brethren to the grace of the Lord. ⁴¹And he was traveling through Syria and Cilicia, strengthening the churches.

Verse 40. As Barnabas and Paul parted, the spotlight followed Paul: **But Paul chose Silas and left. Silas** was a prophet

---

⁹J. B. Rotherham, *The Emphasized New Testament: A New Translation.*
¹⁰J. B. Phillips, *The New Testament in Modern English.*

(v. 32) and one of the "leading men" in the Jerusalem church—perhaps an elder in the congregation (see comments on v. 22). He had come to Antioch with Paul, Barnabas, and others to deliver the letter from the Jerusalem church. While in Antioch, he had done some preaching and teaching, encouraging and strengthening the brethren (v. 32). Apparently, Paul had been impressed with his ability and saw in him a kindred spirit. Therefore, when Paul considered who might replace Barnabas, his thoughts turned to Silas, who had evidently returned to Jerusalem (see comments on vv. 33, 34). Whether he later returned to Antioch or Paul had to send for him in Jerusalem, we do not know.

Silas was perfectly suited for Paul's purpose of visiting the churches established during the first journey. Like Paul, he could speak by inspiration, so he could share the work load. Like Paul, he was a Roman citizen (16:37), so he had the same political rights Paul enjoyed. He also had a qualification making him uniquely suited for the journey: He could confirm the genuineness of the letter from Jerusalem when it was delivered to the congregations (16:4) as he had at Antioch (15:22, 27).

Silas, also known as Silvanus, worked and suffered side by side with Paul through the second journey (16:19, 25, 29; 17:4, 10, 14, 15; 18:5). Second Corinthians 1:19 refers to his work in Corinth. Silas may have been Paul's penman when the apostle wrote the two letters to the Thessalonians from Corinth (1 Thess. 1:1; 2 Thess. 1:1). We do not know what Silas' relationship with Paul was after the second journey. We do know that Silas was later a coworker with Peter and served as the penman for Peter's first epistle (1 Pet. 5:12).

As Paul and Silas left, they were **committed by the brethren to the grace of the Lord.** Once more, in some fashion (formal or informal), the Antioch brethren sent Paul on his way with the blessings of the congregation and the blessings of the Lord.

Verse 41. Barnabas had taken Mark and sailed to Cyprus (v. 39), so Paul did not start by ship as on the first journey. Instead, he and Silas headed north and then west, visiting churches Paul had probably established during his ten or so years in Tarsus (see comments on 9:30; Gal. 1:21): **And he was traveling through Syria and Cilicia, strengthening the churches.** The letter from Jerusalem was addressed to those churches (v. 23); if the epistle had not been previously sent to them, Paul and Silas no doubt delivered it at this time. Paul may have made a visit to his hometown Tarsus while he was in Cilicia.

APPLICATION

Door-Slammers of Today (15:1–35)

In Acts 15, some of the Jewish Christians were trying to slam the "door of faith" shut, requiring Gentiles to become proselytes to Judaism before they could be accepted as Christians. The session in Jerusalem did not settle the matter for all time. It was not long until the same door-slammers (or their spiritual cousins) were traveling far and wide, telling Gentiles that they must be circumcised and keep the Law to be saved. Some of Paul's earlier letters—especially Galatians and Romans—deal extensively with this problem. Unfortunately, the spiritual offspring of these door-slammers have multiplied and continue with us today.

Law-Keeping Door-Slammers. For instance, we still have those today who teach that Christians need to keep all or part of the Old Testament. One religious group goes to the Old Testament to find authority for its holy places, a separate priesthood, the burning of incense, and the burning of candles. Another group goes to Exodus 20 to teach that the Christians' special day of worship is the seventh day, not the first day of the week. Many religious organizations base their ritualistic worship, including the use of instrumental music and choirs, on Old Testament procedures. Some have even used the Law to justify their practice of having multiple wives.

It is hard for some of us to understand how the Judaizing teachers in Acts 15—and the Law-binders of today—could make such a fundamental mistake. From childhood, some of us have seen the simple diagram showing that the old covenant was nailed to the cross (Col. 2:14, 16) and that the new covenant of Jesus went into effect when He died (Heb. 9:16, 17). What could be easier to understand?

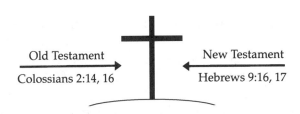

Old Testament
→
Colossians 2:14, 16

New Testament
←
Hebrews 9:16, 17

Regarding the Judaizing teachers in Acts 15, we must remember that Galatians and Romans had not yet been written—and that Jewish Christians were going through a transitional period concerning their understanding of the place of the Law. On the other hand, when we consider Law-binders today, we simply remark that they need to study Paul's letters carefully. In his letter to the Galatians, Paul emphasized that the Law had fulfilled its purpose and that we are no longer under its authority (Gal. 3:16, 19, 24, 25). In Romans, Paul stressed that "by the works of the Law *no* flesh will be justified in His sight" (Rom. 3:20; emphasis added), and in his letter to the Ephesians, he said simply, "*By grace* are ye saved" (Eph. 2:8; KJV; emphasis added).

Tradition-Binding Door-Slammers. Men trying to bind the law of Moses are not the only ones trying to slam the door on our spiritual freedom. The mention of the Pharisees in Acts 15 reminds us that the Pharisees had their manmade traditions that they considered as binding as the Scriptures. Jesus spoke of the teachings of the Pharisees when He said, "They tie up heavy burdens and lay them on men's shoulders . . ." (Mt. 23:4).

Traditions are not necessarily bad within themselves. Many of us have family traditions that give our families roots. In the Lord's church, traditional ways of working and worshiping can be used as long as those methods do not violate the Scriptures. However, when we equate our traditions with the Scriptures and attempt to bind our traditions on others, we are condemned by the words of Jesus in Matthew 15:9: "But in vain do they worship Me, teaching as doctrines the precepts of men."

The religious world today is full of the creeds of men, each of them bound on a segment of society. Some like it so. They find safety in letting others tell them what to do and what to think. It has been said, "There is a kind of security in slavery."

(Note the Israelites' attitude in Num. 11:1–6.) Let none of us exchange our freedom in Christ for the chains of manmade dogmas. Paul wrote, "It was for freedom that Christ set us free; therefore keep standing firm and do not be subject again to a yoke of slavery" (Gal. 5:1).

Jesus' warning against traditionalism is important, but some have taken the teaching to an extreme. They automatically equate "the way we have always done it" with "human tradition." This is true regarding many practices, but not all. Churches of Christ have *always* insisted on the Scriptures being taught, but that does not mean this is a human tradition that can be cast aside. Some activities that have "always been done a certain way" are done that way not because of human tradition, but because of divine tradition (2 Thess. 3:6). Beware of those who lump together everything that is commonly practiced, calling all of it "traditionalism." Each practice must be individually examined in the light of God's Word to decide if it is a human tradition or a divine tradition.

A special word of warning needs to be given in areas of the world just opening up to the gospel (see 20:28–31). Experience in the mission field teaches us that once the Lord's church is established in a new area and flourishes, it will not be long until men come to "spy out [the] liberty which [the new Christians] have in Christ Jesus, in order to bring [them] into bondage" (Gal. 2:4). In Acts 15, those who came to Antioch gained credibility because they were from Jerusalem. Today, some assume that any preacher who comes from America must be doctrinally sound (2 Tim. 4:3), but unfortunately it is not always so. Beware of anyone who tries to bind on the church, rules and regulations that originated in their own fertile imaginations and did not originate with God. In many areas of the Christian experience, we are free to use our best judgment as long as we can do so without violating basic biblical teaching. For instance, when God tells us *what* to do, but does not specify *how* to do it, we are free to use whatever method we think best. Do not allow anyone to slam this door of freedom.

Works-Oriented Door-Slammers. We cannot finish without mentioning one additional type of door-slammer: the salvation-by-works door-slammer. In some ways, this is the most subtle door-slammer of all; unlike those already mentioned, (1) he stresses that we are under the New Testament, not the Old; (2) he decries the traditions of men; (3) he teaches the commands of God as they are found in the New Testament, without addition or subtraction. All this we applaud—so where is the danger? The danger lies in the fact that this door-slammer emphasizes the obedience of man to the exclusion of the grace of God. He substitutes the commands of the Old Testament with those of the New Testament and proclaims that we will be saved by perfectly keeping all God has commanded in the New Testament.

This position is wrong for many reasons. First and foremost, it is wrong because the Bible does not teach it. In his sermon in Acts 15, Peter stressed that all of us are "saved through the grace of the Lord Jesus" (v. 11). This statement implied that Gentiles could not be saved by keeping the law of Moses. It also implies that men cannot be saved by law-keeping in general. Paul stressed this truth in Ephesians 2:8, 9: "For by grace you have been saved through faith; and that not of yourselves, it is the gift of God; not as a result of works, so that no one may boast." This teaching does not exclude the necessity of obeying God (Mt. 7:21–23; Heb. 5:8, 9), but it *does* exclude the possibility that any of us can earn our own salvation. No matter how much we do, we can never put God in our debt (Lk. 17:10). "Salvation is a matter of atonement, not attainment."

Peter said that the salvation-by-works position is wrong because it places "upon the neck of the disciples a yoke which neither our fathers nor we have been able to bear" (Acts 15:10). Even as every honest Israelite had to admit the impossibility of perfectly keeping the law of Moses, so every honest Christian must acknowledge the impossibility of perfectly keeping the commands of Christ. In some ways the requirements of Christ are harder than those of the Old Testament (see the "but I say to you" sections in Mt. 5). Even when we do our best, we will always fall short (Rom. 3:23; 7:15). If we believe that God will not save us unless we obey every commandment perfectly, at best we will be frustrated and at worst we will be devastated. The person who embraces this doctrine will always be saddled with a load of guilt. "Wretched man that I am!" he cries. "Who will set me free . . . ?" (Rom. 7:24). How liberating it is to realize, as implied in Peter's speech, that God does not look for perfection in our lives but for faith in our hearts (Acts 15:8, 9).

The faith God looks for is the kind that desires above all else to do the will of God (Rom. 1:5; Gal. 5:6; Jas. 2:26). Some individuals would reason, "I cannot save myself because I am saved by the grace of God. Therefore, there is no need to obey God." Such a person lacks saving faith; his heart is not right before God. Salvation by grace does not eliminate the need for obedience; but it *does* free us from the fearful bondage of expecting the impossible from ourselves—namely, a sinless life.

Anyone who declares that we must live perfectly to be saved has slammed the door of salvation in our faces; for although we do the best we can, we remain sinful people. Let us thank God for delivering us from salvation-by-works door-slammers.

Visualizing the Jerusalem Meeting (15:1–35)

You may want to take time to emphasize that the meeting in Acts 15 was not a denominational council or conference. The following diagram, illustrating a denominational conference, might be drawn on a chalkboard or an overhead transparency.

Note: The "C" in the diagrams stands for "congregation," and the "D" stands for "delegates." This diagram can be adapted to contrast Catholic Church councils with the Jerusalem meeting.

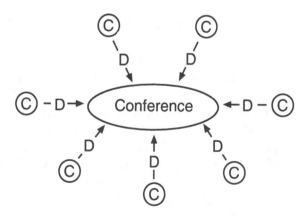

In contrast with the above, the meeting in Acts 15 did not involve (1) uninspired men, (2) representatives, and (3) matters of opinion, but rather (1) inspired men, (2) the "whole church," and (3) a matter of salvation. The following diagram notes that in Acts 15 one church sent men with a question to a church where inspired men resided.

$$\text{©} \xrightarrow[\text{a question}]{\text{men with}} \text{©} \quad \text{with inspired men}$$

The Jerusalem Meeting (15:1–35)

Warren Wiersbe outlined 15:1–35 with three "D's": (1) The Dispute (vv. 1–5), (2) The Defense (vv. 6–18), and (3) The Decision (vv. 19–35). Under the second division, he noted that Peter reviewed the past (vv. 6–11), Paul and Barnabas reported on the present (v. 12), and James related it all to the future (vv. 13–18).

Signing Boldly (15:1–35)

At noon on January 1, 1863, William Henry Seward, Abraham Lincoln's Secretary of State, brought Lincoln the Emancipation Proclamation to be signed. This document proclaimed that all slaves were freed. Lincoln picked up the pen twice, putting it down each time. He said to Seward, "I've been shaking hands since 9:00 this morning and my right arm is almost paralyzed. If my name should go down in history, it will be because of this document. If I sign it now and my hand shakes, they will examine the paper later and say, 'Lincoln hesitated; his heart wasn't in it.' I will not sign it until I can sign it boldly." When at last his hand was steady, he picked up the pen and slowly and firmly signed the document that forever said all men in this nation are free.[11]

When we examine the Acts 15 meeting, we see that Peter, Paul, Barnabas, and James boldly proclaimed that men are free

---

[11]This illustration was taken from Rick Atchley, "The Place of Grace," Sermon preached at the Southern Hills church of Christ, Abilene, Texas, on 13 April 1986.

in Christ. We should proclaim that same freedom with boldness today.

Dealing with Controversy (15:1, 2)

In dealing with church controversy, one must first determine the nature of the disagreement. Are we talking about a doctrinal dispute (as was the case in chapter 15), or are we talking about someone's feelings being hurt (as was the case in chapter 6)? Genuine doctrinal disputes in a congregation are few and far between, but occasionally they do occur. When that is the case, Jude's admonition is appropriate: "Contend earnestly for the faith which was once for all handed down to the saints" (Jude 3). For this reason, "Paul and Barnabas had great dissension and debate" with the false teachers (15:2).

Most congregational controversies involve personalities more than principles. Sometimes there is a difference of opinion on how something should be done. Sometimes someone thinks (rightly or wrongly) that he has been mistreated. In most cases, if the matter is handled scripturally, only a handful of people are involved. Often times, however, the disputants line up people on their sides, and full-scale congregational disputes result. Those who engage in ungodly congregational maneuverings need to remember that high on God's hate-list is "one who spreads strife among brothers" (Prov. 6:16, 19). We usually say that "God hates sin, but not the sinner." In this case, the text says God hates *the individual* "who spreads strife among brothers." Being a spiritual troublemaker is a grievous sin indeed.

If an essential doctrinal principle is involved, we must follow Paul's example and not "yield . . . for even an hour, so that the truth . . . would remain" (Gal. 2:5). On the other hand, if the conflict is over hurt feelings or matters of opinion, let us "pursue the things which make for peace and the building up of one another" (Rom. 14:19). Let us be ready to forget our bruised egos and be prepared to yield to the wisdom of others. The peace and harmony of the church for which Jesus died (Acts 20:28) is infinitely more important than our feelings and opinions.

When controversy arose in the church in Antioch, "the brethren determined that Paul and Barnabas and some others of them should go up to Jerusalem to the apostles and elders concerning this issue" (15:2). This occasion was a special situation involving a biblical principle and inspired men (the apostles). For the brethren in Antioch to check with the apostles in Jerusalem would be basically equivalent to our checking with the New Testament when an issue arises today. We can also draw from the text another general principle: Although each congregation is autonomous (self-ruling) (see the comments on 20:28), it is permissible and sometimes expedient for the leaders of a congregation to call on outside help to resolve an issue.

Usually, this is done indirectly, as those involved in a conflict seek advice from godly men whose judgment they respect. Occasionally, however, direct help is sought. There have been congregational meetings in which respected brethren from the area were asked to mediate between opposing views. Those visiting brethren had no authority to make decisions for the congregations involved, but they could see the situations more clearly than those enmeshed in the controversies. Another "direct" way outside help is sometimes sought is that the leaders of a congregation may ask a guest speaker to preach a lesson or series of lessons on a doctrinal or practical issue that is troubling the congregation. Done with an attitude of humility and love, this can sometimes calm troubled waters.

Handling Conflict (15:1, 2)

The way some "handle" conflict is to ignore it, maybe even denying that any conflict exists. Counselors call this "the withdrawal approach" and say that the person who uses this approach has little or no respect for himself or the one with whom he has the conflict. This approach seldom, if ever, resolves an issue. When false teachers came from Jerusalem (v. 1), Paul and Barnabas did not just ignore the problem, hoping it would go away. Rather, they dealt with it (v. 2). Controversy in a congregation must be dealt with sooner or later—and it is much easier sooner than later (see comments on 6:1–7).

Some individuals take an extreme "withdrawal" approach to conflict, withdrawing themselves permanently from congregations where problems exist. We find no indication that anyone in the Antioch congregation said, "If those church folks are going to fuss and fight, I am leaving!" Before we can help deal with controversy in a congregation, some of us need first to deal with our own attitudes toward controversy. Most of us do not like trouble, but when it shows up in our congregation, we need to help resolve it, not run from it.

Issues or Individuals? (15:6–29)

How many times did Peter name the troublemakers who went to Antioch (vv. 6–11)? The answer is "zero times." Look at the speeches of Paul, Barnabas, and James (vv. 12–21). How many times did those men name the Judaizing teachers? The letter to the church in Antioch mentioned "some of our number ... [who] ... disturbed you" (v. 24), but not one individual was singled out by name. Peter, Paul, Barnabas, and James concentrated on the issues, not individuals. Name-calling seldom produces good. Since inspired writers sometimes mention opponents by name (1 Tim. 1:20; 3 Jn. 9), we cannot discount the possibility that there may be occasions to mention false teachers by name. However, *the Holy Spirit* told New Testament writers the right time to do it. Calling names typically produces great harm. It detracts from the issue, and it can create gulfs as uncrossable as the chasm of Luke 16:26. Learn from our text: Deal with principles, not personalities.

Outlining the Public Meeting (15:6–29)

The public meeting of verses 6 through 29 could be outlined as follows: (1) Peter's Reasoning (vv. 7–11), (2) Barnabas and Paul's Report (v. 12), and (3) James' Recommendation (vv. 13–29).

Do the Prohibitions Apply to Us? (15:20, 29)

Scholars do not agree as to what extent the prohibitions of Acts 15:20, 29 were bound on the early church. Some ("Side 1") say that the prohibitions were only for a special situation. Others ("Side 2") insist that the prohibitions were universal and should be observed today.

Side 2 points to the word "essentials" in 15:28 ("necessary things"; KJV), but Side 1 says that this could mean "essential for Jewish and Gentile Christians to have fellowship" rather than "essential for salvation." Side 2 says, "The fact that the Holy Spirit incorporated the letter in the Book of Acts shows that He intended for us to follow its instructions," but Side 1 insists that this is not necessarily so. Side 1, rather, suggests that the account of Acts 15 has been recorded (1) as an important part of the history of the early church and (2) to teach us in a *general* way how to handle problems.

Side 1 notes that the letter was addressed to a limited audience (15:23), but Side 2 emphasizes that the letter was taken farther than that (16:4, 6). Furthermore, Side 2 observes that each of Paul's letters was addressed to a limited audience (Rom. 1:7; 1 Cor. 1:2), but the instructions in those letters still apply to us today. Side 1 asks, "If the Acts 15 letter was intended to be universal, why did Paul not mention the letter when he wrote to the Galatians about the same subject discussed at the Jerusalem meeting: the binding of circumcision on Gentile Christians? Why, when he wrote to the Corinthian Christians, did he make the eating of meat sacrificed to idols an optional matter instead of absolutely prohibiting it as was done in the Acts 15 letter?" Side 2 replies, "Paul's letter to the Galatians emphasized that the original apostles had contributed nothing to his understanding (Gal. 2:6). It would have been counterproductive to mention the ruling of the original apostles. Paul's letter to the Corinthians began by saying Christians had a right to eat meat sacrificed to idols, but it finished by saying that to avoid causing others to stumble, Christians should *not* eat meat they knew had been sacrificed to idols (1 Cor. 10:23–33). In other words, Paul reached the same basic conclusion given in the Acts 15 letter: "For the sake of others, do not eat meat sacrificed to idols."

Most agree that the New Testament in general condemns fornication and eating meat sacrificed to idols (1 Cor. 10:19–21; 1 Thess. 4:3, 5; Rev. 2:14, 20). The majority of the disagreement, therefore, centers on the prohibition to eat/drink blood, which is not mentioned elsewhere in the New Testament. This practice was condemned before the law of Moses was given (Gen. 9:4) and also in the Law (Lev. 17:8–16). Reasons for this prohibition include the stated theological reasons and an unstated practical reason: to prevent the spread of disease.

Since the eating/drinking of blood was condemned before the Law was given, it seems to be a general principle that God has always desired. Most of us, therefore, do not eat or drink blood. We cannot, however, be dogmatic on the point. "Each person must be fully convinced in his own mind" (Rom. 14:5).

(Even if the prohibition not to eat/drink blood applies today, the prohibition does not forbid blood transfusions as the Jehovah's Witnesses claim.)

The Value of a Letter (15:22–29)

Letters can undoubtedly have value. (Twenty-one of the twenty-seven books of the New Testament are letters.) It is often good to "get everything down in writing." On the other hand, letters can fuel the flames of controversy instead of extinguishing them—especially letters written in the heat of passion. Letters have built-in shortcomings. If the reader misunderstands the intent of the letter, the writer is not there to explain what he really meant. If the letter contains words that can be taken as criticism, those words are not "said" once as they would be in a face-to-face discussion. Rather, the recipient invariably reads them over and over again, becoming more unhappy each time. A third shortcoming is that controversial letters can be saved, filed, and shared with any number of people—spreading the controversy like a prairie fire.

If you are involved in a church controversy, the following advice concerning letters may be helpful: (1) If you *must* write a letter, do so with the sensitivity of those who composed the letter from Jerusalem. As a general rule, do not write a letter while you are upset; or if you do, wait several days before you send it and then reread it carefully and prayerfully several times before sending it. (2) If it is at all possible to talk directly with the other party, do *not* write a letter. Someone may object, "But I can't think when I confront someone. I express myself better in a letter." Then learn from the brethren in Jerusalem: Write your letter, but deliver it *in person*; be there to explain and answer questions as it is read. In your dealings with others, always keep the personal touch.

This discussion says nothing about sending anonymous letters. Surely every Christian realizes that few acts are more cowardly than sending a letter of criticism anonymously.

The Benefits of Controversy (15:30–35)

Believe it or not, good can come from controversy (Rom. 8:28)—if we maintain positive attitudes and handle the matter in the right way. Controversy may bring into the open problems that should have been dealt with long ago. Controversy may force us to restudy issues—and bring us closer to an understanding of the will of God. Controversy may force us to work on relationships that we have neglected. Verses 30 through 35 tell of the positive results from the proper handling of the Acts 15 controversy: (1) There was rejoicing (v. 30); (2) God's Word continued to be preached (v. 32); (3) Relationships between the Jews and the Gentiles were strengthened (v. 33).

Disagreements Between Brethren (15:36–41)

It is tempting to stop and speculate on what Paul and Barnabas could have and should have done. It is hard not to think that if they had followed the principles found earlier in chapter 15, they might have worked out their differences. However, Luke only recorded a brief summary of what happened and did not give sufficient information for us to play judge and jury. We will, therefore, simply look at several basic truths from the story regarding differences between brethren:

(1) *Brethren always have disagreed and always will disagree at times—even good brethren.* It is especially true that there will be disagreements when two strong-willed persons work together—and preachers tend to be strong-willed. Paul and Barnabas were both good men, but they disagreed. Someone has said that if two people always agree, there is no need for one of them. Nothing is wrong with disagreement as long as the disagreement does not get out of control and as long as the disagreement is over matters of opinion. We should agree on basic doctrine (1 Cor. 1:10), but we do not have to agree on matters of opinion (Rom.

14). We cannot, of course, commend the *"sharp* disagreement" between Paul and Barnabas.

(2) *In most disagreements, both parties are partly in the right and partly in the wrong.* When we study the story of Paul and Barnabas' disagreement, invariably we ask the question "Who was right, and who was wrong?" One person says, "I think Paul was right. I've been where he was—and I tell you that you can't lean on a broken straw!" Someone else responds, "No. Barnabas was right—because Mark turned out to be a great worker for the Lord!" Luke does not say who was right and who was wrong. The fact the Antioch brethren gave Paul and Silas a formal send-off (15:40) may imply that they took Paul's side, but that is inconclusive. At least they did not censure him for his position.

Both were wrong in allowing the disagreement to get out of control. In another sense, both were right; Paul and Barnabas were looking at the matter from two different points of view. Paul saw the question of taking John Mark from the standpoint of the mission; Barnabas saw it from the standpoint of the man. Paul was fearful that taking Mark might discourage other team members and might jeopardize the mission. The work of confronting false teachers in Galatia would not be easy, and Paul probably thought there was a possibility that Mark would turn back again. Barnabas was fearful that *not* taking Mark might discourage him and jeopardize the man. "Paul looked at people and asked, 'What can they do for God's work?' while Barnabas looked at people and asked, 'What can God's work do for them?'"[12] *Both* points of view are needed in the work of the Lord.

In the United States, we have a legal tenet like this: "When two people disagree, both cannot be right. One can be right and the other wrong, or both can be wrong, but both cannot be right." Biblically, this tenet may hold true in matters of doctrine, but it does not hold true in matters of opinion. It will greatly enhance our relationships if we acknowledge the right of others to disagree in matters of personal preference—and maybe even admit the possibility, slight though we think it may be, that others could be right.

---

[12]Wiersbe, 466.

(3) *Sometimes, in spite of multiplied efforts, all attempts at reaching an agreement fail, and brethren simply have to "agree to disagree."* We would prefer for this not to be the case, but it is. When this happens, it is not the greatest tragedy in the world, nor necessarily the end of a friendship—as long as both parties conduct themselves as they should.

(4) *Even when brethren cannot agree, they should still act like Christians.* Paul's admonition to the Ephesians should be required reading when strong-willed brethren discuss their differences:

> When you are angry, do not sin, and be sure to stop being angry before the end of the day. . . . When you talk, do not say harmful things, but say what people need—words that will help others become stronger. . . . Do not be bitter or angry or mad. Never shout angrily or say things to hurt others. . . . Be kind and loving to each other (Eph. 4:26, 29, 31, 32; NCV).

Someone has said, "We can disagree without being disagreeable."

How did Paul and Barnabas conduct themselves when they could not agree? First, they did not quit serving the Lord. Too often, one brother becomes upset at another brother and then takes it out on the Lord. Second, they did not try to destroy one another's influence. We find no indication that Paul circulated a letter in Galatia questioning Barnabas' soundness, or that Barnabas sent an article to the *Cyprus Informer* denouncing Paul's lack of compassion. Third, they held no grudges, and since they did not, time probably healed the breach. Paul referred to Barnabas when he later wrote to the Corinthians (1 Cor. 9:6). The reference implies that no hard feelings lingered; it may even indicate that they later worked together again. May God help us to learn from Paul and Barnabas when we disagree with a brother in the Lord.

(5) *If we conduct ourselves as Christians, God can overrule our shortcomings and bring good from the disagreement.* The immediate result of Paul and Barnabas' disagreement was that, not one,

but two mission teams went out. It would be presumptuous to suggest that the Holy Spirit prompted the whole episode to get two teams into the mission field, but it is not out of line to suggest that God overruled the unpleasantness and caused good to come from it (Rom. 8:28). The Paul/Barnabas disagreement has been reenacted many times on modern mission fields: Two men are unable to work together, so they agree that they should work in separate areas. Most of the time, the parting is congenial and the end result is the establishment of two congregations instead of one—congregations in full fellowship with each other.

Because both Paul and Barnabas continued to serve God in spite of their differences, there were also positive long-range results. Both men were blessed by God in their efforts. Exciting and fruitful days were ahead for Paul and his new team of workers. At the same time, Barnabas' efforts to help Mark realize his full potential as a servant of the Lord were unbelievably successful. According to uninspired tradition, Mark went to Alexandria in Egypt and established the work there.[13] Whether that is true or not, we know that Mark was later a coworker with Peter (1 Pet. 5:13) and that he wrote the Gospel of Mark. Eventually, he reconciled with Paul. Mark was with Paul during his first imprisonment in Rome. Paul referred to him as a fellow worker "for the kingdom of God" and noted that Mark had "proved to be an encouragement" (Col. 4:10, 11; see Philem. 24). Most revealing, however, is Paul's plea to Timothy, written during his second imprisonment, shortly before his death: "Only Luke is with me. Pick up Mark and bring him with you, for he is useful to me for service" (2 Tim. 4:11). At one time Paul thought Mark was useless; in the end he found him useful. It is wonderful that God can use imperfect people!

Drawing Chalk Lines (15:36–41)

There is a story about two sisters who long ago had a petty disagreement; neither could remember what it was about. Although they lived in the same house, they had not spoken to each other for years. They had drawn a chalk mark that divided

---

[13]*The Teaching of the Apostles.*

their house in two parts—through the middle of doorways, through the middle of the fireplace. They cooked in the same kitchen, ate at the same table, slept in the same bedroom. At night they could hear one another breathing, but all communication had been destroyed.

"How sad," you might say, but all around the world, families, communities, even churches have chalk marks drawn down the middle. No, we are not speaking of visible chalk marks, but chalk marks of the mind. We refer to people who will have nothing to do with other people because of disagreements of the past. If you ever find yourself in that situation, do all you can to erase those chalk marks. "Do your best to live at peace with everyone" (Rom. 12:18; NCV).

The Dialogue Between Paul and Barnabas (15:37, 38)

Barnabas kept insisting that they should take Mark, while Paul kept insisting they should not. We are not given the exchange, but it is not hard to imagine:[14]

Barnabas: I really think we ought to give Mark another chance.

Paul: No. The Lord said, "No one, after putting his hand to the plow and looking back, is fit for the kingdom of God" (Lk. 9:62).

Barnabas: He also said, "Blessed are the merciful, for they shall receive mercy" (Mt. 5:7).

Paul: This trip won't be easy, and we must be able to depend on everyone who goes. The Wise Man said, "Like a bad tooth and an unsteady foot is confidence in a faithless man in time of trouble" (Prov. 25:19).

Barnabas: If you are going to appeal to the Scriptures, don't forget the stories of David, Jonah, and others. If God is willing to give people a second chance, why shouldn't we?

---

[14]This idea was suggested by an imagined exchange by Rick Atchley, "When Brothers Get Off the Mark," Sermon preached at the Southern Hills church of Christ, Abilene, Texas, on 4 May 1986.

Paul: You wouldn't be standing up for Mark if he weren't your cousin! (See Col. 4:10.)

Barnabas: You aren't my cousin, and I stood up for you in Jerusalem—remember? (See Acts 9:26, 27.)

Rebuilding the Team (15:40, 41)

Being part of a team has value for one who is going to preach the gospel in a new field. When Jesus sent out workers, He sent them in pairs (Mk. 6:7; Lk. 10:1). As a rule, Paul did not attempt to work by himself. Athens was an exception, but that was due to the circumstances—and the results were less than satisfactory (17:16–34). There have been those who took their families into hard fields to work alone. Their courage and dedication were admirable, but often the results were tragic: Workers became discouraged and quit, marriage relationships were impaired, and children were lost to the Lord.

When Paul started on the first journey with Barnabas and John Mark, he probably thought that he was part of a team that would be together indefinitely. However, it was not long until Mark left (13:13). Then, as Paul contemplated the second journey, he and Barnabas had "a sharp disagreement" and went their separate ways (v. 39). Paul had to rebuild the team. Following the example of Paul (1 Cor. 9:24–27), an athletic analogy is used here. If you are interested at all in sports, you know that every few years it is necessary to rebuild a team: In high school and college, players graduate; in the professional ranks, players go to other teams or retire. You also know that it is hard to find quality players to replace those who leave. Paul's rebuilding effort was infinitely more important than rebuilding a sports team; he had to find the right ones, or the Lord's work would suffer. He faced a monumental task.

Paul's second missionary journey was one that took him into far-flung areas he had never dreamed of evangelizing. In the early stages of this journey, Paul gathered around him a new team of coworkers, most of whom would stay with him for the rest of his life. Timothy and Luke continued to work with Paul until his death. They became more than his team; they became his closest friends.

CHAPTER 16

PAUL'S SECOND MISSIONARY JOURNEY (PART 2)

ANOTHER TRAVELING COMPANION (TIMOTHY) (16:1–3)

¹Paul came also to Derbe and to Lystra. And a disciple was there, named Timothy, the son of a Jewish woman who was a believer, but his father was a Greek, ²and he was well spoken of by the brethren who were in Lystra and Iconium. ³Paul wanted this man to go with him; and he took him and circumcised him because of the Jews who were in those parts, for they all knew that his father was a Greek.

Verse 1. With their task in Syria and Cilicia completed, Paul and Silas headed west. Leaving the lowlands of Cilicia, they crossed the rugged Taurus Mountains through the pass known as the Cilician Gates. Although Luke did not give this detail, for all practical purposes this was the only way from Cilicia to Galatia. At last they reached the plateau of Southern Galatia, where Paul had labored on the first journey: **Paul came also to Derbe and to Lystra.** Since Paul came from the east instead of the west, Derbe is mentioned before Lystra. As Paul labored in Derbe, we wonder if anyone asked him about Barnabas—and, if they did, what he answered.

When Paul reached Lystra, **a disciple was there, named Timothy.** If only verse 1 were considered, Timothy could conceivably be from either Derbe or Lystra, although the natural antecedent of "there" is Lystra. However, when verse 2 is also considered, we can be confident that Timothy was from Lystra, for only Lystra and Iconium are mentioned. If Timothy were from Derbe, we would have the unlikely situation of his being well spoken of in Lystra and Iconium, but not in his hometown.

At this point in the narrative we are introduced to the man who became "the dearest friend [Paul] ever knew,"[1] "the son in the faith he never had in the flesh."[2] Timothy was **the son of a Jewish woman who was a believer.** We know from 2 Timothy 1:5 that Timothy's mother was named Eunice and that he also had a godly grandmother named Lois. From his childhood, these two godly women had taught Timothy the Scriptures (2 Tim. 3:15), instilling in him a deep faith in God and His Word (2 Tim. 1:5). It is likely when Paul came to Lystra the first time, Eunice and Lois were converted. Paul never specifically said that Lois had become a Christian as Eunice had, but this is implied in 2 Timothy 1:5. It was probably on that same visit, young Timothy, still a teenager, was also baptized (see comments on 14:20a). McGarvey estimated his age at fifteen on Paul's first missionary journey. Since, almost twenty years later, Timothy was still referred to as "young" (1 Tim. 4:12), he must have been *very* young when he first met Paul.

It should be noted that Eunice and Lois had to "train up [Timothy] in the way he should go . . ." (Prov. 22:6) by themselves—with little or no help from others. Lystra had no synagogue, no rabbi to teach Timothy (see comments on 14:7). Further, Eunice was married to a Gentile husband: Timothy's **father was a Greek.** Since marriages were normally arranged in those days, we assume this was not Eunice's decision, but that of her father. Because Timothy's grandfather is not held up by Paul as a good influence on young Timothy, it can be assumed that he arranged the marriage to a Gentile for financial reasons. Eunice's husband did not share her faith and probably actively opposed the practice of her religion. Since Lois and Eunice are

---

[1]J. W. McGarvey, *New Commentary on Acts of Apostles*, vol. 2 (Delight, Ark.: Gospel Light Publishing Co., n.d.), 47.

[2]Ken R. Durham, "Scenes at Philippi," *Acts, the Spreading Flame* (Searcy, Ark.: Harding University, 1989), 187.

pictured by Paul as exemplary in their love for the Scriptures, the most likely explanation for the fact that Timothy was not circumcised is that his father had forbidden it. In those days, wives normally had no choice but to do what their husbands ordered.

Verse 2. From time to time, missionaries and preachers return to places where they have worked. Invariably, the experience fills them with both sadness and joy. They are saddened to learn of those who have fallen away, but thrilled to see how others have grown spiritually. Paul must have been delighted to see the progress made by the young man Timothy. Still in his late teens or early twenties, he was already **well spoken of by the brethren who were in Lystra and Iconium.** Since Iconium was some distance from Lystra, Timothy had been active in the Lord's service over a wide area. Perhaps he already had a reputation as a preacher. (In the 1950's and 60's, it was not uncommon for young men in their late teens to preach every Sunday for a congregation.) At some point, elders laid their hands on him (1 Tim. 4:14). "[T]here can be no reasonable doubt that this ceremony on the part of the eldership was intended to set him [Timothy] apart to the work of preaching; for there is no other purpose that can account for it."[3] This event probably took place at Lystra and may have occurred before Paul arrived.

Timothy was surely still ragged around the edges, as all young preachers are. In addition to that, he was timid. Many commentators think that passages such as 1 Corinthians 16:10 and 2 Timothy 1:6, 7 suggest this. Yes, the Lord can use timid people, even in teaching and preaching (Phil. 4:13). Timothy also suffered from a variety of physical ailments (1 Tim. 5:23). Nevertheless, Paul saw amazing potential in him and longed to have him as part of his team. Paul desired to do with Timothy what Barnabas wanted to do with Mark: train him for greater service in the kingdom. Perhaps Paul even envisioned Timothy as the man who could someday take his place (2 Tim. 2:2).

Verse 3. Paul wanted this man to go with him. Timothy was still a young man, and his father was probably dead. In the

---

[3]McGarvey, 81.

47

phrase "his father was a Greek," the verb "was" (ὑπῆρχεν, hupērchen; from ὑπάρχω, huparchō) is in the imperfect tense, likely meaning that Timothy's father was alive in the past, but not the present.[4] Therefore, Eunice had to make the decision whether or not to let Timothy travel with Paul. For a moment, put yourself in that mother's place: You can still hear the howling mob crushing the life from Paul. You can close your eyes and still see his broken body covered with blood (14:19, 20). Now this man, who often has to live like a hunted animal, comes to you and says, "I would like your son to come with me and share my life." The fact that Eunice allowed him to go, knowing the dangers involved, fills us with admiration for her.

Timothy joined the team; the twosome became a threesome. Paul then did something startling, almost shocking: **And he took** Timothy **and circumcised him.** Is this the same Paul who fought the Judaizing teachers who said a man had to be circumcised to be a Christian (15:2)? Is this the same Paul who refused to allow Titus to be circumcised when they traveled to the Jerusalem meeting (Gal. 2:3)? Is this the same Paul who wrote to the churches of Galatia, "If you receive circumcision, Christ will be of no benefit to you" (Gal. 5:2)? Is this the same Paul who was carrying a letter from Jerusalem to inform the churches that circumcision was not bound on Christians (16:4)?

We need to understand why Paul would not allow Titus to be circumcised and why he believed it important that Timothy be circumcised. Consider the differences between the two cases. Let us start with Titus: Titus was a Gentile (Gal. 2:3), and the Judaizing teachers were insisting that he be circumcised to be saved (15:1). If Paul had permitted Titus to be circumcised, this would have been tantamount to saying the teachers of error were right—and Paul could not sanction that. Paul did not allow Titus to be circumcised *as a matter of principle.*

On the other hand, Timothy had a Jewish background (16:1), and the matter of his salvation was not in question. Our text

---

[4]I. Howard Marshall, *The Acts of the Apostles*, The Tyndale New Testament Commentaries, gen. ed. R. V. G. Tasker (Grand Rapids, Mich.: Wm. B. Eerdmans Publishing Co., 1980), 259.

tells us why Paul had him circumcised: **because of the Jews who were in those parts, for they all knew that his father was a Greek. Greek** probably just means "Greek-speaking Gentile." Since Timothy's mother was a Jew, Timothy was considered a Jew by Jewish people. Their pragmatic philosophy was "You can't be sure who a baby's father is, but you always know who the mother is. Therefore, if the mother is a Jew, the baby is a Jew." However, since he was not circumcised, he was technically an apostate Jew. As we have seen, when Paul entered a new city, if the town had a synagogue, he started his work there. If Timothy were not circumcised, he would possibly not be allowed in the synagogue.[5] Further, if the Jews thought that Paul countenanced Timothy's apostasy, he would not be allowed in the synagogue either. Paul had Timothy circumcised *as a matter of expediency*. Circumcision itself was a matter of indifference to Paul (Gal. 5:6; 6:15); it was wrong only if it were bound on people as a condition of salvation. Keep in mind that the practice of circumcision predated the Law (Jn. 7:22); it was practiced by the Israelites long before Moses gave the Law. "Timothy's circumcision was a minor surgical operation carried out for practical purposes—his greater usefulness in the ministry of the gospel."[6]

Before we leave the matter of Timothy's circumcision, we should take note of the compliance of the young man himself. Circumcision may have been "a minor surgical operation," but it was still painful—not to mention acutely embarrassing. If Timothy had been like some young people today, he might have said, "Nobody can *make* me do that!" or "Show me the Scripture that says I *have* to be circumcised!" Timothy did not have to submit to the pain and embarrassment; it was his choice. It is doubtful that anyone could have physically forced Timothy to be circumcised. Further, he did not have to submit to circumcision to be saved. He *did* have to submit to circumcision to be Paul's traveling companion—but no one was forcing him to go with

---

[5] F. F. Bruce, *The Book of the Acts*, The New International Commentary on the New Testament, gen. ed. F. F. Bruce, rev. ed. (Grand Rapids, Mich.: Wm. B. Eerdmans Publishing Co., 1988), 304.

[6] Ibid.

Paul. Why did he allow himself to be circumcised? For the good of the work of the Lord and to be a better influence. Rebellious youths who embarrass their families and the church by their dress and demeanor could learn from young Timothy.

Once Timothy was circumcised, Paul was ready to resume his journey with the added advantage of training a young man to continue his work when he was no longer able. Few works are more vital than that of training young men and women to serve the Lord. (Regarding training young women, see Tit. 2:3–5.) In addition, few ways are more effective than one-on-one, on-the-job training. We often refer to this situation as "the Paul-Timothy arrangement."

"THROUGH THE CITIES" (16:4, 5)

⁴Now while they were passing through the cities, they were delivering the decrees which had been decided upon by the apostles and elders who were in Jerusalem, for them to observe. ⁵So the churches were being strengthened in the faith, and were increasing in number daily.

Verse 4. It was time for the team to move on. Perhaps at this time the elders of the Lystra church laid their hands on Timothy (1 Tim. 4:14). At some point, Paul also laid his hands on him (2 Tim. 1:6), no doubt to give him miraculous abilities. Perhaps the elders and Paul had a joint service, setting Timothy apart for the work ahead and preparing him for that work. (It is also possible that Paul did not lay hands on Timothy until later, after Timothy had proven himself.) Can you imagine the farewell scene as young Timothy, holding back tears, pulled himself away from his mother, waved to the brethren at Lystra, then followed Paul and Silas down a dusty road to an unknown future?

The men traveled north, then west, visiting churches established on the first journey—in Iconium, Antioch of Pisidia, and perhaps elsewhere. We are not sure if other congregations were established (see 13:13, 14; 14:24, 25). **Now while they were passing through the cities, they were delivering the decrees which had been decided upon by the apostles and elders who were** in Jerusalem, for them to observe (see comments on 15:23–29). Notice the word **they** in this verse. In 15:40 through 16:3, the singular "he" was used—emphasizing the work of Paul. However, 16:4 emphasizes that "they" delivered the decrees: Silas fulfilled his unique purpose of confirming that the decrees were indeed from the apostles in Jerusalem.

Verse 5. They were passing through the region where once Paul had been chased out of town and where the citizens had tried to kill him. This time, however, the missionaries seem to have had a peaceful ministry—and God blessed their mission. **So the churches were being strengthened in the faith.** This was the primary stated purpose of Paul's visit (15:36). The churches were generally "strengthened in the faith" through the teaching and encouragement given them by Paul and Silas. They were also specifically "strengthened in the faith" by having Judaizing teachers in the area exposed as false teachers. In addition, the churches **were increasing in number daily.** This statement is another one of Luke's "progress reports." Note that when the churches were "strengthened," they increased in number daily.

TO TROAS: THE "MACEDONIAN CALL" (16:6–10)

⁶**They passed through the Phrygian and Galatian region, having been forbidden by the Holy Spirit to speak the word in Asia; ⁷and after they came to Mysia, they were trying to go into Bithynia, and the Spirit of Jesus did not permit them; ⁸and passing by Mysia, they came down to Troas. ⁹A vision appeared to Paul in the night: a man of Macedonia was standing and appealing to him, and saying, "Come over to Macedonia and help us." ¹⁰When he had seen the vision, immediately we sought to go into Macedonia, concluding that God had called us to preach the gospel to them.**

Verse 6. Paul was so encouraged by the success of the work in Phrygia and Galatia that he looked for new fields in which to plant the seed of the gospel. To the west was Asia, the leading and most prosperous province in the eastern part of the Roman

Empire. Paul and his company headed for the heart of Asia, to the city of Ephesus, "that great metropolis in which the East looked out upon the West."[7] It seems obvious from subsequent events that this was their destination (18:19–21; 19:1). To their surprise, God blocked their way, and they had to alter their course. **They passed through the Phrygian and Galatian region, having been forbidden by the Holy Spirit to speak the word in Asia.** We do not know how the Holy Spirit conveyed His message; perhaps it was through prophetic utterance (see 20:23; 21:4, 10, 11). Regardless of the means, God left no doubt in their minds: They were not to go to Asia at this time. Paul did work later in Asia (ch. 19), so this was a "not now" answer rather than an unequivocal "no." God had closed the door for the moment, but He would open it later (1 Cor. 16:8, 9).

Verse 7. And after they came to Mysia, they were trying to go into Bithynia, and the Spirit of Jesus did not permit them. When they reached the region of Mysia, they decided to go north into the rich, important Roman province of Bithynia; but again this was not the Lord's plan. This region was evangelized later, perhaps by Peter (see 1 Pet. 1:1). **The Spirit of Jesus** is the same as "the Holy Spirit" mentioned in verse 6. This unique phrase, found nowhere else in the Scriptures, is perhaps used here to stress that Jesus Himself was personally and vitally involved in the carrying out of His Great Commission.

Verse 8. They could not go south into Asia; they could not go north into Bithynia. Unless they admitted defeat and turned back, the only direction they could go was west. No doubt puzzled and perplexed, they at last reached **Troas**, a Roman colony and busy seaport a few miles from the ruins of ancient Troy. As they stood on the shore, looking out at the beautiful blue of the Aegean Sea, they no doubt wondered why they were there and what God wanted them to do. They did not seem to think that God's plan at that time was for them to evangelize Troas. At least, they evidently did not preach there. Later, a church was established in Troas (20:6–12; see 2 Cor. 2:12). Their

---

[7]F. J. A. Hort, *Prolegomena to Romans and Ephesians* (London: n.p., 1895), 83.

minds probably whirled with questions as they went to bed, but they did not have long to wonder. In the night God gave them their answer.

Verse 9. A vision appeared to Paul in the night (see comments on 10:3). Whether Paul was awake or asleep, we do not know. In the vision, there was **a man of Macedonia.** The translation "a certain man of Macedonia" (NASB 1977) is supported by the original text. The word "certain" (τις, *tis*) has led to speculation as to who this "certain man" might be. We have no idea if this was someone who might be recognized by Paul or not. Macedonia was the northern portion of Greece made famous by Philip II of Macedon and his son Alexander the Great. Macedonia was northwest of Troas, reachable by ship across the upper part of the Aegean Sea.

This man from Macedonia **was standing and appealing to Paul, and saying, "Come over to Macedonia and help us."** Paul was from the eastern part of the Roman Empire, and it seems apparent that the idea of taking the gospel to the West was not part of his immediate plans. Consider these facts: (1) Paul first tried to go into the province of Asia and then the province of Bithynia, both in the East. There was sufficient territory in the East to occupy Paul for years, perhaps for the rest of his life. (2) Paul only headed west when the Lord would not allow him to go elsewhere. (3) Even when Paul was standing on the shore in Troas, looking in a westward direction, it still took a special vision from the Lord to convince him that he could and should take the gospel across the Aegean Sea to a new culture and a new people.

Verse 10. When he had seen the vision, immediately *we* sought to go into Macedonia concluding that God had called *us* to preach the gospel to them (emphasis added). Dr. Luke, the author of Acts, used two personal pronouns to introduce himself into the story. Paul found his fourth team member at Troas.

How did Paul meet Luke? The most natural explanation is that Paul and Timothy went looking for a doctor and found Luke. Between the two of them, they had a range of maladies. Other suggestions include these: Luke was waiting for a ship to return to his hometown of Philippi; Luke was looking for a job as a ship's doctor; Luke headed a delegation from Philippi that went to Troas to try to persuade Paul and the others to come to his town. This last suggestion is highly unlikely. However it happened, in the providence of God, Paul found another man who would be a valuable member of his team.

We could say much about Luke. As noted in the *Introduction, The Penman,* he was a Gentile—probably a Greek (Col. 4:10, 11, 14), traditionally from Antioch—and had not been an eye-witness of Jesus' life (Lk. 1:2). He was a learned and intelligent man, trained as a physician (Col. 4:14); and after Paul laid his hands on him, he was an inspired man. As Paul's traveling companion, he showed himself a brave coworker and a committed church builder (2 Tim. 4:11; Philem. 24).

Luke served in at least two other important roles: He became Paul's personal physician and faithful friend. In 2 Corinthians, Paul spoke both of his mental anguish ("the daily pressure" of caring for "all the churches" [11:28]), and his physical anguish (his debilitating "thorn in the flesh" [12:7–9]). Luke was "the man who kept Paul going." When Paul and company sailed from Troas, the threesome had become a foursome. Paul's ideal team was complete. His companions were a diverse group, including a prophet, a preacher, and a physician, but all were committed to a common cause.

Once Paul received the vision, he wasted no time sharing it with his companions. In the vision, commonly referred to as the "Macedonian Call," the man from Macedonia had simply said, "Come . . . *help* us." Paul and the others, however, concluded that God had called them "*to preach the gospel* to them" (emphasis added). The fact that Luke said, "God . . . called *us* to preach" indicates that to some extent Luke was capable of preaching (see the word "we" in v. 13). Immediately, they started looking for a ship going from Troas to Macedonia. In the providence of God, it was not long until one was available. When one responds to God's call, God will be with him and bless his efforts.

At last the gospel was going to Europe. The ancients recognized a great difference between the East and the West. Even today, travelers notice that the cultures of Turkey (where the ruins of Troas are) and Greece are strikingly different. When Paul and his coworkers answered the Macedonian Call, they *did* open a new field to evangelism. It is possible, even probable, that there were Christians in Rome before Paul went to Macedonia (2:10), but there is no evidence of systematic evangelization of the western part of the Roman Empire until Paul and his companions went to Macedonia.

SAILING TO MACEDONIA (16:11, 12)

¹¹So putting out to sea from Troas, we ran a straight course to Samothrace, and on the day following to Neapolis; ¹²and from there to Philippi, which is a leading city of the district of Macedonia, a Roman colony; and we were staying in this city for some days.

Verse 11. At this point Luke recorded details of the voyage. **So putting out to sea from Troas, we ran a straight course to Samothrace. Samothrace** was a mountainous island about halfway between Troas and their destination. They probably anchored near Samothrace the first night. The fact that they were able to run **a straight course** indicates that the wind was behind them. This trip from Troas to Neapolis took only two days. Later, a return trip over the same course took five days (20:6). God was hastening them to their destination.

It is fascinating to look back and see how seemingly small events affect subsequent history. The voyage from Troas to Macedonia covered about 150 miles and took only two days, but the course of human events was forever changed. If this trip (or one like it) had not been made, churches in the Eastern world would probably be sending missionaries to the Western world today.

The next day, Paul and his company came **to Neapolis.** "Neapolis" combines the Greek word for "new" (νέος, *neos*) with the word for "city" (πόλις, *polis*). Thus "Neapolis" means "New City." Today the city is called Kavalla, which means "mare." Neapolis served as the seaport for Philippi, which was nine or ten miles inland. Running through Neapolis was the famed

Egnatian Way. Parts of this ancient stone highway have been excavated and the ruts worn by ancient vehicles can still be seen. This Roman thoroughfare began at the Adriatic Sea. (Immediately across the Adriatic Sea was Italy and the beginning of the Appian Way that led to Rome [28:15].) The Egnatian Way stretched across Macedonia to Neapolis and on to Byzantium. Byzantium was later known as Constantinople; today it is called Istanbul.

Verse 12. The missionaries wasted no time getting on the famed highway and heading west-northwest for **Philippi.** They would have climbed the ridge north of Neapolis, and then headed down into the plain of Philippi. We have no record that they preached in Neapolis at this time. Paul probably reasoned that if the Word was established in Philippi, it would naturally spread to Neapolis.

Since the man in the vision simply said, "Come over to Macedonia" (v. 9), why did Paul and the others go to Philippi instead of some other part of the province? No doubt, they were depending on the guidance of the Lord. The first ship they found heading to Macedonia went to Neapolis. Since Macedonia stretched to the west of Neapolis along the Egnatian Way, they may have taken this as a sign that they should get on that highway and head across Macedonia, evangelizing major cities as they went. Philippi was the first major city.

Philippi is described by Luke as **a leading city of the district of Macedonia, a Roman colony.** Scholars disagree over the meaning of the phrase **a leading city.** The KJV has "the chief city," but no definite article appears in the original text. The words could not mean the capital of Macedonia, for Thessalonica was the capital of the entire province. The phrase could not even mean the capital of the subdistrict in which Philippi was located, for Amphipolis had that honor. Probably Luke simply meant that, comparatively speaking, Philippi was important in the area in which it was located. Another possibility is that Luke was merely locating the city in the first **district of Macedonia.** Macedonia was divided into four districts, and Philippi was in the first one on the east.

Of greater significance to our study is the phrase **a Roman**

colony. The original text has only "colony," but Luke's readers would have understood that a *Roman* colony was meant. To understand the significance of the phrase "a Roman colony," we need to know something of the history of Philippi.

Philippi was originally the village of Crenides, meaning "springs." (The present-day village of Krinides is near the ruins of Philippi.) Philip II of Macedon became interested in the area because of a gold-bearing mountain there. He fortified the city and renamed it Philippi. Later, a famous battle that determined the fate of the Roman republic was fought in the plains outside Philippi. (Shakespeare referred to this battle in the play *Julius Caesar*.) There, Octavian (Augustus) and Antony defeated Brutus and Cassius, the murderers of Julius Caesar. When Augustus became emperor (Lk. 2:1), he made Philippi a Roman colony. The city was then known as Colonia Julia Augustus Philippensium. Luke used the common name of the city, Philippi. Six cities mentioned in Acts were Roman colonies: Antioch of Pisidia, Lystra, Troas, Philippi, Corinth, and Ptolemais. However, the only one so designated by Luke was Philippi. This was probably not by accident. The words may be the key to the puzzle as to why God did not allow Paul to preach in Asia at the time, but insisted on his coming to Macedonia.

A Roman colony enjoyed many privileges. Among other benefits, the people were self-ruling and did not have to pay taxes to Rome. A Roman colony was, in effect, a piece of Rome transplanted to foreign soil. Rome sent many army veterans to Roman colonies, where they enjoyed special privileges. Having these retired soldiers in their midst reminded the inhabitants of the entire region of the ever-presence of Rome. The citizens wore Roman clothing, spoke Latin instead of Greek, observed Roman customs, and were fiercely patriotic (vv. 20, 21). In some ways a Roman colony was more Roman than the city of Rome. Rome itself had a cosmopolitan character, blending many cultures. For instance, it had many Jews and many synagogues (18:2; 28:17). In contrast, Philippi had few Jews, if any, and probably no synagogue. In Philippi, Paul was immersed in Roman culture in a way he had never been before. We have previously seen Paul in Roman colonies; but these were in the East, and most had the leavening effect of a Jewish synagogue.

Paul's success in this intensely Roman environment may have planted in his mind the idea of evangelizing Rome. Previously, Paul had been satisfied to preach the gospel in a variety of major cities and let the Word spread from them to outlying areas. At some point, he came to the realization that if the work of the Lord were firmly established in Rome, it would not merely spread a few hundred miles in every direction, but throughout the empire. Therefore, he made plans to go to Rome (Rom. 1:9–13; 15:22–29). Perhaps his desire to travel to Rome originated in Philippi. Perhaps that was why God was insistent on Paul's going there. The Macedonian call was more than a call to a single Roman province; it was a cry for help from a world lost in sin. Philippi represented the even greater challenge of reaching the entire Roman Empire.

The missionaries stayed in Philippi **for some days.** We do not know for how long, but during that time Paul and the others converted a number of people (v. 40). They established a church that became a favorite of Paul—the congregation he probably felt closer to than any other. The church at Philippi was the one congregation constantly concerned about Paul's welfare. Later, Paul wrote the Philippians a letter of love (Phil. 1:3–5; 4:1).

IN PHILIPPI: THE CONVERSION OF LYDIA'S HOUSEHOLD (16:13–15)

¹³**And on the Sabbath day we went outside the gate to a riverside, where we were supposing that there would be a place of prayer; and we sat down and began speaking to the women who had assembled. ¹⁴A woman named Lydia, from the city of Thyatira, a seller of purple fabrics, a worshiper of God, was listening; and the Lord opened her heart to respond to the things spoken by Paul. ¹⁵And when she and her household had been baptized, she urged us, saying, "If you have judged me to be faithful to the Lord, come into my house and stay." And she prevailed upon us.**

Verse 13. The congregation began in an inauspicious way.

As far as we know, Philippi had no synagogue. The word προσευχή (*proseuchē*), translated **place of prayer** (see v. 16), is sometimes used in ancient literature to indicate a "synagogue." However, Luke usually used the word συναγωγή (*sunagōgē*) to refer to a Jewish house of prayer. Since only ten men were required to form a synagogue, this tradition indicates there were few Jews in the city, if any. Paul, therefore, could not begin his work by going to the synagogue as he normally did. Knowing Paul, if he and the others arrived in Philippi several days before the Sabbath, they probably did general preaching (as they did in Lystra where there was no synagogue) while trying to find out if there were any Jews in the area.

When the first **Sabbath day** arrived, Luke noted: **We went outside the gate to a riverside, where we were supposing that there would be a place of prayer.** During the Exile, when the Jews could not go to the temple, they formed the habit of gathering beside the nearest river to pray (Ezra 8:15, 21; Ps. 137:1)—perhaps so the river could be used for ceremonial washings. Near Philippi was the Gangites River, about a mile west of the city gates. Other rivers and streams outside Philippi include the Krenides. Paul and the others headed for one of these riversides to see if they could find any believers in the true God.

The text in verse 13 is uncertain at this point. The phrase **we were supposing** (ἐνομίζομεν, *enomizomen*, from νομίζω, *nomizō*) is one possibility. Some Greek manuscripts have "it was customary" (ἐνομίζετο, *enomizeto*) for there to be a place of prayer. Another reading is "it seemed" (ἐδόκει, *edokei*, from δοκέω, *dokeō*) there was a place of prayer.

When they arrived at the river, they found several women who had gathered to pray. We do not know if they were in the open air, under a shelter, or in a house close to the river. Luke did not say whether they were Jews, proselytes, or God-fearers; probably they were either proselytes or God-fearers (see comments on 2:9–12; 10:2). The language used to describe Lydia in verse 14 would suggest this. She is called a "worshiper of God" (see 13:43, 50; 17:4, 17; 18:7). Whether or not the missionaries were disappointed that no men were there, we do not know. Luke simply reported, **We sat down and began speaking to the**

women who had assembled. Jewish teachers normally sat when they taught (Mt. 5:1). Surely the presence of these God-fearing women at the riverside Sabbath after Sabbath was partial reason for God's making sure that Paul and the others reached Philippi when they did. It is noteworthy that a *man* from Macedonia called the missionaries (v. 9), but their first converts were *women*.

Verse 14. Among the women was **a woman named Lydia**, a common name in the first century world. This woman was **from the city of Thyatira**, a city located across the Aegean Sea in the Roman province of Asia. Thyatira lay in the territory of the ancient kingdom of Lydia and was later the site of one of the seven churches of Asia (Rev. 1:11; 2:18–29). We can see a touch of irony in the fact that, after Paul was not allowed to go into Asia (v. 6), his first convert in Philippi was from Asia.

Lydia was a businesswoman who had come from Thyatira to Philippi to sell her wares. She was **a seller of purple fabrics** (πορφυρόπωλις, *porphuropōlis*). *Porphuropōlis* is a compound word combining πορφύρα (*porphura*), "purple," and πωλέω (*pōleō*), "to sell." *Porphura* ("purple") referred to a purple shellfish, as well as the purple dye extracted from the fish. The word *porphura* was also used to refer to fabric dyed with purple; this last usage is the meaning of the word in the New Testament (Mk. 15:17, 20; Lk. 16:19; Rev. 17:4; 18:12). Historically, Thyatira was noted for the production of purple cloth. Purple fabric was outrageously expensive. Only kings and the very rich could afford to wear "the royal purple" (Lk. 16:19). This fact, plus the details that Lydia owned a large house (large enough to occupy herself, her household, and four missionaries) and probably had servants (v. 15), indicates that the Lord had blessed her materially. She was representative of the more wealthy of society in Philippi.

More important is the fact that Lydia was **a worshiper of God** (σεβομένη τὸν θεόν, *sebomenē ton theon*). This phrase is used several times in Acts to refer to God-fearers and proselytes (see comments on v. 13). Worship evidently meant more to her than business. The Sabbath Day was not a sacred holiday in Philippi; it was just another day to make money. Worshiping

God meant that Lydia was willing to close her shop, giving her competition an advantage. Jews in foreign cities closed their shops on the Sabbath; Lydia must have done the same. The indication is that Lydia's servants, who might have kept the shop open, were with her beside the river.

The most important fact about Lydia, however, is that she was willing to listen and learn when God's truth was presented. In many ways Lydia is the feminine counterpart of "righteous and God-fearing" Cornelius, who told Peter, "We are all here present before God to hear all that you have been commanded by the Lord" (10:22, 33). Luke said that she **was listening and the Lord opened her heart to respond to the things spoken by Paul.** The Greek word ἤκουεν (*ēkouen*, from ἀκούω, *akouō*) translated **was listening** is in the imperfect tense, indicating that she kept listening. F. F. Bruce translated the verb as "listened carefully." Although all were speaking (v. 13), **Paul** seems to have been the chief speaker (see 14:12).

We must pause to comment about the words **the Lord opened her heart.** This phrase is unique to the conversion of Lydia; in no other case of conversion has it been said that the Lord opened the hearts of the listeners. What is the significance of this expression?

Verse 14 has been used by Calvinists[8] to "prove" their doctrine of the "direct operation of the Holy Spirit" on the heart of the alien sinner. They believe that a man is born in sin, unable to respond in any way to the call of the gospel until the Holy Spirit performs a miracle on his heart. This doctrine is called "total hereditary depravity." It is not taught in the Scriptures (see Ezek. 18:20; Mt. 18:3). Notice, however, that Lydia was able to listen attentively to Paul *before* her heart was opened; no Calvinist doctrine is taught in the passage. Therefore, we ask again, "What is the significance of this expression?"

It is common for Luke to emphasize that *God* did something when, in actuality, He did it *through an agent.* For instance, when

---

[8]A Calvinist is one who accepts the basic tenets of John Calvin, a prominent religious leader during the Protestant Reformation. Many denominations accept some of Calvin's positions.

Paul and Barnabas returned from the first journey, they reported to the church at Antioch "all things that God had done with them and how He had opened a door of faith to the Gentiles" (14:27; see 15:4). Notice first the words "all things God had done." Then notice the agency used: "with them." God converted many Gentiles—but He did it *through* the preaching of Paul and Barnabas. In 15:12 similar terminology is used, and the agency is indicated by the words *"through* them." For an Old Testament example, notice Psalm 105:41: God "opened the rock"—but He did so *through* the agency of Moses' action (Ex. 17:1–7).

It seems obvious from the text that God opened the heart of Lydia *through* the preaching of the gospel: She "was *listening; . . . to the things spoken by Paul"* (emphasis added). The Macedonian Call served the same purpose in the conversion of Lydia that the direction of the Spirit did in the conversion of the eunuch and the vision did in the conversion of Cornelius: It got the sinner and the preacher together (Rom. 1:16, 22; 10:13–17; Eph. 6:17; Heb. 4:12; Jas. 1:21). Some believe that the phrase "opened her heart" is used to indicate that in some way Lydia had closed her heart. Probably, however, her heart was not closed because of any prejudice she possessed, but simply closed because of her ignorance. A knowledge of the truth opened her understanding. R. C. H. Lenski stated, "The Lord opens the heart, but the hand with which he lifts the latch and draws the door is the Word . . . and the door opens as we heed. . . ."[9] God did not do anything for Lydia that He had not done for all other sinners in the cases of conversion we have studied. ". . . God is not one to show partiality . . ." (10:34). Lydia was saved exactly as all others in Acts were saved: She heard the Word; the Word touched her heart (see 2:37); faith was produced, and obedience followed.

This view still does not explain why Luke chose to use the expression "the Lord opened her heart" instead of stating that Lydia was moved by the Word. Luke probably used this terminology because he saw the hand of *God* in all that had happened: It was *God* who prevented them from going into Asia or Bithynia.

---

[9]R. C. H. Lenski, *The Interpretation of the Acts of the Apostles* (Columbus, Ohio: The Wartburg Press, 1944), 658.

It was *God* who gave them the vision in Troas. Further, *God's* providence brought them to the receptive hearts at the riverside, and *His* Spirit inspired their preaching. It was not Paul, Silas, Luke, or Timothy who opened the heart of Lydia; God alone deserved the credit. Never forget: We may plant and water, but only God gives the increase (1 Cor. 3:6; KJV).

Verse 15. Lydia **and her household had been baptized.** This statement probably indicates that most, if not all, of the other women present by the riverside were part of her household—probably her servants. Water for immersion was readily at hand, and they doubtless went immediately into the river to be baptized into Christ. These women were probably baptized by Silas, Luke, or Timothy. As a general rule, Paul did not do the baptizing (1 Cor. 1:14–17).

Before we leave the riverside, let us examine the phrase **and her household.** Four "household baptisms" are explicitly recorded in the New Testament: Cornelius and his household (10:24, 48), Lydia and her household (16:15), the Philippian jailer and his household (16:31–34), and the household of Stephanas (1 Cor. 1:16; 16:15). A fifth is implied: Crispus and his household (18:8; 1 Cor. 1:14). These "household baptisms" are used as a "proof" by those who attempt to justify infant baptism by the Scriptures. They reason that "surely in at least one of these households, there was an infant." However, in four of the five cases, the text makes clear that all in the household were old enough to respond personally to the preaching (10:33, 43, 44, 46–48; 16:34; 18:8; 1 Cor. 16:15). This fact leaves the baptism of the household of Lydia as their primary "proof."

Does the baptism of Lydia's household prove that infants should be baptized? Consider the assumptions of those who find a baby among those baptized that day: (1) They assume that Lydia was married or had been married. (Today in many societies, you would not automatically assume a woman with a baby was or had been married, but in those days you would.) (2) They assume that she had children. (3) They assume that at least one of her children was an infant. (4) They assume that Luke included that infant in the "household" that was immersed despite the fact that everywhere else Luke stressed that one must believe before being baptized (2:37, 38; 8:36–38). Allow an individual four assumptions, and he can "prove" almost anything. That is *not* the way to discover truth. The text itself gives no reason at all to believe an infant was immersed that day.

A final quality of Lydia's character must be noted: She was hospitable (see Rom. 12:13; 1 Pet. 4:9). After Lydia and her household had been baptized, **she urged us, saying, "If you have judged me to be faithful to the Lord, come into my house and stay."** Paul probably had mixed emotions about accepting the invitation. On the one hand, staying in a Christian home was greatly to be preferred over lodging with pagans. On the other hand, there was the question of propriety: How would it look if four men stayed in a house full of women? Lydia, however, would not take "no" for an answer. Luke said, **And she prevailed upon us.** For the remainder of Paul's stay in Philippi, Lydia's home was his base of operations (v. 40).

IN PHILIPPI: THE HEALING OF A POSSESSED GIRL; IMPRISONED (16:16–24)

[16]It happened that as we were going to the place of prayer, a slave-girl having a spirit of divination met us, who was bringing her masters much profit by fortune-telling. [17]Following after Paul and us, she kept crying out, saying, "These men are bond-servants of the Most High God, who are proclaiming to you the way of salvation." [18]She continued doing this for many days. But Paul was greatly annoyed, and turned and said to the spirit, "I command you in the name of Jesus Christ to come out of her!" And it came out at that very moment.

[19]But when her masters saw that their hope of profit was gone, they seized Paul and Silas and dragged them into the market place before the authorities, [20]and when they had brought them to the chief magistrates, they said, "These men are throwing our city into confusion, being Jews, [21]and are proclaiming customs which it is not lawful for us to accept or to observe, being Romans." [22]The crowd rose up together against them, and the chief magistrates tore their robes off them and proceeded to order them to be beaten with rods. [23]When they

had struck them with many blows, they threw them into prison, commanding the jailer to guard them securely; [24]and he, having received such a command, threw them into the inner prison and fastened their feet in the stocks.

Verse 16. Luke moved immediately to an incident near the end of Paul's initial work in Philippi: **It happened that as we were going to the place of prayer, a slave-girl having a spirit of divination met us, who was bringing her masters much profit by fortune-telling.** Luke continued to use the first person (**we, us**) to indicate that he was present when these events happened. **The place of prayer** probably refers to the banks of the river where the missionaries had met Lydia and the other women (v. 13). Perhaps they were going there to pray; perhaps they were going there to see if they could find other honest hearts. As they went on their way, they met a certain **slave-girl**. To move from the story of Lydia to the story of this slave-girl is to move from the upper class of society to the very lowest class of society. A slave was not considered a person; a slave was property—like one's house, furniture, or tools.

This particular slave had **a spirit of divination**. The Greek text has πνεῦμα πύθωνα (*pneuma puthōna*), "a pythian spirit." "Pythian" is from "python," a very large snake that coils itself around its victims and crushes them. In Greek mythology, the god Apollo had slain the python, and the spirit of the python had then taken control of the female oracle at Delphi. Consequently, when people believed that a woman had powers similar to those of the Delphi oracle, they said she had "the pythian spirit." According to at least one ancient writer, the term "python" was also used to refer to "a ventriloquist," and that fact is often pointed out by modern writers. However, it is possible that they misunderstand what the term "ventriloquist" meant in those days. Today we use the term to refer to one who can "throw his voice," and that would have been a useful skill for a charlatan to have: He could have made it appear that images were speaking, that the gods were speaking from above, and so forth. However, the word "ventriloquism" literally means "to speak from the belly." In Bible times, it probably referred to the superstition that spirits took over the bodies of the oracles and spoke from inside them, that is, from their bellies. Luke's use of the phrase "pythian spirit" does not mean that he believed the superstitious tale; he was using accommodative language. The poor girl had an unclean spirit, such as were recorded earlier in Acts; she was possessed by a demon (see comments on 5:16; 8:7). Apparently, demons instinctively knew some facts mortals did not know, and this unnatural knowledge impressed the crowds. This kind of knowledge is evident in our present story. Under the influence of the unclean spirit, the girl knew that Paul and the others were servants of the Most High God. Note that demons were *not* omniscient (all-knowing). It does not, however, take much to impress those who want to believe in fortunetellers. Thus the demon-possessed girl was able to bring her masters **much profit by fortune-telling**.

Verse 17. When the missionaries met the girl with the unclean spirit, they apparently tried to ignore her. The girl refused to be ignored. She followed them and **kept crying out, saying, "These men are bond-servants of the Most High God, who are proclaiming to you the way of salvation."** Her words remind us of the words of the Gerasene demoniac who called Jesus "Son of the Most High God" (Mk. 5:7). The demon that possessed the slave-girl knew who the missionaries were and their purpose for being in Philippi. The term "most high god" was also used by the Greeks to refer to Zeus. The Greek word σωτηρία (*sōtēria*), translated **salvation**, also had a variety of meanings. It is possible, therefore, that those who heard the girl misunderstood the full significance of her words. However, since the New Testament indicates that demons were very aware of the true God and His servants, it is unlikely that she had pagan concepts in mind as she referred to Paul and the others. James said that "the demons . . . believe, and shudder" (Jas. 2:19).

Verse 18. She continued doing this for many days. Every day, wherever Paul and his companions went, this slave-girl was there, loudly proclaiming to the crowd: "These men are bondservants of the Most High God." Finally, he could stand it no more; **Paul was greatly annoyed.** The phrase "greatly annoyed" is translated from the Greek word διαπονέομαι (*diaponeomai*).

This word also appears in 4:2 when the Jewish leaders were "greatly disturbed" because of the preaching of Peter and John. In both cases where the word is used, there was a constant aggravation. Paul **turned and said to the spirit, "I command you in the name of Jesus Christ to come out of her!"**

This passage produces two questions: (1) Why was Paul annoyed when she was speaking the truth? Paul evidently did not want it to appear that the missionaries had some alliance with a demon-possessed individual. Such an impression could reflect favorably on her and unfavorably on them. During His ministry, Jesus had not allowed demons to testify on His behalf either (Mk. 1:23–25, 34). (2) If this explanation is correct, why did Paul wait so long to cast the demon from her? Perhaps he anticipated the consequences (v. 19). The girl was valuable property. If he cast out the demon, in the eyes of the owners he would be destroying valuable property.

Whatever Paul's thoughts were, he finally took pity on the girl. He commanded the spirit in the name of Jesus to leave— and it did **at that very moment**. Can you imagine how that girl felt? For years, she had been the prisoner of a dark spirit; now she was free! For years, her mind had been the playground of evil; now she was in her right mind (see Mk. 5:15)! We wish we knew what became of her. We would like to think that she acted on the truths she had spoken earlier and became a Christian. Luke, however, immediately shifted the attention from her to her masters (v. 19). Nevertheless, we have seen the change that took place in her life.

Verse 19. The girl's **masters saw that their hope of profit was gone.** Luke used a play on words: In the Greek text, the word ἐξῆλθεν (*exēlthen*, from ἐξέρχομαι, *exerchomai*), translated "came out" in verse 18, is also used in verse 19 where it is translated "was gone." Luke literally said that when the unclean spirit left, their profit left. If you want to make a man your enemy, hit him in his pocketbook.

The owners of the slave-girl **seized Paul and Silas**. We do not know why they seized Paul and Silas and did not seize Luke and Timothy. Probably Paul was the one they were after, and Silas just happened to be with Paul when they grabbed him.

The owners of the slave-girl **dragged them into the market place before the authorities.** The word translated **authorities** (ἄρχοντας, *archontas*) is different from the one translated "chief magistrates" (στρατηγοῖς, *stratēgois*) in verse 20, leading to speculation that they were first taken before minor officials and then before the chief officials. The words, however, could just be two ways of speaking of the same men. The **market place** was the city square, a large expanse of stone paving surrounded by stately columns, marble buildings, shops, and temples. The phrase "market place" does not refer to a noisy bazaar filled with hawkers and shoppers. The biblical "market place" was more like the stately town square of a prosperous city. The Greeks called it "the agora" (ἀγορά); the Romans called it "the forum." The forum in Philippi has been excavated. It is large, about half the length of a U.S. football field. On the north side was a large marble platform used for speech-making and ceremonies. On this occasion, it served as the judgment seat. The Greek word for this platform was βῆμα (*bēma*) (see comments on 18:12).

Verses 20, 21. The masters of the slave-girl brought Paul and Silas **to the chief magistrates.** Once more Luke used exactly the right political term to refer to the local authorities. "Chief magistrates" is translated from στρατηγοί (*stratēgoi*), which means the "generals." This word is an appropriate term for the chief city officials of a Roman colony.

The slave-owners said nothing about the real reason for their citizens' arrest of Paul and Silas—their financial loss. Instead **they said, "These men are throwing our city into confusion, being Jews, and are proclaiming customs which it is not lawful for us to accept or to observe, being Romans."** The accusers of Paul and Silas pulled three effective emotional triggers. The first was decency and order: **"These men are throwing our city into confusion."** To some extent, their coming had upset the city of Philippi. Maintaining public order was a prime objective of Roman law. During Jesus' ministry, the chief priests and Pharisees feared that His following would create such a disturbance that the Romans would come and destroy the Jewish temple and dissolve their nation (Jn. 11:47, 48). The second trigger was anti-Semitism: **"These men are . . . Jews."** Jews were obviously not popular in Philippi; for that matter, they were not favorites anywhere in the Roman Empire. In chapter 18 we read that Jews had been expelled from Rome (v. 2). The third trigger was nationalism: **"These men . . . are proclaiming customs which it is not lawful for us to accept or to observe, being Romans."** Remember that citizens in Roman colonies were often more Roman than those in Rome itself.[10]

Verse 22. A trial in the market place always attracted a crowd (see comments on 17:5). The accusations had been calculated to agitate the listeners and they had the desired effect. **The crowd rose up together against** Paul and Silas. To placate the mob, perhaps to avoid a riot, **the chief magistrates tore** Paul and Silas' **robes off them and proceeded to order them to be beaten with rods.**

The beatings would have been administered by the men called "policemen" in verses 35 and 38. The KJV calls these men "sergeants"; the NIV calls them "officials." None of these translations fully expresses the idea of their function. The Greek word translated "policemen" is ῥαβδοῦχοι (*rhabdouchoi*), which literally means "rod-bearers." The word "rod" (ῥάβδος, *rhabdos*) is combined with the verb "to hold" (ἔχω, *echō*). The Romans called them "lictors." These men accompanied the magistrates and carried with them a bundle of wooden rods tied with red cords. These sticks were about a thumb's thickness. In the center of the rods was an ax. This bundle served representatively as the symbol of Roman authority, and practically as the means of administering instant Roman justice. This symbol—a bundle of sticks with an ax in the middle—exists today in statuary in several parts of Europe. For years, this symbol could be seen on the back of the U.S. dime. It was also the symbol used in Italy during World War II by Mussolini, as he tried to capitalize on the mystique of the long-gone Roman Empire.

Verse 23. In Roman beatings, the guards stripped the clothing from the one to be punished, exposing the back. Often the victim was stripped naked and the rods laid on his body from head to foot. Jewish whippings were limited to thirty-nine stripes

---

[10]Adapted from Durham, 189.

(2 Cor. 11:24); the number of strokes in Roman beatings was at the discretion of the official in charge. Luke said simply that **they . . . struck them with many blows.**

It should be noted that it was illegal to beat a Roman citizen. Cicero said, "It is a misdeed to bind a Roman citizen, a crime to scourge him, almost parricide to put him to death."[11] Why, then, did not Paul and Silas inform the magistrates of their Roman citizenship (v. 37) and escape the mistreatment? Perhaps they tried, but the authorities could not hear them; after all, the circumstances were chaotic. Some have suggested that Paul waited until verse 37 to speak of his Roman citizenship so the fact would carry more political weight. It seems more reasonable that Paul would have tried to identify himself as a Roman citizen when he and Silas were beaten, but for some reason, he was either not heard or not believed. It is possible that the magistrates pronounced the sentence and then immediately left to get away from the ugly scene. Take note of this beating; it has special significance, for it is the first persecution of Christians instigated by Gentiles.

After the beating, **they threw them into prison, commanding the jailer to guard them securely.** We are thus introduced to the third person in chapter 16 whose life was changed by the Lord. It was the practice of Rome to send retired soldiers to populate its colonies, so some speculate that this jailer was a veteran of the Roman army. He represents the sturdy middle class in Philippi.

Verse 24. The jailer was told to "guard [Paul and Silas] securely." Does his excessive zeal in carrying out that charge indicate that he had a touch of the sadistic in his nature? Perhaps, or it may just indicate that he was conscientious about doing his job. At any rate, **he, having received such a command, threw them into the inner prison.** The **inner prison** was without fresh air and light; it was reserved for the most hardened and dangerous of criminals. Think of a dungeon—dark, dank, dirty, rat-infested—and you will not go far wrong. The jailer was not satisfied with that measure of security, however. He also **fastened**

---

[11]Cicero *Against Verres* 2.5.66.

their feet in the stocks. Victims were seated on the floor, their legs spread apart as far as they could go, and then their feet fastened in the stocks. The foot stock was not merely a contraption to constrain; it was also a tool to torture. Whatever else the jailer had learned in the army, he had not learned kindness.

Paul and Silas sat in the oppressive darkness, their feet imprisoned, cramps starting up their legs, unable even to lay back because of the deep bloody gashes on their backs (v. 33). The discomfort and distress were etched on Paul's soul. He later wrote of being beaten with rods (2 Cor. 11:25). This beating at Philippi was only one of the beatings he had to endure. Paul also wrote of his suffering and mistreatment in Philippi (1 Thess. 2:2).

Slowly, so slowly, the hours crept by. When nighttime came, the jailer went to sleep, his slumber undisturbed by any remorse over the mistreatment of his prisoners. The fact that the jailer apparently had his sword on his person (v. 27) indicates he was probably asleep on duty, fully dressed, inside the prison. It is possible, however, that he was asleep in his living quarters nearby, perhaps on the prison grounds, and grabbed his belt and scabbard on his way out of the apartment. After what would have seemed an agonizing eternity to Paul and Silas, the midnight hour arrived.

IN PHILIPPI: THE CONVERSION OF THE JAILER'S HOUSEHOLD (16:25–34)

[25]**But about midnight Paul and Silas were praying and singing hymns of praise to God, and the prisoners were listening to them;** [26]**and suddenly there came a great earthquake, so that the foundations of the prison house were shaken; and immediately all the doors were opened and everyone's chains were unfastened.** [27]**When the jailer awoke and saw the prison doors opened, he drew his sword and was about to kill himself, supposing that the prisoners had escaped.** [28]**But Paul cried out with a loud voice, saying, "Do not harm yourself, for we are all here!"** [29]**And he called for lights and rushed in, and trembling with fear he fell down before Paul and Silas,** [30]**and after he brought them out, he said, "Sirs, what must I do to be saved?"**

³¹They said, "Believe in the Lord Jesus, and you will be saved, you and your household." ³²And they spoke the word of the Lord to him together with all who were in his house. ³³And he took them that very hour of the night and washed their wounds, and immediately he was baptized, he and all his household. ³⁴And he brought them into his house and set food before them, and rejoiced greatly, having believed in God with his whole household.

Verse 25. What if we had been in that inner prison, our backs in shreds, our feet in stocks—what would we have been doing at midnight? Crying? Complaining? Luke wrote, **But about midnight Paul and Silas were praying and singing hymns of praise to God.** Instead of singing "the blues," Paul and Silas sang praises. Do not think that Paul and Silas sang because their bodies had ceased to cry for relief. They sang in spite of their circumstances. Does the fact that Luke mentioned their singing at **midnight** mean that Paul and Silas had to work on their attitude awhile before they could pray and sing? We do not know. Anyone can sing God's praises when things are going well; it takes faith to sing praises to God when everything is going wrong. Faith in God is the key. God remains the same. If He is worthy of our praise when everything seems to be right in our lives, He is also worthy of praise when everything seems to be going wrong. Paul later challenged Christians in Ephesus to sing "to the Lord; *always giving thanks for all things*" (Eph. 5:19, 20; emphasis added). Paul demonstrated that quality in a prison cell in Philippi.

Luke noted that the other **prisoners were listening to them.** The other prisoners had doubtless heard cries and curses from the inner prison; never before had they heard prayers and praise.

Verse 26. The midnight concert was unexpectedly interrupted as **suddenly there came a great earthquake, so that the foundations of the prison house were shaken.** Philippi was located in earthquake territory. Wherever one travels throughout Turkey and Greece today, he can see evidence of massive earthquakes of the past. We do not know what this earthquake would have registered on the Richter Scale, but one that could shake the stone foundations of the prison had to be great indeed. The earthquake was so violent that it sprung the doors and cracked the walls, releasing the bolts that held the prisoners' fetters. **And immediately all the doors were opened and everyone's chains were unfastened.** The earthquake may or may not have been a natural phenomenon, but no one in the prison would have doubted that it was sent from heaven in response to the songs in the night. One way or another, angels were probably involved—as they were in two previous divine releases from prison (5:19; 12:7, 10, 11).

Verse 27. The quake jarred the jailer out of a sound sleep. He sprang to his feet and in the dim light could see the gates ajar. **When the jailer awoke and saw the prison doors opened, he drew his sword and was about to kill himself, supposing that the prisoners had escaped.** If one had charge of a prisoner and allowed that prisoner to escape, Roman law decreed that the one in charge must receive the punishment the prisoner would have received (see comments on 12:19). Apparently, one or more of the prisoners in the jail had been sentenced to die. If they had escaped as the jailer thought, he would be executed in their stead. Deciding to take what he considered "the honorable way out," the warden was about to commit suicide.

This type of thinking was a pagan philosophy, not a biblical philosophy. Suicide has never been "the honorable way out" for God's people. Psychologists tell us that people commit suicide because they believe that every door has been closed to them except the door of death. Children of God know, however, that no matter how bad their situations become, God will always provide a "way of escape" so that they "will be able to endure" their pain (1 Cor. 10:13).

Verse 28. As the jailer raised his sword to plunge it into his chest, **Paul cried out with a loud voice, saying, "Do not harm yourself, for we are all here!"** How could Paul see the jailer and the jailer not see him? How did Paul know that no one had escaped? Since these details were not pertinent to Luke's story, he did not tell us. Perhaps Paul's eyes were better adjusted to the darkness than the jailer's eyes. God may have given Paul supernatural knowledge of the situation.

Verse 29. The jailer was incredulous, so **he called for lights.** This detail indicates that other guards were on duty, or at least were nearby. Then the jailer **rushed in** to see for himself. To his amazement, Paul's words were true. Why did the other prisoners not escape when they had a chance? Perhaps they were momentarily stunned by what had happened. Perhaps Paul asked them to stay and they were afraid not to comply with his request. Perhaps God kept them where they were by His power. Again, this detail is not pertinent to Luke's story, and he did not tell us. The Western Text says the jailer quickly "secured the other prisoners." Then, **trembling with fear he fell down before Paul and Silas.** His soul had been shaken more violently than the prison. When Paul and Silas had been put in his keeping, they had been minor nuisances, petty criminals to be taught a lesson. Now, the dramatic sequence of events convinced him that these men controlled a Force mightier than any he had ever known. At least, he thought that they represented deity of some kind.

Verse 30. He brought them out of the prison, apparently into his own living quarters (v. 32), and asked, **"Sirs, what must I do to be saved?"** His words raise many questions: For instance, exactly what did the jailer mean by **saved**? Did he know enough about scriptural teaching to use the word "saved" as we do; or was this simply a desperate cry by a pagan, fearful of the Power at the missionaries' command, who desired to be saved from the consequences of how he had treated them?

Further, if the jailer did happen to have a proper concept of salvation, why did he think Paul and Silas could supply the answer? Had news of their preaching reached his ears earlier? Had the ones bringing Paul and Silas to the prison told him that the slave-girl had said they were "bond-servants of the Most High God, who are proclaiming . . . the way of salvation" (v. 17)? Had Paul and Silas said something to him as he put their feet in the stocks? Did he simply know instinctively that these men could help him? We cannot give certain answers, but this much is clear: This pagan was shaken to the core. He had stood on the brink of death, looking into its inky darkness, and what he had seen terrified him! "Sirs," he cried, "what must I do to be saved?"

Verse 31. Whatever he meant by the words, they provided

the perfect opening for Paul and Silas. They replied, **"Believe in the Lord Jesus, and you will be saved, you and your household."** Standing before the Council, Peter had stressed that salvation is found only in Jesus Christ, "for there is no other name under heaven that has been given among men by which we must be saved" (4:12). If the jailer was to be saved, it would be through Jesus.

Sometimes people wonder why the jailer was not given the same answer the Jews were given on Pentecost when they asked what to do (2:37): "Repent, and each of you be baptized in the name of Jesus Christ for the forgiveness of your sins; and you will receive the gift of the Holy Spirit" (2:38). Some may ask why he was not given the answer Saul was given in response to his question "What shall I do, Lord?" (22:10): "Get up and be baptized, and wash away your sins, calling on His name" (22:16). Look again at the answers given to the Jews on Pentecost and to Saul: "Repent, and each of you be baptized *in the name of Jesus Christ* for the forgiveness of your sins; and you will receive the gift of the Holy Spirit" (2:38; emphasis added); "Get up and be baptized, and wash away your sins, *calling on His name*" (22:16; emphasis added). To do something in the name of Jesus, or to call on the name of Jesus, presupposes that one knows who Jesus is and believes in Jesus. The jailer did not have that knowledge; he did not have that faith. If he had been told to do something "in the name of Christ," like the blind man, he would have had to ask, "Who is He . . . that I may believe in Him?" (Jn. 9:36).

Verse 32. Paul and Silas soon rectified the jailer's lack of knowledge. **And they spoke the word of the Lord to him together with all who were in his house.** "So faith comes from hearing, and hearing by the word of Christ" (Rom. 10:17). **The word of the Lord** probably included a "word" about the true God (v. 34). It certainly included a "word" about Jesus and the cross. That it also included a "word" about how to benefit from the sacrifice of Jesus, plus a "word" about the life that should follow, is evident from the verses that follow.

Verse 33. And the jailer **took them that very hour of the night and washed their wounds, and immediately he was baptized, he and all his household.** It probably would have been

2:00 or 3:00 a.m. when the jailer and his household were baptized. The fact that the jailer responded **immediately** was proof of *sincerity*; the fact that he **washed their wounds** was proof of *sorrow*; the fact that he was **baptized** was proof of *submission*. Some attempt to prove infant baptism by the fact that the jailer's **household** was baptized. Note, however, that all those in his household who were baptized (v. 33) were first taught (v. 32) and believed (v. 34) (see comments on v. 15).

Verse 34. We do not know where the jailer and his household were immersed. It may have been in some nearby pool. A pool may have been located inside the prison, but there was no problem with the jailer's taking them outside the prison. His charge had been "to guard them securely" (v. 23), not to keep them locked up. They may have gone outside the city to the River Gangites or the Krenides (see comments on v. 13). After the baptism, the jailer **brought** Paul and Silas **into his house and set food before them.** Paul and Silas would not have had anything to eat since their arrest. Once more, Christian hospitality is stressed in Acts. The jailer **rejoiced greatly, having believed in God with his whole household.** He had been saved twice in one night, first from physical death and now from spiritual death. His soul had been imprisoned by sin more securely than the bodies of Paul and Silas had been imprisoned by stocks in the inner cell, but now he was free.

Note that the word **believed** in verse 34 is used in the comprehensive sense, taking in the totality of the jailer's response. Compare the conversion of the jailer to the conversion of Crispus: The statement that Crispus believed (18:8) included his response of baptism (1 Cor. 1:14). The jailer had been told that if he believed, he and his household would be saved (v. 31). He had been taught the Word of the Lord. After he had repented and been baptized, then it was stressed that he *had* believed.

It is not uncommon for denominational preachers to quote the jailer's question in verse 30, then the answer in verse 31, and to stop there as though that were the end of the story. As J. W. McGarvey said, They "leave the jail too soon."[12] When the story

---

[12]McGarvey, 103.

of the jailer's conversion is examined in its entirety, it will be found that he was saved from his sins like all the other examples in Acts: He was taught the gospel; he believed in Jesus; he repented of his sins; he was baptized.

IN PHILIPPI: THE RELEASE FROM PRISON (16:35–40)

[35]Now when day came, the chief magistrates sent their policemen, saying, "Release those men." [36]And the jailer reported these words to Paul, saying, "The chief magistrates have sent to release you. Therefore come out now and go in peace." [37]But Paul said to them, "They have beaten us in public without trial, men who are Romans, and have thrown us into prison; and now are they sending us away secretly? No indeed! But let them come themselves and bring us out." [38]The policemen reported these words to the chief magistrates. They were afraid when they heard that they were Romans, [39]and they came and appealed to them, and when they had brought them out, they kept begging them to leave the city. [40]They went out of the prison and entered the house of Lydia, and when they saw the brethren, they encouraged them and departed.

Verse 35. The conclusion of the story has a touch of wry humor. **Now when day came, the chief magistrates sent their policemen** to the jailer, **saying, "Release those men."** At least one ancient manuscript indicates that the magistrates were upset by the earthquake and decided they had made a mistake in their mistreatment of Paul and Silas. Since, however, the textual evidence is against this addition to the text, we do not know if that was the case or not. The officials probably thought the beating and a night in jail was sufficient to teach these troublesome Jews their place. (See comments on v. 22 concerning **policemen.**)

Verse 36. The jailer, apparently in the company of the officers from the magistrates, **reported these words to Paul, saying, "The chief magistrates have sent to release you. Therefore come out now and go in peace."** Since he told Paul and

Silas to **come out**, they had apparently returned to a cell in the prison at the end of the night to avoid embarrassing their new brother. The jailer was probably glad the ordeal was over.

Verse 37. Paul did not budge from the cell, however. He faced the officers, that is, the policemen (rod-bearers) who had beaten him and Silas (vv. 22, 35, 38) and **said to them, "They have beaten us in public without trial, men who are Romans, and have thrown us into prison; and now are they sending us away secretly? No indeed! But let them come themselves and bring us out"** (see 22:25–29). Apparently, Silas had Roman citizenship just as Paul did. We noted earlier that it was a major crime to beat a Roman citizen. Though the magistrates were chosen locally, if news of their conduct reached Rome, at best they would lose their jobs; at worst they would lose their heads.

Verses 38, 39. The policemen quickly returned and **reported these words to the chief magistrates. They were afraid when they heard that** Paul and Silas **were Romans, and they** personally **came** to the prison **and appealed to them.** The RSV says that "they came and apologized to them." The NCV says that "they came and told Paul and Silas they were sorry." Then, **when they had brought them out, they kept begging them to leave the city.** Try to picture these important officials on their knees, sweat popping from their brows, as they pleaded with Paul and Silas to leave the city with a minimum of fuss.

Before leaving this scene, we should stress that Paul did not insist on his rights as a Roman citizen to spite the rulers of the city (see Rom. 12:17, 19). Rather, he desired to set the record straight for the sake of the young Christians he would leave behind. They would have enough problems (Phil. 1:28–30) without the added embarrassment of having to explain why their founder had been arrested, beaten, and thrown in jail— and then had suddenly left town under a cloud of suspicion. Since Paul went to the trouble to set the record straight, he was later able to return to the city without repercussions from the previous visit (20:1, 2, 6).

Why did these officers take Paul's word regarding his Roman citizenship? Apparently, they did not ask Paul for proof. The indication from secular documents is that one had simply to cry *ciuis Romanus sum*, "I am a Roman citizen." Paul would have been registered as a citizen in Tarsus; but he probably did not carry proof with him, and it would have taken time to send for a certified copy of the registration. If proof was not required, why didn't everyone claim to be a Roman citizen to escape punishment? Falsely claiming to be a Roman citizen was a more serious crime than mistreating a Roman citizen. "Death was the penalty for making a claim to Roman citizenship when it was false; seldom did anyone make a false claim because of the severe penalty."[13]

Verse 40. Paul and Silas were probably ready to move to a new field anyway, so they agreed to comply with the magistrates' request—much to the officials' relief. They did so, however, without haste and with dignity. **They went out of the prison and entered the house of Lydia,** which had served as their base of operations and perhaps even their place of meeting. On this occasion, a number of brethren had gathered there; perhaps they had been having a prayer meeting (see 12:12). **And when** Paul and Silas **saw the brethren, they encouraged them.** Burton Coffman called this "one of the grandest statements in scripture."[14] The evangelists needed encouragement, but instead they encouraged others. The two evangelists were the ones who had been mistreated; yet their concern was not for themselves, but for these vulnerable babes in Christ.

The **brethren** included Lydia's household, the jailer's household, and probably numerous others. Luke recorded no more details concerning the beginning of the congregation. Later, when Paul wrote to the Philippian church from Rome, he addressed his letter "to all the saints in Christ Jesus who are in Philippi, including the overseers and deacons" (Phil. 1:1). "Overseers" is another way of speaking of elders (see comments on 20:28). Perhaps Paul helped to organize the church before he left (see 14:23); perhaps that happened later. Finally, having said

---

[13]H. Leo Boles, *A Commentary on Acts of the Apostles* (Nashville: Gospel Advocate Co., 1941), 268. See Suetonius *Claudius* 25.

[14]James Burton Coffman, *Commentary on Acts* (Austin, Tex.: Firm Foundation Publishing House, 1976), 325.

their farewells, they **departed**. Thus was a congregation established—a congregation that grew more precious to Paul with every passing year (Phil. 1:3–8; 4:1).

As Paul and Silas left to look for honest hearts elsewhere, Luke apparently stayed behind in Philippi to continue working with the young congregation. We reach this conclusion because Luke did not use first person ("we") in the narrative as he told of Paul and Silas' leaving—and we do not see the first person used again until 20:5, 6, when Paul revisited Philippi. Luke's presence in Philippi may help to explain why the Philippian church continued to take a personal interest in Paul after he left. Some also think that Timothy stayed a while longer in Philippi, finally catching up with Paul and Silas in Berea. They arrive at this conclusion because the antecedent of "they" in 16:40 and 17:1 is Paul and Silas. The next place Timothy is mentioned is in Berea (17:14). Of course, Timothy may have left with Paul and Silas without the fact being mentioned.

APPLICATION

Biographical Sketches (Ch. 16)

You may enjoy doing biographical sketches on the traveling companions of Paul: Silas, Timothy, and Luke. Information on Silas can be found in the comments on 15:40. There are details concerning Timothy in the comments on verses 1 through 3. It may be helpful to consult other references (see Rom. 16:21; 1 Cor. 4:17; 16:10, 11; 2 Cor. 1:1, 19; Phil. 1:1; 2:19–23; Col. 1:1; 1 Thess. 1:1; 3:2, 5, 6; Philem. 1; Heb. 13:23). The best references would be the letters Paul wrote to Timothy: 1 and 2 Timothy (especially see 1 Tim. 1:18; 4:12; 2 Tim. 1:2–4, 6; 4:9, 13). A good source on Luke is the *Introduction, The Penman*.

Train Up a Child (16:1)

Timothy was blessed with a godly mother who was concerned about his spiritual welfare. He was "the son of a Jewish woman who was a believer" (v. 1). She and Timothy's grandmother were held up by the apostle Paul as women of great faith—a faith they passed along to Timothy. Paul wrote, "For I am mindful of the sincere faith within you, which first dwelt in your grandmother Lois and your mother Eunice, and I am sure that it is in you as well" (2 Tim. 1:5). From his childhood, these godly women had taught Timothy the Old Testament Scriptures, which were able to give him wisdom that leads to salvation in Christ (2 Tim. 3:15).

How blessed is a child who has parents and grandparents concerned first and foremost about his spiritual welfare! If you are a parent with small children, understand that your greatest responsibility is to rear those children right—and your greatest service to the Lord is to teach them His way. Sometimes parents feel guilty because they do not have the time to serve as do those who have no children; let them know that as they train their children, they *are* serving the Lord. *Grandparents* also need to understand their responsibility to do what they can to influence their grandchildren in the way of the Lord. We do not know what else Eunice and Lois did in the service of God, but these women never did a greater work than rearing a boy who could be used by the Lord.

The Sacrifice of a Mother (16:3)

Paul wanted Timothy to join his missionary team (v. 3). Knowing the difficulties and persecutions that Paul frequently faced, certainly Eunice would have had difficulty letting her son Timothy leave. If you were in Eunice's position, what would you have said? We know what many mothers would have said. In our limited experience, the number one reason men and women have changed their minds about going to the mission field is tearful mothers who cried, "Please don't leave me! I can't stand it if you go that far away!" or "Please don't deprive me of my grandchildren!" What would these mothers do if a battered missionary came to them and said, "I want your child to come and suffer with me"? God bless parents who release their children to the work of the Lord, who say with Eunice, "I would love to keep you here with me, but God's work is more important than my personal desires. As a parent, I reserve the right to worry about you—but I believe that God will watch over you. Go with my blessing."

"All Things to All Men" (16:3)

Paul's circumcision of Timothy (v. 3) is a practical demonstration of his statement in 1 Corinthians 9:

> For though I am free from all men, I have made myself a slave to all, so that I might win more. To the Jews I became as a Jew, so that I might win Jews . . . I have become all things to all men, so that I may by all means save some (vv. 19–22).

A vital principle is found in Acts 16 and 1 Corinthians 9: When we are trying to reach people with the gospel, we need to do everything we can to keep from offending them *as long as we can do so without compromising the truth*. The circumcision of Titus would have compromised the truth. The circumcision of Timothy did not compromise the truth, but it did remove a stigma.

Modern-day illustrations could be multiplied. Many words in common use in America are considered crude, if not vulgar, by other English-speaking countries. When doing mission work, we should refrain from using those words to keep from offending those we are trying to reach. In many countries, the shoes are removed as one enters a house. To fail to do so insults the host. In some countries, it is considered offensive to give someone an object with the left hand. If the missionaries in those countries want to reach those around them, they learn to refrain from using the left hand in that fashion. None of these cases involve questions of compromising the truth. We simply need to avoid erecting needless barriers between ourselves and those we hope to reach with the gospel.

However, deciding whether or not complying with a local custom involves a compromise of truth is not always simple. "It is a wise spiritual leader who knows . . . when to stand firm and when to yield."[15] When faced with a hard decision in this regard, you will want to pray to God for wisdom (Jas. 1:5), and possibly talk with one older and wiser in the faith (Prov. 11:14).

---

[15]Warren W. Wiersbe, *The Bible Exposition Commentary*, vol. 1 (Wheaton, Ill.: Victor Books, 1989), 467.

The Paul-Timothy Arrangement (16:3)

Look around where you worship. Is there a young person you could encourage in the Lord's service? Is there someone you could train, someone you could take with you as you serve the Master? This could be the most significant work you ever do for the King. In times past, some preachers held "Timothy classes" where they taught young men to recite memory verses, lead prayer, and present short sermons.

Knowing the Will of God (16:6–10)

All of us face hard decisions: What should we do with our lives? Should we get married? If so, whom should we marry? Where should we live? You can add to the list. Today God will not give us a vision in the night as He gave Paul, but He still calls us—through His Word, through providentially opening and closing doors, and through the counsel of godly friends. We read, "The steps of a good man are ordered by the Lord" (Ps. 37:23; KJV); and "In all thy ways acknowledge him and he shall direct thy paths" (Prov. 3:6; KJV). If we would know the will of God for our lives, our text suggests that we should respond in certain ways:

(1) *Be ready.* We must be ready to respond immediately to God's call. After Paul saw the vision, Luke said, ". . . *immediately* we sought to go into Macedonia, concluding that God had called us to preach the gospel to them" (v. 10; emphasis added). If you would know God's special plan for your life, you must be ready to respond at once when He calls.

(2) *Be flexible.* We must be flexible, understanding that God's purposes and plans may not always be readily apparent. Paul tried to go south, and God stopped him; he tried traveling north, and God blocked his path (vv. 6–8). Paul and company were surely perplexed regarding what God wanted them to do. Even when they finally reached Philippi, Paul's usual place for beginning his preaching—the synagogue—was unavailable. It was not until they found the women by the riverside that they began to understand why they were there. Even so, as you strive to discover God's will for your life, God's plans for you may not always be readily apparent. You need to be flexible in your think-

ing—and do not get discouraged if God is not in as big a hurry to give you an answer as you are to find it.

(3) *Be mobile.* Instead of waiting for opportunities, we need to be making opportunities. At some point, Paul and his co-workers might have sat down and waited "until God decides to tell us what He wants us to do." Instead, they kept moving, looking for opportunities to serve Him.

(4) *Be humble.* Finally, we need to be humble, believing that if we respond positively to God's call, He will bless us. Paul's plan for the second missionary journey was different from God's. When God's plan became clear, he responded in a positive way—and God blessed his efforts. Souls were saved, and a new continent was opened to the gospel. Even so, some of us may have a hard time recognizing God's answer because it is not what we think it should be. We need to be humble enough to accept God's answer—responding positively once we understand His will.

The "Macedonian Call" (16:9, 10)

There are many kinds of help the church can and should give the world, but the only *unique* help it can give the world is the sharing of the gospel. As we have opportunity, let us do good to all men (Gal. 6:10), but let us never forget our special purpose for existence (Mt. 28:18–20; Eph. 3:10, 11, 21).

If you are already a Christian, you need to respond to the "Macedonian Call." Allow the Lord to open your ears to hear the call from hundreds and thousands of the lost who cry, "Come, help us!" If it seems to you that none are interested, remember Philippi: The city itself may have been cold, but by the river were those waiting to be told. If you will search for them, you will find honest souls, like Lydia and her household, who are seeking for the truth.

If you are not already a Christian, you need to answer the most important call of all: God's call to be saved and to become His special person! Paul stressed in 2 Thessalonians 2:14 that God calls every man through the gospel. The church is made up of "the called-out ones"—in other words, those who have responded to the call of the good news (2:38, 41, 47; KJV). If you have not responded as Lydia and her household did, allow God to open your heart—and be baptized at once, as were Lydia and her household.

Paul's Friend and Physician (16:10)

Luke, the author of the Book of Acts, informs us of his presence with Paul's missionary team by using the first person ("we," "us," v. 10). Luke was both a physician and good friend to Paul (Col. 4:14; see comments on v. 10).

Everyone needs someone he can trust, someone he can train, someone to whom he can turn. Many of us have found the first and last of these in a Christian mate and the second in our children. Whether or not that is your situation, we encourage you to team up with others who share the same convictions and concerns that you have.

> Two are better than one. . . . For if either of them falls, the one will lift up his companion. But woe to the one who falls when there is not another to lift him up. . . . And if one can overpower him who is alone, two can resist him. A cord of three strands is not quickly torn apart (Eccles. 4:9–12).

The Perfect Prospect? (16:11–40)

When Paul later referred to his work in Philippi, he called it "the first preaching of the gospel" (Phil. 4:15); when Paul crossed the Aegean Sea, he thought of it as starting afresh. Some translations insert the words "to you" in Philippians 4:15 ("when I first preached to you"), but "to you" is not in the original text. This new phase of Paul's work is celebrated in the Book of Acts with not one, but two detailed accounts of conversion: the conversion of a businesswoman named Lydia and the conversion of a Roman jailer. Between the two accounts is the story of the demonic slave-girl whose life was forever changed. All three of these individuals were very different from the apostle Paul.

Picture in your mind what you consider "a perfect prospect" for the gospel. If you were looking for someone to teach, what would be the characteristics of that person? Perhaps you will think of some specific individual whom you hope to bring to

Christ. How much is that "perfect prospect" like you? Probably your "ideal prospect" is much like yourself. When we look for someone with whom to share the gospel, we tend to look for someone of our own race, our own educational background, our own social standing, our own marital status. We feel comfortable with people like that.

Daniel Boorstin in *The Discoverers* tells the story of Cape Bojador. It was just a small piece of land along the African coast jutting out in the Atlantic Ocean, but in the fifteenth century, no ship dared to sail past it. Cape Bojador was no more dangerous than many other capes, but terrible rumors had circulated about what lay beyond it—perhaps even the end of the world. It was for the navigators of that day, says Boorstin, simply a "barrier in the mind."[16]

When we look for lives to change, let us have no "barriers in the mind." The challenge is for us to expand our evangelistic vision to see the potential in all people. Acts 16 declares that the gospel is for all and that, with the help of God, anyone's life can be changed—regardless of his or her background.

A Place of Prayer (16:13–15)

A lesson entitled "A Place of Prayer" could include subpoints such as "A Place of Prayer," "A Place of Speaking," "A Place of Listening," "A Place of Obedience," "A Place of Hospitality" (Lydia's offer).

A Certain Woman (16:13–15)

A sermon called "A Certain Woman" (v. 14; NASB 1977) could concentrate on the character of Lydia: a businesswoman, a worshiping woman, a listening woman, an obedient woman, a saved woman, a hospitable woman. In the lesson, stress how vital women are to the Lord's work.

The Importance of Women in the Church (16:13–15)

The church at Philippi was not the only congregation started with God-fearing women. Around the world, hundreds of con-

---

[16]Durham, 192.

gregations are in existence because of the influence and concern of godly women. We do not know of any congregation that could long survive without the continued support of its women. In God's plan, women are not to preach in the assembly (1 Tim. 2:8–15), but never underestimate their indispensable support.

Christian Businesswomen (16:14)

Christian women can be businesswomen. It is preferable that Christian mothers not work outside the home because there are too many neglected children. However, scripturally they can do so as long as they keep their priorities straight—understanding their primary God-given task is to make a home (Tit. 2:4, 5). The worthy woman in Proverbs 31:10–31 engaged in many business ventures, but she did not neglect her family to do so.

Covetousness (16:16–24)

C. Bruce White preached an unpublished sermon on the story of the demonic slave-girl, centering on the greed and covetousness of her owners. He noted that (1) covetousness demeans integrity—the way the girl was treated, (2) covetousness deters the truth—the lies the owners told about Paul and Silas, and (3) covetousness demands injustice—the way Paul and Silas were treated.

Avoiding the Occult (16:16)

Although the spread of Christianity invariably wipes out many irrational beliefs, we have seen a revival of superstition in recent years. (We refer to the Christianity revealed in the New Testament. Some forms of so-called "Christianity" have promoted superstition rather than discouraging it.) Fortunetellers, palm readers, crystal-ball gazers, horoscope interpreters, mediums, self-proclaimed psychics, and so-called "channelers" abound—and all of them prey on the ignorant and unsuspecting. Needless to say, a Christian shuns such people and their practices, encouraging others to do the same.

The Roman Jailer (16:23–40)

The story of the Roman jailer can be narrated with six divisions: (1) Prison—Paul and Silas were cast in the inner cell (vv. 23, 24); (2) Praise—Paul and Silas sang at midnight (v. 25); (3) Power—the Lord sent an earthquake (vv. 26–30); (4) Preaching—Paul and Silas spoke the word of the Lord to the jailer and his household (vv. 31, 32); (5) Pardon—the jailer and his household were saved (vv. 33, 34); (6) Protest—Paul charged the authorities with mistreating Roman citizens (vv. 35–40).

Why Was the Jailer Baptized? (16:25–34)

A title that one can use to preach on the conversion of the jailer is "Why Was the Jailer Baptized?" The story can be narrated and then the question asked, "If Acts 16:30, 31 teaches that we are saved by faith only, why was the jailer baptized?" More specifically, one could ask, "Why was he baptized 'that very hour of the night' if baptism is only an optional ceremony?"

Another way to preach the story of the jailer is with three "C's": (1) The Convicts—Paul and Silas in prison, (2) A Concert—singing at midnight, (3) A Conversion—the jailer and his household believe and are baptized.

Songs in the Night (16:25)

Paul and Silas' singing and praying at midnight has inspired many sermons on "Songs in the Night." (For this phrase, see Job 35:10; Is. 30:29.) Rick Atchley has suggested that we, too, can "sing in the night" of trouble if we (1) put our troubles in perspective, (2) put our treasures in heaven, and (3) put our trust in God.[17]

The Greatest Question of the Ages (16:30)

Many sermons have been preached on "The Greatest Question of the Ages" (v. 30). The jailer's question is broken down into its component parts, and each part provides a main thought: (1) "What"—a Probing Question, (2) "Must"—an Essential Question, (3) "I"—a Personal Question, (4) "Do"—an Active Question, (5) "To Be Saved"—a Timeless Question.

---

[17]Rick Atchley, "Singing in the Pain," Sermon preached at the Southern Hills church of Christ, Abilene, Texas, 20 September 1986.

On the Road to Salvation (16:30, 31)

A visual aid utilizing a road map has often been used with the conversion of the jailer: Pick out a well-known point of origin on the left side of the map (point A) and then a well-known destination on the right side of the map (point B). Mark the road between the two with a heavy line. Finally, pick out two stops along the way and clearly mark those. In Bible class, show the map and suppose that someone started to travel from point A to point B. Before the individual starts the journey, he asks someone the question "How far is it to my destination?" He asks the same question at his first stop and at his second. Although the same question is asked each time, a different answer will be given—because he is nearer to the destination each time. Even so, the same basic question "What must I do?" was asked three times in the Book of Acts (2:37; 16:30; 22:10), but a slightly different answer was given each time (2:38; 16:31; 22:16). No contradiction is involved; the different answers were the result of the inquirers' being at different locations "on the road to salvation."

CHAPTER 17
PAUL'S SECOND MISSIONARY JOURNEY (PART 3)

When Jesus explained the Parable of the Sower, He said that the good soil stood for those "who have heard the word in *an honest and good heart,* and hold it fast, and bear fruit with perseverance" (Lk. 8:15, emphasis added). A great need of our day is for "honest and good hearts." One of the finest descriptions of that kind of heart is found in Acts 17: "Now these [Jews in Berea] were more noble-minded than those in Thessalonica, for they received the word with great eagerness, examining the Scriptures daily to see whether these things were so" (v. 11). Every serious soul-winner looks for honest hearts. This is the kind of heart Paul was looking for as he continued his travels through Greece.

TO THESSALONICA (17:1–9)

¹Now when they had traveled through Amphipolis and Apollonia, they came to Thessalonica, where there was a synagogue of the Jews. ²And according to Paul's custom, he went to them, and for three Sabbaths reasoned with them from the Scriptures, ³explaining and giving evidence that the Christ had to suffer and rise again from the dead, and saying, "This Jesus whom I am proclaiming to you is the Christ." ⁴And some of them were persuaded and joined Paul and Silas, along with a large number of the God-fearing Greeks and a number of the leading women. ⁵But the Jews, becoming jealous and taking along some wicked men from the market place, formed a mob and set the city in an uproar; and attacking the house of Jason,

they were seeking to bring them out to the people. ⁶When they did not find them, they began dragging Jason and some brethren before the city authorities, shouting, "These men who have upset the world have come here also; ⁷and Jason has welcomed them, and they all act contrary to the decrees of Caesar, saying that there is another king, Jesus." ⁸They stirred up the crowd and the city authorities who heard these things. ⁹And when they had received a pledge from Jason and the others, they released them.

Verse 1. As Paul and Silas left, they traveled west on the Egnatian Way, mingling with the festive crowds traveling in the direction of Rome. A day's journey, about thirty miles, would have brought them to **Amphipolis**, the capital of the district in which Philippi was located. Another day's journey, a little less than thirty miles, and they were at **Apollonia**. Both Amphipolis and Apollonia were comparatively small, and the missionaries apparently passed through them without stopping to preach. Paul's general mission strategy was to evangelize population centers and then to let the gospel spread from there to the outlying areas. Amphipolis and Apollonia could be evangelized as the gospel spread from Philippi and Thessalonica (see 1 Thess. 1:8). Their destination, yet another thirty miles, was the capital of Macedonia: **Thessalonica**. The city was named after the sister of Alexander the Great. Thessalonica had sided early with Rome and had been rewarded by being made a "free city." This designation meant that it was autonomous, could mint its own coins, and had no Roman garrison within its walls. It was very much a Greek city instead of a Roman city. Thessalonica was also the principal seaport in that part of the world and a major commercial center rivaling Ephesus and Corinth. This city, now known as Salonika, is still a major seaport of southeast Europe.

The Egnatian Way ran through the middle of Thessalonica, forming its main street. When Paul and Silas arrived in the capital city, they discovered that, unlike Philippi, Thessalonica had a sizable Jewish population. Paul was thus able to begin his work by going to the **synagogue**.

Verses 2, 3. And according to Paul's custom, he went to

them, and for three Sabbaths reasoned with them from the Scriptures, explaining and giving evidence that the Christ had to suffer and rise again from the dead, and saying, "This Jesus whom I am proclaiming to you is the Christ." The fact that Paul went to the synagogue on three consecutive Sabbaths does not mean that they were only in Thessalonica for three weeks. This period of time refers to what Paul did for the first three weeks he was in that city.

Four verbs in these verses outline Paul's approach in preaching to the Jews: (1) He reasoned, (2) he explained, (3) he proved (gave evidence), and (4) he proclaimed. Paul had two aims: to prove from the Old Testament Scriptures that the Christ (the Messiah) had to suffer and rise again, and then to prove that Jesus was that looked-for Messiah. The first of these aims was the hardest, for the Jews found it difficult to believe in a suffering Savior (1 Cor. 1:23). Paul met their objections by **giving evidence**—which translates from a Greek word παρατίθημι (*paratithēmi*), which means "lay alongside." He first quoted Old Testament prophecies and then "laid alongside" those prophecies the facts concerning Jesus. For an example of how he did this, see Paul's synagogue sermon in Pisidian Antioch (13:16–41).

Verse 4. When the seed of the gospel is planted in honest hearts, invariably there will be a harvest (Lk. 8:8). Therefore, **some of them were persuaded and joined Paul and Silas, along with a large number of the God-fearing Greeks and a number of the leading women.** Instead of **joined**, Hugo McCord has "joined company with."[1] The Greek verb is from προσκληρόω (*prosklēroō*), which could mean "threw in their lot with." The Greek word κλῆρος (*klēros*) means "lot."

Notice the word **some**: Only a few Jews became Christians. On the other hand, **a large number** of the Gentile God-fearers became Christians, including many of the "leading women" who attended synagogue services. According to the Western Text, **leading women** refers to the wives of leaders in the city. Many Gentile women were attracted to the morals and ethics of Judaism. As usual, Luke exalted the role of women.

---

[1] *McCord's New Testament Translation of the Everlasting Gospel.*

From Paul's letters to the Thessalonians, it is evident that he and Silas also did much preaching outside the synagogue, to the idol worshipers in the city (1 Thess. 1:9). In those letters, he spoke about how he had preached the Word (1 Thess. 1:6; 2:2, 14), the miracles that he and Silas had performed (1 Thess. 1:5), and how he had learned to love the Thessalonians (1 Thess. 2:7, 8). Since Acts 17:1–4 tells of Paul's first three weeks in Thessalonica and since 17:5–9 tells of the end of his stay, apparently there was an interval of time between verse 4 and verse 5 in which Paul did most of his work in Thessalonica. In the Thessalonian letters, he also mentioned that, while ministering there, he and Silas had supported themselves by doing manual labor (1 Thess. 2:9). More than once, however, they received some financial help from Philippi (Phil. 4:15, 16). Of greatest significance to Paul, however, was the honest response of many Thessalonians to the gospel:

> . . . you turned to God from idols to serve a living and true God, and to wait for His Son from heaven, whom He raised from the dead, that is Jesus, who rescues us from the wrath to come.
>
> . . . we . . . constantly thank God that when you received the word of God which you heard from us, you accepted it not as the word of men, but for what it really is, the word of God, which also performs its work in you who believe (1 Thess. 1:9, 10; 2:13).

Two who responded were Aristarchus and Secundus (Acts 20:4; 27:2). Their names have led to the speculation that Aristarchus was Jewish and Secundus was Greek.

After the Thessalonians became Christians, Paul continued to indoctrinate them (1 Thess. 4:2, 3, 6; 2 Thess. 2:15; 3:10), preparing them for the day he would have to depart. As he taught them, he told them of the trials that were ahead—for them and for him (see Acts 14:22). Later, he wrote, "For indeed when we were with you, we kept telling you in advance that we were going to suffer affliction" (1 Thess. 3:4).

Verse 5. Trouble was not long in coming, because for every honest heart, there are hundreds of hardened hearts. As the success of Paul and Silas continued, the unbelieving Jews became increasingly agitated. **The Jews, becoming jealous** (see 13:45) **and taking along some wicked men from the market place, formed a mob.** The phrase **from the market place** translates a form of the Greek word ἀγοραῖος (*agoraios*), which could be translated as "agora men." The agora (or forum) was the heart of the city—the center of commerce, politics, and religion (see comments on 16:19). Human nature being the same in every age, we are not surprised to learn there were loafers who hung around the area, ready to cause trouble. F. F. Bruce's translation has "some characters who loafed around the agora, ready for mischief."[2] Cicero referred to the "agora men" as "sub-rostrums." The Romans used the word *rostrum* to refer to a speaker's platform; the Greeks called this structure the *bēma* (see comments on 18:12). The sub-rostrums were those who stood beneath the rostrum in the agora, who delighted in harassing speakers. These could be hired to applaud or to heckle. In this chapter they were evidently hired for a more deadly purpose. Luke said that the Jews used these men to **set the city in an uproar.**

Paul and Silas had been staying in the home of a man named Jason (v. 7), so the mob headed in that direction. They attacked **the house of Jason.** We do not know whether Jason was a Christian or not. The fact that the text seems to make a distinction between "Jason" and "some brethren" (v. 6) may indicate that he was not. We are inclined, however, to believe that he was. Some think he was the same Jason mentioned in Romans 16:21. If so, he later traveled to Corinth.

They were seeking to bring Paul and Silas **out to the people.** The word **people** is translated from the word δῆμος (*dēmos*), the word from which we get "democracy," a government by the people. As a free city, Thessalonica was self-governed by a people's council. The mob wanted to haul the missionaries before this council.

---

[2] F. F. Bruce, *The Book of Acts*, The New International Commentary on the New Testament, gen. ed. F. F. Bruce, rev. ed. (Grand Rapids, Mich.: Wm. B. Eerdmans Publishing Co., 1988), 323.

Verse 6. Paul and Silas were either not home, or else brethren had spirited them away as the mob approached. In the providence of God, Paul was often warned of trouble before it happened. Perhaps that was the case here. Frustrated, the Jews grabbed Jason and several new Christians and dragged them before **the city authorities**. This phrase translates the Greek word πολιτάρχας (*politarchas*) which combines the word πόλις (*polis*, "city") with the word ἀρχή (*archē*, "ruler"). Archaeological studies have confirmed that the people's council in Thessalonica was headed by five or six men called "politarchs." For years, skeptics challenged Luke's use of the word "politarchs" since the term was not found in secular writing. Then the Vardar Gate was discovered in Thessalonica with an inscription referring to the six politarchs of the city. Since that time, several similar inscriptions have been found.

When the Jews were before the council, they did not mention their real reason for being upset—their jealousy at the success of the gospel. Instead, they repeated the lies the slave masters had told the officials in Philippi (16:19–21)—that Paul and Silas were troublemakers, acting contrary to the laws and interests of Rome. They began to shout: **"These men who have upset the world have come here also."**

The words of the Jews were designed to harass Paul and Silas. Unwittingly, however, they paid one of the highest compliments ever given to the power of the gospel. The phrase τὴν οἰκουμένην ἀναστατώσαντες (*tēn oikoumenēn anastatōsantes*), translated **upset the world,** can also be translated "turned the world upside down" (KJV, RSV). The phrasing "turn upside down" was used by the fisherman to speak of turning his boat over so he could scrape the bottom, make repairs, recaulk, and paint his boat. What the Jews did not realize was that *sin* had turned the world upside down (Gen. 3) and finally the gospel was turning it right-side up.

Verse 7. The Jews shouted, **"And Jason has welcomed them."** If Jason was a Christian, perhaps he—like Lydia (16:15, 40)—had invited Paul and Silas into his home after being converted. The charge against Jason was that he had aided and abetted these troublesome fellows. They continued their accusation:

"And they all act contrary to the decrees of Caesar, saying that there is another king, Jesus." The Jews should have choked on these words. Claudius Caesar was their avowed enemy (18:2), but they pretended to care about his decrees. The dishonest heart has no limit to its deception.

Two specific charges were made against Paul and Silas *in absentia*: (1) They were causing trouble, and (2) they claimed that Jesus was a king, a rival to Caesar. The same accusation was made against Jesus while He was alive (Lk. 23:2). The first charge was patently untrue; it was the Jews, not Paul and Silas, who had "set the city in an uproar" (v. 5). The second was a deliberate misrepresentation of what the missionaries had preached: Jesus is King (1 Tim. 6:15); but since His kingdom "is not of this world" (Jn. 18:36), He was no rival to Caesar (Mt. 22:21). As part of preaching the Resurrection, gospel preachers made it clear that Jesus had returned to heaven. He could not, therefore, be considered a rival earthly king.

Verse 8. When the Jews told their lies, ignorance and prejudice triumphed in dishonest hearts: **They stirred up the crowd and the city authorities who heard these things.** They may have stirred up the authorities, but Jason and the others were treated mildly, considering the seriousness of the charges. This underscores the fact that there was no concrete evidence for the accusations.

Verse 9. And when they had received a pledge from Jason and the others, they released them. The **pledge** (ἱκανός, *hikanos*) was a bond that Jason and the others had to post, which would be forfeited in the event of further disturbance. Perhaps it was a large sum of money; perhaps it was the deeds to their homes or other properties. Possibly, part of the agreement was the stipulation that Paul and Silas would leave town and not return (see 1 Thess. 2:18).

TO BEREA: A "NOBLE-MINDED" PEOPLE (17:10–15)

[10]**The brethren immediately sent Paul and Silas away by night to Berea, and when they arrived, they went into the syna-**

gogue of the Jews. [11]Now these were more noble-minded than those in Thessalonica, for they received the word with great eagerness, examining the Scriptures daily to see whether these things were so. [12]Therefore many of them believed, along with a number of prominent Greek women and men. [13]But when the Jews of Thessalonica found out that the word of God had been proclaimed by Paul in Berea also, they came there as well, agitating and stirring up the crowds. [14]Then immediately the brethren sent Paul out to go as far as the sea; and Silas and Timothy remained there. [15]Now those who escorted Paul brought him as far as Athens; and receiving a command for Silas and Timothy to come to him as soon as possible, they left.

Verse 10. Whatever the conditions laid down by the authorities, the congregation was concerned about Paul's safety. Under cover of darkness, the Christians **immediately sent Paul and Silas away . . . to Berea.** Paul left with a heavy heart, apprehensive about the safety of the young and vulnerable congregation he left behind (1 Thess. 1:6; 2:14, 15). He knew he could take persecution and keep his faith, but could they?

Berea was about fifty miles west-southwest of Thessalonica, at the foot of the famed Mount Olympus. Paul and Silas would have traveled several miles west on the Egnatian Way and then headed south. Some have suggested that Paul's plan was to continue west on the Egnatian Way, preaching in major cities as he went, until he reached Rome (Rom. 1:13; 15:22). If that were his plan, once more God stepped in to change the plan. Perhaps the brethren sent Paul and Silas to what Cicero called an "out-of-the-way" city, hoping their absence would dissipate the hatred of the Thessalonian Jews. However, since Berea was in the heart of a prosperous and populous region, it is equally possible that Paul already had Berea on the list as his next place to preach.

If the Christians who sent Paul and Silas to Berea thought the preachers would remain incognito until tempers cooled in Thessalonica, they did not know the two men. As soon as **they arrived** in Berea, **they went into the synagogue of the Jews.**

Verse 11. To their pleasant surprise, the synagogue in Berea was filled with honest hearts, not merely among the Gentile God-fearers, but also among the Jews: **Now these** Jews **were more noble-minded than those in Thessalonica, for they received the word with great eagerness, examining the Scriptures daily to see whether these things were so.** Luke was not referring to the people of Berea in general—in contrast to the people of Thessalonica. Rather, in this context, he was contrasting the Jews of Berea with the Jews of Thessalonica (v. 5).

The Jews of Berea were **more noble-minded**. This phrase is translated from a comparative form of the Greek word εὐγενής (*eugenēs*), which can mean "noble" or "noble-minded." The term "noble" was used by the Greeks to refer to those of noble birth. In this passage, it refers to nobility of character. The word may have been deliberately used by Luke to suggest that nobility of character was more important than nobility of birth.

If the work in Thessalonica demonstrated how the gospel should be preached, the work in Berea demonstrated how the gospel should be received. Those who heard Paul and Silas were commended by Luke for four qualities: (1) They were receptive: The Bereans **received the word with great eagerness.** (2) They were diligent: The Bereans met **daily** to study with Paul and to examine the Scriptures. (3) They were cautious: The Bereans had a healthy skepticism. They did not take Paul and Silas' word without checking for themselves. Instead, they examined the Scriptures **to see whether these things were so.** There is a difference between having an honest heart and being gullible. (4) They were loyal—to God and to His Word. The Bereans recognized **the Scriptures** as the final authority in religion. They did not examine what Paul said in light of their previously held beliefs. They did not examine what Paul said in light of what was "practical" or "workable." They examined Paul's teaching in the light of the Scriptures. Luke commended them for checking up on an apostle.

Verse 12. Because the Jews in Berea had honest hearts, **many of them believed.** In Thessalonica "*some* of [the Jews] were persuaded" (v. 4), but in Berea "*many* of [the Jews] believed" (emphasis added). Thus we see the difference between dishonest hearts and honest hearts. These believing Jews were accompanied by **a number of prominent Greek women and men.** Note again Luke's emphasis on the role of women. He listed them before the men in this passage. We do not know how long Paul and Silas stayed in Berea, but once more a congregation of God's people was established. Among the converts was Sopater, who later traveled with Paul (20:4).

Verse 13. Eventually, word of Paul and Silas' success filtered back to Thessalonica. If the anger of the Jews in Thessalonica had cooled, the news that many Jews in Berea had become Christians refueled their wrath. They thought that they were rid of Paul, but he was again preaching his abominable doctrines just forty or fifty miles away. Soon they were on the road to Berea: **But when the Jews of Thessalonica found out that the word of God had been proclaimed by Paul in Berea also, they came there as well, agitating and stirring up the crowds.** A similar incident is recorded in 14:19. They no doubt used the same tactics that had proven successful in Thessalonica.

Verses 14, 15. Since the anger of the mob centered on Paul, Christians determined to send him away—so far away that he could not be reached by the vindictive Thessalonian Jews. **Then immediately the brethren sent Paul out to go as far as the sea; and Silas and Timothy remained there.** Those who accompanied the apostle **brought him as far as Athens; and receiving a command for Silas and Timothy to come to him as soon as possible, they left.** Again he was sent away by the brethren (see 9:25, 30; 17:10), this time all the way to **Athens** in the southern part of Greece called Achaia. Once more it was probably hard for Paul to leave, but he had the satisfaction of knowing that he was leaving behind in Macedonia three new congregations of the Lord. **Silas and Timothy** remained in Berea to help the new Christians there and, at some point, Timothy went back to Thessalonica (1 Thess. 3:2, 6). We do not know if these travels were the brethren's idea, Paul's idea, or the Holy Spirit's idea. Regardless of whose idea they were, Paul did not want Silas and Timothy to stay any longer in those cities than was absolutely necessary.

The wording of some ancient manuscripts raises questions about whether or not **the brethren** had a definite destination in mind when they left with Paul, and whether they traveled to Athens by sea or by land. One textual variant, followed by the KJV, suggests they only pretended to take Paul to the sea to escape from his adversaries—"to go *as it were* to the sea" (emphasis added). It is, however, more likely that they took a ship, sailing around Thessaly and coming to Athens. Traveling by sea would have been just a few days journey.

TO ATHENS: PAUL'S SPIRIT STIRRED (17:16–21)

[16]Now while Paul was waiting for them at Athens, his spirit was being provoked within him as he was observing the city full of idols. [17]So he was reasoning in the synagogue with the Jews and the God-fearing Gentiles, and in the market place every day with those who happened to be present. [18]And also some of the Epicurean and Stoic philosophers were conversing with him. Some were saying, "What would this idle babbler wish to say?" Others, "He seems to be a proclaimer of strange deities," because he was preaching Jesus and the resurrection. [19]And they took him and brought him to the Areopagus, saying, "May we know what this new teaching is which you are proclaiming? [20]For you are bringing some strange things to our ears; so we want to know what these things mean." [21](Now all the Athenians and the strangers visiting there used to spend their time in nothing other than telling or hearing something new.)

For the first time since Paul had been sent out by the church in Antioch, he was alone—alone in one of the most influential cities in the world. Athens was the cultural and philosophical center of the Graeco-Roman world. Paul felt overwhelmed, but this did not keep him from looking for honest hearts.

Many writers refer to his work in Athens as "one of Paul's greatest failures," citing these facts: (1) Luke mentioned only a few responses. (2) The New Testament never refers to a congregation in Athens. (3) Paul had traveling companions from most places he worked (20:4), but no traveling companion from Athens was ever listed. (4) No Christian from Athens was ever named in the greetings in Paul's letters. Considering these facts, it is not hard to understand why some call Paul's work in Athens a failure. However, we believe that the apostle's labors were a success in God's sight because he faithfully proclaimed the good news of Christ. God's messengers are responsible for proclaiming the message, not for producing the hearer's response (1 Cor. 3:5–9).

Verse 16. Much of the glory of Athens was already in the past, but in Paul's day the city was still a force to be reckoned with. Many of the greatest thinkers, orators, and artists who ever lived had made Athens their home. The concept of democracy had been born there. In the process of conquering the world, Alexander the Great and later the Romans had spread Athenian culture and the Greek language. Athens was still considered by many to be the greatest of three university cities in the world at that time. The other two cities were Alexandria in Egypt and Tarsus in Cilicia, Paul's hometown. Paul was familiar with university towns.

If the brethren brought Paul to Athens by ship, which seems likely, they probably said their "good-byes" at the seaport, which was about five miles from the city. As Paul walked to Athens, one of the first sights he would have seen was the Acropolis. "Acropolis" is a transliteration of the Greek word ἀκρόπολις, which combines the word ἄκρον (akron, "high") with the word πόλις (polis, "city"). "Acropolis" means the "high city." In ancient days, most cities of any size had an acropolis, which not only served as the location of temples and libraries, but also was a refuge for the population to flee to in case of attack. The Acropolis in Athens was crowned by the dazzling white and gold Parthenon—considered by many to be the most beautiful building ever fashioned by the hands of men. The name "Parthenon" comes from the Greek word παρθένος (parthenos), which means "virgin." This was the temple dedicated to Athena, who was the patron goddess of Athens and one of three "virgin" goddesses of the Greeks. The more famous statue of Athena was inside the Parthenon, but there was also one outside. This latter image was so tall, according to ancient writers, that even from the seaport one could see the sunshine reflecting off the point of Athena's spear.

Paul had asked the brethren who left him in Athens to tell Silas and Timothy to come to him as soon as possible (v. 15). Perhaps Paul did not plan to begin his work in Athens until the team reassembled. He could not, however, disregard the error and ignorance he saw. Everywhere he turned, he would have observed heathen festivals and processions, sacrifices and celebrations full of superstitious fears. He would have seen the proliferation of idols and temples, including the unfinished temple to Zeus, the largest temple in ancient Greece. Zeus was considered the chief deity of the Greeks (see comments on 14:12). The satirist Pretonius had written that it was easier to find a god than a man in Athens. Paul even passed an altar with the inscription "To an unknown god" (v. 23). Thus **while Paul was waiting for** Silas and Timothy **at Athens, his spirit was being provoked within him as he was observing the city full of idols.**

Paul was not upset merely because of the existence of images; in front of the idols were worshipers and sacrifices that had been left for these gods. Every vase filled with withered flowers, every bowl of rotting fruit represented someone's heart. Today, visitors to Athens classify the ruins of the ancient city as art and architecture. When Paul beheld the idols and magnificent temples, he did not see the beauty of architecture; he saw the ugliness of error. He did not see cultural progress; he saw spiritual pornography. He did not see enlightenment of the mind; he saw ignorance of the soul. (Some today find it difficult to appreciate ancient European cathedrals and other religious structures. Perhaps they contain art treasures, but they are also monuments to man's departure from the divine pattern [1 Tim. 4:1–4].) Paul later wrote, ". . . the things which the Gentiles sacrifice, they sacrifice to demons and not to God" (1 Cor. 10:20).

How could a center of learning also be a center of superstition? Athens was a vivid demonstration of the truth of 1 Corinthians 1:21: ". . . the world through its wisdom did not [and cannot] come to know God." Romans 1:18–32 is a divine commentary on what had happened in that "enlightened" city.

Verse 17. What could Paul do? Silas and Timothy had not yet arrived. We cannot know for certain whether or not Silas and Timothy ever arrived in Athens. The next time they are mentioned in Acts is in 18:5. However, 1 Thessalonians 3:1, 2 probably indicates that Timothy rejoined Paul in Athens, but Paul immediately sent him back to Thessalonica. Some speculate that Silas also rejoined Paul in Athens, but Paul quickly sent him elsewhere, perhaps to Philippi. Both Silas and Timothy eventually rejoined Paul in Corinth. Although his coworkers were not present to support him, Paul began to preach. **So he was reasoning in the synagogue with the Jews and the God-fearing Gentiles, and in the market place every day with those who happened to be present.** The Greek word from διαλέγομαι (*dialegomai*), translated **reasoning**, can also mean "debating." Paul would have debated in the synagogue concerning Jesus' being the Christ; he may also have reprimanded the Jews for their failure to speak out against the idolatry in Athens.

As was his custom, he went to **the synagogue** on the Sabbath (see v. 2). Then, Sunday through Friday, he discussed biblical truths with any who had come to **the market place**—the agora. In other cities, the agora was the cultural, commercial, and religious center (see comments on 16:19). In Athens, it was also the educational center where philosophers met. Socrates, Plato, and Aristotle had taught in the agora of Athens.

Verse 18. Among those who argued with Paul in the agora were adherents of two major schools of thought in Athens: **And also some of the Epicurean and Stoic philosophers were conversing with him.** The Epicureans were followers of the Greek philosopher Epicurus (340–270 B.C.). They are noted today for defining man's purpose for existence as "the pursuit of pleasure." By "pleasure," Epicurean teachers meant the absence of pain and suffering. Regarding religion, Epicureans were materialistic deists: They acknowledged the existence of gods, but thought those deities were so far removed from the world that they could not exercise any influence on its affairs. Although Epicurean teachers did not define pleasure in terms of the senses, the philosophy had no real check on sensuality. Eventually, for some, the position deteriorated into the familiar philosophy "Eat, drink, and be merry, for tomorrow we die" (see 1 Cor. 15:32). Today the word "epicure" is used to refer to one who enjoys extravagance in food and drink.

The Stoics were disciples of the philosopher Zeno (c. 340–265 B.C.). Their name came from the Greek word στοά (*stoa*), which means "porch." (The word *stoa* is used in the original text to refer to "Solomon's portico" at the Jerusalem temple [see comments on 3:11].) Zeno had taught in the "Painted Stoa," located in the agora in Athens, and that was still their principal meeting place. These "porches" were elaborate structures: a covered colonnade, open on at least one side. Stoics believed in duty as the highest good; they emphasized self-discipline and a denial of the flesh. Regarding religion, Stoics were materialistic pantheists: God to them was an impersonal Force permeating everything in the universe. They believed that fate determined everything in their lives and that they should be resigned to accept whatever happened. We use the word "stoic" today to refer to one who appears indifferent to physical or emotional pain.

Epicurean philosophy ultimately deteriorated into extravagance, while Stoic philosophy deteriorated into pride as it exalted the self-sufficiency of man. Though the Epicureans and Stoics represented opposite views in Greek philosophy, the philosophies had much in common: Both exalted man and his capabilities. Neither acknowledged the need for a personal God. Neither believed in a conscious existence after death. Both were uncomfortable with dogmatic statements concerning truth. Thus adherents of both philosophies felt threatened by Paul's teaching.

According to Luke, the response of the philosophers was varied. **Some were saying, "What would this idle babbler wish to say?"** The term **idle babbler** is a translation of the Greek word σπερμολόγος (*spermologos*), a compound word combining σπέρμα (*sperma*, "seed") with λέγω (*legō*, "pick"). Literally meaning "seed-picker," the term referred to worthless birds who survived by picking up seeds here and there. "Seed-picker" was Athenian slang for a religious huckster who picked up ideas from many sources and formulated a worthless hybrid philosophy. That type of individual was common in that day; he is also common today.

Others were saying, **"He seems to be a proclaimer of strange**

deities," because he was preaching Jesus and the resurrection.
Notice Paul's topics. Those who call Paul's efforts in Athens a
failure say that Paul learned there that philosophy was ineffec-
tive, so he changed his approach when he went to Corinth and
began to preach "Jesus Christ, and Him crucified" (1 Cor. 2:1,
2). According to Luke, however, Paul's basic message in Athens
was the same as it was in Corinth: The Greek word translated
preaching is from εὐαγγελίζω (*euangelizō*), which literally means
"preach the gospel" (see comments on 5:42; 8:4). The center of
the "good news" was **Jesus and the resurrection**.

The Athenians grasped Paul's topics, but they struggled with
what he meant. With their mindset, they said Paul was **a proclaimer of strange deities**. Note the plural form "deities." When
Paul preached on "Jesus and the resurrection," they decided he
was teaching on two deities: one named "Jesus" and the other
named "Resurrection." Since many of their gods were personi-
fications of abstract qualities such as truth and beauty, they apparently assumed that ἀνάστασις (*anastasis*, "resurrection") was
the name of a god. In the Greek language, "Jesus" (᾽Ιησοῦς,
Iēsous) is masculine gender, while *anastasis* is feminine gender.
Since pagans often had masculine and feminine manifestations
of their gods, the Greeks might have thought Paul was proclaiming the same concerning his God.

It should be noted that the Greek phrase Ξένων δαιμονίων
(*Xenōn daimoniōn*), translated "strange deities," literally means
"foreign demons." In the minds of the Greeks, a demon was a
person who had died, often a bad person, but whose spirit was
still around. In their thinking, these demons had certain powers, but they were not as powerful as "the Immortals," the gods
and goddesses. They already worshiped thousands of demons,
and now this foreign seed-picker had the audacity to introduce
new ones.

Verses 19, 20. They may have misunderstood Paul, but he
aroused their curiosity. So **they took him and brought him to
the Areopagus**. The name **Areopagus** is derived from two
Greek words: ῎Αρειος πάγος (*Areios pagos*). "Ares" was the name
of the Greek god of war, corresponding to the Roman god Mars,
and *pagos* was the word for "hill." Thus "Areopagus" literally

means "hill [or mountain] of Ares," or to use the more familiar Latin term, "Mars' hill." The hill was and is located just south of the agora, at the foot of the Acropolis. According to Greek mythology, Ares, who was always looking for a fight, was tried on the hill for killing the son of Poseidon and was acquitted. (Poseidon was considered the god of the sea, corresponding to the Roman god Neptune.) At one time, there was a temple to Ares on the hill. The hill became the location of the most ancient and prestigious court in Athens, which took its name from the location: the Areopagus. By New Testament times, this court was not as powerful as it had once been, but it was still influential. On special occasions, the court still met on the hill, but ordinary meetings were held in the Royal Colonnade in the northwest corner of the agora.

Since the name "Areopagus" can refer both to the hill and to the court, questions arise regarding where Paul was taken and why he was taken there: Was he taken to the top of the hill or to the spot in the agora where the court usually met? Some think the phrase "stood in the midst of the Areopagus" (v. 22) favors the court rather than the hill, but we suppose Paul could stand in the middle of the hilltop. According to tradition, the apostle was taken to the top of the hill, possibly to get away from the hustle and bustle of the agora. A massive bronze plaque has been mounted on the side of the hill, with the complete text of Paul's sermon in Greek. It is ironic that, as a whole, the Athenians were unimpressed with Paul's sermon, but now their offspring have put up a plaque commemorating it. Standing on Mars' Hill, to the north one can look 377 feet down into the ancient agora; to the west one can look up 135 feet at the towering Acropolis. If Paul was on the hill of Mars, the philosopher Socrates (c. 470–399 B.C.) was tried and convicted on the same spot as a perverter of the accepted religion. Paul may have had the unique opportunity of telling about the Prince of Peace on the hill dedicated to the god of war.

Regardless of where Paul was taken, the question arises whether this meeting was an informal hearing or a formal trial. The fact that an officer of the court, called an "Areopagite," was converted (v. 34) would indicate that at least some members of the court were present, and it is possible that Paul was on trial as an introducer of foreign gods. The conclusion of the session (vv. 32, 33), however, points to an informal hearing.

When the Athenians reached their destination, whatever it was, they asked Paul, **"May we know what this new teaching is which you are proclaiming? For you are bringing some strange things to our ears; so we want to know what these things mean."**

Verse 21. At this point in the narrative, Luke inserted this editorial note: **(Now all the Athenians and the strangers visiting there used to spend their time in nothing other than telling or hearing something new.) All the Athenians** would not, of course, include working men, but referred to those who crowded the agora every day. **Strangers** also came from all over the world to Athens to study philosophy. Aristotle defined philosophy as "the science which considers truth." The citizens of Athens and visitors alike claimed to be in search of truth; in reality, they were in search of the new and novel. Philosophers have always been better at chasing ideas than reaching conclusions. The natural inclination of Athenians to hear **something new** may not have been commendable, but it gave Paul a perfect opportunity to preach the gospel.

IN ATHENS: THE SERMON ON (OR TO) THE AREOPAGUS (17:22–34)

[22]**So Paul stood in the midst of the Areopagus and said, "Men of Athens, I observe that you are very religious in all respects.** [23]**For while I was passing through and examining the objects of your worship, I also found an altar with this inscription, 'TO AN UNKNOWN GOD.' Therefore what you worship in ignorance, this I proclaim to you.** [24]**The God who made the world and all things in it, since He is Lord of heaven and earth, does not dwell in temples made with hands;** [25]**nor is He served by human hands, as though He needed anything, since He Himself gives to all people life and breath and all things;** [26]**and He made from one man every nation of mankind to live on all the face of the earth, having determined their**

appointed times and the boundaries of their habitation, [27]that they would seek God, if perhaps they might grope for Him and find Him, though He is not far from each one of us; [28]for in Him we live and move and exist, as even some of your own poets have said, 'For we also are His children.' [29]Being then the children of God, we ought not to think that the Divine Nature is like gold or silver or stone, an image formed by the art and thought of man. [30]Therefore having overlooked the times of ignorance, God is now declaring to men that all people everywhere should repent, [31]because He has fixed a day in which He will judge the world in righteousness through a Man whom He has appointed, having furnished proof to all men by raising Him from the dead."

[32]Now when they heard of the resurrection of the dead, some began to sneer, but others said, "We shall hear you again concerning this." [33]So Paul went out of their midst. [34]But some men joined him and believed, among whom also were Dionysius the Areopagite and a woman named Damaris and others with them.

Among the most important questions in life that might be asked are these: "Where did I come from?"; "Why am I here?"; Where am I going?" "Science attempts to answer the first question, and philosophy wrestles with the second; but only the Christian faith has a compelling answer to all three."[3] Heaven's plain answers to man's perplexing questions are recorded in Paul's sermon on Mars' Hill. Only ten verses record this sermon, and it can be read in less than two minutes; but it is one of the greatest sermons ever preached by mortal man.

Verse 22. Paul had been asked to elaborate on his teaching (v. 19). From a human viewpoint, Paul's preaching "success" thus far in Athens had been nonexistent. If any had become believers in response to Paul's teaching in the synagogue, Luke did not mention it. Paul had been labeled an "idle babbler" and "a proclaimer of strange deities" after preaching in the agora.

---

[3]Warren W. Wiersbe, *The Bible Exposition Commentary*, vol. 1 (Wheaton, Ill.: Victor Books, 1989), 473.

As he looked about at those surrounding him on the Areopagus, it was obvious that they were not interested in learning truth, but in satisfying their curiosity. Nevertheless, the apostle did not hesitate.

So Paul stood in the midst of the Areopagus. The KJV, following the Latin Vulgate, has "Mars' hill" here. To many Christians, Paul's sermon in Acts 17 will always be "Paul's sermon on Mars' Hill." On the Areopagus (Mars' Hill) were two white stones. During a trial, the prosecutor stood on one and the defendant stood on the other. Since sound carries upward, these were on the lower end of the hill. If the trial was on the hill, it is possible that Paul stood on or near one of those stones, ready to speak to the intelligentsia of Athens.

How should he proceed? He could not begin as he had in the synagogue of Antioch of Pisidia, with a survey of God's dealings with the Israelite nation (13:17). He could not even reason "with them from the Scriptures" as he had in the synagogue in Thessalonica (v. 2), for his listeners were ignorant of God's Word. *We must always start where people are.* When Jesus faced a woman at a well, He spoke on water—the water of life (Jn. 4:10). When Paul faced self-proclaimed seekers of truth, he spoke on truth— the truth about God and man.

Paul began, **"Men of Athens, I observe that you are very religious in all respects."** The Greek word translated **very religious**, is a comparative adjective form of the compound word δεισιδαίμων (*deisidaimōn*), which combines δείδω (*deidō*, "fear") with δαίμων (*daimōn*, "demon"). The word *deisidaimōn* could mean "demon-fearers," that is, those who reverenced demons. The word "demons" did not automatically have a bad connotation to Paul's listeners as it does to us; the Greeks worshiped demons (see comments on v. 18). Since the city was packed with idols dedicated to these demons, they probably would not have taken the statement as either compliment or criticism, but simply a statement of fact. If Paul was on trial, it was unlawful to compliment this particular court in an effort to influence its verdict. The KJV has "too superstitious," which is probably what Paul personally thought about their idolatry. The apostle may have been playing a word game with his listeners—using a phrase that had one meaning to them and a different meaning to him. However, *deisidaimōn* can simply mean "religion." The word is even used in reference to the Jewish faith (25:19). Thus Paul may have simply been stressing that the Athenians were "very religious," as the NASB indicates.

Verse 23. Paul illustrated what he meant: **"For while I was passing through and examining the objects of your worship, I also found an altar with this inscription, 'TO AN UNKNOWN GOD.'"** Secular historians, including Pausanias in the second century and Philostratus in the early third century A.D., have recorded that altars to unknown deities were not uncommon in that area. Archaeologists found such an altar dedicated "to the unknown god" at the temple of Demeter in Pergamum, located across the Aegean Sea from Athens. There has been considerable speculation on the origin of these shrines. In some cases, when an altar fell into disuse and was later repaired, if the original inscription was gone, perhaps it was given the generic inscription "to an unknown god or gods."

A popular explanation has to do with an event that had occurred years before. A plague had swept through the land, killing hundreds. Thinking the gods were unhappy, the people had sacrificed to their thousands of deities, to no avail. The advice of a wise, old man named Epimenides had been sought. "There must be a god you do not know who is unhappy with you," he had said, suggesting a course of action. They were to turn loose a flock of multi-colored sheep in the vicinity of the sacred plot of ground known as the Areopagus, and pray that the unknown god would cause the sheep that he wanted sacrificed to him to lie down. The people had followed this advice, erecting an altar in every place a sheep had lain down and sacrificing the sheep on that altar. Several Greek writers told of this plague, indicating that the advice was carried out and that the plague ended. At least one of the altars dedicated to that "unknown god" may have survived to Paul's day.

The simplest explanation for the altar may be that some conscientious idol-worshiper was so fearful of leaving out a god that he took no chances, erecting an altar to any god that was unknown. Whatever the reason for the shrine, it served Paul's purposes perfectly. He had been accused of introducing "strange deities" (v. 18); he would show that he preached a God whose existence the Athenians acknowledged, but of whom they admitted ignorance. **"Therefore what you worship in ignorance, this I proclaim to you."**

The word **ignorance** sounds insulting to modern readers. Paul, however, used the same language the Athenians had applied to "the unknown god" (see also v. 30). The Greek word translated "unknown" is from ἄγνωστος (*agnōstos*), a compound word combining α (*a*, a negating prefix) with γνῶσις (*gnōsis*, "knowledge"). The word *agnōstos* indicates a lack of knowledge, that is, ignorance. It is the word from which we get "agnostic," which literally means "one who does not know." An atheist says, "There is no God"; an agnostic says, "I do not know whether or not there is a God." Paul said, in effect, "Listen to me and you will know the God that you thought was unknowable."

Verses 24, 25. When Paul spoke to people who had an inaccurate concept of God, he did not start by telling about Jesus, but about God. Most false religions in the world are based on a false view of God. Remember: You must start where people are, not where you wish they were.

(1) *God made all things.* Paul did not begin with philosophical proofs of the existence of God. Most people believe in something called a "god," as the Athenians did. Rather, Paul's sermon commenced where the Old Testament does (Gen. 1:1) by referring to the **God who made the world and all things in it** (see comments on 14:15–17).

Paul was telling them that they had not made God, but God had made them; they had not made God a home, but He had made them a home—this earth. His words refuted the materialistic concept of the Epicureans that this world came into being as the result of a chance collision of atoms.

Paul proceeded to reveal the God who had made all things: **"Since He is Lord of heaven and earth, [He] does not dwell in temples made with hands; nor is He served by human hands, as though He needed anything."** Paul's words remind us of those of Solomon (1 Kings 8:27) and Stephen (Acts 7:48, 49). Paul was surrounded by the greatest array of pagan temples the world has ever seen. In the distance was the temple of Zeus, one of the largest temples ever built. Below was the agora, packed with idols and temples. Above was the Acropolis with its multiplicity of temples, including the incomparable Parthenon. God, however, had no need of temples, regardless of how beautiful they were. Unlike the lifeless, helpless idols in those temples, God did not need the Athenians to serve Him; rather, they needed His help.

(2) *God made all men*. Paul moved from the generic to the specific. Since God made all things, that means He made us: **"He Himself gives to all people life and breath and all things."** He gives us life initially; then He enables us to continue life by giving us breath; further, He gives us "all things" that sustain life. How much do you need God? Take a deep breath. God enabled you to take that breath—and without it, you would die. Every breath you take is a gift from the Almighty.

Verse 26. Again, God **made from one man every nation of mankind to live on all the face of the earth.** Notice the phrase **from one man.** The word "man" has been supplied by the translators. The original Greek text has ἐξ ἑνός (*ex henos*), "from one" (see NASB 1977). This phrase refers to the creation of Adam and subsequent populating of the earth. (See Gen. 3:20; although this verse refers to Eve, the point is the same.) Due to a variant in some Greek manuscripts, the KJV has "from one blood." This reading is an accurate application of the truth of this verse and has been confirmed by medical science. Regardless of race or origin, the blood of one man is basically the same as the blood of every other man. Differences of blood type have no relationship to race or origin.

If Paul had attacked the Grecian view of God in his previous remarks, here he attacked the Grecian view of man. The Greeks thought of themselves as unique, with a different origin and status than all other men. They grouped mankind into two categories: "Greeks and barbarians." It had to be a blow to their national pride to hear that God "made from one man every nation of mankind [including Greece] to live on all the face of the earth."

In fairness to the Greeks, they were not alone in being condescending. Most ethnic groups thought of mankind as composed of "us" and "them." The Jews' division was "Jews and Gentiles." Roman categories were "citizens and noncitizens." Unfortunately, such prejudicial groupings continue among those unaware that Jesus broke down the barriers between men (Eph. 2:14), so we might all be "one in Christ Jesus" (Gal. 3:26–28). The only categories that really matter are "in Christ" and "outside of Christ."

(3) *God controls all things.* Having asserted God's creation of humanity through one man, Paul added that He **"determined their appointed times and the boundaries of their habitation."** Some have attempted to give verse 26 racial overtones; they say the verse means that "God put every man in his place, and he should stay in that place." Consider, however, that the man who made this statement was a Jew who had grown up in Asia Minor, had been educated in Jerusalem, and was preaching in Europe. He associated with men on all educational and social levels. He obviously was not "staying" in some so-called "divinely predetermined" social or geographical "place." Daniel 2:21 is a good commentary on this verse: "It is He who changes the times and the epochs; He removes kings and establishes kings." In other words, God is in control. Not only did He determine the appointed seasons (14:17), but He also determined the length of the reigns of kings. Not only did He establish geographical boundaries such as oceans, but He also established political boundaries. God did not make the world and then walk away; He was and is active in the affairs of men. Though the Athenians were unaware of it, this Unknown God had given them *their* place of honor in history.

Verse 27. Having revealed what God had done, Paul turned to what man must do.

(1) *Man must seek God.* This verse begins with the words **that they would seek God** (see Deut. 4:29; Mt. 7:7, 8; Heb. 11:6). The word "that" ties this verse with the truths just presented. God made all things and controls all things to encourage us to seek Him. The NIV has "God did this *so* that men would seek him" (emphasis added). We have not been placed in this world to seek position, possessions, or pleasure; we have been put here

to seek God. Jesus gave another purpose for existing: "Let your light shine before men in such a way that they may see your good works, and glorify your Father who is in heaven" (Mt. 5:16). "Seeking God" might be thought of as man's initial purpose; "glorifying God," as man's ultimate purpose. God does not need our service (v. 25), but He does want our fellowship.

We cannot help but wonder if Paul's next words were not a veiled description of the Athenian philosophers: **"if perhaps they might grope for Him and find Him, though He is not far from each one of us."** The philosophers were searching for truth, but—using only human reason—they groped in the darkness. A parallel that comes to mind is blindfolded children at a party, stumbling around the room trying to "pin the tail on the donkey." Without the blindfold, it would be easy; with the blindfold, it is almost impossible. If the philosophers could swallow their pride and acknowledge that the Unknown God had revealed Himself, they could pull off their self-imposed blindfolds and see that "He is not far from each one of us."

Verse 28. How close is God? Paul said that **"in Him we live and move and exist."** Some have accused Paul of expressing a pantheistic concept similar to the materialistic pantheism of the Stoics. However, the Stoic concept of an impersonal Force that permeates nature bears little resemblance to the biblical concept of a personal, omnipresent God who fills heaven and earth, who "upholds [and sustains; NIV] all things by the word of His power" (Heb. 1:3)—including us. Paul's next words were diametrically opposed to the pantheistic concepts of the Stoics.

Knowing that many of his listeners found it hard to conceive of a God who is near, Paul noted that their own writers agreed with his statement: **"as even some of your own poets have said, 'For we also are His children.'"** Paul quoted from two poets. His previous thought had been expressed years earlier in a poem attributed to Epimenides (c. 600 B.C.): "In thee we live and move and have our being." The quotation in Titus 1:12 is also generally attributed to Epimenides. He was highly respected by Grecian philosophers; some Greeks even thought he was inspired. The second quotation, "we also are His children," apparently referred to a line from the writings of Aratus (born 310 B.C.): "For we are truly his offspring." Aratus was a Cilician as Paul was. Paul probably had often heard the words of Aratus quoted during his early schooling in Tarsus. Another poet, Cleanthes, expressed the same idea in slightly different words. It should be noted that the god referred to in these poems was not Jehovah, who was "unknown" to them, but their principal god, Zeus (see comments on 14:12). Paul was not saying that Jehovah is to be identified with Zeus. Rather, he was pointing out that even human philosophy had led to the concept of a close, personal God, and therefore, that his words about the nature of the true God should not be thought unreasonable.

Verse 29. Having spoken of the nature of the Unknown God, Paul moved quickly to the worship of the one true God. How we worship God is always based on our concept of God.

(2) *Man must worship correctly.* Paul had already touched on the subject of worship several times. At the beginning of his lesson, he had noted that they worshiped the Unknown God "in ignorance" (v. 23). He had stressed that God "does not dwell in temples made with hands; nor is He served by human hands" (vv. 24, 25). His statements that one God made all (vv. 25, 26) would lead to the conclusion that all men should worship the same God, and should worship Him in the same way. Now, lest the Athenians had missed the implications of his words, Paul plunged a dagger into the heart of their idolatrous practices: **"Being then the children of God, we ought not to think that the Divine Nature is like gold or silver or stone, an image formed by the art and thought of man."** How could the inferior (man) create the superior (God)? Further, if we who are alive and breathe and move are made in God's image, how can we think that something made of cold, dead, inert matter can be God?

The term **Divine Nature** is translated from the Greek word θεῖος (*theios*) (see 2 Pet. 1:3, 4). The KJV uses "Godhead" here to translate this word, which refers to the distinctive qualities of deity. The old English word "Godhead" might be thought of as "Godhood." Even as "manhood" refers to the qualities of a man that make him a man, so "Godhood" would refer to the qualities of God that make Him God.

Paul's statement was bold, perhaps even reckless. (See 19:23–28 for a later reaction to Paul's teaching on idolatry.) Each Athenian possessed his small idols made of gold and silver, while the city was filled with magnificent idols made of marble—including the image of Athena, fashioned of marble overlaid with precious ivory and gold.

Verse 30. Fearless, Paul rushed on to his conclusion.

(3) *Man must repent.* If his words were true, the superstitious worship of the Athenians was wrong; and if they were to please the one-and-only, true-and-living God, they had no choice but to change: **"Therefore having overlooked the times of ignorance, God is now declaring to men that all people everywhere should repent."** Instead of the word **overlooked**, the KJV has the picturesque term "winked at." The Greek word is from ὑπεροράω (*huperoraō*), a compound word that combines the preposition ὑπέρ (*huper,* "over") with ὁράω (*horaō,* "look"). It means "overlook" or "disregard."

For the third time, Paul used the Greek word indicating **ignorance**: (1) In calling God "unknown," the Athenians had admitted their ignorance of Him (v. 23). (2) They worshiped Him "in ignorance" (v. 23). (3) Now, Paul said that God had tolerated their "ignorance" in days past, but would no more. God was revealing Himself to them; they no longer had any excuse for ignorance (see Rom. 1:20).

Some commentators struggle with the question "To what extent did God overlook their ignorance?" Since we do not know the mind of God (Is. 55:8, 9), it is not a question we can answer. Further, since Paul implied that God no longer overlooks ignorance, it is not a question we need to answer; it has little or nothing to do with how God deals with mankind today. Nevertheless, a simple parallel can be made: When children are small, parents overlook some behavior that they do not overlook when their children grow older. In days past, when mankind was in its infancy, God overlooked some behavior that He no longer overlooks (see Mt. 19:8, 9). God now says to all mankind, "You have been on the earth long enough to know what is right and what is wrong; therefore, I hold you responsible for your actions."

Earlier in Acts, Peter's suggestion that the self-righteous Sanhedrin needed to repent (5:31) had "cut [them] to the quick," and they had sought to kill him (5:33). Now Paul pointed to self-satisfied philosophers and informed them that men with great minds needed to **repent**. To "repent" means "to change one's mind or attitude about sin, as a result of a genuine sorrow for sin, determining to change one's life" (see comments on 2:38; 3:19). Specifically, Paul's listeners needed to turn "to God from idols to serve a living and true God" (1 Thess. 1:9).

Verse 31. Paul had told the Athenians about the past: God had overlooked their ignorance. He had told them about the present: God was "*now* declaring . . . that all people everywhere should repent" (emphasis added). To motivate them, he then told them about the future: **"He has fixed a day in which He will judge the world in righteousness."** The Epicureans thought of life as a road to extinction, the Stoics thought life was a pathway to being absorbed into a divine Life-force, but Paul announced that life is "a journey to the judgment seat of God."[4] Paul started the sermon by asserting that the Unknown God was their Creator; he closed by affirming that the Unknown God would be their Judge. No one knows when the fixed Day of Judgment will be except God alone (Mt. 24:36).

Paul's introductory sermon on "the truth about God and man" was basically finished. Without quoting a single Scripture, Paul had presented one scriptural argument after another. However, he still needed to introduce his most important lesson on "the truth about Jesus." He declared that God would judge the world **"through *a Man* whom He has appointed, having furnished proof to all men by raising Him from the dead"** (emphasis added). That "Man" was Jesus. The fact of the resurrection of Jesus serves many teaching purposes (Rom. 1:4; 1 Cor. 15:20); a lesser-known purpose is that it proves there will be a judgment day.

Paul had been called before the distinguished assembly because he had preached Jesus and the Resurrection (v. 18). As he

---

[4]William Barclay, *The Acts of the Apostles,* The Daily Study Bible Series, rev. ed. (Philadelphia: Westminster Press, 1976), 132.

closed, he came full circle, ending with those two themes. If he had been given the opportunity to speak to the council again, his "second lesson would have unpacked the compressed contents of verse 31. Who was this man of God's appointment? And what were the circumstances of his being raised from the dead?"[5]

Regarding Paul's introductory sermon, why did he speak of Jesus as Judge instead of Savior? Why did he command repentance instead of faith, as was common in gospel sermons? Whatever Paul's reasons, we can be confident of three facts: (1) The Holy Spirit gave Paul the message these specific individuals needed at that specific time (Mt. 10:19). Paul possibly spoke of God as Judge because the Areopagus needed to know that they would be judged even as they were judging him. Paul may have spoken about the need for repentance because of their self-satisfaction. (2) Those who desired to hear more of Paul's preaching (v. 32) would hear about Jesus and the cross (1 Cor. 2:2). (3) The word "repent" in verse 30 stands for the totality of man's response, even as the word "believe" stands for the totality of man's response in similar passages in Acts.

To be consistent, those who argue that baptism is not essential because it is sometimes not mentioned as a condition of salvation should argue that faith in Jesus as Savior is not essential because it is not mentioned as a condition of salvation in Paul's sermon on Mars' Hill. Those who treat the Scriptures fairly know that Paul did not preach "a different gospel" (Gal. 1:6) to the Athenians than he did to others. To be saved from their past sins, they had to respond as all others did: They had to believe in Jesus, repent of their sins, confess their faith, and be buried in baptism (Rom. 6:3, 4).

Verses 32–34. Paul came to Athens looking for honest hearts. Jesus said that honest hearts are like good soil: deep, clean, and fertile (Lk. 8:4–15). For the most part, the soil in Athens was shallow, choked with the weeds of superstition and human reasoning, and dead. Luke wrote, **Now when they heard of the resurrection of the dead, some began to sneer, but others said, "We shall hear you again concerning this." . . . But some men**

---

[5]Bruce, 342.

joined him and believed. The three types of responses listed by Luke are typical of responses to the gospel around the world.

(1) *Some mocked.* When some **heard of the resurrection of the dead,** they **began to sneer.** The KJV has "mocked." Another possibility is "scoffed." Shallow-minded individuals discovered long ago that it is easier to make fun of something new than it is to investigate it; and "if you laugh at it, you can ignore it."

The topic that had broken up the meeting was "the resurrection of the dead." They had listened patiently to Paul's downgrading of their sacred artifacts and had even endured the implication that they needed to repent. When, however, the "out-of-town seed-picker" spoke of a bodily resurrection, they could restrain themselves no longer. The different schools of philosophy agreed on little, but they did agree that the idea of a bodily resurrection was ridiculous. Even those who believed in the immortality of the soul thought of the body as earthly and evil. The Greeks viewed the body as a prison; to escape from the flesh was to attain a state of joy. The thought of raising a dead body to live in again made no sense to them. The attitude of a typical educated Greek might be summed up in a statement by the Greek dramatist Aeschylus (525–456 B.C.): "Once a man is dead and the ground drinks up his blood, there is no resurrection."[6] The word used for "resurrection" in that statement was ἀνάστασις (*anastasis*), the same word used by Paul (see comments on v. 18). The scoffers on Areopagus had a treasure in their grasp, but they let it slip through their fingers.

(2) *Some waited.* Others told Paul, **"We shall hear you again concerning this."** Like Felix, they said, "Go away for the present, and when [we] find time, [we] will summon you" (24:25). Were they really interested, or were they just being politely evasive? We cannot answer that question, but we do know that procrastination is a most dangerous game to play with God (see comments on 24:25).

(3) *Some believed.* At that point, **Paul went out of their midst.** This terminology would indicate that Paul was free to come or go as he pleased, so he was probably not on trial in a formal

---

[6]Aeschylus *Eumenides* 647.

sense. If the trial was on the hill, he descended the steps, leaving them to think about what he had said. Perhaps he left discouraged. First Corinthians 2:1–3 may indicate that Paul's experiences in Athens distressed him. If so, we thank God for verse 34: **But some men joined him and believed, among whom also were Dionysius the Areopagite and a woman named Damaris and others with them.** It was not an abundant harvest, but it was a harvest—and one soul is worth more than all the world.

Among the converts was **Dionysius the Areopagite**. An "Areopagite" was a member of the illustrious Areopagus court. Therefore, Dionysius was one of the elite of the city. According to tradition, Dionysius became a bishop (elder) of the church in Athens. This may be true; other traditions concerning him are less likely. Today in Athens, there is a street named after him. Then there was a woman named **Damaris**. Once more Luke stressed the role of women in the early church. Since he named her, perhaps she was a woman of some influence. Guesses vary as to the identity of Damaris—from "a woman of the street" to "a member of the aristocracy." Much of the speculation assumes that she heard the sermon on (or to) the Areopagus, but Luke did not say that. Perhaps she was a God-fearer who heard Paul in the synagogue. Then there were **others**. Even as Luke gave an abbreviated form of Paul's sermon, he apparently also gave an abbreviated version of Paul's ministry in Athens and the responses to that ministry.

Many commentators insist that no one was baptized in Athens. They base this on Paul's statement to the Corinthians that the household of Stephanas, who lived in Corinth (1 Cor. 1:14–16; 16:17), were "the first fruits of Achaia" (1 Cor. 16:15); both Athens and Corinth were in the province of Achaia. It is possible, however, that Stephanas and his family had been visiting in Athens during Paul's stay there and had been baptized by Paul at that time. There could also be some other explanation for Paul's statement. Some writers believe that the qualifying phrase "in Corinth" is to be understood, indicating "the first fruits of Achaia" as far as *Corinth* was concerned (see comments on 18:8). The statement that some **believed** and **joined** themselves to Paul is typical of Luke's abbreviated reports of conversion in other cities (13:48; 14:1; 17:4, 12); there is no reason to conclude that in verse 34 he meant anything different. It is true that Paul wrote that "not many wise" became Christians (1 Cor. 1:26), but "not many" does not mean "not any."

With few exceptions, commentators confidently assert that Paul established no congregation in Athens—primarily based on the fact that there is no mention in the New Testament of a church in that city. Paul, however, no doubt established many congregations not mentioned by name in the New Testament. Most commentators have a denominational concept of what it takes to constitute a congregation. The Bible teaches that when one obeys the gospel, God adds that individual to the church (see comments 2:47). Luke told of at least half a dozen converts in Athens: The text speaks of "some men [at least 2] . . . among whom was Dionysius . . . [+1] and a woman named Damaris [+1] and others [+ at least 2 more]." "Organized" or "unorganized," those members constituted the church in that city. History records that a strong congregation existed in Athens in the second century. It was Paul who planted the initial seeds for that harvest.

APPLICATION

Reactions to the Gospel (Ch. 17)

Warren W. Wiersbe outlines chapter 17 as follows: (1) Thessalonica—Resisting the Word (vv. 1–9), (2) Berea—Receiving the Word (vv. 10–15), (3) Athens—Ridiculing the Word (vv. 16–34).[7] Using this outline, one could emphasize the importance of how we react to the gospel today, including the sobering reality of the Judgment (v. 31).

Honest Hearts (Ch. 17)

There are many practical lessons we can learn from this chapter: (1) We must continue to preach God's Word. Paul "reasoned . . . from the Scriptures" (v. 2; see also v. 13). (2) Regardless of the results, we must preach God's Word. Paul baptized "some" Jews

---

[7]Wiersbe, 469–72.

at Thessalonica and "many" at Berea, but he preached the same message at both places. We must be faithful in preaching and teaching, and leave the results to God (1 Cor. 3:7). (3) We must encourage our listeners to accept nothing we say merely because we say it. Rather, everything we teach, or anything anyone teaches, must be examined in the light of the Scriptures (v. 11). (4) If we do preach God's Word faithfully, it will stir people up—for good or for ill. Some of us are overcautious; we are fearful of offending someone. A little boy was not far wrong when he said, "The Bible ends with Revolutions."

The apostle Paul kept looking for honest hearts. Honest hearts will accept God's Word when it is preached, but dishonest hearts will not. How can one find honest hearts? Unfortunately, people do not walk around with signs: "I have an honest heart" or "I have a dishonest heart." The only way we know to find honest hearts is to do what Paul and Silas did: Keep telling about Jesus Christ in favorable and unfavorable circumstances (2 Tim. 4:2), and then rejoice when someone responds in a positive way.

Attitudes (17:6)

When the Jews dragged Christians before the authorities in Thessalonica, they made this accusation: "Those that have turned the world upside down are come hither also" (17:6; KJV). These words indict us. Have we "turned the world upside down"? Have we even made it rock a little? Someone has said that to compare the church of the first century to the church of today is to compare the deafening roar of a cannon to the insignificant pop of a toy gun.

We may protest, "If we only knew *why* the early church was able to accomplish what it did, we would do the same." It is not hard to discover "the secret" of the power of the early church. Even a superficial reading of Acts reveals the attitudes they had that gave them success.

Attitude Toward Christianity. To early Christians, Christianity was not an emotional release or something to round out their lives; it was their passion. It was not *a* way of life, but *the* way of life. It was not just a way of looking at certain situations, but a certain way of looking at *all* situations (Gal. 2:20). As a result, early Christians were willing to give their all: They sold their possessions and gave to others (Acts 5). They gave up their homes, their families, their jobs (ch. 8). Some even gave their lives (chs. 7; 12). As a result, the church grew by leaps and bounds. "But surely God doesn't expect that much of us!" you may think. How do you know? What does Christianity mean to you? Are you willing to make any sacrifice to see it reach all the world?

Attitude Toward Life. The attitude of early Christians toward Christianity affected their attitude toward life. They had new life in Jesus (Rom. 6:3–6), and they took that life seriously (Acts 19:19, 20). There could be no compromise. Acts 5:13, 14 gives the result of strong discipline in the early church.

We can never have an impact on the world until those in the world see us acting differently from the world. Many years ago, a preacher sent a request to the chief of the Six Nations tribe of Indians to start a mission among them. The reply was in the form of an oration. Here is an excerpt:

> Brother, we have been told that you have been preaching to the white people in this place. These people are our neighbors. We are acquainted with them. We will wait a little while and see what effect your preaching has upon them. If we find it does them good, makes them honest and less disposed to cheat Indians, we will then consider again of what you have said.

Attitude Toward Others. The love God has for man and the love early Christians had for God and others is evident in the Book of Acts. To the pagans, this was one of the most astonishing qualities of Christianity. In the pagan world, it was "dog-eat-dog": kicking those who were down; ignoring the sick and the helpless; striking back at enemies. In contrast, Christians loved. Rome met Christianity with a sword, but Christianity met Rome with love—and conquered it. This attitude was likely one of the primary reasons for the phenomenal growth of the early church.

Today, we live in a similar world of competition, amid the philosophy "look out for number one." Real Christians, however, still care.

Attitude Toward Teaching. As a result of their attitude toward others, early Christians naturally wanted to share the gospel with all they met (Mt. 28:18–20). Notice that the Great Commission contains four "alls": *all* authority, *all* the nations, *all* Jesus had taught them, and *always*. Wherever they were scattered, early Christians "went about preaching the word" (Acts 8:1, 4). Philip Schaff gave this as the primary reason for the growth of the early church:

> Christianity once established was its own best missionary. It grew naturally from within. It attracted people by its very presence. . . . [E]very congregation was a missionary society, and every Christian believer a missionary, inflamed by the love of Christ to convert his fellow-men. . . . Celsus scoffingly remarks that fullers and workers in wool and leather, rustic and ignorant persons, were the most zealous propagators of Christianity. . . . Women and slaves introduced it into the home-circle. . . . Every Christian told his neighbor, the laborer to his fellow-laborer, the slave to his fellow-slave, the servant to his master and mistress, the story of his conversion, as a mariner tells the story of rescue from shipwreck.[8]

The Sanhedrin said that the apostles had filled Jerusalem with their doctrine (5:28). Have *we* filled our world, our nation, our district, our city, even our own neighborhoods, with the gospel?

Attitude Toward Prayer. Without this final factor, the attitudes of early Christians toward Christianity, toward their lives, toward others, and toward teaching would have amounted to nothing. They recognized their dependence upon God (4:24, 29).

---

[8]Philip Schaff, *History of the Christian Church*, vol. 2, *Ante-Nicene Christianity A.D. 100–325* (n.p., 1883; reprint, Grand Rapids, Mich.: Wm. B. Eerdmans Publishing Co., 1973), 20–21.

Are we known as a people of prayer? If we are not, God help us to repent—and learn to depend on Him.

Conclusion. There may be one last objection: "But they were more successful than we are because it was *easier* back then!" Was it? Consider these words from J. B. Phillips in his preface to *Letters to Young Churches*:

> Without going into wearisome historical details, we need to remember that these letters were written, and the lives they indicate were led, against a background of paganism. There were no churches, no Sundays [set aside by the world], no books about the Faith. Slavery, sexual immorality, cruelty, callousness to human suffering, and a low standard of public opinion, were universal; traveling and communications were chancy and perilous; most people were illiterate. Many Christians today talk about the "difficulties of our times" as though we should have to wait for better ones before the Christian religion can take root. It is heartening to remember that this Faith took root and flourished amazingly in conditions that would have killed anything less vital in a matter of weeks. These early Christians were on fire with the conviction that they had become, through Christ, literally sons of God; they were pioneers of a new humanity, founders of a new Kingdom. They still speak to us across the centuries. Perhaps if we believed what they believed, we might achieve what they achieved.[9]

Our problem today is one of attitude. Millions are on the way to hell, and many do not care. Some who once embraced Jesus have given way to the pull of the world, and many do not care. *God help us to care.*

Searching the Scriptures (17:11)

The Berean Jews were diligent in their pursuit of God's truth.

---

[9]J. B. Phillips, *Letters to Young Churches* (New York: Macmillan Co., 1958), xiii.

126

They constantly evaluated what Paul taught them by examining the Scriptures (v. 11). We need more people today who are ready to receive truth but must be convinced by the Bible that a given teaching is the truth before they accept it. Every individual has a responsibility to evaluate what a preacher or teacher says in the light of God's Word. If it is truth, accept it; if it is error, reject it. This advice is applicable both to those outside the body of Christ and those within it. More errors "than this world has dreamed of" have resulted from men making other men their authority instead of making God their sole authority (1 Cor. 4:6).

Success in God's Eyes (17:16–34)

Some writers think that Paul's efforts in Athens were a failure. After all, Luke recorded that only a few people responded to his preaching; most mocked him or were indifferent. Apparently, Paul did not leave behind a "thriving" church when he left Athens, as he had in other cities. Considering these thoughts, was Paul's work in Athens a failure?

The world measures success superficially— by possessions, achievements, level of education, appearance, influence, and power. Those of us in the church fall into the same trap when we think of success in terms of buildings, crowds, programs, responses, and excitement. What really constitutes "success" in the Lord's work?

If your heart can be stirred by error and ignorance (v. 16). Paul was provoked by what he saw in Athens. Are we provoked by what we see all around us, or have our hearts become hardened to a world filled with sin and lost souls? Some are embarrassed to "get too excited" about what is right and what is wrong; but Jesus was not (Mt. 9:36; Jn. 2:17), and neither was Paul (Rom. 9:1–3). Generally, nothing significant happens in life until someone gets excited. How is your EQ (Excitement Quotient) regarding ignorance and error?

If you do what you can to correct the wrong (vv. 17–19, 21). How would we have responded if we had been Paul? Would we have felt overwhelmed? Would we have been discouraged, ready to give up? Would we have said, "There is nothing I can do. There is just one of me and thousands of them"? Instead of responding negatively, Paul did what he could to remedy the situation. You are a success spiritually if you are a person who does what he can to correct what is wrong. God never expects more than we can do—but He does expect that!

If you teach regardless of results (vv. 19, 20, 22, 32–34). God has commissioned us to teach and preach (Mt. 28:18–20). Preaching and teaching is our business; response is God's business (1 Cor. 3:6, 7). If you continue to teach and preach God's Word faithfully, regardless of results, you are a success in God's eyes.

If you always do your best (vv. 22–31). For a moment, let us look at our own service to the Lord. Do we always give Him our best, or is it possible that we sometimes toss Him the leftovers of our time, our money, our energies, our talents? Regardless of the outcome, you are a success if you always do your best in your labors for the Master.

We often gauge the success of the Lord's work in a given locale with questions like these: "What kind of building do you have?"; "How many are attending?"; "How many have been baptized?" Rarely do we ask the most important question of all: "Is the gospel being preached faithfully?" Read what the Bible has to say about the labors of Jeremiah and the early work of Ezekiel: Both were "failures" from a human standpoint, but both fulfilled their God-given tasks. They were successes in God's eyes—and you will be, too, if you "go and do likewise."

Preaching in Athens (17:16–34)

C. Bruce White called one unpublished sermon on Acts 17:16–34 "The Newest Thing in Athens," while Rick Atchley titled one "What the Know-It-Alls Didn't Know."[10] James O. Baird presented a lesson on Acts 17 at the 1967 Oklahoma Christian College Bible Teachers Workshop entitled "Meeting the Challenge of 1967." The lesson began by noting that the world in Paul's day, like ours, was characterized by change: political change, religious change, moral change. Brother Baird pointed out two extreme responses to change: (1) We can be overwhelmed by it,

---

[10]Sermon preached at Southern Hills church of Christ, Abilene, Texas, 12 October 1986.

or (2) we can go along with it without thinking. Paul did neither: (1) He had a sensitive spirit that could be stirred by what was happening, (2) he did *something*—as opposed to nothing, and (3) he stayed with fundamentals—the topics of "the sermon on Mars' Hill."

Is There Any News? (17:21)

Dino Roussos, a national preacher who labors in Athens, says that Athenians are much the same today; the common greeting in Athens is "What's the news?" He notes, however, that in Paul's day the topic was philosophy, while today it is politics; an Athenian loves to ponder what he would do "if he could run the government for just twenty-four hours."

Paul's Sermon (17:24–31)

You may want to title Paul's sermon "Heaven's Plain Answers to Man's Perplexing Questions," dividing the sermon according to these important questions: (1) "Where did I come from?"—God made me (vv. 24–26); (2) "Why am I here?"—to seek God (vv. 27–29); (3) "Where am I going?"—to the Judgment (vv. 30, 31). These thoughts might also be designated as (1) Man's Origin, (2) Man's Purpose, and (3) Man's Destiny.

Wiersbe outlined Paul's sermon like this: (1) The Greatness of God—He is Creator (v. 24); (2) The Goodness of God—He is Provider (v. 25); (3) The Government of God—He is Ruler (vv. 26–29); (4) The Grace of God—He is Savior (vv. 30, 31).[11]

The God of Creation (17:24)

Paul's words bring to mind marvelous sights such as the vastness of the Grand Canyon, the formations of the Carlsbad Caverns, the majestic Swiss Alps, the amazing Ayers Rock in Australia, the lush greenness of Scotland, an awe-inspiring sunset over the beaches of Hawaii, the glory of a starlit night on any continent. We are filled with wonder when we meditate on the fact that "God made it all!"

Any correct understanding of the purpose of life must be-

---

[11]Wiersbe, 473–74.

gin with an understanding of, and acknowledgment of, the Creator. Thus Satan continues to mount a massive attack against the concept of special creation—and we must zealously oppose the devil's lie that we came into existence by chance.

Brotherhood of Man (17:26)

Since God made each one of us, we have a common Father and we are all brothers. The pictures of our lives are all different: school children running on a playground, teenagers caught up in the latest fashions, an old man with the years engraved on his face, a young mother cradling a baby in her arms, a business executive connecting flights, a beggar seeking his next meal. Each one of us is different, yet all are God's handiwork.

Quoting from Uninspired Sources (17:28)

Paul's "sermon on Mars' Hill" probably reflects his classical education; he was able to quote from secular poets whose writings were respected by his listeners. Two other times that Paul quoted from uninspired writers are found in 1 Corinthians 15:33 and Titus 1:12. From these examples, we draw two conclusions: (1) It is permissible for a preacher to quote from uninspired sources for purposes of illustration or clarification. (2) Since so few examples of this are seen, we conclude that it should be done sparingly. A Bible class lesson or sermon should not be a hodgepodge of quotations from books, magazines, newspapers, and other secular sources. The solemn charge remains: "Preach *the word*" (2 Tim. 4:2; emphasis added). The gospel is still God's power to salvation (Rom. 1:16).

The Call To Repent (17:30)

Repentance was one of the greatest needs of Paul's day, and it is one of the greatest needs of our day. In a book entitled *Whatever Became of Sin?* Karl Menninger, M.D., wrote:

> . . . few clergymen nowadays venture to call for repentance, as did the prophets and John the Baptist and [preachers in the past]. . . . They fear the public reproach of having reverted (as some extremists have) to threats

of fire-and-brimstone damnation. They dread the accusation so much that they don't speak out even what they believe should be heard and heeded by the man in the pew.[12]

The men-pleasers (Gal. 1:10) that Menninger calls "clergymen" may hesitate to call men to repentance, but gospel preachers dare not do so. When Jesus came preaching, the first word out of His mouth was "Repent" (Mt. 4:17).

---

[12]Karl Menninger, *Whatever Became of Sin?* (New York: Hawthorn Books, Inc., 1973), 195–96.

CHAPTER 18

PAUL'S SECOND MISSIONARY JOURNEY (PART 4)—AND HIS THIRD MISSIONARY JOURNEY (PART 1)

A YEAR AND A HALF AT CORINTH (18:1–17)

Paul Finds Aquila and Priscilla (18:1–4)

¹After these things he left Athens and went to Corinth. ²And he found a Jew named Aquila, a native of Pontus, having recently come from Italy with his wife Priscilla, because Claudius had commanded all the Jews to leave Rome. He came to them, ³and because he was of the same trade, he stayed with them and they were working, for by trade they were tentmakers. ⁴And he was reasoning in the synagogue every Sabbath and trying to persuade Jews and Greeks.

Fear is part of the human condition. If you doubt this, look up the words "fear" and "afraid" in a Bible concordance. In the Book of Genesis alone, you will find that at some time or another, every major character was afraid: Adam, Abraham, Sarah, Lot, Isaac, Jacob, Jacob's sons (Gen. 3:10; 15:1; 18:15; 19:30; 20:11; 26:7; 31:31; 43:18). One should note, however, that although it is natural to *be* afraid, it is not natural to *live* in fear as some do. In chapter 18, the indomitable apostle Paul was overwhelmed by fear. However, the Lord helped him conquer that fear and continue to spread the good news of Christ.

Verse 1. Paul had been preaching in Athens, the educational and cultural center of the world. **After these things he left Athens and went to Corinth.** We do not know if Paul went by land or sea; either was possible. **Corinth** was only about forty miles to the west, but Paul might as well have been going to another country. Athens was a small university town; Corinth was one of the commercial centers of the world. Athenians were intrigued with the intellect; Corinthians were fascinated with the flesh. Athenians claimed to search for truth; Corinthians unashamedly pursued pleasure.

When we read of Paul's early work in Corinth in 18:1–8, it appears that victory followed victory. We would suppose that Paul was filled with joy and overflowing with confidence. Verse 9 surprises us, therefore, when we read that the Lord appeared to Paul with this message: "Do not be afraid any longer." The words "any longer" have been added by the translators. However, the present tense used in Jesus' words in the Greek text indicates that Paul's fear was a continuing condition. The words "any longer" are one way of indicating this. "Afraid *any longer*"? We cry out, "But we did not know that he was afraid!" The fact is, however, that Paul was plagued with fear and misgivings when he entered the bustling metropolis of Corinth.

We know this from Paul's correspondence. During his preaching ministry at Corinth, he began his writing ministry in earnest. The only preserved letter of Paul that may have been written before this is Galatians. Thus we have his letters to supplement Luke's account and to fill in some of the blanks. In Paul's correspondence to the Corinthians, he told of his mindset when he entered their city:

> And when I came to you, brethren, I did not come with superiority of speech or of wisdom, proclaiming to you the testimony of God. . . . I was with you in weakness and in fear and in much trembling (1 Cor. 2:1–3).

Why did Paul come to Corinth "in weakness and in fear and in much trembling"? Knowing something of Paul's situation and something of the human spirit, we can make some educated guesses:

As many of us do, Paul probably let events relating to the *past* prey on his mind. The small number of responses in Athens no doubt disturbed him. He left Athens after a relatively short stay—not because he had to, but because he wanted to. Athens was the first city in Greece where he was not forced to leave town. He evidently thought that he could do little good among the Athenian philosophers.

Further, the plight of the fledgling churches established in Philippi, Thessalonica, and Berea weighed on his mind (2 Cor. 11:28). He was especially concerned about the new Christians in Thessalonica, a city from which he had fled for his life. He feared that "the tempter might have tempted [them]" and that his labor would, therefore, be in vain (1 Thess. 3:5).

As we often do, Paul probably let *present* circumstances get him down. His own situation was anything but encouraging. He was still alone. If Silas and Timothy had joined him in Athens as he had requested, he had immediately sent them back to Macedonia (see comments on 18:5). Thus he was all alone, a stranger in a city of around 125,000 people. Further, Paul probably entered Corinth penniless. Further still, it is possible that, in the absence of Dr. Luke, Paul was sick when he came to Corinth; the word "weakness" (ἀσθένεια, *astheneia*) in 1 Corinthians 2:3 could refer to his physical condition. In 2 Corinthians 12:7 Paul spoke of his "thorn in the flesh" as though the Corinthians were familiar with it. Loneliness compounded by poverty and illness can fill the sturdiest heart with fear.

Paul also had to be intimidated to some extent by Corinth itself. The city was large, corrupt, and rich. Some of this wealth was generated by the Isthmian Games, which Corinth hosted every two years in honor of the mythological god Poseidon. The Isthmian Games were ranked with the Olympic Games and the Delphic Games. These games probably explain Paul's use of athletic illustrations in writing to the Corinthians (1 Cor. 9:24–27).

Regarding commerce, Corinth had an ideal location. It was situated on the narrow isthmus connecting the Peloponnesian peninsula with the rest of Greece, "where the sea has almost gnawed Greece in two."[1] All land traffic in Greece had to come

---

[1] Avon Malone, "The Preaching in Corinth," *Acts, the Spreading Flame* (Searcy, Ark.: Harding University, 1989), 199.

through Corinth. Further, dangerous sailing conditions forced most sea trade to come through Corinth. At the tip of the peninsula was Cape Malea with its turbulent waters. Sailors had a proverb: "Let him who thinks of sailing Malea make his will." To save a two hundred mile trip around stormy Malea, most ships coming from Rome sailed to the harbor at Lechaeum, just north of Corinth. There they unloaded and carted their cargo four miles across the isthmus to the harbor at Cenchrea (see comments on vv. 18, 19; Rom. 16:1) just east of Corinth, where the goods were loaded onto another ship. Ships going to Rome reversed the process. Small ships were even towed across the isthmus, completely loaded, on a special stone roadway known as the *diolkos*. (A canal across the isthmus was begun in Nero's day, but was not finished until 1893. Small ships still pass through the canal today.) Thus through Corinth flowed the commerce of the world.

Corinth was not world-renowned for its commercial enterprise, however. It was, rather, famed as the place where, from the viewpoint of the world, one went to "have a good time." Towering over the city was Acrocorinth, 1,886 feet high, crowned by the temple of Aphrodite, the so-called goddess of love. The Romans called this goddess Venus. Secular historians tell of a thousand priestesses, that is, cult prostitutes who plied their trade in the city. These historical references allude to a time earlier than Paul's visit, but the same general practice probably continued in his day (1 Cor. 6:15, 16, 18). Corinth had the dubious distinction of contributing to the language of the day: To "Corinthianize" was to commit fornication; a "Corinthian girl" was a harlot. As late as the seventeenth century, Shakespeare portrayed "a Corinthian" as a drunken rogue.

When Paul looked at Corinth, its sensuality, idolatry, and intellectual arrogance must have been overwhelming. The city was dotted with temples, including the magnificent temple of Apollo, built one hundred years before the Parthenon in Athens. Seven of its original thirty-eight monolithic columns still stand. The intellectual arrogance of Corinth is evident from 1 Corinthians 1:21, 22. The daunting challenge of the city can be seen in Paul's first letter to the Corinthians:

Or do you not know that the unrighteous will not inherit the kingdom of God? Do not be deceived; neither fornicators, nor idolaters, nor adulterers, nor effeminate, nor homosexuals, nor thieves, nor the covetous, nor drunkards, nor revilers, nor swindlers, will inherit the kingdom of God. *Such were some of you* . . . (1 Cor. 6:9–11; emphasis added).

If Athens had been spiritually barren soil, Corinth must have looked like a sun-baked desert.

Finally, as we often are, Paul was probably concerned about what would happen in the *future*. Corinth's commercial success had attracted a large contingency of Jews. This fact meant that the city had a synagogue where Paul could begin his work, but it also meant that trouble was just around the corner. A basic pattern had developed in Paul's work: (1) He would have initial success; (2) strong opposition would arise; (3) he would be mistreated. In other cities, he had been beaten, stoned, put in prison, and forced to leave town. Even the strongest of men begin to be affected by repeated mistreatment.

Verse 2. When Paul was "in weakness and in fear and in much trembling" (1 Cor. 2:3), God did not abandon him. Paul later referred to the Lord as the "God of all comfort, who comforts us in all our affliction . . ." (2 Cor. 1:3, 4). Among other occasions, he probably had in mind how God had comforted him when he came to Corinth. God is not only with us when sunshine overflows our souls; He is also with us when the blackness of despair fills our hearts. God does not forsake us when we are deserted, discouraged, and disillusioned.

What did God do for Paul? According to our text, God providentially supplied him with what he needed to calm his fears. Initially God gave Paul enduring relationships. Friendship can strengthen us when fear threatens to engulf us. **And** Paul **found a Jew named Aquila, a native of Pontus, having recently come from Italy with his wife Priscilla.** Since only Aquila is specifically called **a Jew**, some have speculated that **Priscilla** was a Gentile; but she was probably a Jew as well. **Aquila** is a Roman name meaning "eagle." This man was **a native of Pontus**, a Roman province in northern Asia Minor. Jews from Pontus were present on the Day of Pentecost (2:9). At some point the church was established there (1 Pet. 1:1). Aquila had recently come to Corinth from **Italy** with his wife Priscilla, **because Claudius had commanded all the Jews to leave Rome. Claudius** was mentioned earlier in 11:28. He is the only Roman emperor whose name is mentioned twice in the New Testament.

Secular writers tell of an imperial banishment of the Jews from Rome about A.D. 49. (Aquila and Priscilla probably arrived in Corinth just shortly before Paul.) Most scholars tie this fact to a statement by Suetonius that Claudius banished the Jews because they were "indulging in constant riots at the instigation of Chrestus."[2] "Chrestus" was a common name meaning "kind [one]," but the statement probably referred to a conflict between Jews and Christians over the preaching of Christ. "Chrestus" and "Christus" sound the same. In the production of many literary works, the author dictated to a scribe. The scribe may have been true to what he heard, but wrote a different word. Since Rome considered Christianity a form of Judaism, Christians as well as Jews would probably have been expelled. Certainly, Christian Jews would have been expelled. Some scholars think that the Book of Hebrews was written to a group of Jewish Christians at Rome and that Hebrews 10:32–34 tells of this expulsion, which would have affected those addressed.

We do not know if Aquila and Priscilla were Christians when Paul met them. Both those who believe they were and those who believe they were not base their positions on Luke's silence: "If they were not Christians, why didn't Luke tell of their conversion?"; "If they were already Christians, why didn't Luke call Aquila a Christian instead of a Jew?" The fact that Paul did not list them among those he baptized during his early days at Corinth (1 Cor. 1:14–16) probably argues in favor of their being Christians when he met them. Assuming that they were Christians, Luke probably mentioned the fact that Aquila was a Jew to explain why he and Priscilla were expelled from Rome. If they were not Christians when they first came in contact with

---

[2]Suetonius *Life of Claudius* 25.4.

Paul, daily association with the apostle no doubt soon convinced them that Jesus was the Messiah.

The text says that Paul **found** Aquila; we do not know how that occurred. It has been suggested that Jews of the same guild, an association of people with the same trade, sat together in the synagogue and Paul met Aquila there. Perhaps, in the providence of God, Paul asked for work in the shop of Aquila and Priscilla. However he met them, they became lifelong friends. He later wrote concerning them: "Greet Prisca and Aquila, my fellow workers in Christ Jesus, who for my life risked their own necks, to whom not only do I give thanks, but also all the churches of the Gentiles" (Rom. 16:3, 4). "Prisca" was the formal way to say "Priscilla" (see 1 Cor. 16:19; 2 Tim. 4:19); as a rule, Luke used informal names. When Paul wrote Romans 16:3, 4, Aquila and Priscilla were back in Rome. Some secular writers indicate that the banishment of the Jews from Rome lasted only a year or so.

Verse 3. In addition to giving him dear friends, God also gave Paul work to do. When an individual is discouraged, it is important to keep busy. Doggedly sticking to a routine can dilute fear. Initially, God supplied Paul with physical labor. Paul came to Aquila and Priscilla, **and because he was of the same trade, he stayed with them and they were working, for by trade they were tent-makers.** This reference is the first time we have read of Paul's occupation. Although Paul was trained as a rabbi, he was also taught the trade of tent-making. It was common in those days for a rabbi to learn and practice another trade. The Jews believed this kept rabbis in touch with the realities of life. Paul's native province of Cilicia was noted for producing a cloth of goat's hair that dispelled dampness and was ideal for tents, so it was natural that he should be taught the trade of tent-making. Perhaps Paul's father had trained him to be a tent-maker; sons generally followed the trades of their fathers. It should be noted that the Greek word σκηνοποιοί (*skēnopoioi*), translated "tent-makers," also means "workers in leather." Paul was a skilled craftsman in both cloth and leather.

When Paul first arrived in Corinth, physical labor was apparently a financial necessity. However, even when his financial condition improved, he continued to labor with his hands (1 Cor. 4:12), trying to avoid the accusation that he "preached for money" (1 Cor. 9:11, 12). It was Paul's general policy to support himself wherever he was, taking no pay from those to whom he preached (20:34; 1 Cor. 9:1–18; 2 Cor. 11:7–9; Phil. 4:15–17; 1 Thess. 2:9; 4:11; 2 Thess. 3:8). Nevertheless, as we shall see, he did accept support from other congregations. Further, Paul stressed the right of a preacher to be supported by those to whom he preached (1 Cor. 9:1–18). Paul gave up this right to try to avoid criticism, but his enemies later used his practice to criticize him (2 Cor. 11:7–9). Perhaps they suggested that he would not accept pay because he knew he was not worthy.

Paul not only worked with Aquila and Priscilla, but he also lived in their home. Maybe they owned a shop with living space in the back. It is likely that their quarters became a meeting place for the church in Corinth. Later, in other cities, the church met in the home of Aquila and Priscilla (Rom. 16:3–5; 1 Cor. 16:19).

Verse 4. In addition to providing Paul with the opportunity to work with his hands, God also supplied the opportunity for Paul to fulfill his greater ministry of sharing the gospel. A major commercial city like Corinth invariably had a large Jewish colony, providing a synagogue in which Paul could begin his work. Thus we read that **he was reasoning** from the Scriptures (see 17:2) **in the synagogue every Sabbath and trying to persuade Jews and Greeks.** The **Greeks** would have been "God-fearers," who were repelled by the ungodliness of the city and were seeking something better. The initial thrust of Paul's preaching in the synagogue was probably ". . . giving evidence [from the Scriptures] that the Christ [the Messiah] had to suffer and rise again from the dead . . ." (17:3).

A stone lintel from an old **synagogue** has been found in the ruins of Corinth. The reconstructed inscription on the stone is "synagogue of [the] Hebrews." It has been variously dated from 100 B.C. to A.D. 200, but is probably closer to A.D. 200. This inscription illustrates the presence of a Jewish population in the city of Corinth. The stone was found near the road that led to Lechaeum.

The Lord Comforts Paul (18:5–11)

⁵But when Silas and Timothy came down from Macedonia, Paul began devoting himself completely to the word, solemnly testifying to the Jews that Jesus was the Christ. ⁶But when they resisted and blasphemed, he shook out his garments and said to them, "Your blood be on your own heads! I am clean. From now on I will go to the Gentiles." ⁷Then he left there and went to the house of a man named Titius Justus, a worshiper of God, whose house was next to the synagogue. ⁸Crispus, the leader of the synagogue, believed in the Lord with all his household, and many of the Corinthians when they heard were believing and being baptized. ⁹And the Lord said to Paul in the night by a vision, "Do not be afraid any longer, but go on speaking and do not be silent; ¹⁰for I am with you, and no man will attack you in order to harm you, for I have many people in this city." ¹¹And he settled there a year and six months, teaching the word of God among them.

Verse 5. As Paul labored both physically and spiritually, further encouragement was provided by the arrival of two of his coworkers. If there is anything better than two new friends, it is two old friends. We read that **Silas and Timothy came down from Macedonia.** Upon being left in Athens, Paul had sent word back to Macedonia "for Silas and Timothy to come to him as soon as possible" (17:15). First Thessalonians 3:1–5 indicates that Timothy had joined Paul in Athens, but that Paul had immediately sent him back to Thessalonica to strengthen and encourage the Christians there. It is possible that Paul sent word to Berea for Timothy to return to Thessalonica rather than coming to Athens. The more natural interpretation of 1 Thessalonians 3:1, 2, however, is that Timothy came to Athens as requested and was then sent back to Thessalonica. Perhaps Silas had also briefly rejoined Paul in Athens and then had been sent back to Philippi. This possibility is based on the idea that Silas and Timothy probably brought a contribution from the church at Philippi. Since Timothy came from Thessalonica, it seems reasonable that Silas came from Philippi—and that Paul had sent him there to see how the brethren were faring, even as he had sent Timothy to Thessalonica.

The arrival of Silas and Timothy in Corinth revitalized Paul in several ways. Their presence alone would have been an encouragement. Picture in your mind Paul, Silas, and Timothy laughing and crying together in Priscilla and Aquila's home as they brought each other up-to-date. In addition, Timothy brought good news from the church in Thessalonica. Paul wrote to the Thessalonians, "But now that Timothy has come to us from you, and has brought us good news of your faith and love . . . in all our distress and affliction we were comforted about you through your faith" (1 Thess. 3:6, 7). Also, Silas and Timothy apparently brought a substantial financial gift from the Christians at Philippi. Since Christians in Philippi were the only ones who helped Paul when he first left Macedonia (Phil. 4:15, 16), and since Silas and Timothy apparently brought help from Macedonia (2 Cor. 11:9), that help must have come from Philippi. Paul later wrote to the Corinthians that "when the brethren came from Macedonia they fully supplied my need" (2 Cor. 11:9). This gift made it possible for Paul to devote full time to his first love: the preaching of the gospel. When Silas and Timothy arrived, **Paul began devoting himself completely to the word.** The phrase **began devoting** is translated from the Greek word συνείχετο (*suneicheto*), which is a form of συνέχω (*sunechō*). The word means "be occupied with" or "absorbed in." The KJV has "pressed in the spirit." The sentence could be translated "Paul was pressed by [or "to," or "in"] the word." This statement could mean that the Word of God pressed Paul, as Jeremiah's fire in his bones, to be more bold, or that Paul began to press the Word with greater vigor on his hearers. Many translators and commentators believe the gift from Macedonia enabled Paul to pursue his preaching with greater fervor—as he did not have to work daily with his hands, at least for a while. The NIV has "devoted himself exclusively to preaching" (see NEB, TEV).

The coming of Silas and Timothy apparently prompted Paul to be bolder in his preaching in the synagogue. Previously, he had stressed that the Scriptures taught that the Messiah was to suffer, die, and be raised. Now he carried this line of thought to its conclusion, **solemnly testifying to the Jews that *Jesus* was the Christ**, the Messiah (emphasis added). For an expansion of Paul's basic message in Corinth, see 1 Corinthians 1:18–25; 2:2; 15:1–8.

Verse 6. When Paul proclaimed that Jesus was the Christ, the Jews became hostile. **They resisted** him **and blasphemed** the name of Jesus. When they did this, Paul **shook out his garments and said to them, "Your blood be on your own heads! I am clean. From now on I will go to the Gentiles."** Once more, Paul's statement that he would go to the Gentiles from then on had local significance only. He continued to preach to Jews as he had opportunity (v. 19). Paul's actions and words were rooted in Old Testament symbolism. Earlier, Paul and Barnabas had shaken the dust off their feet as a witness against the Jews in Antioch of Pisidia (13:50, 51); Paul's shaking the dust off his clothing conveyed the same basic message: "You are rejected by God; therefore, I will have nothing more to do with you!" For a similar Old Testament example, see Nehemiah 5:13.

Paul's words that their **blood** was on their **own heads** and that he was **clean**, were from Ezekiel 3 and 33. If God's messenger failed to warn the wicked man, that man would die in his iniquity—but his blood would be required at the hand of the one who failed to warn him (Ezek. 3:18; 33:8). On the other hand, if God's messenger warned the wicked man, the messenger had delivered his own soul—whether or not the wicked man changed his ways (Ezek. 3:19; 33:9). If one who heard a warning ignored it, "his blood [was] on his own head" (Ezek. 33:4; see also Josh. 2:19).

Verse 7. Paul then left the synagogue; but he did not go far, for a man offered him the use of his house, which was next door. We read that Paul **left there and went to the house of a man named Titius Justus, a worshiper of God, whose house was next to the synagogue.** Some have speculated that **Titius Justus** was Titus, who later became a traveling companion of Paul (Tit. 1:4, 5), but this is unlikely. Others think this man was the Gaius whom Paul baptized with his own hands (1 Cor. 1:14), Paul's host in Corinth on a later trip (Rom. 16:23). It was common for Romans to have three names. The term **worshiper of God** in

Acts usually indicates a God-fearer. Titius Justus probably became a Christian at some point; we do not know if this was before or after he invited Paul to use his house. The fact that Paul went to his **house** does not mean that Paul left the home of Aquila and Priscilla to live with Titius Justus. The home of Titius Justus was used as a place to preach to those who wanted to learn more about Jesus.

It is hard not to see a touch of divine irony in the providential provision of a Christian meeting place **next to the** Jewish **synagogue**. Those interested in hearing Paul did not have to vary their Sabbath routine; instead of going into the synagogue, they just went next door. Knowing that Jesus was being preached next door had to make the Jews unhappy, and hearing the Christians in Titius' house praising Jesus, while they were trying to read the Torah, surely filled them with fury.

Verse 8. Results in Athens had been rare (17:32–34), but the responses in Corinth were remarkable. Does this indicate that the immoral are better prospects than intellectuals? Later, the Lord said that He had "many people" in Corinth (v. 10) who would obey the gospel if Paul taught them. Verse 8 tells of the beginning of the harvest. The first convert mentioned is amazing: **Crispus, the leader of the synagogue, believed in the Lord with all his household.**

The **leader of the synagogue** was responsible for the facilities and the services (see 13:15). It is possible that the synagogue in Corinth had more than one ruler, as in 13:15; **Crispus** could have been one and Sosthenes, the other (v. 17). It is more likely, however, that Sosthenes was appointed leader when Crispus obeyed the gospel. There were many things that Crispus had to sacrifice to become a Christian, including his reputation and authority among the Jews in Corinth. If Paul's moving next door upset the Jews, the defection of the top man in the synagogue must have devastated them.

This reference is the fourth **household** conversion recorded in Acts (see comments on 16:15). It should be noted in passing that the phrase **believed in the Lord** is once more used as a comprehensive phrase encompassing all that he did to become a Christian. Paul said in 1 Corinthians 1:14 that Crispus was baptized; in fact, he baptized Crispus with his own hands.

After telling of Crispus' conversion, Luke gave a terse statement regarding those who responded to Paul's preaching in Corinth: **And many of the Corinthians when they heard were believing and being baptized.** Hearing the gospel is an important part of God's conditions of salvation (Rom. 10:17). The Corinthians were saved exactly as all others in the Book of Acts were saved. It is possible that the **many** who believed and were baptized included Stephanas and his household (1 Cor. 1:16), whom Paul later referred to as "the first fruits of Achaia" (1 Cor. 16:15; see comments on 17:32–34). Stephanas and his household were most likely baptized at Corinth, not Athens. The phrase "first fruits of Achaia" should probably be understood by the phrase "as far as Corinth was concerned."

Verses 9, 10. It appears that victory followed victory in Paul's early work in Corinth. These verses, however, inform us that Paul still struggled with negative emotions. Again, there could have been a number of contributing factors: Maybe Paul was concerned that the powerful temptations of Corinth would pull the converts back. It was probably tiring to deal with the egos of the influential people who had been baptized. Perhaps he had been so emotionally exhausted before he came to Corinth that it took him a long time to be revived. There is one definite factor we can deduce from verse 10: Paul dreaded the inevitable mistreatment from the Jews.

God, therefore, gave Paul one last blessing to help him overcome his fear: a special visit and message from Jesus. On the road to Damascus, Jesus had promised Paul that He would reappear to him from time to time (26:16). This occasion was one of those special visits. The other recorded appearances of Jesus to Paul are found in 9:1–6; 22:17, 18; 23:11; 27:23–25; 2 Timothy 4:16, 17.

And the Lord said to Paul in the night by a vision, "Do not be afraid any longer, but go on speaking and do not be silent; for I am with you, and no man will attack you in order to harm you, for I have many people in this city."

145

It was suggested earlier that Paul may have been overwhelmed by the past, present, and future (see comments on v. 1); Jesus addressed all three when He appeared to the apostle. He dismissed the *past*: **"Do not be afraid any longer."** He gave assurance for the *present*: **"Go on speaking and do not be silent; for I am with you."** Jesus also made two solemn promises regarding the *future*, one stated and the other implied. The stated promise was **"No man will attack you in order to harm you."** These words suggest that Paul dreaded the inevitable attack from the jealous Jews. Perhaps he even thought he had done all the good he could in Corinth and was considering leaving before his enemies had a chance to mistreat him. Even strong men can break under constant pressure. Christ gave Paul the solemn promise, however, that although he had been harmed in other cities, he would not be harmed in Corinth.

Connected with the stated promise was an implied one, in Jesus' words **"for I have many people in this city."** God had "many people" in Corinth in a *prospective* sense. The passage does not teach that God has predetermined who will be saved and who will be lost. All the examples of conversion emphasize that each man can accept or reject the gospel. This promise relates to God's pledge that He would take "from among the Gentiles *a people* for His name" (15:14; emphasis added). God, who knows the hearts of men, knew that there were receptive Gentiles in Corinth who would turn to Him if they had the opportunity. God, who knows all things, had perhaps even looked into the future and seen these respond to the preaching of Paul. Jesus, in effect, was promising Paul that if he stayed in the city and continued to preach, many others would be baptized in addition to the "many" who had already been baptized (v. 8). Note that God's protection of Paul was not simply to benefit Paul, but to benefit receptive souls in Corinth—that is, to keep Paul in Corinth where he could preach to these souls.

Verse 11. Jesus' assurances turned Paul's anxiety into anticipation: **And he settled there a year and six months, teaching the word of God among them.** Paul stayed on for a year and a half in Corinth, the second longest period he worked in any city on his missionary journeys. He stayed longer in Ephesus (19:10).

We do not know if this year and a half was in addition to the time he had already spent there. Neither do we know if the time ("many days") in verse 18 is in addition to the eighteen months. Verse 11 is probably a summary statement of all Paul's time in Corinth and includes the other times mentioned—but the possibility remains that Paul's stay was several months longer than a year and a half. We are safe in saying, however, that Paul spent *at least* a year and six months in Corinth, a city that appeared to be the least likely of locations in which to establish the church. Perhaps we spend too much time today conducting soil tests when we need to do more sowing.

During this time, Paul wrote 1 and 2 Thessalonians. First Thessalonians was written shortly after Timothy reported to Paul in Corinth (1 Thess. 3:6). Timothy was then sent to Thessalonica with that letter. When he returned, Paul wrote a follow-up letter. This second letter was almost certainly also written from Corinth. Note that Silas is mentioned in the first verse of 2 Thessalonians; the last place Silas is mentioned in Acts is in Corinth (v. 5).

Paul Appears Before Gallio (18:12–17)

[12]**But while Gallio was proconsul of Achaia, the Jews with one accord rose up against Paul and brought him before the judgment seat,** [13]**saying, "This man persuades men to worship God contrary to the law."** [14]**But when Paul was about to open his mouth, Gallio said to the Jews, "If it were a matter of wrong or of vicious crime, O Jews, it would be reasonable for me to put up with you;** [15]**but if there are questions about words and names and your own law, look after it yourselves; I am unwilling to be a judge of these matters."** [16]**And he drove them away from the judgment seat.** [17]**And they all took hold of Sosthenes, the leader of the synagogue, and began beating him in front of the judgment seat. But Gallio was not concerned about any of these things.**

Verse 12. Often the fulfillment of God's promises comes years later. In this instance, the fulfillment to His promise (v. 10) came immediately. Luke showed how God kept His word—working through a pagan.

But while Gallio was proconsul of Achaia, the Jews with one accord rose up against Paul and brought him before the judgment seat. Gallio was the most important Roman official Paul met on his three journeys. Gallio's brother was the famed Stoic philosopher Seneca, tutor to Nero. He himself was mentioned as a man of considerable influence by a number of imperial writers, including Tacitus, Pliny, and Seneca. The beginning of Gallio's administration as **proconsul** at Corinth can be fixed fairly accurately at July A.D. 51 because of an inscription found at Delphi. This date helps with the chronology of Acts and the dating of the writing of 1 and 2 Thessalonians. We can date Paul's work in Corinth with some accuracy as being from the fall of A.D. 50 to the spring of A.D. 52.

The Jews did not bring Paul before city magistrates as had been the case in other cities, but before the governor of the entire province of **Achaia**, of which Corinth was the capital. An adverse ruling by a powerful man like Gallio would set a precedent for all other Roman provinces. The legal and political significance of this event cannot be overemphasized.

Many believe that **the Jews** brought **Paul** before Gallio when the Roman official first came to Corinth. If so, perhaps they thought that Gallio would initially be concerned with establishing a good relationship with the people of the area and would be impressed with a protest by a large number of citizens. What they could not foresee was Gallio's integrity. It was with **one accord** that the Jews opposed Paul. Here is an example of unity of the wrong sort (see 5:9; 7:57). Unity is important, but not as important as doing the will of God.

The Jews brought Paul **before the judgment seat**. The Greek word translated "judgment seat" is βῆμα (*bēma*). The bema was a raised stage near the center of the agora in Corinth, made of stone and covered with marble. It was used for various public functions, including speaking. If Paul was given the opportunity, he no doubt preached from this platform. Primarily, however, the bema served as the place where court was held. The bema still stands in old Corinth. It is well preserved, with bits of blue and white marble adhering to its rock surface. In front of the bema is a little pillar where the accused stood. Picture Paul standing by that pillar, perhaps chained to it, his fate resting in Gallio's hands.

Verse 13. We are not told how the Jews "brought [Paul] before the judgment seat." Maybe they dragged him there (16:19); perhaps he was summoned by the court. When all participants were present, the Jews solemnly made their charge before the new proconsul: **"This man persuades men to worship God contrary to the law."** Some think the word **law** referred to the law of Moses; the NCV has "our law." Others think the Jews meant Roman law. If they meant the law of Moses, their argument was that since Judaism was a "legal religion" (*religio licita*), the Jews had been promised protection and Paul should be prevented from disturbing them. If they were appealing to Roman law, the Jews were accusing Christians of fostering an illegal religion, which should not be protected by Rome. Either way, they argued that Paul, and by implication all Christians, deserved to be punished by the Roman government.

At that moment, it would have appeared to the skeptic that God's promise was uncertain. The Lord had told Paul that "no man will attack you in order to harm you" (v. 10), but there he was, under attack. Further, in every other city, when the Jews decided to exert their influence against Paul, he had barely escaped with his life (13:50; 14:5, 6, 19; 17:6–10, 13). How could Paul possibly escape harm on this occasion?

Verses 14, 15. Paul was about to open his mouth. He was ready to show the ridiculousness of the charges; he was probably also planning to preach the gospel to Gallio (see chs. 22, 23, 24, 26). Before he could say anything, however, the proconsul spoke.

> **Gallio said to the Jews, "If it were a matter of wrong or of vicious crime, O Jews, it would be reasonable for me to put up with you; but if there are questions about words and names and your own law, look after it yourselves; I am unwilling to be a judge of these matters."**

It seems that in some way Gallio had heard something about the conflict between Jews and Christians. Perhaps, in their accusation, the Jews mentioned specific **words and names**. The "words" would probably have included ones such as "salvation" and "resurrection," while the question of "names" probably revolved around whether "Jesus" was actually "Christ."

For the first time in Paul's frequent battles with the Jews, his enemies were face to face with an honest Roman official whom they could not intimidate. If Gallio had needed political reassurance, he would have found it in the fact that at that moment Jews were out of favor in Rome (v. 2). He probably would have ruled as he did, however, regardless of the situation in Rome. Gallio may have been confused about the fundamental differences between Judaism and Christianity, but this he understood: Whatever the dispute between Paul and the Jews, it was not within his jurisdiction. If the Jews were asking him to make a judgment based on Roman law, as verse 13 likely indicates, he recognized that the problem centered on their own law. He did not hesitate to throw the case out of court.

Verse 16. Imagine the shocked surprise of the Jews as Gallio ordered his officers to clear the court. Those who did not move quickly enough would have received a taste of the lictor's rod (see comments on 16:22, 23, 35, 38). Thus Gallio **drove them away from the judgment seat.**

Verse 17. Luke added a note of irony: **And they all took hold of Sosthenes, the leader of the synagogue, and began beating him in front of the judgment seat.** Luke earlier had spoken of the conversion of Crispus, "the leader of the synagogue" (v. 8); **Sosthenes** had evidently taken his place (see comments on 18:8). Sosthenes was probably abused because, as the leader of the Jews, he had been their spokesman in bringing charges against Paul.

The text is not clear regarding who **they** were who beat Sosthenes. Some ancient texts indicate that "the Greeks" beat him (see KJV). If so, these were probably loafers who hung around the agora (see comments on 17:5) and took advantage of the turn of events to vent their dislike for the Jews. The better manuscript evidence has only "they," with the antecedent of "they" being the Jews (vv. 14–16). Could it be that the Jews turned on their own leader, thinking that if he had handled matters better, they would not have been embarrassed?

Even more peculiar are the words that follow: **But Gallio was not concerned about any of these things.** This statement is generally taken to mean that Gallio was indifferent about the beating of an innocent man. If this understanding is correct, maybe Gallio saw some element of justice in the action. Perhaps he thought that "the punishment fit the crime." However, this interpretation does not seem to harmonize with his personality as depicted by secular writers. It could be that **these things** does not refer to the beating of Sosthenes, but to the charges brought against Paul by the Jews. Barclay suggested that "the real meaning is that [Gallio] was absolutely impartial and refused to allow himself to be influenced" by the Jewish delegation.[3]

Whatever the exact meaning of verse 17, the entire sequence of events was startling. Not only was Paul left unharmed, but he was also vindicated. It has been suggested that Paul's fair treatment at the hands of Gallio may have been a major factor in his later appeal to Rome (25:11). The Jews who had plotted to punish him were themselves punished. God kept His promise—using the most unexpected of resources, a high-placed Roman official. It has also been suggested that Gallio's recognition of Paul's legal innocence bought ten years of peace for the church. Even as Paul's indictment by Gallio would have set a legal precedent for other provinces, so did Paul's release. It would be many years before Jews again attempted to influence Roman authorities to punish Paul.

PAUL RETURNS TO ANTIOCH IN SYRIA BY WAY OF EPHESUS (18:18–22)

[18]**Paul, having remained many days longer, took leave of the brethren and put out to sea for Syria, and with him were Priscilla and Aquila. In Cenchrea he had his hair cut, for he**

---

[3]William Barclay, *The Acts of the Apostles*, The Daily Study Bible Series, rev. ed. (Philadelphia.: Westminster Press, 1976), 137.

was keeping a vow. [19]They came to Ephesus, and he left them there. Now he himself entered the synagogue and reasoned with the Jews. [20]When they asked him to stay for a longer time, he did not consent, [21]but taking leave of them and saying, "I will return to you again if God wills," he set sail from Ephesus.

[22]When he had landed at Caesarea, he went up and greeted the church, and went down to Antioch.

Verse 18. Verses 18 through 22 wrap up Paul's second missionary journey. After Paul's hearing, he **remained many days longer** in Corinth. Luke recorded no details of the apostle's work during these "many days," but we can be sure that the Lord's second promise (v. 10) was realized: As Paul continued to preach and teach, many others became Christians. Since Paul stayed at Corinth longer than most other places, we could say that Corinth was one of the best educated of all the churches with whom he worked. We are amazed, then, to read in 1 Corinthians of all the problems in the church. One writer made a valid note that the Christians in Corinth probably would have had *worse* problems if they had not been so well taught. We must keep in mind the immoral cesspool from which these Christians were pulled.

It is possible that Sosthenes, the ruler of the synagogue who was beaten, was one of those converts. When Paul wrote his first letter to the Christians at Corinth, he mentioned a fellow-worker named Sosthenes who apparently was known to the Corinthians. It would be interesting to speculate that Paul and Crispus visited Sosthenes after his beating, to picture them washing his wounds and telling him about Jesus—but we must leave such ideas in the realm of conjecture. There is an inscription on a stone monument in Corinth with the name "Sosthenes." The name was sufficiently common so we cannot be dogmatic about the identity of the Sosthenes mentioned in 1 Corinthians 1:1.

We know definitely of one other remarkable convert in Corinth. Later, when Paul wrote to Rome from Corinth, he included this greeting: "Erastus, the city treasurer greets you" (Rom. 16:23). Not only did influential Jews in Corinth become Christians, but so did an influential Roman. Second Timothy 4:20 mentions an "Erastus" at Corinth, with the implication that he had traveled with Paul. This person may be the same man. An archaeological find in the ruins of Corinth probably pertains to this official. In the pavement in front of Corinth's magnificent theater, a stone was laid with this inscription in Latin: "Erastus in return for his aedileship laid [the pavement] at his own expense." The work of an *aedile* included the upkeep of city property, managing revenues, and sitting in judgment on commercial and financial cases. Paul used the term "city treasurer" (οἰκονόμος, *oikonomos*) for Erastus in Romans 16:23, which describes the work of an *aedile* in Corinth. Originally the carved-out letters of the inscription were filled with bronze held in place with lead. Today only the hollow letters remain, but they are easily read.

During those "many days," Paul also would have continued to preach the gospel in the region surrounding Corinth, establishing churches throughout Achaia. In 2 Corinthians 1:1, Paul spoke of "all the saints who are throughout Achaia." We know definitely that congregations were established at Corinth (2 Cor. 1:1) and Cenchrea (Rom. 16:1), and we have suggested that a congregation was established at Athens (see comments on 17:34). However, there must have been many more Christians throughout the province. Those "many days" probably would have also been the time when 2 Thessalonians was composed. As Paul continued to work in the area, unharmed by both the Jews and the Roman authorities and blessed with a multiplicity of responses, how often he must have reflected on the promises of Jesus—and how marvelously they were fulfilled.

Paul **took leave of the brethren and put out to sea for Syria.** Having finished his work in Corinth, Paul made plans to return to Antioch of Syria, from where he had started three years earlier. Traveling **with him were Priscilla and Aquila**—his fellow Christians, friends, and fellow tent-makers. Note that Priscilla is mentioned first—as in 18:26; Romans 16:3; and 2 Timothy 4:19—probably an indication of her prominence in the church.

Since only Priscilla and Aquila were mentioned, perhaps Paul left Silas and Timothy in Corinth to continue the work there. The last time we read of Silas in Acts, he was in Corinth (v. 5). Before we lose sight of this man who sang and prayed with Paul in prison, we should acknowledge his invaluable contribution to the second missionary journey. We know little of Silas' subsequent labors, other than the fact that he later worked with Peter (1 Pet. 5:12). We have every confidence, however, that Silas continued as a faithful servant of the Lord.

At the end of verse 18, Luke tossed in a strange little note: **In Cenchrea** Paul **had his hair cut, for he was keeping a vow. Vow** is translated from the Greek word εὐχή (*euchē*). The verb form of this word is found seven times in the New Testament and generally refers to or implies making a request to deity (26:29; 27:29; Rom. 9:3; 2 Cor. 13:7, 9; Jas. 5:16; 3 Jn. 2). The noun form is found only three times in the New Testament: here, in Acts 21:23, and in James 5:15. In James 5:15, it is translated "prayer"; in Acts 18:18 and 21:23, it is translated "vow." Vows are mentioned often in the Old Testament, but only a handful of times in the New Testament.

Vows were serious. They were made voluntarily, but once made, they were binding (Num. 30:2; Deut. 23:21–23). They were thus not to be made rashly (Prov. 20:25). A vow was similar to an oath. The two are treated together in Numbers 30:2. In Matthew 5:33, the Greek word for "oath" (ὅρκος, *horkos*) is translated as "vow" in the NASB. There were, however, differences. For instance, an oath could be made to a man, while a vow was made only to God. As a rule, a vow included a condition, stated or implied, while an oath did not. A vow said, in effect, "God, if You will do this, I will do that," or "Because You have done this, I will do that." "Jews made vows to God either for thankfulness for past blessings . . . or as part of a petition for future blessings."[4]

Regarding the vow in Acts 18, Luke recorded just enough to tantalize us. There is some question regarding who made the vow. Grammatically the words could apply to Aquila, but most agree that the context favors Paul. Again, we cannot be certain what kind of vow it was, although the mention of the cutting of

---

[4]I. Howard Marshall, *The Acts of the Apostles*, The Tyndale New Testament Commentaries, gen. ed. R. V. G. Tasker (Grand Rapids, Mich.: Wm. B. Eerdmans Publishing Co., 1980), 300.

the hair suggests the Nazirite vow or something similar (Num. 6:2, 5). In Acts 21, the vow is definitely a Nazirite vow, but that is not conclusive in this passage. F. F. Bruce thought Paul's vow at Cenchrea was "private" rather than "formal."[5]

The term "Nazirite" basically means "one consecrated." The Nazirite vow was a commitment to totally consecrate oneself to the Lord. The outward expressions of that vow were to let the hair grow, abstain from everything made from grapes, and avoid dead bodies (Num. 6:1–7). For some, the Nazirite vow was life-long (Judg. 13:5), but for most, it was for shorter periods. At the fulfillment of the vow, certain offerings were to be made (Num. 6:13–17). The Law also specified that the vow-maker's hair was to be shaved off in the temple and burned in the fire of the altar (Num. 6:18). By New Testament times, Jewish tradition allowed for the cutting to be done elsewhere, as long as the hair was taken to Jerusalem and the sacrifices were made within thirty days.[6] This allowance was made because of the great number of Jews dispersed outside of Palestine.

Many assume that Paul had taken a short-term Nazirite vow because of thankfulness for God's protection in Corinth, and that the end of the vow coincided with his arrival in Cenchrea. They then assume that the apostle planned to go to Jerusalem when he reached Palestine to take the shorn locks and make the necessary offerings. Others think it possible that the Nazirite vow also commenced with shaving the head, and that the vow in chapter 18 was taken in Cenchrea as part of a petition for a safe journey. Some even suggest that the vow mentioned in Acts 18 was completed in Acts 21, though there is no reason for that assumption. The vow in chapter 21 was that of the four men, not Paul. Furthermore, there is no indication that Paul planned to make sacrifices at the temple until the elders suggested it.

Glance over the last few paragraphs and note the words "could," "possible," "assume," and "suggest." The proliferation

---

[5]F. F. Bruce, *The Book of Acts*, The New International Commentary on the New Testament, gen. ed. F. F. Bruce, rev. ed. (Grand Rapids, Mich.: Wm. B. Eerdmans Publishing Co., 1988), 355.

[6]*Mishna Nazir* 1:3; 3:6; 6:8.

of such words underline the fact that Luke did not give us sufficient information to know for certain what Paul did at Cenchrea
and why he did it. The fact remains, however, that Paul did take
a vow and one that looks suspiciously like the Nazirite vow.
Acknowledging the possibility that he took the Nazirite vow,
we ask, "Is there any reason why he might?" The subject is discussed in more detail in the comments on chapter 21, including
the worrisome aspect of the required sacrifices, but a few observations are in order here:

Keep in mind that, although Paul was a follower of Jesus,
he, like other Hebrew Christians, remained a Jew nationally. As
long as he could do so without leaving the impression that keeping the Law was essential to salvation or that it was bound on
Gentiles, he was not adverse to keeping certain Jewish customs
and ceremonies (see comments on 16:3). Remember also that, as
part of his mission strategy, Paul became "all things to all men,
so that [he might] by all means save some" (1 Cor. 9:22). This
included his fellow Jews:

> . . . I have made myself a slave to all, so that I may win
> more. To the Jews I became as a Jew, so that I might win
> Jews; to those who are under the Law, as under the Law
> though not being myself under the Law, so that I might
> win those who are under the Law (1 Cor. 9:19, 20).

It is possible that Paul had taken a Jewish vow as part of
reaffirming his national heritage in the sight of Jews he was trying to reach in Corinth and the surrounding area. If missing a
few haircuts, avoiding grape products, and shunning corpses
would result in souls being saved, the apostle probably would
not have hesitated to do all three since none of these was inher-
ently wrong within itself.

Verse 19. Paul and his companions sailed from Cenchrea (v.
18), the important Corinthian port on the Saronic Gulf. We later
read of a congregation in Cenchrea (Rom. 16:1), probably established during Paul's labors in Corinth. Their first major stop
was **Ephesus**, the capital of the Roman province of Asia and
almost certainly Paul's intended destination earlier on this sec-

ond missionary journey. God had forbidden him to go to Asia at that time (16:6), but that prohibition had evidently been lifted. Paul used the short time he had in Ephesus to test the receptivity of the Jews. We do not know why he had limited time in Ephesus. Some have suggested that he wanted to get back to Jerusalem in time for the Passover feast or Pentecost. More likely, the ship he was on was scheduled to stay only a few days in the harbor at Ephesus as it unloaded old cargo and loaded new cargo.

Paul **left** Aquila and Priscilla in Ephesus to prepare the soil for his return. It has been speculated that they desired to stay in Ephesus to open "a branch office" for their tent-making enterprise. All we know is that they stayed for a number of years in that area, furthering the cause of Christ (18:26; 1 Cor. 16:19). Paul **himself entered the synagogue and reasoned with the Jews.**

Verses 20, 21. The Jews **asked him to stay for a longer time—** a request not frequently made (see 13:42). Paul **did not consent** to their petition. However, he responded, **"I will return to you again if God wills."** Paul yielded his life to the sovereignty of God (see Mt. 6:10; Rom. 1:10; 15:32; 1 Cor. 4:19; 16:7; Heb. 6:3; Jas. 4:13–15). Note that it *was* the Lord's will, for Paul did return (Acts 19:1). Following the Western Text, the KJV adds these words at the beginning of Paul's answer: "I must by all means keep this feast that cometh in Jerusalem." These words are not supported by the best textual evidence. **Taking leave of them . . . he set sail from Ephesus.**

Verse 22. After sailing about another month, Paul's ship finally landed at Caesarea, the home city of Philip the evangelist and Cornelius the centurion (8:40; 10:1; 21:8). **When he had landed at Caesarea, he went up and greeted the church. The church** may refer to the congregation that met in Caesarea, or it may refer to the church in Jerusalem. The context fits the church in Caesarea better, while the words "went up" and "went down" fit Jerusalem better (8:5; 9:30, 32; 11:2, 27; 13:31; 15:1, 2, 30).

It is possible that Paul went to Jerusalem not only to greet the church, but also to complete a vow (see comments on v. 18). Finally, he **went down to Antioch**; no doubt he once more was warmly received by the congregation there and once more reported "all things that God had done" (14:27) during the three years he and his coworkers had labored in Greece.

THE BEGINNING OF THE
THIRD MISSIONARY JOURNEY (18:23)

[23]And having spent some time there, he left and passed successively through the Galatian region and Phrygia, strengthening all the disciples.

Verse 23. Paul **spent some time** in Antioch. Maybe he stayed there through the winter months, working with the church which had continued to encourage him in his worldwide mission. Later, possibly in the spring, when the roads were again passable, **he left** on his third journey. He probably departed in the spring of A.D. 53. As he left, no doubt he had plans to return to the brethren at Antioch, as he had done at the close of each of his journeys. As he bid them farewell, he was unaware that he would never see their faces again.

We are not told if Paul had traveling companions at the beginning of his third missionary journey, but he seldom traveled alone by choice. Luke later mentioned that Timothy was at Ephesus (19:22); perhaps the young preacher had come from Corinth (see comments on v. 18) and started this trip with Paul. Here are other possibilities: Timothy may have gone from Corinth back to Lystra to see his mother and rejoined Paul there, or Timothy may have sailed from Corinth to Ephesus after Paul arrived in Ephesus. Also, we learn from 2 Corinthians that Titus was apparently with Paul in Ephesus (2 Cor. 2:13; 7:6, 13, 14; 8:6, 16, 23; 12:18); it is possible that Titus also was with Paul as he left Antioch. One of the mysteries of Acts is why Luke never mentioned Titus. As noted earlier, a possible explanation is that Titus was related to Luke. According to uninspired tradition, Titus, like Luke, was from Antioch of Syria (see Gal. 1:21; 2:1), and it would have been natural for him to leave with Paul on this trip.

When Paul and his companions, whoever they may have

been, left Antioch, they followed the same land route Paul and Silas had used at the start of the second journey. They would have headed north from Syria and then west, crossing the Taurus Mountains through the pass called the Cilician Gates, until they reached the plateau of Southern Galatia. They then **passed successively through the Galatian region and Phrygia,** once more visiting the churches established on the first journey. A primary purpose was to see how the Christians were progressing in the faith, so Paul and his fellow workers spent their time **strengthening all the disciples.**

Once more, we wish Luke had given details concerning this part of the journey. If Timothy was with Paul, it is conceivable to imagine a tearful reunion with his mother in Lystra. She probably would have been surprised to see him still alive.

One of Paul's purposes on his third journey was not emphasized by Luke, but it was prominent in the letters he wrote during the journey: He was collecting funds for "the poor among the saints in Jerusalem" (Rom. 15:26). As he passed through Galatia, he gave directions to "the churches of Galatia" to take up a collection "on the first day of every week" for that purpose (1 Cor. 16:1, 2). He probably also made arrangements for representatives from the area to complete the collection and to help deliver the contribution to Jerusalem later (1 Cor. 16:3, 4). Gaius of Derbe later traveled with Paul on this benevolent mission. Timothy also came, representing Lystra (Acts 20:4). Luke's only reference to the special collection is in 24:17.

AN INTRODUCTION OF AN ELOQUENT PREACHER (APOLLOS) (18:24–28)

[24]Now a Jew named Apollos, an Alexandrian by birth, an eloquent man, came to Ephesus; and he was mighty in the Scriptures. [25]This man had been instructed in the way of the Lord; and being fervent in spirit, he was speaking and teaching accurately the things concerning Jesus, being acquainted only with the baptism of John; [26]and he began to speak out boldly in the synagogue. But when Priscilla and Aquila heard him, they took him aside and explained to him the way of

God more accurately. ²⁷And when he wanted to go across to Achaia, the brethren encouraged him and wrote to the disciples to welcome him; and when he had arrived, he greatly helped those who had believed through grace, ²⁸for he powerfully refuted the Jews in public, demonstrating by the Scriptures that Jesus was the Christ.

Verse 24. Before writing about Paul's arrival in the city of Ephesus (19:1), Luke inserted the story of Apollos. He did so to inform us about what happened between Paul's visits to Ephesus, and to prepare us for the situation Paul found when he finally got there.

Now a Jew named Apollos, an Alexandrian by birth, an eloquent man, came to Ephesus; and he was mighty in the Scriptures. The name **Apollos** was a shortened form of "Apollonius." This man was **an Alexandrian by birth.** "By birth" is translated from τῷ γένει (*tō genei*), which in this context means "by nationality," indicating that Apollos was both born and reared in Alexandria (see 4:36; 18:2). Apollos was also **an eloquent man.** The Greek word λόγιος (*logios*), translated "eloquent," can also mean "learned" (see NIV).

Thus we are introduced to Apollos, who became a prominent evangelist in the early church (1 Cor. 3:5, 6; Tit. 3:13). Although his parents were Jewish, he was born in Alexandria, the celebrated city that was one of the educational centers of the world. It had the largest library in the world—almost 700,000 volumes. Alexandria was also a seaport of Egypt, located a few miles from the mouth of the Nile River. The city had been founded by and named after Alexander the Great. Alexandria had a considerable Jewish population; some think that at least one-fourth of its population was Jewish. The Greek version of the Old Testament, the Septuagint, had been produced at Alexandria. Philo, one of the most famous Jewish teachers who ever lived, made Alexandria his home; he was a contemporary of Paul and Apollos. Since Apollos knew the baptism of John (v. 25), he may have also spent some time in Palestine, perhaps studying there as a young man, as Paul had. Their backgrounds were alike in several ways: Paul was born in Tarsus, also a center of learning. Both were extremely talented men who were dedicated to God. Further, both were in error when first mentioned in Scripture.

Apollos possessed many admirable qualities. Luke's description of him indicates that he was well-educated. Being raised in Alexandria and having perhaps spent time in Palestine, he had received the finest secular and religious training available in his day. Further, Luke's references to the eloquence and fervor of Apollos attest to his ability to speak and persuade. Rhetoric, the art of speaking, was an important study in the schools of Alexandria, as it was in schools throughout the Roman world.

Verse 25. Most of all, Apollos is admirable for dedicating his considerable talents to the service of God. He had applied his intellect to the study of the Word. He **had been instructed in the way of the Lord.** The term "the way" is used to refer to Christianity, but the phrase "the way of the Lord" seems to be limited to the teaching of John the Immerser (Mt. 3:3; Mk. 1:3; Lk. 3:4; Jn. 1:23). Apollos was also "mighty in the [Old Testament] Scriptures" (v. 24). He knew the Book—the first requirement for anyone who would call himself a "preacher."

Further, his ability to speak had been dedicated to the proclamation of the Word. He spoke "in the synagogue" (v. 26) about Jesus Christ. Further still, his dedication was such that he was not content with mere performance; rather, he put his *heart* into it. As he preached, he was **fervent in spirit** (see Rom. 12:11). A few "individual" translations render this phrase "fervent in the Spirit," that is, the Holy Spirit. Apollos also spoke "boldly" (v. 26).

When we are introduced to Apollos, his understanding of the will of the Lord was limited. He knew the Old Testament Scriptures (v. 24), including what those Scriptures said about the Messiah (v. 28). To some extent, he was even able to speak and teach **accurately the things concerning Jesus.** We read, however, that he was **acquainted only with the baptism of John.** His knowledge of Jesus was apparently limited to what John the Immerser had known. John had been killed (Mt. 14:1–12) before Jesus promised to build His church (Mt. 16:16–19)—and *long* before Jesus died, was raised, gave the Great Commission, and ascended to heaven. John had spoken of the coming of the Spirit (Mt. 3:11), but he had learned nothing of the fulfillment of that promise (Acts 1:4–8; 2:1–4), the establishment of the church, or Christian worship.

Luke did not explain how Apollos learned of the baptism of John or why his knowledge of the Lord was incomplete. Perhaps Apollos had been in Palestine during the ministry of John and had become a disciple of his (Mt. 3:5, 6), or perhaps he had been taught by one of John's disciples traveling in Egypt. The Western Text may indicate that Apollos learned of John's baptism in Alexandria. J. W. Roberts once said that, according to secular writers, some disciples of John the Immerser did not accept Jesus as the Messiah and continued to teach "John's gospel." If Apollos had become a disciple of John in Palestine, perhaps he had left the country soon afterward to spread the good news as he understood it. At any rate, he had apparently not been in Palestine since the Day of Pentecost (Acts 2), nor had he come in contact with those who had a fuller knowledge of Jesus and His way. Since it had been twenty-five or so years since John had preached, this presents something of a mystery; but it is certainly possible that he did not come in contact with any Christians during all those years. However, the length of the time involved *may* indicate that Apollos had learned of the baptism of John in more recent years from a disciple of John, rather than from John himself years earlier. Therefore, he preached what he knew: the baptism of John.

A few words about the baptism of John are in order. John came in fulfillment of prophecy to prepare the way for the Messiah (Is. 40:3; Mal. 4:5, 6; Mt. 3:1–3; 17:10–13). As part of his preparation, he commanded his listeners to repent and change their lives (Mt. 3:2; Lk. 3:7–14), and he practiced a preparatory baptism (Mt. 3:5, 6). His baptism was an immersion in water (Jn. 3:23) for "the forgiveness of sins" (Mk. 1:4). It was called "a baptism of repentance" (Mk. 1:4; Acts 13:24; 19:4) because it embodied and expressed repentance. Those who came to him were "baptized by him in the Jordan River, as they confessed their sins" (Mt. 3:6). Baptism was so much a part of John's ministry that he was known as "the Baptist [Immerser]" (Mt. 3:1). "Baptist" (βαπτιστής, *baptistēs*) literally means "one who baptizes [immerses]." During John's ministry, his baptism served as a dividing point between those willing to accept God's purposes and those unwilling to accept them (Lk. 7:30).

As far as verse 25 is concerned, the key fact to remember about John's baptism is that it was never intended to be a permanent part of God's plan for the Christian Age. Great Commission baptism is a baptism in the name of the Father, Son, and Holy Spirit (Mt. 28:19, 20; Mk. 16:15, 16) and is to be administered "to the end of the [Christian] age" (Mt. 28:20). It is, therefore, the "one baptism" (Eph. 4:5) which is now part of God's plans and purposes. The baptism of John had no validity after Great Commission baptism began to be preached and practiced (Acts 2). A major shortcoming of John's baptism was that it was predicated upon an incomplete knowledge of Jesus. John could only charge his followers "to believe in Him who was coming after him . . ." (19:4).

Although the baptism that Apollos knew was invalidated, he preached what he believed with conviction and fervor. The opening segment of the next chapter indicates that he even made a number of converts as he preached in Ephesus (19:1–6).

Verse 26. One Sabbath, Aquila and Priscilla went to the synagogue in Ephesus. It is generally assumed that they went to worship. Perhaps they did; as noted before, this was a transitional period. Perhaps, however, they went there for the same purpose Paul had—to find honest hearts they could teach. Aquila and Priscilla were the friends of Paul who stayed in Ephesus as he returned to Antioch of Syria (v. 19). The synagogue was probably the same one in which Paul had received a warm reception (vv. 19–21). When it came time for the lesson, to their surprise, a stranger arose who **began to speak out boldly in the synagogue** concerning Jesus. Like Paul, Apollos apparently began his work in a new community by going to the synagogue.

Priscilla and Aquila were listening to Apollos' message. The Western Text lists Aquila first (see KJV), but the better manuscripts list Priscilla first, again indicating her prominence in the early church. Some believe that she is also listed first so there would be no question about her active involvement in correcting the preacher. In other words, if Aquila and Priscilla took Apollos to their home, Priscilla was not preparing coffee and cookies while Aquila did all the teaching. Note, however, that this is private teaching and in no way justifies a woman's preaching in the assembly.

As the couple listened to the eloquent speaker, it soon became apparent that he knew only the baptism of John and that his knowledge of the Savior was incomplete. After the service, **they took him aside.** This phrase is one possible translation of the Greek word which comes from προσλαμβάνω (*proslambanō*) (see Mt. 16:22). Another possible translation is "they invited him to their home" (NIV). *Proslambanō* is also used in contexts of receiving and welcoming guests (Acts 28:2; Philem. 17), as well as eating food (Acts 27:33). That they took him home for dinner is a reasonable guess. In a private setting, Priscilla and Aquila **explained to** Apollos **the way of God more accurately.** No doubt they started with John's predictions (Mt. 3:11) and showed how those predictions had been fulfilled.

When Acts 18:24–26 is being discussed, this is generally the point at which someone asks, "Did Apollos have to be re-immersed—like the disciples were in the next chapter?" This question is always good for an hour's discussion, and at the end no one is the wiser. Our opinion is that those who had been baptized with John's baptism before the death of Jesus did not need to be re-immersed when the church was established. In other words, God automatically "set them into the church." The classic example is the apostles, all of whom had surely received John's baptism (Lk. 7:29, 30; Jn. 1:25–51; 3:22, 26; 4:1, 2). We doubt that the apostles were baptized in water on the Day of Pentecost. Further, if the word "spirit" in verse 25 refers to the Holy Spirit, this would indicate that Apollos was already a Christian and did not need to be baptized. Among other problems, Luke did not say whether Apollos learned of John's baptism before or after the Day of Pentecost, or whether Apollos was baptized with John's baptism before or after the Day of Pentecost. Most discussions assume that Apollos was baptized with John's baptism *before* the Day of Pentecost, but the text is silent on the point. Again we stress, however, that this entire discussion is a matter of speculation, and the opinion of one should not be bound on another.[7] All we can say with certainty is that if Apollos needed to be baptized, he was; if he didn't need to, he wasn't. It is obvious from our text that this preacher was willing to do whatever was needed to please God.

Verse 27. When some people learn "the way of God more accurately," they refuse to change because they fear what family, friends, or others might say or do. In contrast, Apollos was willing to pay the price in humiliation. He was probably back in the synagogue the next Sabbath, confessing that he had been wrong on several key points, then boldly proclaiming the new truths he had learned.

Sometime later, Apollos **wanted to go across** the Aegean Sea **to Achaia**, the area in Greece where Paul had last worked. This desire probably originated soon after his discussion with Priscilla and Aquila, which would help to explain why the disciples of chapter 19 still knew only the baptism of John. The Western Text indicates that Corinthian Christians visiting in Ephesus heard Apollos preach and invited him to come to Corinth. A more likely scenario is that Aquila and Priscilla told Apollos about the church in Corinth, inspiring him to want to go there. **The brethren encouraged him** to carry out this new work. The term "brethren" indicates that a congregation had been established in Ephesus. "The brethren" would have included Aquila and Priscilla, as well as any converted by them or by Paul on his brief visit. The church was probably already meeting in the home of Aquila and Priscilla (1 Cor. 16:19). The church at Ephesus **wrote to the disciples to welcome him.** This is a good example of sending a letter of introduction from one congregation to another. The names of Aquila and Priscilla at the close of the letter would have carried considerable weight with the church in Corinth, Apollos' destination (19:1).

When Apollos **arrived** in Corinth, he worked both with those who were already Christians and those who needed to become

---

[7]For further study on this question, see J. W. McGarvey, *New Commentary on Acts of Apostles*, vol. 2 (Delight, Ark.: Gospel Light Publishing Co., n.d.), 151–52.

Christians. First, **he greatly helped** those in the church, **those who had believed through grace.** God's grace had given them the opportunity to learn about Jesus and to become Christians. They were saved by grace. Apollos found a ready acceptance among the Christians in Corinth (1 Cor. 1:12; 3:4, 22; 4:6). The Greeks delighted in eloquence; this may be one reason why some preferred Apollos over Paul (1 Cor. 2:1). However, there is no indication that Apollos encouraged any who admired him to form a faction. Paul and Apollos were not rivals; they enjoyed a close relationship (1 Cor. 16:12; Tit. 3:13).

Verse 28. Apollos **powerfully refuted the Jews in public,** using what he had learned from Priscilla and Aquila to good advantage, **demonstrating by the Scriptures that Jesus was the Christ.** These were the same Jews who hated Paul and who had brought him before Gallio (vv. 12–17). Apollos may have had even more success with them than Paul. If this was the case, it shows the value of having preachers in the church with differing talents. Certainly there is no hint of rivalry or jealousy in Luke's words. Paul later wrote the Corinthians: "What then is Apollos? And what is Paul? Servants through whom you believed, even as the Lord gave opportunity to each one. I planted, Apollos watered, but God was causing the growth" (1 Cor. 3:5, 6).

Acts 18:24—19:1 is the first and last time we read about Apollos in the Book of Acts. At some point, he apparently returned to Ephesus, where he became Paul's friend (1 Cor. 16:12). Much later, he and another brother were scheduled to go to Crete where Titus, one of Paul's helpers, was working (Tit. 3:13). Beyond that, we know nothing about the subsequent labors of Apollos. We are confident, however, that he continued to use his considerable talents to spread the good news about Jesus.

APPLICATION

Aquila and Priscilla (Ch. 18)

An interesting lesson could be developed featuring Aquila and Priscilla (vv. 1–2, 24–28). Observe that Priscilla's name is often given before Aquila's, probably indicating that she was not merely an adjunct to Aquila, but worked side by side with him. Other material on this unique couple can be found in Romans 16:3–5; 1 Corinthians 16:19; and 2 Timothy 4:19.

Lessons from Corinth (18:1–11)

Many lessons can be learned from Paul's early work in Corinth: (1) Even the best of God's servants are afraid sometimes—Paul was. We should not be ashamed to admit our fears. (2) When fear fills our hearts, God does not abandon us. Rather, He stays with us and helps us. He helps us in some of the same ways He helped Paul: He gives us friends to encourage us, work to revitalize us, opportunities to challenge us, and promises to sustain us (Rom. 8:28). Jesus told Paul, "I am with you"; He also tells us, "I am with you always" (Mt. 28:20; see Is. 43:5). (3) Even if we are afraid, if we do not forsake God, He will bless us. He blessed Paul, and He will also bless us (2 Tim. 4:17, 18).

No Time To Be Afraid (18:9, 10)

Paul Rogers used a textual lesson on Jesus' words to Paul in 18:9, 10. Following his outline, one could develop his own lesson on this passage: (1) "Do not be afraid any longer"—talk about fear in general. (2) "But go on speaking and do not be silent"—emphasize the need to tell others about Jesus. (3) "For I am with you, and no man will . . . harm you"—speak of Jesus' promise to be with us and protect us (Mt. 28:20; 2 Thess. 3:3).[8]

Saying Good-bye (18:22, 23)

As Paul said farewell to the brethren in Antioch of Syria, beginning his third missionary journey, he had no idea that he would never see them again. Anytime you tell someone "good-bye," understand that it could be for the last time. Never part from someone without making sure that nothing in your relationship will haunt you if you never see him or her again.

Apollos (18:24–28)

You may want to use the information in 18:24–28 to present

---

[8]Paul Rogers, "No Time To Be Afraid," *Preacher's Periodical* 5 (May 1985): 23, 47.

a character study of Apollos. If so, expand on his later work, especially in Corinth. You may want to include the fact that Martin Luther and others believed Apollos to be the author of the Book of Hebrews, since the reasoning in the book is typical of that taught in logic and rhetoric classes in Alexandria. Whether or not this is the case, the fact that some think Apollos was capable of writing such a masterpiece testifies to his ability.

If you decide to preach a series on the conversions in Acts, you could include a sermon on "The Conversion of a Preacher." Remember that "conversion" literally means "change." Here is a simple outline you might use:

>   I. A Preacher Who Needed Conversion
>   A. This preacher had many fine qualities.
>   B. He was wrong on baptism.
>   II. A Preacher Who Was Converted
>   A. He was converted because some cared enough
>   to confront him in his error.
>   B. He was converted because he was big enough
>   to admit that he had been wrong.

Verses 24 through 26 could be used as the basis of a valuable lesson to young preachers. The last point would be "There is always something else you need to learn."

A Preacher I Can't Help Admiring (18:24–28)

A sermon based on Apollos' work in Ephesus could be entitled "A Preacher I Can't Help Admiring." The following four points could be used: (1) He dedicated his talents to the Lord (vv. 24–26); (2) he boldly proclaimed what he believed (vv. 25, 26); (3) he was not too proud to admit that he was wrong (v. 26); and (4) he continued to grow in his service (vv. 27, 28).

Humility (18:24–26)

Let us view this occasion from the standpoint of the preacher. Imagine that you are Apollos, a knowledgeable and eloquent speaker. You preach in the synagogue, pouring out your heart, trying to convince your listeners. After the service, you are exhausted; then a couple invites you home with them. You are beginning to relax in their home, when the conversation turns to your sermon. The couple has the audacity to suggest that your sermon was filled with inaccuracies. How would you react? It would have been easy for Apollos to respond like this: "Who do you think you are, criticizing me? I have studied at Alexandria and in Jerusalem, at the feet of the greatest teachers alive! I know a hundred times more about the Scriptures than you will ever know! Do you presume to instruct me?"

The fact that Priscilla and Aquila were able to explain to Apollos "the way of God more accurately" (v. 26) gives us insight into the heart of Apollos. Although he was well educated, he did not think he knew it all. Although he had convictions and boldly proclaimed them, he also had an open mind and was willing to listen. Most importantly, he loved truth (2 Thess. 2:10); truth was more important to him than his pride. Thus, when Priscilla and Aquila taught him, he was able to admit that he had been wrong. These are rare qualities in a man.

Correcting Error—In Love (18:26)

One could teach an entire lesson on verse 26. The major points would describe how Priscilla and Aquila conducted themselves when they heard someone teach error. (1) They had sufficient knowledge to recognize error when they heard it. (2) They did not believe that it was all right to teach error "as long as one is sincere." (3) They did not say, "We wish Paul were here to instruct him"; they understood that they had as much responsibility to teach as the preacher did. (4) They believed the best of Apollos. They did not consider him a dishonest teacher of error; evidently, they saw him as one who had an honest heart and would be willing to accept instruction. (5) Instead of talking about Apollos to others, they went to him personally (Mt. 18:15). (6) They did not embarrass Apollos publicly; rather, they handled the matter privately, taking "him aside"—probably to their home. (7) They were kind and gentle in their approach (Gal. 6:1). Instead of chiding him for preaching error, they *explained to him the way of God more accurately* (emphasis added). (8) The modifying word "more" in "more accurately" indicates that they acknowledged to Apollos that a great deal of what he taught was "accurate." Thus, instead of attacking Apollos for his error, they built on the truth he already possessed. The result of this kind of approach was a servant of even greater value to the Lord. Special application could be made here to new preachers who are still learning. The sledgehammer tactics often used in "straightening out" young evangelists have so discouraged some that they have given up this noble work.

CHAPTER 19
PAUL'S THIRD MISSIONARY JOURNEY (PART 2)

IN EPHESUS: TWELVE DISCIPLES RE-IMMERSED (19:1–7)

¹It happened that while Apollos was at Corinth, Paul passed through the upper country and came to Ephesus, and found some disciples. ²He said to them, "Did you receive the Holy Spirit when you believed?" And they said to him, "No, we have not even heard whether there is a Holy Spirit." ³And he said, "Into what then were you baptized?" And they said, "Into John's baptism." ⁴Paul said, "John baptized with the baptism of repentance, telling the people to believe in Him who was coming after him, that is, in Jesus." ⁵When they heard this, they were baptized in the name of the Lord Jesus. ⁶And when Paul had laid his hands upon them, the Holy Spirit came on them, and they began speaking with tongues and prophesying. ⁷There were in all about twelve men.

After their work in Galatia and Phrygia was completed, Paul and those with him headed west toward Ephesus. Paul had promised the Jews in Ephesus that he would try to return (18:21), and he was keeping that promise. These Jews were Paul's brethren in Abraham, and he hoped to make them his brethren in Christ.

Verse 1. Thus **it happened that while Apollos was at Corinth** (18:27), **Paul passed through the upper country.** This detail indicates that Paul did not approach Ephesus by the usual trade routes, but rather came by the less-traveled road that came into

171

Ephesus from the north. Then he **came to Ephesus.** Luke's purpose was to get to Ephesus as quickly as possible to tell about Paul's ministry there, perhaps his most significant work in all three journeys.

Ephesus was the jewel of Asia. It was the capital city of that Roman province and the center of trade in that part of the world. Its harbor could accommodate the largest seagoing vessels, and it stood on the main route from Rome to the East. In addition to traders, tourists from all the world flooded Ephesus to visit the temple of Artemis, one of the Seven Wonders of the Ancient World. Ephesus was famous, magnificent, wealthy—and lost in sin (Eph. 2:1, 12).

Upon entering a new city, Paul usually went first into the synagogue, if the city had one, looking for honest hearts. The situation in Ephesus was different. There was already a small church there (see comments on 18:27), probably meeting in the home of Aquila and Priscilla (1 Cor. 16:19). Certainly Paul had a joyful reunion with this couple (see 18:2, 3, 18, 19), while becoming acquainted with the brethren there. As Paul moved about the city, helping and strengthening new Christians, he **found some disciples.** What is the significance of the word "found"? There are several possibilities: (1) It may mean that Paul had been told about the disciples and was looking for them. (2) Perhaps Aquila and Priscilla knew about the men but were not sure how to proceed with them. (3) Maybe the couple had been less successful instructing them than they had been in teaching Apollos—and thus had waited for Paul to resolve the issues involved. (4) The word "found" may simply mean that, in the providence of God, Paul "came across them." We favor this last understanding, but the significant fact is that Paul *did* contact them.

Were these men already Christians? Ordinarily, we would assume they were. Luke normally used the word "disciples" to refer to those who were followers of Jesus (6:1, 2; 9:19, 26, 38; 11:26, 29; 14:20–22; 15:10; 18:23, 27). In this case, however, we have serious problems classifying these twelve men as Christians. When Paul asked them, "Did you receive the Holy Spirit when you believed?" they answered "No" (v. 2). Since the New Testament does not recognize the possibility of being a Christian apart from possessing the Spirit (2:38; Rom. 8:9; Tit. 3:5; Heb. 6:4; 1 Jn. 3:24; 4:13), it is hard to see how these men could be called Christians.

Perhaps Luke used the term "disciples" in its general meaning of "learners and followers" without identifying whom the men followed. It is possible that the Greek word τινας (*tinas*) translated "some" indicates that Luke intended a more general usage. Many early Christians thought that these twelve men were disciples of John the Baptist, not disciples of Jesus. One of the earliest to record this interpretation was John Chrysostom in the fourth century.[1] Other interpretations of the word "disciples" are also possible. One commentator suggested this approach: "The correct explanation of the passage is that Luke has told the story from the standpoint of the principal actor: Paul met some men who *appeared to him* to be disciples."[2] It is possible that Paul knew of the men and their background and had been looking for them, and the questions he asked were calculated to lay bare their spiritual needs. It is more likely that Paul assumed the twelve men *were* Christians, and his questions were based on this assumption.

Verse 2. When Paul found the men, he asked them, **"Did you receive the Holy Spirit when you believed?"** The KJV has "since"; **when** is the better translation. **Believed** is used in the comprehensive sense of their total response to the Lord, including baptism (v. 3). Paul was not asking whether or not they had received the non-miraculous "ordinary gift" of the Spirit when they were baptized; everyone who is scripturally baptized receives that gift (see comments on 2:38). Subsequent verses reveal that Paul's intention when he met the men was to lay his hands on them and give them miraculous gifts (v. 6) if they did not already possess such gifts. Thus the apostle was actually asking, "Did you receive a *miraculous* manifestation of the Holy Spirit when you became Christians?"

---

[1] John Chrysostom *Homilies on Acts* 40.

[2] I. Howard Marshall, *The Acts of the Apostles*, The Tyndale New Testament Commentaries, gen. ed. R. V. G. Tasker (Grand Rapids, Mich.: Wm. B. Eerdmans Publishing Co., 1980), 305–6. (Emphasis his.)

To Paul's surprise, they replied, **"No, we have not even heard whether there is a Holy Spirit."** Alarms must have started going off in Paul's head. He now knew, if he had not known before, that something was wrong with their baptism because the baptism of the Great Commission has many connections to the Holy Spirit: It is in the name of the Father, the Son, *and the Holy Spirit* (Mt. 28:19). Among the blessings connected with this baptism is the reception of the Spirit as a gift (Acts 2:38). Further, being thus baptized is called being "born of water and the Spirit" (Jn. 3:5). Paul often connected conversion with the Spirit: Becoming a Christian was the same as "receiv[ing] the Spirit" (Gal. 3:2). When one was saved, he was "sealed" with the Spirit (Eph. 1:13).

It should be noted in passing that although the phrase **whether there *is* a Holy Spirit** (emphasis added) may be an accurate translation, it does not express the meaning required by the context. Even if the twelve men knew only the teaching of John the Baptist, they should have heard about the Holy Spirit (Mt. 3:11). Also, if they knew anything about the Old Testament, they would have known of the Holy Spirit, for that testament occasionally spoke of God's Holy Spirit (Ps. 51:11; Is. 63:11). The meaning in context is that if the Holy Spirit had *come*, they were unaware of it. The Greek word ἔστιν (*estin*), translated "there is" in verse 2, is found in the past tense (ἦν, *ēn*) in John 7:39, relating to the advent of the Spirit, and is there translated "was . . . given." In the NASB, the word "given" is in italics, indicating that it has been added by the translators to complete the sense. The same word should have been added in Acts 19:2 to convey accurately the sense of the context. The ASV, the forerunner of the NASB, translates the men's words in verse 2, "Nay, we did not so much as hear whether the Holy Spirit was *given*" (emphasis added). The Western Text, which often conveys the understanding of early Christians, has "if any are receiving the Holy Spirit."

Verse 3. Knowing there was something wrong with their baptism, Paul asked the men, **"Into what then were you baptized?"** **Into what** is a literal translation of the Greek text, reminding us that the baptism commanded for the Christian age puts us "into *Christ*" (Rom. 6:3, 4; Gal. 3:27). Note that Paul automatically assumed that they had been baptized. **And they said, "Into John's baptism."** Where had these men learned of John the Baptist's baptism? Some details in the context imply that they had been taught and baptized by Apollos: the proximity of this story with that of the eloquent preacher Apollos, who was "acquainted only with the baptism of John" (18:25), and the fact that Luke made a point of speaking of Apollos when introducing the twelve men (v. 1). Other scenarios are possible, but they are less probable. For instance, Apollos and the twelve men could have been taught and baptized by the same men, presumably some of John's disciples who were traveling in the area. If that were the case, Apollos probably had to be re-immersed even as the twelve did (see comments on 18:25, 26). However, most scholars believe that Apollos was baptized with John's baptism *before* the Day of Pentecost (ch. 2), and that those he taught and baptized were baptized with John's baptism *after* the Day of Pentecost. J. W. McGarvey wrote,

> The most probable answer [as to why these men had to be reimmersed], and the only one which harmonizes with the facts, is that they had been baptized by Apollos, or by some one teaching as he taught, since John's baptism had ceased to be a valid ordinance.[3]

To borrow the words of Richard Oster, these twelve disciples were "post-Pentecost believer[s] with pre-Pentecost instruction."[4] On occasion, people have consulted an outdated map and lost their way. The fault did not lie with the map itself; it had been fine for its day. The problem was that the map had become obsolete and was no longer accurate. In their religious journey, the twelve disciples had been consulting an outdated spiritual map.

---

[3]J. W. McGarvey, *New Commentary on Acts of Apostles*, vol. 2 (Delight, Ark.: Gospel Light Publishing Co., n.d.), 152.

[4]Richard Oster, *The Acts of the Apostles*, Part 2, The Living Word Commentary, ed. Everett Ferguson (Austin, Tex.: Sweet Publishing Co., 1979), 87.

Verse 4. Since the men's understanding was incomplete, their first need was to have their knowledge updated. Paul did not waste his time criticizing those who had taught these men *error*; rather, he spent his time teaching them *truth*. He said, **"John baptized with the baptism of repentance, telling the people to believe in Him who was coming after him, that is, in Jesus."** This reference is the last mention of **John** the Baptist in the Bible. Throughout Acts, Luke invariably gave Holy Spirit-inspired abbreviations of sermons; but regarding Luke's treatment of Paul's instruction to the twelve, the word "abbreviation" is insufficient. Here, Luke employed a heavy-duty compactor. The **baptism** of John would just have been the starting place of Paul's remarks. He would have told them about the One who came after John, **that is, . . . Jesus**: His death, burial, and resurrection; His ascension and sending of the Spirit; the establishing, organizing, and spreading of Jesus' church. The response of the twelve (v. 5) also indicates that Paul carefully contrasted their baptism with baptism in the name of Jesus.

Verse 5. After Paul had finished speaking, the twelve men might have responded in a variety of ways. They could have become angry at the apostle for implying that their baptism was not God-pleasing. If they had been like some today, they would have said, "But baptism is merely symbolic and certainly not worth worrying about. One baptism is as good as another." Their response, however, indicated the honesty of their hearts. The teaching of Paul had revealed that their previous understanding was incomplete and their obedience inadequate. Without hesitation, **when they heard this, they were baptized in the name of the Lord Jesus.**

As we read of the baptism of these men, questions flood our minds: Why was it necessary for them to be re-immersed? In what way was the baptism of John different from baptism in the name of Jesus? Why had John's baptism been invalidated? The second question holds the key to the others: How did John's baptism differ from the one Paul administered?

Most commentators use words such as *"the* difference between the two baptisms was," followed by what they consider the most significant difference. In the context, however, *many* differences are stated or implied. Let us start with Paul's question about the Holy Spirit (v. 2): John's baptism had no promise of the Spirit, while the baptism of the Great Commission did (2:38).

Again, Paul referred to John's baptism as a "baptism of repentance" (v. 4); in other words, it embodied and expressed repentance. On the other hand, it would be appropriate to refer to the baptism of the Christian Age as a "baptism of faith," embodying and expressing faith—specifically our faith in Jesus' death, burial, and resurrection (Rom. 6:3, 4). When people received John's baptism, they confessed their sins (Mk. 1:5); before people are baptized with Jesus' baptism, they confess their *faith* in Jesus (Acts 8:37; see comments on 2:37).

Probably the most significant difference is suggested by Paul's statement that John told "the people to believe in Him *who was coming after him . . .*" (v. 4; emphasis added). The faith of John's disciples pointed *forward* to the coming Messiah, while our faith points *back* to the One who died for us (Gal. 2:20). Since John's disciples looked forward to the coming One, they were ignorant of His death, burial, and resurrection, which is the heart of the gospel (1 Cor. 15:1–4). Consequently, their baptism was not "in the likeness of His death" and "the likeness of His resurrection" as the baptism that Paul taught (Rom. 6:5). They knew nothing of the relationship of baptism to the death of Jesus (Rom. 6:3). They did not know that their sins could be washed away by the blood of Jesus when they were immersed (see comments on 22:16).

Finally, the fact that the twelve were **baptized in the name of the Lord Jesus** reminds us that apparently no name at all was associated with John's baptism. The baptism of the Great Commission, in contrast, is administered in the sacred "name of the Father and the Son and the Holy Spirit" (Mt. 28:19). (Concerning the significance of doing something "in the name of" the Lord, see comments on 2:38.)

In fact, as we closely inspect the two baptisms, we find that they had only a few characteristics in common: Both were by immersion in water (Jn. 3:23; Mt. 3:16; see comments on Acts 8:38), and both were "for the forgiveness of sins" (Mk. 1:4; Lk.

3:3; see comments on Acts 2:38). Even the brief comparison we have made should leave little doubt as to why it was necessary for these men to be immersed a second time, "in the name of the Lord Jesus."

It is significant that the text does not say the twelve disciples were "re-baptized." Since the Greek word βάπτισμα (*baptisma*) translated "baptism" literally means "immersion," it is hard to express ourselves as precisely as we would like. We are trying to make a distinction between a rite that might be *called* "baptism" and genuine Christian baptism. Since the twelve men had been immersed earlier (in John's baptism) and were now immersed for a second time (in the name of Jesus), we have used the term "re-immersed" several times in this chapter. However, they only submitted to the baptism of the Great Commission *once*. The Bible says nothing of "re-baptism." If one has been scripturally immersed, he has been baptized. He has received the forgiveness of his sins, has been added by the Lord to His church, and never needs to repeat that act. On the other hand, though one may have gone through a form *called* baptism, if the ritual did not conform to the New Testament pattern, *he has not been baptized*; he has simply gotten wet. That individual needs to be baptized—for the first and only time.

Verse 6. After being baptized, the twelve would have been welcomed into the fellowship of the little band in Ephesus. As part of that joyful occasion, Paul finally carried out what had apparently been his original intent when he met the men. **And when Paul had laid his hands upon them, the Holy Spirit came on them, and they began speaking with tongues and prophesying.** Paul's action is similar to what Peter and John did when they came to Samaria and **laid** their **hands** on the Samaritans who had become Christians (see comments on 8:17, 18). It was the practice of the apostles to lay their hands on Christians to give them miraculous gifts of the **Holy Spirit.** These gifts allowed Christians to know God's will in the absence of a written New Testament and to be able to function as a church in the absence of an apostle.

One question remains: Why did Luke mention the fact that Paul laid his hands on these men and that they spoke in **tongues**?

Laying hands on new Christians was apparently a common practice with Paul (2 Tim. 1:6), but this is the only time Luke mentions it. For instance, Paul evidently laid his hands on many in Corinth during his ministry there, enabling some to speak in tongues (1 Cor. 1:7; 12:10), but Luke did not record the fact. Why, then, did he tell about it here? Perhaps Luke was drawing some parallel between what Peter did in Samaria and what Paul did in Ephesus. He drew many parallels in Acts between the work of Peter and the work of Paul. Here are some examples: healing a lame man, casting out demons, escaping from prison, and raising the dead. This is common practice in the Scriptures—to show that God is with a successor just as He was with the predecessor (for example, Moses and Joshua, Elijah and Elisha). Again, maybe the fact was recorded to emphasize that these re-immersed men were accepted into the fellowship of the church in Ephesus without reservation—even as the laying on of the apostles' hands in Acts 8 showed that the Samaritans had been accepted (see comments on 8:17). This event is the third scene in the Book of Acts related to tongue-speaking. In all three occurrences, this phenomenon coincides with instruction on the Holy Spirit as new groups are incorporated into the church (2:4; 10:46; 19:6).[5]

Verse 7. There were in all about twelve men. Since Luke said **about** (ὡσεί, *hōsei*), we suppose there could have been eleven or thirteen.

IN EPHESUS: PAUL'S MINISTRY AND PLANS (19:8–22)

Paul's Teaching at Ephesus (19:8–10)

[8]**And he entered the synagogue and continued speaking out boldly for three months, reasoning and persuading them about the kingdom of God. [9]But when some were becoming hardened and disobedient, speaking evil of the Way before the people, he withdrew from them and took away the dis-**

---

[5]Ibid., 88.

ciples, reasoning daily in the school of Tyrannus. ¹⁰This took place for two years, so that all who lived in Asia heard the word of the Lord, both Jews and Greeks.

Verse 8. During his brief visit to Ephesus near the end of his second journey, Paul had spoken in the synagogue and had been urged by the people to stay longer. He had said that he must leave but would return, God willing (18:19–21). He now kept that promise. **He entered the synagogue and continued speaking out boldly for three months.** To be allowed to speak in the synagogue for three months without getting beaten or booted out was a record for Paul. Compare this scene to the three weeks in Thessalonica (17:2, 3). He was probably allowed to continue that long because of the favorable impression he had made on his first visit. It is also possible that he was having less success than usual with the God-fearers, so the Jews became jealous less quickly.

In Paul's synagogue preaching, he was **reasoning and persuading them about the kingdom of God.** The phrase **kingdom of God** is another way of speaking of the Messiah and His kingdom (see 28:31). Paul told the people about Jesus and His church (see comments on 1:3).

Verse 9. Although Paul's initial reception in the synagogue was better than usual, the end result was the same. **Some** of the Jews became **hardened and disobedient.** Some translations have "disbelieving" or its equivalent. The Greek word from ἀπείθεω (*apetheō*) used here refers to disobedience but implies that behind that disobedience was disbelief (see comments on 14:2). Saving faith goes hand in hand with obedience. These people began to speak **evil of the Way before the people.** The Greek word from πλῆθος (*plēthos*), translated **people** or "multitude" (NASB 1977), can also be a technical term for a religious community (4:32; 6:2; 15:12, 30). Thus some translations have "before the congregation" in this verse. The term **the Way** refers to Christianity, following Jesus who is "*the* way" (Jn. 14:6; emphasis added; see comments on 9:2). When unbelieving Jews slandered Jesus in public, Paul decided the time had come to leave the synagogue (see Mt. 7:6). Thus **he withdrew from them and took away the disciples**—that is, those who had embraced his teaching about the Messiah and His kingdom.

In Philippi, Paul had taught on a river bank; in Athens, in the agora; in Corinth, in the private dwelling of Titius Justus. In Ephesus, Paul found a school house in which he could preach.[6] He reasoned **daily in the school of Tyrannus.** Some think the school of Tyrannus was held in a gymnasium. In those days, unlike today, gymnasiums catered both to the body and to the mind; they were places of exercise and instruction. A man named **Tyrannus**, about whom we know nothing else, owned a lecture hall that he rented or loaned to Paul. It is possible that Tyrannus was a Christian and let Paul use the hall free of charge. "Tyrannus" is Latin for "tyrant." If Tyrannus lectured in his own school, maybe this was a nickname he had been given by his students. If so, it was not necessarily an insult. Seemingly harsh nicknames have sometimes been given out of rough affection.

The Western Text adds an interesting note about Paul's teaching: "He taught daily . . . from the fifth to the tenth hour." Although this addition is not found in the better translations, most scholars think that it is probably an accurate statement of the situation. "From the fifth to the tenth hour" would be from 11 a.m. to 4 p.m. People in that part of the world took a break during that part of the day.[7] Citing the work of Lake and Cadbury, F. F. Bruce stated that "more people would be asleep at 1 p.m. than at 1 a.m."[8] A typical work day would be from 7 to 11 a.m., then 4 to 9:30 p.m. During the five-hour break in the middle of the day, when others were resting and the hall was not in use, Paul taught those who wanted to learn of Christ.

Later, Paul noted that at Ephesus he worked with his hands to support himself and his fellow workers (20:34). Further, he taught not only publicly, but also from house to house (20:20)—not just in the daytime, but also at night (20:31). Paul's daily

---

[6]In the early days of the church in the U.S., a preacher would go into a new area, secure the use of a school house, and then have preaching every night. This is how the church was established in hundreds of communities.

[7]Martial *Epigrams* 4.8.

[8]F. F. Bruce, *The Book of Acts*, The New International Commentary on the New Testament, gen. ed. F. F. Bruce, rev. ed. (Grand Rapids, Mich.: Wm. B. Eerdmans Publishing Co., 1988), 366.

schedule, then, may have been something like this: From 7 to 11 a.m., he worked making tents—probably in Aquila and Priscilla's workshop; from 11 a.m. to 4 p.m., he taught God's Word in the school of Tyrannus; from 4 to 9:30 p.m., he made more tents; from 9:30 p.m. to 12 midnight, he taught in homes. This scenario says something about Paul: He loved to *teach* the Word. It also says something about the people of that area: They loved to *study* the Word. Every day while their friends and neighbors were taking a siesta, they were probably listening to Paul.

Verse 10. Paul's instruction in the school of Tyrannus **took place for two years.** This two-year period plus the three months Paul had taught in the synagogue (v. 8), plus perhaps the "a while" period of verse 22 totals the round "three years" figure referred to later by Paul (20:31). This period was his longest stay in any city during his special missionary journeys, indicating the unique opportunities he found in Ephesus (1 Cor. 16:9).

Largely as a result of Paul's efforts, the Word spread not only through Ephesus, but also throughout the Roman province of Asia, **so that all who lived in Asia heard the word of the Lord, both Jews and Greeks.** Paul's enemies later said, "Not only in Ephesus, but in almost all of Asia, this Paul has persuaded . . . a considerable number of people . . ." (v. 26). Probably most, if not all, of "the seven churches" of Asia (Rev. 1:11) were established during this time, plus the congregations in Colossae and Hierapolis (Col. 1:2; 4:13).

Paul did not do all the evangelizing. A wise leader is always multiplying himself by training and motivating others. We noted earlier that Timothy and Titus were associated with Paul in the Ephesian ministry. A brother named Erastus also worked with him (19:22), as did a Christian named Sosthenes (1 Cor. 1:1, 2). Also, two brethren from Colossae—Epaphras and Archippus— were apparently trained and commissioned by Paul (Col. 1:7, 8; 4:12, 13, 17; Philem. 2, 23). It is also possible that "Paul's traveling companions from Macedonia," Gaius and Aristarchus (19:29), worked some with him in the province of Asia—and we must not forget Paul's evangelistic friends Aquila and Priscilla (18:18, 19, 26). Tychicus and Trophimus from Asia later traveled and worked with Paul (20:4); it is probable that they, too, were converted and trained by the apostle.

Paul likely did most of his public teaching of God's Word in Ephesus in the school of Tyrannus (vv. 9, 10). There he taught students who came from throughout the province. They then took the Word back to their home cities. For example, Paul later said that he had not personally visited Colossae, Laodicea, and other cities in that region (Col. 2:1)—including Hierapolis, which was near Laodicea. The gospel was taken to Colossae, and probably to Laodicea and Hierapolis, by a protégé named Epaphras (Col. 1:7, 8; 4:12, 13). Epaphras apparently traveled some with Paul. He was with Paul in Rome (Col. 4:12, 13) and is even called "a fellow prisoner" (Philem. 23).

Magic and the Gospel (19:11–20)

[11]**God was performing extraordinary miracles by the hands of Paul, [12]so that handkerchiefs or aprons were even carried from his body to the sick, and the diseases left them and the evil spirits went out. [13]But also some of the Jewish exorcists, who went from place to place, attempted to name over those who had the evil spirits the name of the Lord Jesus, saying, "I adjure you by Jesus whom Paul preaches." [14]Seven sons of one Sceva, a Jewish chief priest, were doing this. [15]And the evil spirit answered and said to them, "I recognize Jesus, and I know about Paul, but who are you?" [16]And the man, in whom was the evil spirit, leaped on them and subdued all of them and overpowered them, so that they fled out of that house naked and wounded. [17]This became known to all, both Jews and Greeks, who lived in Ephesus; and fear fell upon them all and the name of the Lord Jesus was being magnified. [18]Many also of those who had believed kept coming, confessing and disclosing their practices. [19]And many of those who practiced magic brought their books together and began burning them in the sight of everyone; and they counted up the price of them and found it fifty thousand pieces of silver. [20]So the word of the Lord was growing mightily and prevailing.**

The word "occult" comes from the Latin *occultus*, which

means "hidden," and refers to hidden or concealed mysteries or knowledge. The *American Heritage Dictionary* defines "occult" in this way:

1. Of, relating to, or dealing with supernatural influences, agencies, or phenomena.
2. Beyond the realm of human comprehension; inscrutable.
3. Available only to the initiate; secret.[9]

Deuteronomy 18:9–14 lists several occult practices that might be grouped under three headings: (1) divination—fortunetelling, including astrology; (2) sorcery—including the casting of spells; and (3) spiritualism. All were condemned by God (see Ex. 22:18; Lev. 19:31; 20:6, 27; Is. 47:13, 14). In the book *The Fortune Sellers*, Gary Wilburn grouped modern-day expressions of the occult under the same three headings: (1) fortunetelling—including astrology, tarot cards, palmistry, and psychics; (2) magic— sorcery, including witchcraft and Satanism; and (3) spiritualism —including séances, channeling, and Ouija boards.[10] Though clearly condemned by the Lord, the occult is flourishing today as it flourished in New Testament times.

In Paul's day, Ephesus was one of the centers of occult activity. While the day-to-day life in Athens revolved around intellectualism and everyday life in Corinth revolved around immorality, life in Ephesus revolved around incantations. "Of all ancient Greco-Roman cities, Ephesus . . . was by far the most hospitable to magicians, sorcerers, and charlatans of all sorts."[11] The Ephesians did not suffer so much from mental pride or moral laxness as from mystical obsession.

We noted earlier in chapter 18 that Corinth had the dubious honor of adding to the language of that day; to "Corinthianize" was to commit fornication. Likewise, Ephesus added to the vocabulary: Some collections of magical spells and incantations

---

[9]*American Heritage Electronic Dictionary*, 1992 ed., s.v. "occult."

[10]Gary Wilburn, *The Fortune Sellers* (Glendale, Calif.: Gospel Light Publications, 1972), preface.

[11]Bruce M. Metzger, "St. Paul and the Magicians," *Princeton Seminary Bulletin* 38 (June 1944): 27.

were called Ἐφέσια γράμματα (*Ephesia grammata*), "Ephesian Letters."[12] Centuries later, Shakespeare summed up the reputation of Ephesus in these words:

They say this town is full of cozenage,[13]
As, nimble jugglers[14] that deceive the eye,
Dark-working sorcerers that change the mind,
Soul-killing witches that deform the body,
Disguised cheaters, prating mountebanks,
And many such-like libertines of sin.[15]

The secular references to the "Ephesian Letters" joined with the details of Acts 19 establish Ephesus' preoccupation with the spirit world. In this section, we continue the story of Paul's three years in Ephesus, giving special attention to how God dealt with the dark superstitions that clouded the minds of the people in that city.

Verse 11. Paul had previously faced a sorcerer (13:6–11) and a woman with a spirit of divination (16:16–18), but he never confronted mysticism and superstition on such a scale as it existed in Ephesus. When God commissions a man, He gives that man all he needs to carry out the commission. God had already worked miracles through Paul (14:8–10; see 2 Cor. 12:12), but as Paul faced the magic-oriented, occult-saturated society of Ephesus, the Lord gave him even greater powers: **God was performing** *extraordinary* **miracles by the hands of Paul** (emphasis added). By their nature, all miracles are extraordinary. These miracles, therefore, were *extra*-extraordinary.

Verse 12. The miracles were not extraordinary so much in

---

[12]Ancient writers mentioning these magical texts include: Athenaeus *Diepnosophists* 12.548; Plutarch *Moralia* 706; Clement of Alexandria *Miscellanies* 5.8. Examples of magical texts from Egypt can be found in *The Greek Magical Papyri in Translation*, ed. Hans Dieter Betz (Chicago: University of Chicago Press, 1986).

[13]"Cozenage" refers to deception by fraudulent means.

[14]Since many conjurers included juggling in their acts, "juggling" had become a synonym for conjuring. "Juggling" no longer has this connotation.

[15]Shakespeare *The Comedy of Errors* 1.2.97–102.

the results attained as in the method employed: **So that hand-kerchiefs or aprons were even carried from his body to the sick, and the diseases left them and the evil spirits went out.** Once again, Dr. Luke made a distinction between disease and demon-possession. The text does not say that people brought articles of clothing to Paul for him to bless, but rather that these "handkerchiefs" and "aprons" were "carried from his body." These were probably articles of clothing that had been in contact with Paul's body in the ordinary course of events. The **hand-kerchiefs** were not small squares of cloth with hemmed edges, but large rags used by Paul, probably to wipe the sweat from his face as he made tents. He may have tied the rags around his head as was (and is) the custom. One translator called them "sweat-rags";[16] another, "sweat-bands."[17] The **aprons** probably were the workman's aprons worn by Paul to protect his clothing. These "extraordinary miracles" remind us of those who were healed when they touched Jesus' garments (Mk. 5:25–29; 6:56). We are also reminded of the time the sick waited for Peter's shadow to fall on them (see comments on 5:15).

What God did through Paul was a fulfillment of Jesus' promise in Mark 16:17, 18: "In My name they will cast out demons . . . they will lay hands on the sick, and they will recover." The Lord did those miracles "by the hands of Paul" to let the people of Ephesus know that He was with him in a special way.

Verse 13. Luke described a group of men as **Jewish exorcists, who went from place to place.** "Exorcist" is a transliteration from the compound Greek word ἐξορκιστής (*exorkistēs*), combining ἐκ (*ek*, "out") with ὁρκίζω (*horkizō*, the verb form of "oath"). Incidentally, the Greek word translated "I adjure" later in this verse is *horkizō*. The word *exorkistēs* is generally used to refer to casting demons "out with an oath." Both secular and inspired writers recorded that, in New Testament times, there were Jews claiming the ability to cast out evil spirits (Mt. 12:27; Lk. 11:19). We use the word "claiming" because nothing in the

---

[16]Bruce, 366.

[17]William Barclay, *The Acts of the Apostles,* The Daily Study Bible Series, rev. ed. (Philadelphia: Westminster Press, 1976), 142.

Scriptures forces us to the conclusion that these Jews could actually cast out demons. Jesus' argument in Matthew 12 (Lk. 11) carries equal weight whether or not the Jews could actually cast out evil spirits; the point is that Jesus' accusers *believed* that their fellow Jews could cast out demons.

Verse 13 is the only place the word "exorcist" (*exorkistēs*) is found in the New Testament. The verb form ἐξορκίζω (*exorkizō*) is also found only once and is translated "I adjure [You]" (Mt. 26:63). However, the context of Matthew 26:63 is a trial scene. Therefore, the meaning of the word there is "I put [You] under a solemn oath."

It should be noted that Jesus was not an exorcist. He never used an oath to cast out demons. He merely said, "Be quiet, and come out . . . !" (Mk. 1:25), and the spirits obeyed (see Mt. 8:16; Mk. 5:8; 9:25; Lk. 4:35). Similarly, when the apostles cast out demons, they did not make a production of it. Without ceremony, they said, "I command you in the name of Jesus Christ to come out . . . !" (Acts 16:18)—and that took care of the matter. The so-called "exorcism" rituals of some religious groups are not from God, but originated in the superstitions of the Middle Ages.

Could some Jewish "exorcists" actually cast out demons? It is possible. During New Testament times, not only did the forces of good have miraculous powers, but so did the forces of evil—in a limited capacity. Nevertheless, we are convinced that the seven "exorcists" of Acts 19 were out-and-out frauds like Simon the sorcerer (8:9–13) and Elymas Bar-Jesus (13:6–12). This conclusion is based on the following reasons: (1) Consider their base of operations. An honest man avoids doing business in a den of thieves. These men blended in perfectly with the mystic swindlers of Ephesus. (2) They were described as men "who went from place to place." The KJV has "vagabond"; the NCV has "were traveling around." It can be dangerous for the fraudulent to stay in one place long; they are usually on the move. (3) They decided to use Paul's words to cast out a demon. If they had been having the same success Paul had, why try his "magic words"? (4) As unbelieving Jews, they were aligned with Satan, whether they realized it or not (Rev. 2:9). Jesus said that it would be stupid of Satan to cast out demons who did his service (Mt.

12:26)—and Satan is *not* stupid.

Seeing Paul's success, the sons of Sceva decided to try his "incantation" to see if it would work for them. They **attempted to name over those who had the evil spirits the name of the Lord Jesus.** The superstitious considered certain words to have mystical, magical powers. Scrolls filled with "secret" multi-syllabled gibberish, "guaranteed" to give the owner fantastic powers, brought exorbitant prices (v. 19). The seven sons decided that Paul's "secret word" was **Jesus.** Even some secular practitioners decided that was the case. An ancient document that has been discovered contains the words, "I adjure you by Jesus, the god of the Hebrews."[18] This phrase was part of an incantation used to heal certain diseases. Since these exorcists did not know Jesus personally, they said, **"I adjure you by Jesus whom** *Paul* **preaches"** (emphasis added).

Verse 14. The Jewish "exorcists" were identified as **seven sons of one Sceva, a Jewish chief priest.** The Greek word ἀρχιερεύς (*archiereus*), translated **chief priest,** is usually translated this way only when the word is in the plural form (4:23; 5:24; 9:14, 21; 22:30; 23:14; 25:15; 26:10, 12). In the singular, as the word occurs in this verse, *archiereus* is usually translated "high priest" (4:6; 5:17, 21, 27; 7:1; 9:1; 22:5; 23:2, 4, 5; 24:1). Thus, the KJV has "high priest" here. Since, however, there was never a high priest named Sceva, the NASB translators decided to render the word "chief priest." This term may indicate that Sceva was of the high-priestly family (see comments on 4:6). It is more likely that this designation was a self-assumed title to add weight to his family's fraudulent claims, even as the purveyors of patent medicine in the American Old West often added "Doctor" or "Professor" to the front of their names. "Luke might have placed the words between quotation marks had these been invented in his day."[19]

The use of the number **seven** added to this family's "aura of mystery." The number seven was considered to have special sig-

---

[18]Bruce, 368. See C. K. Barrett, *The New Testament Background: Selected Documents* (New York: Harper & Row Publishers, 1961), 31–33.

[19]Ibid.

nificance—not only by the Jews, but also the superstitious. The "seventh daughter of a seventh daughter" supposedly had the ability to foretell the future.

Verse 15. Wry humor is seen in the demon's reaction: **And the evil spirit answered and said to them, "I recognize Jesus, and I know about Paul, but who are you?"** The spirit spoke through the man in whom he was dwelling (see Mk. 3:11). Demons had limited supernatural knowledge (see comments on 16:17).

Verse 16. And the man, in whom was the evil spirit, leaped on them and subdued all of them and overpowered them, so that they fled out of that house naked and wounded. Instead of **all of them**, some translations have "both of them," which would suggest that only two of the seven tried this experiment. The Greek word from ἀμφότεροι (*amphoteroi*), translated "all of them" in the NASB, usually means "both" or "two or more."

Endowed with superhuman strength (see Mk. 5:2–4), the demon-possessed man attacked the would-be exorcists, forcing them to run for their lives, their clothes torn off, their bodies battered and bruised. The Greek word from γυμνός (*gumnos*), translated **naked,** does not necessarily mean "without clothing." It can mean "inadequately clothed." It seems obvious, however, that the seven men not only lost their dignity, but also lost their modesty. "When they tried to use [the name of Jesus in their ceremony], like an unfamiliar weapon wrongly handled it exploded in their hands."[20] These men failed to understand that it was not some obscure occult quality, but *"faith* in His name" that gave the name of Jesus power (3:16; emphasis added).

Verse 17. Word of the exorcising fiasco spread through the city: **This became known to all, both Jews and Greeks, who lived in Ephesus.** It was obvious that Paul was God-approved and that so-called wonder-workers were God-rejected. One result was that **fear fell upon them all,** even as fear had come upon the church and residents in Jerusalem after God's punishment of Ananias and Sapphira (5:11). Another result was that **the name of the Lord Jesus was being magnified.** Practitioners

---

[20]Ibid.

of magic learned that it could be hazardous to their health to use the name of Jesus rashly.

Verse 18. One of the most important results was that the incident brought some Christians to their senses. Apparently, some Ephesians, steeped in the occult from childhood, had not totally abandoned their heathen practices when they became Christians. Since cultic *magic* had been so vividly contrasted with real *miracles*, **many also of those who had believed kept coming, confessing and disclosing their practices.** The context indicates some kind of public meeting of the church to which non-members could come. Other than that, we are given no details about the whys and wherefores of the service. Notice the continuous action: *kept* **coming, confessing and disclosing. . . .** First one Christian stepped to the front, weeping as he confessed his wrongdoing; then a second; then a dozen more; until finally men and women flooded forward to break forever their ties with the superstitions of the past.

Consider the phrase *disclosing* **their practices.** It was previously noted that the word "occult" literally means "hidden." The stock-in-trade of the world of the occult was (and is) "secret knowledge," supposedly available to a select few. To divulge those secrets was to break all ties with the occult. Even in modern "fun" magic that denies (and decries) supernatural means, an attempt is made to guard the magical "secrets." Normally, the price of a trick is not based on the value of the workmanship but on "how the trick is done." Blatant exposure of magical secrets to the general public can result in a magician's being expelled from a magical society.

Verse 19. Not only were those inside the church affected by the abortive attempt to use the name of Jesus in exorcising, but so were many outside the church. **Many of those who practiced magic** probably included Christians and non-Christians alike, with the majority being unbelievers. These people **brought their books together and began burning them in the sight of everyone.** These **books** were scrolls filled with incantations, spells to bless or curse, recipes for love potions, formulas for casting out spirits, directions for foretelling the future, and so on. **And they counted up the price of them and found it fifty**

thousand pieces of silver. These coins were probably Greek drachmas (see NIV). A drachma was a silver coin which, like the Roman denarius, was worth approximately a day's wages for the common working man. Fifty thousand pieces of silver was a small fortune then, as it would be now. Hundreds, even thousands of scrolls must have been burned. To appreciate the value of that fire, multiply a typical day's wage by fifty thousand. Hundreds of thousands of dollars went up in smoke.

Some may wonder why the people did not sell their scrolls and give the money to the Lord's work. Those who cast their "Ephesian Letters" on the fire were making a statement: They were through with the past, and they wanted all to know it (see Mt. 3:8). In addition, they did not want those ungodly documents to curse any more lives.

Verse 20. As a result, **the word of the Lord was growing mightily and prevailing.** This statement is another one of Luke's progress reports in Acts. The challenge of Ephesus was met in an incredible way.

In Acts 19, we have only highlights of Paul's work in Ephesus. From other references, we get additional insight regarding Paul's triumphs and trials during his three years there. While he was in Ephesus, he wrote, "For a wide door for effective service has opened to me, and there are many adversaries" (1 Cor. 16:9).

The figure of "a wide [or open] door" is used in the Scriptures to refer to opportunity, especially opportunities to preach the gospel (2 Cor. 2:12; Col. 4:3). Paul did not stroll through that door of preaching opportunities; he ran through it. When he finally departed from Ephesus, he left a strong congregation with elders (Acts 20:17) that continued to be a force for good for decades. Furthermore, through the efforts of Paul and his coworkers, "*all* who lived in Asia heard the word of the Lord, both Jews and Greeks" (v. 10; emphasis added). In less than three years, they spread the gospel throughout an area larger than California, establishing ten or so congregations.

A special opportunity Paul had during that time was to continue to encourage congregations established earlier. Second Corinthians 11:28 speaks of Paul's concern for these congregations. No doubt he took advantage of every opportunity to encourage them, even as he encouraged the church at Corinth. For instance, during Paul's work in Ephesus, he maintained contact with the church in Corinth (1 Cor. 5:9),[21] even crossing the Aegean Sea to visit them (2 Cor. 12:14; 13:1).[22]

Paul not only mentioned the fact that a "wide door" had been opened, but he also noted that there were "many adversaries." Later, referring to his days in Ephesus, Paul spoke of "serving the Lord with all humility and with tears and with trials which came upon me through the plots of the Jews" (Acts 20:19). In addition, Paul wrote of the "affliction which came to us in Asia," noting, "We were burdened excessively, beyond our strength, so that we despaired even of life" (2 Cor. 1:8). Paul may have had in mind a severe illness. Perhaps some of the trials mentioned in 2 Corinthians 11:23–27 occurred in Ephesus, such as being beaten by the Jews (v. 24) and being imprisoned (v. 23). Paul spoke of fighting "with wild beasts at Ephesus" (1 Cor. 15:32). This reference is probably metaphorical, using the phrase "wild beasts" to refer to men who acted like wild beasts. As a Roman citizen, Paul could not legally be forced to fight with wild beasts. It is also said that Aquila and Priscilla "risked their own necks" for him (Rom. 16:3, 4). When Paul wrote the Book of Romans, he had been associated with Aquila and Priscilla in two cities: Corinth and Ephesus. Since there is no indication that Aquila and Priscilla had to risk their lives for him in Corinth, the incident probably occurred in Ephesus. When Paul's life was in danger in Ephesus, his friends risked their lives to rescue him. Many believe that the mob scene in the theater (vv. 23–41) is what

---

[21]Some believe that the letter referred to in 1 Corinthians 5:9, which predates 1 Corinthians, has been preserved as part of 2 Corinthians. It is more likely, however, that everything said in the first letter was repeated and expanded in 1 Corinthians and that God, therefore, saw no need to preserve it. The New Testament does not necessarily contain everything that inspired men wrote (Col. 4:16); it does contain everything we need.

[22]These two references mention a *third* visit. This necessitates a second visit between the time Paul left Corinth at the end of the second journey (18:18) and his visit with them at the end of his third journey (20:2, 3). This almost certainly had to be while Paul was living and working in Ephesus.

Paul referred to when he spoke of "fighting wild beasts," but 1 Corinthians was almost certainly written before the events in the theater. Furthermore, Paul did not go into the amphitheater during the riot (vv. 30, 31), so he "fought" with no one. It seems more likely that there was another incident Luke did not tell about.

Paul's Future Plans (19:21, 22)

²¹Now after these things were finished, Paul purposed in the spirit to go to Jerusalem after he had passed through Macedonia and Achaia, saying, "After I have been there, I must also see Rome." ²²And having sent into Macedonia two of those who ministered to him, Timothy and Erastus, he himself stayed in Asia for a while.

Verse 21. After a few years in Ephesus, Paul decided that his work there was done. The gospel had gone throughout the region. Strong churches had been established. Men had been trained. Elders had been appointed in Ephesus to carry on the work there. Paul, therefore, began to make plans: **Now after these things were finished, Paul purposed in the spirit to go to Jerusalem after he had passed through Macedonia and Achaia, saying, "After I have been there, I must also see Rome."**

Luke wrapped the exciting events of Paul's Ephesian ministry in the plain wrapping of the generic phrase **these things**. This terminology could include all the facets of Paul's ministry noted thus far in chapter 19: the re-immersion of the twelve disciples, preaching in the synagogue, teaching in the school of Tyrannus, and performing extraordinary miracles. "These things" would also include the convicting of the magicians as well as the events mentioned in Paul's writings (see comments on v. 20).

Purposed in the spirit can simply mean that Paul was serious about the plans he made, or it can mean that the Holy Spirit was involved in the planning process. Thus the NKJV has "purposed in the Spirit," with a capital "S." Paul's plans were threefold: (1) He planned to go to Jerusalem. The purpose of this trip was to take benevolent help from Gentile Christians to needy Jewish Christians in Jerusalem (Rom. 15:25, 26, 30, 31).

(2) Before going to Jerusalem, he planned a return trip to Macedonia and Achaia, revisiting churches he had established there. It was Paul's practice to revisit churches he had planted (14:22, 23; 15:36, 41; 18:23). Up to this point, as far as we know, with the exception of Corinth, he had not revisited churches established on the second missionary journey. On this trip to Macedonia and Achaia, Paul also intended to complete the benevolent fund for Jerusalem (1 Cor. 16:1, 2; 2 Cor. 8:1–4; 9:1, 2; Rom. 15:26). After taking the special contribution to Jerusalem, Paul probably intended to revisit his "home" congregation in Antioch.

Paul had a pressing reason for visiting one particular congregation in Achaia: the church in Corinth. A delegation had come to Ephesus (1 Cor. 16:8, 9) from Corinth (1 Cor. 16:17), carrying a letter from the congregation. The letter (1 Cor. 7:1) plus the messengers' report (1 Cor. 1:11; 5:1) revealed that the church was overwhelmed by doctrinal and practical problems. It is possible that the coming of the messengers, the arrival of the letter, and the report received from "Chloe's people" were three separate events. However, the simplest scenario is that Chloe, whoever she was, sent the messengers who brought the letter from the church. Filled with sadness (2 Cor. 2:4), Paul dictated a letter to a coworker named Sosthenes (1 Cor. 1:1, 2)—the letter we call "1 Corinthians." We do not know if this is the same Sosthenes mentioned in 18:17. First Corinthians 16:21 indicates that Paul did not write most of the letter with his own hand. Paul's inclusion of a fellow author at the beginning of a letter, usually indicates that he dictated the letter to that individual. The letter addressed the problems in the congregation and promised a personal visit in the near future (1 Cor. 4:19; 16:3–7).

(3) Then Paul planned to start for Rome, the center of the Roman Empire. The word **must** (δεῖ, *dei*) shows how serious he was about these plans; he did not see the matter as optional. This mention is the first time we read of Paul's desire to go to Rome, although he said he had longed to see the brethren there "for many years" (Rom. 15:23; see comments on 16:12) so he

could strengthen them (Rom. 1:11). Paul evidently planned to make Rome his base for evangelizing the West, as he had made Antioch his base for evangelizing the East. He hoped to accomplish God's purposes in Rome and then go to the far western reaches of the empire—to Spain (Rom. 15:22–24).

Acts 19:21 is a pivotal verse in Acts. The last third of the book gives the sequence of events that culminated in Paul's arrival in the city of Rome.

Verse 22. Paul sent the letter to Corinth by the young preacher Timothy (1 Cor. 4:17; 16:10). Luke recorded that, about this time, Paul **sent into Macedonia two of those who ministered to him, Timothy and Erastus.** Probably these two were to do some preliminary work in **Macedonia** before going on to Corinth. Likely they were to prepare for Paul's visit, plus work on the collection for Jerusalem. It is possible that this **Erastus** was the "city treasurer" of Corinth mentioned in Romans 16:23 (see comments on 18:18). If so, this would explain why Paul did not tell the Corinthians that he had sent Erastus; the city treasurer simply "went home" to Corinth. Shortly afterward, Paul sent another young preacher, Titus, to follow up Timothy's work in Corinth (2 Cor. 2:12, 13; 7:5–7; 8:6, 23).[23] In the meantime, Paul **himself stayed in Asia for a while,** taking advantage of the open doors God had given him.

IN EPHESUS: ADVERSARIES (19:23–41)

Demetrius Causes a Disturbance (19:23–27)

[23]**About that time there occurred no small disturbance concerning the Way.** [24]**For a man named Demetrius, a silversmith, who made silver shrines of Artemis, was bringing no little**

---

[23]Other sequences of events are possible. For instance, Paul might have asked Timothy to return to Corinth with the letter. Then Paul could have sent Titus to follow up Timothy's visit and, later, sent Timothy and Erastus to Macedonia on an unrelated trip. As stated before, for some reason Luke never mentioned Titus in Acts. We have to reconstruct his movements from other sources.

business to the craftsmen; [25]these he gathered together with the workmen of similar trades, and said, "Men, you know that our prosperity depends upon this business. [26]You see and hear that not only in Ephesus, but in almost all of Asia, this Paul has persuaded and turned away a considerable number of people, saying that gods made with hands are no gods at all. [27]Not only is there danger that this trade of ours fall into disrepute, but also that the temple of the great goddess Artemis be regarded as worthless and that she whom all of Asia and the world worship will even be dethroned from her magnificence."

This passage brings us to a major incident during Paul's ministry in Ephesus, the final incident that hastened his departure. Although Paul had already decided to leave Ephesus, he probably planned to wait to hear from Titus regarding the Corinthian church before he left (2 Cor. 2:12, 13). The riot made it necessary for him to leave at once. This incident vividly demonstrates what can happen when Christianity adversely hits the pocketbook.

Verse 23. About that time there occurred no small disturbance concerning the Way. Some have speculated that this disturbance took place during the annual festival of Artemis, which occurred about the same time as Pentecost (see 1 Cor. 16:8, 9). **The Way** was one of Luke's favorite terms for Christianity (9:2; 19:9; 22:4; 24:14, 22).

Verse 24. This disturbance was precipitated by **a man named Demetrius.** Another Demetrius is mentioned in 3 John 12; it is unlikely that the two men were the same. Demetrius was **a silversmith, who made silver shrines of Artemis.** No silver shrines of Artemis have been found, but terra-cotta shrines have. We imagine the silver shrines were melted down and the silver recovered when the worship of Artemis declined.

In Ephesus, the goddess **Artemis** was identified with an ancient Asiatic fertility goddess. In some places, Artemis was pictured as a beautiful young huntress surrounded by deer or dogs, but in Ephesus she was depicted as a many-breasted originator and sustainer of life. Some think that the many "breasts" are actually large grapes hung on an apron, but the concept of the giver of life remains. The KJV substitutes the name of the Roman goddess Diana for the Greek goddess Artemis.

Artemis was worshiped as the mother goddess around the world (v. 27). Over thirty different locations that worshiped Artemis have been discovered. However, the center of devotion to her was Ephesus. Citizens of Ephesus thought of the goddess as uniquely theirs; they called her "Artemis of the Ephesians" (vv. 28, 34). The city of Ephesus considered itself "guardian of the temple of the great Artemis" (v. 35).

Inside the temple of Artemis was an image that, according to tradition, "fell down from heaven" (v. 35). This image may have been a meteorite that, to the credulous, resembled Artemis. It is even possible that some creative artist worked on the meteorite to intensify the resemblance. The largest marble temple in the world had been erected just outside the walls of Ephesus to house this crude chunk of rock. This temple, one of the Seven Wonders of the Ancient World, attracted visitors from around the world.

When visitors came to see the temple, like all tourists, they bought souvenirs. They did not merely return home with replicas of the Eiffel Tower or Michelangelo's *David*, as today's tourists do. Rather, they bought little shrines—"models that looked like the temple of the goddess Artemis" (NCV)—and dedicated them in the temple. In their superstitious minds, when they took those shrines home, they brought the presence of Artemis into their houses. As one can imagine, the manufacture of these silver shrines was lucrative. Luke observed that this enterprise, **was bringing no little business to the** local **craftsmen.** However, Paul's preaching made sales plummet.

Verses 25, 26. Demetrius, a shrine-maker, was furious. He gathered the other silversmiths of the area, **together with the workmen of similar trades** and sounded the alarm:

Men, you know that our prosperity depends upon this business. You see and hear that not only in Ephesus, but in almost all of Asia, this Paul has persuaded and turned away a considerable number of people, saying that gods made with hands are no gods at all.

Paul's convictions concerning idolatry were no secret. He proclaimed that God was not "like gold or silver or stone, an image formed by the art and thought of man" (17:29). He dedicated his energies to turning men "from idols to serve [the] living and true God" (1 Thess. 1:9). Paul's message had spread throughout the province of **Asia** (see comments on v. 10). His preaching had its effect; he had **persuaded and turned away a considerable number of people** from the worship of Artemis—which cut into the profits of Demetrius and the other manufacturers of idols. At least Demetrius was honest in his statement to his fellow businessmen; he was not as concerned about his prayerbook as he was his pocketbook.

Verse 27. However, Demetrius was intelligent enough to know that he and the other artisans could not rally public support on the basis of their financial losses, so he bolstered his accusations with religious prejudice and civic pride:

Not only is there danger that this trade of ours fall into disrepute, but also that the temple of the great goddess Artemis be regarded as worthless and that she whom all of Asia and the world worship will even be dethroned from her magnificence.

This section of Acts is unusual in that there are several speeches of uninspired men. Luke allowed pagan lips to witness to the impact of Christianity. No finer testimony to the power of the gospel could be found than the words of Demetrius. If any think that Demetrius overstated the effect of Paul's preaching, it might be noted that forty years later, Pliny the Younger, governor of Bithynia, wrote to the emperor Trajan, complaining that Christianity had caused the temples of the gods to be deserted.[24]

A Riot in Ephesus (19:28–41)

[28]When they heard this and were filled with rage, they began crying out, saying, "Great is Artemis of the Ephesians!"

---

[24]Pliny *Letters* 10.96.

²⁹The city was filled with the confusion, and they rushed with one accord into the theater, dragging along Gaius and Aristarchus, Paul's traveling companions from Macedonia. ³⁰And when Paul wanted to go into the assembly, the disciples would not let him. ³¹Also some of the Asiarchs who were friends of his sent to him and repeatedly urged him not to venture into the theater. ³²So then, some were shouting one thing and some another, for the assembly was in confusion and the majority did not know for what reason they had come together. ³³Some of the crowd concluded it was Alexander, since the Jews had put him forward; and having motioned with his hand, Alexander was intending to make a defense to the assembly. ³⁴But when they recognized that he was a Jew, a single outcry arose from them all as they shouted for about two hours, "Great is Artemis of the Ephesians!" ³⁵After quieting the crowd, the town clerk said, "Men of Ephesus, what man is there after all who does not know that the city of the Ephesians is guardian of the temple of the great Artemis and of the image which fell down from heaven? ³⁶So, since these are undeniable facts, you ought to keep calm and to do nothing rash. ³⁷For you have brought these men here who are neither robbers of temples nor blasphemers of our goddess. ³⁸So then, if Demetrius and the craftsmen who are with him have a complaint against any man, the courts are in session and proconsuls are available; let them bring charges against one another. ³⁹But if you want anything beyond this, it shall be settled in the lawful assembly. ⁴⁰For indeed we are in danger of being accused of a riot in connection with today's events, since there is no real cause for it, and in this connection we will be unable to account for this disorderly gathering." ⁴¹After saying this he dismissed the assembly.

Verse 28. Demetrius' inflammatory words had the desired effect. His listeners **were filled with rage** and **began crying out, saying, "Great is Artemis of the Ephesians!"** The Western Text says that they "ran into the street," shouting their slogan. Rabble-rousers have always found slogans to be convenient substitutes for reason.

Verse 29. The protesters marched through the city, collecting people as they went, until the whole **city was filled with the confusion.** When the numbers swelled, **they rushed with one accord into the theater,** a huge, open-air stadium with seating for 25,000. This structure, along with many others in the ancient city of Ephesus, still stands today. The crowd had become a mob; the demonstration had become a riot.

The instigators had probably planned to sweep up Paul on their march through the city—hoping the mob would kill him—but they did not find the apostle. They did come across **Gaius and Aristarchus, Paul's traveling companions from Macedonia.** We are not sure who this **Gaius . . . from Macedonia** was. Many Gaiuses are mentioned in the New Testament (20:4; Rom. 16:23; 1 Cor. 1:14; 3 Jn. 1). Some believe that the Gaius mentioned in Acts 20:4 is the same as the Gaius in 19:29; the Western Text indicates that the Gaius in 20:4 was from Doberus, a town in Macedonia, rather than Derbe. **Aristarchus** was from Thessalonica, the capital of Macedonia (20:4). He traveled with Paul to Jerusalem, then traveled with him to Rome (27:2). When Paul wrote from Rome, he referred to Aristarchus as his "fellow prisoner" (Col. 4:10; see Philem. 24). We do not know when, where, or why the two men had been **Paul's traveling companions** before verse 29. The mob dragged them into the amphitheater. It was a scene filled with madness; death was in the air. The fate of Gaius and Aristarchus hung by a thread.

Verse 30. When word reached Paul that his friends were in danger, he headed for the amphitheater—probably to offer himself in exchange for the release of his companions. However, **when Paul wanted to go into the assembly, the disciples would not let him.** The Greek word translated **assembly** is not the usual word ἐκκλησία (*ekklēsia*) (see v. 32), but δῆμος (*dēmos*), which literally means "people." *Dēmos* is also translated "assembly" in verse 33. Perhaps Paul thought the group was some kind of council with which he could reason. However, his friends knew there would be no reasoning with the mob, and the Lord's cause could not afford to lose Paul (see 2 Sam. 21:17).

Verse 31. Luke added the note that **also some of the Asiarchs who were friends of** Paul's **sent to him and repeatedly**

urged him not to venture into the theater. The word **Asiarchs** is transliterated from a compound Greek word which means "Asian rulers." Άσιάρχης (*Asiarchēs*) combines the words Άσία (*Asia*, "Asia") and ἀρχή (*archē*, "ruler"). Archaeologists have confirmed that Luke used the right term. These were Asian officials "selected . . . from the more opulent citizens, to preside over the things pertaining to religious worship, and to exhibit annual public games at their own expense in honour of the gods."[25] Their position makes it unlikely that these men had become Christians, but at least they were sympathetic to Paul and the cause he espoused. The fact that these high-placed officials were sympathetic to Christianity is further proof offered by Luke that Christianity posed no threat to society. The phrase **repeatedly urged him** indicates how hard it was to restrain Paul.

Verse 32. Meanwhile, in the amphitheater, **some were shouting one thing and some another, for the assembly was in confusion.** In this verse, **assembly** is a translation of ἐκκλησία (*ekklēsia*), the Greek word usually translated "church." In verses 32, 39, and 41, *ekklēsia* is used in the general sense of an assembly (see comments on 5:11). **The majority did not know for what reason they had come together.** It was a classic mob scene. Benjamin Franklin defined a mob as "a group of persons with heads aplenty but no brain." Most opposition to New Testament Christianity is the result of ignorance.

Verse 33. To illustrate how confused the mob was, Luke said that **some of the crowd concluded it was Alexander, since the Jews had put him forward.** Why were **Jews** present with the crazed idol worshipers? Is it possible that Jewish craftsmen had been making profits off the ignorance of idol worshipers?

The Jews in Ephesus apparently had a "live and let live" policy concerning idolatry, a policy that would never have been approved by God. Who was the **Alexander** the Jews put forward? Paul later referred to an "Alexander the coppersmith" who did him "much harm" (2 Tim. 4:14; see 1 Tim. 1:20). Since Timothy was in Ephesus when Paul wrote 1 Timothy (1 Tim. 1:3), the Alexander mentioned in 1 Timothy 1:20 may have been

---

[25]*The Analytical Greek Lexicon* (London: Samuel Bagster & Sons, 1971), 56.

a native of Ephesus. The fact that Luke mentioned him by name might indicate that readers would have known who he was. Why did the Jews push Alexander, whoever he was, before the mob? Did they want Alexander to make clear that the Jews in Ephesus were not responsible for any trouble Paul may have caused? Whatever Alexander's intention, it was not obvious to the crowd. Perhaps some concluded that Alexander was the instigator of the meeting; others may have thought that he was the one on trial. Alexander would have been **put . . . forward** in the stage area below the tiers of seats. He motioned for quiet, **intending to make a defense to the assembly,** but he never had the opportunity.

Verse 34. When they recognized that he was a Jew, a single outcry arose from them all as they shouted for about two hours, "Great is Artemis of the Ephesians!" According to Josephus, the citizens of Ephesus looked down on the Jews because of their exemption from the military, observance of the Sabbath, strange dietary laws, and other ancestral customs.[26] The Ephesians may have recognized Alexander as a Jew from his appearance and/or clothing.

The crowd was not concerned solely for Artemis. If the confused mob understood that the temple was threatened, then they instinctively understood that their economy was endangered. When a major industry collapses, it affects everyone in the area. Perhaps they too screamed because they felt the pain in their money pouches.

Verse 35. The headquarters for city government were a few blocks from the theater. City officials had to be aware of the riot in the stadium, but no attempt was made to control the crowd until the mob exhausted itself by two hours of maniacal screaming. Then the **town clerk** stepped into the arena and motioned for silence. The Greek term γραμματεύς (*grammateus*) is translated "town clerk." Once again, archaeologists confirm that Luke used exactly the right term. *Grammateus* is usually translated "scribe" and indicates that this city official recorded town business. However, in Ephesus he was much more than a mere sec-

---

[26]Josephus *Antiquities* 14.10.11–19; 16.2.3, 4.

retary. He was "the most important local official and the chief executive officer of the assembly, acting as go-between for Ephesus and the Roman authorities."[27] The Living Bible calls him "the mayor."

This official proved as efficient at quelling a riot as Demetrius had been at inciting one. He started by reassuring those in the amphitheater: **"Men of Ephesus, what man is there after all who does not know that the city of the Ephesians is guardian of the temple of the great Artemis and of the image which fell down from heaven?"** The phrase **guardian of the temple** translates the single Greek word νεωκόρος (*neōkoros*). This is a compound word, joining ναός (*naos*, "temple") and κορέω (*koreō*, "sweep"). *Neōkoros* meant "temple-sweeper," that is, one who cares for the temple. The usual translation is "temple-warden." Cities competed for the honor of being a "temple-warden." The word *neōkoros* appears on the ancient inscriptions and coinage of Ephesus, confirming the city as the guardian of the temple of Artemis. The Ephesians also cared for her **image which**, they believed, **fell down from heaven** (see comments on v. 24).

Verses 36, 37. The official then cautioned them: **"Since these are undeniable facts, you ought to keep calm and to do nothing rash."** The NCV has "Stop and think before you do anything." During the two hours of shouting, the official had done his research; he was armed with facts. He pointed at Gaius and Aristarchus, declaring, **"For you have brought these men here who are neither robbers of temples nor blasphemers of our goddess."**

The clerk first argued that the men brought to the theater were not **robbers of temples** (see Rom. 2:22). In addition to being a center of religious devotion, the temple of Artemis also served as a bank. It was a safety deposit for the money of wealthy citizens. Ministers of the temple collected sacred taxes, lent money, and purchased property in the name of Artemis. The men who were accused had not stolen any of these funds. Neither had they taken or defiled any of the sacred objects related

---

[27]Lewis Foster, notes on Acts, *The NIV Study Bible* (Grand Rapids, Mich.: Zondervan Publishing House, 1985), 1685.

to the worship of Artemis.

The clerk also said that the two Christians were not **blasphemers** of (that is, did not speak against) Artemis. Did he tell a lie? It is possible. Remember (1) that the official was speaking to a confused group, most of whom had no idea what was going on (v. 32); (2) that his purpose was not to defend the men, but to restore order; and (3) that, not being a Christian, he probably would not hesitate to tell a lie if it served his purpose. On the other hand, Demetrius and the other artisans could have challenged him if he had stretched the truth too far. Likely, he was not far off the mark in his statement. While Paul and his fellow-workers had preached that "gods made with hands are no gods at all" (v. 26), they probably had made no personal attack on Artemis. They had not led anti-idolatry rallies or picketed the temple; they had "merely" preached the gospel.

Verse 38. If Demetrius and the other artisans *had* been tempted to protest, the official effectively silenced them by singling them out as perpetrators of the disturbance: **"So then, if Demetrius and the craftsmen who are with him have a complaint against any man, the courts are in session and proconsuls are available; let them bring charges against one another."** The **courts** referred to the local council that met regularly. The **proconsuls** referred to the regional Roman authority. Since there was normally only one proconsul over Asia, the plural form of the word is somewhat of a mystery. Perhaps the word is used in a more general sense to refer to regional authorities.

Verse 39. The official continued: **"But if you want anything beyond this, it shall be settled in the lawful assembly."** This **lawful assembly** was "the regular town meeting of the people" (NCV). The clerk accomplished two purposes with these words. First, he stressed that there was a right and a wrong way to handle complaints—and they had chosen the wrong way. Second, he let the craftsmen know who would be held accountable if there were repercussions.

Verse 40. The official then hinted at possible consequences: **"For indeed we are in danger of being accused of a riot in connection with today's events, since there is no real cause for it, and in this connection we will be unable to account for this**

disorderly gathering." To appreciate the force of these words, we must understand the attitude of Rome toward riots. In the eyes of Rome, few crimes were worse than civil disorder; it was a capital offense to incite a riot. Ephesus was a free city and enjoyed many privileges. Most, if not all, of those could be lost if the disturbance in the theater was reported to Rome. Roman legionnaires could take over the city. The guilty could be imprisoned and even executed—including the town clerk for letting it happen. At the least, fines would be imposed, taxes would be increased, and the guilds would probably be disbanded. In other words, the silversmiths and the rest would be hit in the very pocketbooks they were trying to protect when they started the riot.

Verse 41. When the official finished, the crowd he looked at was far from the unruly mob of minutes before. Luke recorded that **after saying this he dismissed the assembly.** Can you imagine the people—quieted, with heads down—as they left the theater and scurried home? Can you also see the clerk as he wiped his brow, then headed back to city hall to attend to more mundane affairs? He probably thought, "I'm glad I don't have to do *that* every day!" and maybe, "They don't pay me enough for what I have to put up with!"

What happened to Gaius and Aristarchus, Paul's traveling companions who had been dragged into the amphitheater? They were apparently released, probably with the official's apologies. In the next chapter we find at least one of them, Aristarchus, again traveling with Paul (20:4). It is also possible that Gaius also traveled again with the apostle, although the later "Gaius" is said to be from a different location (compare 19:29 and 20:4).

It was another victory for the Way. Once more, believers had been exonerated and their persecutors censured. Luke had shown his readers that it was not Christians, but rather their persecutors, who posed a threat to society.

APPLICATION

How To Grow a Church (19:1–20)

A sermon entitled "How To Grow a Church" could easily be

developed from verses 1 through 20. Drawing a parallel with gardening, the following major points could be made: (1) Make sure the seed is pure (vv. 1–7). (2) Do not be stingy in the sowing (vv. 8–10). (3) Do what you must to prepare the soil before you plant (vv. 11, 12). (4) Be diligent in pulling out weeds (vv. 13–20).

Baptism of John vs. Christian Baptism (19:1–7)

The baptism of John was compared to an outdated map (see comments on v. 3). You may want to have an old, bedraggled map in hand as you use the illustration of the outdated map. If desired, you can pause to make application to today: Some try to use the outdated map of the Old Testament (Heb. 8:7; 10:9); others try to use the outdated map of their own opinions, that is, conclusions based on ignorance (Acts 17:30).

A good way to contrast the baptism of John with the baptism of the Great Commission is to use the chart below.

Baptism Administered by John	Baptism Authorized by Jesus
An immersion in water	An immersion in water
Baptism of preparation	Baptism of fulfillment
Baptism of repentance	Baptism of faith
Preceded by call to repentance	Preceded by preaching of the gospel
Looked forward to Christ (and the cross)	Looks backward to Christ (and the cross)
Confessed sins	Confesses faith in Jesus
Associated with no name	In the name of the Father, Son, and Holy Spirit
For the remission of sins	For the remission of sins
No promise of the Holy Spirit	Promise of the Holy Spirit

When speaking on the essentiality of all three elements of baptism being right (action, subject, and purpose), an object lesson might be helpful. If you can find a three-legged stool, hold it up and ask, "Which of these legs are essential, and which are not?" All three are essential; if one is missing, then, for all practical purposes, the stool becomes worthless. Compare this to baptism with one of the scriptural requirements missing. You may want to loosen one leg of the stool ahead of time. You could pull out the leg as you speak of having one leg gone. Someone could try to sit on the stool with the leg missing. Another possible visual aid would be a combination lock. Note that three steps are necessary to open the lock. Stress that all three steps must be carried out before the lock opens. Even so, all three requirements for scriptural baptism must be fulfilled before that baptism is God-pleasing.

When Is Baptism Not Baptism? (19:1–7)

The story of the twelve men who needed to be re-immersed could be part of a series on conversions in the Book of Acts. Such a lesson would skim over the beginning of the third journey, as Luke did, to get to 19:1. The title of this presentation could be "When Is Baptism Not Baptism?" or "The Conversion of Twelve Disciples Who Had Been Baptized." If this latter title were used, introductory remarks could center on the apparent incongruity of the title: Could "disciples" who had been "baptized" need conversion? Apparently so, according to our text.

Sometimes "baptism" is not baptism. Occasions will arise when individuals who have undergone a rite called baptism still need to be immersed. Since we have no exact parallel today with John's baptism, exactly when this need exists may not be easy to ascertain in all cases. Still, the beginning point of any application must be the truth that not every ritual called baptism is scriptural baptism.

To start our discussion, let us ask, "What is necessary to make a baptism scriptural?" Here is a simple answer, based on our studies in Acts: "It must have the right action, the right person, and the right purpose." *The right action* is an immersion in water. The word "baptism" is a transliterated Greek word literally meaning "immersion" (see comments on 2:38). In Acts 8, the one baptized went down into the water, was baptized, and then came up out of the water (vv. 38, 39). *The right subject* is a person who is mature enough to make a personal commitment of his

207

life, who believes in the Lord, has repented of his sins, and who is willing to confess his faith (2:37, 38; 8:37). The Book of Acts does not authorize the baptism of infants. *The right purpose* is to obtain the forgiveness of sins (2:38; 22:16), to receive the Holy Spirit as a gift (2:38), and to become a member of the Lord's church (2:41, 47).

The first two requirements—the right action and the right subject—do not present undue difficulty as we make application. An individual was either immersed in water or he was not, and he was either old enough to make a personal commitment or he was not. (Of course, if one was old enough to make a personal commitment, there is still the question of whether or not he genuinely believed and repented before his baptism.) Thus, although the idea might be considered insulting by a large segment of "Christendom," if a person was sprinkled as a baby, he still needs to be baptized according to the New Testament pattern.

Where the issue becomes complicated is in the area of purpose. We struggle with the question of exactly what one must know and understand before his baptism is scriptural. Whether or not the question of purpose is complex, it is central to any application we make from Acts 19:1–7. The twelve were grown men (the right subjects) who had been immersed in water (the right action). It was basically in the matter of purpose that their baptism fell short. They knew nothing of the relationship of baptism to the blood of Jesus; they had not been baptized to receive the gift of the Holy Spirit; and they had not been immersed to become members of the Lord's church.

As we consider the question of purpose, we must try to avoid oversimplification. It is tempting to overemphasize a single purpose of baptism. For instance, we have heard it said that if an individual was immersed "for the remission of sins," his baptism is all right. Remember that the twelve disciples had been baptized "for the forgiveness of sins" (Mk 1:4), but they still needed to be re-immersed. Various cults, including the Mormons, immerse adults for the forgiveness of sins, but that alone does not make their baptisms acceptable to God. Among other errors, some of these cults misrepresent the nature of Jesus.

An example of how easy it would be to oversimplify this

question would be to conclude that as long as the baptizer made the pronouncement "in the name of the Lord Jesus" (v. 5), the baptism was scriptural. To be baptized "in the name of Jesus" does not merely refer to invoking the name of Jesus; among other things, it refers to being baptized by Jesus' authority (see comments on 2:38). A baptism different from that authorized by Jesus cannot be done "in His name," even if His name is used as part of the ritual.

The challenge of determining a man's purpose in being baptized is that we are trying to discover what was in that man's heart at that moment, and that is difficult. "For who . . . knows the thoughts of a man except the spirit of the man which is in him?" (1 Cor. 2:11). On the other hand, the writer of Hebrews said that *the word of God* is . . . able to judge the thoughts and intentions of the heart" (Heb. 4:12; emphasis added). We are on safe ground, therefore, when we compare what *the Word* says about the purpose of baptism with the purposes of men.

As we have studied with men and women through the years, they have shared many manmade reasons for baptism. Some were baptized "just because everyone was." Some were baptized to please others. Some were baptized because they were required to do so to get into the denomination of their choice. Some were told that the only purpose of their baptism was to be "an outward sign" of their inward cleansing. Many are not sure why they were baptized, "but it was expected." The purposes given above relate to adult immersion. Those who practice "infant baptism" also have a variety of reasons, ranging from "keeping the child out of limbo" to "having a sweet ceremony to give the baby a Christian name."

When we study one-on-one, it is our practice to compare Christian baptism, including its purpose, with our student's baptism. The student must make the final decision on whether or not he needs to be immersed (or re-immersed), since he alone knows his heart. After an in-depth study, most students decide that, to complete their obedience, they need to be baptized.

Let us hasten to say that we are not insisting that one must know *everything* about baptism before he can be scripturally baptized; nor are we saying that if one's appreciation and understanding of baptism grows over the years, this means he was not scripturally baptized. Paul's words in Romans 6:3–6 no doubt gave the Christians in Rome new insight into the significance of baptism. On the other hand, since we are to "obey from the heart" when we are baptized (see Rom. 6:3, 4, 17, 18), we must have some basic understanding of what scriptural baptism involves and the commitment we are making.

Today's proliferation of manmade rituals called baptism has greatly confused the issue of whether or not individuals have been scripturally baptized. We suppose, however, that the situation of today is not that far removed from the situation Paul found in Ephesus: The coexistence of John's outdated baptism alongside Christian baptism also muddled the issue in Paul's day. The twelve believed that they had been baptized; it is even possible that some Christians thought the twelve had been baptized. The possibility exists that up to the time that Paul arrived, their baptism had been accepted by the Christians in Ephesus, perhaps even by Aquila and Priscilla. Paul's approach to clearing up the confusion was to lay the baptism of the Great Commission alongside John's baptism. It is an approach worthy of imitation today.

Two obvious applications emerge from the story of the twelve men who needed to be re-immersed: (1) We should be straightforward in our teaching, even if the possibility exists that we might hurt someone's feelings by doing so. Paul did not hesitate to tell the twelve that something was wrong with their baptism. If our listeners have honest hearts, they will accept God's Word in the spirit in which we give it (see Eph. 4:15). (2) Each of us needs to compare our religious practices with what the Bible teaches, making whatever adjustments are needed to bring our practices in line with biblical teaching—even if it hurts. The twelve men were willing to do this. Are we?

"Did You Receive the Holy Spirit?" (19:2)

Paul's question "Did you receive the Holy Spirit when you believed?" is a favorite of charismatics today. They use the question as a springboard to preach on the Holy Spirit. Specifically, they preach on the miraculous gifts of the Spirit which they believe are for today. Paul, however, did not follow the question with a sermon on the Holy Spirit, but with a sermon on *Jesus*. The Holy Spirit did not come to exalt Himself, but to glorify Jesus (Jn. 16:14). According to the apostle John, we do not show the presence of the Spirit in our lives by bodily gyrations or unintelligible speech, but rather by confessing "that Jesus Christ has come in the flesh" (1 Jn. 4:2).

Miraculous Tongue-Speaking (19:6)

In 19:6, we have the last mention of miraculous tongue-speaking in the Book of Acts. This might be a good time to say a few words about this phenomenon and related matters.

For many years there has been a movement, sometimes called Pentecostalism, which teaches that the miracles of the New Testament are also for today. In recent years, this "charismatic movement" or "neo-Pentecostalism" has crossed denominational lines.

Many factors have probably contributed to the increased desire for the miraculous. These factors include (1) a reaction to the cold formalism of many "established" churches, (2) a reaction to the uncertainty of the times—some prefer to walk by sight rather than faith (see 2 Cor. 5:7), and (3) a reaction to the multiplied attacks on the Bible. Man needs to believe in *something*; if he thinks he can no longer depend on the Bible, he will turn to the mysterious.

A relatively new development in the charismatic movement has been an increased emphasis on "speaking in tongues" or "glossalalia." "Glossalalia" is a made-up word produced by combining the Greek word for "tongue" (γλῶσσα, *glōssa*) with a Greek word that can mean "speak"(λαλέω, *laleō*).

There are probably a number of reasons why this specific miraculous gift is stressed today. Here are two possibilities: (1) Speaking in tongues is more sedate and thus more acceptable in our "more cultured" age than the frantic exercises that characterized the Pentecostalism of generations past. (2) Speaking in tongues can be more easily demonstrated than healing, handling snakes, or raising the dead.

In spite of the considerable attention given today to tongue-speaking, only five references to the subject appear in the New Testament. Jesus Himself did not speak in tongues. When His disciples asked Him to teach them to pray, He did not teach them "a special prayer language," but taught them to pray after this manner: "Our Father who is in heaven, hallowed be Your name . . ." (Mt. 6:9).

We will look briefly at the five passages on tongue-speaking and consider a few key points. The Greek word *glōssa* is found in each reference and means simply "tongue." Some translators have read their interpretations into the text and have thus rendered the word "ecstatic utterances" in some of the references; but a different Greek word means "ecstatic," and that word is never used to describe this gift.

Mark 16:14–20. Most acknowledge that Jesus did not promise all the gifts in this passage to all believers. Some qualification is needed. In the immediate context, the promise was to the apostles. Regarding the specific gift of tongues, the apostles received this gift (Acts 2), but so did others (Acts 10; 11; 19:1–7; 1 Cor. 12—14). The promise of tongue-speaking was for some believers.

Observe that only one promise concerning speaking in tongues was given by Jesus in Mark 16. Whatever "speaking in tongues" means in passages where the meaning is clear, it also means in passages where the meaning is not as clear.

The purpose of the "signs" (Mk. 16:17, 20)—including speaking in tongues—was to confirm the word (Mk. 16:20). Exactly the same language was used regarding drinking poison as was used regarding speaking in tongues. The gift of speaking in tongues was to last as long as the gift of being unharmed by ingested poison.

Acts 1; 2. On the Day of Pentecost, only the apostles received the gift of speaking in tongues (Acts 1:2–5, 26; 2:1–4, 7, 14, 37; see comments on 2:4). They received that gift by being baptized in the Holy Spirit (1:5; 2:1–4). Some try to make the last part of 2:38 refer to the gift of tongues, but it does not (see comments on 2:38).

The "tongues" the apostles spoke were contemporary languages (2:4, 6, 8, 11). This gift was a sign to those present that they spoke the truth (2:33).

All the miraculous manifestations of Acts 2—the sound of wind, fiery tongues, speaking in tongues—were for the same purpose (2:33). If one should be restored, all should be restored. The special manifestation of speaking in tongues was to last as long as the special manifestations of the wind and fiery tongues.

Acts 10; 11. In these chapters, we read of the first Gentile converts. They spoke in tongues (Acts 10:46; 11:8, 18). These tongues were languages that Cornelius and his household had not studied. This truth is evident because Peter stressed that these Gentiles received the same gift that the apostles received on the Day of Pentecost (11:15, 17; see comments on 11:17). The purpose of the tongue-speaking on the part of Cornelius and the others was to give those present a sign that God had accepted Gentiles just as He had Jews (10:14–18; 11:18).

In the conversion of Cornelius, God used angelic visitations, visions, and speaking in tongues to accomplish His purpose. If we should restore one of these miraculous manifestations, we should restore the others. Speaking in tongues was to last as long as angelic visitations and visions.

Acts 19:1–7. This passage is from the chapter presently under consideration. The recipients of the gift of tongue-speaking were twelve disciples. They received this gift by the laying-on of an apostle's hands (19:6; see comments on 8:18). When Paul laid his hands on the twelve men, "they began speaking with tongues and prophesying" (19:6). Tongue-speaking was to last as long as prophecy, that is, inspired revelation.

If one believes that the gift of speaking in tongues is for today, to be consistent, he must also believe in additional, continuous revelation, such as the Catholics, Mormons, Seventh-day Adventists, Christian Scientists, and others claim to have received. In our experience, those who claim to speak in tongues acknowledge the Bible as their religious authority, but the farther they go into the movement, the less they depend on the objective teachings of the Bible and the more they rely on subjective feelings.

1 Corinthians 12—14. Paul stressed in 1 Corinthians 12 that not all had the same gifts. This implies that only some of the

Corinthians had the gift of speaking in tongues.

First Corinthians 12—14 teaches that the gift of speaking in tongues was given "through the Spirit," with no details given. We must go to other references for details. From those passages, we learn that this gift was bestowed through Holy Spirit baptism (Acts 2:1–4) or the laying on of the apostles' hands (19:6). The means of receiving this gift are not available to us today (see comments on 8:18).

The tongues are not defined in these chapters. Luke's readers needed a definition, but the Corinthians did not. The KJV has "unknown tongues," but the word "unknown" is not in the original text; the word is simply *glōssa*. Nothing in the text compels us to believe that the tongues of 1 Corinthians 12—14 are different from those in Acts 2 and Acts 10—that is, contemporary languages they had not studied.

The gift of tongues was a "sign" to unbelievers (1 Cor. 14:21–25). The term "unbelievers" could refer either to unbelieving Jews or to unbelieving Christians. The text used by Paul in 14:21 is from Isaiah 28, where the prophet said that the coming of the Assyrians would be a sign to unbelieving Israelites, that is, unbelieving children of God. Yes, children of God can fail to believe God. In the setting of 1 Corinthians 14, the gift of tongues is more likely a sign to non-Christian Jews who visited the worship services at Corinth.

First Corinthians 13:8–13 makes clear that miraculous gifts were to cease. Most today would not insist that all the miraculous manifestations of the five passages—including immunity to poison, the mysterious sound of a gale, fiery-tongue apparitions, and angelic visitations—are for today. These and miracles in general were essential to the infancy of the church, but their purpose has been fulfilled. The Word has been confirmed (Heb. 2:3, 4). Today the written Word produces saving faith (Jn. 20:30, 31; Rom. 1:16; 10:17). The temporary and incomplete revelation through miraculous gifts was replaced by the permanent and complete revelation found in the New Testament.[28]

---

[28]For further study on this important topic, see *Truth for Today* 15 (April 1995), entitled "The Holy Spirit."

We would not deny that today some speak in "ecstatic utterances," that is, a flow of unintelligible sound coming forth from their lips, in some cases without their conscious direction. What we do deny is that what is happening today is similar to what occurred in New Testament times, and that it is being done by the power of the Holy Spirit.

Most "tongue-speakers" today admit that their "gift," or something very much like it, can be psychologically induced. Further, they must admit that the "gift" of tongue-speaking also appears in various groups claiming to be Christian which they believe teach false doctrine. Further still, they must admit that some pagan groups also practice "tongue-speaking." Of course, they believe that others do not have a *true* gift from God, while *they* do. *All*, however, must be judged by the same Book, the Bible.

Blessed Hankerchiefs (19:11, 12)

The word "extraordinary" (v. 11) indicates that this manner of healing was the exception rather than the rule, that this was an unusual occurrence even in New Testament times. We mention this because verses 11 and 12 have been a favorite "proof text" of some who prosper by deceiving the poor and sick. If all the handkerchiefs and scraps of cloth that have been "blessed" and sent out by so-called healers were sewn together, they would surely cover a large portion of the world.

The Continuing Challenge (19:19)

As we watch the smoke of the Ephesian bonfire spiraling upward, we need to ask, "What application does God want us to make to our own lives?"

Break Any Ties with Satanic Practices. The most obvious application is that God wants us to break any ties we may have with the occult. Christians should have nothing to do with horoscopes, psychic hotlines, Ouija boards, or even good-luck charms. The superstitious world holds many dangers such as:

(1) The danger of desiring knowledge that God does not want us to have (Deut. 29:29). "Everything pertaining to life and godliness" (2 Pet. 1:3; see Col. 1:28) has been revealed in the Bible

(Jn. 14:26; 2 Tim. 3:16, 17). When we seek answers, we often look for a shortcut instead of the sure way." Remember that the desire for forbidden knowledge resulted in the fall of man (Gen. 3:1–7).

(2) The danger of trying to satisfy morbid curiosities rather than learning eternal truths. Occult "revelations" concentrate on trivia; the Bible tells of sin and salvation, heaven and hell.

(3) The danger of allowing our lives to become man-centered rather than God-centered. The world of the mysterious says, "Your personal problems are important in the scheme of things, and by your own efforts you can solve those problems." The deeper one goes into occultism, the farther he goes from God.

(4) The danger of leaving our minds open to the control of evil. When one enters the supernatural world, he enters the devil's territory. Many occult practices involve a surrender of the will. Every mystical practice gives the devil an opportunity to take control of your life. Ananias allowed Satan to fill his heart with evil (see comments on 5:3); the devil will also fill yours if you let him.

(5) The danger of being led from truth into error, and thus being lost. Satan's purpose in promoting the occult is the same purpose he has in encouraging anything contrary to the will of God: He wants people to follow him and not the Lord; he wants all to spend eternity in hell with him, not in heaven with God. God commands us plainly in His Word to stay away from the devil's playground.

The non-Christian, blinded by "the god of this world" (2 Cor. 4:4), may likely view horoscopes, psychic hotlines, Ouija boards, and good-luck charms as harmless, but the Christian, enlightened by the Word, knows that they are as dangerous as an angry rattlesnake. The Christian policy is "hands-off," without reservation. Dabbling "a little" in the occult is like being "a little" pregnant.

Break All Ties with a Sinful Past. You may be saying, "But I don't have anything to do with the superstitious." Even if you do not, there is still a powerful message to you in our text: Be sure to break all ties with your sinful past.

In theory, all ties with past sins are broken when we repent and become Christians (Acts 2:38). In practice, however, it is hard to turn loose of everything all at once. Many of the Ephesians who had believed still retained ties with their occult past (19:18). Some writers do not believe that the Ephesian Christians were still engaging in sorcery. Whether they were or not, the fact they had held on to their magical scrolls and had not confessed their sins indicated that to some extent they retained ties to the evil realm. Even so, we may still cling to some sin that has a powerful attraction to us. This can range from telling lies to cheating on our income taxes, from entertaining lustful thoughts to perusing pornography.

Several weeks after one young man was baptized, he brought a large box of *Playboy* magazines into the preacher's study. "I can't keep these now that I've become a Christian," he said. Together, he and the preacher disposed of the publications. Several more weeks went by and the young man showed up at the preacher's study again with a large manila envelope in his hand. He laid the envelope on the preacher's desk and said, with a sheepish look, "These are pictures I cut out of the magazines before I gave them to you." It is hard to break all ties with a sinful past.

Some of us may need to have our own private bonfires and "toss into the fire" sinful thoughts and habits we harbor in our hearts and lives.

Conclusion. The Ephesians were wrong in their "hidden" practices, but they were right in believing in a spirit world. Paul later wrote to them:

> Put on the full armor of God, so that you will be able to stand firm against the schemes of the devil. For our struggle is not against flesh and blood, but against the rulers, against the powers, against the world forces of this darkness, against the spiritual forces of wickedness in the heavenly places (Eph. 6:11, 12).

Demons can no longer take control of a man's body against his will, but that does not mean that Satan cannot control our lives if we allow him to do so. The forces of evil can no longer perform miracles any more than the forces of good can, but this does not mean the devil cannot deceive the unwary (Rev. 20:10). Let us be aware that our "adversary, the devil" still "prowls around like a roaring lion, seeking someone to devour" (1 Pet. 5:8). We dare not be "ignorant of his schemes" (2 Cor. 2:11).

If we remain close to the Lord, we need not fear Satan (Jas. 4:7). John gave us this assurance: ". . . greater is He who is in you than he who is in the world" (1 Jn. 4:4). On the other hand, if Christ is *not* in you, then he who is in the world is more powerful than you! This is not a matter to take lightly. You must have the help of Jesus to win the spiritual battle. If you have not yet named His name and put Him on in baptism (Gal. 3:26, 27), you need to do that at once. If, as a Christian, you have retained something in your heart and life that gives Satan a hold on you, you need the courage of the Ephesians: Come before your brethren, "confessing and disclosing [your] practices" (Acts 19:18; see 8:24; Jas. 5:16).

The Ephesian Riot (19:23–41)

The story of the Ephesian riot can be presented with the following outline, inserting points of application along the way: (1) "Diana," Demetrius, and a Disturbance (vv. 23–29); (2) Some Disciples, Imminent Death, and a Defense (vv. 29–34); and (3) Disorder, Danger, and a Dismissal (vv. 35–41).

Demetriuses in the Church? (19:23–27)

Of special significance for our age, is the timely warning not to be overly concerned about money. Money can be an instrument or an idol. It has been said, "When a Christian gets hold of money, it is a terrific thing; when money gets hold of a Christian, it is a terrible thing." We can worship God and use money to further His cause, or we can worship money and use religion to make more money. Step back a moment and look at the anxiety of Demetrius and his friends regarding the almighty drachma; then look into the mirror of self-examination. What is our attitude toward money? How do we react when opportunities are given to help others or to further the cause of Christ?

A preacher was trying to motivate the congregation. He said,

"Brethren, this church has come a long way since we started. When we started, we could barely crawl, but now we can walk." A voice from the back of the building said, "Let it walk, preacher; let it walk!" The preacher was encouraged. "If we commit ourselves, I believe we can run!" he said. The voice said, "Let it run, preacher; let it run!" The preacher got excited. "I even believe that if we put our minds to it, we could *fly* for the Lord! Of course, that would mean we would all need to double our contributions!" The voice from the back said, "Let it walk, preacher; let it walk."

It has been said that the most sensitive part of the anatomy is the pocketbook. Through the years we have never heard anyone say, "I was so embarrassed! I brought someone to worship, and the preacher preached on the gospel [or the church, or love, or baptism]." However, we *have* heard people complain, "I finally got my friend to come with me, and wouldn't you know it—the preacher preached on *giving*. I was never so embarrassed in my life!"

How To Handle Prejudice (19:35–41)

Robert Oglesby has an interesting application of the town clerk's speech. He suggests that the speech is a study in how to handle prejudice and makes application to handling the prejudice we encounter when we teach: (1) The clerk *reassured* the multitude (v. 35). (2) He *discouraged rash action* (v. 36). (3) He made them *look at the real issue* (v. 37). (4) He suggested *orderly action* (vv. 38, 39). (5) He warned them of *possible consequences* (v. 40). (6) He assumed *leadership* (v. 41).[29]

---

[29]Robert Oglesby, *A Group Discussion Study of Acts* (Richardson, Tex.: RKO Publications, 1971), 91–92.

CHAPTER 20
PAUL'S THIRD MISSIONARY JOURNEY
(PART 3)

VISITS TO MACEDONIA, GREECE, AND TROAS (20:1–6)

¹After the uproar had ceased, Paul sent for the disciples, and when he had exhorted them and taken his leave of them, he left to go to Macedonia. ²When he had gone through those districts and had given them much exhortation, he came to Greece. ³And there he spent three months, and when a plot was formed against him by the Jews as he was about to set sail for Syria, he decided to return through Macedonia. ⁴And he was accompanied by Sopater of Berea, the son of Pyrrhus, and by Aristarchus and Secundus of the Thessalonians, and Gaius of Derbe, and Timothy, and Tychicus and Trophimus of Asia. ⁵But these had gone on ahead and were waiting for us at Troas. ⁶We sailed from Philippi after the days of Unleavened Bread, and came to them at Troas within five days; and there we stayed seven days.

When we read the first six verses of chapter 20, they seem merely to be a brief summary of Paul's trip to Greece and back, as he wrapped up his third missionary journey. Like other sections of Scripture that at first seem relatively unimportant and perhaps even dull, these verses, studied in depth, yield rich truths. We will reconstruct the period from Paul's writings during this time: Romans, 1 and 2 Corinthians. It is possible that Luke did not give details of this period because they were already known through those letters.

We find that the passage comprises at least a "year of journey and adventure."[1] F. F. Bruce suggested that the period lasted closer to two years.[2] One of Paul's major concerns during that time might be summarized by his words near the end of chapter 20: "You must help the weak and remember the words of the Lord Jesus, that He Himself said, 'It is more blessed to give than to receive'" (v. 35). At that moment, "the weak" had special reference to "the poor among the saints in Jerusalem" (Rom. 15:26).

From its beginning, the church in Jerusalem had more than its share of needy members. Shortly after its establishment, members who owned property shared with those who had nothing (2:44, 45; 4:32–35; 6:1). When a famine hit, the church in Antioch sent needed help to Jerusalem and Judea (11:27–30; 12:25). When Paul and Barnabas made a special trip to Jerusalem, Peter and other leaders asked them "to remember the poor"—specifically poor Jewish Christians, especially those in Jerusalem. Paul said that he "was eager to do" this (Gal. 2:10).

During Paul's second or third missionary journey, he formulated the idea of making a collection for the Jerusalem church. As with all of Paul's decisions, we are confident that he consulted the Lord before making it. He hoped this Gentile love-offering to Jews would improve relationships between the two segments in the church (2 Cor. 9:11–14). Throughout the third journey, Paul had worked on this collection (1 Cor. 16:1, 2; 2 Cor. 8:10). He was now ready to finish it and take the money to Jerusalem. Keep this purpose in mind as we explore beneath the surface of Acts 20:1–6.

Verse 1. The riot in the theater (19:23–41) convinced Paul that it was time to do what he had already been planning to do: leave Ephesus (19:21, 22). The open door (1 Cor. 16:9) had been slammed shut. Thus, **after the uproar had ceased, Paul sent for the disciples, and when he had exhorted them and taken his**

---

[1]William Barclay, *The Acts of the Apostles*, The Daily Study Bible Series, rev. ed. (Philadelphia: Westminster Press, 1976), 148.

[2]F. F. Bruce, *The Book of Acts*, The New International Commentary on the New Testament, gen. ed. F. F. Bruce, rev. ed. (Grand Rapids, Mich.: Wm. B. Eerdmans Publishing Co., 1988), 381.

leave of them, he left to go to Macedonia.

As Paul left, he was filled with concern. First, there was concern for the Christians he was leaving at Ephesus. **Paul sent for the disciples**—perhaps to see if any had been injured in the riot, maybe to explain why he had not rushed into the theater, and certainly to encourage them before he left. Second, as already suggested, there was an underlying concern for "the poor among the saints in Jerusalem." Paul was traveling **to Macedonia** to gather the collection for those in need. However, another concern must have given Paul sleepless nights—another reason he was heading toward Greece: the problems that threatened to consume the Corinthian church.

Paul had sent Titus to Corinth to follow up Timothy's visit (2 Cor. 2:12, 13; 7:5–7; 8:6, 23). Titus was then to bring Paul word of how the Corinthians were faring. Apparently, Titus' itinerary was to take him from Corinth to Macedonia, then to Troas, and finally on to Ephesus. When Paul left Ephesus on the way to Macedonia, his first stop was Troas (2 Cor. 2:12), where he hoped to rendezvous with Titus.

Troas was the seaport on the Aegean Sea where Paul had earlier received the Macedonian call (16:8–10). During that brief visit, Paul had done little or no preaching there. This time, however, "a door was opened" to him (2 Cor. 2:12); the city was ripe for evangelism. Paul responded to the opportunity in an uncharacteristic fashion: He was so concerned about Corinth that he could not settle down to take advantage of the situation. He later wrote: "I had no rest for my spirit, not finding Titus my brother; but taking my leave of [those in Troas], I went on to Macedonia" (2 Cor. 2:13). This occasion is the only recorded instance when Paul did not take advantage of a God-given opportunity.

Paul hoped to intercept Titus in Macedonia, but Titus was not there. While Paul waited for the young preacher, he worked on the collection for Jerusalem—and was pleasantly surprised by the generosity of the Macedonians (2 Cor. 8:1–5)—but he was still filled with concern. He later wrote, "When we came into Macedonia our flesh had no rest, but we were afflicted on every side: conflicts without, fears within" (2 Cor. 7:5). The "conflicts"

223

were probably with the Jews who had run him out of Thessalonica and Berea. Among other "fears," he was concerned that the Corinthian Christians had reacted poorly to his correspondence. Even Paul had bad days; the Lord does not abandon us when we have bad days.

Finally Titus arrived, bringing good news. In general, the church in Corinth had responded well to Paul's admonitions and warnings. Paul wrote of his relief in these words:

> But God, who comforts the depressed, comforted us by the coming of Titus; and not only by his coming, but also by the comfort with which he was comforted in you, as he reported to us your longing, your mourning, your zeal for me; so that I rejoiced even more (2 Cor. 7:6, 7).

Paul most likely dictated the letter we call 2 Corinthians to Timothy (2 Cor. 1:1) and then sent Titus back to Corinth accompanied by two others (2 Cor. 8:16–24). We do not know who the two unnamed brethren were, nor do we know why Paul did not name them. Names such as Luke, Barnabas, and Timothy have been suggested. Perhaps it was two of the messengers of the churches named in Acts 20:4. One of Paul's purposes in writing 2 Corinthians was to encourage the brethren to finish their contribution for Jerusalem. Paul urged the Corinthians to imitate the generosity of the Macedonians (2 Cor. 8, 9).

Verse 2. After Paul sent the letter, he stayed a while longer in Macedonia, preaching and teaching. We can imagine his joyful reunion with the Christians in Philippi, Thessalonica, Berea, and other places. During this period, he may also have traveled northwestward into the province of Illyricum to preach (Rom. 15:19). Paul's efforts in Illyricum fit better with this visit to Macedonia than with his previous visit. Luke recorded simply that **when he had gone through those districts and had given them much exhortation, he came to Greece.** Since Paul did not anticipate seeing the brethren in Macedonia again, his **exhortation** was probably similar to that found in Acts 20:18–35. The term **Greece** is used here to indicate the province of Achaia.

Verse 3. Luke then noted that **there he spent three months.**

Perhaps he remained there during the winter months, when travel was difficult. Paul spent most of this three months in Corinth, as guest of a brother named Gaius (Rom. 16:23). Some speculate that Gaius is another name of Titius Justus (Acts 18:7).

While in Corinth, Paul wrote his masterpiece, the Book of Romans. It was apparently dictated to Tertius (Rom. 16:22) and probably taken to Rome by Phoebe (Rom. 16:1, 2). This Christian woman lived in Cenchrea, one of the seaports that served Corinth. One interesting note in the book is that Aquila and Priscilla had left Ephesus at some point and traveled back to Rome (Rom. 16:3, 4), perhaps to look after their business interests there. On the surface, Paul wrote in anticipation of visiting Rome (Rom. 1:9–15; 15:22–29). However, he was already aware of dangers he would face when he reached Jerusalem (Rom. 15:31; see Acts 20:22–25; 21:13, 14). By writing to the Romans, he would leave "a concise statement of Christianity" in the heart of the empire, whether he reached there or not.

When Paul wrote Romans, all had gone well in Corinth regarding the collection for Jerusalem. He said that Achaian Christians had "been pleased to make a contribution for the poor among the saints in Jerusalem" (Rom. 15:26). The NCV has "They were happy to do this."

Paul was ready to take the contribution to Jerusalem, but as usual the devil did not let him carry out his plans without a struggle. He had encountered conflict in Macedonia (2 Cor. 7:5); now he had conflict in Achaia. Luke mentioned, almost casually, that **a plot was formed against** Paul **by the Jews.** For other plots of the Jews, see 9:24; 23:16; 25:3; 2 Corinthians 11:26. This plot developed **as he was about to set sail for Syria.** Paul's ultimate goal was to go to Jerusalem, but apparently the ship that was available was headed for **Syria.** His original plan must have been to travel to Syria to report to the brethren in Antioch, and then to travel to Jerusalem to take the gift. These may have been the same Jews who had dragged the apostle before Gallio and had been embarrassed (18:12–17); if they could not destroy Paul by lawful means, they would try unlawful ones. We are not sure what the plot involved. Paul probably planned **to set sail for Syria** from Cenchrea as he had earlier (18:18). It has been suggested that Paul planned to take a chartered Jewish pilgrim ship heading to Jerusalem for the Passover. Since, however, the text says that he planned "to set sail for *Syria*" (where Antioch was), not Palestine (where Jerusalem was), this seems unlikely. Perhaps there was a plot to rob and kill him as he traveled from Corinth to Cenchrea; maybe they planned to grab him at the port or throw him overboard once they were at sea. We do not know if the Jews knew of the collection, but there was probably no way to keep it secret. If the Jews robbed Paul, or had him robbed, his death would seem criminally, and not religiously, motivated.

Verse 4. Paul was probably joined in Corinth by representatives of the various churches who were contributing to the love-offering. Once these "messengers of the churches" (2 Cor. 8:23) added the offerings from their congregations, the contribution was ready. **And he was accompanied by Sopater of Berea, the son of Pyrrhus, and by Aristarchus and Secundus of the Thessalonians, and Gaius of Derbe, and Timothy, and Tychicus and Trophimus of Asia.**

Paul's traveling companions begin with three men from Macedonia. **Sopater of Berea** may be the Sosipater of Romans 16:21, since "Sopater" is a shortened form of "Sosipater." If these passages refer to the same individual, we know definitely this representative was with Paul in Corinth. **Aristarchus . . . of the Thessalonians** was introduced in 19:29, where he was dragged along with Gaius into the theater at Ephesus. In that verse, Luke described Aristarchus as one of "Paul's traveling companions from Macedonia." **Secundus of the Thessalonians** is mentioned alongside Aristarchus. Secundus means "second." He may have been his father's second son—or this name may indicate that he was a slave and "little more than a number." Romans 16:22, 23 mentions Tertius ("third") and Quartus ("fourth").

The list of Paul's companions moves to two men from Lycaonia in South Galatia, including **Gaius of Derbe** (see comments on 19:29) and **Timothy** of Lystra (16:1). Timothy was with Paul in Corinth when he wrote the Book of Romans (Rom. 16:21).

The last two men listed were from the province of Asia. **Tychicus . . . of Asia** was later with Paul in Rome (Eph. 6:21;

Col. 4:7) and traveled with him during his release (2 Tim. 4:12; Tit. 3:12). **Trophimus of Asia** is the one that the Jews later accused Paul of taking into the temple (21:29). He traveled with Paul in the latter part of the apostle's life as well (2 Tim. 4:20).

The churches of Macedonia were represented by Sopater, Aristarchus, and Secundus. The churches of Galatia were represented by Gaius and Timothy. The churches of Asia were represented by Tychicus and Trophimus. No one is specifically named to represent the churches of Achaia. This seems strange, since the one reference to the selection of these representatives is 1 Corinthians 16:3, 4. Perhaps the church in Corinth asked Paul to represent them—or Titus, or the two unnamed messengers of 2 Corinthians 8:18–23, or someone else unnamed.

The men named and others traveled with Paul to take the contribution—but why? Some have suggested that the men served as Paul's bodyguards as he carried a small fortune. This hardly seems likely, since Paul separated himself from the men from time to time on the trip (20:5, 13, 14), and it is more likely that the messengers carried the contribution. Others have supposed that the contribution, which would have been in coins, was distributed among the men and hidden on their persons, so it would not be obvious that they were carrying a large amount of money. One interesting possibility is that Paul was taking prime examples of Gentile Christians to impress Jewish Christians and make them feel better about the fact that the gospel was being preached to the Gentiles. Since most, if not all, of the men named were preachers or preachers-in-training, Paul no doubt took advantage of the opportunity to do some training on the trip to Jerusalem. Another possibility is appealing: A practical purpose of the Gentile delegation's journey to Jerusalem was that these men could say "thank you" *personally* as they put the money in the hands of their Jewish brethren. When working on relationships, it is a good idea to "keep it personal" if possible.

These ideas may or may not have validity—but all that has been revealed is that these men were selected at Paul's request to remove any possibility of him personally profiting from the contribution. When he wrote the Corinthians concerning the collection, he said: "When I arrive [there], whomever you may approve, I will send them with letters to carry your gift to Jerusalem; and if it is fitting for me to go also, they will go with me" (1 Cor. 16:3, 4). Representatives were to be chosen to take their gift to Jerusalem; Paul did not insist on going himself. These same instructions were no doubt conveyed to all the congregations that participated in the contribution (see 2 Cor. 8:19, 23).

Paul was determined to avoid even a hint of scandal. In his follow-up letter to the Corinthians, he spoke of a brother who had been selected to help take the contribution to Jerusalem: "He has also been appointed by the churches to travel with us in this gracious work, which is being administered by us for the glory of the Lord Himself . . ." (2 Cor. 8:19). Then Paul told why he had suggested this arrangement: He was "taking precaution so that no one will discredit us in our administration of this generous gift; for we have regard for what is honorable, not only in the sight of the Lord, but also in the sight of men" (2 Cor. 8:20, 21). Paul was not only concerned about what *God* thought; he was also concerned about what *men* might think.

Verse 5. Once more, in the providence of God, Paul was made aware of the plot against him, so he quickly changed his plans. While his traveling companions proceeded with the plan to board the ship, with instructions to wait for him at **Troas**, Paul himself "decided to return [the long way, traveling overland] through Macedonia" (v. 3). Luke did not say specifically when the messengers parted company with Paul. The scenario mentioned is one possibility. We cannot even be sure that all seven of the men listed went on to Troas. Grammatically, the word **these** in verse 5 could refer to the last two mentioned in verse 4, but all seven probably went on to Troas.

Verse 6. Although Paul's original plan had not been to return to Macedonia, we are confident that he was glad of the opportunity to visit brethren in that area again. Since Paul already knew of the dangers awaiting him in Jerusalem (20:22, 23; Rom. 15:31), it is not hard to imagine the tearful farewells (see Acts 20:22–25, 36–38) as the apostle parted company with those he loved so much.

Finally, Paul tore himself away. Luke wrote, **We sailed from**

Philippi. They would actually have sailed from Neapolis, the seaport that served Philippi (16:11, 12). Their voyage took place **after the days of Unleavened Bread, and** they **came to . . . Troas within five days.** Previously, crossing the Aegean Sea at that point had only taken Paul two days (16:11); that time the winds had probably been favorable, but this time they were probably unfavorable. The term **the days of Unleavened Bread** refers to the Passover; Luke used it to indicate the time of the year, early spring. There is no implication in the text that Luke and other Christians had kept that feast. As a Gentile, Luke would surely not have observed a Jewish celebration.

Luke noted the duration of their visit to Troas: **And there we stayed seven days.** Notice the word **we**; Luke again joined Paul's traveling party. The term "we" could have included more than Luke—Titus and any others not named in verse 4—but it certainly included him. Once more, Luke did not give all the details. Since Paul's original plan had not been to return to Macedonia, it is possible that he had originally planned for Luke to join him and the others in Troas. Another possibility is that Luke was one of the unnamed brethren who had gone with Titus to Corinth (see comments on v. 1), returned to Macedonia with Paul, and then sailed from Philippi. The last time Luke used the first person pronoun was when Paul's company reached Philippi on the second missionary journey (16:11, 12). The implication is that Luke had remained in Philippi, working with the brethren there, until he rejoined Paul at the end of his third missionary journey. From this point on, Luke probably never left Paul's side until his death (Col. 4:14; 2 Tim. 4:11; Philem. 24). It must have been encouraging for Paul to have Luke and Timothy by his side once more.

Although Paul was in a hurry to arrive at Jerusalem by Pentecost (v. 16), he and his friends **stayed seven days** at Troas. "This might be because of a ship schedule, but more likely the delay was in order to meet with the believers on the first day of the week to break bread."[3] Paul stayed seven days in cities on several occasions so he could be with his brethren (21:4; 28:14). Be-

---

[3]Lewis Foster, notes on Acts, *The NIV Study Bible* (Grand Rapids, Mich.: Zondervan Publishing House, 1985), 1685.

cause the trip from Philippi to Troas had taken longer than usual, Paul had missed the Lord's Day meeting with the church in Troas, arriving there on Monday. (Paul, Luke, and any others with them probably met together on shipboard on the first day of the week.) Therefore, he waited a full week to be with his brethren when they came together again. We should not suppose, of course, that Paul and the others simply sat around as they waited. There were at least nine men in Paul's party, most, if not all, of them capable of preaching. A week's preaching campaign by nine-plus men would have borne much fruit.

IN TROAS: A LORD'S DAY MEETING (20:7–12)

⁷On the first day of the week, when we were gathered together to break bread, Paul began talking to them, intending to leave the next day, and he prolonged his message until midnight. ⁸There were many lamps in the upper room where we were gathered together. ⁹And there was a young man named Eutychus sitting on the window sill, sinking into a deep sleep; and as Paul kept on talking, he was overcome by sleep and fell down from the third floor and was picked up dead. ¹⁰But Paul went down and fell upon him, and after embracing him, he said, "Do not be troubled, for his life is in him." ¹¹When he had gone back up and had broken the bread and eaten, he talked with them a long while until daybreak, and then left. ¹²They took away the boy alive, and were greatly comforted.

While Luke quickly passed over some sections of Paul's journey, in other sections he paused to give minute details. In the previous passage (vv. 1–6), Luke rushed through months of activity and adventure. In this passage, Luke methodically gave the facts about a young man who fell asleep in the assembly. Why is this story in Acts? It is surely not there to embarrass a young man who sank "into a deep sleep as Paul talked on and on" (v. 9; NIV). One of the most fascinating aspects of the text is the picture it paints of the congregation in Troas as it met together. The family atmosphere of the early church is most impressive.

Verse 7. On the first day of the week, when we were gathered together to break bread, Paul began talking to them, intending to leave the next day, and he prolonged his message until midnight. Note that Paul did not use being "out of town" and "away from his home congregation" as an excuse not to attend. When he came to a new city, he searched out his brethren and met with them (see comments on 9:26). He wanted to be with his brethren when they met on the first day of the week.

The early church met on **the first day of the week** because Jesus arose from the dead and appeared to His disciples on that day (Lk. 24:1, 7, 13, 21; Jn. 20:19, 26). Justin Martyr later wrote that "Sunday is the day on which we all hold our common assembly, because . . . Jesus Christ, our Savior, on the same day rose from the dead."[4] Justin Martyr, who was born around A.D. 100, is recognized as one of the most important early Christian writers. Statements made in his writings are supported by other ancient documents. For example, Ignatius spoke of those who had come to a new hope, who no longer kept the Sabbath, but lived for the Lord's Day on which Jesus arose.[5] Jews kept the seventh day in memory of the physical creation (Ex. 20:8–11); Christians keep the first day in memory of Christ's death, burial, and resurrection (1 Cor. 11:23–25) that make possible "a new creation" (Gal. 6:15; emphasis added). *Christians* are never instructed to keep the seventh day, "the Sabbath" (see Col. 2:14, 16). It should also be recognized that the church was also established on the first day of the week (Lev. 23:16; Acts 2:1).

Since Luke mentioned lamps burning as they met (v. 8), the church in Troas apparently met at night. The fact that Paul preached **until midnight** would also indicate that the meeting was at night. Since the first day of the week was just another day of work in that society, and since most Christians worked for others, the only time all could meet together was after the day's work was done. Some of these Christians were even slaves (1 Cor. 7:21, 22; 12:13; Eph. 6:5; Col. 3:22; 1 Tim. 6:1; 1 Pet. 2:18).

---

[4]Justin Martyr *Apology* 1.67.7.

[5]Ignatius *Letter to the Magnesians* 9:1–3; see *Epistle of Barnabas* 15:9; Eusebius *Ecclesiastical History* 3.27.5.

Some think that Luke used Jewish reckoning and that the church met on what we think of as Saturday night. The NEB translators apparently thought this, for they used the phrase "Saturday night" in this verse. However, in every other place in the New Testament the same Greek phrase is used (Mt. 28:1; Mk. 16:2; Lk. 24:1; Jn. 20:1, 19; 1 Cor. 16:2), the NEB translators render it "Sunday." Lewis Foster has aptly noted that "there is no indication that Luke [used] the Jewish method of reporting time to tell of happenings in this Hellenistic city."[6] Whether Luke used Jewish or Roman reckoning, the church in Troas met at night on the first day of the week. "The passage does not support the practice of Seventh-Day Adventists who regard sunset on Friday to sunset on Saturday as the Sabbath and the proper day for Christian worship; even if the meeting was on Saturday night, this was not part of the Jewish Sabbath."[7]

When the church came together "on the first day of every week" (1 Cor. 16:2) to worship, the heart of their worship was the Lord's Supper. Note that they came together **to break bread**, not to hear Paul preach. "Even the address of so distinguished an apostle as Paul took second billing on that occasion."[8] The term "break bread" can refer to eating a common meal (Acts 2:46) or to partaking of the Lord's Supper (Mt. 26:26; Acts 2:42; 1 Cor. 10:16). Most scholars agree that the term here "indicates the Lord's Supper, since breaking bread was the expressed purpose for this formal gathering."[9] Some believe that in this verse the term "to break bread" refers to a blending of the Lord's Supper with the *agape*. The *agape* was a "love feast" (Jude 12), that is, a common meal eaten as an expression of fellowship—as was probably the case in Corinth (1 Cor. 11:17–22, 33, 34). In other words, they admit that the term "to break bread" in Acts 20:7 at least *includes* the Lord's Supper. It should be noted, however,

---

[6]Foster, 1685.

[7]I. Howard Marshall, *The Acts of the Apostles,* The Tyndale New Testament Commentaries, gen. ed. R. V. G. Tasker (Grand Rapids, Mich.: Wm. B. Eerdmans Publishing Co., 1980), 326.

[8]James Burton Coffman, *Commentary on Acts* (Austin, Tex.: Firm Foundation Publishing House, 1976), 386.

[9]Foster, 1685.

that there is no indication that the church in Troas had combined the two "meals." If they had, Paul no doubt would have discouraged the practice, as he did in Corinth (1 Cor. 11:17–22, 33, 34).

We are not surprised to learn that "the Lord's Supper" (1 Cor. 11:20) was eaten on "the Lord's day" (Rev. 1:10). Every expression of worship is important, but the uniquely Christian expression of worship is the Lord's Supper. Jews met to study, pray, sing, and give; but only Christians gather around "the table of the Lord" (1 Cor. 10:21) each first day of the week to remember Christ's death, burial, and resurrection. The early Christians observed the Lord's Supper only on the first day of the week, never on any other day.

Early Christians met *every* first day of the week to partake of the Lord's Supper. We can deduce this truth from the passages we have quoted. Since Christians met on every first day of the week (1 Cor. 16:1, 2), and when they met, they gathered *for the purpose of* breaking bread (Acts 20:7), we conclude that every first day they partook of the Lord's Supper. That this is true is confirmed by the testimony of early Christian writers. Early in the second century, these words were written: "On the Lord's own day gather together and break bread and give thanks."[10] Again, we have these words of Justin Martyr, written around A.D. 150:

> And on the day called Sunday, all who live in cities or in the country gather together to one place, and the memoirs of the apostles or the writings of the prophets are read, as long as time permits . . . when our prayer is ended, bread and wine and water are brought, and the president in like manner offers prayers and thanksgiving, according to his ability, and the people assent, saying Amen; and there is distribution to each, and a participation of that over which thanks have been given.[11]

McGarvey stated that "as surely as the disciples met every

---

[10]*Didache* 14:1.
[11]Justin Martyr *Apology* 1.67.7.

Lord's day, they broke the loaf on that day," and then added,

> [The evidence of Acts 20:7] when taken in connection with the universal practice of the church in the second century, and for a long period afterward . . . has proved sufficient to win universal agreement among biblical scholars, that this was the apostolic custom.[12]

If one willingly absents himself from the Lord's Day assembly, he willingly absents himself from the Lord's table. No wonder the writer of Hebrews said that one who sins willfully "has trampled under foot the Son of God, and has regarded as unclean the blood of the covenant by which he was sanctified, and has insulted the Spirit of grace" (Heb. 10:29). In the early days of the church, God's family came together joyfully to partake of the Lord's Supper.

When the church "gathered together to break bread," an important aspect of their worship was the study of God's Word. God's Word was read (Col. 4:16; 1 Tim. 4:13); and if any of the men present were capable of exhortation, there was preaching (1 Tim. 4:13; 2 Tim. 4:1, 2). Luke said that when the church in Troas came together to break bread, **Paul began talking to them.** The Greek word translated "talking" is from διαλέγομαι (*dialegomai*), the word from which we get "dialogue." One translation has "Paul conducted a discussion with them."[13] Lecturing is not the only scriptural method of preaching. The gist of Paul's message would probably have been similar to the charge given to the Ephesian elders a short time later (vv. 17–35).

Preachers are fond of noting that Paul **prolonged his message until midnight.** Paul had much on his heart to share with these Christians, but the brethren probably also encouraged him to keep preaching. We can imagine Paul saying, "That is enough; the hour is late and I know you are tired," only to have his listeners protest, "No! We are not that tired. Preach on, Brother!"

---

[12]J. W. McGarvey, *New Commentary on Acts of Apostles*, vol. 2 (Delight, Ark.: Gospel Light Publishing Co., n.d.), 179.

[13]*McCord's New Testament Translation of the Everlasting Gospel.*

The Christians at Troas were not so much regulated by the clock as by opportunity. Someone has said, "The problem was not to get them to come, but to get them to go home."

Verse 8. Families today have reunions in homes, in rented halls, and in parks. *Where* a family gets together is not a matter of great importance. Likewise, when early Christians came together, the location did not greatly concern them. Sometimes they met in homes (Philem. 1, 2); sometimes they met in public places (Acts 2:46; 5:12). In Troas, they met in a third-floor (v. 9) **upper room**. Since few private dwellings had three floors, this room may have been in an apartment building, such as was common in Rome and in cities that emulated Rome. After all, Troas was a Roman colony.

Why did these Christians meet on the third floor? Maybe the rent was cheaper. Maybe they chose the location to get away from the hustle and bustle of the streets. Perhaps this was the only place they could find. Whatever their reason or reasons, it was not a particularly convenient place to meet. After working all day, the members had to climb three flights of stairs to get to worship. On the occasion detailed in this chapter, they traveled up and down those stairs more than once. This did not concern them. Their *purpose* for meeting was more important than their *place* of meeting.

Luke noted that **many lamps** were in the upper room where they were gathered together. These oil lamps may have caused a depletion of oxygen in the small room.

Verse 9. In the multi-storied tenement block in Troas, **Paul kept on talking.** A crowded room, the lack of oxygen, and the late hour had its effect on one of his listeners. **And there was a young man named Eutychus sitting on the window sill, sinking into a deep sleep.** The words **sinking into** are translated from καταφερόμενος (*katapheromenos*). This Greek word is the present tense of καταφέρω (*katapherō*), indicating that this state of sleep happened gradually. The Greek word translated **sleep** is ὕπνος (*hupnos*), the word from which we get "hypnosis." The name **Eutychus**, meaning "fortunate" or "happy," is appropriate in light of subsequent events. Some think his name indicates that he was a freed slave. Eutychus is called a **young man**

(νεανίας, *neanias*), a general term in the Greek that can mean any age up to forty. He is also referred to in the original text as a "boy" (παῖς, *pais*), a term that usually indicates a young child or youth between the ages of eight and fourteen (v. 12).

We may have been too hard on young Eutychus through the years. There were no child-labor laws in those days; he had probably worked all day before he arrived, exhausted, at the place of meeting. As already suggested, the environment in which they met would have encouraged drowsiness. It is possible that Eutychus was sitting on the uncomfortable windowsill because he had given someone older his seat. Some suggest that he moved to the window to get some fresh air when he felt himself growing sleepy. However, in spite of his youthfulness and the uncomfortable meeting conditions, Eutychus had come to be with the saints—and, in spite of the length of the service, Eutychus did not leave. We should be impressed with a young man who obviously loved the Lord and His church, and who was willing to stay for an extended service.

Nevertheless, disaster was moments away. In those days, windows were simple openings in the walls with shutters that could be opened. Thus there was nothing to restrain Eutychus as he slumped. As Paul continued speaking, Eutychus **was overcome by sleep and fell down from the third floor and was picked up dead.** The service came to an abrupt halt as members jumped to their feet and dashed down the long flight of stairs. Those who have lost a young son or daughter know something of the sadness that overwhelmed them as they stood looking down at the boy's broken body. Luke recorded simply that they were "troubled" (v. 10).

Verse 10. Paul followed the other members **down** the stairs; he was probably older than most of them and moved a bit slower. He also may not have been as anxious as the rest, knowing that he, by the power of God, could raise the boy. When at last he reached the boy, he **fell upon him**, perhaps after the manner of Elijah and Elisha (1 Kings 17:21; 2 Kings 4:34, 35). **After embracing him, he said, "Do not be troubled, for his life is in him."** Paul's words do not mean the boy did not die from the fall. Luke did not write that Eutychus "was picked up *for* dead," or that "they *thought* he was dead." Dr. Luke said that the young man was D-E-A-D (νεκρός, *nekros*) (v. 9). Paul's words meant, rather, that life had returned to the lad (v. 12). This miracle is most impressive. Most likely, shattered bones had to be mended, joints had to be put back in place, ruptured blood vessels had to be repaired, damaged organs had to be rejuvenated, torn and lacerated tissue had to be restored, and the heart had to start pumping again. This incident is one of the many parallels in Acts between the ministries of Peter and Paul: Peter raised Dorcas from the dead (ch. 9), and Paul raised Eutychus.

Paul probably had several reasons for raising Eutychus. First, he was concerned about the boy and the other members of the church in Troas. Second, the miracle confirmed the message just preached (Mk. 16:20). Some see yet another purpose. They point to the parallel between the church's celebrating the death and resurrection of Jesus (Acts 20:7) and the boy's being raised from the dead (vv. 9, 10). Bringing Eutychus back to life validated the faith of the members in the concept of resurrection.

Verse 11. After Eutychus had been revived, Paul and the others returned to the third-story room. **When he had gone back up and had broken the bread and eaten, he talked with them a long while until daybreak.** It is possible that this breaking of bread refers to the same breaking of bread mentioned in verse 7, but it is improbable. Since the Christians in Troas came together "to break bread," it is unlikely that they would have waited hours to partake of the unleavened bread and fruit of the vine while "Paul kept on talking" (v. 9). Surely one of the first things they did was to gather around the Lord's table to remember His sacrifice. After that, they would have been ready to listen to Paul. The breaking of bread in verse 11, which took place hours later, probably refers to a fellowship meal. The text here is similar to that in Acts 2, where the breaking of bread in verse 42 refers to the Lord's Supper, while the same term a few verses later (v. 46) refers to a common meal (see comments on 2:42, 46).

As noted in previous chapters, table fellowship was an important part of the lives of early Christians. Can you imagine Paul and the others returning, exhilarated, to the upper room?

Certainly there was relief in their voices as they spoke of the near tragedy. Someone may have teased Eutychus about falling asleep. That would have been the atmosphere as the food each one had brought was spread together. After giving thanks for the food, for Paul's visit, and for Eutychus' safety, they sat down and ate together. It was a sight that would have amazed the world as Jews and Gentiles, masters and slaves, men and women ate together around a common table—for they were "one in Christ Jesus" (Gal. 3:28).

During their time together, Paul **talked with them a long while until daybreak, and then left.** The Greek word translated **talked** is from ὁμιλέω (*homileō*), whereas the one translated "talking" in verse 7 is from διαλέγομαι (*dialegomai*). *Homileō* is used for relaxed conversation. F. F. Bruce translated the latter part of verse 11, "engaged in much further conversation until dawn."[14] We might paraphrase it by saying, "Paul enjoyed a good visit with them before he left." A few years later, after Paul's release from prison in Rome, he revisited Troas (2 Tim. 4:13).

Verse 12. When the meeting broke up, **they took away the boy alive, and were greatly comforted. They** indicates some members of the church who were apparently responsible for the boy—for his transportation and also for his safety. The NIV has "The people took the young man *home* alive and were greatly comforted" (emphasis added). It could be that the young man's parents were not Christians and the members had promised to get him home safely. For a moment, put yourself in their place as they looked at his shattered body, wondering what they would tell his parents. What joy must have filled their hearts as Paul restored life to the boy! **Were greatly comforted** is a typical understatement by Luke.

ON THE WAY TO JERUSALEM (20:13–16)

[13]**But we, going ahead to the ship, set sail for Assos, intending from there to take Paul on board; for so he had arranged it, intending himself to go by land.** [14]**And when he met**

---

[14]Bruce, 384.

us at Assos, we took him on board and came to Mitylene. [15]Sailing from there, we arrived the following day opposite Chios; and the next day we crossed over to Samos; and the day following we came to Miletus. [16]For Paul had decided to sail past Ephesus so that he would not have to spend time in Asia; for he was hurrying to be in Jerusalem, if possible, on the day of Pentecost.

Verse 13. Paul told his traveling companions to board the ship while he himself walked overland to **Assos**, the next port of call (v. 13). Assos was on the opposite side of the peninsula from Troas—about twenty miles by land, forty miles by ship. Perhaps Paul was not ready to leave when the ship left; he may have wanted to spend a little more time with the brethren in Troas. Perhaps he just wanted to be by himself for a while. Compare this suggestion to Jesus' actions in Mark 6:45, 46. Since Paul had not gone to sleep the night before, he must have had a powerful reason for walking twenty miles instead of sleeping on board the ship.

Verse 14. And when he met us at Assos, we took him on board and came to Mitylene. Paul was now on a ship that stopped at many cities, comparable to a commuter train that stops at almost every town. Later, he got on a ship that made very few stops (21:2), comparable to an express train. **Mitylene** was the harbor on the southeast shore of the island of Lesbos.

Verse 15. Sailing from there, we arrived the following day opposite Chios; and the next day we crossed over to Samos. **Chios** and **Samos** were islands. The Western Text here inserts "and tarried at Trogyllium" (see KJV). **And the day following we came to Miletus. Miletus** was an important seaport. It had been somewhat eclipsed by nearby Ephesus, but it was still a large, important city.

Verse 16. For Paul had decided to sail past Ephesus so that he would not have to spend time in Asia. Paul no doubt would have liked to visit Ephesus, but if he were to reach Jerusalem by the Day of Pentecost, he did not have time to stop: (1) Apparently, the ship Paul was on did not make a scheduled stop in Ephesus. To stop in Ephesus, Paul would have had to disembark at Chios, charter a boat to Ephesus, and then, after his visit, try to find another ship heading for Jerusalem. (2) It would have been impossible for Paul to get away from Ephesus quickly. He had many friends, and Eastern hospitality dictated extended feasts and celebration. (3) Paul could even have found himself in the middle of another riot; he had left Ephesus immediately after one (v. 1).

Paul **was hurrying to be in Jerusalem, if possible, on the day of Pentecost.** He wanted to be in Jerusalem on a feast day. He had already missed the Passover (20:6), and one-third of the time until Pentecost was gone; so he felt a sense of urgency. Why did Paul want to be in Jerusalem for the Day of Pentecost? Perhaps he desired to be there for a variety of reasons: to visit with friends from far and wide, to celebrate his Jewish heritage, to take advantage of the opportunity to preach, and more. However, since he was going to Jerusalem to deliver the collection for the poor, his primary purpose probably related to that contribution. Perhaps the contribution would make a greater impact if more knew about it; perhaps the fact that Jewish Christians from all over Judea would be present would make distribution easier.

IN MILETUS: A SERIOUS TALK
TO THE EPHESIAN ELDERS (20:17–38)

Seven sermons by Paul are recorded in the Book of Acts, excluding his brief words in Lystra (14:14–18). Only one is addressed to Christians—the one recorded in this section.

Paul Reviews His Ministry (20:17–24)

[17]**From Miletus he sent to Ephesus and called to him the elders of the church.** [18]**And when they had come to him, he said to them,**

"You yourselves know, from the first day that I set foot in Asia, how I was with you the whole time, [19]**serving the Lord with all humility and with tears and with trials which came upon me through the plots of the Jews;** [20]**how I did not shrink**

from declaring to you anything that was profitable, and teaching you publicly and from house to house, ²¹solemnly testifying to both Jews and Greeks of repentance toward God and faith in our Lord Jesus Christ. ²²And now, behold, bound in spirit, I am on my way to Jerusalem, not knowing what will happen to me there, ²³except that the Holy Spirit solemnly testifies to me in every city, saying that bonds and afflictions await me. ²⁴But I do not consider my life of any account as dear to myself, so that I may finish my course and the ministry which I received from the Lord Jesus, to testify solemnly of the gospel of the grace of God."

Verse 17. Apparently, Paul had a two- or three-day layover in Miletus as the ship's cargo was loaded or unloaded, or perhaps as repairs were made. He sent a messenger **to Ephesus**, asking **the elders of the church** to come to him at **Miletus**. Paul probably did not go to them because the ship might leave before he got back. If it left before the elders arrived, they would be inconvenienced; but if Paul missed his ship, he would have no way to reach Jerusalem by the feast day. The Ephesian elders traveled about thirty miles to the south to see him; and when they arrived, Paul delivered the great farewell discourse of Acts 20.

Paul's sermon was directed primarily to the Ephesian **elders**. Note that there was a *plurality* of elders in the church in Ephesus. The New Testament never speaks of one elder/bishop/pastor overseeing a congregation (see comments on 14:23). The Greek word translated "elder" is πρεσβύτερος (*presbuteros*). Elders could be called "presbyters." This word is the origin of the denominational name "Presbyterian." The church, of course, should not be designated according to a form of government. *Presbuteros* literally means "older [man]." Chronological age is a factor, but a more important factor is spiritual maturity. An elder needs to be capable of making mature judgments. He needs the capacity to remain levelheaded in crisis situations.

Verse 18. Paul began his farewell message by saying, **"You yourselves know, from the first day that I set foot in Asia, how I was with you the whole time."** Paul frequently reminded others of his way of life, not to boast, but to spur them on in their imitation of Christ (1 Cor. 11:1; Phil. 4:9). On this occasion, he emphasized that his walk with Christ was consistent by using the phrases **from the first day** and **the whole time**. The reference to the province of **Asia** designated the majority of his work on the third missionary journey, which centered in Ephesus (see comments on 19:10). It was this journey that Paul was completing as he headed for Jerusalem.

Verse 19. While Paul ministered in Ephesus for three years (v. 31), he was **serving the Lord with all humility** (see Rom. 12:3; Phil. 2:3–5). The word **serving** is a translated from δουλεύω (*douleuō*), which means "serve as a slave." In verse 24, Paul used a different word to speak of his "ministry" or "service": διακονία (*diakonia*). The word "minister" (διάκονος, *diakonos*) means "servant." A preacher is merely a servant (1 Cor. 3:5; 2 Cor. 3:6; 6:4; Eph. 3:7; 6:21; Col. 1:7, 23, 25; 4:7; 1 Tim. 4:6). He is not the pastor; his task is not to run the church. His task is to preach the Word.

Twice in the sermon, Paul spoke of shedding **tears** (see v. 31), indicating his attitude of compassion. Real men can cry (Jn. 11:35; 2 Cor. 2:4; Phil. 3:18). He also noted the **"trials which came upon** [him] **through the plots of the Jews."** Preaching is not about a life of ease. More than a year previous to this, Paul had written 2 Corinthians 11:23–33, telling about the hardships he had undergone.

Verse 20. He **did not shrink from declaring to** them **anything that was profitable.** The Greek words οὐδέν ὑπεστειλάμην (*ouden hupesteilamēn*), translated **I did not shrink from** were used by the sailor when he said, "I did not lower my sails." Regarding preaching, with Paul it was always "Full speed ahead!" He focused on the subjects that would benefit his hearers the most.

Paul preached and taught everywhere he could: **publicly and from house to house.** His public teaching included the synagogue and the school of Tyrannus (19:8, 9); he also spent time in more private settings. This same method was used by the other apostles earlier in Jerusalem: "And every day, in the temple and from house to house, they kept right on teaching and preaching

Jesus as the Christ" (5:42). The preacher who thinks he needs only to "fill the pulpit" does not understand the scope of the challenge given to him.

Verse 21. Paul stressed that he preached and taught *all* of God's Word. Specific topics mentioned included repentance and faith (v. 21), the gospel (v. 24), grace (v. 24), and the kingdom/ church (v. 25). It is rather unusual to list repentance first and faith second. Normally, people believe in Jesus and then repent of their sins (2:37, 38). Remember, however, that Paul had mainly preached to pagans in Ephesus. He first had to get them to turn "to God from idols" (1 Thess. 1:9), which involved **repentance *toward God*** (emphasis added). He then could teach them about Jesus, so they would have **faith *in our Lord Jesus Christ*** (emphasis added).

Paul preached and taught all of God's Word everywhere he could—to all men. He solemnly testified **to both Jews and Greeks**. He played no favorites. A preacher is ready to help no one until he is ready to help everyone.

Verse 22. Preaching is not about job security. Paul told his listeners, **"And now, behold, bound in spirit, I am on my way to Jerusalem, not knowing what will happen to me there."** Preachers never know from day to day what tomorrow may bring.

The NASB translators thought Paul here referred to his own **spirit**. Many translations have a capital "S" on "Spirit," indicating that they believe Paul was referring to the Holy Spirit. The NCV has "I must obey the Holy Spirit and go to Jerusalem." The meaning is basically the same whether a small "s" or a capital "S" is used: Paul had "purposed in [his] spirit to go to Jerusalem" (19:21), no doubt because he was convinced it was God's will. Therefore, he was determined to go, committed to that end, and would let nothing deter him.

Verse 23. Paul did not know all of the specific details concerning his visit to Jerusalem, but he knew that **bonds and afflictions** awaited him. The **Holy Spirit** could have informed Paul directly, just as He did Philip (8:29). However, the words **in every city** probably indicate that the Holy Spirit spoke to him through prophets in those cities (see 21:10, 11).

Verse 24. The apostle continued, **"I do not consider my life of any account as dear to myself"** (see Mt. 16:25; Mk. 8:35; Lk. 9:24; Phil. 1:23). Paul was consumed with finishing his **course.** He often used athletic imagery, including runners in a race, to portray the Christian life (1 Cor. 7:24–27; Gal. 2:2; 5:7; Phil. 2:16; 3:13, 14; 2 Tim. 2:5). He *did* ultimately finish his course (2 Tim. 4:7).

Paul was consumed with **the ministry which** he **received from the Lord Jesus** (26:15–18), **to testify solemnly of the gospel of the grace of God.** At the beginning of verse 24, the Western Text adds these words: "But I make no reckoning of anything for myself." The KJV translates this statement: "But none of these things move me." We let a multiplicity of things "move" us: We fear criticism, death, failure, illness, loneliness, job insecurity, the future, old age. We let personal difficulties, health problems, and work-related stress get us down. On the other hand, Paul said the only matter that concerned him was fulfilling the commission God had given him—and being faithful to the end.

Paul Admonishes the Ephesian Elders (20:25–35)

[25]**"And now, behold, I know that all of you, among whom I went about preaching the kingdom, will no longer see my face.** [26]**Therefore, I testify to you this day that I am innocent of the blood of all men.** [27]**For I did not shrink from declaring to you the whole purpose of God.** [28]**Be on guard for yourselves and for all the flock, among which the Holy Spirit has made you overseers, to shepherd the church of God which He purchased with His own blood.** [29]**I know that after my departure savage wolves will come in among you, not sparing the flock;** [30]**and from among your own selves men will arise, speaking perverse things, to draw away the disciples after them.** [31]**Therefore be on the alert, remembering that night and day for a period of three years I did not cease to admonish each one with tears.** [32]**And now I commend you to God and to the word of His grace, which is able to build you up and to give you the inheritance among all those who are sanctified.** [33]**I have cov-**

eted no one's silver or gold or clothes. ³⁴You yourselves know that these hands ministered to my own needs and to the men who were with me. ³⁵In everything I showed you that by working hard in this manner you must help the weak and remember the words of the Lord Jesus, that He Himself said, 'It is more blessed to give than to receive.'"

Verse 25. "And now, behold, I know that all of you, among whom I went about preaching the kingdom, will no longer see my face." Paul's statement that they should see his face no more presents a minor problem, since Paul may have revisited Ephesus later (1 Tim. 1:3; 3:14). Consider these thoughts: (1) Since Paul clearly stated that he did not know specifically what would happen to him in Jerusalem (v. 22), his words were probably *his own* conclusion based on the inspired warning that "bonds and afflictions" awaited him (v. 23). Paul expected to die in Jerusalem (v. 24). If he did not, he planned to travel immediately to Rome and make that city his base of operations (Rom. 15:23–25). Either way, he did not expect to be back in Ephesus. (2) Since several years passed before he reached Ephesus (if he did), perhaps those elders had moved or died by that time—so he did not see *their* faces again. (3) The Lord and circumstances often changed Paul's itinerary.

Verse 26. Paul spoke to the elders, insisting that he was **"innocent of the blood of all men."** This language is taken from Ezekiel 3:16–21; 33:1–9 (see comments on 18:6). The NCV has "If any of you should be lost, I am not responsible."

Verse 27. The reason Paul was innocent was that he **did not shrink from declaring to** them **the whole purpose of God** (see comments on v. 20). The preacher's first responsibility is to God. It is not to make people happy, to make them feel good, or to increase the crowds, but to preach "all the counsel of God" (v. 27; KJV).

Verse 28. Having surveyed his work among them, Paul turned to the Ephesian elders' responsibilities by giving them a charge. He began by saying, **"Be on guard for yourselves."** Before the elders could take care of the church, they had to first take care of themselves. Being an elder is first of all about being a *good* person, the kind of person every Christian needs to be (see 1 Pet. 5:3). Paul warned the elders against becoming spiritually overconfident and falling into temptation (see 1 Cor. 10:12; Gal. 6:1).

Next, Paul turned their attention to the church members they were entrusted to defend: **"Be on guard . . . for all the flock."** Being an elder has nothing to do with a position of glory and honor. Paul used as his main illustration the work of a shepherd. Shepherding was a dirty, smelly job; one had to live with sheep. It was a dangerous job; there were wild beasts. It was *not* a glamorous work.

Further, the eldership has nothing to do with establishing an expanding power base. In later years, as the church apostatized, church leaders assumed authority over larger and larger territories. The Ephesian elders had the responsibility of overseeing the church at Ephesus and that alone; this model is the New Testament pattern (see Phil. 1:1; 1 Pet. 5:2). William Barclay said, "[Elders] were the local officials and their authority was confined to the place where they were set apart."[15]

On the other hand, being an elder is about having certain God-given *qualifications*. Paul told the elders from Ephesus that **the Holy Spirit** had made them overseers. The Spirit did this by outlining the qualifications for becoming elders (1 Tim. 3:1–7; Tit. 1:5–9). Although elders are selected and set in place by the members (see comments on 6:1–7), they should feel a *divine* commission. In a real sense *the Holy Spirit* has made them overseers; their primary responsibility is to God (Heb. 13:17).

Serving as an elder is also about accepting *responsibility*. The Greek word translated **overseers** is the plural form of ἐπίσκοπος (*episkopos*). This word is the origin of the denominational name "Episcopalian" (see comments on v. 17). *Episkopos* is a compound word combining the word "over" (ἐπί, *epi*) with a word for "see" (σκοπέω, *skopeō*), to mean "overseer." Incidentally, the noun form σκοπός (*skopos*) is behind our English word "scope," as in "telescope" (to see far) and "microscope" (to see small). It should perhaps be noted that when God gives a man responsibility, He

---

[15]Barclay, 91.

246

also gives him the authority needed to fulfill that responsibility. The term "overseer," therefore, not only involves responsibility, but also involves authority.

One Anglicized form of *episkopos* is "bishop" (see Phil. 1:1; 1 Tim. 3:1, 2; 1 Pet. 2:25 in KJV). The term "bishop" has been so misused by Catholics and others that, for many people, it no longer carries the original concept of "one of the overseers of a local congregation." There is value in pointing out that originally the term "bishop" did *not* mean what it has come to mean. In New Testament times, being an elder was not something different from being a bishop; the terms were used interchangeably and applied to the same "office" (20:17, 28; Tit. 1:5, 7; 1 Pet. 5:1, 2). When we use the word "office" (1 Tim. 3:1), we are not talking about a position as much as a responsibility.

Paul continued by charging the elders **to shepherd** God's people. This responsibility is the heart of his message. The figure employed most in Paul's sermon is that of a conscientious shepherd caring for his flock. The word translated "to shepherd" is the verb form of ποιμήν (*poimēn*), the Greek word for a "shepherd." The Latin translation of this word is "pastor," which is used in the listing of church leaders in Ephesians 4:11. Notice that in Acts 20, "elder" = "bishop" = "pastor." For another passage where all three terms are used interchangeably, see 1 Peter 5:1, 2. The elders, not the preachers, were the shepherds or pastors of the flock. Warren W. Wiersbe wrote,

> The elders/bishops were the "pastors" of the flocks, assisted by the deacons. . . . [I]n the New Testament churches, the three titles elder, bishop, and pastor were synonymous. The qualifications for this office are given in 1 Timothy 3:1–7 and Titus 1:5–9.[16]

The best one-word job description of the function of elders is "shepherding." If you want to know where an elder should concentrate his efforts, think of the responsibilities of a shep-

---

[16]Warren W. Wiersbe, *The Bible Exposition Commentary*, vol. 1 (Wheaton, Ill.: Victor Books, 1989), 451, 486.

herd: He saw that they were fed. The KJV has "feeding" instead of "shepherding" in verse 28 and 1 Peter 5:2. This task was an essential part of the responsibility of a shepherd, but not its entirety. He also guided the sheep. He treated and bound up their wounds. He tried to keep them from straying—and when they did, he brought them back. Furthermore, he had to do all this without favoritism. Paul said, "Be on guard . . . for *all* the flock" (emphasis added). Until a man is ready to shepherd *all* the flock, he is not qualified to shepherd *any* of the flock.

This verse is the only time the expression **church of God** is found in Acts, but it was a favorite with Paul (1 Cor. 1:2; 10:32; 11:22; 15:9; 2 Cor. 1:1; Gal. 1:13; 1 Tim. 3:5). In this verse "God" probably refers to Jesus; some ancient manuscripts have "Lord" instead of "God." Paul qualified "church of God" with the phrase **which He purchased with His own blood.** It is possible for the text here to be rendered "with the blood of His own" (that is, His own Son), but the translation of the NASB is the most natural. This reference is one of the ten or so times in the New Testament that Jesus is referred to as "God."

Verse 28 is the finest statement in Acts on the doctrinal significance of the cross. If we would be saved by the blood, we must be in the church that was purchased with the blood (see Eph. 5:23, 25). Being an elder is about loving the church for which Jesus died. A good elder would never do anything to hurt the church; he would suffer wrong first.

Verse 29. Paul stressed one indispensable shepherding task: protecting the flock. He told the elders that they must remain vigilant because **savage wolves** would come in **not sparing the flock** (see Mt. 7:15; Jn. 10:12).

Verse 30. Inspired and secular history tells us that those "wolves" did enter "the flock" at Ephesus, and from among the leadership, men did **arise, speaking perverse things, to draw away the disciples after them.** The New Testament speaks of six false teachers associated with Ephesus: Hymenaeus and Alexander (1 Tim. 1:19, 20), Phygelus and Hermogenes (2 Tim. 1:15), Philetus (2 Tim. 2:17), and Diotrephes (3 Jn. 9). From the writings of John, we learn that the errors of Gnosticism may have later arisen in Ephesus. "Gnosticism" is the name of a heresy that arose in the second and third centuries, corrupting Christianity with an admixture of Judaism and pagan philosophies. The name comes from the Greek word for "knowledge" (γνῶσις, *gnōsis*) because the leaders claimed to have knowledge unavailable to the uninitiated. Early expressions of this heresy arose toward the end of the first century. The teaching of the Nicolaitans in Ephesus and other places (Rev. 2:1, 6, 12, 15) was probably a form of early Gnosticism. Ultimately, there was a general apostasy (1 Tim. 4:1–5; 2 Tim. 3:3; 4:3, 4). Elders must remain aware of what is happening regarding false teaching, within the church and without. As has been often stated, "The Pope is just an elder gone wrong."

Verse 31. Paul reminded the elders of the gravity of their responsibility to lead the church: **"Therefore be on the alert, remembering that night and day for a period of three years I did not cease to admonish each one with tears."** He again used his own life as a model of diligence and faithfulness (see comments on vv. 18–20). Paul worked **night and day**; he had no 8 a.m. to 5 p.m. job (see comments on 19:9).

Verse 32. The words of this verse would have been a great note for Paul to close on: **"And now I commend you to God."** In his absence, Paul was entrusting the elders to God's protection. The NCV has "I am putting you in the care of God." The apostle also commended them **to the word of His grace.** Being an elder is also about knowing God's Word. When Paul and other inspired men left, how were they to know what to do? He pointed them to the Word. An elder should be "able to teach" (1 Tim. 3:2). Paul emphasized the power of God's Word: "[It] is **able to build you up and to give you the inheritance among all those who are sanctified."**

Verse 33. Paul was not quite finished with his message. Serving as an elder is not about making money or getting ahead in life. It is scriptural for elders to be paid (1 Tim. 5:17, 18), but that is not what being an elder is all about. One qualification of an elder is that he must be "free from the love of money" (1 Tim. 3:3; see Tit. 1:7; 1 Pet. 5:2). Paul urged the Ephesian elders to follow his example and not to covet **silver or gold or clothes.** All of these were status symbols in the first century (see Jas. 5:1–3) and still are in most places today.

Verse 34. Neither is preaching about making money. Paul probably held out his rough, callused hands to the elders as he said, **"These hands ministered to my own needs and to the men who were with me."** The apostle often worked in tent-making alongside his ministry of preaching and teaching (18:1–4). It is scriptural for a preacher to be supported (Lk. 10:7; 1 Cor. 9; 1 Tim. 5:18), but that is not what preaching is all about. Preaching, rather, is about fulfilling one's special ministry.

Verse 35. Paul concluded his words to the Ephesian elders by saying, **"In everything I showed you that by working hard in this manner you must help the weak."** This same teaching is found in Paul's letter to the Ephesians: "He who steals must steal no longer; but rather he must labor, performing with his own hands what is good, so that he will have something to share with one who has need" (Eph. 4:28).

In addition to his own example, Paul supported the need to help the weak by the words of Christ: **"And remember the words of the Lord Jesus, that He Himself said, 'It is more blessed to give than to receive.'"** This is "one of those precious morsels of divine truth, of which many thousands fell from [Jesus'] lips that are not recorded in our brief gospels."[17] (See Jn. 20:30.) Paul here quoted Christ several years before the first Gospel Account was written. Paul had received direct instruction from the Lord after his conversion (Gal. 1:11, 12, 17; see comments on 9:22).

An Emotional Farewell (20:36–38)

[36]When he had said these things, he knelt down and prayed with them all. [37]And they began to weep aloud and embraced Paul, and repeatedly kissed him, [38]grieving especially over the word which he had spoken, that they would not see his face again. And they were accompanying him to the ship.

Verse 36. When he had said these things, he knelt down and prayed with them all. We have spoken so often of "kneel-

---

[17]McGarvey, 193.

ing in prayer" that we may think that was the most common stance in Bible times, but normally men stood when they prayed. When you read in the Scriptures of men kneeling in prayer, invariably there was an emotional climate—sometimes a feeling of guilt or of helplessness. In Miletus, the elders were overcome with sorrow.

Verses 37, 38. And they began to weep aloud and embraced Paul, and repeatedly kissed him. The kiss was a standard form of greeting or farewell in those days; it implied friendship (see Lk. 22:47, 48; Rom. 16:16). They were **grieving especially over the word which he had spoken, that they would not see his face again** (see comments on v. 25).

After weeping and hugging Paul, kissing him again and again, the elders went down **to the ship** to watch him leave. The original language of 21:1 indicates that Paul and the others had to *tear themselves away* from the brethren (see comments on 21:1). We can imagine the elders standing on tiptoe, waving until the ship disappeared from their sight.

APPLICATION

Concern for Brethren (20:1–6)

We have seen, through Paul's example of taking up the collection, the need to be concerned about our brethren. John wrote, "But whoever has the world's goods, and sees his brother in need and closes his heart against him, how does the love of God abide in him?" (1 Jn. 3:17). The phrase "in need" includes physical needs like those of the poor Jerusalem saints, but there are also emotional needs and, most importantly, spiritual needs.

The following five recommendations will be helpful in showing our concern for brethren:

1. Be sensitive; be aware when needs exist.
2. Keep your heart tender when needs exist. It is easy to become hardened. (Some say, "It's their own fault they have these problems.")
3. Make concrete, specific plans on how you can help.
4. Do not be surprised if opposition comes. Do not even

be surprised if it comes from within your own heart.
5. Carry out the plans you make. Remember: If we just *say*, "Be warmed and be filled," our words mean noth- ing (Jas. 2:16).

We cannot read 2 Corinthians without being impressed with the intensity of Paul's concern for his brethren. His soul found "no rest" (2:13; 7:5); he was filled with "fears" (7:5); he was "downcast" (7:6; NIV). We, too, should be consumed with a pro- found concern for our brethren—when they are in want physi- cally, as Paul was moved regarding Christians in Jerusalem, and when they are lacking spiritually, as Paul was affected by the shortcomings of Corinth. Paul's words exhort us all:

> There [should] be no division in the body, but . . . the members [should] have the same care for one another. And if one member suffers, all the members suffer with it; if one member is honored, all the members rejoice with it. Now you are Christ's body, and individually members of it (1 Cor. 12:25–27).

We believe that Paul's primary purpose in taking up the col- lection was to help relationships in the church. If we dedicate ourselves to helping others, we will probably make the greatest contribution possible to peace and harmony in the Lord's body.

What Should We Do About the Poor? (20:1–6)
Many Christians today are indifferent toward the poor. How- ever, the Scriptures provide some pro-active steps for us to take to serve those who are needy.

1. Remember Them:
   "They only asked us to remember the poor—the very thing I also was eager to do" (Gal. 2:10).

2. Honor Them:
   "Listen, my beloved brethren: did not God choose the poor of this world to be rich in faith and heirs of the

kingdom which He promised to those who love Him? But you have dishonored the poor man . . . " (Jas. 2:5, 6).

3. Help Them:
"For Macedonia and Achaia have been pleased to make a contribution for the poor among the saints in Jerusalem" (Rom. 15:26).

"If a brother or sister is without clothing and in need of daily food, and one of you says to them, 'Go in peace, be warmed and be filled,' and yet you do not give them what is necessary for their body, what use is that?" (Jas. 2:15, 16).

4. Teach Them:
"The Spirit of the Lord is upon Me, because He anointed Me to preach the gospel to the poor. He has sent Me to proclaim release to the captives, and recovery of sight to the blind, to set free those who are oppressed . . ." (Lk. 4:18).

5. Invite Them:
"But when you give a reception, invite the poor, the crippled, the lame, the blind . . ." (Lk. 14:13).

Remember the Poor (20:1–6)

The collection was made for the poor among the *saints* in Jerusalem (Rom. 15:26), but you may want to develop a lesson which focuses on all the poor. The Bible has much to say about being sympathetic toward the poor in general. Here are a few passages to get you started: Matthew 19:21; Luke 14:13, 21; 19:8; 2 Corinthians 9:9; James 2:2–6.

Invariably, when we try to do what is right, there will be opposition; the devil will make sure that is the case. When it comes to the matter of helping those in need, conflict will not always come from unbelievers, as in the case of Paul. Sometimes it will come from believers. The collection for the poor among the saints in Jerusalem is used by some brethren today to suggest that only Christians can be helped from "the church treasury" and, even then, only if they are "destitute." However, the purpose of the contribution was not merely to relieve suffering, but to express love and appreciation. If the poor Christians in Jerusalem had been starving, they would have died long before the contribution was completed. We need more such expressions of love, not less—both to members and non-members. Do not let such interference deter you from doing "good to all people, and especially to those who are of the household of the faith" (Gal. 6:10).

Paul's Farewell Tour (20:1–6)

If you want to summarize the conclusion of Paul's third missionary journey, you could preach a lesson on "Paul's Farewell Tour." (When well-known musical artists announce their retirement, they generally make "a farewell tour" of the country.) The main points could be: (1) Farewell to Asia, (2) Farewell to Macedonia, and (3) Farewell to Achaia. You can note that when Paul said "farewell" in one place, he was saying "hello" in another. Thus, when he left Asia, he had plans to say "hello" to Macedonia and Achaia (19:21). When he left Achaia, he had plans to say "hello" to Jerusalem and Rome (19:21, 22). Farewells are sad; but if one remains in God's plan, "farewells" are always followed by "hellos"—even at the end of life! If desired, you can point out that "farewell tours" are not always "final tours"; sometimes the artists decide to cancel their retirement. Paul *thought* he would never see the Christians in Greece and Asia again, but apparently he did.

Handling Money (20:4)

Sometimes men get upset when it is suggested that they take every precaution concerning their handling of money. Some have gotten their feelings hurt and cried, "If they don't trust me, I quit!" Paul did not ask anyone to trust him "just because he was an apostle"; rather, he did all he could so that the offering would not be tainted with rumors of wrongdoing. Judas Iscariot, who betrayed the Lord, had a dishonest reputation when came to handling money. As keeper of the money box, he used "to pilfer what was put into it" (Jn. 12:6).

In recent years, the world has been made aware of religious racketeers getting rich off the unquestioning masses. Some people have concluded that all religion is a racket. We dare not let the world think this way about the religion of Christ. Whenever the Lord's work involves money, we cannot be too cautious. We are to "provide things honest in the sight of all men" (Rom. 12:17; KJV).

A Farewell Service (20:6–12)

Warren W. Wiersbe titled 20:6–12 "A Farewell Service," and divided the text according to these points: (1) The Lord's Day, (2) The Lord's People, (3) The Lord's Supper, (4) The Lord's Message, and (5) The Lord's Power.[18]

Sleeping in Church (20:7–12)

The story of Paul's extended preaching and Eutychus' deep sleep provide modern worshipers with lessons to be learned.

Lessons for Hearers. First, we find lessons for hearers. One of the most obvious lessons is that it can be embarrassing to fall asleep in church. There was once a man who had bruises in his side from his wife's punching him with her elbow to keep him awake. His wife later explained her frustration, "It's not so much that I mind George going to sleep; it's just that his snoring disturbs the other worshipers." Another such story is about a song leader who went to sleep as soon as the preaching began. Not long into his sermon, the preacher paused for dramatic effect. At that moment, the song leader awoke. Hearing only silence, he thought the sermon was over and jumped to his feet and began to lead the invitation song.

Frankly, some, like Eutychus, have good reasons for being sleepy. Some are affected by illness or other physical conditions. Some who take medication must fight going to sleep throughout the service. Some work shift jobs and come to services after working all night. Mothers are sometimes up until the early hours of morning with fussy babies. It is admirable that these

---

[18]Wiersbe, 484–85.

individuals are present in the assembly, fighting to keep their eyelids open.

What about the rest of us? What about those who are sleepy on Sunday morning because they stayed up too late on Saturday night watching TV or visiting with friends? What about those who are simply not interested in spiritual matters? It makes no difference how inspiring the singing is, how uplifting the prayers, how thought-provoking the sermon; they remain glassy-eyed and bored. These are the ones who should concern us. If you find yourself in any of these categories, take note: You may never die from a three-story drop, but your spirituality is plummeting—and spiritual death could be imminent. It is time to wake up and learn to "worship in spirit and truth" (Jn. 4:24)!

Lessons for Preachers. A lesson or two for preachers can also be found in this story. Preachers have been known to point to the fact that Paul preached until midnight to prove that L-O-N-G sermons are scriptural. The term "long" is relative. What is considered long in one area may be considered short in another area and vice versa. By "long," we simply mean what *local hearers* would consider long. Notice, however, that Paul had not been there the Sunday before and would not be there the Sunday after. His situation was considerably different from that of preachers who are with the same people Sunday after Sunday.

The length of Paul's message justifies an occasional long sermon, but it does not justify wearing out our hearers with verbosity week after week. It has been said that the human anatomy has two ends, and that one end can absorb only what the other end can endure. As God's spokesmen, we must work hard to keep our sermons from becoming lullabies.

A Lesson on Environment. We may even see a lesson here on the physical circumstances of the place of meeting. There were "many lamps in the upper room where [they] were gathered together" (v. 8), lamps that probably contributed to a lack of oxygen. One paraphrase says, "It was hot and stuffy in the upstairs room."[19] Where the church meets is not of prime impor-

---

[19]Clarence Jordan, *The Cotton Patch Version of Luke and Acts.*

tance, but there is value in trying to make the place of meeting as conducive as possible to worship. Through the years, poorly ventilated rooms have contributed to lulling saints to sleep.

The Most Important Lesson. The story of Eutychus underlines the fact that physical sleepiness in worship can be a problem and is not to be recommended, but sometimes physical drowsiness is merely a symptom of a more serious problem: *spiritual* slumber. When Paul reprimanded the Corinthians for their abuse of the Lord's Supper, he gave this diagnosis of their spiritual condition: "Many among you are weak and sick, and a number *sleep*" (1 Cor. 11:30; emphasis added). When we speak of "sleeping in church," we should be somewhat concerned if we are talking about the assembly. If, on the other hand, by "church" we mean "the body of Christ," then we should be *greatly* concerned about people "sleeping in church." One of the most important tasks of any preacher is to awaken people from their spiritual slumber. Paul challenged spiritual sleepy-heads: "It is already the hour for you to awaken from sleep . . ." (Rom. 13:11). Again, he wrote, "Awake, sleeper, and arise from the dead, and Christ will shine on you" (Eph. 5:14).

If we imitated the brethren in Troas, it could revitalize us: They were faithful in attendance and in the observance of the Lord's Supper, even at an inconvenient time and place. They had respect for God's spokesman and for God's Word that he preached. We need to walk in their footsteps.

Conclusion. Lessons in this story apply to all listeners. Each needs to do all he can to remain alert during the service so he can really worship. There are lessons here for those of us who preach. We may need to work harder to keep our lessons lively and challenging. The most important lesson, however, is to those whose spiritual interest has waned. "Let us not sleep as others do, but let us be alert and sober" (1 Thess. 5:6).

Meeting with the Church Family (20:7)

Put these facts together: (1) Paul went out of his way to meet with his brethren; (2) the brethren met at an inconvenient time; (3) they came together after they had put in a hard day of work. We conclude that Christians liked to meet with one another

(2:42). Physical families normally enjoy getting together; in fact, if family members do not enjoy being with one another, we call that family dysfunctional. Even so, those in the family of God enjoy being with one another.

Self-examination may be in order. Do you enjoy being with your brothers and sisters in Christ? If you do not enjoy meeting with the family of God, you might want to do some soul-searching about your relationship with your brothers and sisters, and your Father (Heb. 10:25).

The Lord's Day and Supper (20:7)

After years of study, Dr. Willy Rordorf, professor of Systematic Theology at Neuchatel University in Switzerland, concluded that for early Christians, there was no "day of the Lord" without the Lord's Supper, nor was there ever the observance of the Lord's Supper on any other day except on the day of the Lord. Concerning the practice of many denominations of having the Lord's Supper every few months or once a year, he stated: "One of the principal defects in our Sunday worship is this lack of a regular celebration of the Lord's Supper." Again, he said, "We have basically no right to call Sunday the 'Lord's Day,' for the very thing which should make it the Lord's Day, namely the Lord's Supper, is lacking."[20]

A Forgotten Purpose (20:7)

Years ago, two steamboats were headed up the Mississippi River. One captain decided to pass. As he started around the other boat, that boat speeded up—and the race was on. They traveled up the river as fast as they could go. Soon the coal supply of one boat was almost depleted. The captain could not bear the thought of losing the race, so he told his crew to start burning some of their cargo—plump, hickory-smoked hams. The boat burning the hams won the race, but when it docked in the harbor, it had no cargo left to deliver. The captain had forgotten his

---

[20]Willy Rordorf, *Sunday*, trans. A. A. K. Graham (Philadelphia: Westminster Press, 1968), 306.

purpose.[21] Even so, as Christians, we often forget the purposes for which we come together on the Lord's Day.

Meeting Places (20:8)

Owning a meeting place can be beneficial to a congregation: Members know exactly where they will gather from week to week; the building can be adapted to the constantly changing needs of the congregation; to non-members, the church may appear more stable and permanent. Owning a building can also have drawbacks: The cost may drain the financial resources of the members, forcing them to forego many good works; the congregation can become building-oriented and wait for the lost to "come to the services"; a building may make a congregation self-centered and interested primarily in its own welfare.

Some would say that since we have no record of "church buildings" until the third century, it is unscriptural to have such. Often these say we should only meet in homes. Our studies in Acts, however, have shown us that early congregations met in a variety of places; there is no "exclusive pattern" of meeting in homes. Commands to assemble (for example, Heb. 10:25) authorize *a place* to meet, but do not specify the place. The place could be in a home, in a rented hall, under an apple tree, or in a building that the congregation buys or builds. Each congregation must make its own decision concerning the best place for it to meet to fulfill its God-given challenges.

Whether or not the congregation with which you are associated has its own building, the members should be constantly reminded that where they meet is not as important as what they do while they are together—and how they live when they leave.

Raising the Dead (20:10)

The apostle Paul used his miraculous gift to bring Eutychus back to life. Some today claim to have the same power the apostles had, but we will never see the raising of Eutychus duplicated. Newspaper stories have told about "faith-healing"

---

[21]Mark Clairday, "Three Factors to a Successful Church," Sermon preached at the Judsonia church of Christ, Judsonia, Arkansas, n.d.

meetings in which people died from heart attacks or the like. None were brought back to life. People today do *not* have the power of the apostles.

A Fellowship Meal (20:11)

After their period of worship together, the church at Troas enjoyed a time of sharing food and conversation (20:11). The close of this day in Troas corresponds to many services of the Lord's church that have been followed by fellowship meals. The New Testament calls such a meal a "love feast" (Jude 12). The church in Corinth had abused the love feast by combining the Lord's Supper with this feast and making the whole event a drunken brawl (1 Cor. 11). Paul's words to them were not a condemnation of the fellowship meal, but of their abuse of it.

We often call a love feast something more homey: "an all-church fellowship," "a potluck meal," or "dinner on the grounds." Whatever it is called, it is a special time when we get to know each other better, when bonds with one another are strengthened. Families normally enjoy getting together, eating together, and visiting with one another. Even so, members of the early church enjoyed eating and talking with each other. So should we.

Paul's Farewell Speech (20:18–35)

This farewell speech can be easily divided into two parts: Paul's reference to his own work (vv. 18–27) and his charge to the elders (vv. 28–35). The first part concerning Paul's ministry could be used for a sermon entitled "The Work of a Preacher." The second part could be used for a sermon on "The Work of Elders."

Another sermon could be preached on Paul's warning concerning the approaching apostasy (vv. 28–31). It is a matter of history that the apostasy did begin among leaders of the church as they extended the boundaries of their oversight. For other predictions of the apostasy, see Matthew 7:15–23; 2 Corinthians 11:3; 2 Thessalonians 2:1–12; 2 Peter 2:1–3; 3:1–7; Revelation 17:3–6; 18:1–5.

Paul's farewell speech could serve as a text for *your* "farewell" sermon to a congregation. Like Paul, you could first speak of the work you did among them. Then you could give a charge to the congregation in general and the leaders in particular to continue in faithful service to the Lord.

Elders in the Church (20:28)

You may want to make a chart on the different biblical terms for elders in order to impress this key information on the minds of your listeners. The chart might look something like this:

Elders in the Lord's Church

Elders/presbyters	—	Older and more mature (1 Tim. 5:17; 1 Pet. 5:5)
Bishops/overseers	—	Responsible for the congregation (Phil. 1:1)
Pastors/shepherds	—	Caring for the spiritual needs of the members (1 Pet. 5:2, 3)

Overseers (20:28)

Elders had, and still have today, the oversight of *all* the work of the congregation. U.S. President Harry Truman used to say, regarding the running of government, "The buck stops here." Regarding the operation of a local congregation, "the buck stops" with the elders. Elders can, however, secure help in fulfilling their task. Our text contains proof of this: The elders were to "feed the church" (v. 28; KJV); that is, they were to teach the members (Heb. 5:12–14). At the same time, Paul said that *he* taught Christians at Ephesus (v. 20). Did Paul usurp the work of the elders? No, he simply cooperated with them in the great task of teaching. It is scriptural, even necessary, for elders to get men to help them with various responsibilities, even as the apostles did in chapter 6 (see comments on 6:2). At the same time, elders must remember that they, and they alone, are responsible for overseeing the congregation and will one day give an account for their supervision (Heb. 13:17).

CHAPTER 21

PAUL'S THIRD MISSIONARY JOURNEY (PART 4)—AND HIS ARREST IN JERUSALEM

Some people think that they would like to be able to look into the future. However, such an ability might be more of a liability than an asset. What if we knew every tragedy that would come into our lives? It would be hard not to allow this knowledge to hinder our enjoyment of the present.

As Paul headed for Jerusalem, he knew for certain one thing about his future: At the end of this third missionary journey, there would be trouble. When he wrote to Rome from Corinth, he told of his Jerusalem trip and made this request: "Now I urge you, brethren . . . to strive together with me in your prayers to God for me, that I may be rescued from those who are disobedient in Judea" (Rom. 15:30, 31). When he bid farewell to the Ephesian elders in Miletus, he said:

> And now, behold, bound in spirit, I am on my way to Jerusalem, not knowing what will happen to me there, except that the Holy Spirit solemnly testifies to me in every city, saying that bonds and afflictions await me (Acts 20:22, 23).

Paul knew that he definitely would be arrested and might even be killed when he reached Jerusalem (21:13). Why, then, did he go? He was convinced it was God's will that he go—and he was willing to risk everything for the Lord (see comments on 19:21; 20:22). In chapter 21, we will see the completion of Paul's journey to Jerusalem and the increasing tension as he drew closer to that city.

ON TO JERUSALEM BY WAY OF TYRE, PTOLEMAIS, AND CAESAREA (21:1–17)

The Voyage to Tyre (21:1–6)

[1]When we had parted from them and had set sail, we ran a straight course to Cos and the next day to Rhodes and from there to Patara; [2]and having found a ship crossing over to Phoenicia, we went aboard and set sail. [3]When we came in sight of Cyprus, leaving it on the left, we kept sailing to Syria and landed at Tyre; for there the ship was to unload its cargo. [4]After looking up the disciples, we stayed there seven days; and they kept telling Paul through the Spirit not to set foot in Jerusalem. [5]When our days there were ended, we left and started on our journey, while they all, with wives and children, escorted us until we were out of the city. After kneeling down on the beach and praying, we said farewell to one another. [6]Then we went on board the ship, and they returned home again.

Verse 1. Chapter 20 closed with Paul's tearful farewell to the Ephesian elders. Chapter 21 begins with the voyage of Paul and his companions from Miletus on their way to Jerusalem: **When we had parted from them and had set sail. . . .** The Greek word from ἀποσπάω (*apospaō*), translated **had parted**, could mean "had torn away." The NIV has, "After we had torn ourselves away from them." Paul has sometimes been depicted as an austere, aloof individual. A man with those qualities would not have stirred hearts as the hearts of those who knew Paul were moved.

Luke, who was in Paul's company, evidently kept a log of the journey. He recorded, **We ran a straight course to Cos and the next day to Rhodes and from there to Patara.** Luke could have written extensively on the first two stops. The island of **Cos** was the birthplace of Hippocrates (c. 460–377 B.C.) and the home of the world's most famous medical school and the sanctuary of Asclepius, the god of healing. The island of **Rhodes** was known for its cultivation of roses, from which it derived its name. It was also known for the 105-foot-high bronze Colossus that had once stood at its harbor—one of the Seven Wonders of the Ancient World. By the time of Paul's visit, an earthquake had broken the statue, but the ruins of this enormous wonder were still a notable attraction. Luke, however, was not writing a travel brochure. He was telling of Paul's dash to Jerusalem, hurrying to get there before Pentecost (see comments on 20:16).

Verse 2. If Paul's company had continued on the ship they were on—one that stopped at almost every port—there would have been no way for them to reach Jerusalem in time. When they docked in Patara, they were delighted to find an ocean-going vessel bound for Phoenicia. This vessel was probably a much larger ship than the one they had been on. It later took seven days to unload it (vv. 3–6). Phoenicia lay on the eastern end of the Mediterranean Sea, just north of Palestine. From Phoenicia, it would be easy to travel to Jerusalem. Luke wrote, **And having found a ship crossing over to Phoenicia, we went aboard and set sail.**

Verse 3. Unlike their previous coast-hugging craft, this ship headed across the Mediterranean, straight for Phoenicia. Luke said they were sailing **to Syria.** The country of Phoenicia was a region in the Roman province of Syria. On the way, they passed south of the island of **Cyprus,** where Paul and Barnabas had begun the first missionary journey (13:4) about ten years earlier. However, the vessel did not stop until it **landed at Tyre** and docked **to unload its cargo**.

Verse 4. Tyre was the principal city of Phoenicia, an ancient city familiar both to students of secular history and to students of Bible history. Hiram, king of Tyre, furnished cedar for Solomon's temple (1 Kings 5:10). For other Old Testament references to Tyre, see the predictions of Isaiah 23; Ezekiel 26—28; and Amos 1:9, 10. Jesus mentioned Tyre in His preaching (Mt. 11:21) and even visited the area around Tyre (Mt. 15:21; Mk. 7:24).

When persecution by Paul and others had scattered Christians from Jerusalem (Acts 8:1–4), some had gone to Phoenicia (11:19). Probably, the church at Tyre had been established at that time. Years later, on his way from Antioch of Syria to Jerusalem,

Paul had passed through Phoenicia, "describing in detail the conversion of the Gentiles, and . . . bringing great joy to all the brethren" (15:3). Perhaps Paul met some of the brethren in Tyre at that time. It is also possible that Paul and Barnabas had met some of those Christians at Tyre when they took benevolent help from Antioch of Syria to Jerusalem (11:27–30; 12:25).

Paul's ship evidently made good time crossing the Mediterranean; according to John Chrysostom, the journey took only five days.[1] Although still committed to arriving in Jerusalem before Pentecost, Paul apparently now had time to spare. From this point on, he never seems to have been in a hurry. It would take days for his ship to unload in Tyre, but he was not worried. He used the time to deepen his ties with the brethren in that city. Luke wrote, **After looking up the disciples, we stayed there seven days.** The Greek word from ἀνευρίσκω (*aneuriskō*), translated **looking up,** implies a diligent search. The city of Tyre was large, and the church was probably small.

Previously, Paul had thrilled the brethren in that area with an account of the success of the gospel among the Gentiles; he could now bring them an update. Their special time of fellowship would have culminated in gathering around the table of the Lord on the first day of the week. Since they stayed in Tyre a full week, they were there on a first day—and would, therefore, have observed the Lord's Supper (see comments on 20:7).

One concern marred their time together: **They kept telling Paul through the Spirit not to set foot in Jerusalem.** Apparently, one or more of the brethren at Tyre had the gift of prophecy and kept warning Paul of the dangers that awaited him (see 20:23; 21:10, 11).

If we had been in Paul's position, we would have wanted to enjoy association with our brethren without thinking about the future. However, **the Spirit** would not let him forget. "In every city" the Spirit inspired men to remind the apostle that "bonds and afflictions" awaited him (20:23). What a test this must have been to Paul's resolve to carry through on his mission!

Note the admonition of the brethren for Paul **not to set foot**

---

[1]John Chrysostom *Homilies on Acts* 45.

in Jerusalem. It is doubtful that this specific prohibition came from the Holy Spirit—for at least two reasons: (1) Paul had always heeded the Spirit's prohibitions (16:6–8). If the Spirit had plainly told Paul not to go to Jerusalem, he surely would have complied with those instructions. (2) Paul obviously considered himself under divine orders to go to Jerusalem (see comments on 19:21; 20:22), and the Spirit would not contradict Himself. Rather, the Holy Spirit revealed to the brethren at Tyre that hardships awaited Paul at Jerusalem, and it was *their* conclusion that he should not go. The exact words from the Spirit (v. 11) predicted what would happen but did *not* instruct Paul to avoid going to Jerusalem. The Spirit's warning was not intended as a *prohibition* but a *preparation*—preparing Paul for what he could expect in Jerusalem.

Verse 5. The week in Tyre passed quickly. Although formerly Paul had enjoyed only a brief acquaintance with the Christians there, after seven days of fellowship, they parted the closest of friends. Thus has it ever been in God's family. The parting scene is reminiscent of the tearful farewell at Miletus (20:36–38):

> **When our days there were ended, we left and started on our journey, while they all, with wives and children, escorted us until we were out of the city. After kneeling down on the beach and praying, we said farewell to one another.**

With the possible exception of Eutychus (20:9), this reference is the first time **children** have been mentioned in Acts in the context of congregational activities. At this "prayer meeting on the beach," the disciples were **kneeling down** in prayer to God (see comments on 20:36). Entire families had come to tell Paul and his friends good-bye. Tears of men, women, and children mingled as they bid farewell to one willing to risk everything for the Lord.

Verse 6. Then we went on board the ship, and they returned home again. Some see here a hint of loneliness—and an implied contrast: "'We went on board the ship' heading toward danger while 'they returned home again' to safety."

The Prophecy of Agabus (21:7–14)

⁷When we had finished the voyage from Tyre, we arrived at Ptolemais, and after greeting the brethren, we stayed with them for a day. ⁸On the next day we left and came to Caesarea, and entering the house of Philip the evangelist, who was one of the seven, we stayed with him. ⁹Now this man had four virgin daughters who were prophetesses. ¹⁰As we were staying there for some days, a prophet named Agabus came down from Judea. ¹¹And coming to us, he took Paul's belt and bound his own feet and hands, and said, "This is what the Holy Spirit says: 'In this way the Jews at Jerusalem will bind the man who owns this belt and deliver him into the hands of the Gentiles.'" ¹²When we had heard this, we as well as the local residents began begging him not to go up to Jerusalem. ¹³Then Paul answered, "What are you doing, weeping and breaking my heart? For I am ready not only to be bound, but even to die at Jerusalem for the name of the Lord Jesus." ¹⁴And since he would not be persuaded, we fell silent, remarking, "The will of the Lord be done!"

Verse 7. From **Tyre**, the ship traveled south to **Ptolemais**, the southernmost port of Phoenicia, located about ten miles north of Mount Carmel. Ptolemais, a Roman colony (see comments on 16:12), had been called "Acco" in Old Testament times (Judg. 1:31). Later, Ptolemy II of Egypt renamed it. A small congregation, probably established at the same time as the one in Tyre (11:19), met in the city. Some think the phrase **had finished the voyage** indicates that the ship only went as far as Ptolemais, and thus that Paul and the others continued the journey on foot.

And after greeting the brethren, we stayed with them for a day. Luke's language indicates that these brethren were waiting when Paul's ship docked at Ptolemais; the apostle did not have to "look up" these brethren (see v. 4). Word of Paul's itinerary may have reached Ptolemais during the week he and his company spent in Tyre.

If the major theme of 21:1–17 is Paul's willingness to risk everything for the Lord, the minor theme is the desire of early

Christians to be together. Paul made an intense effort to search out his brethren in every city. When he found them, they treated him with genuine hospitality. The unexpected appearance of nine or more brethren (see comments on 20:4) was apparently not considered an imposition. Like Lydia, the Christians of Ptolemais were probably insisting, "If you have judged us to be faithful to the Lord, come into our houses and stay" (see 16:15).

The brethren in Tyre and Ptolemais should be admired for their gracious hospitality. The graciousness of the churches in those cities is especially admirable when we consider that they were the result of the savage persecution in which Paul had participated (8:1–4; 11:19). When the former persecutor showed up on their doorstep, they did not allow past mistreatment to overshadow present fellowship. They welcomed Paul and his friends.

In this section, the major theme and the minor theme are not mutually exclusive. One reason Paul was willing to risk everything for the Lord was that he loved his brethren. He was going to Jerusalem because he hoped to ease the tension between Jewish and Gentile Christians (Rom. 15:22–33). Like Jesus, he was willing to "lay down his life for his friends" (Jn. 15:13).

Verse 8. After a **day** in Ptolemais, Paul and his companions headed south; Luke did not mention whether they traveled by sea or by land. They came to **Caesarea**, the principal seaport of Palestine (see comments on 10:1) where Peter had first preached the gospel to the Gentiles (chs. 10, 11). In addition to the times mentioned in the text (9:30; 18:22), Paul may have visited Caesarea on his trips from Antioch of Syria to Jerusalem and back. The city took on additional significance later, when Paul was imprisoned there for two years (23:31–35; 24:27). At the time of our story, however, it was merely Paul's last major stop before reaching Jerusalem.

Caesarea was a little over sixty miles from Jerusalem, about a two-day journey. Paul stayed there for several days (21:10); estimates range from six to ten days. He did so until it was time to leave for the celebration of Pentecost in Jerusalem. While in Caesarea, Paul stayed with one of the most remarkable hosts of all his journeys. Luke said, **And entering the house of Philip**

the evangelist, who was one of the seven, we stayed with him.

Philip was one of Paul's most remarkable hosts; if anyone had reason to distrust or even to hate Paul, it had to be Philip. He had been a coworker with Stephen (6:5), whom Paul, prior to his own conversion, had helped to execute. Philip was also one of those who had been run out of Jerusalem by Paul (8:1–5). Again, we see Christian graciousness, as Philip invited Paul and his traveling companions into his home.

Philip the evangelist was first introduced in chapter 6 as **one of the seven** men selected to serve tables (6:1–6). When Christians had been driven from Jerusalem, he had gone north into Samaria to preach the gospel (8:4–13). Next, he had traveled south to preach to an Ethiopian nobleman (8:26–39). He had then moved north along the Palestinian coast "preaching the gospel to all the cities until he came to Caesarea" (8:40). Evidently, he had made Caesarea his home, starting his family there.

Philip was called "the evangelist" because this work was his principal pursuit. Compare this descriptive term to "John the Baptist," "Simon the tanner," and others. This passage is one of the three places in the New Testament where the term "evangelist" is found (see Eph. 4:11; 2 Tim. 4:5). "Evangelist" is a variation of the Greek word for "gospel" (see comments on 5:42; 8:4). The word means "gospelizer"—in other words, "one who proclaims the good news." The verb form of the word is found in Acts 8:40, where Philip was *"preaching the gospel* to all the cities" (emphasis added).

The term "evangelist" is sometimes used today to refer to one who travels around preaching the gospel—in contrast with the "preacher," who stays in one place. Evidently, Philip had made Caesarea his home for twenty-plus years and was still known as "the evangelist."

Verse 9. Luke added an interesting biographical note on Philip: **Now this man had four virgin daughters who were prophetesses.** There is no indication that Luke was suggesting a special sanctity in the fact that they were unmarried. These were *not* "the first nuns." In his sermon on the Day of Pentecost, Peter had quoted from Joel 2, where God had promised, ". . . I will pour forth of My Spirit on all mankind; and your sons and your daughters shall prophesy . . ." (Acts 2:17). To "prophesy" was to speak for God by inspiration; the gift of prophecy was bestowed on both men and women (1 Cor. 11:4, 5) by the laying on of the apostles' hands. Women were not to exercise this gift in the public worship assembly (1 Cor. 14:23, 31–37). However, the gift could be exercised in a more private setting.

Why did Luke mention this detail about Philip's daughters? Luke's note may simply have been a detail added by an eyewitness with no significance intended. However, some speculate that the four prophetesses confirmed that difficulties awaited Paul in Jerusalem. Others note that, according to early Christian writings, some of these daughters became well known in the church and were recognized sources of information concerning the early history of the church. They then speculate that they were prime sources for Luke's two-volume work on Christ and the church (see Lk. 1:3). Since Luke ended up with Paul in Rome, he probably stayed close to Paul during his imprisonment in Palestine. Therefore he probably spent much time in or near Caesarea.

Verse 10. As Paul stayed in the home of Philip, once again the peacefulness was shattered by a reminder of what lay ahead. This notice would be the most dramatic of all. **As we were staying there for some days, a prophet named Agabus came down from Judea. Agabus** was not a common name, so this was probably the same prophet from Jerusalem who earlier foretold "that there would certainly be a great famine all over the world" (11:28). This time he came not to predict global disaster, but personal disaster—for Paul.

Verse 11. Like an Old Testament prophet, Agabus reinforced his words with a graphic object lesson (see 1 Kings 11:29–31; 22:11; Is. 20:2–4; Jer. 13:1–11; 27:1–11; 28:1–17; Ezek. 4; 5:1–4; Zech. 11:7–14). Coming to the group of men, Agabus **took Paul's belt and bound his own feet and hands.** Instead of a **belt,** the KJV has "girdle." It was a leather belt or band of cloth that was used to "gird" the outer garment and hold it against the body.

Then Agabus **said, "This is what the Holy Spirit says: 'In this way the Jews at Jerusalem will bind the man who owns this belt and deliver him into the hands of the Gentiles.'"** Later in this chapter, we will see the fulfillment of this prophecy. The Jews did not bind Paul *with the intention* of delivering him to the Gentiles. They intended to kill him personally, but Gentiles, that is, the Roman soldiers, rescued Paul from the mob. The words of the prediction must mean, therefore, that the Jewish binding of Paul *would result in* his being delivered into Gentile hands. This being the case, why did Luke use the terminology he used? Perhaps, he was drawing a parallel between what would happen to Paul and Jesus' prediction of what would happen to Himself in Jerusalem (Lk. 18:32).

Verse 12. Prior to the arrival of Agabus, Luke and Paul's other traveling companions had not sided with those urging him not to go. However, they had probably grown more apprehensive as they came closer to Jerusalem. With Jerusalem about sixty miles away, Agabus' dramatic announcement pushed them over the edge. Luke and the others joined the chorus, pleading, "Don't go! Don't go!" Luke admitted, **When we had heard this, we as well as the local residents began begging him not to go up to Jerusalem.** They probably argued, "We're just two days' journey from Jerusalem. We can take the contribution. You need not put yourself in danger!" They had not listened closely enough to the prediction. The Holy Spirit had not said, "If Paul goes, this is what will happen to him." Rather, the Spirit had said, in effect, "This is what *will* happen." When they begged Paul not to go, whether they realized it or not, they were indirectly asking him to make God a liar.

Verse 13. Paul was surrounded by brethren he loved, with every voice urging him not to go. His beloved Luke was pleading with tears in his eyes; Timothy looked at him with imploring eyes. Not a voice dissented. It was more than the apostle could bear. Paul cried above the clamor: **"What are you doing, weeping and breaking my heart? For I am ready not only to be bound, but even to die at Jerusalem for the name of the Lord Jesus."** The Greek word from συνθρύπτω (*sunthruptō*), translated **breaking,** means "crushing into powder." Unless they ceased, they could destroy his resolve. Paul, of course, did not **die at Jerusalem,** but he was ready to die if that was the Lord's will. For a similar phrase, see Esther's words in Esther 4:16.

Verse 14. When Luke and the rest saw that **he would not be persuaded,** they "gave up" (NIV) and said what they should have said in the first place: **"The will of the Lord be done!"** (See comments on 18:21.)

Some today teach that it is never God's will that any of His children go hungry, get sick, or suffer hardship. Nevertheless, it was His will that Paul go to Jerusalem even though trouble waited. Sometimes personal well-being must be sacrificed for a higher purpose. What purpose could God have in Paul's going to Jerusalem and being arrested there? Let us suggest two: First, it was necessary for Paul to go to Jerusalem, despite the danger, to fulfill a promise made to Peter long ago. Peter had asked Paul to "remember the poor," meaning the poor in Jerusalem and Judea—and Paul had said that he would (Gal. 2:10). At long last, he was keeping his word. There was no way the contribution could be brought to a satisfactory conclusion by remote control. As previously suggested, Paul was risking his life for *peace* between brethren.

Second, it was necessary for Paul to be imprisoned ("bound" means "arrested," v. 13) to fulfill a promise made concerning him more than twenty years earlier. Prior to Paul's baptism, Jesus had said, "He is a chosen instrument of Mine, to bear My name before the Gentiles *and kings* . . ." (9:15; emphasis added). In the ensuing two decades, Paul had preached to thousands of Gentiles but to no kings at all. How could that promise possibly be fulfilled? It was unlikely that any king would come to hear Paul preach or that he would receive a royal command to come to any king's palace. How did God arrange it so that the promise of Jesus would be fulfilled? He allowed Paul to be arrested. In the chapters that follow, Paul preached several times to royalty—always as a prisoner on trial for his life.

The Journey to Jerusalem (21:15–17)

[15]After these days we got ready and started on our way up to Jerusalem. [16]Some of the disciples from Caesarea also came with us, taking us to Mnason of Cyprus, a disciple of long standing with whom we were to lodge.

¹⁷**After we arrived in Jerusalem, the brethren received us gladly.**

Verse 15. Luke continued his narrative: **After these days we got ready and started on our way up to Jerusalem.** These days refers to the days at Caesarea and the days of emotional upheaval. The Greek word from ἐπισκευάζομαι (*episkeuazomai*), translated **we got ready,** refers to packing their luggage, but there may also be the implication that Luke and the rest got their *minds* ready. They resigned themselves to what was to come.

Verse 16. Some of the disciples from Caesarea accompanied them. Perhaps some were Jews who wanted to go to the feast, but their primary purpose was to take Paul and the others **to Mnason of Cyprus.** Mnason was originally from Cyprus, the island where Paul and Barnabas had begun the first missionary journey (13:4–12). He was apparently a Hellenistic Jew who would be more likely to invite Paul and Gentiles into his home than would a Palestinian Jew.

This verse is the only place in the Scriptures we read about Mnason. Luke may have mentioned that he was **a disciple of long standing** to indicate that he was one of the foundational members of the church in Jerusalem with a house in that city—or perhaps Luke mentioned it because he was a source for Luke's twofold history (Lk. 1:3). Maybe it is simply a detail with no particular significance.

Paul and his companions were scheduled **to lodge** with Mnason. These arrangements were probably made during the "some days" Paul and the others spent in Caesarea (v. 10). A few textual difficulties occur at this point. Some manuscripts imply that Mnason came to Caesarea from Jerusalem and then accompanied the group back to Jerusalem (see KJV); other manuscripts suggest that the travelers stayed with Mnason overnight halfway to Jerusalem. The differences do not affect the heart of the story.

It was almost impossible to find lodging in Jerusalem during the feast days when hundreds of thousands of Jewish pilgrims poured into the city. It was an even greater problem for a group that included the most unpopular man in Jerusalem

(21:20–22, 27, 28), plus at least seven despised Gentiles. It was not unheard of for Gentiles to come to the feasts (Jn. 12:20). The large outer court of the temple area was called "The Court of the Gentiles." Nevertheless, unless a Gentile was a "God-fearer," on the way to becoming a Jewish proselyte, he was suspect in Jerusalem.

Mnason had a house big enough to accommodate Paul's party and a heart big enough to invite them to stay. Since Paul's nephew is mentioned later (23:16), some have speculated that Paul's sister owned a house in Jerusalem and that Paul could have stayed with her. Whether or not this is true, we do not know.

Verse 17. Paul and his friends arrived in Jerusalem just a few days before the feast day of Pentecost. Since Pentecost fell on the first day of the week (see comments on 2:1), the Christians in the area would have met on that day to break bread (see comments on 20:7). However, verse 22 of our text implies that there had not yet been a meeting of the Christians in the area (see comments on v. 22). We conclude, therefore, that Paul arrived shortly before the Day of Pentecost. Luke wrote, **After we arrived in Jerusalem, the brethren received us gladly. We** included Luke, Timothy, and at least six other Gentile Christians (20:4, 5). **The brethren** probably consisted of the host, Mnason (v. 16), and a welcoming committee gathered at his home. However, it is possible that verse 17 tells of a first meeting in the home of James, while verse 18 tells of a second meeting when all the elders were present. Perhaps the enthusiastic reception of those present helped to relieve some of Paul's anxieties (see Rom. 15:30, 31). The NIV has "The brothers received us warmly."

Many writers have commented on the similarities between Luke's accounts of Jesus' last journey to Jerusalem and Paul's last trip to the same city. In Luke 9:51 (NASB 1977), we read concerning Jesus: "And it came about . . . that He resolutely set His face to go to Jerusalem" (see also Lk. 9:53; 13:33; 18:31; 19:11, 28). Jesus knew what awaited Him in Jerusalem (Lk. 18:31–33), but He went anyway—knowing it was God's will. Even so, Paul had "set his face to go to Jerusalem" and would not be deterred.

PAUL TRIES TO AVOID CRITICISM (21:18–26)

¹⁸And the following day Paul went in with us to James, and all the elders were present. ¹⁹After he had greeted them, he began to relate one by one the things which God had done among the Gentiles through his ministry. ²⁰And when they heard it they began glorifying God; and they said to him, "You see, brother, how many thousands there are among the Jews of those who have believed, and they are all zealous for the Law; ²¹and they have been told about you, that you are teaching all the Jews who are among the Gentiles to forsake Moses, telling them not to circumcise their children nor to walk according to the customs. ²²What, then, is to be done? They will certainly hear that you have come. ²³Therefore do this that we tell you. We have four men who are under a vow; ²⁴ take them and purify yourself along with them, and pay their expenses so that they may shave their heads; and all will know that there is nothing to the things which they have been told about you, but that you yourself also walk orderly, keeping the Law. ²⁵But concerning the Gentiles who have believed, we wrote, having decided that they should abstain from meat sacrificed to idols and from blood and from what is strangled and from fornication." ²⁶Then Paul took the men, and the next day, purifying himself along with them, went into the temple giving notice of the completion of the days of purification, until the sacrifice was offered for each one of them.

We now come to one of the most perplexing sections in the Book of Acts—the story of Paul's participation in sin offerings in the temple in Jerusalem (21:18–26). By this time, Paul had already written Galatians (see introductory comments on ch. 15), stating, "Therefore the Law has become our tutor to lead us to Christ, so that we may be justified by faith. But now that faith has come, we are no longer under a tutor" (Gal. 3:24, 25). He had also written Romans (see comments on 20:3), in which he emphatically asserted:

Therefore, my brethren, you also were made to die to

the Law through the body of Christ, so that you might be joined to another, to Him who was raised from the dead. . . . For Christ is the end of the law for righteousness to everyone who believes (Rom. 7:4; 10:4).

How could the man who wrote that Christians are no longer under the Law, that Christians were in fact made "dead to the law by the body of Christ" (KJV), that "Christ is the end of the law," still be willing to participate in the sacrifice of sin offerings (Num. 6:11, 14) in "a den of thieves" (Mt. 21:13; KJV)? Commentator Adam Clarke expressed the bewilderment many of us feel:

However we may consider this subject, it is exceedingly difficult to account for the conduct of James and the elders, and of Paul on this occasion. There seems to have been something in this transaction which we do not fully understand.[2]

The whole affair is so incongruous that one scholar could not hide his skepticism:

One could as well believe that . . . Calvin[3] on his deathbed vowed a golden robe to the Holy Mother of God, as that the author of Romans and Galatians stood for seven days in the outer court of the Temple, and subjected himself to all the manipulations with which rabbinic ingenuity had surrounded the vow, and allowed all the liturgical nonsense of that age to be transacted for him by unbelieving priests and Levites.[4]

---

[2]Adam Clarke, *The Holy Bible With a Commentary and Critical Notes,* vol. 5, *Matthew–Acts* (New York: Abingdon Press, n.d.), 860.

[3]John Calvin was a fiery Reformer who spent a lifetime in conflict with the Catholic Church.

[4]This statement, attributed to A. Hausrath, was quoted in Richard Longenecker, *Paul, Apostle of Liberty* (New York: Harper & Row, 1964), 246.

Of course, those of us who believe in the integrity and inspiration of Acts cannot escape the problem of 21:18–26 by denying its historicity. We must struggle with what Paul did and why he did it. Some, like G. Campbell Morgan, have found little that is defensible in Paul's actions: "I hold that Paul made the greatest mistake of his ministry on this occasion."[5] On the other hand, some believe Paul's behavior to be highly commendable, totally compatible with every principle he taught.

Since Luke himself did not commend or condemn Paul's conduct, we cannot be dogmatic in our conclusions. There can be value, however, in trying to understand the passage and looking for principles that are applicable today. We will try to determine exactly *what* Paul did and consider *why* he did it.

Verse 18. Luke wrote, **And the following day Paul went in with us to James, and all the elders were present.** This reference is the last time Luke used first person in the narration until the account of Paul's voyage to Rome (27:1). Perhaps he switched points of view to focus solely on Paul. However, since Luke later traveled with Paul to Rome, he probably stayed in Palestine most or all of the two years Paul was imprisoned at Caesarea. During this time he may have done much of the research for Luke–Acts, his twofold work on the life of Jesus and the early days of the church (Lk. 1:3; Acts 1:1).

Paul and those who came with him had an appointment with the leaders of the church in Jerusalem. That meeting apparently took place at the home of **James**, the half-brother of Jesus, who was considered a pillar in the Jerusalem church (Gal. 2:9; see comments on 15:13). James was probably the only one remaining in Jerusalem who had asked Paul several years before to "remember the poor" (Gal. 2:9, 10), the request that apparently initiated the contribution Paul collected from Gentile churches. It would be natural for Paul to take the contribution to James.

Note the phrase **all the elders**. Throughout Acts, there is a shift from the temporary arrangement of apostles-leadership to

---

[5]G. Campbell Morgan, *The Acts of the Apostles* (Grand Rapids, Mich.: Fleming H. Revell, 1988, reprint), 372.

the permanent arrangement of elders-leadership. We first read about "the apostles" (2:42; 4:35, 37; 5:2; 8:1, 14; 9:27), then about "the apostles and the elders" (15:2, 4, 6, 22, 23; 16:4), and now just "the elders" (21:18; see 14:23; 20:17). We do not know if any of the twelve apostles were in Jerusalem. Perhaps they were preaching in other areas, fulfilling their commission (Mt. 28:19; Acts 1:8). There are many early traditions about the apostles traveling all over the world, preaching the gospel and establishing the church. At any rate, the oversight of the church there had been left in the hands of the elders.

The phrase "James, and all the elders" does not necessarily mean that James was not one of the elders. It certainly does not prove that James was "the bishop" of the church in Jerusalem, having authority over the congregation, in contrast to "the elders," who served in a secondary capacity. A. C. Hervey was grasping at straws when he made this erroneous comment on verse 18:

> Nothing can mark more distinctly the position of James as Bishop of Jerusalem than this visit of Paul to him, and the finding of him surrounded with all the elders of Jerusalem. It is a most distinct evidence of the apostolic origin of the episcopal office.[6]

The words of this Church of England commentator reflect a lack of understanding regarding New Testament teaching on the eldership. In the comments on 20:17, 28, we noted that the terms "elder" and "bishop" were used interchangeably in New Testament times and referred to the same office or work. Hervey was reading into 21:18 a man-made hierarchical system that developed in subsequent centuries.

Luke was not necessarily making a distinction between James and the elders. If an individual were to write, "I went into the house of one of the elders, and all the elders were there,"

---

[6]A. C. Hervey, *The Acts of the Apostles*, vol. 2, The Pulpit Commentary, ed. H. D. M. Spence and Joseph S. Exell, vol. 18 (Grand Rapids, Mich.: Wm. B. Eerdmans Publishing Co., 1950), 172. For a similar comment, see Clarke, 859.

we would not conclude that the first elder mentioned was not part of the group of elders mentioned later. Rather, we would conclude that *all* the elders were present in the home of *one* of the elders. This probably is the case in verse 18, just as Mark Black concluded when he referred to "James and the *other* elders."[7]

Someone may object: "If James was just one of the elders, why was he and he alone mentioned by name?" The answers are because it was his house and because he was well known and highly respected. Note that never again in the narrative is James singled out. From verse 19 through verse 25, collective pronouns ("they," "them," "we") are always used, referring to *all* the elders.

Luke's point was that Paul met with *"all* the elders." It was important that *all* the elders be present and that *only* the elders be present—until some problems were ironed out. Was it Paul's idea or James' idea that all the elders be present? Certainly, both of them wanted all the elders to be present. Paul would have wanted all to be present when the contribution was presented. James would have wanted all to be present to give weight to the "suggestion" that Paul pay the expenses of four men who had taken a vow.

Verse 19. When Paul walked into the presence of the elders, Luke said simply that he **greeted them.** Luke did not linger on that scene because he had other purposes in mind; he wanted his readers to understand the background of Paul's arrest. However, this greeting was a moment of high significance. This was probably the first time for many of the Jerusalem elders to embrace any of their Gentile brethren. This meeting was probably the occasion when Paul and his Gentile companions laid the Gentile love offering "at the feet of" the Jewish elders (see 4:35). From the general response of the elders to Paul (v. 20), we may assume that the contribution was basically well received. Whether or not it improved Jewish-Gentile relationships as Paul hoped, we do not know. It has been suggested that Luke did not tell of the contribution because it did not accomplish Paul's de-

---

[7]Mark Black, "The Vow and the Sacrifices," *Acts, The Spreading Flame* (Searcy, Ark.: Harding University, 1989), 221. (Emphasis added.)

sired purpose—that is, the contribution was a failure. However, using the same reasoning, we could conclude that Paul's letters were all failures since Luke did not mention them. We are on safer ground to note that Luke mentioned what served his purposes and excluded information that did not.

Next, Paul **began to relate one by one the things which God had done among the Gentiles through his ministry.** Both the Greek and the English indicate that Paul took considerable time as he methodically recounted his adventures in the Gentile world. Since Paul had given a report to the elders in Jerusalem after his first journey (15:4), this report probably only covered the second and third journeys. If "the church" in 18:22 refers to the church in Jerusalem, this report may have only covered the third journey. As usual, **God** was given credit for all that was accomplished. Paul did this to give God the glory *and* to emphasize that his ministry had God's approval. At this particular meeting, Paul brought proof of the effectiveness of his ministry. He could point to the stalwart young Gentile brethren who came with him.

The presentation of the contribution, plus Paul's report, signified the successful completion of his third journey. The occasion marked the end of Paul's famous "three missionary journeys." He had traveled thousands of miles over the eastern half of the Roman Empire for more than ten years, establishing congregations in major cities everywhere. It was a moment to savor before a new phase of his ministry commenced.

Verse 20. The elders' reaction to his report must have first gladdened, then saddened Paul's heart. At first, **when they heard it they began glorifying God.** Several facts stand out in their initial response: (1) They saw the hand of God in what Paul had done, and (2) they glorified God, not Paul. (3) The Greek verb ἐδόξαζον (*edoxazon*, from δοξάζω, *doxazō*), translated **began glorifying,** is in the imperfect tense which refers to continuous action in past time. Their praise probably continued for some time. Certainly Paul and the Gentile brethren would have been thrilled with the response of the Jerusalem elders.

The elders' first words to Paul were also encouraging: **"You see, brother, how many thousands there are among the Jews**

of those who have believed." Their use of the term **brother** was a good sign, along with the mention of **thousands** of converts to Christ. The Greek text has μυριάδες (*muriades*), which could also be translated "tens of thousands" or transliterated "myriads." The elders wanted Paul to know that God had not only been working among the Gentiles, but He had also been working among the **Jews.** We do not know whether the elders were referring to the number of Christian Jews who lived in Jerusalem, the number who lived in Palestine, or the number of all Christian Jews who were present in Jerusalem for the feast day. Shortly before this time, Paul had written of his concern for his fellow countrymen (Rom. 9:1–3). As he heard of multiplied thousands of Jews who had become Christians, his heart must have started to soar.

It was not long before he was brought back to earth with a crash—because the elders did not conclude with that positive thought. It is not difficult to identify with Paul in this situation. Perhaps you have presented what you consider a great idea to a friend. When your confidant first responded positively, you were elated. Then came the "but," and you were deflated. Even though the elders did not use the word "but" in their reply, they might as well have. Several translators indicate the switch between the elders' glorifying God and their reply to Paul with the word "then": "Then they said to him. . . ." Apparently, the minds of the elders had been only half on what Paul said; subsequent events show that they had come to the meeting with a hidden agenda.

The elders continued: **"And they** [the thousands of Jewish Christians] **are all zealous for the Law."** Those words must have made Paul uneasy. Paul knew what it meant to be zealous for the Law. He had been zealous for the Law before he had learned better (Gal. 1:14; Phil. 3:5–9). The "converted" Pharisees who had earlier caused trouble had been zealous for the Law (Acts 15:5). Paul perhaps wondered, "What does this have to do with my ministry to the Gentiles and my purpose for being in Jerusalem?"

Verse 21. The elders spoke of rumors that had been spread about Paul:

They (the Jews who had believed) have been told about you, that you are teaching all the Jews who are among the Gentiles to forsake Moses, telling them not to circumcise their children nor to walk according to the customs.

The Greek word, translated **they have been told**, is a form of κατηχέω (*katēcheō*), from which we get "catechize." The rumor had been repeated so often that it was drilled into their minds. Many hateful rumors have been spread about gospel preachers based on others' conclusions, not on what these preachers actually said.

Like most rumors, this one had an element of truth, but in its essence was false. Paul had emphasized that no one, Jew or Gentile, could be justified by the law of **Moses** (Rom. 3:20; Gal. 2:16; 3:11; 5:4) and that circumcision had nothing to do with salvation (Rom. 2:25–29; Gal. 5:6). However, he had *not* launched a campaign to persuade Jews to abandon their Jewishness. The rumor was based on what people thought Paul said, not on what he actually said.

Regarding **the customs**, he had no objection to Jewish Christians keeping Jewish traditions as part of their national heritage—as long as those traditions did not conflict with the truth (see Mt. 15:3) and the Jewish Christians did not bind those traditions on Gentiles (see comments on 15:1, 2). Regarding circumcision, he had insisted on having Timothy circumcised so as not to offend Jews he hoped to reach (see comments on 16:3). His stated policy concerning unbelieving Jews was "To the Jews I became as a Jew, so that I might win Jews; to those who are under the Law, as under the Law . . . so that I might win those who are under the Law" (1 Cor. 9:20).

Verse 22. The rumor was untrue—and the elders *knew* it was untrue. The fact that the rumor was false did not mean that it was not deadly—as Paul well knew. When word had spread in Jerusalem that Stephen's teachings about Jesus would alter the customs (6:14), Stephen had ended up dead and Paul had helped to kill him (7:58—8:1).

Concerning Paul's situation, the elders outlined the predicament as they saw it: **"What, then, is to be done? They will certainly hear that you have come."** The Western Text has "What then? *The assembly must certainly meet,* for they will hear that you have come" (emphasis added). The KJV reflects the Western Text and has "the multitude must needs come together." Some take this to refer to a mob of unbelievers, but the context indicates that the elders were concerned about Christian Jews. The antecedent of **they** is the believing Jews present in Jerusalem (v. 20). The Day of Pentecost, which fell on the first day of the week, was near, perhaps a few hours away. When the first day of the week arrived, all the Christians in the area would gather together to break bread (see comments on 20:7). The elders were asking, "When these thousands come together, already disturbed by what they have heard, and they see Paul and his Gentile friends there, how can we keep tempers from flaring and violence from erupting?"

This occasion would have been an excellent time for the elders to ask *God* the question "What, then, is to be done?" There is no indication that they did. They might have asked Paul what *he* thought they should do, but they did not. At least, they could have discussed the matter with Paul and the others present before reaching a conclusion.

If they had asked us, "What, then, is to be done?" we may have been tempted to tell them to start acting like God's appointed leaders—and personally go to Paul's critics. John Wesley expressed a similar opinion when he said, "James should have told those Jewish Christians: I do not keep the law of Moses; neither does Peter; neither need any of you!"[8] Lloyd Ogilvie revealed his amazement at how the elders handled the matter when he wrote, "Had no one said, 'That's enough! We believe in our brother Paul and know that these rumors are false. There will be no further criticism of his ministry. We trust that the Apostle has faithfully kept what we agree upon'?"[9]

---

[8]Quoted in James Burton Coffman, *Commentary on Acts* (Austin, Tex.: Firm Foundation Publishing House, 1976), 408.

[9]Lloyd J. Ogilvie, *Acts*, The Communicator's Commentary, vol. 5 (Dallas: Word Publishing, 1983), 304.

Verse 23. The elders did not ask their question to solicit input, but merely to set the stage for a prearranged agenda. They had apparently discussed the matter ahead of time and had come to James' house with their plan ready. Their "solution" was to do nothing themselves, but to have *Paul* take care of the matter. They told him, **"Therefore do this that we tell you."** They did not suggest; they commanded. The Greek verb ποίησον (*poiēson*, from ποιέω, *poieō*), translated **do**, is in the imperative mood.

They began their "recommendation" by stating the situation: **"We have four men who are under a vow."** Presumably, the **four men** mentioned were members of the Jerusalem church. It is even possible that the elders had brought the four men to the meeting (v. 26). The **vow** referred to is generally assumed to be the Nazirite vow, since the men had to shave their heads (v. 24). Compare this occasion to Paul's vow mentioned in 18:18. According to Numbers 6:18, the head was shaved at the close of the vow and was to be done at the place of sacrifice. The vow of the four men seems definitely to be the Nazirite vow, while Paul's vow remains something of a puzzle.

The Nazirite vow was a vow of separation and dedication. It could be taken for periods from thirty days to a lifetime. Two who were under the Nazirite vow all their lives were Samson and John the Baptist. Those under this vow were not to cut their hair, were to abstain from anything derived from grapes, and were to avoid dead bodies (Num. 6:2–8). Since verse 26 of our text speaks of "the days of purification" and verse 27 specifies "seven days," most think that the four men had defiled themselves with a dead body, which required a seven-day purification period, after which they had to shave their heads and start their vow all over again (Num. 6:9–12). That period of purification involved time off from work, plus money for the sacrifices involved.

Verse 24. The elders continued their recommendation to Paul, **"Take them and purify yourself along with them, and pay their expenses so that they may shave their heads."** The elders were suggesting that Paul be responsible for all expenses incurred. Writers concern themselves unduly over where Paul got the money to **pay their expenses** since Paul was generally broke. Some have suggested that the elders told Paul to use some of the collection for the saints for this purpose. However, that action would have been misappropriation of funds, and we cannot imagine Paul's agreeing (2 Cor. 8:20, 21). Since Paul later had funds to rent a house in Rome for two years (Acts 28:30), some have speculated that Paul received an inheritance about this time. It is not a matter of great significance. Probably, Paul got the money where he usually did—by working, or from generous brethren.

The elders told Paul to **purify** himself. Paul's own purification was probably a simple ceremonial cleansing to allow him to go into the temple. For typical ceremonial cleansings, see Leviticus 15:1–30. There is no indication that Paul took the Nazirite vow with the men and certainly no indication that he was just then completing a vow taken years before (18:18). Often, when Jews returned from Gentile countries, they went through a ceremonial cleansing process. Perhaps something like this was involved in Paul's purification. Perhaps such a process was required before he could go into the temple and make arrangements with the priests. Paul's going through a purification process at the same time as the four would further demonstrate in the minds of the elders Paul's dedication to the Law.

There is no need to get bogged down in the details of the vow or exactly what occurred in verses 23 through 27. As is often the case, Luke apparently compressed the events, so we cannot be exactly sure what happened. Luke's purpose was not to give details concerning the four men's vow, but to explain how Paul ended up in prison. As far as our study is concerned, the most significant aspect of the Nazirite vow is that it involved sacrifices, including *sin offerings*. After a man had purified himself, to resume his vow he had to bring two turtledoves or pigeons to the priest, and the priest offered "one for *a sin offering* and the other for a burnt offering" to "make *atonement* for him concerning *his sin*" (Num. 6:11; emphasis added). When the man finally completed the vow, among other sacrifices he was to bring a "ewe-lamb a year old without defect *for a sin offering*" (Num. 6:14; emphasis added).

After "advising" Paul to pay the expenses of the four men,

the elders said, **"And all will know that there is nothing to the things which they have been told about you, but that you yourself also walk orderly, keeping the Law."** Did James blush a little when he and the other elders spoke of **keeping the Law?** Eight or more years before, during a special meeting in Jerusalem, James and the elders had concurred with Peter when the apostle referred to the Law as "a yoke which neither our fathers nor we have been able to bear" (15:10). James was present when Peter made the statement (15:13) and in verse 25 of our text, the elders identified themselves as those who wrote the letter composed during the Acts 15 meeting. Now they were "asking" Paul to convince fellow Christians that he was still committed to and willing to shoulder that unbearable yoke.

Verse 25. The elders apparently realized that their proposal could be taken as a retraction of the decision reached at that earlier meeting, for they hastened to confirm that they stood by that judgment: ***"But concerning the Gentiles who have believed, we wrote, having decided that they should abstain from meat sacrificed to idols and from blood and from what is strangled and from fornication"*** (emphasis added; see comments on 15:20). In other words, "Our request does not involve Gentile Christians. What we are asking you to do, Paul, is for the benefit of Jewish Christians only."

We can sympathize with the elders in Jerusalem. Living in the heart of Judaism, they faced an almost impossible task. Jews in general have never made a distinction between their religion and their race. Under the Old Covenant, civil and religious laws were blended. The Law of Moses controlled how they functioned as a nation, as well as their religious activities. The fusion of religion and race for the Jews was true in Bible times; it is still true for many conservative Jews today. To the average Jew, asking him to give up the Law was asking him to give up being a Jew. No doubt the elders thought, "If we speak out against the Law, we will have trouble in the congregation, and we will never be able to influence our friends and neighbors."

On the other hand, we cannot help but think that the Jerusalem elders were overly accommodating both to their society and to the Law-binding faction in the church (15:5; Gal. 2:11, 12). It is doubtful that the elders encouraged aggressive preaching such as Paul did in Jewish synagogues everywhere—preaching that had gotten him beaten and expelled from those synagogues (see 2 Cor. 11:24). In chapters 22 and 23, we will see Paul's sermons to Jews in Jerusalem and their leaders, sermons that stirred their anger. Obviously, they had not been hearing that kind of preaching from the Jewish Christians in Jerusalem. The challenge to live "at peace with all men" (Rom. 12:18) without compromising the truth (Prov. 23:23) is never easy. It was not easy in Jerusalem; it is not easy where you live.

Verse 26. How did Paul respond when the elders told him what to do? Did he protest, "Who are you to order me around?" Did he declare, "You are the leaders of this congregation. Taking care of this matter is your responsibility, not mine"? Did he object, "It is true that I have a policy of becoming as 'under the Law' in certain circumstances, but that policy is for the purpose of winning *unbelieving* Jews, not for the purpose of pampering Jewish Christians"? (See 1 Cor. 9:20.) Did he note that the proposed course of action might be used by Law-binders (Acts 15:5) as "proof" that Paul agreed with them?

The elders had pushed Paul into a corner. The apostle had come to Jerusalem to promote peace in the brotherhood, but the elders were telling him that his arrival was promoting disharmony. He was in a no-win situation. If he refused to go along with the elders' plan, he could be accused of encouraging discord in the church; if he complied with their proposal, he could be accused of inconsistency.

Luke did not record Paul's mental or verbal response to the elders' plan. His purpose was to set down succinctly the sequence of events resulting in Paul's arrest. He simply reported the surprising, almost inexplicable, sequel:

> **Then Paul took the men, and the next day, purifying himself along with them, went into the temple giving notice of the completion of the days of purification, until the sacrifice was offered for each one of them.**

It appears that **the men** were present at the meeting, or at least that they were brought in when the elders made their "suggestion." On the following day, Paul took them into **the temple**. The word "temple" (ἱερόν, *hieron*) in this context refers to the sacred part of the temple, not merely the temple complex which included the Court of the Gentiles.

PAUL ARRESTED (21:27–36)

[27]When the seven days were almost over, the Jews from Asia, upon seeing him in the temple, began to stir up all the crowd and laid hands on him, [28]crying out, "Men of Israel, come to our aid! This is the man who preaches to all men everywhere against our people and the Law and this place; and besides he has even brought Greeks into the temple and has defiled this holy place." [29]For they had previously seen Trophimus the Ephesian in the city with him, and they supposed that Paul had brought him into the temple. [30]Then all the city was provoked, and the people rushed together, and taking hold of Paul they dragged him out of the temple, and immediately the doors were shut. [31]While they were seeking to kill him, a report came up to the commander of the Roman cohort that all Jerusalem was in confusion. [32]At once he took along some soldiers and centurions and ran down to them; and when they saw the commander and the soldiers, they stopped beating Paul. [33]Then the commander came up and took hold of him, and ordered him to be bound with two chains; and he began asking who he was and what he had done. [34]But among the crowd some were shouting one thing and some another, and when he could not find out the facts because of the uproar, he ordered him to be brought into the barracks. [35]When he got to the stairs, he was carried by the soldiers because of the violence of the mob; [36]for the multitude of the people kept following them, shouting, "Away with him!"

The Day of Pentecost had passed, but the streets were still thronging with people from all over the world who had come to Jerusalem for the feast. The feast of Pentecost was a one-day feast, but most who came long distances prolonged their stay in

Jerusalem beyond the single day. Some were buying provisions for the long trip home. Others were enjoying a final visit with friends they would not see until the following year. A few were simply reluctant to leave the place they called "the city of God." In the northeast quarter of the city, where the great temple was, others lingered with a deadlier motive: Their evil eyes scrutinized Paul's every move, looking for any excuse to harm him. Soon they would find that excuse; then Paul would have to face one of the most dangerous moments of his life.

Verse 27. The four men would not be allowed to enter the temple until their seven-day purification was completed, but Paul's ceremonial cleansing would take only a day or so. Refer again to Leviticus 15:1–30 for the type of ceremony involved in ceremonial cleansings. He could go into the temple on their behalf, making arrangements for the sacrifices to be offered at the end of their days of purification.

Two more facts should be noted: (1) Paul did not complete what he started. *When the seven days were almost over,* **the Jews from Asia, upon seeing him in the temple, began to stir up all the crowd and laid hands on him** (emphasis added). Non-Christian Jews grabbed Paul before the sacrifices were actually offered; the sacrifices came at *the end* of **the seven days.** Did God have a hand in the timing, to keep Paul from actually participating in a blood sacrifice? It is an interesting thought.

These **Jews** were probably from Ephesus in the province of **Asia,** where Paul had recently worked for almost three years. They had rejected his preaching (19:8, 9), plotted against him time and again (20:18, 19), and even participated in a riot provoked to dispose of the apostle (19:33)—all to no avail. Now they saw an opportunity to be rid of him at last. Probably, the gathering also included Jews from Galatia, Macedonia, and Achaia—all the places where Jews had attempted to kill Paul. If the Jews from Asia had not instigated this, probably Jews from another area would have done something similar. It is even possible that some had followed Paul to Jerusalem for this very purpose.

(2) Instead of preventing trouble as the elders had hoped, Paul's action precipitated trouble. We do not know if his trips

to the temple eased Jewish believers. Since the Jews from Asia grabbed Paul near the end of the seven-day period, a first-day-of-the-week meeting of Christians in Jerusalem would have taken place between the time Paul met with the elders and the time he was taken captive. What happened at that meeting? Was it tumultuous, or did reason prevail? We would like to know—but, again, it was not Luke's purpose to satisfy our curiosity. However, we do know that Paul's trips to the temple enraged Jewish unbelievers—and resulted in his imprisonment.

The Jews from Asia, upon seeing Paul in the temple, borrowed the tactics of a fellow Ephesian, Demetrius, and **began to stir up all the crowd.** It has been suggested that Alexander and the other Jews who had been in the amphitheater in Ephesus (19:33, 34) may have been the instigators of this riot in Jerusalem. If so, they had learned well from Demetrius and the other silversmiths.

Verse 28. Laying hands on him, the Jews cried out, **"Men of Israel, come to our aid!"** Paul was probably in the Court of the Women when they located him. In the southeast corner of that court were the chambers where individuals stayed while completing the Nazirite vow. The Asiatic Jews grabbed the apostle and shouted, **"This is the man who preaches to all men everywhere against our people and the Law and this place."** The Greek text has simply "the people" (see KJV), but the term used by a Jew would mean "the Jews," hence the NASB translation **our people**. Three things were sacred to the Jewish people: their nation, their Scriptures, and their temple. Paul was accused of dishonoring the first, destroying the second, and defiling the third. There is some irony in the fact that Paul was charged with defiling the temple when he was undergoing purification so he would *not* defile the temple. Those accusations had served the Jews well in the past; they had been used against Jesus (Mk. 14:56–64; Jn. 2:19) and Stephen (Acts 6:11, 13, 14). In both cases, the accused had been executed.

They continued their charge: **"And besides he has even brought Greeks into the temple and has defiled this holy place."** Notice that one man (Trophimus, v. 29) had multiplied into **Greeks** (plural). Did the Jews from Asia assume that the four men who were completing the Nazirite vow were also Gentiles? Keep the exact charges in mind. Later Paul would challenge the Jews to prove their charges and make their case (24:19).

Verse 29. The grounds for the Jews' accusation were based on the fact that **they had previously seen Trophimus the Ephesian in the city with him. Trophimus** was one of the Gentiles who had traveled with Paul to Jerusalem to deliver the special contribution (20:4). Since he was from Ephesus, the Asiatic Jews probably knew him by sight. Now they **supposed that Paul had brought him into the temple.**

To understand why this was a deadly supposition, we must know several facts about the temple (see comments on 3:2). The word **temple** in this passage refers to the sacred part of the temple, the inner courts, just as in verses 26 and 27. Gentiles were allowed to go into the part of the temple complex called the Court of the Gentiles, but they were *not* allowed to go farther. At each entrance leading from the Court of the Gentiles into the sacred courts, there was a warning; two of these inscriptions in Greek have been discovered. The warning read: "No man of another nation [is] to enter within the fence and enclosure around the temple, and whoever is caught will have himself to blame if death ensues." Paul likely had this imagery in mind when he later wrote that Christ "made both groups [Jew and Gentile] into one and broke down the barrier of the dividing wall" (Eph. 2:14). The apostle wrote these words to the Christians at Ephesus; this city was the hometown of Trophimus, the man that Paul was accused of taking beyond the barrier. As a major concession to the Jews, the Romans had given the temple officials authority to immediately kill anyone who violated the sanctity of the temple, even a Roman citizen. If Paul had taken a Gentile into the sacred courts, it was a capital offense.

The Asiatic Jews had no reason for supposing that Paul had desecrated the temple, and neither do we. A man trying to appease Law-keepers would not do something so senseless unless he was a fool—and Paul was no fool. Some have suggested that Trophimus may have inadvertently wandered into one of the sacred courts. I. Howard Marshall noted, "The possibility that

Trophimus might have wandered of his own freewill into the forbidden area is about as unlikely as that someone should wander into the private rooms in the Kremlin for the purpose of sightseeing."[10] When you hate someone, however, you are ready to assume the worst.

If Paul had really been guilty of taking Trophimus into the sacred courts, they should have called the temple guards to their aid. Those officials had the authority to arrest Paul and any Gentile intruders and have them summarily executed. Instead, the Jews from Ephesus asked the crowd for help—indicating that they knew they had no real case against him.

Verse 30. Word spread like wildfire through the crowded streets. **Then all the city was provoked, and the people rushed together.** On a previous Day of Pentecost, people had come from all over Jerusalem to hear the apostles preach (ch. 2). Now, about twenty-seven years later, people pressed into the temple to see an apostle die.

And taking hold of Paul they dragged him out of the temple—in other words, out of the sacred part of the temple into the Court of the Gentiles. This court was the only location in that part of the city large enough to accommodate the crowd. This action was roughly equivalent to dragging a church member from a meeting place during a worship service. They hauled him from the Court of the Women because if they killed him on holy ground, his blood would pollute the temple (see 2 Kings 11:15, 16; 2 Chron. 24:21). They would not hesitate to destroy an innocent man, but they did not want to defile a piece of property.

After describing their actions, Luke added this note: **And immediately the doors were shut.** Perhaps the words were simply to add detail; the temple guards may have shut the doors to the Court of the Women to prevent further pollution or so the worshipers would not be further disturbed. Many commentators, however, see a symbolic significance in the words.

---

[10]I. Howard Marshall, *The Acts of the Apostles,* The Tyndale New Testament Commentaries, ed. R. V. G. Tasker (Grand Rapids, Mich.: Wm. B. Eerdmans Publishing Co., 1980), 348.

For Luke himself, this may have been the moment when the Jerusalem temple ceased to fill the honorable role hitherto ascribed to it in his twofold history. The exclusion of God's message and messenger from the house once called by his name sealed its doom: it was now ripe for the destruction which Jesus had predicted for it many years before (Lk. 21:6).[11]

> . . . the act of closing the gates symbolically signified that the temple was of no importance to the Gentile Christian [segment of the] church and within time—after A.D. 70—would be meaningless to the Jewish Christian segment as well.[12]

Verse 31. If Paul had been guilty as charged, he should have been taken outside the city by the temple guards and stoned (7:58; see Lev. 24:10–14). Instead, the mob began savagely and senselessly to beat him to death (v. 32). Paul had only minutes to live when God stepped in with a divine reprieve. **While they were seeking to kill him, a report came up to the commander of the Roman cohort that all Jerusalem was in confusion.** Ironically, God used an irreligious power to subdue a religious people. This incident was the second time God used the Romans to rescue Paul from a Jewish mob (see 18:12–17). One purpose for civil government is to protect the innocent (Rom. 13:3, 4).

Palestine in general and Jerusalem in particular was a major headache to Roman occupation forces. The privilege of governing the area might be compared to the dubious honor of sitting atop a seething volcano. Never was the situation more volatile than during the major feast days, when hundreds of thousands of Jews packed into Jerusalem. On such occasions, additional military forces occupied the city, ready for trouble.

Those forces were barracked in the Fortress Antonia, which

---

[11]F. F. Bruce, *The Book of Acts*, The New International Commentary on the New Testament, gen. ed. F. F. Bruce, rev. ed. (Grand Rapids, Mich.: Wm. B. Eerdmans Publishing Co., 1988), 410.

[12]Simon J. Kistemaker, *Exposition of the Acts of the Apostles*, New Testament Commentary (Grand Rapids, Mich.: Baker Book House, 1990), 770.

was located at the northwest corner of the temple mount. This structure was an old Jewish fortress which had been rebuilt by Herod the Great and renamed in honor of Mark Antony, Herod's Roman friend and patron. The fort, which towered above the temple, was fifty feet tall—with watch towers rising an additional fifty feet. Watchmen could survey all areas of the temple, along with much of the city.

The local officer in charge of security was a **commander** named Claudius Lysias (23:26). The Greek word χιλίαρχος (*chiliarchos*), translated "commander," refers to one having charge of six hundred to a thousand men. On that day this commander was interrupted by the news he dreaded most: **All Jerusalem is in confusion.** Some have suggested that the news came from one or more of the men with shaved heads who had been with Paul. Since, however, the word was not "they are killing an innocent man," but rather "all Jerusalem [is] in confusion," the word probably came from the watchmen on the towers. The fortress was connected to the outer court of the temple by two flights of stairs.

Verse 32. Giving orders quickly, he hurried to the steps. **At once he took along some soldiers and centurions and ran down to them.** The commander took along at least two centurions, who each had authority over one hundred men. If all of these were present, at least two hundred soldiers were called into action. The sight of a few hundred legionnaires would have momentarily frozen the crowd: **And when they saw the commander and the soldiers, they stopped beating Paul.**

Verse 33. Claudius, who had been schooled in riot control, promptly assessed the situation. He saw that the fury of the mob was directed toward one battered and bloodied man. Quickly, he **came up and took hold of him,** not so much to protect him as to quell the riot. The commander's later report stretches the truth beyond recognition (23:26, 27). Assuming the man to be the source of the furor, the commander **ordered him to be bound with two chains** to two of his soldiers. This arrest fulfilled the prophecy that bonds awaited Paul in Jerusalem (20:22, 23; 21:10, 11). Also, this action fulfilled the prophecy that he would be delivered into the hands of the Gentiles (21:11).

Paperwork has ever been the mainstay of bureaucracy. See the report the commander finally wrote in 23:25–30. It was important to know what Paul had done because, according to Roman law, a Roman citizen could not be held without hearing the charges against him (see 25:26, 27). Knowing he would have to report the incident, the commander **began asking who he was and what he had done.** Since ἐπυνθάνετο (*epunthaneto* from πυνθάνομαι, *punthanomai*) is in the imperfect tense, the word may indicate that he asked again and again.

Verse 34. Next, Luke describes the disordered suppositions of the mob: **But among the crowd some were shouting one thing and some another** (see 19:32). Most had no idea what Paul had been accused of, but they assumed it had to be horrendous to cause such a commotion. They would have agreed with the modern proverb "Where there's smoke, there's fire."

It was soon obvious that the officer would discover nothing helpful. **When he could not find out the facts because of the uproar, he ordered him to be brought into the barracks.** If those who started the commotion were still present, either they did not speak up, or else they could not be heard above the crowd. It has been suggested that they may have slipped away when they saw the soldiers approaching. Paul was to be taken into the **barracks**, where he could be imprisoned and interrogated. Paul was now the prisoner of Rome; he would remain a prisoner to the end of Acts.

Verse 35. When he got to the stairs, he was carried by the soldiers because of the violence of the mob. As those guarding Paul started for the stairs, the murderous mob saw their prey escaping and turned violent. Alarmed, the soldiers picked Paul up and shoved their way through the crowd. Perhaps Paul, in his weakened state, was not walking as fast as the soldiers wanted, or perhaps the soldiers lifted the apostle above the reach of the crowd. This undignified ride had to rank with Paul's escape in a basket as a highlight of embarrassment to him (see comments 9:23–25).

Verse 36. The people began to chant, **"Away with him!"** They meant: "Away with such a fellow . . . for he should not be allowed to live!" (22:22). A few feet from that spot, another mob had used the same words to demand the death of Jesus (Lk. 23:18; Jn. 19:15). We wonder where the "many thousands of Jews" that believed (v. 20; KJV) were while all this was going on. We also wonder where the four men under a vow (v. 23) were. It looks like another occasion when everyone forsook Paul except the Lord (see 2 Tim. 4:16, 17).

PAUL'S OPPORTUNITY TO DEFEND HIMSELF (21:37–40)

³⁷**As Paul was about to be brought into the barracks, he said to the commander, "May I say something to you?" And he said, "Do you know Greek? ³⁸Then you are not the Egyptian who some time ago stirred up a revolt and led the four thousand men of the Assassins out into the wilderness?" ³⁹But Paul said, "I am a Jew of Tarsus in Cilicia, a citizen of no insignificant city; and I beg you, allow me to speak to the people." ⁴⁰When he had given him permission, Paul, standing on the stairs, motioned to the people with his hand; and when there was a great hush, he spoke to them in the Hebrew dialect. . . .**

Verse 37. When they reached the top of the stairs, the apostle spoke. **As Paul was about to be brought into the barracks, he said to the commander, "May I say something to you?"** In the midst of confusion, one had remained calm—the man covered with his own blood. Compare these events to those surrounding the stoning of Stephen (7:54–60). Had Paul learned from the man he had helped to kill? Observing military etiquette, he asked permission to speak.

When the officer heard Paul, he was startled. **"Do you know Greek?"** he asked. We are not sure why Paul's words in Greek surprised him. It was common for Jews to speak Greek, the universal language of the day. It is possible that the words were not so much a surprise as "a revelation" to the commander. The beginning of the next sentence could be translated, "Surely, then, you are the Egyptian." Egyptians spoke Greek. When Paul spoke in Greek instead of Aramaic, the commander may have jumped to the conclusion that he was an Egyptian rebel they had been looking for. On the other hand, perhaps it was not so much that Paul spoke Greek as the quality of Greek he spoke; Paul's words were those of an educated man.

Verse 38. The commander revealed his own supposition: **"Then you are not the Egyptian who some time ago stirred up a revolt and led the four thousand men of the Assassins out into the wilderness?"** According to the Jewish historian Josephus, about three years earlier, an **Egyptian**, claiming to be the Messiah (see Mt. 24:26; Acts 5:36, 37), had led an army to the top of the Mount of Olives.[13] He had threatened to cause the walls of Jerusalem to collapse like the walls of Jericho, after which he and his army would wrest the city from the Romans. The Roman governor, Felix, had attacked the rebels. Four hundred had been killed and two hundred captured, but the Egyptian himself had escaped. Since that time, he had been high on the Romans' "most wanted" list. Apparently, this officer thought that the agitator had fallen into his hands.

The Roman commander referred to **four thousand men** in that **revolt**. In an account written earlier than the one cited above, Josephus wrote that the Egyptian led 30,000 men to the top of Mount Olivet.[14] The difference in figures might be accounted for by the fact that Josephus and the commander spoke of two different events. If there is a contradiction, it is more likely that the Roman officer was correct than Josephus, who sometimes exaggerated. This fact is obvious from the smaller figures (four hundred killed, two hundred captured) given in Josephus' previous account.

The Assassins translates the word σικάριοι (*sikarioi*), which can be transliterated "Sicarii." The word "Sicarii" means "daggermen," from the Latin word *sica*, which means "short dagger." The Sicarii were, as the NASB indicates, assassins. The KJV has "murderers"; the Jerusalem Bible has "cutthroats." They mingled with the crowds during festivals to get close to pro-Roman adversaries. They would secretly thrust their daggers into their

---

[13]Josephus *Antiquities* 20.8.6.
[14]Josephus *Wars* 2.13.5.

enemies, then blend with the horrified crowd. They were part of the general Jewish rebellion that finally resulted in the destruction of Jerusalem.

Verse 39. Paul quickly assured him that he was not the man the authorities sought: **"I am a Jew of Tarsus in Cilicia, a citizen of no insignificant city."** Paul did not mention at this time that he was also a Roman citizen (see 22:25). At that time, one could have dual citizenship: both local citizenship and Roman citizenship. As a Jew, he had a right to be in the temple. As a citizen of Tarsus—a city of cultural and political preeminence—he was a responsible individual, unlikely to stir up trouble.

Paul then made a request that must have astounded the official: **"I beg you, allow me to speak to the people."** The natural reaction for one who had just been beaten half to death would have been, "Get me out of here! I've seen all of this crowd I ever want to see." Paul said, "Let me talk to them." One of the apostle's purposes for coming to Jerusalem was "to testify solemnly of the gospel of the grace of God" (20:24); this would be his first opportunity.

Verse 40. The commander gave Paul **permission** to speak—probably because he thought he would finally discover what the disturbance was all about. **Paul, standing on the stairs, motioned to the people with his hand.** Imagine Paul standing at the top of the stairway that led to the Antonia Fortress, the soldiers between him and the crowd below. His torn clothing was likely covered with dust and blood, his face cut and bruised. Nevertheless, he had a divine dignity about him as he raised **his hand** to get their attention (see 13:16; 26:1). Apparently, the commander allowed at least one of Paul's chained hands (v. 33) to be loosened. **And when there was a great hush, he spoke to them in the Hebrew dialect.** The **Hebrew dialect** was Aramaic. The unruly throng of Jews below became quiet as Paul spoke to them in their native tongue.

APPLICATION

"No Reserve, No Retreat, and No Regrets" (21:10–14)

There was a man named Bill Borden who was a son of a

wealthy family. When he decided to go to China as a missionary, his friends thought he was crazy. When he contracted a disease on the way to China and died, they thought he had thrown his life away for nothing. However, at his bedside, they found this note: "No reserve, no retreat, and no regrets."

Paul would have understood that sentiment. In the face of grave danger, he was determined to go to Jerusalem. In the chapters which follow, the apostle was imprisoned, mistreated, and largely cut off from the work he loved; but he did not quit. Whatever the circumstances, he remained committed to his Lord.

Paul's Belt (21:10, 11)

In presenting Agabus' prophecy concerning Paul, you may enjoy using this attention-getter: Bring a belt to class—the wider, the better. Hold it up at the beginning of the class and say, "This represents different things to different people. To a man, it is a means of holding up his trousers. To a child, it may represent parental punishment. To Paul, however, it was a symbol of imprisonment." Demonstrate how Agabus used Paul's belt.

"Your Will Be Done" (21:12, 13)

After hearing Agabus' prophecy, the brethren begged Paul not to go to Jerusalem (21:12). This instance is probably as close as Paul ever came to backing down on a commitment he had made to God—all because he had friends who begged him not to keep that commitment. They did not do it from bad motives; they were just concerned about Paul. Paul, however, was more concerned about the plans and purposes of God (see Mt. 16:23).

If you risk anything for the Lord, do not be surprised if your friends call you crazy and urge you to renounce your commitment. Some of these friends may be as close to you as Luke and Timothy were to Paul. We have known young men who wanted to preach until well-meaning friends talked them out of it. We have known men and women determined to work through the problems in their marriages until friends convinced them they "didn't have to put up with those indignities any longer." We have known those who had a burden on their hearts to go and teach the lost in other countries until they were dissuaded by friends. Most of these friends did not act from evil intentions; they were simply concerned about people they loved. What they did not understand is that to the Christian, personal well-being is not as important as being faithful to one's commitment to the Lord. When you make a commitment to God that involves risk, put yourself in His hands and leave the outcome to Him. Do not let friends weaken your resolve. We are not saying that you should never listen to the counsel and advice of friends (Prov. 24:6), especially Christian friends. Previously, Paul had often listened to the advice of Christian friends who urged him to stay away from dangerous situations (see 19:30, 31). On this occasion, however, Paul's friends were asking him to disobey God. Never let anyone, even a close friend, talk you out of doing what *God* wants you to do.

To some extent, doing the will of God always entails risks. God never gives easy assignments. Christianity is not for the fainthearted (Rev. 21:8). Unlike the artificial risks taken by jaded thrill-seekers, in the end, risks taken for God are no risks at all— for He never forsakes us and is always working behind the scenes. "He Himself has said, 'I will never desert you, nor will I ever forsake you,' so that we confidently say, 'The Lord is my helper, I will not be afraid. What will man do to me?'" (Heb. 13:5, 6). "And we know that God causes all things to work together for good to those who love God, to those who are called according to His purpose" (Rom. 8:28).

Even if your life is threatened as was Paul's, you can face death with the confidence that "you will receive a rich welcome into the eternal kingdom of our Lord and Savior Jesus Christ" (2 Pet. 1:11; NIV). If you are a faithful Christian, you cannot lose.

Do you know the most terrible risk a man can take? It is to refuse to obey the will of God. There are some who know that God wants them to confess their faith in Jesus and be baptized, but friends are trying to talk them out of it, just as Paul's friends tried to talk him out of going to Jerusalem. We should never let anyone talk us out of obeying God's will for our lives.

Did Paul Do Right or Wrong? (21:17–26)
When Paul went to Jerusalem, he went expecting trouble

(20:22, 23; Rom. 15:30, 31). He was prepared for the possibility that the pride of the Jewish Christians would not allow them to accept the contribution from Gentile Christians. He knew that he could expect harassment from former associates who considered him a traitor. The Spirit had told him that he would be arrested. As he walked through the streets of Jerusalem, he must have looked over his shoulder constantly, wondering where the trouble would come from. Then he walked into an elders' meeting, where he felt safe—and there it was!

> . . . and they said to him, "You see, brother, how many thousands there are among the Jews of those who have believed, and they are all zealous for the Law; and they have been told about you, that you are teaching all the Jews who are among the Gentiles to forsake Moses, telling them not to circumcise their children nor to walk according to the customs. What, then, is to be done? They will certainly hear that you have come. Therefore do this that we tell you. We have four men who are under a vow; take them and purify yourself along with them, and pay their expenses so that they may shave their heads; and all will know that there is nothing to the things which they have been told about you, but that you yourself also walk orderly, keeping the Law" (21:20–24).

To our amazement, the apostle complied with their extraordinary demand:

> Then Paul took the men, and the next day, purifying himself along with them, went into the temple, giving notice of the completion of the days of purification, until the sacrifice was offered for each one of them (v. 26).

Knowing that those sacrifices included sin offerings, we cry out, "Why, Paul?" Questions fill our minds: Did Paul do right or wrong? Would it be all right today to offer sacrifices, especially if we were Jews? These are the questions with which we will grapple.

Man's Conflicting Words. Let us start with the question "Did Paul do right to comply with the elders' demand?" No consensus of opinion exists on this issue—even among respected Christian scholars. For the purposes of this study, we will arbitrarily group a myriad of viewpoints under four headings:

(1) An Unqualified "Yes." A few answer the question with an unqualified "Yes." They believe that Paul and the elders were absolutely right in all they did, that their approach would be right anywhere anytime, and that they should be commended and emulated. This group points to Paul's action as a striking example of what he meant when he said, "I have become all things to all men, so that I may by all means save some" (1 Cor. 9:22), and a perfect illustration of Paul's teaching in Romans 14 to bear with weak brethren.

As evidence that Paul and the elders were right in all they did, the first group notes that Luke nowhere condemned their action, and that Paul's conscience was clear regarding his part in the incident (23:1). This group believes that Paul's deeds underline the importance of getting along with people, and some even teach that his behavior proves that promoting peace is more important than defending a doctrinal position.

We can agree with some aspects of this position, but not all. We can probably learn something from this account regarding trying to avoid offense, but to applaud the elders and Paul for everything they did seems far-fetched.

Paul's policy to "become all things to all men" was designed to win unbelievers, not to placate believers. Even as far as unbelievers in Jerusalem were concerned, Paul's participation in temple service was not likely to win him any popularity contests or make it easier for him to preach to the Jews (see 9:29; 22:17–21).

Romans 14 refers to practices that were matters of indifference. Some things commanded by the Law were insignificant items that did not affect New Testament teaching, including resting on the seventh day and dietary laws, but it is hard to see how making a sin offering can be lightly dismissed as "a matter of indifference." It is suggested by some that sacrifices offered during feast days were made by Christians merely as ceremony.

It is difficult, however, to imagine Paul, who had been such a stickler for the Law, having such an attitude.

Regarding any proof that the elders and Paul did not do wrong, the evidence this group uses is less than convincing. Bible writers do not always pause to commend or condemn; note Moses' treatment of Noah's drunkenness in Genesis 9:20, 21. It is true that Paul said that he had not violated his conscience, but that statement also covered the period when he persecuted Christians (Acts 8:1, 3). Paul's words prove that he did not *intentionally* do wrong in obeying the elders' dictates; it does not prove that his behavior cannot be questioned.

Certainly those who teach that getting along with men is more important than obeying God go too far. James himself later emphasized that purity, whether moral or doctrinal, is more important than peace. He wrote, "But the wisdom from above is first *pure*, then *peaceable* . . ." (Jas. 3:17).

(2) A Qualified "Yes." A second group—perhaps the largest group—would qualify their "yes" by saying, "Paul did right *under the circumstances.*" They do not all agree on the exact mitigating circumstances but believe that Paul did the best he could in light of the situation. Some of the circumstances often listed have already been discussed: the incredible pressure from outside and inside the church on both the elders and Paul, Paul's determination to be "all things to all men," and so on.

Three other circumstances are often emphasized: First, there was the uniqueness of Judaism. In the New Covenant, a distinction is made between civil authority and religious authority. We are to "render to Caesar the things that are Caesar's; and to God the things that are God's" (Mt. 22:21; see 1 Pet. 2:17). We are to obey the laws of the land (Rom. 13:1–7) as long as those laws do not violate the laws of God (Acts 5:29). In contrast to that, under the *Old* Covenant, civil authority and religious authority were blended. The law of Moses combined religious and civil laws. The laws for the Israelites controlled not only their religious activities, but also all of their functions as a nation. Therefore, as noted earlier, most Jews had a hard time distinguishing between their religion and their race. Most Jews likely looked on sacrifices as part of their national heritage—at least until the temple was destroyed in A.D. 70. This factor ties in with the next one.

Second, there was a transitional period. Legally, the Law had been nailed to the cross (Col. 2:14, 16)—including the laws about sacrifices. Practically, God gave the Jews time and opportunity to make the transition from Judaism to Christianity. God did not "owe" the Jews this courtesy; thus the phrase "a grace period" is appropriate. Thus, while some passages speak of the Law as being abolished when Jesus died (for example, Eph. 2:14, 15), some speak of the Law as gradually passing away. For instance, Hebrews 8:13 speaks of the first covenant as "obsolete," then says: "But whatever is becoming obsolete and growing old is ready to disappear" (see 2 Cor. 3:7–11). Matthew Henry noted, "The ceremonial law . . . was dead, but not buried."[15] When did God finally "bury" the Law? Most agree that God signaled the end of the transitional period when He allowed the destruction of the temple in A.D. 70. If this is true, the Jews were still in the transitional period in A.D. 57 when Paul went into the temple. This factor parallels the next factor.

Third, there was a gradually-given revelation. God did not reveal His will all at once, but rather as needed and as people could assimilate it. For instance, Peter's words on the Day of Pentecost included Gentiles as part of God's overall plan (Acts 2:39), but Peter did not understand that until God gave him a special vision (ch. 10). It has been suggested that even though Paul had written Galatians and Romans, he did not grasp the logical application of the teachings of those books to sacrifices. Several years later, God inspired the author of Hebrews to reveal the end of the Jewish sacrificial system. We do not know exactly when Hebrews was written. Since it speaks of priests offering sacrifices (10:11), it was probably written before the destruction of the temple in A.D. 70. We are fairly safe in asserting that it was written several years after Paul's arrest in Jerusalem in A.D. 57. The author of Hebrews wrote, "In whole burnt offerings and sacrifices for sin You have taken no pleasure"; "Now where there is forgiveness . . . there is no longer any offering

---

[15]Matthew Henry, *Commentary on the Whole Bible*, one vol. (Grand Rapids, Mich.: Zondervan Publishing House, 1961), 1723.

for sin" (Heb. 10:6, 18). God's revelation is now complete (2 Pet. 1:3; Jude 3), but it was not when Paul went into the temple.

This position that Paul did right "under the circumstances" may be the correct one; certainly the factors listed above are all found in the Scriptures. Nevertheless, we find it difficult to say that Paul did right when he was willing to offer a sacrifice for *sin*—after Jesus had offered the perfect sacrifice for sins. Most who hold this second position are aware that this difficulty deserves special attention. Adam Clarke, one who recognized the difficulty, compared the sacrifices to our paying taxes since "the ministers of state were chiefly maintained by these."[16] Another compares the sacrifices to our paying a fine when we violate the law of the land.

Our problem is the way the law of the Nazirite vow reads: One of the birds brought by the vow-maker was to be offered as "a sin offering" to "make atonement for him concerning his sin . . ." (Num. 6:11). We sometimes use the phrase "make atonement" to refer to a man's relationship with his fellow man, but what did the phrase in Numbers 6 mean to the Jews? Surely, in their minds, it referred to a man's relationship with his God. Perhaps Paul understood that the sacrifices offered had nothing to do with his soul's salvation, but would the priests have understood that? Would the unbelieving Jews who saw Paul make arrangements for the sacrifices have understood that? We cannot help but think that, at least, Paul's action was questionable.

(3) A Qualified "No." We are more comfortable with the position of those—a sizable number—who cannot defend what Paul did, but can sympathize with his predicament. This group believes that the circumstances noted were significant factors in Paul's action but do not justify his involvement in offering blood sacrifices.

Most in this group avoid the word "sin." Rather, they generally use the word "mistake." They vary regarding how serious the "mistake" was, but that seems the preferred term. As noted in the comments, it was G. Campbell Morgan who said that Paul "made the greatest mistake of his ministry on this occasion."

---

[16]Clarke, 861.

Keep in mind that we are not required to justify every action of Bible figures, even the best. Elders were—and are—fallible, and even inspired men made mistakes in action (Gal. 2:11–14). Paul himself noted that he was a sinner (Rom. 3:23) and not perfect (Phil. 3:12). For an example of Paul's acknowledging wrongdoing, see Acts 23:5.

(4) An Unqualified "No." A few—perhaps the smallest group of all—insist that Paul did wrong and that there was absolutely no excuse for what he did. This group could be right, but the position seems to violate the basic principle of putting the best possible construction on the actions of others (1 Cor. 13:7).

God's Conclusive Word. Since God did not see fit to tell us how He viewed Paul's action, we should be hesitant to speak dogmatically regarding where Paul's action falls on the right-wrong scale. However, regarding the second question raised earlier about offering sacrifices today, God *has* spoken—and we should listen. God has said that it would *not* be all right for Paul or anyone else to offer blood sacrifices today.

(1) A Definitive Assertion. Some time after Paul spent a week in the temple, God caused the Book of Hebrews to be written—perhaps by Paul or one of his friends.[17] Hebrews was written to Hebrew (that is, Jewish) Christians who were tempted to return to their old ways. The author argued that everything in Christianity is better, so it would be foolish—even disastrous—for them to return to Judaism.

Regarding the question under consideration, key chapters are Hebrews 7–10. In chapters 7 and 8, the writer noted that the Aaronic priesthood had been abolished. In chapters 9 and 10, he stressed that the sacrifice of Christ superseded that of dumb animals. For the moment, let us look at one section concerning the offering of sacrifices:

For it is impossible for the blood of bulls and goats to take away sins. Therefore, when He comes into the world, He says, "Sacrifice and offering You have not desired,

---

[17]See David Roper, "Hebrews: A Word of Encouragement," *Truth for Today* 14 (July 1993): 37–38.

but a body You have prepared for Me; in whole burnt offerings and sacrifices for sin You have taken no pleasure." "Then I said, 'Behold, I have come (in the scroll of the book it is written of Me) to do Your will, O God.'" After saying above, "Sacrifices and offerings and whole burnt offerings and sacrifices for sin You have not desired, nor have You taken pleasure in them" (which are offered according to the Law), then He said, "Behold, I have come to do Your will." He takes away the first in order to establish the second. By this will we have been sanctified through the offering of the body of Jesus Christ once for all. . . . For by one offering He has perfected for all time those who are sanctified. And the Holy Spirit also testifies to us; for after saying, "This is the covenant that I will make with them after those days, says the Lord: I will put My laws upon their heart, and on their mind I will write them," He then says, "And their sins and their lawless deeds I will remember no more." Now where there is forgiveness of these things, there is no longer any offering for sin (Heb. 10:4–18).

Coffman noted, "With the rescue of Paul by Lysias from the temple mob, there is no record that any Christian ever afterward even so much as set foot in the Jewish temple again."[18]

(2) A Decisive Action. In case anyone did not get the message, God settled the matter for all time when, a few years later, He allowed the temple to be destroyed. Coffman suggested, "The Lord knew that the hold of [the temple's] forms and sacrifices would have such a force upon all the Jews, that rather than their being able to tear away from them, God would tear them away from the Jews."[19] Referring to the destruction of the temple, Clarke said that "God abolished the Mosaic dispensation, by rendering in the course of his providence, the observance of it *impossible*."[20]

---

[18]Coffman, 8.
[19]Ibid., 408.
[20]Clarke, 859. (Emphasis his.)

The destruction of the temple and the cessation of sacrifices in A.D. 70 had been foretold long before. Daniel had said that the holy place would be trampled (Dan. 8:13), that the city and the sanctuary would be destroyed (9:26), that the sacrifices and grain offerings would be stopped (9:27), and that "the regular sacrifice" would be "abolished" (12:11). The prophet had spoken of terrible tribulation, using terms like "desolations" and "abominations" (9:26, 27). Over six hundred years later, as Jesus was leaving the temple, He had startled His disciples by saying that "not one stone here will be left upon another, which will not be torn down" (Mt. 24:2; see Mt. 24:21). When asked about this statement, He referred to Daniel's prophecy, saying that they would "see the abomination of desolation which was spoken of through Daniel the prophet, standing in the holy place . . ." (Mt. 24:15).[21] About forty years later, the Roman army leveled Jerusalem—including the temple. When that happened, the Jewish sacrificial system "became a dead issue."[22] It might also be noted that the Jews themselves later settled the matter of having Christian Jews attending synagogue services; in the final decade of the first century, they added the prayer that "the Nazarenes and the heretics might perish as in a moment and be blotted out of the book of life."[23]

Today, whether Jews or Gentiles, we are to approach no priest on earth, but rather our "great high priest . . . Jesus the Son of God" (Heb. 4:14), "who has taken His seat at the right hand of the throne of the Majesty in the heavens" (Heb. 8:1). We are not to offer up sacrifices of bulls and goats (Heb. 10:4), but rather we are to "offer up a sacrifice of praise to God, that is, the fruit

---

[21]In Matthew 24:3, the disciples thought they were asking one question, for they assumed that the destruction of the temple would come at the end of the world. In reality, they were asking about the destruction of the temple and *also* about the end of the world. Thus, the first part of the chapter is primarily about the destruction of Jerusalem, while the last part is primarily about the end of the world.

[22]Richard Oster, *The Acts of the Apostles*, Part 2, The Living Word Commentary, ed. Everett Ferguson (Austin, Tex.: Sweet Publishing Co., 1979), 124.

[23]Quoted in Bruce, 428.

of lips that give thanks to His name" (Heb. 13:15) for giving us the perfect sacrifice of Jesus (Heb. 9:26).

Conclusion. After exploring Paul's participation in the offering of sacrifice in the temple, we are still inclined to say with Clarke: "There seems to have been something in this transaction which we do not fully understand."[24] One conclusion is obvious, however: Old ways die hard. It has always been so. The elders at Jerusalem struggled with this truth. Paul struggled with it. We struggle with it today. We must constantly keep in mind that the most important consideration is not whether something is old or new, but whether it is right or wrong—and what determines that is God's Word.

Practical Lessons from Paul and the Elders (21:17–26)

Even with the difficulties surrounding verses 17 through 26, there are many lessons we can learn regarding relationships in the church. One is that what one member does affects all the members. Another is that no matter what you do, you will not please everyone. A third is that there will always be some who are ready to believe the worst and to spread their beliefs to others. Balancing out those negative thoughts is the example of Paul, who was concerned about what others thought and was willing to do whatever it took to promote harmony in the church. We can learn from Paul to love the church in spite of its imperfections.

We can also learn lessons regarding advice—both giving it and receiving it. On the one hand, we should be cautious about giving advice; it is far too easy to tell others what to do when their lives, and not ours, will be affected. We wonder if the elders ever regretted putting pressure on Paul. Over the next five years, did any of them ever say, "If it hadn't been for us, Paul wouldn't be in prison. He would be out preaching the gospel"? On the other hand, we should be cautious about accepting advice. All advice should be doubly weighed—in the inspired balances of God's truth and in the practical balances of possible consequences.

---

[24]Clarke, 860.

Perhaps most important, this passage can teach us lessons regarding God's wisdom and God's graciousness. Whether or not Paul made a mistake, God used the situation for His plans and purposes. The incident fulfilled the prophecy that imprisonment awaited Paul in Jerusalem (20:22, 23) and initiated the sequence of events that later resulted in Paul's reaching Rome. It is comforting to know that as long as our motives are pure and our hearts are stayed on Him, God can work in our lives even when we make errors in judgment.

Rumors (21:21)

Rumors are insidious things. Shakespeare called them "foul whisperings."[25] A breeder of horses named one speedy steed "Rumors." When asked why he had given this peculiar name to his horse, he grinned and said, "Because rumors travel fast."

Dangerous Suppositions Today (21:27–40)

The Asiatic Jews, the mob, and the Roman commander were not the first to be guilty of making false suppositions. Mary and Joseph "supposed [Jesus] to be in the caravan, and went a day's journey" without Him (Lk. 2:44). Some supposed that the apostles were drunk on the Day of Pentecost (Acts 2:15). When the earthquake woke up the jailer, "he drew his sword and was about to kill himself, supposing that the prisoners had escaped" (16:27). (For other examples of Bible suppositions, see Mk. 6:49; Lk. 12:51; 13:2, 4; 19:11; Jn. 11:31; 13:29; 20:15; Acts 14:19; 27:13.)

As disastrous as those assumptions might have been, of greater concern are suppositions such as these: Some suppose that they will be saved because of their religious background (Mt. 3:9); some "suppose that godliness is a means of gain" (1 Tim. 6:5); some suppose that they can pass judgment on others while committing the same offenses themselves, yet escape the judgment of God (Rom. 2:3).

Assumption did not die with those who lived in the first century. Dangerous suppositions abound today.

---

[25]Quoted in Herbert V. Prochnow and Herbert V. Prochnow, Jr., *A Dictionary of Wit, Wisdom, & Satire* (New York: Popular Library, 1964), 116.

Suppositions Relating to Principles. Of special concern are the many presuppositions held in the religious world. Bobby Duncan wrote about this situation some years ago:

> . . . the doctrine of "salvation by faith only" could grow out of the fact that one reads . . . one of the many passages which teach that salvation is by faith, and then, without considering other passages that deal with the subject, jumps to the conclusion that salvation is by faith only. One may read that "salvation is not of works," and then jump to the conclusion that one cannot do anything to be saved. He may read that sinners are saved by the blood of Christ, then jump to the conclusion that the church is a non-essential institution.
>
> [He] may read that "Christ tasted death for every man," then jump to the conclusion that all people will be saved. He may read that "whosoever shall call upon the name of the Lord shall be saved," then jump to the conclusion that to be saved, all an alien [sinner] must do is pray for forgiveness of sins. He may read a passage that teaches that believers are not condemned, then jump to the conclusion that it is impossible for Christians to fall from grace. . . . All these false doctrines can be avoided simply by considering all the facts before coming to a conclusion. . . . [O]ne does not have the truth on any Bible subject until he has all the Bible says about the subject.[26]

Suppositions Relating to People. In many of our lives, however, the more deadly suppositions are those we make about others. Once a man was hoeing his garden while sitting in a chair. A passerby thought, "That's the laziest man I ever saw!" Then he noticed a pair of crutches leaning against the gardener's chair—and his face turned red.

---

[26]Bobby Duncan, "Paul in the Temple and in Prison at Jerusalem," *Studies in Acts* (Denton, Tex.: Valid Publications, 1985), 203.

In an article titled "Assumptions," Chris Smith observed that there is often a great gulf between what we suppose and what is true:

> How often do we assume our information is correct, only later to find out we were wrong?
>
> *Assumption:* "She thinks she's better than everyone else."
>
> *Truth:* She's shy, wishes she had more friends, and wonders why she doesn't.
>
> *Assumption:* "The elders did nothing about it!"
>
> *Truth:* The elders held two special meetings about it, prayed extensively, made the best decision possible, and told no one because of respect for confidentiality.
>
> *Assumption:* "Wilma's really upset! She told Wilbur, who told Josephine, and she told me. . . ."
>
> *Truth:* Who knows?! Ask Wilma.
>
> Can we always double-check our information? Perhaps not. It is too time consuming. Should we be careful about making assumptions? When it concerns people, absolutely! A person's reputation is too valuable a commodity to ruin through incomplete information, half truths, and gossip.[27]

When the Roman commander found out the facts of Paul's case, he was surprised. We, too, might be surprised if we knew what others had to deal with day after day. Someone has written, "The crosses people bear are seldom in sight."

Jesus said long ago: "Do not judge so that you will not be judged. For in the way you judge, you will be judged . . ." (Mt. 7:1, 2). Certainly we want other people to believe the best of us, and love demands that we put the best construction on the actions of others (1 Cor. 13:7).

---

[27]This article originally appeared in the bulletin of the Duncanville church of Christ, Duncanville, Texas, early in 1995.

CHAPTER 22
PAUL'S IMPRISONMENT AT JERUSALEM (PART 1)

PAUL'S DEFENSE (22:1–21)

This chapter contains the second account of Paul's conversion found in Acts. The first was in chapter 9; a third is in chapter 26. This account differs from the one in Acts 9 in that it is told from Paul's point of view. Each account was adapted for the intended audience. The three accounts supplement each other.

Paul, the Persecutor (22:1–5)

¹"Brethren and fathers, hear my defense which I now offer to you."

²And when they heard that he was addressing them in the Hebrew dialect, they became even more quiet; and he said,

³"I am a Jew, born in Tarsus of Cilicia, but brought up in this city, educated under Gamaliel, strictly according to the law of our fathers, being zealous for God just as you all are today. ⁴I persecuted this Way to the death, binding and putting both men and women into prisons, ⁵as also the high priest and all the Council of the elders can testify. From them I also received letters to the brethren, and started off for Damascus in order to bring even those who were there to Jerusalem as prisoners to be punished."

Verse 1. As he stood on the stairs overshadowing the Court of the Gentiles, Paul began, **"Brethren and fathers, hear my defense which I now offer to you."** Compare Paul's opening words with those of Stephen in 7:2. Since Stephen was referring to members of the Sanhedrin when he said **brethren and fathers**, some wonder if members of the Council were present in the murderous crowd in chapter 21. It is possible, perhaps even probable. Of course, Paul's reference to "fathers" could simply be a respectful acknowledgment of the older men in the crowd. He acknowledged those present as family by calling them "brethren." This designation is not a reference to *Christian* brethren, but rather to his fellow Jews (see comments on 9:17). Paul began his defense by identifying with his listeners.

The Greek word translated **defense** is ἀπολογία (*apologia*), a compound word combining ἀπό (*apo*, "from") with λόγος (*logos*, "word" or "reason"). *Apologia* is the word from which we get "apology." This "apology," however, is neither an acknowledgment of wrongdoing nor an appeal for forgiveness, but it is what Peter had in mind when he said to be ready "to make a defense to everyone who asks . . . an account for the hope that is in you" (1 Pet. 3:15). The study of arguments in favor of the Christian faith is called "Apologetics." *Apologia* is found eight times in Acts, and seven of those occurrences are in chapters 22 through 26 when Paul defended himself again and again before both Jews and Romans (22:1; 24:10; 25:8, 16; 26:1, 2, 24). It has been suggested that the final one-fourth of Acts could serve as a legal defense as Luke showed again and again that Paul was not guilty of breaking any law of Rome. The "apologetic purpose" of Acts is discussed in the *Introduction, The Purpose, apologetic.*

Verse 2. And when they heard that he was addressing them in the Hebrew dialect, they became even more quiet. Paul had spoken to the commander in Greek (21:37), but he spoke to his fellow Jews in their native tongue, Aramaic (see comments on 21:40). Most, if not all, of them would have understood Paul if he had spoken in Greek. Paul, however, wanted to establish rapport with them.

Verse 3. When Paul had faced Jews in synagogues throughout much of the Roman Empire, he had "reasoned with them from the Scriptures . . . saying, 'This Jesus whom I am proclaiming to you is the Christ'" (17:2, 3). We might expect to read that he did the same in Jerusalem, but the situation was different.

These people were crying for his blood; he first had to win their confidence before they would listen to him about Jesus.

Paul wanted them to know that *he understood them.* Like them, he had been brought up to revere the Law. Since he had not lived in Jerusalem in more than twenty years and many did not know him personally, he reviewed his Jewish heritage. **"I am a Jew, born in Tarsus of Cilicia."** However, he quickly assured his listeners that being born in Tarsus did not mean he had a pagan mentality; he had been **brought up in** Jerusalem. In this city he had been **educated under Gamaliel.** The Greek text has παρὰ τοὺς πόδας *(para tous podas),* "at the feet of" (see KJV). In those days, students literally sat on the floor at the feet of their teachers, who sat on benches or chairs. Gamaliel, who had died only five years earlier, was considered one of the greatest rabbis who had ever lived (see comments on 5:34). Paul's religious credentials could not be faulted.

Although Paul did not directly address the charges against himself, he showed that they had no factual basis. Two charges against Paul were that (1) his preaching spoke against the Jewish people and (2) he dishonored the Law (21:28). In Paul's opening remarks, he said, in effect, "On the contrary, I am proud to be a Jew, and I have always had a profound respect for the Law." (For a third charge against Paul, see comments on v. 17.)

Having been educated **strictly according to the law,** Paul was **zealous for God**—how zealous, he would soon tell them. Before he did so, he added the astonishing words **"just as you all are today."** He complimented the zeal of those who, moments before, had been zealously beating him to death. Paul's compliment to these Jews was similar to his compliment to the Athenians (17:22). Both compliments focused on certain positive facts, leaving other truths unspoken for the moment. For a full statement of Paul's feelings about the zeal of the Jews, see Romans 10:2, which had been written a few months earlier.

Verse 4. Paul let them know that he even understood why they wanted to kill him—because in the past he had felt the same way about Jews who had become Christians: **"I persecuted this Way to the death, binding and putting both men and women into prisons"** (see comments on 9:1). The term **Way** is again used in reference to Christianity (see comments on 9:2).

Verse 5. Paul's former persecution of Christians was no secret to the leaders of the Jewish people. Concerning those facts, Paul said, **"The high priest and all the Council of the elders can testify."** "Elders" here does not refer to elders of the church, but to older Jewish leaders. **The Council of the elders** is one way to refer to the Sanhedrin. Caiaphas had been the high priest during the time when Paul was persecuting Christians (see comments on 4:6). When Paul spoke on the steps of the Fortress Antonia, the **high priest** was Ananias (23:2). It is possible that some present members of the Sanhedrin—perhaps even the high priest—had been part of the Council that had commissioned Paul to go to Damascus. If so, these could confirm his words. It is also possible that Paul was suggesting *the records* of the Sanhedrin would confirm what he was saying. It was from the Jewish leaders that Paul **received letters to the brethren, and started off for Damascus in order to bring even those who were there to Jerusalem as prisoners to be punished** (see comments on 9:2). As mentioned earlier, the **brethren** referred to were fellow Jews, not Christian brethren.

Paul's Conversion in Damascus (22:6–16)

⁶"But it happened that as I was on my way, approaching Damascus about noontime, a very bright light suddenly flashed from heaven all around me, ⁷and I fell to the ground and heard a voice saying to me, 'Saul, Saul, why are you persecuting Me?' ⁸And I answered, 'Who are You, Lord?' And He said to me, 'I am Jesus the Nazarene, whom you are persecuting.' ⁹And those who were with me saw the light, to be sure, but did not understand the voice of the One who was speaking to me. ¹⁰And I said, 'What shall I do, Lord?' And the Lord said to me, 'Get up and go on into Damascus, and there you will be told of all that has been appointed for you to do.' ¹¹But since I could not see because of the brightness of that light, I was led by the hand by those who were with me and came into Damascus.

¹²"A certain Ananias, a man who was devout by the stan-

dard of the Law, and well spoken of by all the Jews who lived there, [13]came to me, and standing near said to me, 'Brother Saul, receive your sight!' And at that very time I looked up at him. [14]And he said, 'The God of our fathers has appointed you to know His will and to see the Righteous One and to hear an utterance from His mouth. [15]For you will be a witness for Him to all men of what you have seen and heard. [16]Now why do you delay? Get up and be baptized, and wash away your sins, calling on His name.'"

Verses 6–8. Paul, after stressing that he understood them, asked them, in effect, to try *to understand him*. On his trip to Damascus, the farthest thing from his mind had been becoming a follower of Jesus—but something astonishing had happened on the road. He had not gone looking for the Lord, but the Lord had come looking for him (see comments on 9:3–5).

> But it happened that as I was on my way, approaching Damascus about noontime, a very bright light suddenly flashed from heaven all around me, and I fell to the ground and heard a voice saying to me, "Saul, Saul, why are you persecuting Me?" And I answered, "Who are You, Lord?" And He said to me, "I am Jesus the Nazarene, whom you are persecuting."

Paul did not use the word "resurrection," but most listeners would understand that Paul was saying that Jesus was not dead, thus that He had been raised. The official position in Jerusalem was that the body of Jesus had been stolen (Mt. 28:11–15). Paul's account showed the story to be a lie—and no one protested.

Verse 9. Paul continued his narration, **"And those who were with me saw the light, to be sure, but did not understand the voice of the One who was speaking to me"** (see comments on 9:7). Some of those who had accompanied Paul from Jerusalem to Damascus probably still resided in Jerusalem and could verify the truthfulness of his statements. Of greater significance, was the change in Paul. How could his hearers explain the startling transformation in his life if he had *not* seen Jesus in a vision?

Verse 10. Paul then had said, **"What shall I do, Lord?"** This question was a cry for relief from the burden of guilt: "What shall I do, Lord, to make amends for, and to be forgiven of, my misguided zeal?" It was even more than that. Up to that point in his life, Paul had thought that he knew exactly who he was, where he was going, and how he was going to get there. Suddenly, his life had been turned upside down. His self-image had been demolished, his agenda destroyed. He no longer had any plans for the future. He was thus also asking, "What shall I do, Lord, with the rest of my life?" Until we are willing to ask that question, Jesus can never make a difference in our lives.

The Lord had told Paul, **"Get up and go on into Damascus, and there you will be told of all that has been appointed for you to do"** (see comments on 9:6). He had been convicted on the road and converted in Damascus.

Verses 11–13. The apostle continued the remarkable account: **"But since I could not see because of the brightness of that light, I was led by the hand by those who were with me and came into Damascus"** (see comments on 9:8). Then Paul told his audience about a preacher named **Ananias.** He was **a man who was devout by the standard of the Law, and well spoken of by all the Jews who lived** in Damascus. Ananias was also a Christian, but Paul spoke of aspects of his character which would make a favorable impression on his Jewish audience. After some discussion with the Lord (see comments on 9:10–16), Ananias had come to Paul and said, **"Brother Saul, receive your sight!"** At that moment, Paul **looked up at him,** having his sight restored (see comments on 9:17, 18).

Verses 14, 15. Then Ananias had said, **"The God of our fathers has appointed you to know His will and to see the Righteous One and to hear an utterance from His mouth."** Ananias was referring to the vision of Jesus that Paul had seen on the road to Damascus. **The Righteous One** was a term for the Messiah (3:14; 7:52; 1 Jn. 2:1; see Is. 53:11), of whom Paul was an eyewitness. The phrase **a witness . . . of what you have seen and heard** is one of the best biblical descriptions of the primary meaning of the word "witness" (see comments on 1:7, 8). Seeing the resurrected Lord and hearing His voice was foundational for Paul's apostleship and ministry (1 Cor. 9:1; 15:8).

Paul knew that the real reason he was hated by the Jews was that he preached to Gentiles. Specifically, he was hated because he preached that Gentiles could be saved without first becoming Jewish proselytes. He wanted the crowd to understand that it was not his idea—but the Lord's—to go to the Gentiles. The Lord had hinted at this through the words of Ananias which were spoken to Paul: **"You will be a witness for Him *to all men"*** (emphasis added). Ananias did not specifically mention Gentiles, but they would be included in "all men."

Verse 16. Paul's divine mission began with his own obedience to the gospel. Ananias said, **"Now why do you delay? Get up and be baptized, and wash away your sins, calling on His name."** Paul did not hesitate to obey the command to be **baptized** (see comments on 9:18). Baptism is spoken of as a "washing" in other contexts as well (1 Cor. 6:11; Eph. 5:26; Tit. 3:5; Heb. 10:22). The nature of this "washing" is spiritual, not physical (1 Pet. 3:21). It was at this point that Paul was cleansed from his **sins** by the blood of Christ (see comments on 2:38).

Calling on his name involves an acceptance of all that Christ is. Some ways in which this is expressed during the baptismal ceremony are (1) the confession of His name before the baptism and (2) the invoking of His name during the baptism. We must also continue "to call on His name" *after* being baptized. (See the description of Christians in 9:14; see also Mt. 10:32, 33.)

Paul Is Sent to the Gentiles (22:17–21)

[17]**"It happened when I returned to Jerusalem and was praying in the temple, that I fell into a trance,** [18]**and I saw Him saying to me, 'Make haste, and get out of Jerusalem quickly, because they will not accept your testimony about Me.'** [19]**And I said, 'Lord, they themselves understand that in one synagogue after another I used to imprison and beat those who believed in You.** [20]**And when the blood of Your witness Stephen was being shed, I also was standing by approving, and watching out for the coats of those who were slaying him.'** [21]**And He said to me, 'Go! For I will send you far away to the Gentiles.'"**

Verse 17. Paul was ready to speak of his divine commission. He skipped over his three years in Damascus and Arabia, and came to his first trip back to Jerusalem after his conversion (9:26–30; Gal. 1:18): **"It happened when I returned to Jerusalem and was praying in the temple, that I fell into a trance."** Some think that Paul had this vision during a later visit (11:27–30; 12:25), but it seems to fit best with his first visit after his conversion (9:26–30). The third charge against Paul was that he had preached "to all men everywhere" against the temple (21:28). On the contrary, when he returned to Jerusalem after his conversion, one of the first places he visited was the temple. There he prayed, and there he saw the Lord. Any unbiased person could recognize that the charges were false.

Verses 18–20. Paul told of his vision:

> **And I saw Him saying to me, "Make haste, and get out of Jerusalem quickly, because they will not accept your testimony about Me." And I said, "Lord, they themselves understand that in one synagogue after another I used to imprison and beat those who believed in You. And when the blood of Your witness Stephen was being shed, I also was standing by approving, and watching out for the coats of those who were slaying him."**

Like Peter when he saw the vision of clean and unclean animals (10:13, 14), Paul had argued with the Lord. This parallel is one of many between the lives of Peter and Paul included by Luke in Acts. Paul had said, in effect, "Lord, surely they will accept my testimony when they remember what I used to do and see how I have changed." For Paul's persecution of the church, see comments on 8:3. For his participation in the stoning of Stephen, see comments on 7:58; 8:1.

Verse 21. Paul had wanted to stay in Jerusalem with his fellow Jews rather than going elsewhere. However, the Lord had been aware that, instead of listening to Paul, his former associates would consider him a traitor and try to kill him (9:29). The Lord's response to Paul's hesitation left no room for argument:

"Go!" Then He had emphasized Paul's special commission: **"For I will send you far away to the Gentiles."** The Lord chose Paul to be the "apostle to the Gentiles" (see Gal. 2:7, 8). In addition to addressing unbelieving Jews, some writers think that Paul may also have been making a defense to any *Christian* Jews in the crowd who resented his ministry to the Gentiles.

A PERPLEXED COMMANDER (22:22–30)

22They listened to him up to this statement, and then they raised their voices and said, "Away with such a fellow from the earth, for he should not be allowed to live!" 23And as they were crying out and throwing off their cloaks and tossing dust into the air, 24the commander ordered him to be brought into the barracks, stating that he should be examined by scourging so that he might find out the reason why they were shouting against him that way. 25But when they stretched him out with thongs, Paul said to the centurion who was standing by, "Is it lawful for you to scourge a man who is a Roman and uncondemned?" 26When the centurion heard this, he went to the commander and told him, saying, "What are you about to do? For this man is a Roman." 27The commander came and said to him, "Tell me, are you a Roman?" And he said, "Yes." 28The commander answered, "I acquired this citizenship with a large sum of money." And Paul said, "But I was actually born a citizen." 29Therefore those who were about to examine him immediately let go of him; and the commander also was afraid when he found out that he was a Roman, and because he had put him in chains.

30But on the next day, wishing to know for certain why he had been accused by the Jews, he released him and ordered the chief priests and all the Council to assemble, and brought Paul down and set him before them.

Verse 22. The word "Gentiles" was as far as Paul got in his narrative. He probably planned to tell how God had blessed his work among the Gentiles. Almost certainly he intended to make an appeal to his hearers to believe in the resurrected Lord. He never had that opportunity. When Paul said "Gentiles," the mob erupted. **They listened to him up to this statement, and then they raised their voices and said, "Away with such a fellow from the earth, for he should not be allowed to live!"** The Greek word λόγος (*logos*), translated **statement,** can also be translated "word" (see KJV). The text could be translated: "And they heard him as far as to *this word* [Gentiles]." Paul's last statement was explosive only because of the word "Gentiles."

Verse 23. Luke noted that **they were crying out and throwing off their cloaks and tossing dust into the air.** We do not know the precise significance of their actions. Perhaps they threw off their cloaks preparing to stone Paul (see v. 20), but all they could find to throw was dust (see 2 Sam. 16:13). Perhaps they simply "vented their rage like maddened beasts,"[1] tossing up dust as an enraged bull paws the ground. It has also been suggested that their action was similar to Paul's shaking the dust off his garments to indicate that those who opposed him had been rejected (13:51; 18:6). All we know is that when they heard the word "Gentiles," they went berserk. Paul was specifically charged with taking Greeks, that is, Gentiles, into the sacred part of the temple (21:28). The mention of Gentiles apparently brought this fact back to the minds of Paul's hearers.

Verse 24. If the Roman commander had hoped to discover the cause of the disturbance from Paul's speech (21:37, 40), he was disappointed. He probably did not understand Aramaic, and even if he did or had someone to translate for him, he probably wondered why the word "Gentile" triggered such a violent reaction. He was as much in the dark at the end of Paul's defense as at the beginning.

Frustrated, **the commander ordered him to be brought into the barracks** to quieten the mob. Then he ordered that Paul **should be examined by scourging so that he might find out the reason why they were shouting against him that way.** This was standard operating procedure for the Romans. They did not expect a criminal to tell the truth unless it was beaten out of

---

[1]J. W. McGarvey, *New Commentary on Acts of Apostles,* vol. 2 (Delight, Ark.: Gospel Light Publishing Co., n.d.), 220.

him. Throughout history, many cruel methods have been devised to force "the truth" from those under suspicion.

Other than crucifixion, **scourging** was the most cruel punishment meted out by the Romans. Four or five leather thongs were attached to a stout wooden handle. Imbedded in the thongs were bits of bone and metal. When wielded by a zealous executioner, the scourge opened the flesh at every lash, exposing muscles and bones. Many thus **examined** were crippled for life; some died; few survived in their right minds. Paul had been beaten many times (2 Cor. 11:24, 25), but he had never undergone Roman scourging.

Verse 25. The commander did not accompany the execution party to the torture chamber; perhaps he had no stomach for the ordeal. The chamber may have been the same place Jesus had been scourged at the orders of Pilate (Mt. 27:26; Mk. 15:15; Jn. 19:1). Paul's clothing was stripped from him; then he was tied to the flogging pillar. Often both the hands and the feet were bound to the pillar. If this scenario was the case, this event may have been part of the fulfillment of Agabus' acted-out prophecy (21:11).

As the wielder of the flagellum prepared to strike, the apostle spoke to the officer in charge: **But when they stretched him out with thongs, Paul said to the centurion who was standing by, "Is it lawful for you to scourge a man who is a Roman and uncondemned?"** The statement **they stretched him out with thongs** could mean that they hoisted him into the air with the thongs, but the more common procedure was to be stretched over the whipping post. As in the case of the beating in Acts 16 where Paul did not reveal his **Roman** citizenship until later, we have to ask, "Why now? Why not earlier?" Again, we cannot answer with certainty. Perhaps he did not have opportunity before. Maybe he waited for maximum effect.

This instance is the second time in Acts that Paul insisted on his rights as a Roman citizen (see 16:37). A third occasion is found in 25:11. Each time Paul did so, it was not so much to benefit him personally as to benefit the cause of Christ (see comments on 16:38, 39; 25:10–12). In Acts 22, Paul announced his citizenship because the Lord's cause would not be helped, but hurt, by his death. Paul was not a masochist; he harbored no "martyr complex." He was ready to die if it was the Lord's will (21:13; Phil. 1:21, 23), but he had no desire to throw his life away needlessly.

Verse 26. Paul's simple question turned the torturers into the tortured. It was against the law to bind and scourge a Roman citizen (see comments on 16:23); he knew it, and they knew it. They also knew that they could lose their positions and perhaps their lives if they proceeded with the beating, if Paul actually was a Roman citizen. The centurion wasted no time finding the commander: **He went to the commander and told him, saying, "What are you about to do? For this man is a Roman."**

Verse 27. Alarmed, **the commander came and said to him, "Tell me, are you a Roman?" And he said, "Yes."** Paul's answer may have been somewhat hard to believe. According to the apocryphal *Acts of Paul and Thecla*, Paul was "baldheaded, bowlegged, strongly built, a man small in size, with meeting eyebrows, with a rather large nose." According to W. M. Ramsay, "This plain and unflattering account of the apostle's personal appearance seems to embody a very early tradition."[2] At his best, the small, balding Jew did not appear overly impressive (2 Cor. 10:10). Now, standing stripped, his body covered with old scars (Gal. 6:17) and fresh cuts and bruises, he looked more like a three-time loser than a refined Roman citizen.

Verse 28. We can hear skepticism, or possibly surprise, in the official's voice as he replied, **"I acquired this citizenship with a large sum of money."** Legally, Roman citizenship was acquired by being born in Rome or a Roman colony, or by having citizenship bestowed by the government for unusual service rendered. It could also be acquired illegally by bribing officials, which is evidently what the commander had done. Since the commander's first name was Claudius (23:26) and since it was a common practice to take the name of the one bestowing freedom, many assume that the commander obtained his citi-

---

[2]Quoted in A. T. Robertson, "Paul, the Apostle," *The International Standard Bible Encyclopedia*, ed. James Orr (Grand Rapids, Mich.: Wm. B. Eerdmans Publishing Co., 1960), 4:2277.

zenship when Claudius was emperor (A.D. 41–54). This type of bribery reached scandalous proportions under Claudius.[3] The commander was probably thinking, "How could a Jewish vagabond ever come up with that much cash?" **"But,"** Paul answered calmly, **"I was actually born a citizen."**

The fact that Paul was born in Tarsus had not made him a Roman citizen; Tarsus was a free city, but not a Roman colony. Therefore, his father or grandfather before him must have been a citizen. How that citizenship was obtained, we do not know. Presumably, an ancestor of Paul had rendered special service to the Roman government—perhaps to Pompey or Mark Antony, both of whom had ties with Tarsus. The alternative to this would be that one or the other had obtained citizenship through bribery, an unlikely act for a strict Pharisee.

Roman citizenship was highly prized in New Testament times. The truth of this statement is apparent from the fact that the Roman commander had paid "a large sum of money" to acquire that citizenship. A Roman citizen had rights not enjoyed by everyone. Paul's Roman citizenship . . .

> . . . availed for him not in one city only, but throughout the [Roman] world and secured for him everywhere certain great immunities and rights. Precisely what all of these were we are not certain, but we know that . . . exemption from shameful punishments, such as scourging with rods or whips, and [especially] crucifixion, was secured to every [Roman] citizen; also the right of appeal to the emperor with certain limitations.[4]

Many of the rights of a Roman related to the legal system, including the right to trial, the right to know the charges against oneself, and the right to face one's accusers (25:16)—plus the right to appeal to Rome if one believed that he was not being

---

[3] Dio Cassius *History* 60.17.5, 6.

[4] G. H. Trever, "Citizenship," *International Standard Bible Encyclopedia,* ed. James Orr (Grand Rapids, Mich.: Wm. B. Eerdmans Publishing Co., 1960), 1:661.

treated fairly (25:10–12). Some of us take such rights for granted, but they were precious in Paul's day.

Verse 29. Something in Paul's voice or demeanor left no question in the minds of those who heard him: He was what he claimed to be. **Those who were about to examine him immediately let go of him.** We can see them scrambling to loose him, fumbling at the leather cords with trembling fingers. J. W. McGarvey aptly observed: "We can but admire the majesty of a law, which, in a remote province, and within the walls of a prison, could thus dash to the ground the uplifted instruments of torture under the simple declaration, 'I am a Roman citizen.'"[5]

In connection with Paul's claim to Roman citizenship in Philippi (ch. 16), we again struggle with the question of why the authorities seem to have taken Paul at his word. Did Paul carry a first-century equivalent of an identification card—perhaps a birth certificate? (See comments on 16:38, 39.) It has been suggested that the situation in Jerusalem was different from that in Philippi. Paul may have had proof of citizenship somewhere in the city. Further, the commander had Paul in custody long enough to send to Tarsus for verification if desired.

Even the commander **was afraid when he found out that he was a Roman, and because he had put him in chains.** Cicero had said that it was a misdeed to bind a Roman citizen. Later, however, Paul was bound by chains for two years in Rome itself (28:20). Perhaps the commander's fears were not because he had bound Paul with chains when he arrested him, but because Paul had been bound with thongs preparatory to being scourged (v. 25). In verse 29, the original text simply has "he had bound him" (αὐτὸν ἦν δεδεκώς, *auton ēn dedekōs*), rather than "had put him in chains" (see KJV). If the beating had taken place, the commander would probably have lost the citizenship that had cost him so much—maybe even his life. He was no doubt relieved that tragedy had been averted—but had to be even more perplexed. Why did Paul, this innocuous Jew/Roman, arouse so much hatred?

Verse 30. The commander of the Roman occupation forces

---

[5]McGarvey, 221–22.

in Jerusalem had bound Paul, and now he was in a bind. A Roman citizen was in his custody, and it was against Roman law to hold a Roman citizen without informing him of the charges. However, he had no idea what the man had done wrong. The commander had already made three attempts to discover the truth: While rescuing the man from the mob, he had asked the rioters what the problem was, but no one seemed to know. He had given the captive permission to speak to the crowd, but he was no wiser after the man had finished. When he started to beat the truth out of the prisoner, the man had shocked the officials by informing them that he was a Roman citizen.

The officer must have spent a sleepless night trying to decide on a course of action. By morning, he thought he knew the solution. Since the source of the conflict was obviously religious in nature and not political, he would place the matter before the theological experts in the city. **But on the next day, wishing to know for certain why Paul had been accused by the Jews, he released him and ordered the chief priests and all the Council to assemble, and brought Paul down and set him before them.**

Since Paul remained a prisoner, the phrase **he released him** does not mean the commander released him from custody. It probably just means that he had him brought from his cell. The **chief priests** and **the Council** (Sanhedrin) (see comments on 4:1, 5) were commanded to **assemble**. The Sanhedrin met under the authority of Rome. Therefore, the Roman commander had a right to order them to gather together.

The Fortress Antonia towered above the temple complex and was reached by a stairway from the Court of the Gentiles (see comments on 21:31, 35, 40). Paul was **brought down** the stairs. We are not sure whether this was an official meeting of the Sanhedrin or an unofficial meeting, whether they met in their usual place or elsewhere. Note that the commander apparently remained for the meeting (23:28, 29). He was responsible for Paul's safety and for seeing that he did not escape (see 12:18, 19; 16:27). If the commander was present, the Council did not meet in the sacred part of the temple.

Paul's body no doubt throbbed with pain from the beating received the day before in the temple courts, but we can be confidant that he stood straight before the supreme court of the Jewish people. He stood where Peter, John, and the other apostles had stood; where Stephen had stood; where his Lord had stood. Years ago, Paul had sat with the Council (see comments on 7:58; 9:1)—now he stood before them and learned what it was like to look into their cold, hard faces. Some of the faces he recognized; many he did not. A number of the men who had been on the Council more than twenty years earlier would still be alive. Also, some of the young Jewish men who had been Paul's associates would have been selected to the Council by this time.

APPLICATION

Lessons for Preachers and Listeners (Ch. 22)

Every preacher has had an experience similar to Paul's. His sermon is going well; he can tell by the expressions on his listeners' faces that they appreciate his message. Then he speaks a word or makes a statement—perhaps one he considers harmless—and suddenly the faces grow dark and cold. These "loaded" words or topics are like spiritual land mines. They lie hidden, unseen and unknown to the unwary preacher until, in his ignorance, he touches on them—and then they explode in his face. It is obvious that some would take him out and stone him if they were not so civilized—or if it were not illegal.

There is a lesson here for listeners. The word "Gentile" was the hated word for Paul's hearers. Is there a word that touches a nerve, a phrase we cannot stand, a Bible topic that makes us uncomfortable, even angry? The Jews in the temple court revealed the prejudice and intolerance in their hearts by their response to the word "Gentile." The words and themes that upset us may say more about our hearts than we realize. An application can be made here to "loaded" words and topics relevant to the audience. Perhaps the challenge to give liberally or the challenge to make a total commitment of life to the Lord is not popular. Perhaps certain moral issues touch raw nerves. Perhaps no one wants to talk about prejudices that exist. Maybe some church "issues" involve words that make some members angry. Note that unscriptural words and concepts *should* make us unhappy, but we are discussing words that are either biblical or at least harmless in themselves. Listeners should be encouraged to examine their hearts to see if they are open-minded.

There are also lessons here for preachers. As we read Paul's sermon to the crowd, we are impressed with how far he went to avoid offending his listeners. He used Jewish terminology throughout his speech. Other than the Lord's self-identification, he never used the name "Jesus." He did not mention that Ananias was a Christian or that "the Lord" who appeared to him in the temple was Jesus. Why, then, did he eventually use the offensive word "Gentiles"? Because there is a difference between avoiding offense and compromise. Paul wanted to avoid irritating the Jews as far as he could, but he would not compromise. The Lord had said, "I will send you far away to the Gentiles," so that is what Paul reported. When you teach, you can only go so far in trying not to antagonize your students. Men-pleasers will avoid a "word" that offends at all cost; if, however, that "word" is *God's* Word, God-pleasers will preach the truth, no matter what the cost (Gal. 1:10; 2 Tim. 4:1–4).

On the Steps of Fortress Antonia (22:1–21)

Paul's sermon on the steps of Fortress Antonia may be divided into three parts: (1) His Early Conduct (vv. 3–5); (2) His Exciting Conversion (vv. 6–13, 16); (3) His Exacting Commission (vv. 14, 15, 17–21).

Our Apology (22:1–21)

The biblical word "apology" has nothing to do with what we today call "apologizing." Too many who claim to be Christians are ashamed of their faith—and think that they must apologize for their convictions. A Bible apology is not an acknowledgment of wrong, but an argument for right. There are several lessons from our text regarding making "a defense to everyone who asks . . . an account for the hope that is in you" (1 Pet. 3:15):

1. *Be ready.* Sooner or later, like Paul, you will be called on to defend your faith—so prepare yourself sooner, rather than later.

2. *Be courteous.* Shortly before this arrest, Paul had written, "Never pay back evil for evil to anyone. . . . Do not be overcome

by evil, but overcome evil with good" (Rom. 12:17–21). He had written it, but could he live it? With a crazed Jewish mob crying for his blood and insensitive Roman soldiers ready to shred his flesh, he was severely tested. He met the test, remaining calm and courteous. Those who challenge your faith may be unpleasant, but you do not have to be.

3. *Be personal.* You may not know all there is to know about the Bible or be able to answer every question that can be asked, but you can tell others how you became a Christian. Paul's message was basically a recitation of his conversion experience. You will want to continue to learn more about the Bible so that you will grow more adept in defending the faith, but always keep your message personal.

4. *Be Christ-centered.* Although Paul told of his conversion, his purpose was not to call attention to himself, but to the Lord. The name "Jesus the Nazarene" reminded his listeners about the One who had been crucified, and Paul's account of the vision on the road informed them that this same Jesus had been raised. We are not to convert people to ourselves, but to Jesus.

5. *Be flexible.* Paul's basic message was always the same, but his approach on this occasion was different from his approach in the synagogues. Know those who challenge you, and adapt your defense accordingly.

6. *Be challenging.* After Paul told what Jesus had done, he told what man should do. If Jesus was the Messiah, then every man should respond as he had: Each should "Get up, and be baptized, and wash away [his] sins, calling on His name" (v. 16). Then each should commit his life to the Lord. As you defend your faith, your purpose is not to win arguments, but souls. Challenge all who are present to make the same commitment to the Lord that you have made.

7. *Be consistent.* Your defense can be convincing only if your life is consistent with your words. Paul was ready to die for his faith. Can people see that you are ready to live for yours?

8. *Be sensible.* Even though we should be ready to suffer for our faith, we should also exercise common sense. Paul was not willing to suffer when his suffering would not advance the cause of Christ. He did not hesitate to insist on his rights as a Roman

citizen. You do not have to take abuse from unbelievers. Remain courteous, but walk away.

9. *Be persistent.* After you have done your best, do not be disappointed if you fail to convince those who challenged your faith. Paul did not convince the mob. In the next four chapters of Acts (chs. 23—26), three more sermons of Paul are recorded, plus one personal study. As far as the record goes, not a single person was converted, but the apostle was doing what God wanted him to do. If you keep on sharing your faith, you will be doing what God wants you to do, whether or not you see "results." Never, never give up.

Demanding Rights (22:25)

As we consider Paul's rights as a Roman citizen, one aspect is puzzling: Apparently, he sometimes insisted on his rights as a citizen and at other times did not. It is obvious that Paul occasionally insisted on his rights from the incidents in chapters 16, 22, and 25. The fact that he did not always demand his rights may be less obvious.

Consider one of Paul's statements concerning abuse he had undergone. After saying that he had been "beaten times without number," he gave two examples: "Five times I received from the Jews thirty-nine lashes. Three times I was beaten with rods" (2 Cor. 11:23–25). Beating with rods was a Roman punishment. In Acts 16:22, 23, Paul was beaten with rods by Roman authorities in Philippi, but the other two occasions were not recorded by Luke.

When Paul gave up his rights, he was consistent with his teaching in his epistles. Paul taught that *a Christian should be willing to give up rights if doing so would help the cause of Christ.* Note, for instance, his words to the Corinthians: He directed them to give up their legal right to sue a brother because of the detrimental effect this was having on the influence of the church. "Why not rather be wronged?" he wrote. "Why not rather be defrauded?" (1 Cor. 6:7). Paul stressed his own willingness to give up the right to eat meat if it caused his brother to stumble (1 Cor. 8:13). First Corinthians 8—10 is on the subject of eating meat sacrificed to idols. Often the best meat on sale in the public market had first been offered to idols. This presented a problem for new Christians who were formerly idol worshipers; it was hard for them to blot out the source of the meat as they ate it. He also stated that for the good of the congregation he had given up the right to be paid by the church in Corinth (1 Cor. 9:1–23).

Freedom (22:27, 28)

Paul's use of Roman citizenship could be illustrated by comparing it to the rights that Americans enjoy. You may want to find a copy of the U.S. Bill of Rights to use as a visual aid. You may also be able to find reproductions of Norman Rockwell's famous paintings of "The Four Freedoms."

Citizenship (22:27, 28)

Citizenship is a precious gift often taken for granted. Two aspects of citizenship should be emphasized: the rights of citizenship and the responsibilities of citizenship. All the words in the New Testament relating to "citizens" or "citizenship" are derived from πόλις (*polis*), the Greek word for "city." The English word "citizen" is derived from the word "city."

The Rights of Citizenship. With Paul's attitude toward rights in mind, there are some lessons each of us can learn:

(1) Be thankful for any rights you have. Some rights are "natural" or "human" rights. The U.S. Declaration of Independence lists the most basic of these as "life, liberty, and the pursuit of happiness." Note that *happiness* is not the right of every citizen—only the right to *pursue* happiness. Then there are rights guaranteed by the state. The U.S. Bill of Rights, the popular name given to the first ten amendments to the U.S. Constitution, lists such rights as freedom of speech, freedom of religion, freedom of the press, and the right to assemble. These are sometimes called "The Four Freedoms." Another right guaranteed by the Bill of Rights is "the right to a speedy and public trial." This right is spelled out in the sixth amendment. The wording is similar to the rights previously mentioned in the comments concerning Roman citizens: the right "to be informed of the nature and cause of the accusation," the right "to be confronted with the

witnesses against oneself," and so on.

(2) Paul's example teaches that a Christian can scripturally take advantage of his rights as a citizen—especially when it contributes to the ongoing of the kingdom. Here is something to think about: Paul knew what the law was and what his rights were. Some basic knowledge of the law can be valuable for Christians.

(3) The most important thing in life is *not* to "get what one has coming." All over the world, angry people are shaking their fists and shouting, "I want what is best for me. I know my rights, and I insist on them—so my life can be improved!" What the world needs is more citizens shaking their heads and saying, "I want what is best for my country. I know my rights, but I insist on making the sacrifices needed so that my nation can be strengthened." Especially does the world need Christians willing to give up their rights if it will fortify their families, the church, and the society in which they live.

The Responsibilities of Citizenship. Imbedded in the principle that citizens have certain rights is the inescapable conclusion that citizens also have certain responsibilities. If one is unwilling to accept the responsibilities, he should not insist on the rights.

For instance, citizens have responsibilities to the government: Our basic responsibility to the government might be summarized in three words—*pay, pray,* and *obey*: (1) We are to *pay* our taxes. Jesus made this clear in Matthew 22:17–21, and Paul reemphasized it in Romans 13:6, 7. (2) We should *pray* for all government officials (1 Tim. 2:1, 2). (3) We must *obey* the laws of the land. An exception must be made when the laws of the land violate the laws of God (Acts 5:29). In addition to the plain teaching of Paul (Rom. 13:1–5), Peter wrote, "Submit yourselves for the Lord's sake to every human institution, whether to a king as the one in authority, or to governors. . . . For such is the will of God . . ." (1 Pet. 2:13–15).

Another way of expressing our basic responsibility as citizens is that we should be *good* citizens. Concerning civil government, the apostle Paul wrote, "Do you want to have no fear of authority? Do what is good and you will have praise from the same" (Rom. 13:3). Peter also wrote,

> Submit yourselves for the Lord's sake to every human
> institution, . . . as sent by him for . . . the praise of those
> who do right. For such is the will of God that by doing
> right you may silence the ignorance of foolish men (1 Pet.
> 2:13–15).

When Paul stood before the Sanhedrin, he said, "Brethren, I
have lived my life with a perfectly good conscience before God
up to this day" (Acts 23:1). The Greek word translated "lived"
is derived from *polis*. Literally, the apostle said, "I have lived *as
a citizen* with a perfectly good conscience before God up to this
day" (emphasis added). Whether one considered Paul's Roman
citizenship, Tarsus citizenship (21:39), or Jewish citizenship, he
pled innocence regarding their charges—whether religious or
civil.

Much of God's will for Christians contributes directly to the
strength of a nation: Work for a living (2 Thess. 3:10); take care
of your own (1 Tim. 5:8); respect the rights of others (1 Cor. 13:5);
build strong homes (Eph. 5:22—6:4); live peaceable lives (Rom.
12:18); and so forth. The greatest contribution any Christian can
make to his nation is to be righteous (Prov. 14:34).

Throughout Acts, Christians were represented as those who
did not start riots, plan insurrections, or revolt. Others committed such acts and then blamed Christians, but Christians themselves were God-fearing, law-abiding citizens. Luke wanted the
world to know that a good Christian was a good citizen.

Conclusion. We hope you are able to say, "I'm *glad* I am a
citizen of my country." We also hope you act like it by being the
best citizen you can be.

As important as earthly citizenship is, we must realize that
heavenly citizenship is infinitely more important. The Philippians were proud to be citizens of a Roman colony, but Paul
wanted them to know that "our citizenship is in heaven, from
which also we eagerly wait for a Savior, the Lord Jesus Christ"
(Phil. 3:20). He told the Christians at Ephesus, "You are fellow
citizens with the saints" (Eph. 2:19). We may just be "strangers

and exiles on the earth" (Heb. 11:13), but our "names are recorded in heaven" (Lk. 10:20; see Heb. 12:23; Rev. 13:8; 20:12, 15; 21:27).

Space does not permit the listing all of our *rights* as citizens of the heavenly kingdom, but here are a few: We have the right to call God Father (Mt. 6:9). We have the right to claim God's promises (Heb. 8:6; 2 Pet. 1:4). We have the right to cherish God's blessings (Eph. 1:3). As citizens, we are traveling to that "better country . . . a heavenly one" (Heb. 11:16; see Heb. 13:14).

Closely related to our rights are our *responsibilities*. When Paul told the Philippians that their "citizenship is in heaven" (Phil. 3:20), he challenged them: "Conduct yourselves in a manner worthy of the gospel of Christ" (Phil. 1:27). Literally, he said, "Be sure to conduct yourselves *as citizens.*"[6] Living as citizens of the Lord's kingdom includes consulting God's Word (Acts 17:11), cheering the fainthearted (2 Cor. 1:3, 4), congregating with the saints (Heb. 10:25), and combating evil (1 Tim. 6:12).

You may not have had a choice regarding earthly citizenship, but you do have a choice regarding heavenly citizenship. You decide whether or not you want the rights of heavenly citizenship and whether or not you are willing to accept the responsibilities of heavenly citizenship. If you are not a citizen in God's kingdom, the church, let us beg you to be "born again" (Jn. 3:3) by being immersed in water as the Spirit-inspired Word directs (Acts 2:38). Jesus said, "Unless one is born of water and the Spirit he cannot enter into the kingdom of God" (Jn. 3:5).

If you are already a citizen of His kingdom, let us urge you to "keep seeking the things above, where Christ is, seated at the right hand of God. Set your mind on the things above, not on the things that are on earth" (Col. 3:1, 2). On the other hand, if you are a citizen of the kingdom but are no longer a *good* citizen, then "remember from where you have fallen, and repent and do the deeds you did at first . . ." (Rev. 2:5; see Acts 8:22).

---

[6]*Berkeley Version of the New Testament* (emphasis added).

Chapter 23

Paul's Imprisonment at Jerusalem (Part 2)—And His Imprisonment at Caesarea (Part 1)

Jesus was delivering His last public discourse in the temple courts. Near the close, He paused and looked around at Jerusalem and its inhabitants. Then, with heavy heart, He said farewell to the city that had rejected Him:

> Jerusalem, Jerusalem, who kills the prophets and stones those who are sent to her! How often I wanted to gather your children together, the way a hen gathers her chicks under her wings, and you were unwilling. Behold, your house [that is, the temple] is being left to you desolate! For I say to you, from now on you shall not see Me until you say, "Blessed is He who comes in the name of the Lord!" (Mt. 23:37–39).

About 1000 B.C., King David had captured Jerusalem (Jebus) and made it his capital. He had moved the ark to the city, and his son Solomon had later built the temple there. Jerusalem had become known to the Israelites as "the city of God." After the destruction of Jerusalem by the Babylonians in 586 B.C., the Jews in captivity had mourned the city. As soon as possible, they had rebuilt it. For a thousand years, Jerusalem had been the center of the religious, social, and political life of the Jewish people. Nevertheless, because of its constant rebellion against God, Jesus announced that its days as God's holy city were numbered.

Luke devoted as much space to Paul's last few days in Jerusalem as he did to any of the missionary journeys, in spite of the fact that "no new churches were established" and "no theological or ecclesiastical problems [were] solved."[1] Many commentators believe Luke had a reason for this. Some are convinced that "the importance of these chapters is found in their illustration of Israel's rejection of the Gospel."[2]

> Luke devotes considerable space to the record of Paul's last visit to Jerusalem, not because the visit was important in itself, but because it showed the final rejection of the Gospel by Jerusalem.[3]

> [O]ne of the purposes . . . was to show people . . . that God was through with Judaism, and that the Jewish nation, as a nation, was through with God. . . . The things we see here alone would vindicate God in bringing upon Jerusalem the awful destruction foretold by the Lord in Matthew 24, Mark 13, and Luke 21. The Jews were filling up the measure of their fathers, and demonstrating that they were the children of them who had killed the prophets (Matt. 23:31–32).[4]

> The people of the nation had already been involved in three murders: John the Baptist, Christ, and Stephen. They would have committed a fourth had not God delivered Paul through the intervention of the Roman guard. . . . Israel was now set aside; . . . its period of probation was over.[5]

The Bible teaches that Jehovah is a patient God, but there is a limit to His patience. He will tolerate disobedience only so

---

[1]George E. Ladd, *The Young Church: Acts of the Apostles* (Nashville: Abingdon Press, 1964), 78.

[2]Ibid., 79.

[3]George E. Ladd, *Acts*, The Wycliffe Bible Commentary (Nashville: The Southwestern Company, 1962), 1164.

[4]Bobby Duncan, "Paul in the Temple and in Prison at Jerusalem," *Studies in Acts* (Denton, Tex.: Valid Publications, 1985), 199–200.

[5]Warren W. Wiersbe, *Wiersbe's Expository Outlines on the New Testament* (Wheaton, Ill.: Victor Books, 1992), 341.

long. Then He says, "That's enough! You will go no further!" In this chapter, we will see some of the final events that made God say "That's enough!" to the city of Jerusalem.

PAUL BEFORE THE SANHEDRIN (23:1–10)

Paul Confronts the High Priest (23:1–5)

¹Paul, looking intently at the Council, said, "Brethren, I have lived my life with a perfectly good conscience before God up to this day." ²The high priest Ananias commanded those standing beside him to strike him on the mouth. ³Then Paul said to him, "God is going to strike you, you whitewashed wall! Do you sit to try me according to the Law, and in violation of the Law order me to be struck?" ⁴But the bystanders said, "Do you revile God's high priest?" ⁵And Paul said, "I was not aware, brethren, that he was high priest; for it is written, 'You shall not speak evil of a ruler of your people.'"

Verse 1. The Roman commander had brought Paul before the Sanhedrin to find out what crime had been committed (22:30). During a formal trial, one of the first orders of business was the reading of charges against the accused. That procedure had been waived when Jesus was tried (Mt. 26:59–62) and when the apostles were tried (Acts 4:5–7) because the Council had no charges to bring. They hoped the words of the accused would provide them with a formal charge. Their strategy was likely the same in Paul's trial; he was allowed to speak first in hopes that he would condemn himself by his speech. Apparently, the charge that he had desecrated the temple (21:28) was not brought up, indicating that they realized it was unsubstantiated.

When Paul had spoken to the mob, he had gotten their attention with a wave of his hand (21:40); now he was **looking intently at the Council** until the assembly grew quiet and every eye was fastened on him. This strategy is an effective way to get the attention of a noisy crowd. Other reasons have also been suggested for Paul's intent look, including "sizing up the crowd," (that is, seeing whom he recognized), seeing who looked sympathetic, and so forth. Some have even suggested that the words simply indicate Paul was nearsighted.

Boldly, he said, **"Brethren, I have lived my life with a perfectly good conscience before God up to this day."** Paul started his speech by identifying with his Jewish audience as **brethren** (see 13:26, 38; 22:1, 5; 28:17). Some have suggested that Paul intentionally insulted the Council by not addressing them more formally as "brethren and fathers" (see 7:2), but it is unlikely he would immediately court the displeasure of this group that held his life in their hands.

The Greek word translated **have lived my life** is from πολιτεύω (*politeuō*), which refers to "living as a citizen." The related noun πολίτης (*politēs*, "citizen") is the word from which we get "politics." Paul was saying that he had lived as a good Jewish citizen and had not broken the Law. He had lived **with a perfectly good conscience before God up to this day** (see 24:16; 2 Cor. 1:12; 1 Tim. 3:9). Paul was not saying he was sinless. The conscience guides aright only to the extent that it is rightly guided—that is, to the extent it has been rightly taught. Paul was simply saying that he had always lived according to what he *thought* was right. Even when persecuting Christians, Paul believed he was doing God a service (26:9). He was saying, "I know in my heart that I am not guilty of the things I have been accused of. I stand before you innocent of all charges!" It has been suggested that Paul picked up where he was forced to leave off when he was speaking to the mob the day before (22:21, 22). It is certainly possible, maybe even probable, that some members of the Sanhedrin had heard him speak to the mob.

Verse 2. The **high priest**, who officiated at such gatherings, reacted to Paul's audacious words by commanding **those standing beside him to strike him on the mouth**—both to punish him and to silence him. It was easier for the high priest to strike Paul than to answer him—for the high priest had no provable accusation to bring against him. Jesus had also been struck on the mouth during His trials (Jn. 18:22).

The high priest's name was Ananias. He should not be confused with "Annas the high priest" (4:6) or one of the Ananiases introduced earlier in Acts (5:1; 9:10). According to historians,

Ananias the high priest was one of the most ungodly and un-scrupulous men ever to hold that position. He stole tithes from his own priests to make himself richer, and had people mur-dered so he could stay in power.[6] He was "notorious as a glut-ton, a thief, a rapacious robber, and a quisling in the Roman service."[7]

Verse 3. The savage blow did not silence the apostle. He lashed back: **"God is going to strike you, you whitewashed wall! Do you sit to try me according to the Law, and in viola-tion of the Law order me to be struck?"** The Law was clear that no one was to be punished until he had been tried and found guilty (Lev. 19:15; Deut. 25:1, 2). Even the oral law said, "He who strikes the cheek of an Israelite, strikes, as it were, the glory of God."[8] Hebrews 5:1, 2 tells how the high priest *should* have conducted himself:

> For every high priest taken from among men is ap-pointed on behalf of men in things pertaining to God, in order to offer both gifts and sacrifices for sins; he can deal gently with the ignorant and misguided, since he himself also is beset with weakness.

Paul's reference to a **whitewashed wall** was familiar to his audience. The prophet Ezekiel had compared false prophets to crumbling walls that had been whitewashed to cover their flaws (Ezek. 13:10–16). Paul accused his tormentor of hypocrisy. His statement is comparable to Jesus' calling the Pharisees "white-washed tombs which on the outside appear beautiful, but in-side . . . are full of dead men's bones" (Mt. 23:27).

The apostle's prediction that **God** would **strike** Ananias for his cruelty came true in less than ten years, when the high priest was assassinated in A.D. 66 by Jewish Zealots because of his pro-Roman sentiments.[9] Does this mean that Paul spoke the first

---

[6]Josephus *Antiquities* 20.9.2, 4.

[7]William Barclay, *The Acts of the Apostles*, The Daily Study Bible Series, rev. ed. (Philadelphia: Westminster Press, 1976), 164.

[8]Ibid.

[9]Josephus *Wars* 2.17.9.

part of verse 3 by inspiration? If he later apologized for the last part of verse 3, it is hard to see how part of Paul's statement could be inspired and part not. Probably, he was voicing the general truth that those who disobey God will ultimately be punished by God, a truth familiar to all who know the Scriptures.

Verses 4, 5. The assembly was shocked at Paul's pointed words. **"Do you revile God's high priest?"** they asked. Paul was taken aback. **"I was not aware, brethren,"** he said, **"that he was high priest; for it is written, 'You shall not speak evil of a ruler of your people.'"** The quotation was from Exodus 22:28. Once more Paul demonstrated that instead of speaking against the Law (21:28), he had a profound respect for it.

Scholars wrestle with two questions. The first is: How could Paul not know he was speaking to the high priest? Some suggest that the apostle's eyesight was not the best (see Gal. 4:15; 6:11). Others think that since this meeting had been called by the Roman government, Ananias was not sitting in his usual place and was not wearing his high-priestly garb. Still others are convinced that since Paul had been in Jerusalem only a few times in the previous two decades, he did not know the high priest by sight. We do not know the explanation. Any or all of these factors may have been involved, and perhaps others we have not considered.

The second question ties closely with the first: Was Paul really apologizing, or were his words merely spoken in irony? Those who believe Paul spoke with irony insist that he was saying, "I did not recognize Ananias as high priest, *for surely a true high priest would not conduct himself in this manner.*" We prefer to take Paul's words at face value. A basic principle of biblical interpretation is that words should be taken in their most obvious meaning unless there is a compelling reason to take them otherwise. There is no convincing reason to take Paul's words in any other way than their natural, normal, usual meaning. Regarding the idea that Ananias was not a *worthy* high priest and that Paul, therefore, refused to accept him as such, one must remember that there were many unworthy high priests before him. When God tells us to respect a position, the worthiness of the one holding that position is not a factor. Paul's quotation from

Exodus fits better with an apology than with irony.

We believe that Luke was simply revealing the humanity of Paul. Surely, at some time or another, all of us have been caught off guard by the callousness of another and, instead of turning the other cheek (Mt. 5:39), have treated others as we were treated. Further, we believe that Paul was genuinely sorry when he realized what he had done, and his apology was sincere. In that, he is an example for us all. However, it should be noted that Paul did not say he had misrepresented the truth; his words were 100 percent accurate. Rather, he was wrong in maligning one who was considered God's leader. Even when we cannot respect the person, we can respect the position.

Since Paul had once been closely associated with the Sanhedrin, perhaps he actually thought he might get a fair hearing from them. The hatred on the face of the high priest and the increasing animosity in the assembly drove any such thought from his mind. Now his main concern was to get out of the Council alive. Incidentally, the high priest Ananias' hatred for Paul later caused him to pursue the apostle, even to Caesarea (24:1; see 25:2, 3).

The Council Divides over the Resurrection (23:6–10)

⁶But perceiving that one group were Sadducees and the other Pharisees, Paul began crying out in the Council, "Brethren, I am a Pharisee, a son of Pharisees; I am on trial for the hope and resurrection of the dead!" ⁷As he said this, there occurred a dissension between the Pharisees and Sadducees, and the assembly was divided. ⁸For the Sadducees say that there is no resurrection, nor an angel, nor a spirit, but the Pharisees acknowledge them all. ⁹And there occurred a great uproar; and some of the scribes of the Pharisaic party stood up and began to argue heatedly, saying, "We find nothing wrong with this man; suppose a spirit or an angel has spoken to him?" ¹⁰And as a great dissension was developing, the commander was afraid Paul would be torn to pieces by them and ordered the troops to go down and take him away from them by force, and bring him into the barracks.

Verse 6. Paul knew well the composition of the Sanhedrin. Sadducees were in the majority, but many Pharisees were also present—a vocal minority. Paul also knew well the doctrinal differences between the two sects (see comments on v. 8). Thus **perceiving that one group were Sadducees and the other Pharisees, Paul began crying out in the Council, "Brethren, I am a Pharisee, a son of Pharisees; I am on trial for the hope and resurrection of the dead!"** The fact that Paul had to cry out indicates that the assembly was becoming noisy. Perhaps they were even on the verge of attacking him.

Some have objected to Paul's words **"I am a Pharisee."** Keep in mind that (1) Paul was referring to what was commendable in the position of the Pharisees; he certainly was not referring to the Pharisaic abuses condemned by Jesus. (2) He was emphasizing the way he had been reared (26:5). To Paul, his Pharisaic upbringing was something he had put behind him (Phil. 3:1–11), but it was a definite part of his past. The phrase "a son of" was a Hebrew expression that meant "partaking of the nature of." Therefore, Paul's words **"a son of Pharisees"** could mean his ancestors were Pharisees, or it could mean he embodied all that the word "Pharisee" implied.

The phrase **the hope and resurrection of the dead** is a literal translation of the text. This expression means "the hope of [or, in] the resurrection of the dead." Paul had not been charged with preaching Christ's resurrection (21:28), but he knew the reason the leaders of the Jews hated Christians was because they preached that Jesus had been raised from the dead (see 4:2). When Paul said that he was on trial "for the hope and resurrection of the dead," he was forcing the real issue into the open. Throughout his trials, he would insist that the charges against him were contrived and the real issue was the resurrection (24:21; 26:6–8, 21–23; 28:20).

Verse 7. Did Paul anticipate how explosive his words would be? Some have suggested that Paul was simply trying to get the Pharisees on his side in an effort to receive a fair hearing concerning the resurrection of Jesus. Probably, what actually happened was what Paul intended, but we cannot know for sure. At any rate, God used what happened in the meeting to keep

Paul safe. As Paul uttered the words of verse 6, **there occurred a dissension between the Pharisees and Sadducees, and the assembly was divided.**

Verse 8. Among the many differences between the Sadducees and the Pharisees, there were three very important ones. (For more information on the Sadducees, see comments on 4:1; 5:17.) **The Sadducees say that** (1) **there is no resurrection** (see Lk. 20:27), (2) **nor an angel,** (3) **nor a spirit.** However, **the Pharisees acknowledge them all.** The Pharisees' belief in the spiritual realm is illustrated in the next verse, where they conceded that "a spirit or an angel" may have spoken to Paul.

Verse 9. And there occurred a great uproar; and some of the scribes of the Pharisaic party stood up and began to argue heatedly, saying, "We find nothing wrong with this man; suppose a spirit or an angel has spoken to him?" The Pharisees had their own grievances against Paul, but they could **find nothing wrong** with his statement about the resurrection or even the possibility that he may have received a heavenly vision. At the end of verse 9, some Greek manuscripts have, "Let us not fight against God" (see KJV). These words are not found in the earliest manuscripts of Acts. They are probably a reflection of another Pharisee's earlier words (5:39).

The statement of the Pharisees did not so much indicate that they were *for* Paul as that they were *against* the Sadducees—and were thrilled to have an opportunity to goad them. Paul's words had the same effect as the man who turns two wild beasts at each other's throats to keep them from devouring him.[10]

Once more, that distinguished body was thrown into a turmoil (see 7:54–58). We can see those aged Jews in their resplendent robes, screaming at each other as the Roman officials looked on in amazement. At the center of the storm was Paul. On one side were the Sadducees, grabbing at him with murder in their eyes. On the other side were the Pharisees, trying to tear him away from them.

Verse 10. For the third time, the Roman officer had to step in

---

[10]This idea was adapted from J. W. McGarvey, *New Commentary on Acts of Apostles,* vol. 2 (Delight, Ark.: Gospel Light Publishing Co., n.d.), 226.

to save Paul's life. **And as a great dissension was developing, the commander was afraid Paul would be torn to pieces by them.** He quickly sent for reinforcements, ordering **the troops to go down and take him away from them by force, and bring him into the barracks.**

AN ENCOURAGING VISION (23:11)

[11]**But on the night immediately following, the Lord stood at his side and said, "Take courage; for as you have solemnly witnessed to My cause at Jerusalem, so you must witness at Rome also."**

Verse 11. Paul had been returned to his prison cell. It was dark, but he could not sleep. G. Campbell Morgan called that night "one of the darkest . . . in the history of Paul."[11] The buffeting the apostle had received in the Council chambers had aggravated the wounds he had received when the mob beat him and had given him fresh aches and pains. The greatest pain, however, was in his heart. Since Luke gave an abbreviated account, as usual, we should be cautious about indicting the church at Jerusalem—but as far as the record goes, he received no help or support from the local congregation during his troubles in Jerusalem. We wish we could read that "prayer for him was being made fervently by the church to God" as it had been for Peter (12:5), but we cannot.

Luke did not tell of Paul's mental state, but it is not hard to reconstruct: He must have been *discouraged*; his cherished plans to improve relationships between Christians had apparently come to nothing. He was surely *disappointed*; he had hoped his fellow Jews would listen to him, but they refused. He had to be *doubtful*; it looked as if there were no way he would ever reach Rome. In his heart, hope had withered.

The Lord, however, is the great rekindler of hope. During His appearance to Paul on the road to Damascus, He had prom-

---

[11]G. Campbell Morgan, *The Acts of the Apostles* (Grand Rapids, Mich.: Fleming H. Revell, 1988), 379.

ised that He would appear to him from time to time (26:16). At least twice before, the Lord had kept that promise when Paul's spirits were at low ebb and danger was near (22:17–21; 18:9, 10). Now the Lord came to him again: **On the night immediately following** Paul's appearance before the Sanhedrin, **the Lord stood at his side.** The phrase "stood at his side" can be taken both literally and symbolically—to indicate that the Lord had not forsaken him. In 2 Timothy 4:16, 17, Paul said, "At my first defense no one supported me, but all deserted me . . . But the Lord stood with me and strengthened me. . . ."

The Lord said, **"Take courage."** The KJV has, "Be of good cheer." He felt Paul's pain (Heb. 4:15) and took care of every area of concern. Paul was *discouraged* over how the situation had turned out, so Jesus brought him a message of *courage*. Warren Wiersbe wrote,

> Jesus often spoke these words during His earthly ministry. He spoke them to the palsied man (Matt. 9:2) and to the woman who suffered with the hemorrhage (Matt. 9:22). He shouted them to the disciples in the storm (Matt. 14:27), and repeated them in the Upper Room (John 16:33). As God's people, we can always take courage in times of difficulty because the Lord is with us and will see us through.[12]

Theoretically, Paul had been defending himself in Jerusalem; practically, he had been witnessing to the Lord's cause. The apostle was *disappointed* because he thought he had failed to convince his fellow Jews, so Jesus gave him a message of *commendation*: **"You have solemnly witnessed to My cause at Jerusalem."** Paul's task was not to convert, but to preach. This he had done, and the Lord acknowledged his efforts. Obvious "success" is not the only indication that we are pleasing to the Lord. If we faithfully discharge our commission, we make the Lord happy.

---

[12]Warren W. Wiersbe, *The Bible Exposition Commentary*, vol. 1 (Wheaton, Ill.: Victor Books, 1989), 495.

Paul was *doubtful* about the future, so Jesus presented him with a word of *confidence*: **"You must witness at Rome also."** For the first time, Paul knew for certain that he would reach Rome. The Spirit had informed him that "bonds and afflictions" awaited him in Jerusalem (20:22, 23), but beyond that the Spirit had said nothing. Now, when it seemed his path to Rome had reached a dead end, the Lord opened a superhighway straight to the capital city.

The Lord did not promise Paul comfort, freedom, or success. He promised only that Paul would reach Rome—but that was all the apostle needed. When the vision faded, Paul's body still ached, and he was still surrounded by prison walls. He still had no idea how he would reach Rome, but none of that mattered. Now he had the Lord's promise. He had fanned the dying embers of Paul's expectations; the flames of hope once more burned brightly in his breast.

It has been suggested that the words "so you must witness at Rome also" could be "the title for the last third of the Book of Acts. Beginning with the sixteenth chapter, the central theme is Paul's progress westward toward Rome."[13]

A MURDEROUS CONSPIRACY EXPOSED (23:12–22)

The Jews Form a Conspiracy (23:12–15)

[12]When it was day, the Jews formed a conspiracy and bound themselves under an oath, saying that they would neither eat nor drink until they had killed Paul. [13]There were more than forty who formed this plot. [14]They came to the chief priests and the elders and said, "We have bound ourselves under a solemn oath to taste nothing until we have killed Paul. [15]Now therefore, you and the Council notify the commander to bring him down to you, as though you were going to determine his

---

[13]Halford E. Luccock, *The Acts of the Apostles in Present-Day Preaching* (Chicago: Willett, Clark & Co., 1942), 152.

case by a more thorough investigation; and we for our part are ready to slay him before he comes near the place."

Verse 12. The Lord's promise was immediately and severely tested. Even as the Lord spoke to Paul of his future, the apostle's enemies were considering how they might prevent him from having a future. Frustrated that Paul had slipped through their fingers in the Court of the Gentiles and again in the Council chambers, the Jews devised a plan they thought was foolproof. **When it was day, the Jews formed a conspiracy and bound themselves under an oath, saying that they would neither eat nor drink until they had killed Paul.** Compare this incident to 1 Samuel 14:24 and 2 Samuel 3:35. For a pagan parallel, see 1 Kings 19:2. Their oath would have been something along these lines: "May the Lord do to us and more also, if we eat or drink before we kill Paul." Are we shocked that God's name would be invoked in connection with such a murderous purpose? Jesus had promised His followers that "a time is coming when anyone who kills you will think he is offering a service to God" (Jn. 16:2; NIV).

Verse 13. There were more than forty who formed this plot. Who were the forty Jews who bound themselves with an oath? Were they the Hellenistic Jews who had tried to kill Paul two decades earlier (9:29)? Were they the Asiatic Jews who had started the riot in the temple a few days before (21:27)? Were they from the Sadducees whom Paul had enraged in the Council (23:6–9)—or at least Sadducee sympathizers? Perhaps all of these and more were involved, for Paul's enemies among the Jews were numerous.

Verse 20 notes that the leaders of the Council agreed to this murderous plot. We have to agree with Warren Wiersbe, who said, "Jerusalem was certainly far from God when more than forty men could conspire in the name of religion to slay a godly Jew" and when "even the chief priests and elders were a part of the crime!"[14] Throughout chapters 21, 22, and 23, there is a stark contrast between the pagan Roman commander Claudius Lysias,

---

[14]Wiersbe, *Wiersbe's Expository Outlines on the New Testament*, 343.

who tried to discover the truth, and the religious Jewish leaders, who dealt in deceit and destruction. The Jewish leaders proved once and for all that their hearts could not be touched with the gospel. They judged themselves unworthy of eternal life (see 13:46).

Verse 14. Those plotting against Paul **came to the chief priests and the elders and said, "We have bound ourselves under a solemn oath to taste nothing until we have killed Paul."** Their plot required the cooperation of the leaders of the Sanhedrin, but knowing the blood-stained reputation of the high priest and his friends (see comments on v. 2), they did not hesitate to approach them concerning their assassination plot.

Verse 15. The plotters continued, **"Now therefore, you and the Council notify the commander to bring him down to you, as though you were going to determine his case by a more thorough investigation."** It is not necessary to suppose that the Pharisees who had defended Paul the previous day were party to this plot. Note that the scribes are never mentioned; most of the scribes were Pharisees. The Sanhedrin was under the control of the Sadducees. The plan was probably to call a meeting of the Sanhedrin and propose that the commander be asked to bring Paul before them again, without mentioning the plot to kill Paul. The Pharisees would probably have agreed to this. The schemers concluded, **"And we for our part are ready to slay him before he comes near the place."** Those who made this plot, plus those in the Council who agreed to go along with it, thus admitted the innocence of Paul. They knew that Paul would never be convicted in a fair trial.

The plot was simple. A representative of the Council would apologize to the Roman commander for the disturbance of the previous day and ask for another opportunity, assuring the officer that the commotion would not be repeated. Since the official was still perplexed regarding Paul's offense, he would probably welcome another opportunity to discover the truth. The forty conspirators would mingle with the crowd in the temple, having razor-sharp daggers hidden in the folds of their robes. As Paul was hustled through the Court of the Gentiles by a small detachment of soldiers, the assassins would converge on them, knives flashing. In moments, the blood of Paul would mingle on the pavement with the blood of his protectors and his murderers. The Western Text adds at the end of verse 15, "even if we must die for it." It has been often pointed out that it is possible to assassinate almost anyone as long as the assassin is willing to give his life to do it. These fanatics hated Paul so much that they were willing to sacrifice their lives to end his. When the deed was announced to the Council, the high priest would shake his head, announce his horror that such a thing had taken place in the temple courts, and dismiss the assembly. It was a plot sure to succeed.

The wise man had proclaimed: "There is . . . no plan [of man] that can succeed against the Lord" (Prov. 21:30; NIV)—and Jesus had assured Paul that he would reach Rome. How, then, could the plot be averted? Would the Lord arrange a *miraculous* escape for Paul? God had proven Himself adept at miraculous jail breaks (5:19; 12:7; 16:26). This action was not to be the Lord's arrangement in chapter 23. Rather, Paul would be protected by God's *providential* care.

The Plot Is Reported to the Commander (23:16–22)

[16]But the son of Paul's sister heard of their ambush, and he came and entered the barracks and told Paul. [17]Paul called one of the centurions to him and said, "Lead this young man to the commander, for he has something to report to him." [18]So he took him and led him to the commander and said, "Paul the prisoner called me to him and asked me to lead this young man to you since he has something to tell you." [19]The commander took him by the hand and stepping aside, began to inquire of him privately, "What is it that you have to report to me?" [20]And he said, "The Jews have agreed to ask you to bring Paul down tomorrow to the Council, as though they were going to inquire somewhat more thoroughly about him. [21]So do not listen to them, for more than forty of them are lying in wait for him who have bound themselves under a curse not to eat or drink until they slay him; and now they are ready and waiting for the promise from you." [22]So the commander let

the young man go, instructing him, "Tell no one that you have notified me of these things."

Verse 16. In God's providence, **the son of Paul's sister heard of their ambush, and he came and entered the barracks and told Paul.** How Luke's words arouse our curiosity! F. F. Bruce called this "one of the most tantalizing incidents in Acts, for all who are interested in Paul's private life and family relationships."[15] This verse is the only certain reference to Paul's family in the Bible. The term "kinsmen" in Romans 16:7, 21 probably refers to fellow Jews (see Rom. 9:3).

Who was this nephew? Why was he in Jerusalem? Perhaps, like his uncle before him, he had been sent to Jerusalem as a student. Maybe his family had come to Jerusalem for the feast of Pentecost and had not yet returned home. Some think that his sister had a house in Jerusalem, but if this were the case and they were friends, it is hard to understand why Paul stayed with Mnason (21:16). Was Paul's nephew a Christian? When Paul became a Christian, his conversion probably alienated him from his family (see Phil. 3:7, 8), but for some reason this nephew was concerned about what happened to him. When Paul returned to Tarsus after his conversion (9:30), had he been able to convert some of his family, including his sister? If the nephew had come to Jerusalem to study, had he come in contact with Christians and been converted, or at least become sympathetic to the Christian cause? If he had not been converted, perhaps the young man simply considered Paul "family" and hated to see him killed.

How did Paul's nephew learn of the proposed ambush? Perhaps he simply heard a rumor; it is hard to keep a matter secret when forty-plus people know about it. Since, however, he (1) heard about it almost at once and (2) was able to repeat the plot almost word for word (compare verses 12 through 15 with verses 20 and 21), it is more likely that he actually overheard the

---

[15]F. F. Bruce, *The Book of Acts,* The New International Commentary on the New Testament, gen. ed. F. F. Bruce, rev. ed. (Grand Rapids, Mich.: Wm. B. Eerdmans Publishing Co., 1988), 432.

plans being made. The NASB 1977 has this alternate reading for **came**, relating this verb to the first part of the sentence: "Or, *having been present* with them." In other words, Paul's nephew heard about their plot because he was in their company. Some believe that Paul's sister had married into a high-priestly family and thus that her household would be privy to such information. It has also been suggested that word of the plot reached the church and that they sent the young child to bring Paul word. This scenario is perhaps the most unlikely of the various possibilities.

None of this information was important to Luke. What was important was that the young man learned of the plot and came directly to Paul with the news. Once Paul had told the Romans that he was a Roman citizen, he apparently received preferential treatment, including being allowed to have visitors (see 24:23; 28:30). It was common practice for one imprisoned to have to rely on friends for food and other necessities of life (see Mt. 25:36, 40; Heb. 10:34; 13:3).

Verses 17–19. Naturally, Paul was concerned by his nephew's report. We read,

> **Paul called one of the centurions to him and said, "Lead this young man to the commander, for he has something to report to him." So he took him and led him to the commander and said, "Paul the prisoner called me to him and asked me to lead this young man to you since he has something to tell you." The commander took him by the hand and stepping aside, began to inquire of him privately, "What is it that you have to report to me?"**

Something about the young man, perhaps the look on his face, immediately convinced the Roman officer that he had a message of consequence. He led him to one side so all could not hear. The Greek words νεανίας (*neanias*) and νεανίσκος (*neaniskos*) are used to describe Paul's nephew as a **young man**. This detail and the fact that the commander led him **by the hand** have caused many scholars to conclude that he was little more than a boy. After all, a Roman soldier would be unlikely to lead an older teenage or adult male by the hand. Even if Paul's nephew were a boy, he was still old enough to communicate accurately all the details of the plot. He was brave indeed to bring such a dangerous message to the prison.

Verses 20, 21. This young man did not hesitate to give a Roman officer instructions:

> **And he said, "The Jews have agreed to ask you to bring Paul down tomorrow to the Council, as though they were going to inquire somewhat more thoroughly about him. So do not listen to them, for more than forty of them are lying in wait for him who have bound themselves under a curse not to eat or drink until they slay him; and now they are ready and waiting for the promise from you."**

The words **ready and waiting** should not be taken to mean that the request had already been made and that they were waiting for the commander's answer. The words simply mean they were "ready and waiting" to put the plan into action. They did not want to fast any longer than they had to! Probably, the request would have come early the next morning.

The Roman officer had probably been commander of that post long enough to know that this scheme was exactly the type of action the Jews were capable of plotting. Perhaps he also had much experience in deciding whether people were telling him the truth or lies. Even as the boy spoke, the commander was considering his options. As soon as he dismissed Paul's nephew, he had made his decision about how to proceed. One option was to agree to the Council's request. If the commander did that, he would be rid of a pesky problem—but it would be a blot on his record to lose a prisoner, plus he was a conscientious man. Some ancient manuscripts add at the end of verse 24: "For he was afraid lest the Jews should seize him [Paul] and slay him, and he afterwards be accused of taking money [that is, a bribe for allowing Paul to be lynched]." Paul was a Roman citizen who should be protected.

Another option would be to pretend to agree to the San-hedrin's plan and then send enough soldiers to kill the would-be assassins. That, however, could bring on a riot—the type of explosive situation he was to avoid. The only viable option was to get the prisoner out of town, as quickly and quietly as possible.

Verse 22. Having made up his mind, the commander quickly dismissed the informant, **instructing him, "Tell no one that you have notified me of these things."** He did not want the Council to know that he had learned of their plot before he acted, or they might try to thwart his plan. Neither did he want them to know he had learned of their plans afterward, or they might revolt. His actions had to look like standard military and political policy.

PAUL TAKEN TO CAESAREA (23:23–35)

A Letter from Claudius Lysias (23:23–30)

[23]**And he called to him two of the centurions and said, "Get two hundred soldiers ready by the third hour of the night to proceed to Caesarea, with seventy horsemen and two hundred spearmen."** [24]**They were also to provide mounts to put Paul on and bring him safely to Felix the governor.** [25]**And he wrote a letter having this form:**

[26]**"Claudius Lysias, to the most excellent governor Felix, greetings.**

[27]**"When this man was arrested by the Jews and was about to be slain by them, I came up to them with the troops and rescued him, having learned that he was a Roman.** [28]**And wanting to ascertain the charge for which they were accusing him, I brought him down to their Council;** [29]**and I found him to be accused over questions about their Law, but under no accusation deserving death or imprisonment.**

[30]**"When I was informed that there would be a plot against the man, I sent him to you at once, also instructing his accusers to bring charges against him before you."**

Verse 23. Quickly the official put his plan into action: **And**

he called to him two of the centurions and said, "Get two hundred soldiers ready by the third hour of the night [about 9:00 p.m.] to proceed to Caesarea, with seventy horsemen and two hundred spearmen." The Greek word δεξιολάβοι (*dexiolaboi*), translated **spearmen**, is an ambiguous term that means "holding in (or throwing with) the right hand." This word apparently refers to soldiers armed with a weapon that could be held in or thrown with the right hand. Some translations have "light-armed troops."

The commander sent 470 men to escort one prisoner—probably about half of the regiment under his command. The Greek term used to designate this commander indicates that he had from six hundred to a thousand men under his command (see comments on 21:31). We have seen "the lengths to which the Jews would go to eliminate Paul"; now "we see the lengths to which the Roman government would go in order to administer impartial justice."[16] Some skeptics doubt Luke's veracity on this point; they scoff at the idea that so many men would be dispatched to protect one prisoner. These were, however, troubled times in Palestine. The commander did not want merely to send enough men to defeat the forty fanatics if the soldiers were attacked; he wanted to send enough men so that none would *dare* attack them. Paul was to be taken to **Caesarea**, the headquarters of the Roman forces of occupation and the home of the Roman governor (see comments on 10:1). Caesarea appears often in the Book of Acts (8:40; 9:30; 10:1, 24; 11:11; 12:19; 18:22; 21:8, 16).

Verse 24. The two centurions **were also to provide mounts to put Paul on and bring him safely to Felix the governor.** Instead of **mounts**, the KJV has "beasts," which is a vague translation. These animals could have been horses or mules. Since Paul was accompanying "horsemen" (ἱππεῖς, *hippeis*) (v. 23), we assume that his mount was a horse (ἵππος, *hippos*). It is possible that a horse was provided for Paul because, after his mistreatment, he was in no condition for a sustained march. It is also possible that this was a concession to one whom the commander

---

[16]Barclay, 166.

recognized to be innocent. At any rate, they would probably be able to travel faster on the first part of the journey—and definitely on the latter part of the journey—if Paul were mounted. Note that "mounts" is plural. Were the extra mounts to assure that Paul would always have a fresh mount? Was one of the mounts for the soldier who would be chained to Paul? Were extra mounts necessary to carry Paul's belongings? It is possible that some of Paul's friends and "fellow prisoners" were also moved at the same time, such as Luke and Aristarchus (see 27:2; Col. 4:10). Once more, we must say that we do not know.

We must pause to ask some questions: Was it a fluke that of all the people in Jerusalem, the one who overheard the plot was concerned enough about Paul to warn him? Was it happenstance that Paul was treated with deference so he could both receive guests and also send word to the commander? Was it only coincidence that the one commanding the fortress was the kind of man who would be agreeable to listening to a young man, and one conscientious enough to protect Paul—whatever the cost? Was it mere chance that Paul was sent to Caesarea, where he would have the opportunity to appeal to Caesar (25:11) and thus at last reach Rome? To ask these questions is to answer them: No; all of this was the result of the marvelous providence of God.

Verse 25. And he wrote a letter having this form. While arrangements were being made to transport the prisoner, the commander composed **a letter** (ἐπιστολή, *epistolē*) to the governor. It was not an easy letter to write, since he had no clear idea of what Paul had supposedly done wrong. The Greek word translated **form** is τύπος (*tupos*), the word for "pattern." The letter follows the standard form or pattern for letters in those days, especially official correspondence. Luke may have used the word to let us know that he gave an abbreviated form of the letter. Critics accuse Luke of "making up" the letter, insisting that there was no way he could know of its contents. It is possible, however, that the letter was read in Paul's hearing after he arrived at Caesarea. More importantly, Luke was inspired by the Holy Spirit—and we are sure God knew the contents.

Verse 26. The letter begins with a common greeting which first identifies the author and then the recipient: **"Claudius Lysias, to the most excellent governor Felix, greetings."** The Roman commander introduces himself as **Claudius Lysias** (see comments on 22:28). This instance is the first mention of the commander's name in the story (see 24:22). The name "Lysias" indicates that he was a Greek by birth. The letter's recipient is given the honorable epithet **most excellent** (see Lk. 1:3; Acts 24:3; 26:25). This title was given to a special order of Roman citizens, the equestrians ("knights"). It was also applied to other Roman officials, such as **governor Felix.**

Verses 27, 28. The commander began the body of his letter:

> **When this man was arrested by the Jews and was about to be slain by them, I came up to them with the troops and rescued him, having learned that he was a Roman. And wanting to ascertain the charge for which they were accusing him, I brought him down to their Council.**

The letter is a fascinating example of how facts can be manipulated to put the one telling the tale in the best light possible. It was true that the commander had rescued Paul, but he did not rescue him because he was a Roman citizen. Rather, he arrested him to break up a riot. He did not learn that Paul was a Roman citizen until he started to beat him—a fact conveniently left out of the narrative.

Verse 29. However, Luke did not include this letter—the only secular letter found in the New Testament—to embarrass a Roman official, but rather to immortalize these words: **"And I found him to be accused over questions about their Law, but under no accusation deserving death or imprisonment."** To the words **their Law,** the Western Text adds "concerning Moses and a certain Jesus." The commander's words support the conclusion that the charge of defiling the temple had not been raised during Paul's "trial" before the Council (see comments on v. 1)— for desecration of the temple *was* a capital offense. As confused as the commander might have been about what Paul had done, he could see that the disagreement was theological and not political. Concerning Roman law, he was convinced that Paul was undeserving of either death or imprisonment. This fact is another parallel with the trials of Jesus (Jn. 18:38). Remember that Luke was writing for a Roman official (see the *Introduction, The Patron*). He probably wanted to make clear that the consistent Roman position on Christians was that they were not guilty of violating any laws of Rome (see the *Introduction, The Purpose, apologetic*). Paul was no criminal and should be set free.

Verse 30. "When I was informed that there would be a plot against the man, I sent him to you at once, also instructing his accusers to bring charges against him before you." When the officer sent the letter, he probably had not yet instructed Paul's accusers to go to Caesarea to bring charges against him. Surely he would save this task until the next day, when he knew Paul was safely beyond their reach. His plan was probably to wait until the Council came to him with the request to bring Paul before them. Then he would express his regret that he had already sent Paul to Caesarea and suggest that they go there if they wanted to pursue the matter. This suggestion apparently prompted the high priest's visit to Caesarea in 24:1. According to the Western Text, the commander told Paul's accusers to go to Caesarea (see comments on 24:8).

Paul Delivered to Caesarea (23:31–35)

[31]**So the soldiers, in accordance with their orders, took Paul and brought him by night to Antipatris.** [32]**But the next day, leaving the horsemen to go on with him, they returned to the barracks.** [33]**When these had come to Caesarea and delivered the letter to the governor, they also presented Paul to him.** [34]**When he had read it, he asked from what province he was, and when he learned that he was from Cilicia,** [35]**he said, "I will give you a hearing after your accusers arrive also," giving orders for him to be kept in Herod's Praetorium.**

Verse 31. When all was ready, the small army left the city and marched through the hilly, shadowy region northwest of

Jerusalem. The movement of troops in and out the city was probably a common sight and aroused no suspicions. Paul had 470 guards. More importantly, he had the Lord watching over him. The men traveled as quickly as possible through the area of potential trouble. **So the soldiers, in accordance with their orders, took Paul and brought him by night to Antipatris.** Once again, Paul had been smuggled out of town under the cover of darkness (see 9:25; 17:10). The Old Testament name of **Antipatris** was Aphek (1 Sam. 4:1). The city had been rebuilt by Herod the Great and renamed after his father, Antipater. Antipatris was a military station situated on the border between Judea and Samaria, about thirty-five miles from Jerusalem, a little over halfway to Caesarea.

Verse 32. But the next day, leaving the horsemen to go on with him, they returned to the barracks. As the commander had hoped, they eluded Paul's enemies by leaving at night. Once they reached Antipatris, the rough, mountainous terrain where they could be ambushed was behind them; the land before them was open and flat. Therefore, the next day, probably after a brief rest, the four hundred soldiers and spearmen returned to Jerusalem to resume their peacekeeping duties, leaving the seventy horsemen to take Paul on to Caesarea.

Since all in the party were on horses, the final twenty-five miles to Caesarea would have been covered quickly. As he rode along, Paul was retracing the route he and his companions had taken less than two weeks before (21:15–17). He must have marveled over all that had happened in those few days and how the situation had turned out.

Verse 33. At last, the group reached **Caesarea.** If any Christians saw Paul surrounded by seventy-plus mounted legionnaires, they must have been amazed how soon the prophecy of Agabus had been fulfilled (21:10, 11). When Paul's armed escort reached the governor's palace, they **delivered the letter to the governor** and **also presented Paul to him.** We can imagine Paul, weary and dust-covered from his trip, chained hand and foot, yet filled with calm assurance as he stood before Governor Felix. For the first time, but not the last, the little Jew faced the most powerful political figure in Palestine.

Verse 34. After the governor read the letter from the commander, he must have looked the weary traveler up and down, wondering how such a harmless-looking Jew could cause so much trouble. Finally, he asked Paul what **province** he was from. Determining where people should be tried was apparently a complicated matter involving the type of province, who was the governing authority in a given province, and so forth. Probably, the deciding factors in Felix' decision to try the case included these: (1) Cilicia was a Roman province; (2) Paul was a Roman citizen; (3) the offense had occurred in Felix' province; (4) if the governor made the Jews go to Cilicia to bring their accusations against Paul, that would make them unhappy—something he did not care to do (see 24:27). **When** Felix **learned that** Paul **was from Cilicia**, a Roman province, he decided that he could legitimately deal with the case.

Verse 35. Felix dismissed Paul with an offhand promise: **"I will give you a hearing after your accusers arrive also."** Felix' declaration was made in response to the statement in the commander's letter that he was instructing Paul's accusers to bring their charges against Paul before Felix (v. 30). These accusations are recorded in 24:5–9.

Paul was not put in the common prison, but in **Herod's Praetorium.** "Praetorium" is a transliteration of the Greek word πραιτώριον (*praitōrion*), a term used for "official" residences in several locations (Mt. 27:27; Mk. 15:16; Jn. 18:28, 33; 19:9; Phil. 1:13). This particular praetorium was a palace built by Herod the Great which retained his name. It now served as the official headquarters of the Roman governor. In the providence of God, this was to be Paul's "safe house" for the next two years (24:27).

What about those forty-plus would-be assassins who had vowed not to eat or drink until Paul was dead? Can you imagine how frustrated they were to learn that their plot had been foiled and Paul was again out of reach? If they were conscientious about their vow, they got very hungry! Since the Jews were adept at reneging on vows they regretted taking, we doubt that these men missed many meals. Ideally they at least learned that "no plan . . . can succeed against the Lord" (Prov. 21:30; NIV)—but this is unlikely.

APPLICATION

The Rejection of Jerusalem (Ch. 23)

In chapter 23, Luke focuses on Jerusalem's rejection of the gospel which is illustrated by the Jewish leaders' desire to murder the apostle Paul. Jesus had anticipated the final rejection by Jerusalem and the ultimate consequences. As punishment for her sins, Jerusalem would be destroyed by the Romans (Lk. 21:20); the city would cease to be part of God's eternal plan. Jesus told the Samaritan woman at the well, "An hour is coming when neither in this mountain [of Gerizim] nor in Jerusalem will you worship the Father" (Jn. 4:21). Today, instead of looking to the earthly city of Jerusalem, we come "to Mount Zion and to the city of the living God, the heavenly Jerusalem . . ." (Heb. 12:22), in other words, to the throne of God, where Jesus now reigns over His kingdom.

We can draw a number of truths from these passages. One is that our premillennial friends are wrong when they teach that Jerusalem still has a place in God's cosmic plans and will one day again be the center of God's religion. On a more personal level, however, is the truth that if we persist in rejecting God, at some point He will reject us—completely and finally. The wise man said, "A man who hardens his neck after much reproof will suddenly be broken beyond remedy" (Prov. 29:1). When God gives a person the opportunity to hear and obey the gospel, he can respect that opportunity or reject it. Respecting God's way brings deliverance and delight; rejecting it results in danger and disaster. To continue to reject God's way is to mock Him, and God refuses to be mocked (Gal. 6:7).

God's Providence, Man's Hope (Ch. 23)

It is tragic to lose hope. We have been with individuals when they lost hope that their health would improve, that a loved one would recover, that a mate would return. We have seen their shoulders slump, their faces sag, their eyes glaze over. When hope is all that keeps us going, it is devastating to conclude "There is nothing to hope for" (Job 6:11; NCV).

At one time, Paul had hoped to go to Rome (Acts 19:21; Rom.

15:22–29), but that hope had been crushed. A few days after his arrival in Jerusalem, he had been attacked and then arrested. Now he was imprisoned, and the Jews continued to plot his death. It looked like a hopeless situation: If he stayed in prison, he had no ministry; if he were released, he would certainly be killed. His hope of reaching Rome flickered and all but died.

In Acts 23, we find the rebirth of Paul's hope. The apostle received reassurance that the Lord was in control of his life and that he would bear witness to Christ in Rome (v. 11). A consideration of God's providence in our lives will invariably enhance our hope as well. G. C. Brewer, a well-known gospel preacher from the past, was once asked, "Do you believe in the special providence of God?" He replied, "What other kind is there?"

The noun "providence" is rarely found in our English Bibles. However, the verb "provide" is frequently used in reference to God's care. The noun occurs in Acts 24:2 where it refers not to God's providence, but to the foresight of a Roman official. The English word "providence" comes from Latin and means literally "seeing ahead," that is, anticipating. The compound Greek word πρόνοια (*pronoia*), translated "providence," means almost the same: "thinking before or ahead [of time]." Both the English and Greek words refer to making provision ahead of time. Of course, humans make preparations all the time. It is reassuring to know that God does the same for His people.

Providence is God working through natural law rather than through the suspension of natural law, that is, through miracles. Someone has called providence "God's hand in the glove of history." In the story of Paul's last visit to Jerusalem, we see God's providence at work again and again. Was it merely coincidence that a Roman commander was immediately at hand when Paul was mobbed in the temple court? Was it only "lucky" that Paul escaped the Roman scourging because he was a Roman citizen? Did it "just happen" that the commander was a conscientious official who respected Paul's rights as a citizen? Was it by chance that Paul's nephew overheard the plot on his uncle's life? No, our God is in control.

When we teach that God does not work miraculously today, we are often accused of limiting God. However, those who believe that God cannot work unless He works miraculously are the ones who limit God. Acts 23:12–35 does not mention God once, nor does any miracle occur. However, the hand of God is apparent in all that takes place.

The fact that God is in control helped Paul keep his hope alive. Augustine said, "Trust the past to the mercy of God, the present to His love, and the future to His providence."[17] From day to day, we may not be able to tell that God is at work in our lives, but we can rest assured that He is. Ed Wharton noted, "God's providence in our lives is a book which like some languages can only be read backwards, and then only by Bible believers."[18] No matter what happens, trust in Him. Learn to say with the psalmist, "You are my hope; O Lord God, You are my confidence . . ." (Ps. 71:5).

When night is the darkest and hope has almost vanished, the Lord can rekindle our hope. No, the Lord will not come to us in a vision with a promise that every dream will be realized. However, He gives us a message of courage, commendation, and confidence: His message of courage is "Wait for the Lord; be strong and let your heart take courage . . ." (Ps. 27:14). His message of commendation is "Well done, good and faithful servant" (Mt. 25:21; KJV). His message of confidence is "This is the confidence which we have before Him, that, if we ask anything according to His will, He hears us" (1 Jn. 5:14). Maybe not everything in our lives is right, but this is right: God loves us and cares for us and will cause all things in our lives "to work together for good to those who love God, to those who are called according to His purpose" (Rom. 8:28).

The Plot Against Paul (23:12–35)

The plot that the Jews formed against Paul can be divided into three sections: (1) A Plot Made (vv. 12–15), (2) A Plot Exposed (vv. 16–22), and (3) A Plot Foiled (vv. 23–35).

---

[17]Quoted in Wiersbe, *The Bible Exposition Commentary*, vol. 1, 496.

[18]Ed Wharton, *The Action of the Book of Acts* (Dallas: Gospel Teachers Publications, 1977), 54.

CHAPTER 24

PAUL'S IMPRISONMENT AT CAESAREA (PART 2)

The last seven chapters of Acts tell of Paul as a prisoner—briefly in Jerusalem (22:24), then two years in Caesarea (23:33–35; 24:27), followed by at least two years in Rome (28:16, 30). Paul was no stranger to prison life. He had been imprisoned often (2 Cor. 11:23). Luke recorded an earlier imprisonment—when Paul and his coworker Silas were beaten and then put in stocks in Philippi (Acts 16). Never before, however, had the apostle had to endure confinement day after day, week after week, month after month, year after year. Since he was used to an active, vigorous lifestyle, this had to be one of the greatest trials Paul ever experienced. However, he maintained a positive, upbeat attitude throughout this trying period. He was able to have this attitude *after* the Lord appeared to him with a message of assurance (23:11).

PAUL'S TRIAL BEFORE FELIX (24:1–23)

The Accusation Against Paul (24:1–9)

¹After five days the high priest Ananias came down with some elders, with an attorney named Tertullus, and they brought charges to the governor against Paul. ²After Paul had been summoned, Tertullus began to accuse him, saying to the governor,

"Since we have through you attained much peace, and since by your providence reforms are being carried out for this nation, ³we acknowledge this in every way and everywhere, most excellent Felix, with all thankfulness. ⁴But, that I may not weary you any further, I beg you to grant us, by your kindness, a brief hearing. ⁵For we have found this man a real pest and a fellow who stirs up dissension among all the Jews throughout the world, and a ringleader of the sect of the Nazarenes. ⁶And he even tried to desecrate the temple; and then we arrested him. [We wanted to judge him according to our own Law. ⁷But Lysias the commander came along, and with much violence took him out of our hands, ⁸ordering his accusers to come before you.] By examining him yourself concerning all these matters you will be able to ascertain the things of which we accuse him." ⁹The Jews also joined in the attack, asserting that these things were so.

Paul had been brought to Caesarea and delivered to Governor Felix, who imprisoned him in Herod's Praetorium (23:23–35). Now, in chapter 24, Luke recorded Paul's first trial in Caesarea—one of many trials he had to undergo during the approximately five years he spent in prison. These five years include Paul's confinement at Jerusalem, two years at Caesarea (24:27), two years in Rome (28:30), and any subsequent time.

Verse 1. After Paul was safely away from Jerusalem, the commander informed the Sanhedrin that the prisoner had been taken to Caesarea. It was probably with great satisfaction that the officer told them that if they wanted to pursue the matter, they would have to travel to Caesarea and present their case before Governor Felix (see comments on 23:30). The Jewish leaders must have been enraged to have Paul escape their clutches again, but they were not ready to admit defeat. Within days, they were prepared again to try to eliminate him. **After five days the high priest Ananias came down with some elders, with an attorney named Tertullus, and they brought charges to the governor against Paul.**

The phrase **after five days** probably means that Paul had been in Caesarea five days, but it could mean five days had passed from the time the Jews learned that he was gone. The **high priest Ananias** once again led the Jews in their attack against Paul (see comments on 23:2). The old priest probably was unhappy about traveling the sixty-plus miles to Caesarea, but he was willing to suffer any discomfort to exterminate Paul. The **elders** would have been other members of the Council. They **came down** from Jerusalem to Caesarea. Jerusalem was about 2,400 feet above sea level (see comments on 15:30), while Caesarea was on the coast. As they came to accuse Paul, they brought **an attorney** with them. The Greek word ῥήτωρ (*rhētōr*), translated "attorney," means "orator" (see KJV); this man was trained in legal persuasion. Incidentally, the English word "rhetor" means "a teacher of rhetoric." "Rhetoric" is "the persuasive use of language." This orator was named **Tertullus**, a diminutive form of the Latin word for "third." We do not know if he was a Roman or a Hellenistic Jew. They probably secured the services of a skilled speaker because (1) Tertullus would be more familiar with Roman law and (2) they surely would have choked on the flattery that needed to be spoken. When this party arrived in Caesarea, **they brought charges to the governor against Paul.**

Verses 2, 3. They were ushered into the presence of Antonius Felix, the Roman governor (procurator) of Judea. From time to time, Judea was governed by procurators, who were representatives of Rome. Pilate was one of these (Mt. 27:2). The only other governors named in Acts are Felix (chs. 23, 24) and Festus (chs. 25, 26). After **Paul** had been brought in, **Tertullus** started the proceedings by addressing Felix with "nauseating flattery":[1]

> **Since we have through you attained much peace, and since by your providence reforms are being carried out for this nation, we acknowledge this in every way and everywhere, most excellent Felix, with all thankfulness.**

In truth, Felix had put down several rebellions. (For an example, see comments on 21:38.) However, he had done so with

---

[1]William Barclay, *The Acts of the Apostles*, The Daily Study Bible Series, rev. ed. (Philadelphia: Westminster Press, 1976), 168. For God's attitude toward flattery, see Proverbs 26:28.

a ruthlessness that enraged even moderate Jews. Most citizens of Judea would say that whatever peace existed was in spite of him, not because of him. Felix, however, was both judge and jury—and Tertullus would say anything to win him to their side.

Verse 4. The smooth-tongued attorney continued: **"But, that I may not weary you any further, I beg you to grant us, by your kindness, a brief hearing."** Tertullus spoke as if compliments would weary the governor! After his opening remarks, the lawyer brought three charges against Paul—charges as counterfeit as his flattery.

Verse 5. First was a *personal* charge: **"For we have found this man a real pest."** The phrase **a real pest** is translated from the Greek word λοιμός (*loimos*), which can also mean "a plague" or "pestilence." In other words, "Paul is a first-class troublemaker, not the sort any right-thinking person would allow to live."

Next came a *political* charge: Paul is **"a fellow who stirs up dissension among all the Jews throughout the world, and a ringleader of the sect of the Nazarenes."** This charge would be the one of greatest interest to Felix, since he was commissioned by the Roman government to keep the peace. The accusation had an element of truth in it, for disorder had occurred in many places Paul had been (13:50; 14:5, 19; 17:5–9, 13; 18:12–16; 19:23–41). To imply, however, that Paul had instigated the trouble was untrue.

Note the phrase **a ringleader of the sect of the Nazarenes.** The Greek word translated **sect** is αἵρεσις (*hairesis*), the word from which we get "heresy." This verse is the only place in the Scriptures the term "Nazarenes" is used to refer to Christians. It was a designation used by the Jews to mean "a follower of Jesus of Nazareth" (see Mt. 2:23; 21:11; 26:71; Mk. 1:24; Lk. 4:34; 18:37; Jn. 1:45). It was a term of derision: "Can any good thing come out of Nazareth?" (Jn. 1:46). There is no authority in this passage for followers of Jesus to refer to themselves as "Nazarenes." Since Tertullus called this despised group a "sect," he was probably suggesting that Christianity was an illegal religion (see comments on 18:13) and should be abolished by Rome.

Verse 6a. Finally, the attorney made a *pious*, that is, religious charge: **"And he even tried to desecrate the temple."** Originally, the Jews from Asia had shouted that Paul *had* desecrated the temple (21:28); now that charge had been softened to "he . . . *tried to* desecrate the temple"—a charge more vague and thereby harder to prove or disprove. As noted before, Rome had given temple authorities the right to execute any who defiled the temple (see comments on 21:28, 29).

Verses 6b–8a. Tertullus added:

And then we arrested him. [We wanted to judge him according to our own Law. But Lysias the commander came along, and with much violence took him out of our hands, ordering his accusers to come before you.]

The mob scene of chapter 22 could hardly be referred to as a formal arrest preparatory to a fair trial. When we compare Luke's record of Paul's arrest (21:27–40) with the commander's version in his letter (23:25–30) and the lawyer's version in his prosecution (24:5–8), we can easily understand the confusion often found in court. The lawyer did not know that Felix had in his possession a statement from Lysias that he had to rescue Paul from the Jews as they were trying to kill him (23:27).

Note the bracket before the phrase "We wanted to" in verse 6 and the bracket after the phrase "to come before you" in verse 8. The end of verse 6, all of verse 7, and the beginning of verse 8 are not included in many ancient manuscripts. Since there is insufficient textual evidence for the genuineness of this reading, most translations do not include it but relegate it to brackets, a footnote, or something similar. The KJV, following the Western Text, has the passage without brackets. Regarding his own translation in his commentary on Acts, Simon Kistemaker explained, "The Western reading has a ring of authenticity. Hence, I do not wish to bar its inclusion but judiciously place it within brackets."[2] F. F. Bruce agreed: "The tone of the Western addition is so thoroughly in accord with the rest of Tertullus's

---

[2]Simon J. Kistemaker, *Exposition of the Acts of the Apostles*, New Testament Commentary (Grand Rapids, Mich.: Baker Book House, 1990), 883.

speech that one is inclined to accept it as genuine."[3]

Verse 8b. Having tried his best to prejudice the governor against Paul, Tertullus concluded: **"By examining him yourself concerning all these matters you will be able to ascertain the things of which we accuse him."** If the passage in brackets is included, Tertullus may refer to examining the Roman commander. Some think Felix' words in verse 22 about sending for Lysias are in response to Tertullus' suggestion in verse 8, and thus that the reference in verse 8 is to examining *Lysias* to find out what really happened. However, the attorney probably referred to examining Paul. The personal pronouns in verses 6b through 8a all refer to Paul. J. W. McGarvey thought this language was a hint that the Jews wanted Paul to be "examined by scourging" (22:24).[4] Either way, the attorney expressed his confidence that when Felix had all the facts, he would find the evidence in their favor.

Verse 9. At that point, the high priest and the elders added their voices. **The Jews also joined in the attack, asserting that these things were so.** No formal witnesses were called to testify against Paul. This strategy may have been used to avoid inconsistent testimony (see Mk. 14:56, 59). Instead, the Jews tried to sway the governor by giving their "amens" to the words of their attorney, Tertullus. They also probably hoped Paul would incriminate himself by his own defense.

Paul's Defense (24:10–23)

[10]**When the governor had nodded for him to speak, Paul responded:**

"Knowing that for many years you have been a judge to this nation, I cheerfully make my defense, [11]since you can take note of the fact that no more than twelve days ago I went up to

---

[3]F. F. Bruce, *The Book of Acts*, The New International Commentary on the New Testament, gen. ed. F. F. Bruce, rev. ed. (Grand Rapids, Mich.: Wm. B. Eerdmans Publishing Co., 1988), 441.

[4]J. W. McGarvey, *New Commentary on Acts of Apostles*, vol. 2 (Delight, Ark.: Gospel Light Publishing Co., n.d.), 235.

Jerusalem to worship. [12]Neither in the temple, nor in the synagogues, nor in the city itself did they find me carrying on a discussion with anyone or causing a riot. [13]Nor can they prove to you the charges of which they now accuse me. [14]But this I admit to you, that according to the Way which they call a sect I do serve the God of our fathers, believing everything that is in accordance with the Law and that is written in the Prophets; [15]having a hope in God, which these men cherish themselves, that there shall certainly be a resurrection of both the righteous and the wicked. [16]In view of this, I also do my best to maintain always a blameless conscience both before God and before men. [17]Now after several years I came to bring alms to my nation and to present offerings; [18]in which they found me occupied in the temple, having been purified, without any crowd or uproar. But there were some Jews from Asia—[19]who ought to have been present before you and to make accusation, if they should have anything against me. [20]Or else let these men themselves tell what misdeed they found when I stood before the Council, [21]other than for this one statement which I shouted out while standing among them, 'For the resurrection of the dead I am on trial before you today.'"

[22] But Felix, having a more exact knowledge about the Way, put them off, saying, "When Lysias the commander comes down, I will decide your case." [23]Then he gave orders to the centurion for him to be kept in custody and yet have some freedom, and not to prevent any of his friends from ministering to him.

Verse 10. If the Jews intended for the governor to interrogate Paul, they were disappointed. Instead, the governor simply **nodded for him to speak**, and Paul began his response. Instead of beginning with flattery (vv. 2, 3; see 1 Thess. 2:5), Paul simply referred to Felix' experience in dealing with the Jews: **"Knowing that for many years you have been a judge to this nation, I cheerfully make my defense."** Compare these words with those in 26:2, 3. With the help of the Lord, the apostle remained unflustered, master of the situation. Jesus had promised:

> ... they will lay their hands on you and will persecute
> you, delivering you to the synagogues and prisons, bring-
> ing you before kings and governors for My name's sake.
> It will lead to an opportunity for your testimony. . . . I
> will give you utterance and wisdom which none of your
> opponents will be able to resist or refute (Lk. 21:12–15).

Verse 11. As Paul stood before a governor, he laid hold of
Jesus' promise. He first answered the charge that he was an agitator: **"You can take note of the fact that no more than twelve
days ago I went up to Jerusalem to worship"**—not to cause
trouble. The simplest way to take Paul's time reference is that
he had gone to Jerusalem only **twelve days** before. Since this
trial was taking place on the fifth day after Paul came to Caesarea
(v. 1), Paul only spent seven days in Jerusalem. Some think that
one week is inadequate for all that happened and believe that
the twelve days refers only to the time he was in Jerusalem, including the days he spent imprisoned. Either way, much of the
twelve days he had been in jail, leaving little time to cause
trouble. There had not been enough time for Paul to work up a
rebellion, and further, since the events happened only a short
time ago, Felix would have no problem locating eyewitnesses
who could tell him what really happened. The phrase **to worship** could refer to temple worship, to meeting with his fellow
Christians in the area, or to both. Paul's point was that he came
to Jerusalem for peaceful, not disruptive, purposes.

Verse 12. Paul added, **"Neither in the temple, nor in the
synagogues, nor in the city itself did they find me carrying on
a discussion with anyone or causing a riot."** Paul had been
unusually reticent in Jerusalem, probably trying to placate the
Jerusalem elders who were concerned that his presence might
cause problems (21:22). It is also possible that Paul was honor-
ing an agreement he had made with James, Peter, and John (Gal.
2:9).

Verse 13. The apostle then put his accusers on the spot: **"Nor
can they prove to you the charges of which they now accuse
me."** The Council had no firsthand knowledge of the charges
they made; they dealt only in hearsay. They had brought no wit-

nesses, just a smooth-tongued orator. An accusation was not evidence.

Verse 14. Paul did, however, plead guilty to one charge: He acknowledged he was indeed a Christian. **"But this I admit to you, that according to the Way which they call a sect I do serve the God of our fathers."** Paul said that *the Jews* called Christianity **a sect;** he himself did not. The church has never been and never will be a sect. The KJV has "heresy" here, but the same Greek word used in this verse is translated "sect" in verse 5. Notice the phrase **God of *our* fathers** (emphasis added). Paul still identified with the Jews, even with his accusers. He believed **everything that is in accordance with the Law and that is written in the Prophets.** He had not rejected the Jewish Scriptures; he in fact believed those Scriptures foretold the coming of the Messiah and His kingdom. "Paul and the early Christians did not see themselves as 'former Jews' but as 'fulfilled Jews,'"[5] the true offspring of Abraham (Gal. 3:29).

Verse 15. Regarding what had been "written in the Prophets," he added, **"having a hope in God, which these men cherish themselves, that there shall certainly be a resurrection of both the righteous and the wicked."** Although the New Testament often speaks of the resurrection of both the righteous and the wicked (see Jn. 5:28, 29), this instance is the only time Paul did. Usually, when Paul spoke or wrote of the resurrection, his emphasis was on the righteous (see 1 Cor. 15; 1 Thess. 4:13–18). However, he often mentioned the judgment of both the righteous and the wicked, which presupposes the resurrection (Rom. 2:5–11; 2 Cor. 5:10; 2 Thess. 1:6–10; 2 Tim. 4:1). In the Old Testament, the prophet Daniel had spoken of the resurrection (see Dan. 12:2, 3). Since the Sadducees did not believe in the resurrection of the dead, some of the elders who had come were apparently Pharisees who did believe. Thus Paul could speak of **"a hope . . . which *these* men cherish themselves"** (emphasis added). The high priest was a Sadducee, as probably were others with him. However, they would hesitate to challenge Paul

---

[5]Warren W. Wiersbe, *The Bible Exposition Commentary,* vol. 1 (Wheaton, Ill.: Victor Books, 1989), 500.

on the resurrection in front of the governor because they would want to present a united front to Felix.

Verse 16. Since the concept of the resurrection presupposes a day of reckoning, a day when all will stand before God and give an account, Paul said, **"In view of this, I also do my best to maintain always a blameless conscience both before God and before men."** In other words, "I stand before you, Felix, an innocent man!" The phrase **do my best** comes from the Greek verb ἀσκέω (*askeō*), which indicates practice and self-discipline. The KJV has "I exercise myself." The Cotton Patch Version has "I constantly give myself workouts." This spiritual "exercise" is more important than physical exercise (1 Tim. 4:7, 8). Concerning Paul's **blameless conscience**, see comments on 23:1.

Verse 17. One accusation remained unanswered, the specific charge of trying to defile the temple. Paul began his explanation of what actually happened: **"Now after several years I came to bring alms to my nation and to present offerings."** If 18:22 refers to a visit to Jerusalem ("he went up"), it had been five years or so since Paul had visited Jerusalem. If that verse does not refer to a visit to Jerusalem, it had been even longer since Paul had been in the city. In other words, in all that time he had not been in Felix' territory, stirring up trouble.

One of the reasons Paul came to Jerusalem was to help his people. **Alms** refers to benevolent help (see 3:2, 3, 10; 10:2, 4). The gift Paul brought was for specific Jews (Christian Jews in Jerusalem)—but for Jews nevertheless—so his statement that he brought alms to his **nation** was accurate. Verse 17 is the only direct reference in Acts to the collection Paul made (see comments on 19:21; 20:3, 4). The term **offerings** could refer to sacrifices in the temple, but there is no indication that Paul intended to offer any sacrifices until the elders suggested it (21:23, 24). If he had planned to do so, that idea would have served their purpose better than their suggestion. The term "offerings" may just refer to the love-offering brought to the Jewish Christians. In 2 Corinthians 9:12, we see that one purpose of the contribution was to produce "many thanksgivings to God."

Felix must have picked up on the terms "alms" and "offerings." He apparently thought, "This Jew is a man of means and

376

influence; perhaps he can lay his hands on more funds" (see v. 26).

Verses 18, 19. Paul continued: **"They found me occupied in the temple, having been purified** [see 21:26], **without any crowd or uproar."** Those facts could be verified by temple records. **"But there were some Jews from Asia—who ought to have been present before you and to make accusation, if they should have anything against me."** A break in the thought in the original text is indicated in the NASB by a dash. Paul broke off what he was saying at that point. Throughout the account of this trial, both in Tertullus' charge and in Paul's defense, Luke captured the nuances of normal speech.

Some Jews from Asia were the ones who originally charged Paul with defiling the temple (21:27, 28). If the charges were true, they should have been there as witnesses for the prosecution. Where *were* the Jews from Asia? Probably, they simply faded from sight once they failed in their attempt to kill Paul. Even if they were still in the vicinity of Jerusalem, the Jewish delegation to Caesarea did not dare bring them because they had no proof of their accusation. Again, Paul established that the Jewish leaders could not prove the charges they had brought against him (see v. 13).

Verses 20, 21. Paul concluded with a direct challenge to the members of the Sanhedrin:

> **Or else let these men themselves tell what misdeed they found when I stood before the Council, other than for this one statement which I shouted out while standing among them, "For the resurrection of the dead I am on trial before you today."**

Paul was not saying that his statement was a **misdeed**, nor was he apologizing for the statement. What he meant was this: "The only thing I am guilty of is doing the job I was told to do"—that is, "I am guilty of nothing."

We can imagine the faces of the high priest and the elders turning purple with embarrassment and rage. When Paul stood before the Council, they had not indicted him of breaking any law. If believing in the resurrection was a crime, then all the Pharisees in the Council were also guilty. Rather, the assembly had erupted into violence after his crying out, **"For the resurrection of the dead I am on trial before you today"** (see 23:6–10). They had no answer for Paul, at least none they cared to voice before Felix. Paul stood before his accusers victorious, waiting for the governor's decision. He should have been set free.

Verse 22. It was mentioned earlier that the Jewish leaders were unaware that Felix had in his hands the report from the Roman commander Claudius Lysias. They also did not realize that the governor had some understanding of Christianity. Luke said Felix had **a more exact knowledge about the Way.** The Greek word ἀκριβέστερον (*akribesteron*), translated **more exact,** is a term of comparison. The word also appears in 18:26 where Aquila and Priscilla taught Apollos the way of God "more accurately." In the present context, the phrase could mean a more exact knowledge "than the Jews realized" or "than the Jewish leaders had" or "than most people had." How Felix had learned about **the Way,** Luke did not say. Perhaps a Roman officer named Cornelius (ch. 10) had shared his faith with the governor. Perhaps Felix had heard Philip the evangelist as he "preached Jesus" (8:35) in Caesarea (8:40; 21:8). Perhaps as governor, he had simply made it his business to know what was going on. Apparently, however, Felix' knowledge had reached only his head and not his heart. He had seen the light, but preferred to live in darkness.

Even if his knowledge did not change his life, it did keep Felix from being deceived by the Jewish delegation. Paul was obviously guilty of nothing "deserving death or imprisonment" (23:29) and should have been released. This fact is another parallel between the trials of Jesus and the trials of Paul. Both were found innocent again and again, but still not released. The governor did not release Paul because he was more concerned about getting along with the Jews (v. 27) than with justice. Further, he was already considering how he might lay his greedy hands on the funds Paul had mentioned (v. 26).

Therefore, Felix put off the Jewish delegation, saying, **"When**

Lysias the commander comes down, I will decide your case."
No indication is given that Felix called Lysias or that the commander ever came to Caesarea to be interrogated about the case.
Felix already had the officer's report and had no need to call
him. The governor's words were merely an excuse not to make
a decision, a pretext for procrastination. Felix seemed inclined
to put things off (see v. 25). The Jewish leaders decided to drop
the case until Felix was replaced (25:1, 2).

Verse 23. In the meantime, Felix **gave orders to the centurion for** Paul **to be kept in custody and yet have some freedom, and not to prevent any of his friends from ministering
to him.** The apostle's situation was probably similar to that later
in Rome, where he was kept chained (28:16, 20) but could welcome "all who came to him" (28:30). Paul spent the next two
years this way (24:27). During that time, Paul must have wondered what God's plan was. He seemed no closer to Rome, and
he surely missed traveling and preaching. Perhaps he did some
writing and preaching in his cell, as he later did in Rome (28:31).
However, as far as we know, no such letters are preserved from
this period. Some have suggested that the "prison epistles"
(Ephesians, Philippians, Colossians, and Philemon) were written from Caesarea, but it seems more probable that they were
written from Rome (see Phil. 4:22). It has also been suggested
that Paul wrote Hebrews while imprisoned at Caesarea. However, since we cannot be sure who wrote Hebrews, this idea must
remain speculation. Paul's confinement may have been a blessing from God, giving him time to recover from the physical and
mental abuse he had received over the previous two decades.

Many writers think the two-year hiatus gave Luke time and
opportunity to research and write his Gospel Account and the
first part of Acts. Since Luke was with Paul when the apostle
reached Jerusalem (21:17), and since he was with Paul two years
later when Paul left for Rome (27:1), it is assumed that he stayed
in the general area for the two years. During those months, Luke
could have interviewed many of the main players in the drama
of the life of Jesus and the early days of the church in Jerusalem
(see Lk. 1:3). He may have spent long hours with Paul review-
ing his ministry and journeys. Burton Coffman said:

In the matter of Luke's painstaking investigations and interviews of eyewitnesses of the glorious beginnings of Christianity, one may behold the gracious Providence which overruled the injustice suffered by the apostle Paul, providing in that suffering and delay the occasion for the indispensable writings of the beloved physician Luke.[6]

Whatever God's purposes were, Paul resigned himself to them. Later, it was from a prison cell that he wrote, "Rejoice in the Lord always; again I will say, rejoice!" (Phil. 4:4).

"WHEN I FIND TIME": THE NON-CONVERSION OF FELIX (24:24–27)

[24]But some days later Felix arrived with Drusilla, his wife who was a Jewess, and sent for Paul and heard him speak about faith in Christ Jesus. [25]But as he was discussing righteousness, self-control and the judgment to come, Felix became frightened and said, "Go away for the present, and when I find time I will summon you." [26]At the same time too, he was hoping that money would be given him by Paul; therefore he also used to send for him quite often and converse with him. [27]But after two years had passed, Felix was succeeded by Porcius Festus, and wishing to do the Jews a favor, Felix left Paul imprisoned.

Verses 24 through 27 comprise a classic case of procrastination in the Book of Acts: the non-conversion of Governor Felix. In the earlier part of the chapter, Paul was on trial for part of a day; in these verses, Felix was "on trial" for two years.

Verse 24. But some days later, after Paul had been returned to protective custody, **Felix arrived with Drusilla, his wife who was a Jewess.** As part of his duties as governor, Felix had to travel—making inspection tours of the area, courtesy visits to

---

[6]James Burton Coffman, *Commentary on Acts* (Austin, Tex.: Firm Foundation Publishing House, 1976), 462–63.

other officials, and the like. Returning from such a trip, the governor and his wife arrived in Caesarea. It is possible that the word **arrived** simply means that they traveled from where they were staying in Caesarea to where Paul was imprisoned. However, since the governor usually lived in the Praetorium and that was where Paul was imprisoned, the most natural meaning of "arrived" is that they had been out of town and returned.

Before we go further, a thumbnail sketch of this illustrious couple might be in order.[7] Felix had been born a slave in the household of Antonia, the mother of Claudius. Antonia became fond of Felix and his brother Pallas and freed them. Pallas became a favorite of Claudius and, after Claudius became emperor, exerted great influence in the empire. It was through Pallas' influence that Felix was first given a place of authority in Samaria and then became procurator of Judea. Felix was one of the few ex-slaves in history to rise to such a post. The name **Felix** means "happy." It is probably a name he took after he was freed from slavery. However, as we shall see, he was not a very happy man.

Felix had the position, but he did not have the disposition to govern. The Roman historian Tacitus said that "with every kind of cruelty and lust, [Felix] exercised the authority of a king with the temper of a slave."[8] One writer characterized the governor as cruel, corrupt, covetous, and compromising.[9] Felix governed during a period of great unrest in Judea. A man of tact and diplomacy might have defused the situation, but Felix had neither quality. Historians say that his ruthless rule was a major factor in the Jewish rebellion less than a decade later—the rebellion that resulted in the destruction of Jerusalem.

The woman sitting by the side of the governor was his match both in self-centeredness and in unbridled lust. **Drusilla** was a member of the infamous Herod family (see comments on 12:1). Her father had killed the apostle James (12:1, 2). Her great-uncle

---

[7]See Josephus *Wars* 2.12.8–13.7; *Antiquities* 20.7.1–8.9; Tacitus *Annals* 12.54.
[8]Tacitus *History* 5.9.
[9]G. Campbell Morgan, *The Acts of the Apostles* (Grand Rapids, Mich.: Fleming H. Revell, 1988 ed.), 388.

had killed John the Baptist (Mt. 14:1–12) and mocked Jesus (Lk. 23:6–12). Her great-grandfather had tried to kill the baby Jesus (Mt. 2). Drusilla was called **a Jewess** because her great-grandmother was Mariamne, who was from a famous Jewish family. Mariamne was one of Herod the Great's wives and the mother of Aristobulus, the line through which Drusilla came. Drusilla had a brother, Herod Agrippa II, and a sister, Bernice, who are introduced in chapter 25.

Historians are unanimous in praising Drusilla's sensual beauty. Clovis Chappell said she was "as fair outwardly" as she was "rotten inwardly."[10] Drusilla was the governor's third **wife**. All of Felix's marriages were social-climbing achievements; all three wives were of royal birth. One was a granddaughter of Antony and Cleopatra. Felix had seduced Drusilla from her husband when she was only sixteen. She was not yet twenty, but she was old in the ways of the world.

In the present context, Felix and Drusilla had come back to Caesarea. As they were catching up on the news, the name of Paul came up—and Drusilla apparently expressed an interest in meeting him. The Western Text adds that Drusilla "asked to see Paul and hear him speak, so wishing to satisfy her [Felix] summoned Paul." Why would Drusilla want to hear Paul? Did she wish to be entertained on an otherwise dull evening? Sin quickly bores. If a profligate from ancient Babylon should be resurrected in our ungodly age, he would merely yawn and say, "I've seen it all before." Or, did she have a sincere desire to learn more about the Way? We would hope that her interest was genuine.

Whatever the reason, Felix **sent for Paul.** C. C. Crawford pictured the scene like this:

> Felix orders him brought up from the guardroom to tell them more about the faith in Christ. . . . Clank, clank drags the chain up the marble stairway, and Paul walks into their presence, the stench of the prison emanating from his clothes, a little man only about sixty years old,

---

[10]Clovis G. Chappell, *Values That Last* (New York: Abingdon Press, 1939), 10.

but looking as if he might be eighty. He bows courteously to the governor and the beautiful woman by his side. At their request, he begins to present the first principles of the faith.[11]

When Paul stood before Felix and Drusilla, he could have impressed them with discourse on many topics: Greek philosophy, ancient mythology, wonders he had seen in his travels. Paul, however, was not interested in winning their applause, but their souls. As corrupt as they were, God wanted Felix and Drusilla to be saved (2 Pet. 3:9). They were hard cases, but no harder than others who had come to a saving knowledge of Christ: for example, Simon the sorcerer, the Philippian jailer, and Paul himself. He spoke to them concerning **faith in Christ Jesus.** Since Drusilla had a Jewish background, the apostle probably began with Old Testament prophecies and explained their fulfillment in Jesus' life (see 17:2, 3). He surely spoke of the crucifixion and resurrection of Jesus, and the necessity of trusting in Him for salvation (4:12; 2:37, 38).

Verse 25. Then Paul's discourse took an unexpected turn. His presentation became painfully personal as he pointed out that faith in Jesus has moral implications and ethical demands. On occasion, we have heard people say, "Preacher, you've stopped preaching and started meddling." Sooner or later, good preaching is meddling;[12] preaching has to get down to where we live.

Paul's presentation was relevant, reproving, relentless, and risky. Luke recorded the apostle's three-point sermon outline: **He was discussing** (1) **righteousness,** (2) **self-control and** (3) **the judgment to come.** During Paul's trial before Felix, three accusations had been made against him (24:5, 6)—accusations that were patently false. Now, in effect, three accusations were leveled against Felix and Drusilla—accusations that were painfully true.

---

[11]C. C. Crawford, *Sermon Outlines on Acts,* rev. ed. (Murfreesboro, Tenn.: Dehoff Publications, 1956), 230.

[12]Adapted from Lloyd J. Ogilvie, *Acts,* The Communicator's Commentary, vol. 5 (Dallas: Word Publishing, 1983), 310.

To a couple whose names were synonymous with injustice and wrongdoing, Paul spoke of "righteousness." **Righteousness** was one of Paul's favorite words; he used it almost sixty times in his letters. The Greek word δικαιοσύνη (*dikaiosunē*), translated "righteousness," can refer to doing right. The psalmist said to the Lord: "All Your commandments are righteousness" (Ps. 119:172). Jesus said that "it is fitting for us to fulfill all righteousness" (Mt. 3:15). The word can also refer to being counted as right in God's eyes (Phil. 3:9). Abraham's faith "was credited to him as righteousness" (Rom. 4:3). Righteousness also carries the idea of "justice," being equitable and fair—qualities to which the governor and his wife were strangers.

Simply put, Paul preached on sin—specifically that Felix and Drusilla were sinners in need of the grace of God. Jesus said that the Holy Spirit would "convict the world concerning sin and righteousness" (Jn. 16:8). Most do not object to a preacher's preaching about sin as long as he is merely "against it." Paul, however, became uncomfortably personal.

To two people who were preoccupied with lustful living, Paul spoke of "self-control." The Bible has much to say about **self-control**. Self-control is part of the fruit of the Spirit (Gal. 5:23), one of the Christian graces (2 Pet. 1:6; see 1 Cor. 9:25; Tit. 1:8). The Greek word ἐγκράτεια (*enkrateia*), translated "self-control," is a compound word which means "inward strength." Both the English word "self-control" and the Greek word *enkrateia* refer to self-discipline, the inner strength to master one's desires, the capacity to crucify "the flesh with its passions and desires" (Gal. 5:24). One with self-control abstains from that which is wrong.

In Paul's day, the Greek word translated "self-control" also "frequently denoted *sexual* purity that is maintained by exercising restraint in one's conduct"[13] (see 1 Cor. 7:9). This message could have put Paul in danger, since he preached it to a couple living in indisputable sexual sin (1 Cor. 7:10) with no sense of shame. When John the Baptizer preached a similar message to Drusilla's great-uncle, John lost his head (Mt. 14:4, 10). It was, however, a message Felix and Drusilla needed to hear—and

---

[13]Kistemaker, 852 (emphasis added).

Paul did not hesitate to preach it.

Paul had a third truth to explain. He had to answer the question "What difference does it make whether or not one lives right or is self-disciplined?" Felix and Drusilla could have said, "Paul, you've lived a godly, disciplined life—and where has it gotten you? You stand before us in chains and a prison tunic. But we've lived as we pleased, and we sit on thrones in royal robes!" They needed to understand that God does not settle all accounts in this life.

Thus, to a pair who lived for the moment, Paul spoke of "the judgment to come." Paul stood before the thrones of Felix and Drusilla, but he wanted them to understand that they would one day stand before an eternal throne in **judgment** to account for their self-indulgence and dissipation (Rom. 14:12; 2 Cor. 5:10; Rev. 20:11–15). Paul had proclaimed this same message to the Athenians:

> God is now declaring to men that all people everywhere should repent, because He has fixed a day in which He will judge the world in righteousness through a Man whom He has appointed, having furnished proof to all men by raising Him from the dead (Acts 17:30, 31).

During Paul's trial, we were not surprised at his response to the accusations: He immediately began to defend himself. When Paul, in effect, accused Felix and Drusilla of unrighteousness, self-indulgence, and indifference toward the judgment, the governor's response was unexpected, even startling. From the ruler, we might have expected indifference, ridicule, or even anger. For a moment, he was struck dumb and could do nothing but "tremble" (v. 25; KJV). **Felix became frightened;** the ASV has "Felix was *terrified*" (emphasis added).

Clovis Chappell imagined being present and observing the scene:

> As I watched him, I saw him clinch his fists until his knuckles grew white, and his nails bit into the palms of his hands. I saw the big beads of perspiration break out on

his face. I saw him shake like a man in the grip of a heavy chill.[14]

Knowing what we know of Felix, it is difficult to conceive that he had a touchable conscience; but apparently he did. He caught sight of his true self in the mirror of God's Word (Jas. 1:23–25)—plus a glimpse of eternity—and what he saw scared him to death.

Incidentally, there is no indication that Drusilla trembled or was otherwise touched by Paul's message. If this beautiful young woman was ever interested in the gospel, she quickly lost interest when she learned that accepting it would require her to change her lifestyle.

It was the moment of truth for Felix, his golden opportunity. If the governor had cried out in desperation, "Brother, *what shall I do?*" (see 2:37), his life—and his eternity—might have turned out differently. Instead, he cried, "*Wait!*" While his fear was not sufficient to make him turn from evil to righteousness, it was enough to make him cut the interview short, saying, **"Go away for the present, and when I find time I will summon you."** Felix has been used as an example of "the sorrow of the world" (2 Cor. 7:10). We seldom "*find* time" for what is really important; rather, we must "*make* time." Compare this response to that of the Athenians in 17:32. During Paul's trial before Felix, the governor had put off making a decision (v. 22); as Felix stood on trial before the Lord, he again put off making a decision. "He adjourned his own case."[15]

Felix probably had his "reasons" for delaying a decision that day: It was getting late; he and Drusilla were tired from traveling; he had other matters on his mind—the Jews were constantly on the brink of revolt. No doubt, it seemed reasonable to him that "later" would be a better time to consider what Paul had said. The fact remains, however, that by procrastinating, Felix lost the opportunity of a lifetime.

The KJV has "When I have a *convenient* season, I will call for

---

[14]Chappell, 18.
[15]Morgan, 388.

thee" (emphasis added). The NIV reads similarly: "When I find it convenient, I will send for you." It is never "convenient" to change a sinful lifestyle, give up a lucrative position, and put away a beautiful wife.

Verse 26. As the days went by, Felix did find time to meet with Paul again: **therefore he also used to send for him quite often and converse with him.** We find no indication that Drusilla ever had any interest in listening to Paul again. However, the governor no longer called for Paul to hear "about faith in Christ Jesus" (v. 24). If he ever trembled again in Paul's presence, Luke did not record it. Felix had missed "his opportunity to allow the Lord to fill the emptiness of his things-oriented, power-hungry, money-grasping heart."[16] His spiritual "window of opportunity" had closed. The spark of decency flickering in Felix had been quenched. His heart had become as hard as the iron bars imprisoning Paul (see Heb. 4:7). All spiritual interest was gone.

At the same time too, the governor sent for the apostle, **hoping that money would be given him by Paul.** We can imagine Paul trying to talk about Jesus with Felix interrupting: "Yes, that is all very interesting, but what you said earlier about bringing alms to the Jews is even more interesting" (see comments on v. 17). We can see Felix looking at him with mock sympathy: "I hate to see you like this, Paul, when it is so unnecessary. You have friends with financial resources, right? I am a reasonable man. Arrangements could be made. . . ."

The KJV and NKJV, reflecting later manuscripts, have an additional phrase: "that he might loose [or, release] him." With or without these words, it is obvious that Felix, hoping for a generous bribe, dangled the thought of freedom before Paul. Since Felix was a ruler with a royal wife and a brother who was one of the richest men in Rome, a modest bribe would not have sufficed. Taking bribes was forbidden by Roman law, but bribery was nevertheless a fact of life with officials like Felix.

The biblical teaching on bribery is clear (see Ex. 23:8; Deut. 16:19; 2 Chron. 19:7; Ps. 15:5) and this story is a powerful application of that teaching. If ever a situation existed in which a

[16]Ogilvie, 328.

bribe might be justified, this was it. Paul's friends could have reasoned that God would surely desire for Paul to be free to preach and teach, that "this one time" it would be expedient to buy off a corrupt official. Paul had friends with money; but, significantly, no bribe was forthcoming. "The end" never "justifies the means" when "the means" violates God's Word.

Verse 27. The days slipped into weeks and the weeks into months, until **two years** had gone by. Apparently, the second hearing promised by Felix (v. 22) never took place. Words passed between Felix and Paul, but no money. At the end of the two years, **Felix was succeeded by Porcius Festus, and wishing to do the Jews a favor, Felix left Paul imprisoned.** The only legal action **Felix** could take was to release Paul, so once more he opted to do nothing—consistent to the end. Spiritually, Felix left as the one imprisoned, while Paul was free in Christ. After **imprisoned**, a few ancient manuscripts add "for the sake of Drusilla." Perhaps Drusilla walked in the footsteps of her aunt Herodias in the matter of holding grudges against one whose words had condemned her (Mk. 6:19).

From secular sources we know that Felix was deposed by Nero and summoned to Rome in A.D. 59. Verse 27 is, therefore, a key reference in working out the chronology of Acts: Paul had been arrested in Jerusalem two years earlier in A.D. 57; he started for Rome shortly after Festus became governor (c. A.D. 60) and was there for two years (28:30), so the book closes about A.D. 62.

History is clear on why Felix was replaced and why he was anxious for the goodwill of the Jews:

> There was a longstanding argument as to whether Caesarea was a Jewish or a Greek city and Jews and Greeks were at daggers drawn. There was an outbreak of mob violence in which the Jews came off best. Felix dispatched his troops to aid the Gentiles. Thousands of Jews were killed and the troops, with Felix's consent and encouragement, sacked and looted the houses of the wealthiest Jews in the city.
>
> The Jews did what all Roman provincials had a right

to do—they reported their governor to Rome. That was why Felix left Paul in prison, even though he was aware that he should be liberated. He was trying to curry favour with the Jews.[17]

Regarding Felix' efforts to appease the Jews, Barclay said, "It was all to no purpose. He was dismissed from his governorship and only the influence of his brother Pallas saved him from execution."[18] Felix was banished to Gaul (France) where he died. Drusilla and their son later perished in the eruption of Mount Vesuvius, ending the sad tale of a couple who tried to gain the world and thereby lost their souls (Mt. 16:26). The sadness of this tale is intensified when one recalls a memorable day when the two listened to Paul speak of his Lord. "For all sad words of tongue or pen, the saddest are these: 'It might have been!'"[19]

APPLICATION

An Application from a Preacher (Ch. 24)
A congregation was in need of an evangelist. One of the elders was trying to find out what kind of preacher the church wanted. To do this, he composed a letter and read it to the congregation as though it had been received from an applicant:

Gentlemen:
Understanding that you are in need of a preacher, I would like to apply.

I have many qualifications that I think you would appreciate. I have been blessed to preach with power and have had some success as a writer. Some say that I am a good organizer. I have been a leader in many places I have gone.

Some, however, have some things against me. I am over fifty years old. My health is not the best, but I

---

[17]Barclay, 171. See Josephus *Wars* 2.13.7; *Antiquities* 20.8.7, 9.
[18]Ibid.
[19]John Whittier, *Maud Muller*, 53.

manage to get a good deal done. I have never preached in one place for more than three years at a time. Most of the congregations I have preached for have been small. I have generally had to work at my trade to help pay my way. I'm afraid I'm not too good at keeping records (I have been known even to forget whom I baptized).

I have not gotten along too well with the religious leaders in several towns. In fact, some of them threatened me, took me to court, and even attacked me physically. In several places I had to leave town hurriedly when my work caused riots and disturbances. I have even been in jail three or four times, but not because of any wrongdoing.

If you can use me, I shall do my best for you even if I have to work to help with my support.

After reading the letter, the elder asked the members if they were interested in the applicant. They all agreed that he would never do for the congregation there. They did not want an unhealthy, contentious, trouble-making ex-convict as a preacher, and they were insulted that his application had been presented. One, however, did ask the preacher's name. The elder replied, "The apostle Paul."

Sermons from Paul's Trial (Ch. 24)
C. Bruce White covered chapter 24 in one lesson: (1) A False Witness (vv. 1–9); (2) A Fair Answer (vv. 10–23); (3) A Firm Sermon (vv. 24, 25); (4) A Fearful Response (vv. 25–27).

Warren Wiersbe divided the chapter according to principal characters: (1) Tertullus: False Accusation (vv. 1–9); (2) Paul: Faithful Answers (vv. 10–21); (3) Felix: Foolish Attitudes (vv. 22–27).[20]

Imprisoned, Yet Free (Ch. 24)
A centurion in the Fortress Antonia referred to the apostle as "Paul the prisoner" (23:18). That phrase describes Paul throughout the last seven chapters of Acts. Paul called himself

---

[20]Wiersbe, 497–502.

"the prisoner of Christ Jesus" and "the prisoner of the Lord" (Eph. 3:1; 4:1). Note that Paul did not consider himself the prisoner of *Rome*, but "the prisoner *of the Lord.*" Paul was reconciled to his lot because he believed he was where the Lord wanted him to be; he believed the Lord knew best and would work things out.

Some Christians are actually in prison. Many more feel imprisoned by circumstances, by forces beyond their control. If you feel that way, are you reconciled to your situation as Paul was, or do you fret and worry over conditions you cannot change? Once you have done all you can, are you willing to leave matters in the hands of God?

In working with inmates, we have found many behind prison walls who were free in Christ (Rom. 8:2; Gal. 5:1), both spiritually and emotionally. Outside the prison, we have found multitudes imprisoned by sin (Rom. 6:17) and by their own fears (see Lev. 26:17). Being free or being imprisoned by life is basically a state of mind. Those who trust in the Lord find the words of Richard Lovelace to be true: "Stone walls do not a prison make, nor iron bars a cage."[21]

Procrastination (24:24–27)

A preacher introduced a sermon on "Procrastination" by saying, "This is a much needed subject . . . and I've been intending to preach on it for several months . . . but for some reason, I've kept putting it off."

All of us are guilty of putting off tasks, especially tasks we do not enjoy. Students put off writing term papers; husbands put off doing household repairs; Americans put off filling out their income tax forms until the April 15 deadline.

While many jobs we put off are trivial in nature, some tasks and decisions we put off matter greatly. Someone has written:

He was going to be all that a mortal should be—tomorrow.
No one would be kinder or braver than he—tomorrow.
But the fact is he died and faded from view,

---

[21]Quoted in Christopher Morley, ed., *The Shorter Bartlett's Familiar Quotations* (New York: Permabooks, 1953), 223.

And all that he left when his living was through
Was a bundle of things he intended to do—tomorrow.[22]

It is a significant matter to put off becoming a Christian. The story is often told that Satan once held a conference with his demons. He announced his concern about the number becoming Christians and asked if any had a suggestion on how they might slow the trend. One demon said, "We could tell people there is no heaven, so there is no need for them to become Christians." "No, that won't work," said Satan. "All who believe in God know there is something beyond this life—an existence with God Himself." Another demon spoke up: "We could tell people there is no hell, so they have nothing to worry about if they don't become Christians." Satan sighed. "That won't work either. Anyone who looks at the injustice in the world knows that there has to be a time when everything is made right." Finally, one demon suggested, "We could tell people that they should become Christians, that there *is* a heaven and a hell—but that *there is no hurry.*" Satan laughed and said, "Perfect! That will cause more to be lost than any other message we could preach!" The story is fiction, but the message is not: The idea that "there is no hurry" has sent millions to face God unprepared.

Edward Young said, "Procrastination is the thief of time."[23] It is also the thief of souls. An old English proverb declares that "One of these days is none of these days." A preacher once commented that "Someday is not on the calendar."[24] The Bible declares: "Do not boast about tomorrow, for you do not know what a day may bring forth" (Prov. 27:1; see Lk. 12:19–21; Jas. 4:13, 14).

The dangers of procrastination are great: (1) One may die before he has another opportunity; (2) the Lord may return; (3) the heart may become hardened. Every time one refuses the gospel invitation, his heart becomes a little harder. The Lord's invitation is urgent. "For He says, 'At the acceptable time I lis-

---

[22]Quoted in Paul Rogers, "Three Responses at Athens," *Preacher's Periodical* 5 (May 1985): 20.

[23]Quoted in Morley, 438.

[24]Jeff Taylor, sermon preached at the Judsonia church of Christ, Judsonia, Arkansas, on 11 February 1996.

tened to you, and on the day of salvation I helped you.' Behold, now is 'the acceptable time,' behold, now is 'the day of salvation'" (2 Cor. 6:2). "Today if you hear His voice, do not harden your hearts" (Heb. 4:7). Someone has said, "One day will be your last day to obey the gospel." Today may be that day.

The Heaviest "Wait" (24:24–27)

If you teach on Felix, here is an attention-getter to use as you begin: At the top of the chalkboard write, "The Heaviest Weight in the World." Beneath that, sketch an elephant, weights used by weight-lifters, and other heavy items. Ask the class what they think "the heaviest weight in the world" is. Then change the word "Weight" to "Wait" and note that the heaviest "wait" is to wait on *obedience*.

You could also use a chalkboard presentation with a simple outline: (1) An Ungodly Audience, (2) A Fearless Preacher, (3) A Searching Sermon, and (4) Disappointing Results. As you talk about the "audience," sketch Felix and Drusilla on the board. As you discuss the "preacher," draw Paul in chains. When you come to the "sermon," list Paul's three points. Finally, highlight the "results" by writing on the board "Frightened, but Waited" or "Trembled, but Waited for 'A Convenient Season'" (KJV).

"Felix, Example of Sinners" (24:24–27)

William Smitty suggested these ideas for a sermon entitled "Felix, Example of Sinners": (1) Felix, like *some* sinners, had a "more perfect knowledge" of the truth. (2) Felix, like *all* sinners, came to the crossroads of decision. (3) Felix, like *many* sinners, turned away from the messenger and the message of God. (4) Felix, like *multitudes* of sinners, never again found a "convenient season" for hearing and believing the Word of God.[25]

Preaching Against Sin (24:25)

Even though it was risky, Paul did not hesitate to proclaim "righteousness, self-control and the judgment to come" to a

---

[25]William H. Smitty, *300 Sermon Outlines From the New Testament* (Nashville, Tenn.: Broadman Press, 1983), 46.

couple absorbed in sin (v. 25). We need a revival of this kind of preaching today. The world has no greater need, for it has lost the sense of sin. Renowned writer and poet Phyllis McGinley observed, "People are no longer sinful. They are only immature or underprivileged or frightened or, more particularly, sick."[26] Whether the world likes it or not, sin is still sin, and "the wages of sin" is still spiritual death (Rom. 6:23).

Once, when U.S. President Calvin Coolidge returned from a church service, he was asked the preacher's topic. The President, not known for being talkative, replied, "Sin." The inquirer persisted: "What did he say about it?" Coolidge answered, "He was against it." Most do not object to a preacher speaking "against sin," as long as he does not get too specific and personal. Paul spoke very personally to Felix and Drusilla about the sin in their lives.

Today, we need men with the courage to preach on all the sins covered by Paul. For instance, we need those who will preach against the sexual sin that saturates our society (see 2 Tim. 4:1–4). Multiplied thousands commit fornication and adultery with little or no thought of the immediate or eternal consequences (Rom. 13:9; 1 Cor. 6:18–20; Gal. 5:19–21). It remains true that "the one who commits adultery . . . is lacking sense" (Prov. 6:32).

In many pulpits today, the judgment is also a shunned topic. People want to believe that after this life a glowing heavenly welcome committee will greet one and all. The widely publicized "near-death experiences" of our day (many, if not most, of them suspect) would leave the impression that after death all men will have a happy, even ecstatic existence. The Bible teaches otherwise (Mt. 7:13, 14). The writer of Hebrews emphasized,

> It is appointed for [all] men to die once and after this comes *judgment*. . . . For if we go on sinning willfully . . . there no longer remains a sacrifice for sins, but a certain terrifying expectation of judgment and the fury of a fire which will consume the adversaries. . . . For we know

---

[26]Quoted in Wiersbe, 501.

Him who said, "Vengeance is Mine, I will repay." . . . It is a terrifying thing to fall into the hands of the living God (Heb. 9:27; 10:26, 27, 30, 31; emphasis added).

Other passages on this topic include 2 Thessalonians 1:1–9; 1 Peter 4:17–19; 2 Peter 2:9–14; 3:3–10.

CHAPTER 25

PAUL'S IMPRISONMENT AT CAESAREA (PART 3)

As we read chapter 25, we find many details that parallel the previous chapters: Paul on trial, a weak governor, a vindictive Council, a diabolical plot. Reading this chapter is like re-reading a book or watching a rerun on television. There are details we have either forgotten or did not notice the first time. Even so, as we cover material similar to that seen earlier in Acts, there will be new thoughts and truths to discover.

PAUL, IN HIS TRIAL BEFORE FESTUS, APPEALS TO CAESAR (25:1–12)

Festus in Jerusalem (25:1–5)

¹Festus then, having arrived in the province, three days later went up to Jerusalem from Caesarea. ²And the chief priests and the leading men of the Jews brought charges against Paul, and they were urging him, ³requesting a concession against Paul, that he might have him brought to Jerusalem (at the same time, setting an ambush to kill him on the way). ⁴Festus then answered that Paul was being kept in custody at Caesarea and that he himself was about to leave shortly. ⁵"Therefore," he said, "let the influential men among you go there with me, and if there is anything wrong about the man, let them prosecute him."

Verse 1. The story opens as the account in chapter 24 did. One of the key participants is a Roman governor—a different individual, but a Roman governor nevertheless. The last verse of chapter 24 stated, "Felix was succeeded by Porcius Festus" (24:27). This chapter begins, **Festus then, having arrived in the province.**

We do not know much about **Festus.** He was apparently a member of one of the noble families in Rome. The historian Josephus described him as wise, fair, and agreeable. We would agree that he was more just and moderate than his predecessor or his successors. Like his predecessor Felix, Festus attempted to rid the province of Judea of robbers and assassins. Both men also tried to placate the Jews. Festus died after only two years in office. He was followed by Albinus and Florus, who were both evil men. The rule of Florus in Judea intensified the animosity which led to the Jewish revolt in A.D. 66.[1]

Initially, we are impressed with Festus' determination to be a good governor. Only **three days** after he arrived in the country, he **went up to Jerusalem from Caesarea.** Festus had many reasons to meet immediately with the Jewish leaders in Jerusalem: He needed to pay his respects (v. 13). He also needed to get to know them. Remember that they were the ones who had gotten Felix removed from office! He needed to find out their greatest concerns and assure them that he would address these. He needed their cooperation if he were to meet his greatest challenge—to reverse the tide of political and social unrest in Judea.

Verse 2. When Festus arrived in Jerusalem, he was met by a cast we have often seen on the stage in Acts: **the chief priests and the leading men of the Jews**—in other words, the Sanhedrin. In the two years since the last trial, the president of the Council had changed. Ananias, that "whitewashed wall," had been "struck by God" from office. However, he still exerted considerable influence and would probably have been among "the chief priests" mentioned. Later he was "struck" dead (see comments on 23:2, 3). According to the historian Josephus, Ishmael was now the high priest. This man was cut from the same cloth as Ananias; he, too, was ruthless and self-seeking.[2]

---

[1]Josephus *Antiquities* 20.8.9—9.5; 20.11.1; *Wars* 2.14.1—16.5.
[2]Josephus *Antiquities* 20.8.8.

When Festus sat down to discuss affairs of state with the Jewish leaders, he probably expected talk of the sagging economy, the rising crime rate, perhaps even what they considered to be Roman injustices. Instead, to his surprise, the top item on their agenda was an unresolved court case—concerning an aged tentmaker Felix had left rotting in jail in Caesarea (24:27). The Jewish leaders **brought charges against Paul.**

Festus later reported what happened in Jerusalem: "When I was at Jerusalem, the chief priests and the elders of the Jews brought charges against [Paul], asking for a sentence of condemnation upon him" (v. 15). The phrase "a sentence of condemnation" translates the Greek word καταδίκη (*katadikē*) that refers to "a guilty verdict."[3] We realize that Festus was putting himself in as good a light as possible when he told what had happened (see comments on vv. 17, 18, 20), but we are inclined to believe Festus for at least two reasons: (1) The governor's words do not contradict Luke's original account; rather, they supplement it. (2) The requests of the Jewish leaders as reported by Festus are consistent with their known hatred of Paul. Festus also said the Jews were "loudly declaring that he ought not to live any longer" (v. 24). Perhaps they asked him to turn Paul over to them. In verse 24, the Western Text adds "that I should hand him over to them for punishment without any defense." We can hear them saying to Festus, "Felix should have released that troublemaker to us, but the crafty politician knew nothing of justice!"

They wanted Festus to render a guilty verdict without a trial, but he "answered them that it is not the custom of the Romans to hand over any man before the accused meets his accusers face to face and has an opportunity to make his defense against the charges" (v. 16). Regardless of what horrendous crimes the imprisoned man had committed, Roman law said he had the right to a fair trial. This right was one of the grandest principles of Roman jurisprudence, even though the Romans sometimes fell short of their ideal.

---

[3]Simon J. Kistemaker, *Exposition of the Acts of the Apostles*, New Testament Commentary (Grand Rapids, Mich.: Baker Book House, 1990), 875.

Verse 3. The Council members must have been surprised to find themselves dealing with a Roman who had a sense of justice. However, they had an alternate plan ready. They would agree to a trial if the governor would hold it in Jerusalem. They began urging him, **requesting a concession against Paul, that he might have him brought to Jerusalem.** It seemed a reasonable request. The governor could hold court in either Caesarea or Jerusalem (see Jn. 19:13), so why not Jerusalem?

Note the word **concession.** The Greek word χάρις (*charis*), translated "concession," is rendered "favor" in most translations (see KJV, ASV, RSV, NIV). The NASB translates the word *charis* as "favor" later in our text (v. 9). Kistemaker pointed out that "in the singular . . . the word *favor* reveals a *quid pro quo* (something for something) exchange."[4] The Jews presented this ultimatum to the governor: "If you want us to help you, then you help us first. Give us Paul!" The pressure put on the new official was incredible. It has been suggested that they probably even tried to bribe Festus. Since Festus' predecessor could be bought (24:26), they would assume the same about him.

On the surface, the Jews were requesting justice. Beneath the surface, they were plotting an injustice—for they were, **at the same time, setting an ambush to kill** Paul **on the way.** This story line sounds familiar. Two years earlier, the leaders of the Sanhedrin had planned to ask the Roman commander to bring Paul to them, secretly plotting for their co-conspirators to overwhelm his guard and kill the apostle (23:12–15). This time, armed men would hide in the hill country of Judea to ambush Paul and his escort as they neared Jerusalem. Some or all of these schemers might have been the same men who had previously bound themselves with an oath to kill Paul (23:12, 13). On this occasion, Festus was unlikely to provide the massive escort that Claudius Lysias had sent (23:23).

Time can diminish bitterness in the heart, but only if the heart's possessor turns loose of his anger (see Eph. 4:31). The Jewish leaders had unceasingly stoked their hatred, and it blazed higher than ever before (Heb. 12:15). The plot in chapter 23 had

---

[4]Ibid., 862.

originated with the forty; then they had taken their plan to the Council. This time, the deadly plot originated with the Council itself.

Verses 4, 5. If Lysias was still commander in Jerusalem, he may have told Festus about the assassination plot of two years earlier. However, there is no indication that the governor knew about that plot. If he had, he surely would have mentioned it in his private conversation with Agrippa (vv. 14–21). Festus may not have been aware of the Jews' plot, but he knew a power play when he saw it. The Jewish leaders were trying to take advantage of the inexperience of a new ruler who had a natural desire to get his regime off to a good start. Compare this to the Jews' approach to Gallio in Corinth (see comments on 18:12).

> **Festus then answered that Paul was being kept in custody at Caesarea and that he himself was about to leave shortly. "Therefore," he said, "let the influential men among you go there with me, and if there is anything wrong about the man, let them prosecute him."**

Festus was saying, "As a concession to you, I will re-open the case, but never forget that I am the governor. You must fit in with my plans, not I with yours."

Once more the providence of God was demonstrated (Prov. 21:1), for if the governor had agreed to bring Paul to Jerusalem, the life of the apostle would have been forfeited. As John Wesley noted, "By what invisible springs does God govern the world! Festus' care to preserve the imperial privileges was the means of preserving Paul's life."[5]

Paul Appeals to Caesar (25:6–12)

> **[6]After he had spent not more than eight or ten days among them, he went down to Caesarea, and on the next day he took**

---

[5]Quoted in James Burton Coffman, *Commentary on Acts* (Austin, Tex.: Firm Foundation Publishing House, 1976), 467.

his seat on the tribunal and ordered Paul to be brought. ⁷After Paul arrived, the Jews who had come down from Jerusalem stood around him, bringing many and serious charges against him which they could not prove, ⁸while Paul said in his own defense, "I have committed no offense either against the Law of the Jews or against the temple or against Caesar." ⁹But Festus, wishing to do the Jews a favor, answered Paul and said, "Are you willing to go up to Jerusalem and stand trial before me on these charges?" ¹⁰But Paul said, "I am standing before Caesar's tribunal, where I ought to be tried. I have done no wrong to the Jews, as you also very well know. ¹¹If, then, I am a wrongdoer and have committed anything worthy of death, I do not refuse to die; but if none of those things is true of which these men accuse me, no·one can hand me over to them. I appeal to Caesar." ¹²Then when Festus had conferred with his council, he answered, "You have appealed to Caesar, to Caesar you shall go."

Verse 6. After the Jewish leaders reluctantly agreed to Festus' counter-offer, the governor quickly wrapped up his visit to Jerusalem. Then, **after he had spent not more than eight or ten days among them, he went down to Caesarea**, the Jewish leaders traveling with him (v. 5). The KJV, based on a different text, has "more than ten days." "Not more than eight or ten" is preferred, but the variation is insignificant.

To demonstrate his desire to cooperate with the Jews, Festus cleared his calendar **and on the next day he took his seat on the tribunal and ordered Paul to be brought.** The **tribunal** was the βῆμα (*bēma*), the judgment seat (see KJV), the symbol of Roman authority (see comments on 18:12). Although it could have been inside the Praetorium, the *bēma* was probably located in a courtyard. Compare this picture to John 18:28. Festus was determined to dispose of the matter efficiently and decisively. He later declared, "So after [the Jews] had assembled here, I did not delay, but on the next day took my seat on the tribunal and ordered the man to be brought before me" (v. 17).

When the soldiers came to get Paul, the apostle must have been surprised, even shocked. He had already been tried and found innocent by the former governor (24:26). There was no need for another trial.

Verse 7. Once Paul was present, Festus gave the Jewish leaders permission to present their case. This time they did not have an orator to represent them (see 24:1). Rather, they all **stood around** Paul, **bringing many and serious charges against him.** The accusations might have been new to Judge Festus, but they were the same tired complaints of chapters 21 and 24 with a slight variation: a political twist. We know this because of Paul's reply in verse 8. For details on the charges, see comments on 21:28 and 24:10–21. Notice the parallels between this scene and 17:5–8. Their charges remained accusations **which they could not prove** under cross-examination (see 24:13).

The scene was confused, even chaotic. The proper procedure was for the prosecutors to remain seated until they presented their case (v. 18). Then they were to speak in turn, one at a time. Instead, all the leaders from Jerusalem crowded around Paul (v. 7), pouring out their hatred. At the same time, local Jews from Caesarea were shouting from the audience that Paul "ought not to live any longer" (v. 24).

What could the Jews expect to accomplish by this hysterical outburst? Knowing that they would never indict Paul on their fallacious and fictitious charges, they evidently hoped to intimidate a new governor who was concerned about maintaining order in the land.

Verse 8. By this time, Festus must have been cursing Felix for leaving this particular case unresolved. Dispensing Roman justice among the Jewish people was not as simple as he had supposed. After restoring order, the governor allowed Paul to speak. Luke summarized Paul's defense in a few words: **"I have committed no offense either against the Law of the Jews or against the temple or against Caesar."** Apparently, the Council had again accused Paul of sin, sacrilege, and sedition: *sin*—breaking **the Law of the Jews;** *sacrilege*—defiling **the temple;** and *sedition*—stirring up trouble for Rome. Since the Jews had no proof for their charges, the only way Paul could be convicted was if he admitted his guilt. When he pleaded "not guilty," he should have immediately been declared innocent by Festus.

However, in connection with the third charge, a new word had been used: **Caesar**. This imperial title had not surfaced in Paul's Judean trials, and its appearance in verse 8 is no mere coincidence. The focus was shifting from Palestine to Rome, from subordinates to the top man (see 27:24).

Luke's words feature the Roman emperor nine times in this chapter. The word "Caesar" is used six times (vv. 8, 10, 11, 12, 21). The Greek word translated "Caesar" is Καῖσαρ (*Kaisar*). Originally, "Caesar" was a designation given to Gaius Julius [Caesar], but it then became a title for Roman rulers. Luke uses the title "Emperor" twice (vv. 21, 25). The Greek word translated "Emperor" is Σεβαστός (*Sebastos*), the Greek equivalent of the Latin word "Augustus" (see KJV). The term "Augustus" was a title meaning "the majestic, awe-inspiring one." After Octavian accepted the title "Augustus," other emperors followed suit (see Lk. 2:1). The title "lord" is used once (v. 26). The Greek word translated "lord" is κύριος (*kurios*). When applied to the emperor, it sometimes implied deity, especially if it was coupled with the word "god" (θεός, *theos*). The current emperor, Nero, gloried in such titles. Christians could not conscientiously refer to the emperor as "lord" in a *divine* sense. For the child of God, there is only "one Lord" (Eph. 4:5).

In addition to pleading "not guilty" to the three charges, Paul again pled "guilty" to believing in the Resurrection (see 24:20, 21), boldly proclaiming that Jesus was alive (25:19).

Verse 9. When Paul finished, Festus was bewildered and confused (v. 20). Unlike Felix, Festus did not have "a more exact knowledge about the Way" (24:22). As he later recounted, both sides sounded to him like nonsense:

> When the accusers stood up, they began bringing charges against [Paul] not of such crimes as I was expecting, but they simply had some points of disagreement with him about their own religion and about a dead man, Jesus, whom Paul asserted to be alive (25:18, 19).

Two facts were crystal clear to the governor: First, the issue was a religious one, not a political one. Having come to that conclusion, Gallio had thrown the case out of court (18:14–16), and Festus should have done the same. Second, Paul was not a criminal. The governor later admitted, "I found that he had committed nothing worthy of death" (25:25). Those two facts should have settled the matter. Festus should have announced from his judgment seat, "I find the defendant 'not guilty'"—but he did not.

The governor was between the proverbial rock and hard place. On the one hand, he dared not find Paul guilty for fear of Rome. Paul was a Roman citizen and had certain rights. If it were reported to Rome that Festus had punished an innocent Roman citizen, he would be severely penalized. On the other hand, he dared not find Paul innocent for fear of the Jews. In less than two weeks at his new post, his lofty ideals had been crushed. Like many other politicians before and after him, he ended up concerned with what was politically expedient.

Surrounded by stony-faced Jewish leaders who could make or break his administration, Festus considered his options. It is not hard to imagine his thought processes: "A Jewish religious question is at the heart of this unpleasantness, so the best place to resolve it would be at the center of the Jewish religion, Jerusalem. This decision would make the Council members happy, and I need them on my side. On the other hand, this move would make the prisoner nervous. So I'll assure him that I'll stay in charge."

Luke stated that Festus made the proposal because he was **wishing to do** *the Jews* **a favor** (emphasis added). Once more, a weak bureaucrat decided to use Paul as a political pawn (see 24:27). Festus turned to Paul and said: **"Are you willing to go up to Jerusalem and stand trial before me on these charges?"** The words **before me** may have sounded like a concession in Paul's favor, but the proposition could not possibly benefit him. The proposal was illegal, illogical, and ill-advised. It was *illegal* because Paul had been found innocent twice. In the United States and in other countries today, there is a law of "double jeopardy," which says that once a man has been found innocent of a specific crime, he cannot be tried again for that same crime. Festus evidently did not even believe in protection from "triple jeopardy." It was *illogical* because if no decision had been reached in two previous trials, why should a third trial produce a different result? Finally, from Paul's viewpoint, the plan was decidedly *ill-advised*. If Festus could be intimidated by a handful of Jewish leaders, he would be more intimidated surrounded by thousands demanding Paul's death. Further, who knew what deviltry the Jews were up to? Paul had suffered too often from their plots (9:24; 20:3; 23:14) to trust them now.

Do not be misled by the fact that Festus *asked* Paul if he was **willing to go up to Jerusalem** (emphasis added). "A governor's query [was] tantamount to his decision."[6] The governor was not giving Paul a choice. He was telling the apostle that he *would* be going to Jerusalem. This fact is obvious from Paul's response: "No one can hand me over to them [the Jewish leaders]." If Paul had been given the option of saying, "No, thank you; I prefer not to go to Jerusalem," it would not have been necessary for him to appeal to Caesar (see 28:19).

Verses 10, 11. At this point, our story takes a twist. Instead of a rerun, it becomes a reminder, a reassurance that God always provides a "way of escape" (1 Cor. 10:13). His life hanging in the balance, Paul faced the most powerful man in Palestine (see Jn. 19:10)—and said, "No":

> **I am standing before Caesar's tribunal, where I ought to be tried. I have done no wrong to the Jews, as you also very well know. If, then, I am a wrongdoer and have committed anything worthy of death, I do not refuse to die; but if none of those things is true of which these men accuse me, no one can hand me over to them. I appeal to Caesar.**

Our text tells of a power struggle between a Roman governor and a Roman citizen—and, with the help of God, the citizen prevailed. The Living Bible paraphrases Paul's words like this:

---

[6]Ernst Haenchen, paraphrased by I. Howard Marshall, *The Acts of the Apostles*, The Tyndale New Testament Commentaries, gen. ed. R. V. G. Tasker (Grand Rapids, Mich.: Wm. B. Eerdmans Publishing Co., 1980), 384.

No! I demand my privilege of a hearing before the Emperor himself. You know very well I am not guilty. If I have done something worthy of death, I don't refuse to die! But if I am innocent, neither you nor anyone else has a right to turn me over to these men to kill me. *I appeal to Caesar* (emphasis theirs).

A Roman citizen had the right to appeal to Caesar if he believed that his case was being mishandled. A few exceptions were made to this right, such as cases involving murderers or thieves who had been caught in the act. However, the right to appeal was one of the basic rights of Roman citizenship. Originally, a citizen appealed to the people. Later, the appeal was to the Roman senate, who represented the people. After that, it was to the emperor, who was supposed to be the people's representative. When a citizen said, *"Caesarem appello,"* immediately the matter was taken out of the hands of his judge. These two Latin words are substituted in the original text with the Greek equivalent: Καίσαρα ἐπικαλοῦμαι (*Kaisara epikaloumai*). Richard B. Rackham made this observation concerning the powerful effect of Paul's words "I appeal to Caesar": "Thus by uttering two words . . . Paul was able to deliver himself altogether out of the power of the Jews."[7]

The Caesar at the time of Paul's appeal was Nero, who had come to the throne in A.D. 54. Knowing Nero's history of bloodshed, we may think it strange that Paul would desire to put his life in his hands. Keep in mind, however, that the first five years of Nero's reign were considered a "golden age" by the Romans. During that time, he was under the influence of Seneca, who was Gallio's brother (see comments on 18:12), as well as others. "There was little in A.D. 59 that gave warning of the events of A.D. 64 and 65."[8] In these later years, the emperor Nero began his persecution of Christians.

---

[7]Richard B. Rackham, *The Acts of the Apostles*, Westminster Commentaries, ed. Walter Lock (London: Methuen & Co., 1901) 452.

[8]F. F. Bruce, *The Book of Acts*, The New International Commentary on the New Testament, gen. ed. F. F. Bruce, rev. ed. (Grand Rapids, Mich.: Wm. B. Eerdmans Publishing Co., 1988), 454.

Festus must have been surprised by Paul's response. Although every Roman citizen had the right to appeal to Rome, few availed themselves of it because of the embarrassment and inconvenience. To enter the capital city under armed guard was no man's ambition. Further, the average man could not afford the time involved in travel, plus the stay in Rome waiting for his case to come up for trial (see 28:30).

Verse 12. Flustered, Festus **conferred with his council** to see what he should do. The Greek text has simply "the council" (see KJV). Do not confuse this with the Jewish Council. This council was the governor's advisory board. Since no executive can be an expert in every field, most have advisory boards or "cabinets" filled with experts on different aspects of government. They no doubt told him that Paul was within his rights—and that, as Rome's representative, the governor had no choice. Likely embarrassed, Festus returned to the tribunal and pronounced the ancient formula: *"Caesarem appellesti; ad Caesarem ibis"*—**"You have appealed to Caesar, to Caesar you shall go."**

As Festus spoke those words, he probably had mixed emotions. He was probably smarting from the unexpected rebuff from a "nobody." He was definitely nervous about how to handle the affair in a way that would not reflect on his administration. He was probably also relieved because soon this bothersome creature and burdensome case would no longer be his responsibility. The governor "ordered [Paul] to be kept in custody" until arrangements could be made to "send him to Caesar" (v. 21). At last, Paul was on his way to Rome!

As we consider Paul's appeal, several questions come to mind: Since Paul was aware of his right to appeal to Caesar, why had he not exercised that right before, thus bypassing two years of imprisonment in Caesarea? Why did he finally insist on his rights at the time he did? Apparently, up to the moment that Festus spoke about returning to Jerusalem, Paul thought he had more than one option for getting to Rome. One door open to him was an appeal to Caesar, but that was the least preferred door. Notice 28:19, where Paul said, "I was *forced* to appeal to Caesar" (emphasis added). Paul did not want to go to Rome as a prisoner. According to Philippians 1:12–17, brethren in Rome had mixed emotions about Paul's imprisonment. Some were apparently embarrassed by his chains. Rather, he wanted to walk into Rome a free man—free to go where he wished, free to preach where he would. It is possible that Paul had interpreted Jesus' promise of going to Rome (23:11) to mean that he would be released so that he could travel. Paul had earlier misinterpreted the Spirit's warning (20:22–25); he could also have misinterpreted Jesus' promise. During the two years that Felix had him in custody, Paul had reason to believe he could be released at any time. When Felix left the country without releasing Paul, one door closed in his face (24:27). In addition to the times Paul was found innocent and should have been set free, he probably expected to be released when Felix left Palestine. Often, when a governor left office, one of his final acts of clemency was to release any prisoner concerning whom he had not made a decision regarding punishment.

When the governorship was given to Festus—a man who had neither an understanding of the craftiness of the Jews nor an appreciation of Christianity—other doors began to shut. Finally, when the governor informed Paul that he would be taken to Jerusalem, only one doorway remained open: an appeal to Caesar. Paul dashed through that door before it also closed.

Did Paul make a mistake when he appealed to Caesar? Didn't King Agrippa later say to Festus, "This man might have been set free if he had not appealed to Caesar" (26:32)? Agrippa made that statement, but it was the personal opinion of one who had no jurisdiction in the case. Further, Agrippa made it considerably later (25:13, 14). If Paul had not thwarted the governor's plans with his appeal, Luke would have been writing the apostle's obituary before Agrippa and Bernice ever arrived in Caesarea. Festus believed in taking action without delay (vv. 6, 17) and would have sent Paul back to Jerusalem immediately. In Acts 28:19 the Western Text has Paul saying, "I was forced to appeal to Caesar . . . that I might deliver my soul from death." There is also another reason for believing that Paul did not make a mistake in appealing to Caesar: When the apostle faced his accusers, he generally allowed the Spirit to speak through him (see Mk. 13:11).

By appealing to Caesar, Paul had the opportunity to preach to King Agrippa (26:1; see 9:15). By appealing to Caesar, Paul remained under Roman protection until he was safely out of the country (see 25:21). By appealing to Caesar, Paul was later able to extend the influence of the gospel into Caesar's palace (Phil. 4:22). By appealing to Caesar, Paul even got to preach to Nero's tribunal, and most likely to the emperor himself (Acts 9:15; 27:24). It is even possible that it was God who "forced" Paul to appeal to Caesar (28:19), so Paul could present the case for legalizing Christianity before the imperial court. Once more the providential hand of God can be seen.

TWO VISITORS COME TO CAESAREA (25:13–27)

Festus Relates Paul's Story to Agrippa (25:13–22)

¹³Now when several days had elapsed, King Agrippa and Bernice arrived at Caesarea and paid their respects to Festus. ¹⁴While they were spending many days there, Festus laid Paul's case before the king, saying, "There is a man who was left as a prisoner by Felix; ¹⁵and when I was at Jerusalem, the chief priests and the elders of the Jews brought charges against him, asking for a sentence of condemnation against him. ¹⁶I answered them that it is not the custom of the Romans to hand over any man before the accused meets his accusers face to face and has an opportunity to make his defense against the charges. ¹⁷So after they had assembled here, I did not delay, but on the next day took my seat on the tribunal and ordered the man to be brought before me. ¹⁸When the accusers stood up, they began bringing charges against him not of such crimes as I was expecting, ¹⁹but they simply had some points of disagreement with him about their own religion and about a dead man, Jesus, whom Paul asserted to be alive. ²⁰Being at a loss how to investigate such matters, I asked whether he was willing to go to Jerusalem and there stand trial on these matters. ²¹But when Paul appealed to be held in custody for the Emperor's decision, I ordered him to be kept in custody until I send him to Caesar." ²²Then Agrippa said to Festus, "I also

would like to hear the man myself." "Tomorrow," he said, "you shall hear him."

Verse 13. While arrangements were being made for Paul's trial, Festus had two royal visitors: **King Agrippa and Bernice arrived at Caesarea and paid their respects to Festus.**

King Agrippa is known in history as Herod Agrippa II. His father, Herod Agrippa I, was the Herod of Acts 12 who killed James and tried to kill Peter. His great-grandfather was Herod the Great, who instigated a search-and-destroy mission against the baby Jesus. Agrippa was the last of the Herod dynasty; he is sometimes called "the last of the Herods" (see comments on 12:1).

Agrippa was only seventeen when his father died, so he had not been given his father's widespread domain. Rather, a few years later, he was given an insignificant territory north of Palestine. Over the years, he had been granted additional land, but his kingdom was trifling compared to that of his father. However, he had considerable influence among the Jewish people. He had Jewish blood, and Rome made him legal guardian of the temple in Jerusalem, giving him the right to select the high priest. For all practical purposes, he was the secular head of the Jewish faith. In chapter 24 we encountered a sister of Agrippa, Drusilla, who was married to Governor Felix (24:24).

Agrippa was a typical Herod and lived for self-gratification. His most notorious escapade was living in open sin with his beautiful sister, Julia **Bernice,** even though the Law clearly condemned incest (Lev. 18:1–18; 20:11–21). According to ancient writers, this relationship "was a scandal among Jews and Gentiles alike."[9]

Bernice had married Marcus, royalty from Alexandria. After his death, she married her uncle, Herod of Chalcis. A remarkable number of marriages took place in the Herod family between uncles and nieces. When Herod of Chalcis died, she came to live with her unmarried brother, serving as his queen. She

---

[9]Henry E. Dosker, "Herod," in *The International Standard Bible Encyclopedia*, gen. ed. James Orr (Grand Rapids, Mich.: Wm. B. Eerdmans Publishing Co., 1960), 3:1383.

was designated as "queen" on several ancient inscriptions. At one point, she remarried—apparently to quell the rumors about incest—but she could not stay away from Agrippa. She soon deserted her husband and returned to her brother. Later, after the destruction of Jerusalem, she and Agrippa went to Rome where she had an affair with Titus. She would have married him except for a great outcry by the citizens of Rome.[10] Agrippa was about thirty-two at the time of our story; Bernice was a year younger.

Since Agrippa had the title of **king**, it might seem that he was Festus' superior, but the opposite was true. While Agrippa had inherited the title from his illustrious father, he had not inherited his territory. It was to his advantage to cultivate a relationship with a high-ranking Roman official. Thus, as Festus began his administration, Agrippa and Bernice came "to welcome" him (25:13; RSV) and to congratulate him on his appointment.

For Agrippa and Bernice, traveling to **Caesarea** was a homecoming. The city had been built by their great-grandfather Herod the Great. Everywhere was evidence of Herod's fondness for construction: great marble buildings, magnificent marble pavements and statuary (see comments on 10:1). Caesarea had also been the capital of their father's reign, a regime rivaling that of Herod the Great—and perhaps surpassing it. As Herod Agrippa II came into town, could he have thought, "This should be all mine"? When Agrippa and Bernice finally reached the Praetorium, bittersweet memories must have flooded their thoughts. This place was their childhood home. It was also where their father had died an agonizing death fifteen years earlier (12:20–23).

The two would have been shocked if they had been told their visit was in fulfillment of a prophecy of Jesus:

> But beware of men, for they will hand you over to the courts and scourge you in their synagogues; and you will even be brought before governors *and kings* for My sake,

---

[10]Josephus *Antiquities* 19.5.1; 19.9.1; 20.7.3; Juvenal *Satires* 6.156; Suetonius *Life of Titus* 7.

as a testimony to them and to the Gentiles (Mt. 10:17, 18; emphasis added).

Paul had spoken before governors, Felix and Festus; now God was setting the stage for him to speak before a king, Agrippa.

Verse 14. Festus probably greeted Agrippa and Bernice warmly for the sake of their family name. The name Herod still carried weight. A religious/political party called "the Herodians" existed in the country (Mk. 3:6; 12:13). Festus would have also received Agrippa and Bernice warmly because of the king's role in the religious life of Judea. Even though Agrippa did not rule over Judea, Rome had given him guardianship over the temple in Jerusalem and the right to appoint the high priest. Agrippa could make Festus' challenge of governing the Jews easier or more difficult.

As the days went by, the governor decided that the young king's visit might turn out to be beneficial to him. Agrippa could perhaps give him insight into the puzzling matter of the little Jewish tentmaker tucked away in a locked room in the palace. Like Drusilla (24:24), Agrippa was a descendant of a Jewish princess named Mariamne (see comments on 12:1) and was considered a Jew. He was Rome's resident expert on Jewish matters (26:3, 27). Thus, after Agrippa and Bernice had spent **many days there, Festus laid Paul's case before the king, saying, "There is a man who was left as a prisoner by Felix."** The governor explained Paul's situation to the king, admitting that he was "at a loss" how to proceed (v. 20). Once again, skeptics wonder "how Luke knew" about a private conversation between the governor and the king. They suggest that Luke "invented" Festus' words. It is possible that servants who were present were sympathetic to Christianity (see Phil. 4:22). More important, Luke was inspired—and *God* knows what goes on in royal chambers (2 Kings 6:12).

Verses 15, 16. Festus' account of the case allows us to see it from a Roman viewpoint, specifically from the viewpoint of a Roman who was ignorant of Judaism and Christianity. His words are a study in how facts can be manipulated to put the speaker in the best light. Compare his words with Lysias' account of

413

what happened in Jerusalem (see comments on 23:25–30). Festus said:

> **And when I was at Jerusalem, the chief priests and the elders of the Jews brought charges against (Paul), asking for a sentence of condemnation against him. I answered them that it is not the custom of the Romans to hand over any man before the accused meets his accusers face to face and has an opportunity to make his defense against the charges.**

Though confused, Festus had discerned that the issue was religious in nature, not political. As Gallio had told the Jews, these were "questions about words and names and [their] own law" (18:15). Rome had a policy of non-interference in local religious laws and practices as long as they did not conflict with Roman law. Festus would have subscribed to the slogan "One religion is as good as another," with this addendum: ". . . and none of them worth much." Like many others in public office, the governor was ignorant of religious matters and determined to stay that way.

Verses 17, 18. Festus continued, **"So after [the Jewish leaders] had assembled here, I did not delay, but on the next day took my seat on the tribunal and ordered [Paul] to be brought before me"** (see comments on v. 6). Festus was comparing his conscientiousness with Felix' laxness. **"When the accusers stood up, they began bringing charges against him not of such crimes as I was expecting"** (see comments on vv. 7, 8). Festus probably expected charges of murder, major theft, or the like.

Verse 19. Instead of bringing charges that Paul violated Roman law, the Jewish leaders **simply had some points of disagreement with him about their own religion and about a dead man, Jesus, whom Paul asserted to be alive.** Why did Festus say *"their own religion"* (emphasis added) to one with a Jewish background, that is, King Agrippa? Perhaps he did not want to identify his royal visitor with the injustice of the Jewish leaders. Perhaps it was a slip of the tongue.

The word **religion** is δεισιδαιμονία (*deisidaimonia*), a form of the Greek word translated "religious" in 17:22. The word can mean "demon-worship" and is translated "superstition" by the KJV (see comments on 17:22). Since Festus would not insult his Jewish guest deliberately, "religion" is probably the better translation. It is possible that he had a double meaning in mind as Paul may have had in 17:22.

Governor Festus realized that the heart of the conflict was whether or not someone named **Jesus** was really **alive**. As we read his assessment of the primary point of disagreement, we are both impressed and distressed. We are impressed that the governor was astute enough to recognize the significance of the question: "Is Jesus alive or dead?" Some who claim to be Christians today, even some preachers, do not think the Resurrection is a key issue. Some of these denominational preachers have said, "Whether or not Jesus actually arose from the dead is unimportant; what *is* important is that early Christians *thought* He did."

Although Festus grasped the issue, we are distressed at the nonchalant, almost frivolous, way he dismissed the topic: a **"disagreement . . . about a dead man, Jesus, whom Paul asserted to be alive."** Thus "a Roman magistrate could speak of the most glorious truth in the Christian religion."[11] The governor showed the kind of appreciation for the Resurrection that an earthworm has for a diamond or a pig has for the stars. How much Festus missed by not having a curious mind and an open heart!

Verse 20. Festus continued to lay Paul's case before King Agrippa: **"Being at a loss how to investigate such matters, I asked whether he was willing to go to Jerusalem and there stand trial on these matters."** Festus conveniently failed to mention that his motivation for suggesting Paul be tried in **Jerusalem** was to please the Jews (see comments on v. 9). The phrase **at a loss** could be used to describe Festus' state of mind in general (see vv. 26, 27). He was hoping that the young king could give him insight.

Verse 21. **"But when Paul appealed to be held in custody for the Emperor's decision, I ordered him to be kept in cus-**

---

[11]Albert Barnes, *Acts*, Notes on the New Testament (Grand Rapids, Mich.: Baker Book House, 1953, reprint), 344.

tody until I send him to Caesar." The phrase **held in custody** suggests that one reason Paul appealed to Caesar was to be protected by Rome until he got out of Palestine. Whether or not this thought was in Paul's mind, in God's providence it was a practical result of Paul's appealing to Caesar.

Verse 22. Agrippa's interest must have been aroused by the mention of Paul. Although the followers of Jesus were unknown to Festus, they were well known to Agrippa. The cruel history of the Herods was inexorably intertwined with the blessed history of the spread of Christianity (see comments on 12:1). Living in Palestine, Agrippa would have heard of "the renegade Jew" who was Christianity's best-known advocate (see 26:26). The king would not have gone to a synagogue to hear Paul preach, but here was an opportunity for first-hand information—an opportunity he could not resist. **Then Agrippa said to Festus, "I also would like to hear the man myself."** Agrippa probably had many motivations for wanting to hear Paul—curiosity, the desire to break the tedium of a state visit—but perhaps a tiny corner of his heart harbored a desire to learn about Jesus.

Festus was happy to grant Agrippa's request. By granting it, he could accomplish several items on his own agenda: (1) He could honor his guests. (2) He could provide another day's entertainment for them. It was difficult to come up with something novel every day. (3) He could protect himself. If Festus had trouble with Rome, he would have well-known witnesses who could testify that he had done everything possible to provide justice in Paul's case.

The problem was not that Festus had nothing to write, but that he had nothing to write that would make sense in Rome. He had accusations, but no evidence. He had charges, but none that would interest the emperor. Therefore, he quickly assured Agrippa: **"Tomorrow,"** . . . **"you shall hear him."**

Word had probably reached Paul that two members of the Herod family were in the palace. He would not have been surprised to hear that they wanted to see him beheaded (see Mt. 14:3–12), but he must have been amazed to learn that King Agrippa wanted to hear him preach. J. W. McGarvey tried to imagine Paul's excitement:

Could it be true that the gulf between Christ and this bloodiest of families . . . was so nearly bridged that one of them . . . really desired to hear the gospel? . . . The bare possibility of winning a Herod over to the cause of Christ must have thrilled his soul.[12]

Of all those who needed to be prodded back to the Lord's way, Agrippa and Bernice must have been near the top of the list.

Festus Introduces Paul (25:23–27)

[23]So, on the next day when Agrippa came together with Bernice amid great pomp, and entered the auditorium accompanied by the commanders and the prominent men of the city, at the command of Festus, Paul was brought in. [24]Festus said, "King Agrippa, and all you gentlemen here present with us, you see this man about whom all the people of the Jews appealed to me, both at Jerusalem and here, loudly declaring that he ought not to live any longer. [25]But I found that he had committed nothing worthy of death; and since he himself appealed to the Emperor, I decided to send him. [26]Yet I have nothing definite about him to write to my lord. Therefore I have brought him before you all and especially before you, King Agrippa, so that after the investigation has taken place, I may have something to write. [27]For it seems absurd to me in sending a prisoner, not to indicate also the charges against him."

Verse 23. Paul probably did not get much sleep the night before he appeared in front of the governor and the king. Finally, the day dawned when he would have the opportunity to try to convert Agrippa. **On the next day . . . Agrippa came together with Bernice amid great pomp.** The Greek word translated **pomp** is φαντασία (*phantasia*), which means "show, display." This word, from which we get "fantasy" and "fantastic," was used to refer to elaborate pageantry and is rendered "pag-

---

[12]J. W. McGarvey, *New Commentary on Acts of Apostles*, vol. 2 (Delight, Ark.: Gospel Light Publishing Co., n.d.), 248–49.

eantry" in this verse in some translations.

Agrippa and Bernice **entered the auditorium accompanied by the commanders and the prominent men of the city.** The story reads like an eyewitness account. It is possible that the distinguished Dr. Luke was invited to the occasion. Picture the scene in your mind: The **auditorium** was probably the elegant Hall of Audience built by Herod the Great. The walls were adorned with heavy tapestries. Marble pillars reached from the floor to the elaborately carved ceiling. The room, decorated with flags and banners, was packed with the greatest who were dressed in ornate finery. Around the walls was "a solid phalanx of the tall Roman legionnaires on ceremonial guard."[13]

Trumpeters likely sounded as a dazzling parade swept into the auditorium. First came the most **prominent men** of the area—influential civic and business leaders—accompanied by powerful Roman **commanders.** Each of these officers had authority over a thousand men (see comments on 21:31). Josephus said that five auxilary cohorts were posted at Caesarea,[14] which indicates that five commanders were also there. Then, possibly after a double blast of the trumpets, Festus ushered in his celebrated guests. Agrippa and Bernice dressed in royal splendor as their father had (see comments on 12:21). The couple were likely adorned with purple robes and golden circlets. Bernice's beauty would have been enhanced by sparkling jewels in her hair and on her wrist. Not to be outdone, Festus would have been in the scarlet governor's robe, worn on state occasions. It was undoubtedly a magnificent display of glitter, glamour, and earthly glory.[15]

Some have suggested that the Sanhedrin was present, but this is unlikely. They would have gone home many days before, for "several days" had passed (vv. 13, 14). However, it is possible, even probable, that a number of Jews were present among the

---

[13]William Barclay, *The Acts of the Apostles*, The Daily Study Bible Series, rev. ed. (Philadelphia: Westminster Press, 1976), 175.

[14]Josephus *Antiquities* 19.9.2.

[15]These terms were used in G. Campbell Morgan, *The Acts of the Apostles* (Grand Rapids, Mich.: Fleming H. Revell Co., 1988), 391.

influential men of the area. After all, Caesarea was in Palestine.

Festus gave the order and **Paul was brought in.** The contrast must have been startling. The apostle stood before the imposing assembly in his drab garb, chains on his wrists clinking when he moved (26:29). He was a creature to be pitied: his flesh scarred, his body bowed with decades of strain and abuse. That is, one might have pitied him until looking into his eyes—for his eyes burned with an inner flame. As was written in Hebrews, Paul could "confidently say, 'The Lord is my helper, I will not be afraid. What will man do to me?'" (Heb. 13:6). The apostle had met the Lord on the road to Damascus; he had been commissioned by the Lord; he had surrendered his life to the Lord. He could boldly face anything and anyone.

Verse 24. Festus addressed his guests and introduced Paul:

King Agrippa, and all you gentlemen here present with us, you see this man about whom all the people of the Jews appealed to me, both at Jerusalem and here, loudly declaring that he ought not to live any longer.

After greeting the king, Festus mentioned the **gentlemen.** He used the specific Greek word for "men," ἄνδρες (*andres*), instead of the generic word ἄνθρωποι (*anthrōpoi*), which can mean "people." Festus used this exclusive language even though women were present, including Bernice. Since he surely did not mean to insult one of his royal guests, this was probably the formal way to address such a meeting.

Festus fell into the same trap many fall into today. All the Jews *he had talked to* had denounced Paul, so he said, *"All ... the Jews"* (emphasis added) wanted Paul dead. How easy it is to declare, *"Everyone* thinks this or that!" Festus was careful to place the blame for the dilemma on others: on Felix (v. 14), on the Jews (v. 24), on Paul (26:32), on anyone except himself.

Verse 25. Festus began the proceedings with a candid admission: **"But I found that he had committed nothing worthy of death; and since he himself appealed to the Emperor, I decided to send him."** Actually, he had no decision to make— Paul's appeal took the matter out of his hands—but he wanted to appear decisive to those assembled.

Verse 26. Most important, the governor hoped to get help in writing his official report to Rome.

> **Yet I have nothing definite about him to write to my lord. Therefore I have brought him before you all and especially before you, King Agrippa, so that after the investigation has taken place, I may have something to write.**

Roman officials would expect a written report to be sent with a prisoner when he was remanded to the supreme court.[16] This letter would be sent to the Roman emperor himself, referred to in this verse as **my lord** (see comments on v. 8). However, Festus had no idea what to write.

Verse 27. **"For it seems absurd to me in sending a prisoner, not to indicate also the charges against him."** More absurd was the governor's failure to release Paul—especially after he "found that he had committed nothing worthy of death" (v. 25). Festus' public admission that Paul was innocent came too late to help him, but it was no doubt beneficial to other members of the church in that area.

APPLICATION

Sermons from Paul's Trials (Chs. 25, 26)

If you wish to preach a single sermon on Paul's trials in chapter 25, Warren W. Wiersbe suggests three main points:[17] (1) Paul Appeals to Caesar (vv. 1–12); (2) Paul Perplexes Festus (vv. 13–22); (3) Paul Faces Royalty (vv. 23–27).

If you prefer to cover chapters 25 and 26 in one sermon, Wiersbe has a sermon entitled "Paul the Defender" with these divisions:[18] (1) Conciliation: Festus and the Jewish Leaders (25:1–

---

[16]*Digest* 49.6.1.

[17]Warren W. Wiersbe, *Wiersbe's Expository Outlines on the New Testament* (Wheaton, Ill.: Victor Books, 1992), 347–49.

[18]Warren W. Wiersbe, *The Bible Exposition Commentary*, vol. 1 (Wheaton, Ill.: Victor Books, 1989), 50.

12); (2) Consultation: Festus and Agrippa (25:13–27); (3) Confrontation: Festus, Agrippa, and Paul (26:1–32).

The Confident Apostle (Ch. 25)

Paul's trials can be summarized under seven headings:[19] (1) *Unmerited confinement.* Paul should have been released, but he remained in prison. (2) *Unexplained delay.* We read, "But after two years had passed. . . ." Those words in 24:27 take only a second or two to read, but they took twenty-four months to live. Jesus had promised Paul that he would go to Rome (23:11), but He had not mentioned a two-year delay. (3) *Unrelenting attack.* The two-year waiting period did not soften the hatred of the Jews. They continuously desired to kill Paul. (4) *Untrue accusations.* The charges against Paul were either imaginary or inaccurate. (5) *Unfair exploitation.* Felix first tried to use Paul to get a bribe; then he tried to use him to placate the Jews. Festus also tried to use Paul to gain the Jews' good will. (6) *Unworthy judges.* It would be hard to imagine a more unsavory lot than the Sanhedrin, Felix, Festus, and Agrippa; yet these presumed to judge him. (7) *An uncertain future.* Paul must have often wondered, "How can I preach in Rome if I can't even get out of Caesarea?" Even after he appealed to Caesar, he had to be uncertain concerning the outcome of his trial before the emperor. Despite all of these setbacks, Paul remained confident in the Lord and fulfilled his mission as an apostle.

God Protects His Saints (Ch. 25)

The story of Paul demonstrates to us the marvelous way God protects His saints. Paul wrote in 1 Corinthians 10:13:

> No temptation has overtaken you but such as is common to man; and God is faithful, who will not allow you to be tempted beyond what you are able, but with the temptation will provide the way of escape also, so that you will be able to endure it.

---

[19]These seven points are taken from Rick Atchley, "Resigning to Refining," Sermon preached at the Southern Hills church of Christ, Abilene, Texas, on 5 April 1987.

The Greek word in 1 Corinthians 10:13 translated "temptation," πειρασμός (*peirasmos*), is used two ways in the New Testament. It is used for "temptation" as in 1 Corinthians 10:13, and it is used for "trial" as in James 1:2. These two uses are determined by the context. "Temptations," allurements to do evil, come from the devil (Mt. 4:3; 1 Cor. 7:5; 1 Thess. 3:5), not God (Jas. 1:13). "Trials" can come as tests from the Lord but are always intended to strengthen our faith, not destroy it. The devil tempts us to do wrong; God tries us to build up our faith. Each temptation has a way of escape; each trial comes with an avenue through which we can become stronger.

Paul said much about temptations, or trials, in 1 Corinthians 10:13. Trouble comes to everyone; no one is exempt. The troubles we have are not unique; others have had the same problems in the past. Most importantly, when trials come, the Christian can be confident that God is in control. We have seen evidence of this in our studies again and again; God's providential care of Paul cannot be denied. We have witnessed "prison bonds, avarice, evil political motives and hatred . . . used by God to fulfill his great purpose among those who . . . fit into his plans by faith."[20]

Paul gave two promises regarding trials in 1 Corinthians 10:13: First, God not only allows trials, but He also limits them. "God is faithful, who will not allow you to be tempted [or tried] beyond what you are able." God knows your strengths and your weaknesses, and He "will not permit you to be tempted more than you can stand" (NCV). For an illustration of this principle, see the first two chapters of Job. God allows trials to make us stronger.

Did you ever hear a Christian try to excuse his sin by saying, "I just couldn't take it anymore"? Such a statement reflects poorly on God's faithfulness. If it became *impossible* for that individual to "take it anymore," then God allowed him to be tested beyond his capability—and God was not faithful! The truth is, if we do not "take it anymore," it is because we do not *want* to

---

[20]Ed Wharton, *The Action of the Book of Acts* (Dallas: Gospel Teachers Publications, 1977), 57.

"take it anymore," not because we *cannot* "take it anymore." Paul had more tribulations than most of us will ever have, but he did not complain, "Lord, You've given me more than I can bear."

The second promise is vividly illustrated in chapter 25. God not only puts a limitation on our problems, but He also provides the means to be victorious over them. "With the temptation [He] will provide the way of escape also, that you may be able to endure it." The Greek word ἔκβασις (*ekbasis*), translated "the way of escape," literally means "the way out." This term was used by first-century soldiers to tell of being surrounded with defeat inevitable—when suddenly a gap opened in the enemy's ranks, and they were able to escape.

The nature of "the way of escape" depends on three factors. One is the nature of the trouble. The means of escape relates to the problems we face. Paul's "way of escape" from an assassination plot in Jerusalem was to report the plot to a conscientious Roman commander. His "way of escape" from being sent back to Jerusalem was to appeal to Caesar. Second, God knows the capabilities of those who are having trouble. He tailors both the problems and the solutions to fit us. Paul's "way of escape" was to use his Roman citizenship, a privilege that many first-century Christians did not have. Joseph is an interesting illustration of the second factor. Regarding sexual temptation, God's "way of escape" for some is to give them strength to resist, but God's "way of escape" for Joseph was for him to run away (Gen. 39:12). Third, the "way of escape" depends on God's plans and purposes for the one in trouble. The KJV has "*a* way to escape," but the NASB more accurately has "*the* way of escape"—in other words, the way consistent with God's design.

When we are overwhelmed with trouble, we may not recognize God's "way of escape." Often, it is not the way *we* would have devised, not what *we* want. In Caesarea, God's "way of escape" for Paul was not what he desired; he wanted to go to Rome as a free man, not as a prisoner. Nevertheless, an appeal to Caesar was *God's* "way out," whether that was Paul's first choice or not. Even so, when we are burdened with trials, we would prefer that God's "way of escape" involve a removal of those trials. God, however, may have permitted those trials in order to make us better people (Jas. 1:2–4). In that case, His "way of escape" will involve learning to live with our problems and to rely more on Him for our strength. For instance, if you have an unhappy marriage, you may wish that God would give you a "way out" of your marriage—when God's "way of escape" may involve your working harder on making your mate happy.

To prepare yourself for tribulations that will come your way, engrave these two truths in your mind: (1) A way of escape is always available—if we will only look for it. God has promised that it will be so. He took care of Paul; He will take care of us. (2) A victory is always possible—if we will only claim it. God does not force us to go through the open exit. It is up to us to take advantage of it. If we allow God to work in our lives by humbly surrendering to His will, trials can never get the best of us.

Confidence in the Risen Lord (25:19)

Many in the world have little hope or confidence to face life's challenges. However, Christians should have a radically different outlook and approach to living. As we consider the trials endured by the apostle Paul, we need to reflect on his confidence and the confidence we should have as well.

His Confidence. What sustained Paul through all his undeserved trials? His faith. Faith was the "shield" with which he was "able to extinguish all the flaming arrows of the evil one" (Eph. 6:16). He had faith in his God. When he at last stood before Agrippa, he said, "So, having obtained help from God, I stand to this day" (Acts 26:22). Paul wrote, "If God is with us, no one can defeat us" (Rom. 8:31; NCV). He also had faith in the promise of Jesus that he would someday preach in Rome (Acts 23:11). We would suggest, however, that in a special way, it was his faith in *the Resurrection* that gave him courage to go on. He may not have understood the reason for his troubles, but this he understood: His Savior was alive and active and in control. Regardless of what happened to him, even if he at last died at the hands of Caesar, all would be right; the Resurrection guaranteed it. As he wrote to the Christians at Corinth, ". . . Christ has been raised from the dead, the first fruits of those who are asleep" (1 Cor. 15:20). ". . . thanks be to God, who gives us the victory through our Lord Jesus Christ" (1 Cor. 15:57).

Our Confidence. Like Paul in prison, some of you are confined, through no fault of your own. Perhaps you are confined by a disability or stuck in a job with no hope of advancement. Some are fretting because of unexplained delays. You have been waiting for some positive development in your life—and it seems it will never come. Some are under unrelenting attack. You have done all you can to placate an adversary, but he is determined not to be reconciled. Some are victims of untrue accusations. Your efforts to clear your name have left you exhausted. Some have been exploited. You know what it is like to be used by others; you have been used and abused by a friend, an employer, or a mate. Some are being criticized by others unqualified to do so. Perhaps they are jealous of what you have accomplished. All of us face an uncertain future (Jas. 4:14).

How can we, like Paul, keep going in the face of trials? Faith is the key. "This is the victory that has overcome the world— our faith" (1 Jn. 5:4). Write these words where you can refer to them often: "When you are face to face with the unknown, rely on that which you *do* know." You may not know why life has collapsed around you, but this you can know: God loves you and will help you, and things will work together for good (Rom. 8:28; Heb. 13:6; 1 Jn. 4:10). You can also know that Jesus is alive and working in your life: "Blessed be the God and Father of our Lord Jesus Christ, who according to His great mercy has caused us to be born again to a living hope through the resurrection of Jesus Christ from the dead" (1 Pet. 1:3). You can be certain that someday He will return to take you home.

> . . . we will all be changed, in a moment, in the twinkling of an eye, at the last trumpet; for the trumpet will sound, and the dead will be raised imperishable, and we will be changed. For this perishable must put on the imperishable, and this mortal must put on immortality. But when this perishable will have put on the imperishable, and this mortal will have put on immortality, then will come

about the saying that is written, "Death is swallowed up in victory" (1 Cor. 15:51–54).

When everything else goes wrong in your life, cling to the certainty of the Resurrection.

The Resurrection in Paul's Apologies (25:19)

One of the most fascinating cathedrals to visit is Westminster Abbey in London. It is remarkable—not because of the coronations held there, but because of the famous people buried there: royalty, political leaders, military giants, famous artists. A wide range of vocations and avocations are represented, but the tombs have one thing in common—on each are the words "Here lieth the body of," followed by a familiar name. Walter B. Knight made this observation:

> How different it was at the tomb of Jesus. There it [was] not "Here lieth the body of Jesus," but the spoken epitaph of the angel: "He is not here: for he is risen." Earthly greatness usually ends with the grave. The greatest demonstration of Jesus' power began at the grave where He conquered death.[21]

The resurrection of Jesus was a focal point of Paul's preaching. In Athens, "he was preaching Jesus and the resurrection" (Acts 17:18). He told the Romans: "Christ Jesus is He who died, yes, rather who was raised" (Rom. 8:34). He wrote the Corinthians: "If Christ has not been raised, your faith is worthless; you are still in your sins" (1 Cor. 15:17).

We are not surprised, then, to find the Resurrection a focal point of Paul's "apologies" in chapters 23 through 26. In each of the four "trials," he emphasized the Resurrection. We put the word "trials" in quotation marks because it would be hard to think of the fiasco in the Council chambers as a proper trial, and certainly Paul's defense before Agrippa was not actually a trial.

---

[21]Walter B. Knight, *Knight's Treasury of Illustrations* (Grand Rapids: Mich.: Wm. B. Eerdmans Publishing Co., 1963), 314.

Nevertheless, most scholars refer to all these as "trials." In each Paul was on trial for his faith, if not for his life. In trial number one, Paul cried out to the Sanhedrin, "I am on trial for the hope and resurrection of the dead!" (23:6). During the second trial, Paul told Felix, "This I admit to you, that . . . I do serve the God of our fathers . . . having a hope in God . . . that there shall certainly be a resurrection of both the righteous and the wicked" (24:14, 15). In the course of trial three, Paul's presentation of the resurrection of Jesus was so powerful that even though Festus did not understand it, it made an indelible impression on his mind (25:19). In trial four, Paul asked King Agrippa and other distinguished guests, "Why is it considered incredible among you people if God does raise the dead?" (26:8; see 26:22, 23).

If we were to lift the Resurrection from chapters 23 through 26, we would have the story of the mistreatment of a Roman citizen. Because the Resurrection is included, we have a forceful testimony to its power in the life of Paul. "The unifying theme [of these chapters] is the resurrection and what belief in the victorious Lord can do to make us strong and bold in the most excruciating pressures of life."[22]

Some consider the resurrection of Christ an impossibility. However, if one believes the other events recorded in Scripture, there is no difficulty accepting the truth of the Resurrection. If God could create a world from nothing, if God could instill life in Adam, if He could change a man like Paul, how simple for Him to raise Jesus from the dead! "Christ *has* been raised from the dead, the first fruits of those who are asleep" (1 Cor. 15:20; emphasis added).

Regarding Jesus' resurrection, are you as confused as Festus or as confident as Paul? To you, is the Resurrection just a "disagreement . . . about a dead man, Jesus, whom Paul asserted to be alive" (25:19), or is the Resurrection a living truth that has changed your life? "If Christ has not been raised, then our preaching is vain, your faith also is vain"; "If the dead are not raised, let us eat and drink, for tomorrow we die" (1 Cor. 15:14,

---

[22]Lloyd J. Ogilvie, *Acts*, The Communicator's Commentary, vol. 5 (Dallas: Word Publishing, 1983), 339–40.

32). On the contrary, if Christ *has* been raised, this changes everything!

A V.I.P. (Very Important Person) (25:23, 24)

King Agrippa and Bernice, along with the notable leaders of Caesarea and the Roman army commanders, entered into the auditorium. They came with great pomp and pride to hear from an accused apostle of Jesus. When they had taken their places, Governor Festus introduced them to Paul.

We should not feel sorry for the apostle. It was he, not those in the distinguished audience, who dominated the scene. It was he, not they, who was the "Very Important Person" of that occasion. It is he, not they, whose name has become a household word. Someone has said, "Wouldn't they be surprised to learn that the only reason we have heard of them is because, on that day, their lives intersected with a prisoner named Paul?"

Never be jealous of the lifestyles of the rich and famous (see Mk. 10:42–44). Outward grandeur is fleeting; "the lust of the flesh and the lust of the eyes and the boastful pride of life" are "passing away." In contrast, "the one who does the will of God lives forever" (1 Jn. 2:16, 17). We are reminded of Moses, who "refused to be called the son of Pharaoh's daughter, choosing rather to endure ill-treatment with the people of God than to enjoy the passing pleasures of sin" (Heb. 11:24, 25).

CHAPTER 26
PAUL'S IMPRISONMENT AT CAESAREA (PART 4)

When the Lord appeared to Paul on the road to Damascus, He said, "It is hard for you to kick against the goads" (see 26:14). Jesus used an agricultural figure that was well known in that time, and is still familiar to farmers today. The goad was a stick about six to eight feet long, pointed on one end. When the farmer plowed with a one-handle plow, he carried the goad in his free hand. With it, he could make his ox speed up or turn from side to side. Sometimes, an unruly ox would kick back at the farmer, but all he got for his trouble was another prod—harder than before. It *was* hard to kick against the goad.

The Greeks and the Romans used the phrase "to kick against the goad" to refer to fighting against the will of their "gods." For Paul, the words were an indictment that he had been fighting against the will of the true God. Jehovah had another direction for him to go, but he had been fighting God's plan for his life—and it had been hard. In chapter 26, we will see Paul's account of how God had "prodded" him in a direction that caught him by surprise—and how he used that story to "goad" a royal listener into facing spiritual realities.

PAUL'S DEFENSE BEFORE KING AGRIPPA
(26:1–27)

Paul's Opening Remarks (26:1–8)

¹Agrippa said to Paul, "You are permitted to speak for your-

self." Then Paul stretched out his hand and proceeded to make his defense:

²"In regard to all the things of which I am accused by the Jews, I consider myself fortunate, King Agrippa, that I am about to make my defense before you today; ³especially because you are an expert in all customs and questions among the Jews; therefore I beg you to listen to me patiently.

⁴"So then, all Jews know my manner of life from my youth up, which from the beginning was spent among my own nation and at Jerusalem; ⁵since they have known about me for a long time, if they are willing to testify, that I lived as a Pharisee according to the strictest sect of our religion. ⁶And now I am standing trial for the hope of the promise made by God to our fathers; ⁷the promise to which our twelve tribes hope to attain, as they earnestly serve God night and day. And for this hope, O King, I am being accused by Jews. ⁸Why is it considered incredible among you people if God does raise the dead?"

Verse 1. In chapter 25, an illustrious assembly had gathered to hear Paul. Since the occasion was not a formal trial, but an informal hearing, and since Agrippa desired to hear Paul, Festus allowed Agrippa to conduct the interview. **Agrippa said to Paul, "You are permitted to speak for yourself."**

From a worldly standpoint, Paul stood before the most magnificent audience he had ever been privileged to address. Some men would have been shaking in their sandals, but not Paul. The Western Text adds that he was "confident, and encouraged by the Holy Spirit." **Then Paul stretched out his hand.** He often waved his hand as he began his sermons. Some think, however, that this time it may have been in a salute to the governor and king. Next the apostle **proceeded to make his defense,** which, before that distinguished audience, was his longest and most polished in structure and language.

Verses 2, 3. Paul first expressed his happiness concerning the king's hearing of his case. He said, **"In regard to all the things of which I am accused by the Jews, I consider myself fortunate, King Agrippa, that I am about to make my defense before you today."** Paul's stated reason for considering himself

fortunate was that at last he stood before one who understood the situation and who could understand him. He considered Agrippa **an expert in all customs and questions among the Jews.** Paul probably had in mind the controversy in Jewish circles concerning Jesus. He was not engaging in flattery; ancient Jewish writers have confirmed Agrippa's grasp of Judaism.

Paul also had an unstated reason for being happy to stand before the king. He desired with all his heart to convert him. As far as Paul was concerned, he had an audience of one—**Agrippa**. He obviously considered Festus a lost cause (see Mt. 7:6). Paul included all of the audience twice in his remarks (26:8, 29), but his focus was on Agrippa. No other sermon in Acts is so personal. Paul repeatedly addressed Agrippa by name, by title, and with the singular pronoun "you" (vv. 2, 3, 7, 13, 19, 27, 29).

The apostle added, **"Therefore I beg you to listen to me patiently."** Unlike Tertullus, Paul did not claim that he would be brief (see 24:4). Chapter 26 can be read aloud in less than five minutes—proof again that Luke gave an inspired digest of the sermons he recorded. On the surface, Paul's defense seems mainly a dialogue about his experiences. However, his words were not a defense of himself, but a defense of a resurrected Lord (see 2 Cor. 4:5).

Verse 4. Paul spoke of his days as a young man in the Jewish faith. He said that his youth was **"spent among [his] own nation."** The word **nation** from ἔθνος (*ethnos*, "people") could refer to the Jewish community in Tarsus; more likely, it refers to the Jewish community in Judea (see comments on 9:1).

Verse 5. To let his listeners know that he respected the Jewish faith, Paul stated, **"I lived as a Pharisee"**; this way of life was **the strictest sect of** the Jewish **religion.** Festus had said that "all . . . the Jews" condemned Paul (25:24). Paul countered that if "all [the] Jews" (v. 4) told the truth, instead of condemning him, they would commend him.

Verses 6, 7. With reference to his life as a Pharisee, Paul introduced the themes of the **hope** of the **fathers** and the resurrection, for the Pharisees believed the Old Testament promises and also believed in the resurrection of the dead (23:6, 8). Paul did not directly address the specific charges against him in his defense. However, his presentation emphasized that he would not mistreat Jews, disparage the Law, or defile the temple.

Paul mentioned the **"promise to which our twelve tribes hope to attain."** Notice the phrase **twelve tribes**. The myth of "ten lost tribes" has hatched many false doctrines. As I. Howard Marshall remarked, "The idea that only returned exiles from Judah and Benjamin (the southern part of the kingdom) composed the Jewish people in New Testament times is a myth that dies hard (but see, for example, Lk. 2:36)."[1] Although the ten northern tribes (Israel) were captured by the Assyrians in 722 B.C., these tribes were not "lost" or wiped out. Jesus talked about all twelve tribes (Mt. 19:28). James did also (Jas. 1:1), as did the apostle John (Rev. 7:4–8; 21:12). F. F. Bruce commented, "The myth of the ten lost tribes plays no part in the biblical record."[2]

Paul insisted the real reason he was on trial was that he actually believed what most Jews claimed to believe. The original "hope of the promise made by God to [the] fathers" was the hope of the coming Messiah (see comments on 2:30, 31), the "seed" of Abraham (Gen. 12:3; 22:18; Gal. 3:16, 19). As time went by, the original "hope" was expanded. By New Testament times, the Jews hoped for the restoration of the glory of Israel, which they believed the Messiah would accomplish (Lk. 1:67–79; Acts 1:6; 3:20, 21).

Intertwined with the hope of restoration was the hope of the resurrection (Lk. 7:18–23).[3] Daniel 12:2 says, "Many of those who sleep in the dust of the ground will awake, these to everlasting life, but the others to disgrace and everlasting contempt." Similar texts include Job 19:25–27; Psalm 16:10; Isaiah 26:19; Hosea 6:2. To passages like these should be added the examples

---

[1]I. Howard Marshall, *The Acts of the Apostles*, The Tyndale New Testament Commentaries, gen. ed. R. V. G. Tasker (Grand Rapids, Mich.: Wm. B. Eerdmans Publishing Co., 1980), 392.

[2]F. F. Bruce, *The Book of Acts*, The New International Commentary on the New Testament, gen. ed. F. F. Bruce, rev. ed. (Grand Rapids, Mich.: Wm. B. Eerdmans Publishing Co., 1988), 463.

[3]For an explanation of how these hopes developed, see William Barclay, *The Letters to the Corinthians*, The Daily Study Bible Series, rev. ed. (Philadelphia: Westminster Press, 1975), 139–40.

of those who were raised from the dead in Old Testament times (1 Kings 17:23; 2 Kings 4:35; 13:21). When Lazarus died, Martha spoke of the hope of the average Jew: "I know that [Lazarus] will rise again in the resurrection on the last day" (Jn. 11:24).

The resurrection was a basic hope of the Pharisees and all other Jews who believed both the Law and the Prophets. The Sadducees, who did not believe in the resurrection of the dead, accepted the five books of Law, but not the Prophets. Paul was well aware that the Sadducees were the chief instigators behind his present troubles, but nevertheless, he still expressed surprise: **"And for this hope, O King, I am being accused by Jews."** F. F. Bruce caught the spirit of Paul's words in this phrase: "by Jews, of all people."[4]

Verse 8. Paul turned to the rest of his audience, asking, **"Why is it considered incredible among you people if God does raise the dead?"** Instead of **you people**, the Greek has only "you" (see KJV), but the pronoun is plural, indicating that Paul momentarily addressed the entire crowd rather than Agrippa alone. The NASB indicates this shift by adding the word "people." Perhaps more than one listener jumped in his seat as Paul jabbed in all directions with his verbal goad.

Paul's words applied to all those present. Most Gentiles believed in a powerful God (or gods) who had created all things (17:24, 25). If **God** could make the world, why should they consider it **incredible** that He could **raise the dead**? Paul's words especially applied to any Jews present, including Agrippa. If God had raised others from the dead, why should they doubt that God had raised Jesus? Of course, the Resurrection will always seem incredible to those who believe only their limited senses, trust only their faulty reasoning, and rely only on themselves.

Saul's Persecution and Conversion (26:9–18)

[9]**"So then, I thought to myself that I had to do many things hostile to the name of Jesus of Nazareth. **[10]**And this is just what I did in Jerusalem; not only did I lock up many of the saints in

---

[4]Bruce, 463.

prisons, having received authority from the chief priests, but also when they were being put to death I cast my vote against them. [11]And as I punished them often in all the synagogues, I tried to force them to blaspheme; and being furiously enraged at them, I kept pursuing them even to foreign cities.

[12]"While so engaged as I was journeying to Damascus with the authority and commission of the chief priests, [13]at midday, O King, I saw on the way a light from heaven, brighter than the sun, shining all around me and those who were journeying with me. [14]And when we had all fallen to the ground, I heard a voice saying to me in the Hebrew dialect, 'Saul, Saul, why are you persecuting Me? It is hard for you to kick against the goads.' [15]And I said, 'Who are You, Lord?' And the Lord said, 'I am Jesus whom you are persecuting. [16]But get up and stand on your feet; for this purpose I have appeared to you, to appoint you a minister and a witness not only to the things which you have seen, but also to the things in which I will appear to you; [17]rescuing you from the Jewish people and from the Gentiles, to whom I am sending you, [18]to open their eyes so that they may turn from darkness to light and from the dominion of Satan to God, that they may receive forgiveness of sins and an inheritance among those who have been sanctified by faith in Me.'"

Verse 9. Having challenged the assembly, Paul admitted he had once been where they were. As a Pharisee, he had believed theoretically in the resurrection of the dead, but rejected the possibility that Jesus had been raised. Paul thought he **had to do many things hostile to the name of Jesus of Nazareth.** The **name of Jesus** referred to all He was and all He taught (see comments on 2:38).

Verse 10. Paul then went on to **lock up many of the saints** (see comments on 9:13). His use of the word **saints** in this context indicated that he now realized they were innocent of the charges for which they were imprisoned.

Verse 11. He also **tried to force them to blaspheme.** Paul's words could mean that he caused Christians to confess that Jesus was deity, which would be blasphemy to *a Jew*. However, the fact he had to **force** them fits better with the idea that he tried to get them to deny Jesus, which would be blasphemy to *a Christian*. The imperfect tense of ἀναγκάζω (*anankazō*) used here is translated in the NASB as "I *tried* to force [them]" (emphasis added). Paul thus admitted that he was less than successful in his efforts—which probably made him even more hostile toward Christians.

Agrippa probably was surprised to learn that Paul had once persecuted Christians with as much zeal as—or more than—his own family, the Herods. The apostle's words were surely "intended to start within the astonished young man the question: How did this persecutor come to undergo so great a change?"[5] Paul's speech before Agrippa includes the third account of his conversion found in Acts (see chs. 9, 22).

Verses 12–14. Paul told Agrippa what brought about the change in his life: As he was **journeying to Damascus** to persecute Christians, **a light from heaven, brighter than the sun,** enveloped him and his companions. When they had **all fallen to the ground,** he heard **a voice** speaking to him in **the Hebrew dialect, "Saul, Saul, why are you persecuting Me? It is hard for you to kick against the goads"** (see comments on 9:1–4).

All that had happened in Paul's life, including being reared as a resurrection-believing Pharisee, had been the Lord's prodding him to accept Jesus (see Gal. 1:15). Paul had *not* been goaded by an uneasy conscience (23:1). He had stubbornly resisted—to his own hurt and harm. The apostle perhaps wanted Agrippa to realize that his own family had been kicking **against the goads** for over sixty years. The Herod family's contact with Jesus and His followers through the years had given them a unique opportunity to know the Lord and follow Him—if only they had possessed honest hearts (Lk. 8:15). If the king had been honest, he would have admitted that it had often been hard to kick against God's goading; his father's excruciating death was a case in point (see comments on 12:23).

Verse 15. Paul continued his narrative: Surrounded by the

---

[5]J. W. McGarvey, *New Commentary on Acts of Apostles*, vol. 2 (Delight, Ark.: Gospel Light Publishing Co., n.d.), 252–53.

heavenly light, he asked with trembling voice, **"Who are You, Lord?"** The answer came back, **"I am Jesus whom you are persecuting"** (see comments on 9:5). The divine goad turned into a sword that pierced his heart, a scalpel that reshaped his life.

Verse 16. The risen Lord charged him, **"But get up and stand on your feet; for this purpose I have appeared to you, to appoint you a minister."** The Greek word translated **minister** is not the usual word, διάκονος (*diakonos*), but rather ὑπηρέτης (*hupēretēs*), a word that indicates "one who serves a higher will." The apostle was also to be a **witness** to the resurrection of Christ (see comments on 22:14, 15). Jesus appeared to Paul to qualify him to be an apostle (see comments on 1:21, 22).

Verse 17. Throughout Paul's ministry, Christ would also be **rescuing** him. He would especially rescue Paul from **the Jewish people**. The Greek simply has τοῦ λαοῦ (*tou laou*), "the people," but this term was often used to speak of the Jewish people, as it does in this context.

Verse 18. Jesus was sending Paul to Jews and Gentiles alike **to open their eyes**. This language from Isaiah 35:5; 42:6, 7 originally referred to future salvation. Through the death and resurrection of Christ, it had become a present reality. The gospel would empower both Jews and Gentiles to **turn from darkness to light** (see Rom. 13:12; 2 Cor. 4:6; Eph. 5:8; 1 Thess. 5:5) **and from the dominion of Satan to God** (see Col. 1:12–14). This message would enable them to receive the **forgiveness of sins** (see comments on 2:38; 3:19) and **an inheritance** among the saints, being set apart **by faith** in Jesus.

Paul Preaches the Resurrection (26:19–23)

[19]**"So, King Agrippa, I did not prove disobedient to the heavenly vision, **[20]**but kept declaring both to those of Damascus first, and also at Jerusalem and then throughout all the region of Judea, and even to the Gentiles, that they should repent and turn to God, performing deeds appropriate to repentance. **[21]**For this reason some Jews seized me in the temple and tried to put me to death. **[22]**So, having obtained help from God, I stand to this day testifying both to small and great, stat-**

ing nothing but what the Prophets and Moses said was going to take place; ²³that the Christ was to suffer, and that by reason of His resurrection from the dead He would be the first to proclaim light both to the Jewish people and to the Gentiles."

Verse 19. Now Paul aimed his goad at the young king's heart, stating, **"So, King Agrippa, I did not prove disobedient to the heavenly vision."** Implied was the question "How could I do otherwise?" If Paul could not do otherwise, then neither should Agrippa.

Verse 20. Paul had been obedient to the Lord's commands; he had been baptized at once (22:16; 9:18). He had also been obedient to the Lord's commission— he **kept declaring** the need to repent **both to those of Damascus first, and also at Jerusalem and then throughout all the region of Judea.** Paul did not preach throughout all of Judea during his first trip to Jerusalem (Gal. 1:18, 22–24). However, he had other opportunities when he made later trips to Jerusalem (12:25; 15:2–4). The apostle preached **even to the Gentiles, that they should repent and turn to God, performing deeds appropriate to repentance.**

Paul had preached on "righteousness" and "self-control" to an unrighteous and indulgent Roman governor (24:25); now, he preached on **repentance** to an impenitent Jewish king. Agrippa, the acclaimed "expert in all customs . . . among the Jews" (v. 3), surely knew that the Law said, "If there is a man who takes his sister . . . it is a disgrace; and they shall be cut off . . ." (Lev. 20:17). Although it was dangerous to do so, Paul jabbed relentlessly, in effect urging the king to "repent and turn to God, performing deeds appropriate to repentance."

Verse 21. Agrippa needed to understand that if he changed, the Christian life would not be easy. Paul continued, **"For this reason,"** not because of some trumped-up charge, but for preaching salvation to the Gentiles apart from the Law, **"some Jews seized me in the temple and tried to put me to death."** Even so, the king's friends might turn on him if he committed his life to Jesus.

Verse 22. Agrippa also needed to know that the Lord would stand by him if he made such a commitment. Thus Paul quickly added, **"So, having obtained help from God, I stand to this day."** Jesus had told him to "stand" (v. 16), and he had continued to **stand**—with God's help. The strength Paul had received would also be available to the king. By depending on the Lord, Paul had been able to carry out His commission, **testifying both to small and great, stating nothing but what the Prophets and Moses said was going to take place.**

Verse 23. Paul preached **that the Christ was to suffer, and that by reason of His resurrection from the dead He would be the first to proclaim light both to the Jewish people and to the Gentiles.** In the original Greek text, it is not clear what the word πρῶτος (*prōtos*), **first**, should modify. The NASB applies the word to the proclamation of the gospel. The KJV has "That Christ . . . should be the first that should rise from the dead," making this passage similar to 1 Corinthians 15:20 and Colossians 1:18. Jesus was not the first ever to be raised from the dead, but He *was* the first to be raised with a resurrection body, never to die again.

Probably Paul quoted Deuteronomy 18, Isaiah 53, and other passages to prove that the Messiah would die and be raised, and that the good news would then be preached to both **Jewish people** and **Gentiles.** Probably Paul also said, "This Jesus whom I am proclaiming to you *is* the Christ" (17:3; emphasis added). The next logical step would have been to ask Agrippa whether or not he was willing to accept what Moses and the Prophets had written (v. 27). Before Paul could do so, he was interrupted.

Paul Challenges Agrippa (26:24–27)

[24]**While Paul was saying this in his defense, Festus said in a loud voice, "Paul, you are out of your mind! Your great learning is driving you mad."** [25]**But Paul said, "I am not out of my mind, most excellent Festus, but I utter words of sober truth.** [26]**For the king knows about these matters, and I speak to him also with confidence, since I am persuaded that none of these things escape his notice; for this has not been done in a corner.** [27]**King Agrippa, do you believe the Prophets? I know that you do."**

Verse 24. Festus has been out of view since turning the proceedings over to Agrippa at the first of the chapter. Apparently, as Paul's sermon continued, he had become increasingly agitated. **Festus said in a loud voice, "Paul, you are out of your mind! Your great learning is driving you mad."** Regarding the phrase **great learning,** perhaps Festus had been told of Paul's rabbinic education (see comments on 22:3). Perhaps he had seen Paul endlessly studying his parchments in his cell (see 2 Tim. 4:13). Perhaps he was simply impressed with Paul's skillful use of words in his presentation.

Festus' outburst catches us off guard, but his words do not surprise us. A man so shallow that he could dismiss the debate over the greatest truth of the ages as a "disagreement . . . about a dead man, Jesus, whom Paul asserted to be alive" (25:19) would have no trouble dismissing the greatest proponent of that truth as a madman. The one acting like a lunatic was Festus.

Verse 25. Calmly, Paul answered, **"I am not out of my mind, most excellent Festus." Most excellent** is a title of honor (see comments on 23:26). Paul's language is another example of respecting the position when we cannot respect the person. Paul added, **"But I utter words of sober truth."** Paul *had* been insane before he accepted Jesus (v. 11). Although it is not obvious in the English, in the Greek the words "enraged" (v. 11), "out of your mind" (v. 24), "mad" (v. 24), and "out of my mind" (v. 25) are all variations of the Greek word μαίνη (*mainē*), the word from which we get "maniac," "manic," and "mania." However, now he was "in his right mind" (see Mk. 5:15).

Verse 26. The apostle turned back to Agrippa, saying, **"For the king knows about these matters, and I speak to him also with confidence, since I am persuaded that none of these things escape his notice; for this has not been done in a corner."** Christianity was no secret order; the gospel had been shouted from the roof tops (Mt. 10:27). Agrippa's birth had coincided with the beginning of Jesus' personal ministry; he had probably been fed stories about Jesus and the apostles along with his baby food. He could validate all Paul had said. However, to do so would put him in the precarious position of taking sides with the prisoner against his host. Thus he remained silent.

Verse 27. If Agrippa thought his silence would deter Paul, he was mistaken. The apostle pressed him, saying, **"King Agrippa, do you believe the Prophets? I know that you do."** If the young ruler said he did not believe the Prophets, he would lose the respect and support of the Jewish people. If he said he did **believe the Prophets,** Paul's next question would surely be "Are you therefore willing to accept that Jesus is the One of whom the Prophets spoke?"

"ALMOST PERSUADED?": THE
NON-CONVERSION OF AGRIPPA (26:28, 29)

[28]**Agrippa replied to Paul, "In a short time you will persuade me to become a Christian."** [29]**And Paul said, "I would wish to God, that whether in a short or long time, not only you, but also all who hear me this day, might become such as I am, except for these chains."**

Verse 28. Agrippa had to say *something;* everyone in the hall was waiting for his response. At last he spoke, **"In a short time you will persuade me to become a Christian."** This occurrence is the second time the term **Christian** has appeared in Acts. Evidently, it was a commonly used designation for followers of Jesus. There is no indication that Agrippa used the word in a derogatory fashion (see comments on 11:26).

We wish we knew how Agrippa said those words: the tone of his voice, the expression on his face, the posture of his body. The original text can be interpreted any number of ways, as is evident from the differing translations. A rough translation of the original would be: "In a little, you persuade me to make a Christian." The Greek word for "make," ποιέω (*poieō*), could also be translated "act." "Little" could refer to time or means (little effort or little persuasion). Without knowing how Agrippa said those words, we cannot know whether or not he was sincere. Some believe Agrippa was *sincere* (see KJV); others think that while the king was *sympathetic* to Paul's position, he was not yet totally convinced (see NIV); still others are sure that Agrippa was being *sarcastic* (see RSV).[6] Since Agrippa was kindly disposed toward Paul before, throughout, and even after Paul's speech (25:24; 26:1, 32), we can probably eliminate sarcasm as an option. Exactly how near conversion the king was, we will never know.

Verse 29. Whatever Agrippa meant, Paul accepted his words at face value. The fact that Paul seemed to take Agrippa seriously is probably the strongest argument for believing that Agrippa was sincere in what he said. Paul used Agrippa's words for the most powerful and eloquent appeal found in Acts, saying, **"I would wish to God, that whether in a short or long time, not only you, but also all who hear me this day, might become such as I am."** When Paul mentioned everyone present, perhaps he swept with his hand to include Bernice, Festus, the guests, even the soldiers. Observe that Agrippa spoke of becoming "a Christian" while Paul spoke of becoming **"such as I am."** Paul's life defines what a Christian should be (see 1 Cor. 11:1; Phil. 3:17; 4:9). Perhaps Paul held up a manacled wrist as he said **"except for these chains."** Thirty or more years earlier, Paul had not hesitated to bind both men and women (9:2; 26:10), but now he would wish this on no one.

NEXT STOP: ROME (26:30–32)

[30]The king stood up and the governor and Bernice, and those who were sitting with them, [31]and when they had gone aside, they began talking to one another, saying, "This man is not doing anything worthy of death or imprisonment." [32]And Agrippa said to Festus, "This man might have been set free if he had not appealed to Caesar."

Verse 30. Evidently, Agrippa thought he had said too much. Abruptly, he **stood up** along with **the governor and Bernice, and those who were sitting with them.** When prominent individuals such as these stand up, one knows the interview is over.

---

[6]Jimmy Allen, *Survey of Acts*, vol. 2 (Searcy, Ark.: By the Author, 1986), 138.

Verse 31. As soon as Festus and his guests were free from Paul's pleading eyes, **they began talking to one another** about him. The unanimous verdict was: **"This man is not doing anything worthy of death or imprisonment."** It was a victory for Paul, but not the victory he desired. He wanted to vindicate Jesus; instead, he had vindicated himself. He wanted to win their souls; instead, he had won their favor. Luke continued to accumulate official statements of Paul's innocence (see the *Introduction, The Purpose, apologetic*).

Festus, however, was no nearer composing his letter to Rome; he still had no charges against Paul (see 25:26, 27). We do not know what Festus finally wrote, but we can be sure the governor placed any blame for mishandling the case on anyone except himself. Apparently, the ruler's report was favorable to Paul since he was treated well both on the trip and in Rome itself (28:16, 30, 31).

Verse 32. Chapter 26 has a final note—an almost unbelievable occurrence. A Herod would surely never commend a follower of Jesus. A Jewish leader aligned with the high priest could not conceivably speak a good word about Paul; yet Herod Agrippa II, who had selected the high priest who was obsessed with killing Paul, did both. **And Agrippa said to Festus, "This man might have been set free if he had not appealed to Caesar."** Once Paul had appealed to Caesar, the governor's only option was to send him to Caesar (see comments on 25:10, 11). The "last of the Herods" had been impressed with the man and his message. We are left wondering what might have been.

APPLICATION

Paul Preaches to Agrippa (Ch. 26)

Paul had an unstated reason for being happy to stand before King Agrippa. He desired with all his heart to convert him. Convert Agrippa? Convert an unprincipled Herod? Convert one who callously flaunted his incestuous relationship before everyone? Surely that rascal was beyond redemption! Paul did not think so (see 2 Pet. 3:9).

To appreciate the thrust of Paul's sermon, imagine these two face to face: The old man in the chains, the young man in robes; the excited preacher, the empty prodigal; one near the end of his journey, the other near the beginning. Perhaps Paul saw something of his former self in Agrippa: young, rich, and headstrong; full of potential but headed in the wrong direction; knowing the Law while ignorant of its purpose; opposing Christianity without investigation. Did the thought enter Paul's mind that Agrippa was about the age he had been at the time of his conversion? (See comments on 7:58.) We do not know, but this we do know—if Paul had his way, before the day was done, the young king would be a Christian (vv. 28, 29).

Paul's Zeal (26:9–29)

In connection with the account in Acts 26, Mark Clairday emphasized the *zeal* exhibited by Saul/Paul—both before and after his conversion. He spoke of (1) Paul's "misguided zeal" (vv. 9–11)—when he was persecuting Christians, (2) Paul's "redirected zeal" (vv. 19–23)—as a result of the Lord's appearance, and (3) Paul's "evangelistic zeal" (vv. 27–29)—as he tried to convert Agrippa.

Jesus' Commission to Paul (26:16–18)

Jesus appeared in a blaze of light to Saul of Tarsus on the road to Damascus. He commanded Saul,

> But get up and stand on your feet; for this purpose I have appeared to you, to appoint you a minister and a witness not only to the things which you have seen, but also to the things in which I will appear to you; rescuing you from the Jewish people and from the Gentiles, to whom I am sending you, to open their eyes so that they may turn from darkness to light and from the dominion of Satan to God, that they may receive forgiveness of sins and an inheritance among those who have been sanctified by faith in Me (vv. 16–18).

Paul was to be a witness, "not only to the things which [he had] seen"—a reference to Jesus' appearance to Saul on the road—"but also to the things in which [Jesus would] appear to [him]." The Lord made other appearances to Paul (18:9, 10; 22:17–21; 23:11; see 2 Cor. 12:1–4, 7). Jesus' promise of "rescuing [Paul] from the Jewish people and from the Gentiles" was one of divine protection that no doubt contributed to Saul's amazing courage as he spread the gospel. Some believe that 26:16–18 is a summary of *all* Jesus said to Saul, in person *and* through Ananias. Since, however, Paul's speech to Agrippa seems to indicate that Jesus said all this when He appeared to him on the road, it is included at this point.

No greater challenge has ever been given than the one Christ gave Saul on the road. Scholars have debated *why* Jesus appeared to Saul, but the Lord Himself gave His reason: "For *this* purpose," He said to Saul, "I have appeared to you" (v. 16; emphasis added). That purpose can be broken down into three parts. Each purpose is preceded by the word "to" in the NASB text:

First, Jesus appeared to Saul to qualify him *as a witness*—"to appoint you a minister and a witness" (v. 16). One of the qualifications of an apostle was to be a witness of the Resurrection (1:21, 22). Later, when Paul listed Christ's resurrection appearances, he said, "And last of all, as to one untimely born, He appeared to me also. For I am the least of the apostles" (1 Cor. 15:8, 9). "Am I not an apostle?" he wrote to the same church. "Have I not seen Jesus our Lord?" (1 Cor. 9:1).

Second, Jesus appeared to Saul to qualify him to be a witness *to the Gentiles*—Jesus spoke of "the Gentiles, to whom I am sending you" (v. 17). Paul has been called "the apostle to the world," but his *special* ministry was to the Gentiles. This occasion was the first time it was plainly stated in the Book of Acts that Gentiles were included in the Lord's master plan. We know that Gentiles were included in Jesus' challenge to be "witnesses . . . even to the remotest part of the earth" (1:8). Gentiles were included in Peter's statement that "the promise is . . . for all who are far off" (2:39). Gentiles were included in the promise given to Abraham, quoted by Peter in 3:25: "And in your seed all the families of the earth shall be blessed." However, it was not until the Lord appeared to Saul that Gentiles were specifically mentioned. For those of us who are non-Jews, it is certainly a moment worth celebrating.

Third, Jesus appeared to Saul to qualify him to be a witness to the Gentiles *"to open their eyes"* (v. 18; emphasis added). Verse 18 is one of the grandest statements in the Scriptures on the task of winning souls. As soul-winners, our task is fivefold: "[1] To open [the] eyes [of sinners] [2] so that they may turn from darkness to light [3] and from the dominion of Satan to God, [4] that they may receive forgiveness of sins [5] and an inheritance among those who have been sanctified by faith in [Jesus]."

In summary, Christ's stated purpose for appearing to Saul was to qualify him to be the apostle to the Gentiles. It is true that the appearance of Jesus produced faith in Saul's heart and started the conversion process. It was unlikely that any Christians would have approached Saul to preach to him. This fact is obvious from Ananias' later reaction (9:13, 14). However, Jesus said that the unique purpose for which He appeared to Saul was not to save him, but to send him as a witness to the Gentiles. Saul, or Paul, later wrote of this commission in Romans 11:13, "I am the apostle *of the Gentiles*" (KJV; emphasis added; see Gal. 2:6–9).

The Man Who Was Ignorant (26:24)

Although the emphasis in chapter 26 is on King Agrippa, Festus is also noteworthy. A sermon could be preached on "The Man Who Was Ignorant—and Proud of It." The text would be 26:24, where Festus spoke despairingly of Paul's "great learning." (1) Festus was ignorant of the difference between Judaism and Christianity (25:19)—some today do not distinguish between the Old and New Covenants. (2) He was ignorant of the resurrection of Christ (25:19)—many today do not recognize the essentiality of the bodily resurrection of Jesus. (3) He was ignorant concerning God's servant (25:24, "this man")—who he was, what he stood for, what he taught. Many are ignorant of the Bible and its teachings. (4) He was ignorant of spiritual values (26:24)—this is true of our materialistic world. (5) He was ignorant of personal responsibility (25:14, 24; 26:32)—most of us like to shift the blame for our sins. Finally, (6) he was ignorant of the consequences of failing to respond.

A Waste of Time? (26:27–32)

As we watch a disappointed Paul being led back to his cell, we might be tempted to say, "That was a waste of time. That was one of the finest sermons Paul ever preached, and not a single person was converted." On reflection, we realize that it was not a waste of time: Agrippa and the others present had been shown the light; it was not Paul's fault if they closed their eyes. Agrippa and the rest had been shown the way to freedom; Paul was not to blame if they remained in the slavery of sin. Paul had preached Jesus to them; they were now without excuse.

Those outside of Christ need to put themselves in Agrippa's place, feeling the jabs from the Lord's goad as He tries through His Word to change the direction of their lives. Application can also be made to those who are already Christians: God may be trying to "goad" them into lives of greater service—into being more like Paul. Like Paul, we should plead, "I would wish to God, that . . . not only you, but also all who hear me this day, might become such as I am"—a Christian, a follower of Jesus (26:29).

In the end, each individual must decide whether or not he will respond to the Lord. He can be like Paul, who was not "disobedient to the heavenly vision" (v. 19), or he can be like Agrippa, who stood up and walked away. Which will it be?

Almost Persuaded (26:27–29)

The classic approach to this non-conversion is a sermon on "Almost Persuaded" or "Almost—But Lost," using the phrasing of 26:28 (KJV) and the familiar song "Almost Persuaded." Paul Rogers had a sermon titled "Almost Persuaded," with these main points: (1) The Setting, (2) The Danger of Knowing and Rejecting the Right, and (3) The Importance of a Decision.[7] Another thought that could be developed is: "There are two kinds of people: 'almost' Christians and 'altogether' Christians." One other related sermon could be entitled "Not Far From the Kingdom" (see Mk. 12:34).

---

[7]Paul Rogers, "Almost Persuaded," *Preacher's Periodical* 5 (May 1985): 26.

A Rich Young Ruler (26:27–29)

One way to study concerning Agrippa would be to preach on "A Rich Young Ruler," comparing Agrippa with the rich young ruler of Matthew 19 (see Mk. 10; Lk. 18). In some ways they were alike and in other ways they were different, but, in the end, both missed the greatest opportunity of their lives.

CHAPTER 27

PAUL'S JOURNEY TO ROME (PART 1)

Acts 27 is a remarkable chapter. It is a detailed account of a few weeks' voyage that took months—a thrilling adventure filled with raging seas, a shipwreck, and a narrow escape.

What was Luke's purpose for including this episode? Luke loved a good story, but that hardly seems sufficient justification for a writer who was normally miserly with his words. The answer can probably be found in Luke's primary purpose in the last part of the book: telling how Paul reached Rome. Then, underlying the theme of "How Paul Reached Rome" is another: "How Satan Tried To Prevent Paul From Reaching Rome."

When Paul wrote to the church in Thessalonica, he said, "But we, brethren . . . were all the more eager with great desire to see your face. For we wanted to come to you—I, Paul, more than once—*and yet Satan hindered us*" (1 Thess. 2:17, 18; emphasis added). Paul had been prevented from going to Thessalonica by malicious Jews, unfavorable circumstances, and distance—but he understood that those were tools used by Satan.

If Satan did not want Paul to return to Thessalonica, how much more he would not want the apostle to reach Rome! If Paul reached Rome, he could use the imperial city as a base from which to spread the gospel into all the world—and Satan could not tolerate that. We have seen the devil use every means available to prevent Paul from realizing his dream to "see Rome" (19:21): troublemakers from Asia, puzzled soldiers, unscrupulous Jewish leaders, determined assassins, indecisive Roman governors. Through it all, however, God had been with Paul. The devil was thwarted, not Paul. In spite of Satan's best, or perhaps worst, efforts, the apostle was on his way to the city of Rome (27:1).

Did Satan admit defeat? Never! Rather, his rage apparently reached cosmic proportions. In chapter 27 and the first part of chapter 28, we will see the devil try anything to keep Paul from completing his journey: foolish men, fragile ships, and the fury of nature, such as violent winds, angry waves, treacherous sandbars, even a poisonous snake. How could Paul survive this onslaught? The same way he endured Satan's attacks in Jerusalem and Caesarea: through God's providential care and through his faith in God.

Commentators are fond of noting that "we see another side of Paul in chapter 27," as though that was Luke's purpose for telling the story. It is true that we see Paul in a different role: as a leader among non-Christian men. However, Luke's emphasis was not on Paul, but on Paul's God. Luke makes it clear that it was *humanly impossible* for the ship to survive the storm, thus showing that it was necessary for God to step in.

Therefore, Luke's purpose in writing chapter 27 was twofold: (1) to show how God continued to work in the life of Paul, and thereby (2) to demonstrate that even the forces of hell could not hinder God's plans and purposes.

THE JOURNEY BEGINS (27:1–8)

¹**When it was decided that we would sail for Italy, they proceeded to deliver Paul and some other prisoners to a centurion of the Augustan cohort named Julius. ²And embarking in an Adramyttian ship, which was about to sail to the regions along the coast of Asia, we put out to sea accompanied by Aristarchus, a Macedonian of Thessalonica. ³The next day we put in at Sidon; and Julius treated Paul with consideration and allowed him to go to his friends and receive care. ⁴From there we put out to sea and sailed under the shelter of Cyprus because the winds were contrary. ⁵When we had sailed through the sea along the coast of Cilicia and Pamphylia, we landed at Myra in Lycia. ⁶There the centurion found an Alexandrian ship sailing for Italy, and he put us aboard it. ⁷When we had sailed**

slowly for a good many days, and with difficulty had arrived off Cnidus, since the wind did not permit us to go farther, we sailed under the shelter of Crete, off Salmone; ⁸and with difficulty sailing past it we came to a place called Fair Havens, near which was the city of Lasea.

Verse 1. After Paul appealed to Caesar (25:11), Festus kept him in custody while he made arrangements to send him to Rome (25:21). These arrangements would have taken time: They had to find a ship going to Rome, and an official escort had to be secured. In the name of efficiency, officials normally waited until they could transport several prisoners at once. For Festus, however, the hardest part of the preparation was writing a report to the emperor (25:26, 27).

In August, A.D. 59, preparations to transport Paul to Rome were finally completed. The year A.D. 59 agrees with the chronology in connection with Felix' leaving and Festus' arriving in Palestine. That date also agrees with "the fast" (Day of Atonement), which was so late in the year that sailing became hazardous. The month of August is derived by working backward from verse 9 (see comments on v. 9).

Luke begins, **When it was decided that we would sail for Italy. . . .** The first thing that is noticed in this phrase is the word **we**. Luke had traveled with Paul to Jerusalem (21:17) and would travel with Paul to Rome. Glancing ahead to the second verse, we notice that "Aristarchus, a Macedonian of Thessalonica," another of Paul's friends who had gone with him to Jerusalem (20:4), was also on board. Scholars struggle with how Luke and Aristarchus were allowed to accompany Paul, conjecturing that they voluntarily registered as Paul's slaves or that Luke signed on as ship's physician while Aristarchus traveled as Paul's attendant. The solution is probably so obvious that it is overlooked: Luke and Aristarchus likely just paid for passage on the ship. Passengers paid fares to travel on cargo ships (21:3). The two Alexandrian ships to which the centurion later transferred his prisoners (v. 6; 28:11) surely had paying passengers aboard (v. 37).

Before sailing **they proceeded to deliver Paul and some**

other prisoners for transport. The Greek word from ἕτερος (*heteros*), translated **other**, means "others of a different kind." The other **prisoners** may have been condemned criminals being transported to Rome so they could be thrown to wild beasts for the amusement of the crowds. Their fatal future would explain the guards' intention to kill them in the wake of the shipwreck (see comments on v. 42). Such was the cruel world in which they lived.

Paul was delivered **to a centurion of the Augustan cohort named Julius.** A **centurion** was the commander of one hundred men, although it is doubtful that so many were accompanying Julius on this trip. A **cohort** was a regiment of between six hundred and one thousand men (see comments on 10:1). The **Augustan** cohort had some connection with the "August one," that is, the emperor. Some think this was an "imperial . . . cohort, whose officers and men traveled throughout the empire on escort and courier duties."[1] This possibility might explain why, even though **Julius** was "only" a centurion, he had considerable authority on the ship.

Festus and the local Roman officers probably turned the responsibility of Paul over to Julius in a ceremony. Possibly, King Agrippa was still in Caesarea and was present as the governor handed his official report to Julius for him to deliver. Evidently Festus carefully explained to Julius that Paul was an uncondemned Roman citizen who should be given preferential treatment.

Verse 2. Formalities completed, Paul and the others boarded the ship, and they cast off. They probably left from Caesarea, which was the principal seaport of Palestine and the city where Paul had been imprisoned for two years. Luke said, **And embarking in an Adramyttian ship, which was about to sail to the regions along the coast of Asia, we put out to sea.** Adramyttium was a city situated on the west coast of the province of Asia, not far from Troas. The **ship** was probably a coastal vessel heading back to its home port. Unable to find a ship sailing to

---

[1]John Pollock, *The Apostle: A Life of Paul* (Wheaton, Ill.: Scripture Press Publications, 1985), 274.

Italy, they started north along the **coast**, planning to change vessels when they found one headed toward Rome. If all went well, they should reach Rome by late October.

The group was **accompanied by Aristarchus, a Macedonian of Thessalonica** (see comments on v. 1). Paul later referred to **Aristarchus** as "my fellow prisoner" (Col. 4:10); he, too, may have been arrested and then appealed to Caesar. However, in our present text, Aristarchus seems distinct from the "other prisoners" (v. 1). We cannot be sure whether the term "fellow prisoner" in Colossians 4:10 means that he had been arrested or simply refers to a self-imposed confinement so he could minister to Paul (see Philem. 24). Even if Aristarchus was later a prisoner in Rome, we cannot be sure he was when they made the trip to Rome.

Verse 3. Luke reported, **The next day we put in at Sidon,** a trading stop in Phoenicia about seventy miles north of Caesarea. While in port, most of the prisoners would have remained chained below deck, but **Julius treated Paul with consideration and allowed him to go to his friends and receive care**, accompanied by a soldier no doubt. Dr. Luke used a medical term, ἐπιμέλεια (*epimeleia*), for receiving **care**. This reference could merely be Luke's usual phraseology, or perhaps Paul needed medical attention beyond what Luke could give him on board ship. Those **friends** were probably fellow Christians (see Jn. 15:15; 3 Jn. 14). Once more the graciousness of Christians is seen, considering that the church in Sidon had likely been established because Paul had driven Christians out of Jerusalem (8:1–4; 11:19; see comments on 21:3, 7). Perhaps Paul had met them on earlier trips through Phoenicia (12:25; 15:3) or when he had spent a week in Tyre on his way to Jerusalem (21:3, 4). Maybe he had never met them before. It made no difference; a fellow Christian should always be a friend (Prov. 17:17).

Verse 4. From Sidon **we put out to sea and sailed under the shelter of Cyprus because the winds were contrary.** The phrase **sailed under the shelter of** is translated from the Greek word ὑποπλέω (*hupopleō*). The KJV has "we sailed under." The NIV uses the nautical term "to the lee of." "Lee" means "the side sheltered from the wind." Prevailing **winds** in the summer were from the west, so they could not sail directly into the Mediterranean. The west wind had helped Paul make a fast journey across the Mediterranean two years earlier, when he was on his way to Jerusalem (see comments on 21:2–4). Now, he and the others wanted to go in the opposite direction, and the west wind was **contrary** to the way they needed to go. Since ships were not designed to sail against the wind (v. 15), they headed north to sail around the island of Cyprus where they could be partially protected.

Paul was heading to Rome in accordance with God's stated purpose, yet he encountered contrary winds. As all experienced life-travelers have learned, "contrary winds" blow from time to time.

Verse 5. As they traveled north of Cyprus, they passed spots familiar to Paul, possibly making some trading stops as they traveled along the coast. They **sailed through the sea along the coast of Cilicia,** where Paul's hometown, Tarsus, was located, **and Pamphylia,** where he and Barnabas had landed on the first missionary journey (13:13). After about two weeks of traveling, they **landed at Myra in Lycia,** a province in southwest Asia Minor. Traveling from Sidon to **Myra** along the coast would normally take ten to fifteen days. The Western Text adds that the trip thus far had taken fourteen days.

Verse 6. Myra was a principal port on the route of grain ships traveling from Egypt to Rome. Since these ships could not sail against winds from the west, they would head north to Myra and from there make their way to Italy. At Myra, **the centurion found an Alexandrian ship sailing for Italy** with a cargo of wheat (v. 38). The home base of this **ship** was Alexandria, Egypt (see 28:11). Egypt was the principal supplier of grain to Rome. These grain ships were huge. One ancient historian told of such a ship which was 180 feet by 45 feet by 43 feet.[2] Josephus wrote of another such ship which carried 600 persons in addition to its cargo.[3] The ship on which Paul sailed was able to accommodate 276 persons in addition to its cargo (v. 37). A few ancient

---

[2]Lucian *The Ship.*
[3]Josephus *Life* 3.

manuscripts have 76, but the majority have 276. Many of these vessels were under contract to the Roman government, which would give a representative of Rome, such as Julius, special status. Still hoping to reach Rome by October, the **centurion** transferred everyone to the larger ship.

Verse 7. They sailed west along the coast of Asia Minor. Conditions did not improve; in fact the weather deteriorated. They **sailed slowly for a good many days, and with difficulty** until they **arrived off Cnidus,** at the southern tip of the Roman province of Asia. From Myra to **Cnidus** was about 170 miles. The **good many days** would probably have been ten to fifteen days. They had hoped to sail across the sea to Greece (Achaia), but **the wind did not permit** them **to go farther.**

Again, the protection of an island was sought—this time the island of **Crete,** many miles to the south. Cretans had been present on the Day of Pentecost (2:11) and Paul later worked in Crete (Tit. 1:5). However, Cretans had a poor reputation in Bible times (Tit. 1:12). After more days of difficult sailing, they rounded the Cape of **Salome** on the east end of the island and started west along the southern coastline **under the shelter of** Crete (see comments on v. 4).

Verse 8. After moving "along the coast with difficulty" (NIV), they finally **came to a place called Fair Havens**—a harbor halfway along the island, **near which was the city of Lasea.** There they anchored, impatiently waiting day after day for a change in the wind.

WARNED BY PAUL (27:9–12)

⁹**When considerable time had passed and the voyage was now dangerous, since even the fast was already over, Paul began to admonish them,** ¹⁰**and said to them, "Men, I perceive that the voyage will certainly be with damage and great loss, not only of the cargo and the ship, but also of our lives."** ¹¹**But the centurion was more persuaded by the pilot and the captain of the ship than by what was being said by Paul.** ¹²**Because the harbor was not suitable for wintering, the majority reached a decision to put out to sea from there, if somehow**

they could reach Phoenix, a harbor of Crete, facing southwest and northwest, and spend the winter there.

Verse 9. Since **considerable time had passed . . . the voyage was now dangerous.** Every day, the goal to reach Rome by late October looked less attainable. The **dangerous** season for sailing the Mediterranean occurred sometime between mid-September and mid-November. After mid-November, sailing ceased until spring; constantly overcast skies made navigation impossible (see comments on v. 20). The ship was now in the dangerous period; **even the fast was already over.** The **fast** referred to the Jewish Day of Atonement (Lev. 16:29; 23:26, 27), which, according to Sir William Ramsay, in A.D. 59 fell on October 5.[4]

Those on board knew that time was slipping away. The season during which travel was impossible was rapidly approaching, so those in charge of the ship discussed what to do (v. 11). They decided that Fair Havens "was not suitable for wintering" (v. 12): It was open to the sea; the ship would be exposed to the weather, and some of the cargo might become water-soaked. Further, there was no large city in which they could winter in comfort; the nearby "city of Lasea" (v. 8) was small. On the other hand, Phoenix lay only forty miles farther west. It was a major city with a protected harbor. Both they and their ship would fare better there during the long winter months.

Verse 10. When Paul heard that they were considering leaving Fair Havens, he was upset. Luke does not record how he heard of it. Maybe Paul was a part of the conference. Possibly word was passed around the ship. Since he later indicated that his protest was to all on board (v. 21), perhaps he heard a public announcement in response to which he registered his protest to all who were listening. Paul was possibly "the most experienced traveler on board that ship."[5] Luke recorded eleven voyages the apostle made on the Mediterranean (not counting the trip to

---

[4]W. M. Ramsay, *St. Paul the Traveller and the Roman Citizen* (Hodder & Stroughton, 1895), 322.

[5]William Barclay, *The Acts of the Apostles*, The Daily Study Bible Series, rev. ed. (Philadelphia: Westminster Press, 1976), 182.

Rome), covering at least 3,500 miles—and Paul made some trips that Luke did not record: He had been shipwrecked three times and had spent "a night and a day . . . in the deep" (2 Cor. 11:25). Paul, therefore, did not hesitate to tell everyone what he thought: **"Men, I perceive that the voyage will certainly be with damage and great loss, not only of the cargo and the ship, but also of our lives."**

Was Paul's statement inspired? Probably Paul's words were a strong conviction based on his experiences in the past: (1) Paul did not ascribe them to a heavenly source, as he did a later announcement (v. 23). (2) The Greek word from θεωρέω (*theōreō*), translated **perceive**, can mean "to perceive from past experience." (3) Subsequent events did not happen precisely as they were predicted as there was no **loss** of life (vv. 22, 44). Of course, on occasion God has announced a disaster and then modified the outcome in response to prayer (see Num. 14:11–24).

Verse 11. Julius, the highest ranking official on board, was unimpressed. He **was more persuaded by the pilot and the captain of the ship than by what was being said by Paul.** The Greek word ναύκληρος (*nauklēros*), translated **captain**, could indicate the owner of the ship (see KJV, NIV). The owner of a ship often served as the captain. The **centurion** probably thought, "What do you know about it, Mr. Tentmaker/Rabbi? If the experts think we can make it, who are you to argue?"

Verse 12. Because the harbor was not suitable for wintering, the majority reached a decision to put out to sea from there. Is this a **majority** of those in the conference or a majority of those on board ship? Since Paul later apparently reprimanded all on board (v. 21), perhaps those in charge had asked everyone what they thought about the **decision** to sail to Phoenix and had been backed by the majority. The disastrous consequences that followed were not Paul's fault, but the fault of others. The sailors hoped **somehow they could reach Phoenix, a harbor of Crete, facing southwest and northwest, and spend the winter there.** This **harbor** should probably be identified with modern Phineka, which preserves the name **Phoenix** and satisfies the description in the text. Luke's point was that the harbor was protected from winter blasts, which came from the east and northeast.

ADVENTURES ON THE SEA (27:13–44)

A Storm Hits the Ship (27:13–20)

¹³**When a moderate south wind came up, supposing that they had attained their purpose, they weighed anchor and began sailing along Crete, close inshore.** ¹⁴**But before very long there rushed down from the land a violent wind, called Euraquilo;** ¹⁵**and when the ship was caught in it and could not face the wind, we gave way to it and let ourselves be driven along.** ¹⁶**Running under the shelter of a small island called Clauda, we were scarcely able to get the ship's boat under control.** ¹⁷**After they had hoisted it up, they used supporting cables in undergirding the ship; and fearing that they might run aground on the shallows of Syrtis, they let down the sea anchor and in this way let themselves be driven along.** ¹⁸**The next day as we were being violently storm-tossed, they began to jettison the cargo;** ¹⁹**and on the third day they threw the ship's tackle overboard with their own hands.** ²⁰**Since neither sun nor stars appeared for many days, and no small storm was assailing us, from then on all hope of our being saved was gradually abandoned.**

Verse 13. At first, it seemed that the majority had made an excellent decision—for the wind change they had been looking for came. **When a moderate south wind came up, supposing that they had attained their purpose, they weighed anchor and began sailing along Crete, close inshore.** There is often "the calm before the storm."

Verse 14. A few hours from their destination, disaster struck. **But before very long there rushed down from the** towering Cretan mountains **a violent wind, called Euraquilo.** The Greek word τυφωνικός (*tuphōnikos*), translated **violent**, is a form of the word from which we get "typhoon." **Euraquilo** was the sailor's name for a typhoon-like "Northeaster." "Euraquilo" is a hybrid word combining the Greek word for "east wind" with the Latin word for "north wind." The KJV has a different spelling of the word, but the meaning is the same.

Verse 15. Blown from the shelter of Crete, the ship had access to no more harbors, just open sea. **When the ship was caught in it and could not face the wind, we gave way to it and let ourselves be driven along.** The ship was at the mercy of the wind and the waves.

Verse 16. After being driven southeast for several hours, they ran **under the shelter of a small island called Clauda.** Taking advantage of the momentary lull, all worked feverishly to make the vessel as seaworthy as possible. Even Luke pitched in to help secure the lifeboat which was pulled behind the ship. Remembering the struggle, he said, **We were scarcely able to get the ship's boat under control.** The small **boat** would sink or be dashed to pieces if left in the water, and it might be needed later to reach shore. When pulled in, it was probably already partially swamped.

Verse 17. After they had hoisted the boat **up, they used supporting cables in undergirding the ship.** These **cables** were ropes or chains placed around the hull and tightened with winches to hold the vessel together in the storm. No one knows in exactly what direction the cables were placed or which method was used to circle the hull, but there are many fascinating possibilities. The sailors feared **that they might run aground on the shallows of Syrtis.** The **shallows of Syrtis** were sandbars stretching off the coast of North Africa—a ship graveyard feared by sailors. Though the area was many miles to the south, they knew how far a ship could be driven in a storm. Before Paul's ship finally reached land, they were driven five hundred miles to the west. The shallows of Syrtis were much closer than that to the south.

They let down the sea anchor, hoping it would slow the ship. The Greek word σκεῦος (*skeuos*), translated **sea anchor,** can mean many things. It is the same word used in verse 19: "the . . . tackle" (see comments on v. 19). Opinions differ as to what the word means in verse 17. Some think the sailors lowered the mainsail (KJV; NEB), since this is standard practice during a storm. By this time, the ship had been blown past the protection of the little island; they could do nothing but **let themselves be driven along.**

Verse 18. If those on board had hopes that the storm would soon blow itself out, they were disappointed. **The next day** they still **were being violently storm-tossed**. The passengers and crew heard the howling winds, the creaking timbers, the straining ropes. They saw the swirling black clouds, the angry waves that washed across the deck. The ship pitched up and down on the raging sea, and they struggled to keep their footing. The salty spray stung their faces, and they gagged on salt water. Storms are painfully real. Desperate times call for desperate measures, so **they began to jettison the cargo.** Their livelihood depended on the **cargo**, but they were more concerned about their lives than their livelihood.

Verse 19. And on the third day they threw the ship's tackle overboard with their own hands. To lighten the ship, they cast **overboard** everything they did not absolutely need. The Greek word σκεῦος (*skeuos*), translated **tackle**, is sometimes used in the New Testament to refer to household furnishings (Mt. 12:29; Mk. 3:27; see comments on v. 17). In addition to throwing overboard extra tackling, the crew possibly tossed tables, chairs, and chests into the sea. A few manuscripts have "with *our* own hands" (KJV), but most manuscripts have **with *their* own hands** (emphasis added).

Verse 20. The storm continued. **Neither sun nor stars appeared for many days**. They had no compass in those days, no sextant to reckon their position. Navigation was dependent on the **sun** by day and the **stars** at night. Therefore, they had no idea where they were. For all they knew, they could founder on the shallows of Syrtis at any moment, or crash into a hidden reef.

Day after miserable day, night after terrifying night, they rose and fell in mountainous seas. The main cargo of wheat had become thoroughly waterlogged—the sacks too heavy and sodden to move in a pitching ship, and all the time increasing in weight.

> The water level rose, the ship settled lower, until by the eleventh or twelfth day of the storm "all hope of our being saved was abandoned." Foundering was inevitable

now—a matter of a few days at most even if the storm abated—and would mean the loss of all hands if they abandoned ship.[6]

For nearly two weeks, the storm battered the ship and its occupants until both were ready to break apart. Luke wrote, **No small storm was assailing us, from then on all hope of our being saved was gradually abandoned.**

Paul Encourages the Crew (27:21–26)

[21]**When they had gone a long time without food, then Paul stood up in their midst and said, "Men, you ought to have followed my advice and not to have set sail from Crete and incurred this damage and loss.** [22]**Yet now I urge you to keep up your courage, for there will be no loss of life among you, but only of the ship.** [23]**For this very night an angel of the God to whom I belong and whom I serve stood before me,** [24]**saying, 'Do not be afraid, Paul; you must stand before Caesar; and behold, God has granted you all those who are sailing with you.'** [25]**Therefore, keep up your courage, men, for I believe God that it will turn out exactly as I have been told.** [26]**But we must run aground on a certain island."**

Verse 21. Here is the low point of the story. The men were soaked, numb with cold, exhausted to the bone, weak from hunger. **They had gone a long time without food.** "The storm had deprived them of the means, the time, and the inclination to prepare or to eat any regular meals."[7] Even Luke included himself in his portrait of despair: "*We* finally gave up all hope of being saved" (v. 20; NIV; emphasis added). Did the word "we" also include Paul? Perhaps. When the angel appeared to Paul, he admonished him, "Do not be afraid" (v. 24). Even the strongest can be beaten to their knees when battered hard enough and long enough by the storm.

---

[6]Pollock, 280.

[7]Orrin Root, ed., *Standard Bible Commentary: Acts* (Cincinnati, Ohio: Standard Publishing Co., 1966), 196.

When Paul was forced to his knees by hopelessness, he began to pray. In his night of despair, he received a promise from God. The next morning, the apostle hastened to share that message of hope. **Then Paul stood up in their midst and said, "Men, you ought to have followed my advice and not to have set sail from Crete and incurred this damage and loss."** Paul's purpose was not so much to scold them, as to urge them not to make the same mistake again.

Verses 22, 23. Then his words of confidence rang above the howling of the storm: **"Yet now I urge you to keep up your courage, for there will be no loss of life among you, but only of the ship. For this very night an angel of the God to whom I belong and whom I serve stood before me."** Usually the Lord Himself appeared to Paul. An **angel** was perhaps sent rather than Jesus because Paul's pagan shipmates would be more likely to understand "an angel said to me" than "Jesus said to me." The message of hope, however, was basically the same (see 18:9, 10; 23:11).

Verses 24, 25. Paul repeated the angel's words: **"'Do not be afraid, Paul; you must stand before Caesar; and behold, God has granted you all those who are sailing with you.'"** This message added one new note to Jesus' previous assurance: Jesus had said that Paul would definitely go to Rome (23:11); the angel said that in Rome **Paul** would definitely **stand before Caesar.** Based on this divine message, Paul exhorted his shipmates: **"Therefore, keep up your courage, men, for I believe God that it will turn out exactly as I have been told."**

Paul had apparently been praying not only for his own safety, but also for the safety of all on board—and God answered his prayer. God had not **granted** all on board to Paul in the sense that all would become Christians, but in the sense that their lives would be spared. F. F. Bruce commented, "Human society has no idea how much it owes, in the mercy of God, to the presence of righteous men and women."[8] For other examples of how the

---

[8]F. F. Bruce, *The Book of Acts*, The New International Commentary on the New Testament, gen. ed. F. F. Bruce, rev. ed. (Grand Rapids, Mich.: Wm. B. Eerdmans Publishing Co., 1988), 488.

godly help preserve the ungodly, see Genesis 18:26–32; 30:27; 39:5.

Verse 26. God's promise contained good news and bad: Their lives would be spared, but the ship would be lost. Paul added, **"But we must run aground on a certain island."** God promised they would be saved, but that did not mean it would be easy. Hard times were ahead—but God's promise would sustain them.

The Crew Must Stay Together (27:27–32)

²⁷**But when the fourteenth night came, as we were being driven about in the Adriatic Sea, about midnight the sailors began to surmise that they were approaching some land.** ²⁸**They took soundings and found it to be twenty fathoms; and a little farther on they took another sounding and found it to be fifteen fathoms.** ²⁹**Fearing that we might run aground somewhere on the rocks, they cast four anchors from the stern and wished for daybreak.** ³⁰**But as the sailors were trying to escape from the ship and had let down the ship's boat into the sea, on the pretense of intending to lay out anchors from the bow,** ³¹**Paul said to the centurion and to the soldiers, "Unless these men remain in the ship, you yourselves cannot be saved."** ³²**Then the soldiers cut away the ropes of the ship's boat and let it fall away.**

Verse 27. The angel had told Paul that the ship would "run aground on a certain island" (v. 26). That "certain island" was Malta (28:1), about five hundred miles west of where the storm first struck. Malta is a dot in the Mediterranean. As the ship was driven this way and that (27:27), how could it possibly connect with that tiny bit of land? God was the navigator. God was using the same wind that threatened to destroy the ship and its passengers to guide them to that destination (see Rom. 8:28). God does not abandon His own; He continues to work in their lives.

But when the fourteenth night came, the ship was **being driven about in the Adriatic Sea.** This body of water is not to be confused with the Adriatic Sea between Greece and Italy. According to ancient writers, **Adriatic Sea** was one of the designations of the east central section of the Mediterranean. **About midnight the sailors began to surmise that they were approaching some land.** They could probably hear the sound of waves breaking on a beach.

Verse 28. The sailors **took soundings** to try to locate their position. **Soundings** were taken with weighted ropes that had knots a fathom (about six feet) apart. They **found it to be twenty fathoms** (120 feet)**; and a little farther on they took another sounding and found it to be fifteen fathoms** (90 feet). Here was more good news and bad news: The good news was that they were nearing land; the bad news was that danger lurked in the darkness.

Verse 29. Fearing that we might run aground somewhere on the rocks, they cast four anchors from the stern. They probably used most of the **anchors** on board to keep from running aground on hidden **rocks.** Normally, ships were anchored from the bow (the front of the ship), not the **stern** (the back). Since, however, the wind was blowing toward the land, they anchored the ship where the storm would keep it facing the shore. Having done what they could to protect the ship, they **wished for daybreak.** Literally, "they prayed for the day."

Verse 30. Sometime in the night, the tension overwhelmed the frightened sailors. They forgot the time-honored code of remaining with the ship; they forgot about everyone but themselves. **On the pretense of intending to lay out anchors from the bow** they **let down the ship's boat into the sea**, intending to row to shore—a desperate plan almost certain to fail in the stormy darkness.

Paul, who was on deck, had enough experience with ships and storms not to be deceived by the sailors' charade. Anchoring the ship from the **bow** when it had already been anchored from the stern was unnecessary and could even cause damage to the vessel. Thus, **as the sailors were trying to escape from the ship,** Paul spoke up.

Verse 31. Paul said to the centurion and to the soldiers, "Unless these men remain in the ship, you yourselves cannot be saved." Without the sailors to navigate the next day, they had little hope of survival. Other conditions may have made it necessary for them to stay on board. Perhaps God's promise that there would be "no loss of life" (v. 22) presupposed that all would stay together.

Verse 32. The soldiers quickly **cut away the ropes of the ship's boat and let it fall away,** effectively eliminating further attempt at desertion. The next day they probably wished they had the boat to use in getting to shore, but their drastic action served its purpose at the time.

Paul Urges the Crew to Eat (27:33–38)

[33]**Until the day was about to dawn, Paul was encouraging them all to take some food, saying, "Today is the fourteenth day that you have been constantly watching and going without eating, having taken nothing.** [34]**Therefore I encourage you to take some food, for this is for your preservation, for not a hair from the head of any of you will perish."** [35]**Having said this, he took bread and gave thanks to God in the presence of all, and he broke it and began to eat.** [36]**All of them were encouraged and they themselves also took food.** [37]**All of us in the ship were two hundred and seventy-six persons.** [38]**When they had eaten enough, they began to lighten the ship by throwing out the wheat into the sea.**

Verse 33. As the night wore on, the confidence of all on board faded; if experienced sailors were frightened, should not all be terrified? Just before **the day was about to dawn,** Paul took charge again, initiating a three-step program to raise spirits.

Step one was to strengthen their bodies—for that which affects the body invariably affects the spirit. People who are experiencing serious emotional upheavals often have physical problems that contribute to their emotional conditions. **Paul was encouraging them all to take some food, saying, "Today is the fourteenth day that you have been constantly watching and going without eating, having taken nothing."** They had probably eaten a few bites now and then, but no regular meals (see comments on v. 21). It is even possible that the pagan crew and passengers had been fasting to appease their gods, a common practice in those days.

Verse 34. Paul continued, **"Therefore I encourage you to take some food, for this is for your preservation."** In other words, "You need your strength if you are to survive."

Step two was to strengthen their spirits—for that which affects the spirit invariably affects the body. He again expressed God's promise, assuring them that **"not a hair from the head of any of you will perish."** This expression was well-known (1 Sam. 14:45; 2 Sam. 14:11; 1 Kings 1:52; Lk. 21:18).

Verse 35. Step three was perhaps the most important. He demonstrated that *he* believed the promise; he showed that *he* really believed God was with them. Thus he strengthened their souls—for that which affects the soul invariably affects both body and spirit. Paul **took bread and gave thanks to God in the presence of all, and he broke it and began to eat.** This breaking of bread was not the Lord's Supper, but rather a common meal.

Verse 36. Paul's calmness was as contagious as the sailors' fear had been. **All of them were encouraged and they themselves also took food.** What a sight that must have been! One little missionary giving thanks to God for a predawn breakfast catered for three Christians and 273 heathens.

Verse 37. Luke waited until now to mention, **All of us in the ship were two hundred and seventy-six persons** (see comments on v. 6). Perhaps someone did a head count at that point to see how much food to bring out for breakfast or so they could make sure all were accounted for after they were on shore.

Verse 38. Paul's practical conduct during the storm is impressive. God had promised that all on board would be saved, but Paul did not believe that excused him from doing what he could: When spirits were low, he tried to encourage the others on board. When sailors were needed for navigation, he prevented them from leaving the ship. When all aboard were fatigued, he urged them to eat. **When** the crew **had eaten enough,** their strength returned and their hope revived. They prepared for the dawn and **began to lighten the ship by throwing out the wheat into the sea.** They tossed overboard what was left of the cargo (see v. 18), so the **ship** would sit higher in the water and be able to run closer to shore.

Land Is Reached (27:39–44)

[39]**When day came, they could not recognize the land; but they did observe a bay with a beach, and they resolved to drive the ship onto it if they could.** [40]**And casting off the anchors, they left them in the sea while at the same time they were loosening the ropes of the rudders; and hoisting the foresail to the wind, they were heading for the beach.** [41]**But striking a reef where two seas met, they ran the vessel aground; and the prow stuck fast and remained immovable, but the stern began to be broken up by the force of the waves.** [42]**The soldiers' plan was to kill the prisoners, so that none of them would swim away and escape;** [43]**but the centurion, wanting to bring Paul safely through, kept them from their intention, and commanded that those who could swim should jump overboard first and get to land,** [44]**and the rest should follow, some on planks, and others on various things from the ship. And so it happened that they all were brought safely to land.**

Verse 39. This verse begins, **When day came. . . .** Bad nights do pass and morning comes. In the daylight, **they could not recognize the land; but they did observe a bay with a beach.** This incident seems to be one of those rare occasions when the traditional spot is the correct location. Most authorities believe that "St. Paul's Bay" on the northeast coast of Malta is where Paul and the others reached shore. The crew **resolved to drive the ship onto it if they could.** Land was in sight, but they were still far from safety.

Verse 40. Continuing their preparation, the crew took three more steps: (1) They cast **off the** four **anchors** (v. 29) and **left them in the sea,** because they would not need them again. (2) **At the same time they were loosening the ropes of the rudders.** Ancient ships often had two steering paddles or **rudders** located at each corner of the stern, joined by a pole where they could be managed by one steersman. During the storm, these rudders had been raised from the water and tied down. Now they were loosened so that the ship could be steered. (3) They hoisted **the foresail to the wind** to help them steer and to provide some wind thrust. The **foresail** was a small sail at the front of the ship used as much for steering as for propulsion, unlike the main sail, which was mainly for propulsion. They were as ready as they were likely to get, so they headed **for the beach.** The KJV, based on different Greek manuscripts, gives slightly different details in verse 40, but these are insignificant.

Verse 41. They hoped to get close to shore, but **striking a reef where two seas met, they ran the vessel aground.** Two strong currents flowing from opposite directions had piled up sand and/or rocks under the water which the sailors could not see. These reefs, or strips of sand or rocks just below the surface, still exist at the traditional "St. Paul's Bay" in Malta. **The prow stuck fast and remained immovable, but the stern began to be broken up by the force of the waves.** The sailors were unable to move the **prow,** the tip projecting from the front of the ship. Meanwhile the strong **waves** were tearing up the **stern.**

Verse 42. As the ship began to disintegrate, again panic reigned. This time the soldiers, not the sailors, panicked. Military law dictated that if a prisoner escaped, the one responsible for guarding him could receive the prisoner's punishment (see comments on 12:19; 16:27). Some prisoners might escape in the confusion and none of the soldiers desired to be "lion fodder," (see comments on v. 1). Thus **the soldiers' plan was to kill the prisoners, so that none of them would swim away and escape.** They planned to **kill** Paul along with the other **prisoners.**

Verse 43. As the soldiers looked at Paul with murder in their eyes, his life again hung in the balance—but the Lord had promised him that he would stand before Caesar. This time God intervened through Julius, the centurion. Evidently, the Roman officer had not only been instructed to give Paul special treatment, he had also been impressed with his conduct in a time of crisis. Thus, **the centurion, wanting to bring Paul safely through, kept them from their intention.** There is no indication that the **centurion** was concerned about any of the rest of the prisoners. The other prisoners owed their lives once more to **Paul.** Perhaps the centurion accidentally heard of the soldiers' plan and stopped them, or perhaps the soldiers asked permission to kill the prisoners and Julius said "No." The latter seems more likely.

Julius gave orders to abandon ship. He **commanded that those who could swim should jump overboard first and get to land.** It has been suggested that he probably had the soldiers who could **swim** to leave first, so they could collect the prisoners as they arrived on shore.

Verse 44. And the rest should follow, some on planks, and others on various things from the ship. Paul, as the survivor of three shipwrecks, may have given Julius this strategy. Paul had probably survived "a night and a day . . . in the deep" (2 Cor. 11:25) by clinging to debris from the **ship** which sank.

When all jumped into the water and struggled to reach shore, **they all were brought safely to land.** When the last waterlogged man struggled onto the beach, they made a second head count and found that 276—the original number (v. 37)—were alive. As Paul predicted, there was "*no* loss of life"; not even "a hair from the head" of any had perished (vv. 22, 34; emphasis added). Coincidence could not explain it; statistical analysis would call it impossible. Nevertheless, it was true. When God makes a promise, not one word of it will fail (see 1 Kings 8:56).

APPLICATION

Hopelessness (Ch. 27)

Luke capsuled the hopelessness of those on board the storm-tossed ship in these words: "All hope of our being saved was . . . abandoned" (v. 20). We struggle with the feeling of hopelessness that can come when we are battered by the storms of life day after day. In such a state of mind, we often cry out, "Why? Lord, why do You allow these storms?" By glancing ahead to the end of our story, we could give some answers regarding why God allowed Paul to end up in a storm: Surviving the storm probably made Paul stronger in his faith. He had another dramatic demonstration that God cares for His own. Further, the storm gave Paul opportunities he would not have had otherwise. For instance, he had the opportunity to demonstrate his confidence in the Lord. Paul even had the opportunity to tell 273 pagans about the true God! Probably—after they were safely on shore—they were even ready to hear about Jesus. In the end, the storm benefited both Paul and others. Note, however, the phrase "in the end." *While* the storm was raging, those benefits were *not* obvious. Even so, when trials overwhelm us, it is sometimes hard to see how good can possibly come from our trouble. What should we do when we are driven to our knees by the storm? Do as Paul did (v. 24): Pray as you have never prayed before (Phil. 4:6; Jas. 5:13)—and trust in the Lord who knows more about storms than we will ever know (2 Cor. 1:9, 10; 2 Tim. 1:12).

The Storms of Life (Ch. 27)

Forces of hell today cannot hinder God's plans and purposes. Satan continues to try to destroy us and to defeat God's purpose for our lives (1 Pet. 5:8). Each of us needs God's help to survive. Chapter 27 can give us confidence as we face our own storms of life. Luke was not speaking allegorically as he wrote of a terrible storm hurled against the merchant ship bound for Italy; the waves were real, the danger genuine. Nevertheless, few commentators can resist a comparison or two between Paul's journey to Rome and our own journey through life. Chapter 27 is as an exciting adventure, but it has parallels with our own experiences in life. Like Paul's trip, most of our lives have good days and bad—and the unexpected can happen at any moment.

"It Is Well With My Soul" (Ch. 27)

In 1873, a businessman from Chicago, Horatio G. Spafford, decided to take his family on a vacation to Europe. He booked passage on a French liner, but, at the last minute, business prevented him from going. He put his wife and four daughters on the ship, planning to join them later in Europe. On November 22 the liner was rammed by another vessel. In twelve minutes, the ship sank to the bottom of the ocean, killing 226 people, including Spafford's four daughters. Nine days later, when the survivors reached England, his wife sent him a two-word cable: "Saved alone." He immediately booked passage on another ship to go to England to be with his wife. One night the captain called him to his cabin. "As nearly as I can tell," the captain said, "we are over the spot where the ship sank with your daughters." Spafford returned to his cabin. There, in "the valley of the shadow of death," he wrote a song that has brought us great comfort:

When peace like a river attendeth my way,
When sorrows like sea billows roll;
Whatever my lot, Thou hast taught me to say,
"It is well, it is well with my soul."[9]

God Is the God of Nature (Ch. 27)

Since many passages, especially in Psalms, emphasize that God is the God of nature (including storms), a lesson could include a philosophical discussion of God's part and Satan's part in natural disasters. According to the Book of Job, God *allows* natural disasters in order to make us better, while Satan uses them to try to destroy us physically and spiritually. This issue is complex and troubles many Christians. It is wise to be prepared for questions that may be asked. Chapter 27 illustrates the truth of 1 Corinthians 10:13, as well as the Book of Job, that God *limits* Satan in what he can do—and that God always provides a "way of escape" which we can use or refuse.

"Fair Havens" (27:8)

Application can be made concerning "fair havens" in our lives—times and places of temporary respite from the "contrary winds" that blow.

Making Bad Decisions (27:12)

If there was ever a classic example of how to make bad decisions in life, the resolve to keep sailing in 27:12 is it: Ignore the advice of the godly (Prov. 1:5; 19:20; Rev. 3:18); listen to "experts"

---

[9]Horatio G. Spafford, "It Is Well With My Soul," *Songs of Faith and Praise*, comp. and ed. Alton H. Howard (West Monroe, La.: Howard Publishing Co., 1994).

more concerned about profit and pleasure than people and principles (Prov. 12:5; 1 Cor. 3:18–20); and go along with the majority (Ex. 23:2; Mt. 7:13). Sometimes we bring our storms on ourselves (Jon. 1:12), but sometimes others are at fault. We may suffer not because of personal misjudgment, but because—like Paul—we are outvoted.

Gifts and Responsibility (27:13–44)

Acts 27:13–44 illustrates the relationship of God's grace and human responsibility. God "gave" everyone on board to Paul, but the apostle still needed to do what he could to ensure that they reached shore safely. Here is a vivid illustration you may want to use: Show a blank check to your class. Ask each to suppose that you made out the check to him, *giving* him a large sum of money which he did not earn. However, when he received the check, it would be necessary to cash the check and use the money to take advantage of the gift. Even so, salvation is a gift; but we must obey God, doing what we can to appropriate that gift.

Surviving the Storm (27:13–44)

Everyone has either been in a storm, is in one now, or will eventually be in one: domestic storms, financial storms, business storms. As the storms rage, we run aground on the shoals of suffering, sink in the troubled waters of failure, find ourselves off course emotionally and spiritually, and lose hope. Day after day without light, we are driven to our knees. Let us see how Paul survived the storm—and how you can survive yours. When the storms of life hit, you need to know that you are not alone.

Here are five suggestions for surviving the storm:[10] (1) Expect the possibility of a storm—so the storm will not catch you by surprise. (2) Express the promises of God—so the storm will not overtake you unprepared. (3) Exhibit the presence of God—so the storm will not find you unprotected. (4) Expedite the plan of God—so the storm will not show you disobedient. (5) Expe-

---

[10]Adapted from Jack Graham in a "Power Point" television sermon entitled "How To Defeat the Darkness."

rience the peace of God—so the storm will not leave you without reward.

(1) If we would weather the storms of life, we must first *expect the possibility of a storm*. We must be mentally prepared for the fact that they will come. Although Paul was exactly where he was supposed to be—on the way to Rome to testify for the name of Jesus—contrary winds still blew. Ultimately, the storm came. Rain falls on the righteous and the unrighteous (Mt. 5:45); storms break around the heads of both the good and the evil. Storms do not mean that you have been abandoned by God; they are simply a part of life—and sometimes they are part of God's plan to make you a better person. If they force you to your knees, maybe that is where you needed to be.

(2) If we would weather the storms of life, we need to *express the promises of God*. First, we need to express these promises to ourselves, over and over again, to impress them upon our minds and hearts. We may even want to write them out and post them where we can see them every day. If you are presently struggling with a storm in your life, you may want to make these words of the psalmist your motto: "Why are you in despair, O my soul? And why have you become disturbed within me? Hope in God, for I shall again praise Him for the help of his presence" (Ps. 42:5). Then, as Paul did, we need to share those promises with others. God has a message of hope for us. We will not have a heavenly visitor as Paul did, but we have God's "precious and magnificent promises" (2 Pet. 1:4; see Heb. 8:6)— and the message remains the same: "Take courage" (Ps. 27:14; Jn. 16:33). The problem is not that the Lord has left us without assurance (see Ps. 34:18; 145:18; Is. 41:10; 43:1–5; Rom. 8:38, 39). The problem is that too often we lack the faith of Paul who said, "I believe God, that it will turn out *exactly* as I have been told" (Acts 27:25; emphasis added; see Jn. 20:27). With that kind of faith, you can weather any storm.

(3) If we would weather the storms of life, we must *exhibit the presence of God in our lives*. We should let others see that we believe God's promises—and that no matter what happens, we are confident that we have not been abandoned. We can say with Paul, "We are afflicted . . . but not crushed; perplexed, but not

despairing; persecuted, but not forsaken; struck down, but not destroyed" (2 Cor. 4:8, 9). When you are in the midst of a storm, remember that you are not the only one battered by life (1 Cor. 10:13). Pray for others as well as for yourself (Jas. 5:16); nothing will sink a man faster than self-centeredness.

(4) If we would weather the storms of life, we need to *expedite God's plan*—whatever it may be. We must do what *we* can to survive the storm. When told to swim to shore, do you suppose Paul protested, "Wait a minute! You don't expect me to jump out into that cold turbulent water, do you? The Lord promised me that I would be safe! The Lord promised me that I would reach Rome! I am going to wait right here until the Lord rescues me"? Paul was probably one of the first ones in the water. It is not hard to envision him struggling against the waves, swimming or holding onto a piece of broken mast, striving to keep his head above water, choking on salt water, fighting his way toward shore, until at last he lay exhausted on the beach, gasping for breath. Paul understood something all of us need to understand: Even when God promises us victory over the storms of life, we still have a battle ahead. God has a plan for our lives. He will help us accomplish it; but He does not do for us what we can do for ourselves. If His plan calls for us to jump into icy waters and swim for our lives, He does not want us to say, "But, Lord, I can't swim!" He expects us to grab the life preserver of faith and jump. If you would survive the storms of life, be ready to expedite the plan.

(5) If we would weather the storms of life, we must *experience the peace of God*. If we express the promises, will our problems vanish like the proverbial puff of smoke? Probably not. Paul's announcement of God's message of hope did not calm the sea. The clouds did not lift so that the sailors could get their bearings. Nothing changed outwardly; the storm continued to rage. The change was *within*—a change in attitude. Surely this change made all the difference in the world to Paul and to the others who believed. When we put our trust in the Lord's promises during the storms of life, seldom is there outward change; circumstances remain much the same. The real difference is within: We come to know "the peace of God, which

surpasses all comprehension" (Phil. 4:7).

Batten Down the Hatches (27:17)

You can learn from those sailors of long ago: When tempests hit your life, do what you can to minimize the damage, "batten down the hatches," and prepare to ride out the storm. "Batten down the hatches" is a nautical term meaning "cover and secure all deck openings (with battens)." As a figure of speech, it means "make everything as secure as you can."

Anchors of Faith (27:23–29)

We could summarize the faith (vv. 23–25) which enabled Paul to survive the storm in the following way: (1) I recognize God's presence—"stood before me"; (2) I am God's possession—"to whom I belong"; (3) God has given me a purpose—"whom I serve"; (4) God has given me a promise—"you must stand before Caesar."[11]

The incidental mention of "four anchors" (v. 29) has fascinated sermonizers. There are many sermons based on four spiritual "anchors" that can keep us off the rocks. Since the only spiritual anchor mentioned in the Scriptures is "hope" (Heb. 6:19), the lists are highly subjective. Lloyd Ogilvie's suggestion seems the most sensible. He said, "Perhaps you have your own set [of anchors] to keep you off the rocks. . . . [I]t is crucial to list the four *which have worked for you*. Encourage people [then] to identify their [own] anchors."[12]

---

[11]Adapted from Rick Atchley, "Anchors for the Anxious," Sermon preached at the Southern Hills church of Christ, Abilene, Texas, on 19 April 1987.

[12]Lloyd Ogilvie, *Acts*, The Communicator's Commentary, vol. 5 (Dallas: Word Publishing, 1983), 349; emphasis added.

CHAPTER 28
PAUL'S JOURNEY TO ROME (PART 2)

ADVENTURES ON AN ISLAND (MALTA)
(28:1–10)

Paul Is Bitten by a Viper (28:1–6)

¹When they had been brought safely through, then we found out that the island was called Malta. ²The natives showed us extraordinary kindness; for because of the rain that had set in and because of the cold, they kindled a fire and received us all. ³But when Paul had gathered a bundle of sticks and laid them on the fire, a viper came out because of the heat and fastened itself on his hand. ⁴When the natives saw the creature hanging from his hand, they began saying to one another, "Undoubtedly this man is a murderer, and though he has been saved from the sea, justice has not allowed him to live." ⁵However he shook the creature off into the fire and suffered no harm. ⁶But they were expecting that he was about to swell up or suddenly fall down dead. But after they had waited a long time and had seen nothing unusual happen to him, they changed their minds and began to say that he was a god.

Chapter 28 begins with Paul and the other voyagers shipwrecked on the island of Malta. Take a moment to look at the map of Paul's journey to Rome (see the *Appendix, Paul's Journey to Rome*). As you look at this map, mentally draw a straight line from Caesarea, where the journey began, to Rome, where the journey ended. Now compare that line with the actual route his ships took: north, up the coast; west, close to the coast of what is now Turkey; south to the island of Crete and then west to Fair Havens; finally, south, then west as the ship was "driven to and fro" (27:27; ASV) until it grounded on a reef off the coast of Malta. Only after considerable delays and detours did the voyagers head north again, toward Rome.

When Paul found himself on the island of Malta, he was not where he wanted to be. He wanted to be in Rome (19:21). After his arrest in Jerusalem, the Lord had assured him that he would witness at Rome (23:11). The apostle had appealed to Caesar and started toward the capital city. On the journey, God had promised him that he would stand before Caesar (27:24). Paul had every right to expect to be in Rome. Instead, he found himself stuck on a tiny island, miles from the capital, with winter coming on and no possibility of getting off the island until spring.

Verse 1. We can imagine Paul lying exhausted on the beach, gasping for breath, while waterlogged survivors struggled ashore. The 276 men were most likely soaked, hungry, and shivering—huddling together and looking like human debris tossed up from the ocean. As they watched the churning sea slowly dismantle their ship, what do you suppose their thoughts were? The ship's owner may have had tears in his eyes because the ship and cargo were lost, but we imagine most of them, including Paul, were just thankful to be alive.

When the survivors of the wreckage had a chance to look around, they learned that they had not reached Italy. Luke recorded, **When they had been brought safely through, then we found out that the island was called Malta.** They may have **found out** their location from a closer inspection of the terrain, but they were probably informed by the inhabitants who met them. The island was known as **Malta.** "Melita" (KJV) is a transliteration of the name in the original text: Μελίτη (*Melitē*). Today, the island is known as Malta. It is one of three inhabited islands, along with two uninhabited large rocks, which comprise the country of Malta. The rugged little island of Malta, eighteen miles long and eight miles wide, is located fifty-eight miles south of Sicily, in the Mediterranean Sea between Italy and North Africa. It was settled by Phoenician traders, but in

218 B.C. it came under Roman rule. "Malta" meant "refuge" in the Canaanite language; the name was perhaps given by Phoenician sailors who had found refuge on the island. Luke may have been saying, "We recognized that this island of refuge was well named." The island now provided refuge for Paul and his fellow travelers.

Verse 2. The Christian may not know what tomorrow's journey will bring, but he knows who travels with him. Thus he has "peace in every circumstance" (2 Thess. 3:16; see Ps. 29:11; Jn. 14:27; 16:33; Rom. 1:7; 2:10; Col. 3:15). God was watching over Paul and his fellow travelers, so Luke was able to report, **The natives showed us extraordinary kindness.** The word **extraordinary** is translated from the Greek phrase οὐ τὴν τυχοῦσαν (*ou tēn tuchousan*), meaning "not the ordinary." A similar phrase is found in 19:11 to describe the "extraordinary" miracles God performed through Paul. In this verse, the Greek phrase describes the extreme kindness shown to the apostle. The word **kindness** is translated from the Greek word φιλανθρωπία (*philanthrōpia*), from which we get "philanthropy," which literally means "love of mankind."

Those who had been shipwrecked were in need of this "special" hospitality. **Because of the rain that had set in and because of the cold,** the natives of Malta **kindled a fire and received us all.** It was late October or early November. The temperature would have been around 50°F (10°C) in that part of the Mediterranean—chilly enough for one who is soaked, exhausted, and standing in a driving rain. After the waterlogged voyagers had been rocked violently for two weeks by the storm-tossed sea, it must have been comforting to warm up next to a fire.

In that day it was not uncommon for landlocked pirates to wait for shipwrecks and then prey on the victims. Sometimes they killed them; sometimes they made slaves of them; always they robbed them and stole the cargo from the doomed ship. It was therefore a pleasant surprise for these men to be treated so hospitably by the natives of Malta.

A word needs to be said about the term **natives.** Since the KJV has "barbarians" (v. 4; see v. 2), some picture those who welcomed the ship as a band of friendly savages. The KJV has an accurate translation here since the Greek text has βάρβαροι (*barbaroi*), but today the term "barbarians" leaves the wrong impression. "To the Greek, the barbarian was a man who said *barbar*, that is, a man who spoke an unintelligible foreign language and not the beautiful Greek tongue."[1] In Luke's day, the term "barbarian" did not mean uncultured, crude, or unsophisticated as it does today; it simply meant that the individual preferred to speak his own native tongue. In fact, as part of the Roman province of Sicily, Malta was highly civilized. "In Paul's day the island was known for its prosperity and residential architecture."[2] Today 96 percent of the population of Malta is literate, one of the highest percentages in the world. The NIV designation "islanders" is a good description of those who received Paul and his fellow shipmates with kindness.

Verse 3. Paul . . . gathered a bundle of sticks and laid them on the fire. William Barclay said, "Paul was a man who could not bear to be doing nothing; there was a bonfire to be kept alight and Paul was gathering brushwood for it."[3] J. W. McGarvey observed, "Paul was not a preacher after the style of a modern clergyman, who is particular not to soil his hands with menial labor, and who expects everybody to be ready to serve him, while he preserves his dignity and looks on."[4] The apostle had spent a lifetime working with his hands (20:34); he was not too good to gather firewood. There is no task too insignificant for the servant of God who has the attitude of Christ Jesus (Phil. 2:1–13).

As Paul was laying the sticks on the fire, **a viper came out because of the heat and fastened itself on his hand.** Because of the cold, the snake had been lying dormant in a stack of brush which Paul had picked up for the fire. Some writers have proposed that if Paul had poor eyesight, as suggested by Galatians

---

[1]William Barclay, *The Acts of the Apostles*, The Daily Study Bible Series, rev. ed. (Philadelphia: Westminster Press, 1976), 187.

[2]Richard N. Longenecker, *The Acts of the Apostles*, The Expositor's Bible Commentary, ed. Frank E. Gaebelein, vol. 9 (Grand Rapids, Mich.: Zondervan Publishing House, 1981), 563.

[3]Barclay, 187.

[4]J. W. McGarvey, *New Commentary on Acts of Apostles*, vol. 2 (Delight, Ark.: Gospel Light Publishing Co., n.d.), 275.

4:15; 6:11, this may have prevented him from seeing the snake in the sticks. However, there are many people who have had similar experiences, including getting bitten, even though their eyesight was perfect. It could happen to anyone. The heat of the fire had revived the serpent, and it had struck at Paul. Now it hung grotesquely from his hand, its fangs buried in his flesh.

Some skeptics are willing to admit that some kind of snake incident occurred, but they suggest that the snake did not really bite Paul. If this assertion is true, then how did the viper hang from Paul's hand? Vipers do not coil, and they have no hands with which to cling. A viper can hang on to a hand only if its fangs are imbedded in the flesh. The fact that Malta no longer has any poisonous snakes or the forest mentioned earlier has caused other skeptics to dismiss the entire "snake story." Today, however, Malta is one of the most densely populated spots on earth: three thousand people per square mile. That fact alone is sufficient to account for the disappearance of the habitat of many wild creatures and, thus, the creatures themselves.

Verse 4. When the islanders saw the viper dangling from Paul's hand, they said to each other, **"Undoubtedly this man is a murderer, and though he has been saved from the sea, justice has not allowed him to live."** Somehow, they had learned that Paul was a prisoner. His chain surely would have been removed before he jumped into the sea; but perhaps it had been refastened to his wrist. Probably, the islanders learned from the other survivors that Paul was a prisoner. They did not know, however, the specific crime of which he had been accused. When they saw him bitten, they concluded that he must be guilty of a heinous crime and that the deadly snake was an instrument of the gods to make sure he did not escape unscathed. They were probably familiar with several ancient legends concerning men who had escaped the sea only to be killed in some other way by the gods. In one legend, a man was killed by the gods with a snakebite.[5] The word **justice** translates the Greek word δίκη (*dikē*) and should probably start with a capital "J." Pagan people often personified abstract concepts as gods or goddesses. For this

---

[5]*The Greek Anthology* 7.290.

reason, the Athenians misunderstood Paul's teaching on Christ and the Resurrection (see comments on 17:18). The islanders were probably referring to the Greek goddess Dike or her Phoenician counterpart.

Verse 5. Paul **shook the creature off into the fire and suffered no harm.** When Jesus sent out the Seventy, He told them, "Behold, I have given you authority to tread on serpents and scorpions . . . and nothing will injure you" (Lk. 10:19). When He gave the Great Commission, He promised the apostles: "These signs will accompany those who have believed: in My name . . . they will pick up serpents . . ." (Mk. 16:17, 18). Paul was simply performing one of "the signs of a true apostle" (2 Cor. 12:12). This incident is the sole New Testament example of the fulfillment of the promise of "picking up serpents" without being harmed—and this was accidental, not deliberate. Snake-handling cults of today are misapplying the Scriptures, testing God (Mt. 4:7), and subjecting their bodies to unnecessary risks (1 Cor. 3:17).

Verse 6. But they were expecting that he was about to swell up or suddenly fall down dead. The Greek word from πίμπρημι (*pimprēmi*), translated **swell up,** was another medical term used by Luke.

> When a venomous snake strikes, its poison enters the bloodstream, breaks down the capillaries, and causes massive internal hemorrhage. The affected area begins to swell and, if the poison is sufficiently powerful, the victim will die almost instantly.[6]

Some skeptics admit that the snake bit Paul but say it was not poisonous. The islanders, who knew the region, recognized the snake as a deadly species. On what basis would we deny their conclusion—unless we are just determined not to believe in the miracles of the Bible?

After the natives **had waited a long time and had seen noth-**

---

[6]Simon J. Kistemaker, *Exposition of the Acts of the Apostles*, New Testament Commentary (Grand Rapids, Mich.: Baker Book House, 1990), 949.

ing unusual happen to him, they changed their minds and began to say that he was a god. People tend to swing from one extreme to the other. McGarvey called this scene "Lystra reversed."[7] At Lystra, the people first thought Paul and Barnabas were gods and then tried to kill Paul (14:8–20). On this occasion, however, Paul did not shout, "I am also a man of the same nature as you!" (see 14:15)—probably because there was no attempt to worship him here, as there had been at Lystra. Paul remained unruffled whether people said he was a god or a murderer.

The deadly viper was probably one of Satan's last efforts to keep Paul from reaching Rome; the "serpent of old" (Rev. 12:9) had used a snake before to accomplish his aims (Gen. 3). God, however, used the incident for His own purposes. He demonstrated to all who had been on the ship that "Paul was not only a heaven-directed man with a God-given message but also a heaven-protected man."[8]

Paul Heals Publius (28:7–10)

[7]Now in the neighborhood of that place were lands belonging to the leading man of the island, named Publius, who welcomed us and entertained us courteously three days. [8]And it happened that the father of Publius was lying in bed afflicted with recurrent fever and dysentery; and Paul went in to see him and after he had prayed, he laid his hands on him and healed him. [9]After this had happened, the rest of the people on the island who had diseases were coming to him and getting cured. [10]They also honored us with many marks of respect; and when we were setting sail, they supplied us with all we needed.

Verse 7. In the providence of God, the spot where Paul and the rest were cast ashore was near the estate of the most important man on Malta. The NASB calls him the leading man of the island. The Greek text has τῷ πρώτῳ τῆς νήσου (tō prōtō tēs

---

[7]McGarvey, 276.
[8]Longenecker, 564.

nēsou), literally "the first [man] of the island." The words "leading man of the island" could be capitalized, for this was "a provincial administrative title [as] verified in two Graeco-Roman inscriptions."[9]

Luke recorded that this Rome-appointed governor of Malta named **Publius . . . welcomed us and entertained us courteously three days.** The scene thus shifted from a storm-swept beach to a cozy apartment in the governor's residence. We do not know how many Luke included in the word **us.** It is possible that Publius was able to house most or all of the survivors in the various facilities on his estate until other arrangements could be made. After mentioning the **three days** spent as guests of Publius, Luke did not tell where they stayed during the remainder of the three months they spent on the island. Apparently, after that time, more permanent lodging was found for Paul and the rest of those shipwrecked.

Verse 8. As Paul was entertained by Publius, we might expect him to enthrall his host and others present with a dramatic account of the storm and shipwreck. Instead, he apparently listened to his host and drew from him the burdens of his heart. The apostle learned that **the father of Publius was lying in bed afflicted with recurrent fever and dysentery.** The NASB uses the phrase **recurrent fever** to translate the plural Greek word πυρετοῖς (*puretois*), which means "fevers." The word **dysentery** is transliterated from the Greek word δυσεντέριον (*dusenterion*). This language is another example of Luke's use of medical terms. The governor's father apparently had Malta fever, a debilitating disease that could persist for two or three years. It was discovered in 1887 that Malta fever is caused by a microorganism in the milk of Maltese goats. This disease is known by different names in different parts of the world. The scientific name is brucellosis. This disease causes "chills, fever, weight loss, joint and muscle pains, and an enlarged spleen. Serious complications such as encephalitis may also arise."[10]

---

[9]Richard Oster, *The Acts of the Apostles*, Part 2, The Living Word Commentary, ed. Everett Ferguson (Austin, Tex.: Sweet Publishing Co., 1979), 174.
[10]*Grolier Multimedia Encyclopedia*, 1995 ed., s.v. "Brucellosis."

After learning of the sickness of Publius' father, **Paul** went **in to see him**. He looked down at the suffering man, then knelt in prayer, asking God's help. Convinced that God wanted the man well, he laid his hands on him and healed him. He probably then called Publius and the rest of the family (see 9:41). How the household must have rejoiced!

Verse 9. It did not take long for word of the miraculous healing to spread throughout the small island. Soon, **the rest of the people on the island who had diseases were coming to him and getting cured.** This scene is reminiscent of the healing service at Capernaum after word spread concerning Jesus' healing of Peter's mother-in-law (Mk. 1:32–34; Lk. 4:40, 41). The healings on Malta are among the last, if not the last, miracles ascribed to Paul. The gifts of healing and miracles were perhaps gradually fading from the ministry of the apostle. God had performed "extraordinary miracles" through the hands of Paul at Ephesus (19:11), as well as healing numerous people on the island of Malta. However, when Paul wrote from Roman imprisonment two years later, he noted that Epaphroditus had been "sick to the point of death" (Phil. 2:27). He later reported that he had left Trophimus sick at Miletus (2 Tim. 4:20).

It is worth noting that the words **to him** are not found in the Greek. The original text simply says, "the rest . . . came up [or to] and were cured" (see KJV). Note also that the Greek word from θεραπεύω (*therapeuō*), translated **cured** (v. 9), is different from the word ἰάομαι (*iaomai*), translated "healed" (v. 8). The word *therapeuō* ("cured," v. 9) can mean "to treat medically."[11] Our English word "therapy" derives from this word. These details, coupled with the fact that Luke was among those later honored by the islanders (v. 10), has led to speculation that Luke ministered alongside Paul: Luke with his medicine, Paul with his miracles. Barclay suggested that the passage may give us "the earliest picture we possess of the work of a *medical missionary*."[12]

---

[11]Fritz Rienecker, *A Linguistic Key to the Greek New Testament*, ed. Cleon L. Rogers, Jr. (Grand Rapids, Mich.: Zondervan Publishing House, Regency Reference Library, 1980), 343.

[12]Barclay, 189 (emphasis his).

Let us, however, focus on Paul's work during the three months on Malta. Luke did not mention that the apostle preached, but it is hard to imagine that he did not. God had prepared the hearts of those who came from the ship by demonstrating that Paul was His spokesman and by sparing their lives; God had prepared the hearts of those on the island by protecting Paul from the serpent and by giving him power to heal. God never wastes an opportunity.

The apostle had a starting place with those from the ship who had come to recognize his leadership. He also had a starting place with the islanders: Although their world-view was pagan, they still believed in the concept that some things are right and some are wrong, as well as the concept that evil should be punished (v. 4). He could move from those concepts to preach about the Savior who can save us from judgment.

When Paul healed, he surely did so in the name of Jesus (see 19:13). It would have been natural to tell the healed that the Jesus who had made them well physically could also heal them spiritually. Throughout the Gospel Accounts and Acts, healing was never an isolated event. The miracles authenticated the messenger of God, whether Jesus or the apostles, who then shared the message.

Uninspired tradition says that Paul evangelized the island of Malta and that, when he left, the church met in the home of Publius. We are inclined to believe the first part of the tradition at least. Some writers conclude that Paul had no conversions on the island of Malta "because Luke did not mention any." However, neither did Luke mention any conversions in Rome, but we know from other writings that there were conversions in the capital city (Phil. 1:12, 13; 4:22; Philem. 10). Luke may not have mentioned conversions on Malta or in Rome because that was not his purpose.

Perhaps Paul was also able to reach some who had been on the ship. We would especially like to think that any prisoners condemned to die in Rome (see comments on 27:1) would go to meet their fate with hope in their hearts.

Verse 10. Luke recorded, **They** (the islanders) **also honored us with many marks of respect.** The original text has πολλαῖς τιμαῖς ἐτίμησαν (*pollais timais etimēsan*), literally, "with many honors they honored us." The Greek words used could refer to "honorariums," that is, money given in appreciation. Sometimes, though not often, the word τιμή (*timē*), translated "honor," refers to financial support (see 1 Tim. 5:17). However, it is hard to believe that Paul would have accepted money for his efforts. Probably, Luke was merely conveying the growing respect the islanders had for Paul and the other followers of Jesus (see 2:47; 5:13).

During the three months on the island, the centurion located another Alexandrian grain ship that would take them on to Italy (see comments on v. 11). At last the time came for Paul and the rest to leave. When Paul had arrived at Malta, he had not been where he wanted to be; after three months, it was probably hard for him to tear himself away. Ninety days earlier, all had been lost in the storm; Paul and his colleagues had stood on the beach with nothing except the soggy clothing on their backs. Now, new friends supplied him and his shipmates with what was needed to complete their trip to Rome. Luke painted the parting farewell with a single vivid stroke: **And when we were setting sail, they supplied us with all we needed.**

THE JOURNEY CONTINUES; THE ARRIVAL AT ROME (28:11–16)

[11]At the end of three months we set sail on an Alexandrian ship which had wintered at the island, and which had the Twin Brothers for its figurehead. [12]After we put in at Syracuse, we stayed there for three days. [13]From there we sailed around and arrived at Rhegium, and a day later a south wind sprang up, and on the second day we came to Puteoli. [14]There we found some brethren, and were invited to stay with them for seven days; and thus we came to Rome. [15]And the brethren, when they heard about us, came from there as far as the Market of Appius and Three Inns to meet us; and when Paul saw them, he thanked God and took courage.

[16]When we entered Rome, Paul was allowed to stay by himself, with the soldier who was guarding him.

In this section, we will see the apostle Paul reach the city of Rome at last. At Ephesus, he had told the brethren, "I must . . . see Rome" (19:21). In writing to the Christians at Rome, he had spoken of going to Spain and then said, "For I hope to see you in passing, and to be helped on my way there by you, when I have first enjoyed your company for a while" (Rom. 15:24). After Paul's arrest in Jerusalem, Jesus had assured him, "As you have solemnly witnessed to My cause at Jerusalem, so you must witness at Rome also" (23:11). On the tempestuous voyage to Rome, an angel had told him: "Do not be afraid, Paul; you must stand before Caesar" (27:24). These words of expectation and promise were finally coming to their fulfillment.

Verse 11. Paul and his companions had spent **three months** on Malta—perhaps November, December, and January. We do not know why God wanted Paul on the island for three months. Was it a time for Paul to rest and recuperate? Was it a time to hone skills that had become rusty during the apostle's two-year hiatus in Caesarea? Did God just want those on the island to have an opportunity to become Christians? Whatever God's reasons for the delay, Paul had responded gracefully.

During the winter months, Julius, the Roman centurion responsible for getting Paul and the other prisoners to Rome, had booked passage on another **Alexandrian ship** (see 27:6). This vessel **had wintered at the island**, probably in the port of Valletta, a major Mediterranean port and chief city on the island's northwestern coast.

Since the ship had been within three or four days' sailing time from its destination when forced to stop for the winter, the owner would have been anxious to complete the trip. At the earliest opportunity, he resumed his journey. Sailing on the Mediterranean itself did not resume until sometime in March, but coastal sailing, one- or two-day journeys, could begin early in February if the wind was favorable.

Regarding the ship, Luke added a peculiar note: **which had the Twin Brothers for its figurehead.** The Greek word Διοσκούροι (*Dioskouroi*), translated "Twin Brothers," means "sons of Zeus." According to Graeco-Roman mythology, Castor and Pollux (see KJV) were the twin sons of Zeus (Jupiter). The constellation Gemini (Twins) is named for the mythical brothers, who were considered the patron deities of sailors. For an inspired comment on such superstitions, see 1 Corinthians 8:4–6. The Alexandrian ship had a painted carving of the twins on its prow. Luke's note establishes that he was present; it is a careful detail of an eyewitness. His note also underlines the superstition that confronted first-century evangelists—and the superstition faced today by many around the world. The passengers of the previous Alexandrian ship should have been impressed by this fact: The so-called gods of seafarers had done nothing for them. Rather, they owed their lives to the *true* God, the "one God, the Father, from whom are all things" (1 Cor. 8:6; see Acts 27:24).

Verse 12. During the earlier part of the journey, contrary winds had been a hindrance (27:4). Now, the ship progressed to its destination without major difficulty. It first sailed northeast sixty miles to Syracuse, the capital of Sicily. Luke wrote: **After we put in at Syracuse, we stayed there for three days.** Those responsible for the ship perhaps spent the three days transacting business, but they were probably waiting for a favorable wind before they proceeded through the Strait of Messina. The strait was known for dangerous tidal currents and whirlpools. Near Rhegium (v. 13) were the legendary whirlpool of Charybdis and the rock of Scylla. At this point, the crew needed a strong wind to carry them seventy miles to their next port in twenty-four hours.

Verse 13. They were finally able to leave Syracuse. **From there** they **sailed around and arrived at Rhegium,** a town at the toe of the Italian boot. From Rhegium, they could sail up the coast to the commercial harbor at Puteoli, two hundred miles north. **Sailed around** probably indicates that a sailing maneuver called tacking was necessary. J. B. Phillips' translation has "tacked around."[13] Tacking is a zig-zagging maneuver used by sailors that enables them to sail into the wind.

A day later a south wind sprang up, which sped them on

---

[13]J. B. Phillips, *The New Testament in Modern English.*

their journey. Sailing along the west coast of Italy, they would have passed "Vesuvius, belching smoke over the unsuspecting city of Pompeii at its foot."[14] Pompeii was later buried under a thick layer of lava and ash from Vesuvius in A.D. 79. Making excellent time, **on the second day** they **came to Puteoli.** Puteoli was a principal port between the Bay of Naples and Rome. Paul and the rest disembarked at this bustling port. They would walk the final seventy-five miles to Rome.

Verse 14. As Paul stood on the dock of Puteoli, he apparently was filled with anxiety (see v. 15). Nearby were the yachts of the wealthy, symbolic of the worldliness of Rome. To the north were warships, symbolic of the might of Rome. In addition to these secular challenges, he had to be concerned about how he would be received by the brethren as he walked into Rome as a prisoner.

God again proved to be "the Father of mercies and God of all comfort" (2 Cor. 1:3). The apostle was pleasantly surprised to find **some brethren** at Puteoli. The gospel had apparently spread from Rome to the port city. The brethren invited Paul and his companions **to stay with them for seven days.** Perhaps Paul arrived on a Monday and the Christians wanted him to stay for the breaking of bread the following Sunday; this is what had happened in Troas (see comments on 20:6, 7). At any rate, a full week would include a Lord's Day, at which time Paul could enjoy the fellowship of brethren from all over the area. As at Sidon earlier (27:3), the centurion permitted Paul to be with his friends.

Why Julius, the Roman centurion, allowed their journey to be postponed a week when they were so near Rome is a mystery. Did he have business to conduct? Did he have to re-outfit his unit since they had lost everything in the storm? Was he awaiting orders from Rome? None of these possibilities would explain a break lasting seven days. He probably agreed to a week's delay as a personal favor to Paul. Surely he was impressed with the apostle. Possibly he had been affected by the

---

[14]Bernard R. Youngman, *Background to the Bible,* Book 4, *Spreading the Gospel* (London: Hulton Educational Publications, 1956), 90.

gospel and had become a Christian. Other soldiers became Christians, including Cornelius (ch. 10) and some in the praetorian guard (Phil. 1:13).

After a week in the port city, Paul and others in the official party started north on the Appian Way, the most famous of all Roman roads. It was named after Appius Claudius Caecus, who started the work in 312 B.C. and paid for part of the road himself. Appius was an important Roman official called a "censor"— one of two officials responsible for taking the public census and supervising public behavior and morals. What a sight that must have been: solemn Roman soldiers, sullen convicts, and smiling Christians marching on the famed Appian Way! **And thus,** Luke wrote, **we came to Rome.**

Verse 15. During the seven days in Puteoli, word reached Christians in Rome that Paul had arrived in the country. Immediately, a number of them set out to meet him. In the last chapter of Romans, Paul had named twenty-six friends in Rome; those friends were probably among two groups that headed south.

When Paul and the rest had completed half of their journey, they were met by the two welcoming committees. Luke wrote, **And the brethren, when they heard about us, came from** Rome **as far as the Market of Appius and Three Inns to meet us.** Rest stops had been established along the Appian Way for weary travelers, and clusters of enterprises had grown up around the stops. One resting station, forty-three miles from Rome, was the **Market of Appius.** The NASB translates Ἀππίου Φόρου (*Appiou Phorou*) as the "Market of Appius," while the KJV has "Appii forum." In most cities, the forum was the primary place for conducting business; therefore, it could be referred to as a "marketplace." Another resting station, ten miles closer to the capital city, was named **Three Inns.** The NASB translates Τριῶν Ταβερνῶν (*Triōn Tabernōn*) as "Three Inns," while the KJV has "three taverns." A tavern in the first century roughly corresponds to an inn or hotel today in that it included rooms in which to spend the night.

Why did some of the Christians from Rome stop after thirty-three miles, while others continued on another ten miles? One preacher humorously suggested that the *younger* Christians walked forty-three miles, while the *older* Christians were tired after thirty-three. Perhaps it was simply planned that way so that Paul would get a double welcome. The Greek word ἀπάντησις (*apantēsis*), translated **meet** in this verse, "was almost a technical term for the official welcome of a visiting dignitary which went out from the city to greet [Paul] and to escort him for the last part of his journey."[15] Paul's apprehensions vanished as he was given a hero's welcome. **And when Paul saw them, he thanked God and took courage.** We can imagine the tears flowing as he was greeted by friends old and new.

Verse 16. Luke concluded the account of the trip by noting, **When we entered Rome, Paul was allowed to stay by himself, with the soldier who was guarding him.** This verse is the last of the **we** passages in Acts, which indicate Luke's presence with Paul. The Western Text has "When we arrived at Rome, the centurion delivered the prisoners to the captain of the guard." This reference is to prisoners other than Paul, for Luke continued by noting that the apostle was **allowed to stay by himself.** Rather than being placed in the common prison, Paul was allowed to live in "rented quarters" (v. 30) under house arrest, chained (v. 20), watched by a succession of military guards. "By himself" probably indicates that Luke, Aristarchus, and other Christians were not allowed to stay in his quarters, although they could visit him. The preferential treatment given to Paul indicates that Festus' report was favorable. We do not know if the written report survived the shipwreck; but even if it did not, Julius could convey the substance of it. Probably the centurion also added his own favorable comments.

Paul had finally reached the city he had long desired to visit. As he was led through its streets to his place of confinement, what did he see and think? As usual, Luke's account does not satisfy our curiosity. Paul was not there as a tourist, but as a witness for the Lord (23:11). Let us, however, consider the chal-

---

[15]F. F. Bruce, *The Book of Acts*, The New International Commentary on the New Testament, gen. ed. F. F. Bruce, rev. ed. (Grand Rapids, Mich.: Wm. B. Eerdmans Publishing Co., 1988), 502.

lenge facing Paul in that largest and most splendid of ancient cities.

Today's visitor to Rome can still walk on the worn stones of the Appian Way through the gate Paul must have entered. He can still see the remains of the thousands of pagan temples which filled the city at that time, in addition to looking down on the magnificent ruins of the forum—the commercial, social, religious, and political center of the city. He can touch the golden milestone that marked the distance to every part of the empire and stand on Palatine Hill, where Nero had his palace. Almost two thousand years have passed since Paul was led into Rome, but one can still imagine that wealthy and wicked "Mistress of the World." Picture the colorful crowds of Paul's day: the powerful rich who controlled the empire, the indolent poor who cried for free bread, the busy slaves who supplied necessary products and services. Paul and other Christians faced an overwhelming challenge when they came to Rome to preach the gospel.

It was not, however, too great a challenge for God, who rules in the affairs of men. In His plans and purposes, the center of the political kingdom could also be a center from which the good news of His kingdom could spread throughout the populated world. If all roads led to Rome, they also led *from* Rome—"to the remotest part of the earth" (1:8). How significant, then, are the words "and thus we came to Rome" (v. 14)! Paul's journey to that city, begun years earlier, had finally come to an end, and a new phase of God's evangelistic program had begun.

AWAITING TRIAL (28:17-31)

Paul Reviews His Appeal to Ceasar (28:17-22)

[17]After three days Paul called together those who were the leading men of the Jews, and when they came together, he began saying to them, "Brethren, though I had done nothing against our people or the customs of our fathers, yet I was delivered as a prisoner from Jerusalem into the hands of the Romans. [18]And when they had examined me, they were willing to release me because there was no ground for putting me

to death. ¹⁹But when the Jews objected, I was forced to appeal to Caesar, not that I had any accusation against my nation. ²⁰For this reason, therefore, I requested to see you and to speak with you, for I am wearing this chain for the sake of the hope of Israel." ²¹They said to him, "We have neither received letters from Judea concerning you, nor have any of the brethren come here and reported or spoken anything bad about you. ²²But we desire to hear from you what your views are; for concerning this sect, it is known to us that it is spoken against everywhere."

Earlier we had two examples of how to tell a story to make *self* look as good as possible: 23:26–30 and 25:14–21. Paul's speech in this section is an example of how a story can be related to make *others* look good and to gain goodwill.

Verse 17. Paul's usual procedure was to take the gospel to "the Jew first and also to the Greek" (Rom. 1:16). In a new city, he invariably began his preaching ministry in the Jewish synagogue (17:1–3). Rome had a large Jewish population and at least ten synagogues, but Paul did not have the option of going to any of them. Still, he was not deterred in fulfilling his mission. If he could not go to them, he would invite them to come to him.

After a few days of resting and probably renewing acquaintances, Paul **called together those who were the leading men of the Jews**—the elders of the synagogues, the scribes, the heads of leading Jewish families. He wanted to discover whether or not they were filled with the hatred that characterized the Jews in Jerusalem. He also wanted to reassure them that he had not come to cause trouble. Most important, he hoped to win some of them to Jesus (Rom. 9:1–5; 10:1).

When **they came together**, Paul began by identifying with his listeners, calling them **brethren**. He then denied any rumors that he had committed offenses against their **people or the customs of** their **fathers**. These were two of the recurring accusations made against him. He denied the charges in case they had heard them. Nevertheless, though the apostle was innocent, he was a prisoner of Rome. Paul softened the account of his mistreatment. A Roman rescue from a murderous mob of Jews

(21:31–33) became **"delivered as a prisoner from Jerusalem into the hands of the Romans."**

Verse 18. Paul continued, **"And when they had examined me, they were willing to release me because there was no ground for putting me to death."** The officials who had spoken with Paul had found him innocent of breaking any Roman laws. The commander Lysias had written that none of the charges against Paul deserved "death or imprisonment" (23:29). Later, the reason the Roman governor Felix had left Paul in prison was not based upon the apostle's guilt, but Felix' desire for a bribe and "to do the Jews a favor" (24:26, 27). The next governor, Festus, had realized that the Jews' charges against Paul were "points of disagreement . . . about their own religion" (25:19); Paul "had committed nothing worthy of death" (25:25). Although having no jurisdiction in the case, King Agrippa had commented that Paul should have been a free man (26:32).

Verse 19. Paul would therefore have been released if the Jewish leaders had not been so persistent. He explained, **"When the Jews objected, I was forced to appeal to Caesar, not that I had any accusation against my nation."** Paul made a distinction between his listeners and those who had wronged him. When he referred to abuse, he did not speak of "you Jews" but **the Jews**, that is, the Jews back in Judea. At every turn, the Jewish leaders in Judea had accused Paul, desiring to kill him. When the Roman officials would not judge him worthy of death, the Judean Jews had tried to take matters into their own hands. They had convinced Festus to send Paul back to Jerusalem for trial (25:9), where they would be waiting in ambush along the way (25:3). Paul had therefore been **forced** to appeal to the highest Roman court (25:11).

Paul assured his listeners of his goodwill; he had no **accusation** to bring. The Jewish leaders in Rome would have been especially interested in his assurance that he would bring no legal counter-charges against the Jewish nation. A decade before, clashes between Jews and Christians had resulted in the expulsion of all Jews, including Jewish Christians, from Rome under the emperor Claudius (18:2). The Jews would not want a repetition of that troubling period.

Verse 20. Paul concluded his introductory remarks by saying, **"For this reason, therefore, I requested to see you and to speak with you, for I am wearing this chain for the sake of the hope of Israel."** He probably lifted his hand to emphasize the chain hanging from his wrist. He again identified with his hearers. All Jews knew what it meant to suffer persecution for the hope of Israel. This phrase referred primarily to the coming of the Messiah and the restoration of the Israelite nation. This hope also included the resurrection of the dead. Paul continually insisted that he was imprisoned because of his faith in the resurrection (see 23:6; 26:6, 7).

In verses 17 through 20, Paul emphasized three points: (1) He had committed no crimes against the Jews; (2) the Romans had nothing against him; (3) he had no charges to press against the Jews.

Verse 21. The reply of the Jewish leaders was cautious but fair. They began, **"We have neither received letters from Judea concerning you, nor have any of the brethren come here and reported or spoken anything bad about you."** We are surprised to learn that the Jews in Jerusalem had sent no word to Rome concerning Paul. Some have suggested that there had not been enough time for word to reach Rome from Jerusalem, but evidently the Jewish leaders in Rome thought that sufficient time had elapsed for their fellow Jews in Jerusalem to contact them if they desired to do so. As far as we know, the Jerusalem Jews never did send word to Rome. They probably did not bother, since they knew they had no real case against Paul. Perhaps they were happy just to know that he was imprisoned hundreds of miles away, unable, they thought, to hurt their cause. Further, once the apostle was gone, other crises probably demanded their attention—specifically, the growing anarchy in Palestine against Roman rule.

Verse 22. Although the Roman leaders had heard nothing bad about the apostle, they had heard negative reports concerning the cause he espoused. Unlike some, they were willing to investigate the matter. They told Paul, **"But we desire to hear from you what your views are; for concerning this sect, it is known to us that it is spoken against everywhere."** Like other

Jews before, these men thought Christianity was another **sect within Judaism** (see comments on 24:5, 14). Genuine Christianity has always been treated with contempt; Satan will make sure that New Testament Christianity is **spoken against everywhere**.

Paul Preaches to the Jews (28:23–29)

²³**When they had set a day for Paul, they came to him at his lodging in large numbers; and he was explaining to them by solemnly testifying about the kingdom of God and trying to persuade them concerning Jesus, from both the Law of Moses and from the Prophets, from morning until evening.** ²⁴**Some were being persuaded by the things spoken, but others would not believe.** ²⁵**And when they did not agree with one another, they began leaving after Paul had spoken one parting word, "The Holy Spirit rightly spoke through Isaiah the prophet to your fathers,** ²⁶**saying,**
   'Go to this people and say,
   "You will keep on hearing, but will not understand;
   And you will keep on seeing, but will not perceive;
   ²⁷**For the heart of this people has become dull,**
   And with their ears they scarcely hear,
   And they have closed their eyes;
   Otherwise they might see with their eyes,
   And hear with their ears,
   And understand with their heart and return,
   And I would heal them."'
²⁸**Therefore let it be known to you that this salvation of God has been sent to the Gentiles; they will also listen."** ²⁹**[When he had spoken these words, the Jews departed, having a great dispute among themselves.]**

Verse 23. At the end of their first meeting, the Jewish leaders **set a day for Paul** so they could give him a further hearing. When that day arrived, he had a full house: **They came to him at his lodging in large numbers.** Some think that the **lodging** here is not the same location as the "quarters" of verse 30. We see no reason to doubt that they are the same. Paul must have been excited. The Jews probably expected an orientation session, but he planned to make it an evangelistic service. As Jesus had promised, he would have the opportunity to testify in Rome (23:11).

Paul began with a message of hope—as he taught concerning the King and His kingdom. His explanations and testimony focused on **the kingdom of God** (see comments on 1:3). He tried to persuade them that **Jesus** was the long awaited Messiah by appealing to **the Law of Moses** and **the Prophets** (see comments on 17:2, 3). He pressed his case **from morning until evening,** from sunrise to sunset. During this time, people were probably coming and going.

Verse 24. Some were being persuaded by the things spoken, but others would not believe. As usual, some accepted Paul's message and some did not (see 13:45–48; 14:1, 2; 17:4, 5, 12, 13, 32–34; 18:6–8).

Verse 25. An argument arose between the believers and the non-believers: **They did not agree with one another.** The argument grew more heated as the day wore on (v. 29). Near the end of the day, Paul spoke a **parting word** of judgment, quoting from Isaiah. He introduced the quotation by saying, **"The Holy Spirit rightly spoke through Isaiah the prophet to your fathers."** This statement strongly supports the inspiration of the Book of Isaiah (see 1:16; 4:25). In verse 17, Paul had identified himself with the Jewish leaders by saying *"our* fathers." However, when they rejected his message about Jesus, he distanced himself from them by saying *"your* **fathers"** (emphasis added).

Verses 26, 27. The quotation from Isaiah reads:

"Go to this people and say, 'You will keep on hearing, but will not understand; and you will keep on seeing, but will not perceive. For the heart of this people has become dull, and with their ears they scarcely hear, and they have closed their eyes; otherwise they might see with their eyes, and hear with their ears, and understand with their heart and return, and I would heal them.'"

The prophet's words from Isaiah 6:9, 10 emphasize the danger of trifling with God's Word. If a man continually refuses to accept God's message, a time will come when he is so hardened that he cannot accept it.

Isaiah applied these words to the hardhearted Israelites in his day. Later, Jesus applied them to the Jews who rejected Him and His words (Mt. 13:14, 15; Mk. 4:12; Lk. 8:10). The apostle John used Isaiah's prophecy to make the same application (Jn. 12:40). When writing the Book of Romans, Paul applied the passage to his fellow Jews who were unwilling to accept the Messiah (Rom. 11:8). In Acts 28:26, 27, we see that Paul spoke these words to unbelieving Jews in Rome. The calloused hearts of Israelites remained the subject.

Earlier, it was suggested that the Jews' rejection of Paul and the gospel in Acts 21—25 marked the beginning of the end for Jerusalem, which was destroyed by the Romans in A.D. 70. Some also think that Acts 28 marks "the definitive rejection" of the Jews as a people[16]—that Paul's message was the last stern warning the Jewish nation received. They may be right. Luke took sixteen verses to tell of Paul's two years in Rome. All but three of those verses tell of the Jews' rejection of the gospel. Luke did not waste space, so the event must be significant. The purpose suggested seems the most likely.

Verse 28. After quoting Isaiah, Paul added, **"Let it be known to you that this salvation of God has been sent to the Gentiles; they will also listen."** Paul may simply have been affirming that the Gentiles would be more receptive than the Jews had been. "History . . . gives unassailable testimony to the apostle's assertion that *the Gentiles will listen* to the preaching of *salvation.*"[17] It is possible, however, that Paul's words have a deeper significance: He might have been declaring that he was no longer "under obligation to go 'to the Jews first.'"[18] It is noteworthy

---

[16]Ibid., 508.

[17]Oster, 180 (emphasis his).

[18]I. Howard Marshall, *The Acts of the Apostles*, The Tyndale New Testament Commentaries, gen. ed. R. V. G. Tasker (Grand Rapids, Mich.: Wm. B. Eerdmans Publishing Co., 1980), 425.

that Paul did not use the phrase "to the Jew first" in any of his Prison Epistles or in his later epistles, 1 and 2 Timothy and Titus. I. Howard Marshall wrote, "Luke may well be presenting [Paul] as an example for the church generally to follow."[19] Today, when we go into a new community, we are under no obligation to preach first to the Jews before we take the gospel to non-Jews.

Verse 29. Paul's mention of the Gentiles in verse 28 brought the session to a halt. "They began leaving after Paul had spoken one parting word" (v. 25)—the word of judgment. Some translations include this thought found in the Western Text: **When he had spoken these words, the Jews departed, having a great dispute among themselves.** The NASB places the verse within brackets.

As in other cities, Paul and his message had been rejected by the Jews in Rome. This time, however, the Jews could not force him out of town or stone him to death (13:50; 14:5, 19), for he was protected by the Roman government. God works in mysterious ways.

Paul Preached Unhindered (28:30, 31)

[30]**And he stayed two full years in his own rented quarters and was welcoming all who came to him,** [31]**preaching the kingdom of God and teaching concerning the Lord Jesus Christ with all openness, unhindered.**

Verse 30. As Luke wrapped up his account of Paul's stay in Rome, he wrote, **And he stayed two full years in his own rented quarters.** We are not sure why this much time went by before Paul's case was heard. Perhaps, as noted earlier, his accusers sent no word. Perhaps the court docket was that far behind. Whatever the reason, Paul was allowed to stay in "his own rented quarters" during that time. Rome was likely responsible for Paul's care and keeping during his stay in Rome. It is possible that the apostle rented his own quarters so he could have more freedom in how the facilities were used. His lodging was

---

[19]Ibid.

perhaps paid for by Christians in Rome and elsewhere. Financial help came from Philippi during this period (Phil. 2:25; 4:10–18).

As already noted, Paul had some privileges, but he was still confined to his quarters, chained day and night (vv. 16, 20; Eph. 6:20). As the days passed into weeks, the weeks into months, and the months into years, he must have longed to walk the streets, to preach in the forum. He must have wondered why God had brought him to Rome and then kept him confined. We cannot know the mind of God, but here are some possible purposes to consider:

(1) If Paul had not been confined, he probably would have spent little time in Rome itself. The church was already established there, and he did not like to "build on another man's foundation" (Rom. 15:20). His plan had been to make a brief visit to Rome and then to travel on to Spain (Rom. 15:24) and other places.

(2) Paul's extended confinement resulted in the gospel's reaching into the emperor's palace. Paul told the Philippians: "My imprisonment in the cause of Christ has become well known throughout the whole praetorian guard . . ." (Phil. 1:13). The praetorian guard was an elite body of soldiers kept "for the purpose of guarding the emperor, and keeping prisoners awaiting trial in the imperial court."[20] Every four to six hours, the soldier guarding Paul was relieved by another soldier. Every twenty-four hours, four to six soldiers were responsible for Paul. Over two years, potentially hundreds of soldiers were exposed to the gospel. As the apostle taught others, his guard had no choice but to listen. When Paul and the soldier were alone, it is doubtful that the conversation was merely about the weather or the Olympic Games. Over the two-year period, some of those soldiers probably became Christians. When their duties took them into the palace, they took the gospel with them. Paul could write to the church in Philippi, "All the saints greet you, *especially those of Caesar's household*" (Phil. 4:22; emphasis added). Eventually, Paul would have the opportunity of presenting his case before Nero himself (27:24).

---

[20]McGarvey, 287.

(3) During Paul's ministry in Rome, because of his imprisonment, he was protected by the crown. In Philippians 1:12, he
acknowledged the wisdom of God's arrangements: "My circumstances have turned out for the greater progress of the gospel."
The apostle was allowed to keep open house: He was **welcoming all who came to him**—Jews and Gentiles, Christians and
non-Christians alike.

Verse 31. As people came to him, Paul was **preaching the
kingdom of God and teaching concerning the Lord Jesus Christ
with all openness, unhindered.** Compare the language of this
verse with verse 23. The full title **the Lord Jesus Christ** encom-
passes all the wondrous truths concerning our Lord and Master. The Greek word παρρησία (*parrēsia*), translated **openness,**
refers to preaching candidly, clearly, and confidently.[21]

The key word in the closing verse is **unhindered**. In the original text, this word is placed at the end of the verse for emphasis,
and the NASB translators also placed it there. In the heart of
this vast empire, the gospel was unhindered by those who sought
to suppress it: unhindered by Roman authorities, unhindered
by Jewish leaders, unhindered by Satan. The good news of Jesus
could flow freely from the capital city to all parts of the far-flung
empire.

God answered prayers and blessed the efforts of Paul. In
addition to the impact on the soldiers in the praetorian guard
and the conversion of some in Caesar's household (Phil. 1:13;
4:22), we know of one other conversion in Rome: a runaway
slave named Onesimus, who fled to the capital city and somehow came in contact with Paul (Philem. 10–21). No doubt many
others were saved in Rome and the surrounding areas because
Paul was able to preach and teach without hindrance.

In addition to teaching orally, Paul extended his influence
through writing. Some of his finest epistles were written during
this period of time: Ephesians, which tells of Christ and His
church; Philippians, Paul's love letter to the church at Philippi;
Colossians, in which Paul's words combat heresy by exalting

---

[21]Adapted from John R. W. Stott, *The Message of Acts* (Downers Grove,
Ill.: Inter-Varsity Press, 1994), 400.

Jesus; and Philemon, a personal letter to a friend. In all these letters, Paul referred to being imprisoned (Eph. 3:1; 4:1; Phil. 1:13; Col. 4:3, 18; Philem. 1, 9, 13). There are many ties between these letters: The same people were with Paul, the same individuals delivered the letters, and more. These factors lead us to conclude that they were all written at the same time from the same place. Since, in one of them, Paul made mention of "Caesar's household" (Phil. 4:22; see Phil. 1:13), most believe they were written from Rome during Paul's first imprisonment there.

These letters add much to our knowledge of Paul's time in Rome. Old friends were with Paul, such as Luke and Timothy (Phil. 1:1; 2:19–23; Col. 1:1; 4:14; Philem. 24). Worth special mention is John Mark, who had been reconciled with the apostle (Acts 13:13; 15:36–40; Col. 4:10; Philem. 24; 2 Tim. 4:11). Other coworkers included Aristarchus, who had traveled with Paul to Rome, as well as Epaphroditus, Tychicus, Justus, Epaphras, and Demas (Eph. 6:21; Phil. 2:25; Col. 1:7; 4:7, 10–14; Philem. 23, 24; see 2 Tim. 4:10). Many were surely sent by Paul to take the gospel to all parts of the empire.

The Prison Epistles also inform us that Paul remained concerned about the churches he had directly or indirectly helped to establish (Phil. 4:1)—and that he tried to maintain contact with them. These congregations included churches such as those in Colossae and Laodicea which had probably been established as a result of his work in nearby Ephesus, even though the apostle had not personally preached in those cities (Col. 1:7, 8; 2:1; 4:16). Some congregations sent representatives to Rome (see Phil. 4:18). Paul also sent messengers to the churches to inform them of his condition and to report their spiritual needs to him (Eph. 6:21; Phil. 2:19, 23, 25–30; Col. 4:7–10).

Perhaps of greatest interest is the insight the letters give regarding Paul's mental state. He spoke of "conflicts," "sufferings," and a great "struggle" (Phil. 1:30; Col. 1:24; 2:1). He was feeling the effects of age and the constant abuse he had received (Philem. 9). Of special concern to him were brethren in Rome who were "preaching Christ even from envy and strife . . . thinking to cause [him] distress in [his] imprisonment" (Phil. 1:15, 17). Through all his problems, Paul maintained a positive attitude: "I can do all things through Him who strengthens me" (Phil. 4:13; see Col. 1:29). Regardless of what the future held— whether he was released or sentenced to die—he was prepared (Phil. 1:19–24, 27; 2:17). He expected to be released (Phil. 1:25, 26; 2:24; Philem. 22), but being released was not a matter of personal importance to him.

Always, Paul's greatest concern was for the spread of the gospel. He asked for prayers "that God [would] open up to [them] a door for the word . . . that [he] may make it clear in the way [he] ought to speak" (Col. 4:3, 4). Paul may have been especially thinking about the possibility of preaching to Nero himself. He wrote with rejoicing:

> Now I want you to know, brethren, that my circumstances have turned out for the greater progress of the gospel, so that my imprisonment in the cause of Christ has become well known throughout the whole praetorian guard and to everyone else, and that most of the brethren, trusting in the Lord because of my imprisonment, have far more courage to speak the word of God without fear (Phil. 1:12–14).

Acts 28:31 is Luke's final progress statement in Acts. It may be intended to summarize all that had happened since the previous progress statement in 19:20. It certainly summarizes the events of chapter 28. However, it leaves many questions unanswered: What happened when Paul made his defense before Caesar? Was he convicted or released? Was he able to complete his plans to go to Spain with the gospel? To those who are caught up in the story of Paul, Luke's ending is a letdown.

The "abrupt" ending of the book has led to speculation concerning a sequel. Did Luke intend to write a sequel that he never wrote? Did he write a sequel that has been lost? We find no indication that Luke intended to write a third volume. Why, then, did he—under the guidance of the Spirit—end Acts the way he did? Luke's major purpose was not to write a biography of Paul, but to tell how the gospel reached and prospered in Rome itself. If we keep this purpose in mind, we see the ending not as a disappointment, but as a shout of victory. In spite of every obstacle, God accomplished His purpose.

Luke's final word "unhindered" is the key word, the most important word. Paul's hand was chained, but his tongue was free. He could not move freely, but the gospel could. He was imprisoned, but the Word was not (2 Tim. 2:9). On that note of triumph, with the prospect of the gospel spreading throughout the world, Luke laid down his pen.

APPLICATION

The Fine Art of Hospitality (28:1–15)

Abraham was resting at the door of his tent during the heat of the day. When he raised his eyes, he saw three strangers who appeared as though from nowhere. Jumping to his feet, he bowed low and spoke to them:

> My lord, if now I have found favor in your sight, please do not pass your servant by. Please let a little water be brought and wash your feet, and rest yourselves under the tree; and I will bring a piece of bread, that you may refresh yourselves; after that you may go on, since you have visited your servant . . . (Gen. 18:3–5).

While a servant washed the visitors' feet, Abraham told Sarah to prepare bread. He ran to the herd, picked his best calf, and told a servant to prepare the meat. Then he went back to the men to entertain them while a feast was being prepared. During the meal, the mysterious strangers surprised Abraham by announcing that he and Sarah would have a child the next year, though both were past the age for childbearing. After the meal, Abraham started walking down the road with them as good hosts did. As he did so, he discovered that they were messengers from God (Gen. 18:16–33). This incident from the Old Testament is highlighted in the New Testament: "Do not neglect to show hospitality to strangers, for by this some have entertained angels without knowing it" (Heb. 13:2).

Hospitality is an important biblical teaching. In a great chapter on practical Christianity, Romans 12, Paul included these words: "contributing to the needs of the saints, practicing hospitality" (Rom. 12:13). One qualification for an elder is that he must be hospitable (1 Tim. 3:2; Tit. 1:8). Peter said, "Be hospitable to one another without complaint" (1 Pet. 4:9).

Do we really know what hospitality means? When individuals invite others into their homes, we call them "hospitable." In the biblical sense, perhaps they are or perhaps they are not. The Greek word φιλόξενος (*philoxenos*), translated "hospitable," combines a word for "love" (φίλος, *philos*) with the word for "stranger" (ξένος, *xenos*). Thus the Greek word literally means "stranger-lover." The English word "hospitable" comes from the Latin word for "guest" (*hospes*). The meaning of the English word is broader than the Greek word it translates.

Consider again the classic example of Abraham's entertaining the three men: He had never met them before; they were strangers. Biblical hospitality is not reciprocation; it is not entertaining friends who will entertain us in return; it is not giving parties. Rather, *it is showing kindness to individuals who may never have the means or opportunity to repay the kindness* (see Mt. 5:46, 47).

Throughout the Old Testament, special provision was made by God for the stranger:

> You shall not oppress a stranger, since you yourselves know the feelings of a stranger, for you also were strangers in the land of Egypt (Ex. 23:9).

> Nor shall you glean your vineyard, nor shall you gather the fallen fruit of your vineyard; you shall leave them for the needy and for the stranger . . . (Lev. 19:10).

> The stranger who resides with you shall be to you as the native among you, and you shall love him as yourself, for you were aliens in the land of Egypt . . . (Lev. 19:34).

(See Deut. 26:12; Job 31:32; Ps. 146:9; Jer. 22:3; Zech. 7:10.) The Old Testament also warns against being taken advantage of by strangers (Ps. 109:11; Prov. 11:15). We should be hospitable; we should not be gullible.

The New Testament continued the emphasis on being kind to strangers: At the Judgment, the Lord will say to those on His right, "I was a stranger, and you invited Me in" (Mt. 25:35), while He says to those on the left, "I was a stranger, and you did not invite Me in" (Mt. 25:43). Again, among the qualifications of special female servants are these words: ". . . if she has shown hospitality to strangers . . ." (1 Tim. 5:10). These were widows who devoted themselves to serving the body and were, therefore, supported by the church.

Hospitality is a recognition of the fact that all of us at some time or another are strangers. We should treat others as we ourselves would like to be treated. Abraham knew what it was like to be a stranger, to be the outsider. He told the inhabitants of Canaan, "I am a stranger and a sojourner among you" (Gen. 23:4). Think of when you have been a stranger. Perhaps you were like the poet who wrote,

I, a stranger and afraid
In a world I never made.[22]

You may agree with Thomas Wolfe: "Which of us is not forever a stranger and alone?"[23] Each of us has been "a stranger and alone." Therefore, we should reach out to those who are isolated.

If the classic Old Testament example of hospitality is Abraham and the three strangers, the classic New Testament example is found in Acts 28. Many children have learned about biblical hospitality by studying a lesson on how the natives of Malta were kind to Paul. Acts 28:1–15 is a gem in the setting of the account of Paul's struggles to reach Rome.

Paul, his friends, and his shipmates had reached the shores of Malta, a tiny island in the Mediterranean Sea. As we skim through the three months that followed (28:11), we will see some

---

[22]A. E. Housman, *Last Poems* 1922, 9, st. 12, quoted in *Bartlett's Familiar Quotations: Expanded Multimedia Edition*. Executive Producers: Luyen Chou, Ludmil Pandeff. Little, Brown, and Co. and Warner Book, 1995.

[23]Thomas Wolfe, *Look Homeward, Angel*, 1929, quoted in *Bartlett's Familiar Quotations: Expanded Multimedia Edition*.

examples of what it means to "love strangers."

Islanders were kind to strangers (vv. 1–7). Someone on Malta had seen the foundering ship. Word had passed, and many natives were waiting on the beach. It was common for islanders to kill shipwreck victims and steal their valuables. Luke, however, noted that "the natives showed us extraordinary kindness; for because of the rain that had set in and because of the cold, they kindled a fire and received us all" (v. 2). Those from the ship were strangers to the islanders, but they were strangers in need. The citizens of Malta expressed hospitality.

A major reason for the hospitality of the natives becomes clear in verse 7: Luke said, ". . . the leading man of the island, named Publius . . . welcomed us and entertained us courteously three days." Publius, the governor of Malta, was himself a hospitable man and set the example for the other citizens. When you find a hospitable people, you will invariably find a leader who has demonstrated what it means to be hospitable. This influence is one reason elders in the Lord's church must be hospitable, according to 1 Timothy 3:2 and Titus 1:8. If they are not hospitable, most likely the congregation will not be hospitable either.

Paul was kind to strangers (vv. 8–10). The islanders were not the only ones who showed their love and concern for strangers. As Paul visited with Publius, he learned that his father was sick with Malta fever. Immediately, "Paul went in to see him and after he had prayed, he laid his hands on him and healed him" (v. 8). When word spread of that healing, those who were sick came from all over the island to Paul, and perhaps to Dr. Luke, and were cured (see comments on v. 9).

The motivation for hospitality is not reciprocation, since the recipients often have neither the means nor the opportunity to reciprocate. Sometimes, however, help flows in both directions— not because it is planned that way, but because it simply happens. Paul was able to help those who had helped him. Further, Luke noted that the natives "also honored us with many marks of respect." Later, he said, "When we were setting sail, they supplied us with all we needed" (v. 10). Paul and his companions had arrived on shore with little more than the clothes on their backs; the grateful citizens of Malta supplied them with what they needed to continue their journey to Rome.

Brethren were kind to a stranger (vv. 11–15). We have used the word "stranger" with its common meaning: one we have never met before, one with whom we have no relationship. Occasionally, the Bible uses the word to refer to children of God who need encouragement. For instance, in Leviticus 25:35, Moses wrote, "Now in case a countryman of yours becomes poor . . . then you are to sustain him, like a stranger or a sojourner. . . ." Again, in the New Testament, John spoke of helping brethren "especially when they are strangers" (3 Jn. 5).

As Paul made his way to Rome, he met brethren, some of whom he had probably never met before—and they encouraged him by their acceptance. Acts 28:15 says, "And the brethren, when they heard about us, came from [Rome] as far as the Market of Appius and Three Inns to meet us; and when Paul saw them, he thanked God and took courage."

Using this expanded concept of "stranger," we can probably think of many we do not know as well as we should—people whom we need to help and encourage in our communities, in our workplaces, in the congregations we attend, and maybe even in our own homes.

Conclusion. Let us make some final observations about biblical hospitality:

(1) Hospitality often involves inviting people into our homes and feeding them, as was the case with Abraham, but it is not confined to that. Being a "stranger-lover" means that we are sensitive to others' needs and that we supply those needs. In Acts 28, we saw strangers with a variety of needs: the need for a warm fire, a place to stay, health, and encouragement. The "stranger-lovers" in this chapter were kind to supply those needs.

(2) True hospitality is expressed not in the magnitude of the help offered, but in the warmth of the help offered. The idea that one must be extravagant to be hospitable has done more to discourage hospitality than any other single factor. One woman lamented, "I used to have the mistaken idea that being hospitable meant nearly killing myself in preparations, so when the time came for guests, I felt more like going up to bed than an-

swering the door."[24] Many of the expressions of hospitality in our text cost little or nothing—building a fire to welcome the shivering survivors of the shipwreck, traveling down the Appian Way to greet Paul—but these expressions were priceless to the recipients. Modern examples could include stopping to help fix a stranger's flat tire, being supportive of a stranger in a hospital waiting room, sitting up with a sick neighbor one barely knows.

(3) Hospitality is not so much a sharing of possessions as it is a sharing of yourself. Someone has defined "hospitality" as "the creation of a free and friendly space where we can reach out to strangers and invite them to become our friends."[25] The woman who confessed that she was exhausted by the time her guests arrived learned this lesson: "The main purpose [of hospitality] is not to feed your guests—they can eat at home. More important than food is your willingness to share a part of yourself—your love, your kindness, your generosity—and your guests can only get this from you!"[26]

This message is entitled "The Fine Art of Hospitality." For some of us, should it be titled "The *Lost* Art of Hospitality"? May God help each of us to become a "lover of strangers."

A Final Word (28:11–31)

Acts 28:11–31 is Luke's final word regarding the history of the early church. This passage can be divided into three sections: (1) A Final Word About Paul's Trip to Rome (vv. 11–16); (2) A Final Word About Paul's Message to the Jews (vv. 17–29); (3) A Final Word Regarding the Gospel (vv. 30, 31).

The actual "final word" in the text is the word "unhindered" (v. 31). Luke stressed that Paul and his message were unhindered:

1. By Delay (v. 11).
2. By Superstition (v. 11).

---

[24]Beverly LaHaye, *The Spirit Controlled Woman* (Eugene, Oreg.: Harvest House Publishers, 1976), 93.

[25]Henri H. M. Nouwen, *Reaching Out* (New York: Doubleday & Co., 1975), n.p.; quoted in *The Answer* (Dallas: Word Bibles, 1993), 17.

[26]LaHaye, 62.

3. By the Weather (vv. 12, 13).
4. By Apprehension (vv. 14, 15).
5. By Intimidation (vv. 14, 16).
6. By Confinement (vv. 17–23).
7. By Rejection (vv. 23–29).
8. By Chains (v. 30).
9. By Roman Authorities (vv. 30, 31).

Paul's Attitude About His Imprisonment (28:20)

The terms used by Paul to refer to the reason(s) for his imprisonment are fascinating. To the Council, he insisted, "I am on trial for the hope and resurrection of the dead" (23:6; 24:21). Before King Agrippa, he said, "I am standing trial for the hope of the promise made by God to our fathers" (26:6). When he arrived in Rome, he told the Jewish leaders, "I am wearing this chain for the sake of the hope of Israel" (28:20).

When Paul wrote his Prison Epistles, he declared that he was a "prisoner . . . for the sake of you Gentiles" (Eph. 3:1) and "the prisoner of the Lord" (Eph. 4:1). He spoke of "my imprisonment in the cause of Christ" (Phil. 1:13), "my sufferings for your sake" (Col. 1:24), and "the mystery of Christ, for which I have also been imprisoned" (Col. 4:3). In his letter to Philemon, he again said he was "a prisoner of Christ Jesus" (Philem. 1, 9) and spoke of "my imprisonment for the gospel" (Philem. 13).

Paul did not view his bonds as "a miscarriage of justice" or "an [undeserved] punishment from the Lord." Rather, he viewed them as part of God's greater plans and purposes—designed in some way to spread the gospel, to help him mature in Christ, and to glorify his Lord.

The next time you feel "imprisoned" by a situation beyond your control or "bound" by apparently unsolvable problems, it may help if you think of yourself not as the victim of circumstances, but as "a prisoner of [and for] the Lord." God may have a purpose for your dilemma as He did for Paul's (Rom. 8:28).

"This Is Not the End" (28:30, 31)

On November 10, 1942, Winston Churchill addressed a worried audience. For days, Hitler's Luftwaffe had been bombing

London. What could the British Prime Minister say to give hope to an embattled people? Slowly, he growled these immortal words: "Now this is not the end. It is not even the beginning of the end. But it is, perhaps, the end of the beginning." We may adapt his words: Acts 28:30, 31 is not the final word on the spread of the gospel; it is only the final word on the *beginning* of the spread of the good news.

What will be the final word on our own lives regarding the gospel? Have we contributed to the spreading of the gospel throughout the world as Paul did? Have we even contributed to the spreading of the gospel through our neighborhoods? How tragic if the final word should be "He thought only about himself; he was concerned only about himself; he lived only for himself." "For what will it profit a man, if he gains the whole world and forfeits his soul? Or what will a man give in exchange for his soul?" (Mt. 16:26).

Continuing Acts
The Rest of the Story

THE CONTINUING ACTS OF PAUL

Although Luke ended Acts with Paul left in prison, three books in the New Testament provide glimpses of Paul's subsequent activities. These books, 1 and 2 Timothy and Titus, were written to two young evangelists who had worked and trained under Paul.

What *did* happen to Paul after Acts 28:31? Eusebius, "the father of church history" (c. A.D. 275–339), wrote, "After defending himself successfully, it is currently reported that the apostle again went forth to proclaim the Gospel, and afterwards came to Rome a second time, and was martyred under Nero."[1] The facts, as we know them, agree with the idea that Paul was imprisoned *twice* in Rome, and that between those imprisonments he made another journey.

First, we can see many differences between "the Prison Epistles" (Ephesians, Philippians, Colossians, and Philemon) and 2 Timothy. When Paul wrote 2 Timothy, he was also imprisoned (2 Tim. 1:8; 2:9), but consider the differences between that letter and the Prison Epistles: The tone of the Prison Epistles is basically cheerful, but the tone of 2 Timothy is basically somber. When Paul wrote the Prison Epistles, he was surrounded by friends; but when he wrote 2 Timothy, he had been forsaken by all except Luke (2 Tim. 4:11). When Paul wrote the Prison Epistles, he expected to be released (Phil. 1:25, 26; 2:24; Philem. 22); but

---

[1]Eusebius *Ecclesiastical History* 2.22.

when he wrote 2 Timothy, he expected to die (2 Tim. 4:6, 7). These and other differences lead us to believe that Paul was imprisoned in Rome not once, but twice.

Second, certain events and journeys described in the letters to Timothy and Titus find no place in the chronology of Acts. J. W. McGarvey listed several examples:

> Among these are his leaving Timothy in Ephesus to counteract the influence of certain teachers, while he went into Macedonia (I. Tim. i. 3); his leaving Titus in Crete to set in order the things that were wanting there (Tit. i. 5); his visit to Miletus when he left Trophimus there sick (II. Tim. iv. 20); and his journey toward Nicopolis to spend the winter (Tit. iii. 12).[2]

When Paul wrote his letter to Titus and his first letter to Timothy, he was free from Roman chains. He had recently left Timothy in Ephesus (1 Tim. 1:3), and it seems that he had left Titus in Crete after spending some time there (Tit. 1:5). Paul wanted to meet with Titus again in Nicopolis, where he intended to spend the winter (Tit. 3:12). We know that Titus later went to Dalmatia (2 Tim. 4:10), but we are uncertain if Paul and Titus met as planned before Titus continued his journey.

At the writing of 2 Timothy, Paul was again in prison in Rome and had already faced one trial (2 Tim. 4:16, 17). He probably had not been imprisoned long, for the available evidence suggests that he had traveled recently. Paul had left his cloak and some parchments at Troas (2 Tim. 4:13), and he had parted not long before with friends in Miletus and Corinth (2 Tim. 4:20). He may also have been in Ephesus (2 Tim. 4:14, 15; see 1 Tim. 1:3, 20), and he likely had encountered trouble there. Second Timothy was apparently Paul's last letter. Its words, which serve as Paul's last will and testament, are interwoven with touching appeals, ringing charges, and the note of triumph, even in the

---

[2]J. W. McGarvey, *New Commentary on Acts of Apostles*, vol. 2 (Delight, Ark.: Gospel Light Publishing Co., n.d.), 292.

face of imminent death.[3]

Paul's re-arrest probably occurred around A.D. 67. Uninspired tradition says he was beheaded that year in Rome, at Nero's order.

Finally, references were made by early uninspired writers to Paul's release from his first imprisonment and to his subsequent journeys. For instance, Clement of Rome (c. A.D. 96) said that Paul "taught righteousness to the whole world" and reached "to the extreme limit of the west."[4] The Muratorian Canon (c. A.D. 170–190), an early manuscript fragment that lists New Testament books, spoke of Paul's journey when he "went from the city [Rome] to Spain."[5] Even though such references are not inspired, when viewed in the light of the scriptural evidence they take on a degree of significance.

We know that Paul had intended to go to Spain if possible (Rom. 15:24, 28), and the church historian Eusebius implied that Paul was at some point released from his Roman imprisonment. From the information available, we can piece together a probable sequence of events after Acts 28:31 (see the *Appendix, Paul's Final Travels: A Possible Reconstruction*). At some point, perhaps soon after the close of Acts, Paul finally stood before Nero and made his defense (27:24). The apostle's great speeches before Felix, Festus, and Agrippa probably outline the gist of his defense. During the trial, the complimentary reports of Governor Festus and Julius the centurion would have weighed heavily in Paul's favor. Evidently, he was pronounced innocent and released about A.D. 62.

Since Paul had a long-held dream to preach Christ in Spain (Rom. 15:24, 28), this country was likely one of his first destinations. He definitely visited Crete (Tit. 1:5), where he left Titus; and Miletus (2 Tim. 4:20), where he had to leave Trophimus,

---

[3]R. N. Longenecker, "Paul, the Apostle," in *The Zondervan Pictorial Encyclopedia of the Bible*, ed. Merrill C. Tenney (Grand Rapids, Mich.: Zondervan Publishing House, 1975), 4:657.

[4]*1 Clement* 5.

[5]"Translation of the Muratorian Fragment" in *The New Schaff-Herzog Encyclopedia of Religious Knowledge*, ed. Samuel M. Jackson (Grand Rapids, Mich.: Baker Book House, 1977), 8:56.

who was ill. From Miletus, he could have gone inland to Colossae to visit his friend Philemon (Philem. 22). He had thought he would never see the Ephesian elders again (20:25). How he must have rejoiced when God gave him another opportunity to visit with them (see 1 Tim. 1:3)! Paul left Timothy in Ephesus to help the church there, while he traveled on to Macedonia (1 Tim. 1:3).

On his way to Macedonia, Paul stopped at Troas. There he left a cloak and his parchments with a friend (2 Tim. 4:13), probably intending to return to pick them up later. When the apostle reached Macedonia, he surely spent as much time as possible with those he loved in Philippi (Phil. 2:23, 24). As he traveled through Macedonia, he likely wrote his first letter to Timothy and his letter to Titus. Paul, almost seventy years old, was preparing the younger men to carry on the work when he was gone. First and Second Timothy and Titus are often called "the pastoral epistles" because today denominational preachers are usually designated as "pastors." As we have seen, however, the term "pastor" in the Bible applies not to the preacher, but to the elders (see comments on 20:28). It is better to refer to 1 and 2 Timothy and Titus as "the evangelistic epistles." Paul may also have visited Corinth (2 Tim. 4:20), but his ultimate destination was Nicopolis, a Roman colony in western Greece, where he planned to spend the winter (Tit. 3:12).

As Paul traveled and preached, momentous events were occurring in Rome—events that ultimately resulted in his re-arrest and death. On July 18, A.D. 64, a fire broke out in the capital city.

> Of the fourteen sections into which the city was divided, ten were scorched and virtually destroyed. Everywhere palaces, temples, and altars were in ashes. Even the Circus Maximus, large enough to seat 200,000 people was destroyed.[6]

Most present-day historians do not blame Nero for burning the city; the fire probably started accidentally. However, angry

---

[6]Paul Rogers, "At the End of Paul's Life," *Preacher's Periodical* 5 (May 1985): 27; see Tacitus *Annals* 15.38–41.

citizens of Rome, knowing of Nero's ambitious plans to rebuild the capital and his recent irrational actions, began to accuse the emperor. To shift attention from himself, Nero made Christians the scapegoat. Tacitus, a Roman historian (A.D. 55–120), wrote of Nero's actions:

> To get rid of the rumour, Nero put in his place as culprits . . . the men whom the common people hated . . . and called Christians. . . . [T]hey were dressed up in the skins of wild animals to perish either by the worrying of dogs, or on crosses, or by fire. . . . [W]hen daylight failed they were burnt to serve as lights by night. Nero had thrown open his gardens for that spectacle and was giving a circus performance. . . .[7]

Tacitus also reported that Nero had Christians beheaded, cast to lions, and thrown from a high stone pillar.

A vicious persecution of believers thus began. As one of the foremost proclaimers of the faith, Paul would have been a prime target of that persecution. He was probably seized about A.D. 67, perhaps at Nicopolis (Tit. 3:12), and dragged to Rome. During this imprisonment Paul did not live "in his own rented quarters" in Rome as before (Acts 28:30). Instead, early writers tell us that he was confined to the Mamertine Prison—a foul stone pit with a small hole cut in the high stone ceiling for ventilation and light.

In that dim light, using pen and parchment supplied by an unknown benefactor, Paul wrote his last words to his beloved Timothy. As a Roman citizen, the apostle had been allowed his day in court, but since he had been deserted by his supporters and falsely accused by his enemies, Paul had little hope of a second acquittal (2 Tim. 4:16). There is disagreement regarding "the first defense" mentioned by Paul in 2 Timothy 4:16, but this phrase probably referred to a recent occurrence—perhaps the preliminary hearing before the actual trial. Believing that death was imminent (2 Tim. 4:6–8), the apostle pled with the

---

[7]Tacitus *Annals* 15.44.

young preacher Timothy:

> Make every effort to come to me soon. . . . Pick up
> Mark and bring him with you, for he is useful to me for
> service. . . . When you come bring the cloak which I left
> at Troas with Carpus, and the books, especially the
> parchments. . . . Make every effort to come before winter
> (2 Tim. 4:9, 11, 13, 21).

During winter, travel would be impossible, and Paul did not
expect to be alive the following spring.

According to uninspired tradition, Paul was beheaded at
Rome in A.D. 67/68.[8] When the executioner severed his head
from his body, at last the aged apostle's soul was free to depart
and be with his Lord (Phil. 1:23). As we conclude our exami-
nation of the life and ministry of Paul, his words linger in our
minds:

> For I am already being poured out as a drink offering,
> and the time of my departure has come. I have fought
> the good fight, I have finished the course, I have kept
> the faith; in the future there is laid up for me the crown
> of righteousness, which the Lord, the righteous Judge,
> will award to me on that day; and not only to me, but
> also to all who have loved His appearing (2 Tim. 4:6–8).

THE CONTINUING ACTS OF OTHER
FIRST-CENTURY CHRISTIANS

During the last half of the Book of Acts, Luke primarily recorded the work of Paul. This emphasis does not mean that
Christians elsewhere were idle. Peter and the other apostles continued to travel, telling the story of Jesus (9:32). According to
uninspired tradition, the apostles traveled to much of the civilized world with the gospel. Although not inspired, these traditions are in harmony with Christ's commission to the apostles

---

[8]Eusebius *Ecclesiastical History* 2.25.

(Mt. 28:18–20; Mk. 16:15, 16; Acts 1:8) and with Paul's statement to the Colossians that ". . . the gospel . . . has come to you, just as *in all the world* also it is constantly bearing fruit and increasing . . ." (Col. 1:5, 6; emphasis added). These traditions also agree with the fact that in the latter part of Acts most of the apostles were apparently no longer in Jerusalem (see comments on 9:26, 27; 12:17; 15:4; 21:18).

Early Christian writers said that the apostle John spent most of his final years in Ephesus. We know definitely that Peter traveled as far as Antioch (Gal. 2:11) and Babylon (1 Pet. 5:13). Babylon existed in the first century as a small town on the Euphrates, and Peter may have been there when he wrote his first letter, although many are convinced that "Babylon" was a cryptic way of referring to Rome. According to uninspired tradition, Peter died in Rome.

Others, not apostles, were also spreading the good news (11:19). Preachers such as Apollos continued to be active (1 Cor. 16:12; Tit. 3:13). On at least one journey, Peter was accompanied by two of Paul's former traveling companions, Silas and Mark (1 Pet. 5:12, 13).

Men guided by the Holy Spirit, as was Paul, put their words into writing in order to build faith and to strengthen Christians. Luke wrote his Gospel Account and Acts in the early 60's. About the same time, Matthew and Mark recorded their accounts of the life of Christ. Inspired church leaders were writing letters to Christians and congregations as Paul did: James, the half-brother of Jesus, wrote a book to Jewish Christians on practical Christianity. Another half-brother of Jesus, named Jude (or Judas), wrote a short letter urging Christians to ". . . contend earnestly for the faith . . ." (Jude 3). Shortly before his death (2 Pet. 1:13–15), Peter wrote two epistles: the first about suffering persecution with dignity, and the second to warn Christians of false teaching. Those four letters—James, 1 and 2 Peter, and Jude—were probably written in the 60's.

Near the end of the first century, the apostle John wrote five books dealing with special problems that had arisen. His Gospel Account exposed the erroneous teaching that Christ had not come "in the flesh" (Jn. 1:1, 14; see 2 Jn. 7). His first letter to

Christians dealt with the practical consequences of that error (1 Jn. 1:1; 2:1). His second and third letters were notes sent to individuals; among other concerns, they warned against encouraging those who taught error (2 Jn. 7–11). John also penned the final book of the New Testament, but for this writing he was primarily the Lord's secretary (Rev. 1:1, 9–11). That final book, the Book of Revelation, was to encourage Christians who were being persecuted (Rev. 2:10).

The church was persecuted from its beginning. Many in addition to Paul died in the first century for their faith. In the first decades of its existence, the church was mainly persecuted by the Jews. Stephen was stoned to death by the Jewish Council (7:58–60); Christians, both men and women, were put to death during Saul's persecution of the church (22:4; 26:10); and the apostle James was beheaded by King Herod (12:2). According to uninspired tradition, another who died at the hand of the Jews was James, the half-brother of Jesus:

> Ultimately, he incurred the wrath of the rich, corrupt leaders of the Jews [in Jerusalem]. Using the excuse that he was a breaker of the law, they threw him [down] from the [roof of the] temple, stoned him, and then ended his life with a club. It is said that he died with a prayer on his lips for his murderers.[9]

Later, the chief persecutor of the church became the Roman government, beginning with Nero's persecution in A.D. 64/65. The Jews also continued to persecute Christians as they had opportunity (Rev. 2:9, 10); but after the destruction of Jerusalem in A.D. 70, they were no longer capable of a unified effort. Peter's letters concerning mistreatment may have been written during Nero's persecution. According to uninspired tradition, many of the apostles died during that violent period, as well as other Christians mentioned in the Book of Acts. The best-known tradition is that of the death of Peter, who was scourged and sen-

---

[9]David Roper, "James: Practical Christianity," *Truth for Today* 14 (July 1993): 39; see Eusebius *Ecclesiastical History* 2.23.

tenced to die by crucifixion. According to the story, Peter, believing he was unworthy to die as his Lord had, asked to be crucified head down.[10]

At first, Christians were not condemned as Christians, but for specific crimes. In addition to the original charge of arson, they were also accused of sedition, sorcery, incest, even cannibalism. Most of these accusations originated because people misunderstood Christian teaching and practice: Teaching on the kingdom became sedition; the exercise of spiritual gifts became sorcery; love for other Christians, who were called "brothers and sisters," became incest; symbolically partaking of the Lord's body in the Lord's Supper became cannibalism. At the heart of society's hatred of Christianity was the Christian's intolerance of other religions and their gods. Followers of Jesus were labeled "atheists" and "haters of mankind." Soon Christians were blamed for every disaster that occurred, whether natural or man-made. No evidence was required for their conviction:

> At the outset [of Nero's persecution], a trial was required, but soon as a consequence [of the many charges made] the trial could be dispensed with, the Christians being "recognized as a society whose principle might be summarized as *odium generis humani* [hatred of mankind]." A trial became unnecessary; the religion itself involved the crimes. . . .[11]

A second general persecution by the Roman government occurred under the emperor Domitian (A.D. 81–96), the younger son of Vespasian. There is disagreement over the extent of Domitian's persecution, but many respected writers believe it to have been even more widespread than that of Nero. Ray Summers wrote,

---

[10]Eusebius *Ecclesiastical History* 3.1; *Acts of the Holy Apostles Peter and Paul*.

[11]S. Angus, "Roman Empire," *International Standard Bible Encyclopedia*, ed. James Orr (Grand Rapids, Mich.: Wm. B. Eerdmans Publishing Co., 1960), 3:2607.

[U]nder Domitian, Christianity had to enter a struggle of life or death with the imperial power.... The forms of punishment were many. Some were put to death, some were exiled, some were tortured into a confession of the divinity of the emperor, some had their property confiscated, some received combinations of these measures.[12]

The Book of Revelation was probably written during the latter part of Domitian's reign (A.D. 94–96). The book urges Christians to "be faithful, even if you have to die" (Rev. 2:10; NCV) and speaks of "Antipas, My witness [martyr]" who was killed at Pergamum (Rev. 2:13). Revelation also tells of others "... who had been slain because of the word of God, and because of the testimony which they had maintained" (Rev. 6:9). It depicts a harlot called "Babylon the Great," who was "drunk with the blood of the saints, and with the blood of the witnesses [martyrs] of Jesus" (Rev. 17:1–6). Since the harlot sat upon "seven mountains" (Rev. 17:9), it would be hard not to identify her as the city of Rome which was built on seven hills.

According to tradition, one of those killed during Domitian's persecution was Paul's friend and companion Timothy. During the persecution, John, the only apostle still living, was banished to the isle of Patmos, where he received "the Revelation of Jesus Christ" (Rev. 1:1, 9). After the death of Domitian, it is said that John returned to Ephesus, where he died a natural death when he was almost one hundred years old.

Did the fierce persecution of Rome destroy the spirit of the church? Did "the acts" of God's people cease? Tertullian, a second-century Christian writer, described the result of the persecution by the Roman government:

We are a people of yesterday, and yet we have filled every place belonging to you, cities, islands, castles, towns, assemblies, your very camp, your tribes, palace, forum ...

---

[12]Ray Summers, *Worthy is the Lamb* (Nashville: Broadman Press, 1951), 83–85.

nothing whatever is achieved by each more exquisite cruelty you invent, on the contrary it wins men for our school. We are made more as you mow us down. The blood of Christians [or martyrs] is seed.[13]

THE CONTINUING ACTS OF CHRISTIANS THROUGH THE YEARS

During the second and third centuries, "the seed" of the blood of Christian martyrs was sown liberally throughout the Roman Empire. John Foxe, in the famed *Foxe's Book of Martyrs*, listed ten general persecutions under the Roman emperors.[14] During the persecution under the emperor Trajan, Ignatius was brought to Rome and there devoured by wild beasts in the arena. During the persecution under Marcus Aurelius, aged Polycarp, a disciple of John, was sentenced to death after refusing to curse Christ. He exclaimed, "Eighty and six years have I served Him, and He never did me any injury: how then can I blaspheme my King and my Saviour?"[15] About that same time, Justin Martyr was killed for his faith. During the persecution under the emperor Severus, another noted leader, Irenaeus of Lyons, was beheaded. Other persecutions listed by John Foxe occurred during the reigns of Maximus, Decius, Valerian, and Maximian.

There are many other stories of Christians who suffered during the early centuries of the church's existence. While some of these stories have been embellished by early Christian writers, the core truth remains that many believers were martyred for their faith in Jesus Christ.

Again, we ask: Did such treatment destroy the church? Did "the acts" of God's people cease? One writer made this comment:

---

[13]Quoted in Vera E. Walker, *A First Church History* (London: Student Christian Movement Press, 1936), 17.

[14]Marie Gentert King, ed., *Foxe's Book of Martyrs* (Old Tappan, N.J.: Fleming H. Revell Co., 1968), 13–31.

[15]*Martyrdom of Polycarp* 9.

The church was born in the midst of persecution and for the first three hundred years never escaped its palling shadow. Yet in spite of, and perhaps often because of, persecution the church continued to grow. The fires of persecution purged the church of those whose commitment was only lukewarm, thus keeping the church from an easy accommodation with the world about it.[16]

A powerful witness to the attitude of early Christians can be found in the catacombs of Rome. The catacombs are a maze of underground tunnels and rooms running for miles beneath the city of Rome. Christians buried their dead there and sometimes fled there for safety. The sides of the tunnels—where the dead are buried—are covered with pictures and inscriptions. If you could walk through those tunnels, you would see pictures drawn by early Christians of the dove, the anchor, the crown, and other symbols of the faith. You would see depictions of Jesus as the Good Shepherd. What you would not see are pictures of torture or inscriptions of anger against their persecutors. There is "no sign of mourning, no expression of vengeance; all breathes of gentleness, benevolence, and love."[17]

The last great persecution of Christians by Roman emperors was under Diocletian. In 303, Diocletian and an associate, Galerius, began to issue a series of edicts to destroy church buildings, to imprison church leaders, to force all Christians to sacrifice, and to confiscate the Christian Scriptures. Timothy, a young deacon, and Maura, his wife of three weeks, were crucified side by side because they refused to give up a copy of the Bible so it might be burned.

Diocletian and Galerius had waited too long for their radical measures, for by that time the church had grown large enough to force recognition. In 311, Galerius ended the persecution. In 313, the "Edict of Milan" by Constantine and Licinius

---

[16]*Handbook of Church History,* The Living Word Series (Austin, Tex.: R. B. Sweet Co., 1964), 17.

[17]Unknown author, quoted in Theodora W. Wilson, *Into the Arena* (London: William Collins Sons and Co., 1944), 102.

gave Christianity full legal status. In 323, when Constantine the Great became sole ruler, the persecution of the church by the Roman Empire ended. Someone has said, "Rome met Christianity with a sword, and Christianity met Rome with love—and love won." The end of persecution by the Roman government does not mean that all persecution against Christians ceased. Those who stand up for God's way always have been and always will be persecuted in some way (2 Tim. 3:12).

The attainment of legal recognition turned out to be a mixed blessing, for the influence of Constantine accelerated the apostasy foretold by Jesus and the inspired writers (see Mt. 24:24; Acts 20:28–31; 2 Thess. 2:3–12; 1 Tim. 4:1–3; 2 Tim. 4:1–4; 2 Pet. 2:1–3). At this point, however, we cannot trace that apostasy or dwell on the doctrinal errors that arose in the context of the church. Rather, we want simply to stress (1) that regardless of how corrupt the church became, there were always "the faithful few" and (2) that the faithful continued to "act" for God. One historian made this observation:

> Christianity spread as a sort of holy contagion. Its path can be traced along the main lines of commerce. . . . Once planted in a town, it tended to spread insensibly to the adjacent district and strike fresh roots. . . . Pliny, speaking of the northern seaboard province of Bithynia-Pontus, refers to the "large numbers" of Christians "of every age and rank and from both sexes." "For," says he, "the contagion of this superstition has permeated not only towns, but also villages and country"; so that temples are deserted, rites unobserved, victims [sacrificial animals] unbought. . . .
>
> In the East, Edessa, the capital of a small Graecized native kingdom beyond the Euphrates, N.E. from Antioch, had about 200 A.D. a Christian king. . . . From Alexandria . . . the Gospel spread both through Egypt and further west to Cyrene. In the West itself, the two great areas added were Proconsular Africa, with Carthage as capital, and South Gaul, with Lyons as centre. . . . Of Spanish Christians we hear first about the end of the

[second] century; while as to the most distant provinces, like Britain, . . . we may infer some Roman . . . Christians.[18]

The names of some missionaries in the succeeding centuries have been immortalized. Of course, the names of most of the faithful Christians who spread the Word through the years—often having to suffer for their faithfulness—were never recorded in the annals of men. However, God knew who they were, and He continued to record "the acts" of His people.

THE CONTINUING ACTS
OF GOD'S PEOPLE TODAY

If space permitted, we could continue to write of the church's constant struggle through the years to maintain her purity and fidelity to God. Further, we could tell of the godly Christians we have known, men and women around the world dedicated to the Lord and to His Word. However, we must be content with emphasizing that the Lord continues to walk among the churches (Rev. 1:13, 20; 2:1), that He still "knows" about all of His children (Rev. 2:2, 9, 13, 19), and that He still records their "acts."

APPLICATION

"Chapter 29"
Several preachers and teachers have presented a follow-up lesson to the Book of Acts called "Chapter 29." They use this title to stress that chapter 28 of Acts was not the end of the story of "the acts" of God's servants. You might want to use that title for a lesson on the "continuing acts" of God's people.

Acts To Be Continued
A sister in Christ wrote the history of a local congregation in their church bulletin. Each week she concluded her article with

---

[18]J. Vernon Bartlet, *Early Church History* (London: The Religious Tract Society, 1894), 19–20; see Pliny *Letters to Trajan* 10.96.

the words "To be continued." When those words were read, members knew she was not finished with her series; there was more to come.

If such a literary device had been in use in Luke's day, he could have placed one after the words of Acts 28:31, for Acts records only *the beginning* of the work of spreading the gospel. That task was, and is, "to be continued" by each succeeding generation of God's people. The events Luke recorded in the Book of Acts were exciting. However, we should not think that the excitement was over simply because Luke laid down his pen. The excitement continued in the days that followed; it *should* be continuing today.

Those of us who teach Acts have a major concern: We fear that a study of Acts will be viewed simply as first-century history rather than a twenty-first-century mandate to "go and do likewise."

It has been suggested that we should learn "the lesson of the *Queen Mary*." The *Queen Mary* was one of the greatest ocean liners of all time. Initially, she was a magnificent passenger ship. During World War II, she was called into service as a troop ship; as such she was constantly under threat by Nazi submarines. Today, she is docked in the harbor at Long Beach, California. Her great engine has been removed, along with other sailing equipment. Souvenir shops line her deck. Larger rooms are used for conventions; cabins are rented as hotel rooms. Actors play the parts of the crew. The great sailing vessel has become a museum piece. Throughout Acts, we have seen the Lord's church launched. What a magnificent beginning it was, as God's people carried the gospel to all the populated earth! If we are not careful, however, the church can become a museum piece—a monument to the past—rather than God's continuing force for good in the world.

APPENDIX

CHARTS, MAPS, AND ARCHAEOLOGY

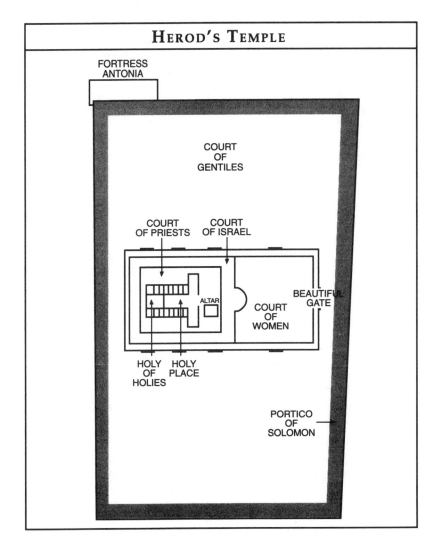

HEROD'S TEMPLE

FORTRESS
ANTONIA

COURT
OF
GENTILES

COURT
OF PRIESTS

COURT
OF ISRAEL

ALTAR

COURT
OF
WOMEN

BEAUTIFUL
GATE

HOLY
OF
HOLIES

HOLY
PLACE

PORTICO
OF
SOLOMON

SPEAKING IN TONGUES: A COMPARISON	
NEW TESTAMENT TIMES	TODAY
1. *Languages* they had not studied.	1. Generally a collection of *sounds* called "ecstatic utterances."
2. *Contemporary* languages that conveyed meaning.	2. Sometimes bits of modern languages or claims concerning some "forgotten language."
3. Only one interpretation possible.	3. Often, "interpretations" vary.
4. Emphasis on *public* demonstration.	4. Emphasis on *private* devotional use.
5. Nothing to do with *maturity* or spiritual growth.	5. Stressed as a sign of growing maturity and a source of greater maturity.
6. Did not prove speaker in God's favor.	6. Considered proof of God's acceptance.
7. Basically a "sign" to *others*.	7. Considered a "sign" to *self*.
8. Used to confirm the Word.	8. Leads men to subjective authority, away from the objective authority of the Bible.
9. A unique sign from God.	9. Can be psychologically induced.
10. Could not be duplicated by non-Christians.	10. "Ecstatic utterances" found in pagan religions, in false sects.
11. No emphasis on all speaking in tongues.	11. *All* are urged to seek this "gift."
12. Specific instructions given for use in assembly: only with an interpreter, only a few in order, no women speaking, etc.	12. Often, every New Testament instruction is violated.
13. Given *temporarily* for a special purpose—to *cease*.	13. Considered a *permanent* part of God's arrangement for the Christian Age.
14. Not emphasized.	14. Greatly emphasized.

ROMAN EMPERORS THROUGH THE FIRST CENTURY

1. Gaius Julius Caesar, 49–44 B.C.
   a. Formed First Triumvirate with Pompey and Crassus, 59 B.C.
   b. Crossed Rubicon to defeat forces of Pompey, 49 B.C.
   c. Assassinated by Brutus and Cassius (44 B.C.), in an effort to save the Republic from Julius' dictatorial powers.
   d. Four months after his death, a comet appeared at games held in his honor. The Senate proclaimed him "the Divine Julius."
2. Roman Civil Wars, 44–31 B.C.
   a. Octavian formed Second Triumvirate with Mark Antony and Lepidus, 43 B.C.
   b. Death of Brutus and Cassius at Battle of Philippi, 42 B.C.
   c. Forces of Octavian defeat forces of Antony at Actium, 31 B.C.
3. Octavian/Augustus, 31 B.C.–A.D. 14.
   a. Great nephew, adopted son, and at age 19 heir of Julius Caesar.
   b. Octavian, with the consent of the Senate, assumes the name Augustus, a title implying a special relationship to the gods, 27 B.C.
   c. Maintained the fiction of Republican Rome managed by the Senate while holding the power himself.
   d. A shrewd ruler who gave the Empire efficient organization and a stable system of laws.
   e. Inaugurated the *Pax Romana*, the Peace of Rome.
   f. Jesus of Nazareth was born during his reign.
4. Tiberius, A.D. 14–37.
   a. Stepson whom Augustus adopted and made his heir.
   b. The last 11 years of his reign, he ruled Rome while living on the island of Capri in the Bay of Naples.
   c. Appointed Pilate procurator of Judea.
   d. Ruled the Empire during the ministry and death of Jesus.
   e. A deeply conservative Roman, he refused to accept divine honors. Unlike his two predecessors, the Senate did not declare him divine after his death.

5. Gaius/Caligula, A.D. 37–41.
    a. Son of the military leader Germanicus, received the name Caligula, "little boots," in the army camp of his father.
    b. A descendant of Augustus and a great nephew of Tiberius, he was adopted by the Emperor and at age 26 inherited power.
    c. Soon intoxicated by power, he claimed to be a god and proposed that his horse be elected consul.
    d. Insisted that a statue of Zeus in his own likeness be erected in the Jewish temple at Jerusalem.
    e. Assassinated in A.D. 41 before the Jerusalem temple was desecrated. The Senate cursed his memory.
6. Claudius, A.D. 41–54.
    a. A 50 year-old uncle of Caligula, made emperor by the praetorian guard.
    b. Crippled and ill-favored, Augustus had been ashamed for him to appear in public.
    c. Added most of Britain and other domains to the Empire.
    d. Expelled Jews from Rome in A.D. 49. Ruled through most of the active ministry of Paul.
    e. An able administrator, organized efficient government for the Empire.
    f. Poisoned by his fourth wife, Agrippina after she persuaded him to make Nero, her son by a previous marriage, his heir instead of his son Britannicus.
7. Nero, A.D. 54–68.
    a. Became Emperor at age 17. Did well during his first years under the guidance of the philosopher Seneca and the military commander Burris.
    b. Warming to his power, within six years he contrived the murder of his advisors, Seneca among them, Britannicus, his mother, and his wife Octavia.
    c. Shocked aristocratic Romans by entering poetry and theatrical contests, as well as chariot races.
    d. When Rome burned in A.D. 64, he placed the blame on Christians and killed many of them.
    e. War with the Jews broke out in A.D. 66. After initial successes by the Jews, the Roman general Vespasian systematically destroyed all resistance.
    f. A revolt of legions in Spain and Gaul led to his suicide.

8. Year of the Four Emperors, A.D. 69.
   a. Marked the end of the Julio-Claudian Emperors, so called because all those from Augustus to Nero wore the family name of Julius or Claudius.
   b. Galba, Otho, and Vitellius in turn managed to get control of armies, allowing each to be Emperor for a few months.
   c. Leaving the Judean War, Vespasian was declared Emperor by his army in Egypt. Came to Rome and assumed the power.
9. Vespasian, A.D. 69–79.
   a. His son Titus took command of the legions in Judea and destroyed Jerusalem in A.D. 70.
   b. Established a harmonious working relationship with the Senate.
   c. A wise and good Emperor, he engaged in a massive rebuilding program in Rome.
10. Titus, A.D. 79–81.
    a. Son of Vespasian who finished the Roman war in Judea, reducing Jerusalem to ruins and ashes.
    b. Erected a great monument, the Arch of Titus, in Rome to commemorate his victory over the Jews. The monument still stands.
11. Domitian, A.D. 81–96.
    a. A younger son of Vespasian whose political and administrative powers fell considerably below those of his father.
    b. Increasing tensions between the Emperor and the Senate.
    c. During the last year of his reign he insisted on being addressed as a god.
    d. Oppressed several religious and ethnic groups, including Jews and Christians.
    e. Oppression of Christians accelerated, especially in Asia Minor where the Christians were more numerous.
    f. The last of the Flavian Emperors. Flavius was the family name of Vespasian, Titus, and Domitian.
    g. After his death, the Senate cursed Domitian's memory as they had Nero's. The Senate named the next Emperor.

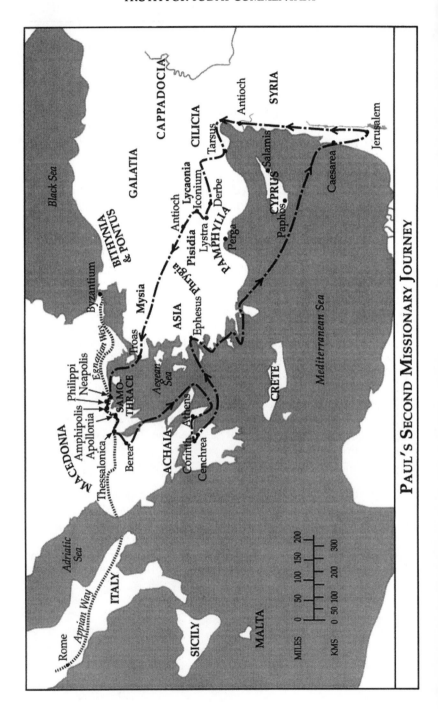

PAUL'S SECOND MISSIONARY JOURNEY

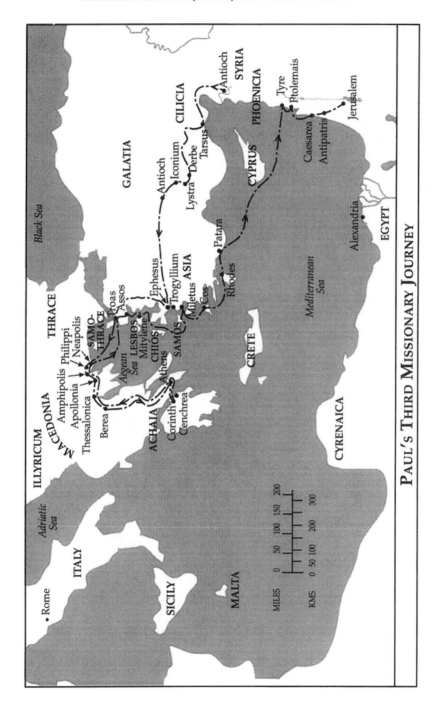

PAUL'S THIRD MISSIONARY JOURNEY

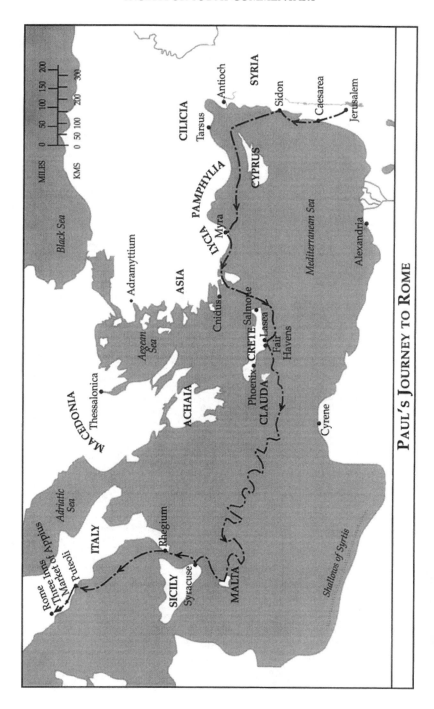

PAUL'S JOURNEY TO ROME

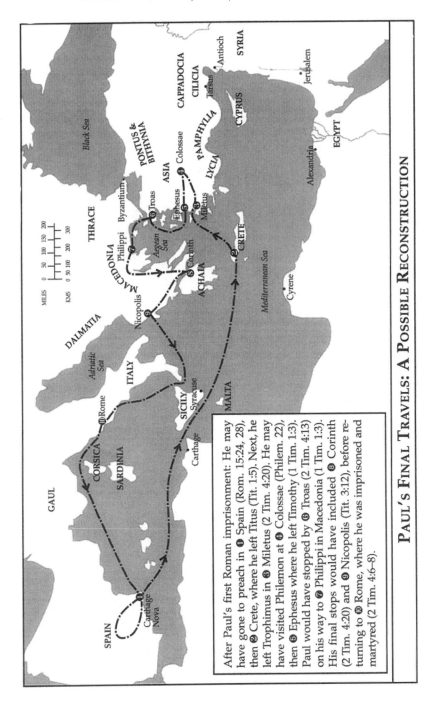

PAUL'S FINAL TRAVELS: A POSSIBLE RECONSTRUCTION

After Paul's first Roman imprisonment: He may have gone to preach in ❶ Spain (Rom. 15:24, 28), then ❷ Crete, where he left Titus (Tit. 1:5). Next, he left Trophimus in ❸ Miletus (2 Tim. 4:20). He may have visited Philemon at ❹ Colossae (Philem. 22), then ❺ Ephesus where he left Timothy (1 Tim. 1:3). Paul would have stopped by ❻ Troas (2 Tim. 4:13) on his way to ❼ Philippi in Macedonia (1 Tim. 1:3). His final stops would have included ❽ Corinth (2 Tim. 4:20) and ❾ Nicopolis (Tit. 3:12), before returning to ❿ Rome, where he was imprisoned and martyred (2 Tim. 4:6–8).

PHILIPPI. The Egnatian Way, a major Roman road that would have been used by Paul in traveling to the Macedonian cities of Philippi, Amphipolis, Apollonia, and Thessalonica (16:12; 17:1).

PHILIPPI. The market place (*agora*), with a sixth-century church building (background). The Philippian church began in the first century with the conversion of the households of Lydia and the jailer (16:15, 33).

PHILIPPI. Prison complex, containing the cell below.

PHILIPPI. Traditional prison cell of Paul and Silas (16:23–25).

ATHENS. Statue of Athena, the patron goddess of Athens.

ATHENS. The Acropolis with the Parthenon dedicated to Athena.

ATHENS. The marketplace (*agora*) where Paul preached (17:17), with the Acropolis (upper left) and Mars' Hill (upper right). Mars' Hill is the traditional site of Paul's sermon to the Areopagus (17:22).

ATHENS. Reconstructed Stoa of Attalos in the marketplace.

CORINTH. "Synagogue of the Hebrews" Inscription (2nd–3rd century A.D.). Paul began his mission work in the Jewish synagogue at Corinth (18:4), just as he had in other cities.

CORINTH. Erastus Inscription: "Erastus in return for his aedileship laid [the pavement] at his own expense." He was a public official and a Christian (Rom. 16:23).

542

CORINTH. The judgment seat (*bēma*) where Paul was brought before Gallio (18:12). Acrocorinth (background) where the Temple of Aphrodite was located.

EPHESUS. Ruins of the Temple of Artemis, of which the city of Ephesus was "guardian" (19:27, 35). Only one column has been reconstructed.

EPHESUS. Statue of Artemis of the Ephesians (19:27).

EPHESUS. Theater where the riot took place (19:29), viewed from above, along with Arcadius Street which terminated at the harbor.

JERUSALEM. Model of the Herodian Temple, viewed from the north-east. Antonia Fortress is located on the right ("the barracks," 21:37).

JERUSALEM. Temple Warning Inscription (21:29): "No man of another nation [is] to enter within the fence and enclosure around the temple, and whoever is caught will have himself to blame if death ensues."

CAESAREA. Theater, which, according to Josephus, was the place where Herod was praised by his audience as a god (12:21–23).

CAESAREA. Herodian harbor from which Paul began his turbulent trip to Rome (27:1, 2). This journey followed his two years of imprisonment in Caesarea (24:27).

ROME. Arch of Titus, celebrating Jerusalem's destruction (A.D. 70).

ROME. Relief inside the Arch of Titus, featuring the triumphal procession with items plundered from the Jewish Temple, including the lampstand (*menorah*).

ROME. The Colosseum.

SELECTED BIBLIOGRAPHY

GENERAL

Allen, Jimmy. *Survey of Acts*. 2 vols. Searcy, Ark: By the Author, 1986.

Ash, Anthony Lee. *The Acts of the Apostles*, Part 1. Living Word Commentary, ed. Everett Ferguson. Austin, Tex.: Sweet Publishing Co., 1979.

Barclay, William. *The Acts of the Apostles.* The Daily Study Bible Series, rev. ed. Philadelphia: Westminster Press, 1976.

Boles, H. Leo. *A Commentary on Acts of the Apostles.* Nashville: Gospel Advocate Co., 1941.

Bruce, F. F. *The Book of Acts.* The New International Commentary on the New Testament, gen. ed. F. F. Bruce, rev. ed. Grand Rapids, Mich.: Wm. B. Eerdmans Publishing Co., 1988.

Cloer, Eddie, ed. *Acts, The Spreading Flame.* Searcy, Ark. Harding University, 1989.

Coffman, James Burton. *Commentary on Acts.* Austin, Tex.: Firm Foundation Publishing House, 1976.

Foster, Lewis. Notes on Acts. *The NIV Study Bible.* Grand Rapids, Mich.: Zondervan Publishing House, 1985.

Hervey, A. C. *The Acts of the Apostles.* 2 vols. The Pulpit Commentary, ed. H. D. M. Spence and Joseph S. Exell, vol. 18. Grand Rapids, Mich.: Wm. B. Eerdmans Publishing Co., 1950.

Kistemaker, Simon J. *Exposition of the Acts of the Apostles.* New Testament Commentary. Grand Rapids, Mich.: Baker Book House, 1990.

Ladd, George E. *Acts.* The Wycliffe Bible Commentary. Nashville: The Southwestern Company, 1962.

_____. *The Young Church: Acts of the Apostles.* Nashville: Abingdon Press, 1964.

Lange, John Peter. *Commentary on Acts.* Vol. 1. Grand Rapids, Mich.: Zondervan Publishing House, 1866.

Lenski, R. C. H. *The Interpretation of the Acts of the Apostles.* Columbus, Ohio: Wartburg Press, 1944.

Longenecker, Richard N. *The Acts of the Apostles.* The Expositor's Bible Commentary, ed. Frank E. Gaebelein, vol. 9. Grand Rapids, Mich.: Zondervan Publishing House, 1981.

_____. *Paul, Apostle of Liberty.* New York: Harper & Row, 1964.

Luccock, Halford E. *The Acts of the Apostles in Present-Day Preaching.* Chicago: Willett, Clark & Co., 1942.

McClish, Dub, ed. *Studies in Acts.* Denton, Tex.: Valid Publications, 1985.

McGarvey, J. W. *New Commentary on Acts of Apostles.* 2 vols. Delight, Ark.: Gospel Light Publishing Co., n.d.

Marshall, I. Howard. *The Acts of the Apostles.* The Tyndale New Testament Commentaries, gen. ed. R. V. G. Tasker. Grand Rapids, Mich.: Wm. B. Eerdmans Publishing Co., 1980.

Morgan, G. Campbell. *The Acts of the Apostles*. Grand Rapids, Mich.: Fleming H. Revell, 1988.

Ogilvie, Lloyd J. *Acts*. The Communicator's Commentary, vol. 5. Dallas: Word Publishing, 1983.

Oster, Richard. *The Acts of the Apostles*, Part 2. The Living Word Commentary, ed. Everett Ferguson. Austin, Tex.: Sweet Publishing Co., 1979.

Pollock, John. *The Apostle: A Life of Paul*. Wheaton, Ill.: Scripture Press Publications, 1985.

Ramsay, W. M. *St. Paul the Traveller and the Roman Citizen*. Grand Rapids, Mich.: Baker Book House, 1975.

Roberts, J. W. *Acts of Apostles*, Part 1. Austin, Tex.: R. B. Sweet Co., 1967.

Root, Orrin, ed. *Standard Bible Commentary: Acts*. Cincinnati: Standard Publishing Co., 1966.

Stott, John R. W. *The Message of Acts*. Downers Grove, Ill.: Inter-Varsity Press, 1994.

Swindoll, Charles R. *The Strength of an Exacting Passion*. Anaheim, Calif.: Insight for Living, 1992.

Trenchard, E. H. *A New Testament Commentary*. Grand Rapids, Mich.: Zondervan Publishing House, 1969.

Wharton, Ed. *The Action of the Book of Acts*. Dallas: Gospel Teachers Publications, 1977.

Wiersbe, Warren W. *The Bible Exposition Commentary*. Vol. 1. Wheaton, Ill.: Victor Books, 1989.

BIBLE TRANSLATIONS

The Acts of the Apostles. Trans. C. H. Rieu. Penguin Books, 1957.

The Amplified New Testament. Grand Rapids, Mich.: Zondervan Publishing House, 1958.

The Bible: A New Translation. Trans. James Moffatt. New York: Harper & Brothers, 1954.

The Cotton Patch Version of Luke and Acts. Trans. Clarence Jordan. Clinton, N. J.: New Win Publishing Co., 1969.

The Emphasized New Testament: A New Translation. Trans. J. B. Rotherham. Grand Rapids, Mich.: Kregel, 1959.

The Holy Bible; American Standard Version. Thomas Nelson & Sons, 1901.

The Holy Bible; Authorized King James Version. Colorado Springs, Colo.: International Bible Society, 1987.

The Holy Bible; New Century Version. Dallas: Word Bibles, 1991.

The Holy Bible; New International Version. Grand Rapids, Mich.: Zondervan Publishing House, 1978.

The Holy Bible; New King James Version. New York: American Bible Society, 1990.

The Holy Bible; Revised Standard Version. Nashville: Thomas Nelson, Inc., 1972.

The Holy Bible; Today's English Version. New York: American Bible Society, 1976.

The Interlinear Greek-English New Testament: The Nestle Greek Text With a New Literal English Translation. Trans. Alfred Marshall. London: Samuel Baxter & Sons, Ltd., 1958.

The Living Bible: Paraphrased. Trans. Kenneth N. Taylor. Wheaton, Ill.: Tyndale House Publishers, 1971.

McCord's New Testament Translation of the Everlasting Gospel. Trans. Hugo McCord. Henderson, Tenn.: Freed-Hardeman College, 1988.

New American Standard Bible. Anaheim, Calif.: Foundation Publications, 1995.

New American Standard Bible. Nashville: Holman Bible Publishers, 1977.

The New English Bible. New York: Oxford University Press, 1971.

The New Testament: A New Translation. Trans. Olaf M. Norlie. Grand Rapids, Mich.: Zondervan Publishing House, 1945.

The New Testament: A Translation in the Language of the People. Trans. Charles B. Williams. Chicago: Moody Press, 1966.

The New Testament: An American Translation. Trans. Edgar J. Goodspeed. Chicago: University of Chicago, 1948.

The New Testament in Modern English. Trans. J. B. Phillips. New York: The MacMillan Company, 1958.

The New Testament in Modern Speech. Trans. Richard Francis Weymouth. New York: Harper & Brothers, n.d.

The New Testament in the Language of Today. Trans. William F. Beck. Concordia Publishing House, 1963.

The New Testament in the Translation of Monsignor Ronald Knox. New York: Sheed and Ward, 1944.

The New Testament of Our Lord and Saviour Jesus Christ. Trans. John Broadus. United Bible Society, n.d.

The Simple English™ Bible. New York: International Bible Publishing Co., 1980.

Twentieth Century New Testament. Trans. B. F. Westcott and F. J. Hort. Chicago: F. H. Revell, 1902.

HAVE YOU HEARD . . .
ABOUT TRUTH FOR TODAY?

What are the big missionary needs of our time? Those who study missionary evangelism point to two paramount needs that are ever present in the mission field.

THE BIG NEEDS OF WORLD EVANGELISM

First, they tell us that educating and maturing the national Christian man so that he can preach to his own people in their own language is of supreme importance. Giving this type of assistance to the national man will help to make our missionary efforts more self-supporting and more enduring. We appreciate one of our own preaching to us, and so do other peoples of the world. When we consider the work "our work," we approach it with greater care and will sacrifice more for it. This principle holds true in all cultures.

Christianity can flourish in any nation and culture, in any time or circumstance, if we will let it. When it is established through national preachers, it is far more likely to grow and blossom in the lives of the national people and not become an effort that is totally dependent upon American support.

After the Restoration Movement began in America, it did not take the early preachers long to realize that they had to teach young men to preach if the movement was really to grow. Thus, very early in the history of the Restoration Movement, schools were established. Wisdom suggested that route.

Christians should be grateful for every mission effort that is going on, such as campaigns, medical missions, and television presentations. However, we must not overlook the surpassing value of providing educational opportunities overseas that will assist a man in becoming capable of preaching effectively to his own people. This approach is absolutely vital to the ongoing success of the overall missionary work of the church.

Second, those who have researched missionary evangelism tell us that we need to make available biblical literature that provides an understanding of the Bible on the level of the people. Those whom the missionary is seeking to teach need their own copies of the Bible and assistance in understanding the Scriptures. They require guidance so they can grow quickly and accurately in their comprehension of the Bible. (See Acts 8:30, 31.)

When Tex Williams, the director of World Bible School, was on Harding University's campus sometime ago, he spoke to students about mission work. As a guest lecturer, he told one of the mission classes that the greatest need of Africa is Christian literature. "Without this literature," he said, "they simply cannot become Christians and grow into Christian maturity as they should." There is possibly one exception to this principle. The exception would be places where there is the presence of well-grounded men of faith continually teaching and preaching. This exception obviously applies to only a few places around the world. Even then, biblical literature is needed to support the teaching done.

Let us all consider carefully these two obvious missionary needs. Our efforts must be geared to meeting them. Not to address them is to ignore the clear results of the research that has been done in mission evangelism.

ADDRESSING THESE NEEDS

An effort is currently being made to address both of these big missionary needs. It has been designated the Truth for Today World Mission School (TFTWMS). Started in 1990 as a work under the oversight of the Champions church of Christ in Houston, Texas, it has proven to be a wonderful way to combine three methods of evangelism and thus minister to these supreme needs.

First, TFTWMS is a unique preacher school. An education in the Scriptures is mailed to the national preacher. The work started with 1,460 native preachers enrolled from 110 nations. Now literature is mailed to 22,000 people in 155 nations. These preachers were recommended to the school by World Bible School teachers, missionaries, campaigners, and the national preachers themselves. The school has enjoyed amazing growth.

Second, it is a printed preacher school. Every two months, the men enrolled receive the equivalent of three hundred pages of expository studies on the Scriptures. It is believed that the expository type of study crosses cultures better than other types of study. The materials sent give a thorough treatment of the New Testament book or Old Testament book being studied. It is designed to keep the national preacher enrolled in the school until he receives a study of each of the New Testament and Old Testament books, as well as *Cruden's Concordance*, *Smith's Bible Dictionary*, and several important special studies.

Picture two normal-sized books that are 150 pages in length, and you have the equivalent of the amount of material that is sent to these men every two months. The entire curriculum calls for these men to receive books that are 150 pages in size, that cover the entire Bible, and that include special studies on leadership, building sermons and Bible lessons, and soul-winning.

Third, in addition to sending expository studies to these men, a flexible, on-site preacher school is sometimes used as a follow-up to the printed material. This on-site school is literally taken to where the men are. Preachers and teachers go into a country and study with the national preachers in that location for two or three weeks. Students are provided with food and a syllabus for the classes they attend. They stay at that location day and night for the entire length of the school. They thus enjoy fellowship with other preaching brethren and are given opportunities to ask questions and receive feedback on problems they are facing.

The printed preacher school and the on-site school answer the big need of giving the national man an opportunity to prepare himself to preach to his own people in their own language. Since this work is accomplished to some extent through the printed page, it also answers the need of providing Christian literature for these teachers and preachers who are in desperate need of it.

THE STRONG POINTS

This unique missionary effort has strong points that should be immediately recognized. First, it provides an education to national men inexpensively. Expository materials can be sent to each of these men every two months in a cost-efficient way. Money for missions is hard to find or raise; what missionary money we have should be used to the maximum. TFTWMS sends an education to hundreds of national men with a small amount of money.

Second, the thrust of this work is to educate national men in their own land. Bringing these men to the United States for an education is very expensive. Often, when the national man tastes of the blessings of America, he does not want to return to his land. It is almost essential, therefore, that a way be found through which the national preacher can receive an education in his own country.

Third, this effort can reach out to hundreds of national men quickly. All of these men are in need of assistance now! How can we get it to them? This method is one of the most practical ways of immediately getting materials to them.

Fourth, it allows the national man to receive an education over a period of time. Because the education comes in the form of printed matter, they have access to the material for months and even years. These men need time to comprehend and assimilate the studies. The printed page offers them that opportunity. They can read and re-read it. They can easily store it. They can share it with others. It can be retained in their possession for as long as ten to fifteen years.

PICTURING THE EFFECTIVENESS

Picture 22,000 men (and thousands more as the work grows) in 155 nations of the world, going out to preach in their own languages to their own people. They are committed to Christ but have had little teaching upon which to build. Furthermore, these men will never have the opportunity to study in the United States to enable them to preach more accurately and faithfully. They have few books, if any. Picture yourself in this type of situation. What would you need?

Can you imagine how these men would be assisted if they received materials on every Old Testament and New Testament book? Can you imagine how encouraging it would be to them to be able to attend a two- to three-week preacher school in their community? Can you picture them in a school, taking several courses in Bible studies, having fellowship with other preachers, having opportunities to have their questions answered, and getting assistance regarding the problems they are facing? Can you not see how these opportunities would increase their effectiveness in leading souls to Christ and in edifying those who have become Christians?

HELPING THOSE WHO HAVE NOT HEARD

In order to help those who have never heard the gospel to become Christians, a special book was designed in 1998 by TFTWMS. It contains three hundred plus pages on how to become a Christian. The reader of the book is introduced to God, Christ, the Holy Spirit, the Bible, the earthly life of Jesus, the death, burial, and resurrection of Jesus, the establishment of the church, and how one can live for Christ today as a member of His church. Then, in the last two hundred pages of the book, there is a complete copy of the New Testament (NASB).

Thousands of these books have been sent to Africa, the Eastern European countries, and other places. The success rate has been very high—almost amazing. The book, 512 pages in length, can be printed and sent to someone in another country for $1.63. It is an attempt to bring together the very message that any Christian would want to provide for someone who has not heard the gospel.

Plans are being made every year to cover a large area of the earth with these books. Before printing, the book is culturally adapted for the specific area into which it is being sent.

HOW CAN YOU HELP?

Your help is needed to maintain this missionary effort that has become one of the largest, most cost-effective and productive efforts. Here is a two-part challenge for every Christian:

First, would you challenge the church where you worship and with whom you work to give a one-time contribution to this work? Even a small contribution will go a long way in providing teaching materials and on-site training for these national preachers.

Second, could you give a one-time contribution to this work? This contribution, of course, would have to be above and beyond your regular contribution to the local congregation of which you are a part. We are not asking anyone to interrupt his commitment to the work of the local congregation. The church needs more works, not fewer works. This effort is designed to strengthen every missionary activity and does not seek to detract from any one of them.

You would be surprised how much can be done if we all do a little extra. No one person has a lot of light, but if we put our lights together, we can have a big light that will reach out into all of the world. Would you decide today to dig a little deeper and give a little extra for this wonderful method of world evangelization?

CONTRIBUTIONS NEEDED

Contributions should be made out to Truth for Today World Mission School and sent to 2209 S. Benton, Searcy, AR 72143. Will you assist us in providing study materials for native preachers? This work is under the oversight of the Champions church of Christ in Houston, Texas.

Eddie Cloer